COMMUNICATION IN HISTORY

THIRD EDITION

COMMUNICATION IN HISTORY

TECHNOLOGY, CULTURE, SOCIETY

David Crowley

McGill University
McLuhan Program in Culture and Technology,
University of Toronto
The InterNet Group

Paul Heyer

Simon Fraser University
McLuhan Program in Culture and Technology,
University of Toronto

An imprint of Addison Wesley Longman, Inc.

New York • Reading, Massachusetts • Menlo Park, California • Harlow, England
Don Mills, Ontario • Sydney • Mexico City • Madrid • Amsterdam

Editor-in-Chief: Priscilla McGeehon
Acquisitions Editor: Donna Erickson
Marketing Manager: John Holdcroft
Project Coordination and Text Design: York Production Services
Cover Designer/Manager: Nancy Danahy
Cover Photo: Brian Benhnke/Illustration Works, Inc.
Full Service Production Manager: Richard Ausburn
Print Buyer: Denise Sandler
Electronic Page Make-up: York Production Services
Printer and Binder: The Maple-Vail Book Manufacturing Group
Cover Printer: Coral Graphic Services, Inc.

Library of Congress-in-Publication Data
Communication in history / [edited by] David Crowley, Paul Heyer.—3rd ed.
    p.   cm.
    Includes biographical references and index.
    ISBN 0-8013-3133-1
    1. Communication—History.   I. Crowley, D. J. (David J.), 1945-
    II. Heyer, Paul, 1946-
p90.C62945 1998
302.2'09—dc21   98-28839
                                                                            CIP

Please visit our website at http://longman.awl.com

ISBN 0-8013-31331

345678910—MA—0100

FOR *Don Theall*
Teacher, Scholar, Friend

CONTENTS

P A R T   V I I   TV Times   259

P A R T   V I I I   New Media and Old in the Information Age   301

PART V Image Technologies and the Emergence of Mass Society 171

PART VI Radio Days 213

Preface

Why does a new communication medium—the alphabet, printing, broadcasting, computer communication—come into being? What impact does it have on the media that precede it? How does a new medium exert influence on the everyday life of society? And how, in turn, can society and culture influence media practices?

These are some of the questions *Communication in History* has been trying to address for the past decade. During that time numerous students and colleagues have told us that the subject area is becoming increasingly vital to their interests and professional development. Thanks to their encouragement and the support of Addison-Wesley Longman, we have created this new and expanded third edition. The new edition features more coverage of major media developments in the past, such as the role of printing in the rise of the modern state, and an expanded examination of communication in our own era of proliferating media forms—television, video, digital technology, the Internet, and cyberspace. We have created this rich canvas using selections from writers considered to be at the vanguard of their respective fields. The goal of this new edition, however, has changed little from previous versions: to invite students to consider the development of human behavior and social experience as, in part, a response to the uses and consequences of communication media in the wider context of human history. The text lays out a journey that will help reveal how media have been influential both in maintaining social order and as powerful agents of change.

The issues raised by the role of media in history are, of course, broad-based, too broad we think to be easily encompassed in a single author textbook. From the beginning, we felt that the best way to go was with an anthology featuring an exemplary list of contributors, whose research relates directly to or complements one another. As with past editions, all the contributors try to tell us something about the characteristics and the human consequences of particular media and their development. It should not be surprising that the contributors come from a variety of disciplines. The history of communication, although most at home in the disciplines of communication and journalism, draws from and has relevance for a variety of fields, including architecture, archeology, anthropology, history, literary criticism, and sociology.

We have divided the third edition into eight sections, beginning with prehistory and ending with the contemporary information era. At times, contributors in a given section will cite each other's work as well as the work of a contributor in another part of the book. As a result, we think you will find considerable unity within and among the eight sections of the text.

To further help students appreciate these connections, and to afford an overview of the history of communication, we have provided a general introduction. Each of the eight sections also includes an introductory essay whose purpose is to provide a rationale for the particular section, an explanation of key concepts and transitions, and to cite background material that might help the reader better appreciate the individual essays. At the end of the volume, we have included a short list of Suggestions for Further Reading.

New to This Edition

- Twelve new selections include Lewis Mumford's "The Invention of Printing," Pat Aufderheide's "Music Videos," and Mark Poster's "The Net as a Public Sphere."

- Five new selections on the technology, style, and emerging issues of digital communication relate contemporary concerns with earlier developments in communication history.

- More selections by contemporary scholars such as Susan Sontag, Janet Murray, and Robert Logan provide an updated view of communication's history.

- "Two Cultures—Television Versus Print," a conversation between cultural critics Neil Postman and Camille Paglia offers students a lively debate on an issue of current interest.

- A startling look into the unfolding relationship between cyberspace and urban architecture is provided in "Softcities," by William J. Mitchell.

Finally, we wish to mention a few of the many individuals who provided encouragement, and often assistance, for this ongoing project. Our thanks go to Alison Beale, Anouk Belanger, Bill Buxton, Ian Chunn, Hart Cohen, Derrick de Kerckhove, Jane Dickson, Bruce Ferguson, Jim Fowles, Kathleen Galarneau, Robert Graham, Lynne Hissey, Richard Herbert Howe, Jesse Hunter, Liss Jeffrey, Stephen Kern, Bill Leiss, Rolly Lorimer, Oya Majlesi, Shauna McCabe, David Mitchell, Jean Ogilvie, John Rowlandson, Lise Ouimet, Firoozeh Radjei, Gertrude Robinson, Wik Rowland, Leslie Shade, Brian Shoesmith, Ed Slopek, Graham Thompson, Phil Vitone.

For their assistance, we would like to thank the National Archives of Canada, the Instructional Communications Centre at McGill, the McLuhan Program in Culture and Technology at the University of Toronto, and the InterNet Consulting Group of Ottawa. Our thanks go as well to our editor, Donna Erickson, and to Kwon Chong at Longman and Lori Ann Smith at York Production Services for production support.

We would also like to thank our reviewers for their thoughtful and constructive commentaries: Robert Arnett, *Mississippi State University;* John Erickson, *University of Iowa;* Alfred Lorenz, *Loyola University;* William McKeen, *University of Florida;* William Petkanas, *Western Connecticut State University;* Paul Soukup, *Santa Clara University;* Monica Strom, *University of Wisconsin—Parkside.*

David Crowley
Paul Heyer

COMMUNICATION
IN HISTORY

The Media of Early Civilization

Painted limestone Stella, from the twelfth Egyptian dynasty, about 1955 B.C. *Metropolitan Museum of Art.*

Whenever the term "media" or "communications" is mentioned, many of us envision the pervasive technology of today's world. Students of communication may range farther back historically and think of the newspaper over the past two hundred years, the invention of the printing press in the fifteenth century, or perhaps the origins of the alphabet in ancient Greece. Communications media, however, are older—much older. In this part of the text we will look at some key aspects of their development, from the early prehistoric context to the complex writing systems of ancient Mesopotamia and Egypt.

What was the first communications medium? This question may be impossible to answer scientifically. However, it is not impossible to imagine. Almost as soon as our prehistoric ancestors made tools of wood, bone, and stone to help them physically adapt to a changing environment, they probably made "tools for thought" as well. Perhaps the earliest device of this kind was a simple stick, notched to indicate the number of deer in a nearby herd, or some rocks or logs arranged to mark the importance of a given territory. What was important was the process. Humankind enlarged its sphere of *communication* by creating *communications*.

Communication is an exchange of information and messages. It is an activity. About one hundred thousand years ago, our early ancestors communicated through nonverbal gestures and an evolving system of spoken language. As their world became increasingly complex, they needed more than just the shared memory of the group to recall important things. They needed what is sometimes called an extrasomatic memory, a memory outside of the body. Thus an increase in "communication" led to "communications," the development of media to store and retrieve the growing volume of information. The microchip of today is one such medium, a direct descendant of our hypothetical notched stick.

The later prehistoric period, from about 50,000 to 10,000 B.C., has recently begun to yield impressive evidence of both communication and communications. Alexander Marshack explores this in our first essay "The Art and Symbols of Ice Age Man." Marshack is an archaeologist engaged in a reexamination of some of the so-called art of the Old Stone Age. He looks at bone tools, figurines, and the famous cave paintings that were found in Western Europe and date from the end of the last Ice Age. Unlike previous researchers, who often saw these artifacts as ritual magic or "art for art's sake," Marshack argues for more: Could they not constitute a systematic attempt at using symbols to record information about the natural environment—in other words, communications media?

Some readers will remain skeptical. Nevertheless, the strength of his argument resides not in the provability of any of its interpretations, but in the way he has added a new direction to earlier research. Much more work must and will be done.

Clearly, the relationship between writing and civilization is on Marshack's mind, even if it is not an explicit theme in his essay. We could say that he is dealing with the indirect, early beginnings of script. The more immediate origins of this phenomenon are traced in Denise Schmandt-Besserat's contribution, "The Earliest Precursor of Writing." Like Marshack's, her argument is based not on the discovery of new archeological remains, but on reinterpreting earlier finds in a new communications way. She begins where Marshack leaves off, about twelve thousand years ago, and continues to the fourth millennium B.C. and the rise of the great Near Eastern civilizations, Sumer and Egypt, which are often said to have been made possible through the invention of writing.

Schmandt-Besserat provides compelling evidence for her contention that before the emergence of writing, several Old World societies were keeping records of economic output and trade through the use of fired clay tokens one to three centimeters in size. Readers will be shown some fascinating archaeological detective work as she comments on traditional interpretations of these artifacts as charms, toys, or tools and then suggests an alternative communications view. In so doing, she notes that many of the tokens resemble the characters known as *ideograms*—conventionalized signs that do not look like what they represent. Ideograms were the basis of the first known writing system, the Sumerian, which arose in 3500 B.C. Thus, if one accepts her hypothesis, the tokens are an abstract form of three-dimensional communications, which evolved into more efficient two-dimensional writing in response to social and economic changes necessitating a more complex way of life: civilization.

Our next excerpt, which is by Harold Innis, deals with what happened in the realm of communications and culture after the establishment of empires in Egypt and Mesopotamia. Innis (1894–1952) was a Canadian political economist turned communication theorist. The communication ideas that he acquired in training at the University of Chicago surfaced periodically in his early economic writings. However, it was the work he produced shortly before his death, *Empire and Communications* (1950) and the *Bias of Communication* (1951), that marked his transformation to communications historian. More than any other twentieth-century figure, Innis argued that this field merits disciplinary or subdisciplinary status. Although he explored almost every facet of the communications/history question, the bulk of his project dealt with the role of media in the organization of ancient empires and early Western civilization.

Innis elaborated his history of communication around a series of core concepts, several of which are used in the excerpt we have included. Perhaps the most significant one pertains to time and space. Innis argued that each of the major Old World civilizations had a specific cultural orientation that was temporal or spatial. This orientation derived in part from the nature and use of the dominant medium it employed. For example, stone in ancient Egypt was a durable, time-biased medium, favoring a centralized absolute government of divine kingship. This bias was further evident in the use of hieroglyphic writing to produce astonishingly accurate calendars, around which the agricultural cycle pivoted. With the coming of papyrus, a light, portable, space-biased medium that was suitable for administration over distance, the complexion of Egypt changed. The priestly class expanded its power as the acquisition of new territories gave rise to an extended empire needing an administrative bureaucracy versed in the new communications.

Our next selection, by Marcia Ascher and Robert Ascher, deals with an area of communications history that has been almost completely ignored by major scholars in the field: ancient New World civilizations. The Aschers focus on the Incas, who, unlike other New World states—the Maya and Aztec, for example—did not have writing. But is not writing essential to civilization and a complex state-level organization? Ascher and Ascher debunk this still prevalent misconception. They convincingly show that it is not writing per se that allows for civilization, but some medium for the keeping of records that can function in an efficient and comprehensive manner. The quipu served this purpose among the Incas of ancient Peru. The quipu was a series of cords of different length, thickness, and colors that were knotted and braided. Each of these elements constituted information, the kind used to record crop production, taxation, a census, and a variety of other kinds of information.

An intriguing point that is relevant to the excerpt by the Aschers and the one preceding it by Innis is that the quipu, being a light, portable medium, was suitable for administration over distance and indeed was heavily used in this manner by the expansionist Inca empire. This is a classic example of Innis's notion of a space-biased medium, although Innis did not consider the Incas. Ascher and Ascher, however, were influenced by him, and their research sustains this interesting and useful concept.

The quipu notwithstanding, most of the world's early civilizations came into being using writing as their dominant medium of communication. In our final selection, Andrew Robinson discusses the variety of writing systems that developed in the ancient world. Although these systems may have differed widely in form, they functioned in similar ways to monitor the information necessary for the maintenance of a complex society. Robinson also shows us that some of the principles used in ancient scripts, such as hieroglyphics, are still with us in everything from road signs to computer keyboards. What further examples can you add to his list?

1 THE ART AND SYMBOLS OF ICE AGE MAN

Alexander Marshack

Alexander Marshack, from his base at the Peabody Museum of Archaeology and Ethnology at Harvard University, initiated an important rethinking of the art and artifacts of prehistory. He has published a major book, The Roots of Civilization, *and numerous articles on the subject, with the promise of more to come.*

Prehistory is mute. We have no record of the languages, the myths, or the lore of the scattered hunting cultures that existed for tens of thousands of years before the rise of farming and the development of the early agricultural civilizations. History, according to the accepted definition, began with writing, with recorded languages written on clay, stone, and papyrus, languages we have learned to decipher and to read, if not to speak. These ancient writings gave us the names and dates of kings, priests, dynasties, cities, battles, gods, and goddesses, as well as a record of the sale of sheep, cows, land, grain, and labor. History, by this definition, began only about 5,000 years ago with the development in Mesopotamia, Egypt, and Asia of early forms of pictographic writing.

But man began making images and keeping symbolic records more than 25,000 years before the invention of true writing. He began during the last Ice Age, not long after modern man, or *Homo sapiens*, appeared in Europe, about 35,000 B.C. The steps from these prehistoric images and symbol systems to writing and history are only now beginning to be scientifically explored and discussed.

Equally important, the efforts by still earlier forms of man toward the making of images are beginning to be tentatively discussed. It is now clear, for instance, that long before modern man appeared in Europe, Neanderthal man was making and using symbols and images. The artifacts from this earlier period are still few and our understanding of them is tenuous. But they are there, and the study of them has begun.

In 1964, the Hungarian archaeologist Laszlo Vertés published a photograph of an unusual small oval object that had been carved by a Neanderthal man about 45,000 years ago from a section of woolly-mammoth tooth. After carefully carving the object and beveling one edge for easier handling, the artist painted the shiny surface with red ocher.

The Neanderthal plaque was found near Tata, Hungary, almost 100 years after the carved and engraved animal images made by later Cro-Magnon hunters began to be excavated in rock shelters of France. These Cro-Magnon images, illustrating extinct species like the mammoth and woolly rhinoceros, were hard for 19th Century Europeans to accept as valid and they were difficult to understand, in much the same way that the Neanderthal Tata plaque is hard to accept or to understand today. When a skeleton of Cro-Magnon man was found in 1868, researchers realized that, physically, the hunter of animals during the Ice Age was exactly like modern *Homo sapiens*. At that time the animal images were interpreted as hunting magic, and it was suggested that they were used by our apparently crude ancestors in primitive ritual to ensure the supply of food. Since the images were considered to be either magic or art or merely decoration, they were not systematically studied by archaeologists.

When I examined the Neanderthal Tata plaque and the animal images of Cro-Magnon man under a low-power microscope to see how they were carved and how the artifacts had been used, I was startled by the many new facts I found. The Neanderthal plaque had been carefully carved and beveled, but the microscope revealed that all marks of carving and scraping were missing. Instead, the edges of the plaque

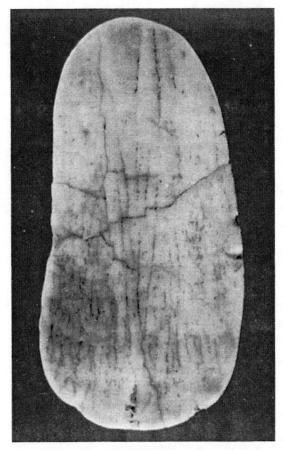

Neanderthal plaque, carved mammoth tooth. Tata, Hungary, c. 45,000 B.C. *Reprinted by permission of the author.*

had been polished and worn by repeated handling. The microscope showed that the bone was not a tool, which would have shown most wear at the points of friction and use. Actually, it was an intentionally carved and painted symbolic object, an artifact apparently manufactured for nonutilitarian ritual use, and it had been kept and used for a long period. How was it used and for what purpose? We do not know.

For more than a century archaeologists believed that Cro-Magnon man had invented symbolic artifacts. It was known that Neanderthal man used red ocher, that he used animal bones, antlers, and skulls as symbols, and that he

buried his dead with grave goods—in one case even with flowers. But there was a tendency among archaeologists to consider Neanderthal man as not yet fully human, though he had a brain volume as large or larger than that of modern man and he made exquisite tools of stone. There was even a dispute as to whether he had any form of language, the belief being that the making of symbolic images and the development of modern language belonged only to fully modern human types.

When I put the earliest animal carvings of Cro-Magnon man under the microscope, I found that they had also been used for long periods of time, much like the symbolic plaque from Tata. The beautiful two-and-a-half-inch-long horse of mammoth ivory from the site of Vogelherd, Germany, is the earliest known example of animal sculpture, dating from about 30,000 B.C. The carefully carved ear, nose, mouth, and mane had been worn down by persistent handling. At some point during this use, a fresh angle or "dart" had been engraved in its flank, apparently representing an act of specialized or ritual killing.

The plaque and horse are among the earliest known intentionally manufactured symbolic human artifacts. The analysis of the two artifacts provides us with a new kind of data for the perpetual debate on the possible reasons for the emergence of art and symbol. There have been many theories about their origins. One, proposed by the Abbé Henri Breuil, the man who began the scientific study of Ice Age art early in the 20th Century and who has been called "the father of prehistory," is that art began as doodling. On the soft clay walls of limestone caves in France and Spain are panels of interlacing finger scrawls that look like random "macaronis." Occasionally such macaronis form an image that look like an animal. According to Breuil, it was by the occasional recognition of an animal form among such random doodlings that art was born. Unfortunately the sophisticated Vogelherd horse, which is carved of ivory, is at least 5,000 or 10,000 years older than the oldest cave macaronis. The symbolic Neanderthal plaque from Tata, which is not an animal image, was certainly not derived from doodling. Besides, the limestone caves of France and Spain are geographic phenomena limited to that part of Europe. Images and symbols were made during the Ice Age wherever the hunters lived, from Spain to Siberia, in areas where there are no caves and therefore no cave macaronis or cave art.

Psychologists working with chimpanzees have made suggestions similar to those of Breuil. A chimpanzee can scribble and doodle lines and forms on a piece of paper. A female chimpanzee, Mojo, once made an image that she and the researchers who were training her, Allen and Beatrice Gardner, recognized as a bird. The problem with such data concerning the capacity of the chimpanzee to make, name, or use images is that the chimpanzees are being encouraged to make and are being taught to recognize and name images. Naming and the use of named images in communication is an evolved aspect of human culture and behavior and is not a normal aspect of chimpanzee culture and behavior. The chimpanzee capacity for such near-human behavior is apparently present, but since it is neither functional nor adaptive for chimpanzees in the wild, it has not been selected for evolutionary genetic development.

Many animals show capacities under human training and testing that are non-functional in their normal environments and that therefore remain as mere potential capacities in the species. The use of the chimpanzee capacity for visual abstraction and symbol recognition does not produce chimpanzee art. It produces an essentially learned and human-type image based on human naming. The naming of objects is a form of classification, differentiation, and consequently of description. This is possible only in a human context where such differentiations have become cultural and functional. A baby can babble, but the babbling does not lead to speech unless it develops in a culture that uses speech. Similarly, without a cultural context, doodling does not lead to art.

Mammoth ivory horse, earliest known animal carving. Vogelherd, Germany, c. 30,000 B.C. *Reprinted by permission of the author.*

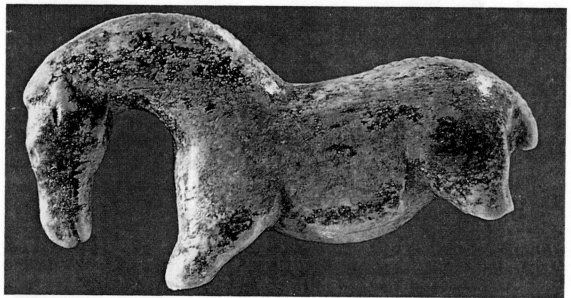

This is important for discussing the possible origins of art and symbol. If we go back to the Tata plaque and the Vogelherd horse, we find that we are not dealing with objects or images but with symbolic artifacts that were made to be *used,* and apparently to be used at the proper time and in the proper way. Such use implies a cultural tradition, and it was this tradition that made the artifacts possible, meaningful, and useful. I assume, then, that Neanderthal man had a human-type culture. The plaque was not the result of an idiosyncratic, individual effort at carving or aesthetic expression, that is, an instance of doodling. In some form or another, the plaque had a name and a cultural use.

If we consider the Vogelherd horse as a late example in a slowly developing human tradition of making and using symbols, then the difference between the plaque, which we cannot name or explain, and the horse, which we can name but cannot explain, is not so great. It was not the shape of the artifact but the creation and use of artificial images and symbols as part of the cultural process that was truly human and revolutionary.

What Cro-Magnon man had apparently achieved was a more complex symbolic culture and social organization than Neanderthal man. Cro-Magnon marked or noted social and cultural processes with a greater range of symbols and images, each of which had some special meaning in the culture. These images and symbols were apparently used as we use images and symbols today—to mark rituals and ceremonies, to indicate differences in age, sex, and rank, to signify important processes, and to stand for parts of myths and stories. Images, in other words, were made to be used. It was this form of image use that, in a sense, erupted in the efflorescence of Ice Age art. But it was not an artistic revolution; it was a cultural revolution.

From the terminal period of the Ice Age cultures of Europe at the Italian site of Paglicci comes the image of a horse engraved on a horse pelvis. Microscopic examination of the image indicates that the horse had been symbolically killed 27 times. This was signified by the engraving in and around the horse of feathered darts and spears, each made by a different engraving point and in a different style, apparently over a considerable period of time. Clearly, the horse never died. Like the Vogelherd horse, this horse was a symbol that could be used at the proper time and in the proper way.

Archaeologists first interpreted such images of killed animals as products of magic intended to ensure success in the hunt. In simple hunting magic an animal image is made and then "killed." Its "death" usually terminates the use of the image that had been made for that hunt. Here, however, the image continues to be used. It has become a symbol, not of one horse or of one hunt and meal, but of all horses and perhaps of a horse myth as well. As in many hunting cultures that kill animals for diverse ritual purposes, the Paghcci horse may have had nothing to do with hunting. An important spirit animal could, for instance, have been symbolically sacrificed, even by the act of killing the image, for a curing, a birth, an initiation ceremony, or even a death.

Analyses of Ice Age animal images have shown that they were used for many different purposes. The analysis of two painted horses in the cave of Pech-Merle, France, painted about 5,000 years before the end of the Ice Age, clearly demonstrates these periodic multiple uses of the animal image. There are no darts that signify killing in the Pech-Merle horses. The artist outlined a horse in black paint on a rock that was shaped like a horse. Infrared analysis indicates that over a period of time this empty horse outline was filled with red and black spots made of many different pigments and ochers. The horse was used, but not necessarily "killed." When the horse was filled, additional spots, along with hand prints, were placed around it, again suggesting a use of the image and wall rather than a killing. After this section of the wall was filled, a

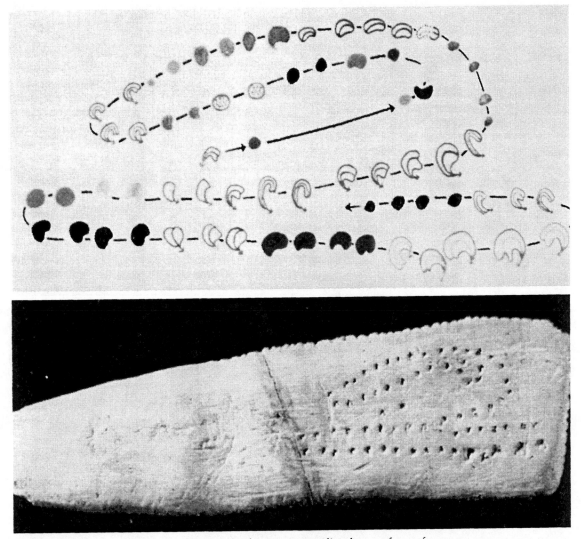

Cro-magnon bone tool and magnified sketch of engraving, earliest known form of notation, may mark phases of the moon. Blanchard, France, c. 28,000 B.C. *Reprinted by permission of the author.*

second horse outline was made and the process of marking it with spots was begun again. In addition, within the first horse is painted a large red fish—a pike—and on its chest is a huge perfect circle made with a different ocher. Neither of these images is related to a killing of the horse. They could be symbolically related to the horse in some context involving the seasons or the sun. We do not know what these uses and symbols (darts, hand prints, signs, and fish) entailed, but they do *not* seem to have been involved in simple hunting magic.

This use of the horse image without any indication of a killing of the animal is documented

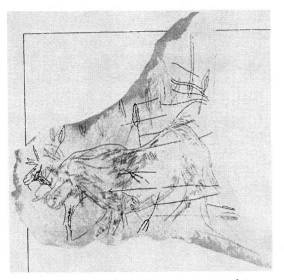

Horse engraved on pelvis. The twenty-seven darts and spears depicted were each incised by a different point and in a different style, indicating ritual reuse of the engraving. Paglicci, Italy, end of the Ice Age. *Reprinted by permission of the author.*

throughout Ice Age art. A simple example will show why such usage escaped archaeological attention. A broken fragment of reindeer antler from the Ice Age site of Kesslerloch, in Switzerland, is engraved with a horse head. Since the fragment was neither a tool nor a costume piece, the horse head cannot be considered decoration. Microscopic examination of the image shows that the head had been renewed twice by engraving schematic horse muzzles on the front of it, each muzzle faintly engraved by a different tool. The image was being used, but the horse was not being "killed." This usage escaped attention because, without the aid of a microscope, the image appeared to be merely a horse head.

There is another class of Ice Age marking and symbol that is completely different from the recognizable animal image. From the same early Ice Age period as the Vogelherd horse, comes a small shaped bone reminiscent of the Tata plaque. It is about the same size as the Tata plaque and was found in a Cro-Magnon rock shelter at Blanchard, France. Microscopic analy-

sis indicated that the plaque, unlike the one from Tata, had in fact been used as a tool. The front end was broken by persistent pressure and the back is highly polished where it sat in the palm of the hand while being used. The plaque was a pressure flaker that had been used, apparently for a long time, to sharpen the point or edge of stone tools. It was probably made for that purpose and may have been carried about in a pouch or pocket.

The microscope showed that during its use the plaque had been engraved with 29 sets of marks, each set made at a different time with a different point and in a different style. The accumulation had slowly formed a serpentine image. It was almost as though someone, 25,000 years before the development of writing and arithmetic, was keeping a record of some process or series of events and was structuring it in a manner that he could "read." After some arithmetic tests, I found that the twists and turns corresponded to the changing phases of the moon, all the full moons falling at the left, all the half moons in the middle, and all the crescents at the right. The fit was perfect for an observational lunar notation. There is no proof, of course, that it was a lunar notation, but clearly it was some form of notation. There is no evidence of arithmetic counting in the sequence, but many primitive people without a knowledge of arithmetic notice the changing periods of the moon and sun and stars.

If the cultural origins of art were based not on doodling or an aesthetic expression but on the manufacture of meaningful images that were intended to be made and used at the right time and in the right way, perhaps the origins of notation or record keeping were also related to the developing complexity of man's symbolic and economic life. If the economic and ritual activities of prehistoric man had to be performed at the right time, then images, symbols, and notations together may have served as a means of structuring these periodic cultural activities.

An example of how the tradition of accumulating meaningful images developed comes

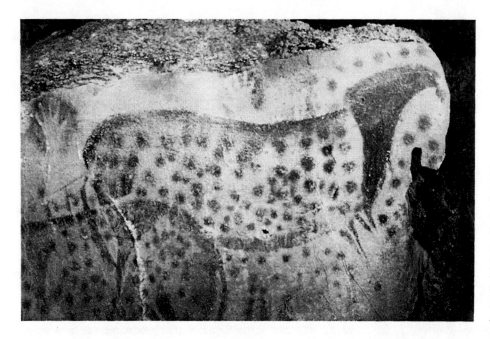

Pech-Merle spotted horse. The outline was filled with spots over a period of time, and hand prints and more spots were added later. France, c. 14,500 B.C. *Reprinted by permission of the author.*

from the end of the Ice Age, about 11,000 to 10,000 B.C. A decorated shaft straightener or "pierced bâton," as they are sometimes called, was found in the 19th Century at the French shelter of Montgaudier. (A shaft straightener is a long bone with a hole at one end. A spear is put through the holes of two such straighteners, which are then used as handles to bend the shaft, often over a fire.) It was only when I examined it by microscope a few years ago that it became clear that it had engraved on one face a bull and cow seal, a male salmon with a hook on the lower jaw that it develops only after leaving the Atlantic and beginning its spawning run upriver, a flower in full bloom, and three plants in full leaf. The bull seal collects his harem of cows in the early spring, at the same time that the salmon arrive for their spawning run. On the reverse face of the bâton there are two serpents that mate in the spring. The full composition contained related images of spring. Into this composition was engraved one small, crude, schematic ibex or wild goat head with an "X" on its head as though it had been symbolically killed in a ritual related to the coming of spring. None of the other animals had killing marks, though salmon and seal were surely hunted.

Images and symbols, according to this theory, were markers of periodic and continuous cultural processes, of rites, and of repetitive myths and stories, whereas notations of whatever sort were apparently means of recording the passage of time in terms of culturally significant events. In the case of the Blanchard pressure flaker, the notation had apparently been used to mark the days or nights and the different phases of the moon. But a lunar notation could also have been achieved by marking a sequence of images illustrating the crescent, half, full, half, and crescent moons. That too would have been a non-arithmetical lunar notation.

In the early period of the Ice Age, images like the Vogelherd horse and notations like the serpentine Blanchard image occurred separately. They were distinct symbol systems and they were made separately, much as we may have writing on one page, an image on another, and a column of numbers on yet another. Toward the

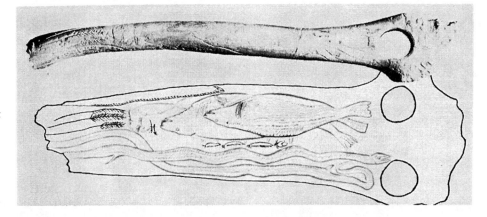

Engraved antler bâton; the seal, salmon, serpent, and plants suggest the spring season. Montgaudier, France, c. 10,000 B.C. *Reprinted by permission of the author.*

last stages of the Ice Age, however, one begins to find complex accumulations and compositions in which many different systems are combined and used together: images, signs, symbols, and notations. The spotted horses in the cave of Pech-Merle are an indication of this trend. But a similar process had begun to appear on artifacts found in the habitation shelter.

Some years after I had studied the Vogelherd horse and the Blanchard bone, which were from the early Cro-Magnon period and about 30,000 years old, I came upon a fragment of engraved reindeer antler, which was about 15,000 years old, from the French rock shelter of La Marche. It had been a practical tool, a pressure retoucher and flaker like the Blanchard bone, and its front end was rounded and broken back from use. A microscopic study of the piece of antler showed that it had once been a different type of tool, perhaps a shaft straightener with a hole at one end, but that the original tool had snapped during use and the fragment had been reshaped to its present form.

When it had been a shaft straightener, the La Marche antler fragment was engraved on one face with an accumulation of notations and with a horse image. The remnants of the horse and the notation were still visible. After it became a pressure flaker it was again engraved with one horse and an accumulation of notations, this time on the other face. What was fascinating was that the notations were accumulated in horizontal rows that proceeded downward from the tip. Each set or group of rows had been engraved by a different point. Usually the sets were made with a changed direction of engraving by reversing the antler for the marking of each set. The microscope suggested that the notations had been accumulated for a long time, perhaps over many months. Arithmetic tests indicated that the total came to seven-and-a-half lunar months.

The horse, which is located below the notations, is a pregnant mare that had been used and reused a number of times. It has three ears, three eyes, and two backs, all made by different points, which suggests that it had been renewed periodically, probably during the period of notational accumulation and use of the tool. There were also sets of darts engraved around the horse, each set made by a different point, suggesting that it had been ritually or symbolically killed a number of times.

The man using this piece of antler as a practical tool probably kept it with him to sharpen his stone points and perhaps carried it in a pouch. During this period he also marked the available free surface of the object, using two separate but culturally related symbol systems. Conceptually, if we took the Vogelherd horse and the Blanchard notation and combined them,

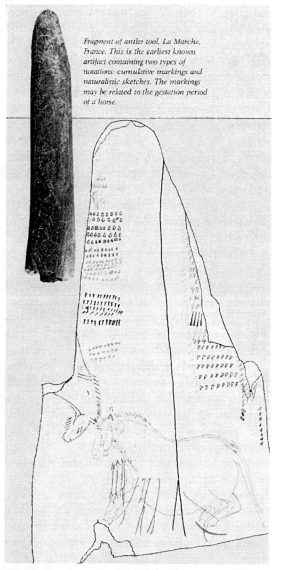

Fragment of antler tool, La Marche, France. This is the earliest known artifact containing two types of notations: cumulative markings and naturalistic sketches. The markings may be related to the gestation period of a horse.

Fragment of antler tool, earliest known artifact containing two types of notation: cumulative markings of naturalistic sketches. The markings may be related to the gestation period of a horse. LaMarche, France. *Reprinted by permission of the author.*

we would have a repeatedly used horse and a periodically accumulated notation that looked like the La Marche antler. This combining of separate symbol systems as the Ice Age devel-

oped was one of the great intellectual achievements of man. Separate symbol systems and different types of imagery, each of which had a different specialized meaning and each of which was used differently, could be combined or associated. We do this when we use writing and numbers under a chart and then provide an image or graph to which the writing and numbers refer: These are three separate symbol systems within a single context. Ice Age man was apparently doing the same.

A test of the notations on the antler suggested that they might be nonarithmetic, observational lunar notations. The pregnancy period of a horse is 11 months. Whether the notations were related to the duration of a mare's pregnancy, we cannot tell; but we do know that for the engraver the notational accumulation and the renewal and "killing" of the horse image were somehow related.

The concept of symbols, images, and notations serving functionally as markers for periodic and continuous cultural processes and recognitions is new in the field of prehistoric archaeology. If it is a valid concept, we may have found one of the intellectual and cultural threads that leads eventually to true writing and to history. But these Ice Age symbol and image systems were not writing and arithmetic: We do not have history. We cannot decipher these Ice Age systems precisely and accurately and thus learn the dates, names, myths, or rituals to which they refer. Despite this we are able to state that the intelligence involved in the development and use of these images and symbols for cultural purposes is the same as we have today.

One can perhaps assume that the images of animals, the shaft straighteners, the tool retouchers, and the notations associated with them were made and used by men. We can make no such assumption concerning the female images of the Ice Age. Two types of female image come from the early period in France. The best known are the often magnificent "Venus" figurines, such as the famous Venus of Lespugue, carved of mam-

Carved mammoth ivory "Venus," Lespugue, France, c. 25,000 B.C. *Reprinted by permission of the author.*

moth ivory. These Venus figurines have exaggerated hips and breasts, tiny feet, bent knees, and no faces. Similar images that date from the Ice Age have been found in Italy, Austria, Czechoslovakia, and the Ukraine. Images of naked females in a somewhat different style have been found at Ice Age sites in Siberia. These images often show the polish of long use and, at times, the remains of red ocher, which indicates that they were often symbolically painted. They have been called fertility images, but their actual meaning and use have not been discovered.

A second type of female image from the early period is the carved vulva image. Vulva shapes of this type are today found in rock engravings from Africa and Australia to South America. In France they are found carved on large blocks of limestone in an Ice Age habitation site. A careful analysis has shown that, like the animal images, these female images were made to be used. They are often overmarked with strokes and gashes as if they had been used in ritual.

By the end of the Ice Age the Venus figurines and vulva images essentially disappeared, but the tradition of making female images on stones in the habitation site continued. In this late period it is not the vulva shape but schematic female outlines, with no head or feet and with exaggerated buttocks, that have accumulated on limestone and slate slabs in the habitation site. Like the earlier vulva carvings, these female images were repeatedly marked and overmarked and sometimes overengraved. Were these accumulations of female images made by women? Were they related to female processes and phases? We do not know. But these studies are beginning to give us new kinds of data and to make such questions possible. Whatever their meaning, we have evidence once again of a ritual use of image and symbol in the Ice Age that could have helped prepare the way for the development of true record keeping.

The prehistoric past may be silent, but the silent images are, ever so tentatively, beginning to speak.

2 THE EARLIEST PRECURSOR OF WRITING

Denise Schmandt-Besserat

Denise Schmandt-Besserat is an archaeologist working at the University of Texas at Austin. Her work on early symbol systems leading to the origin of writing is currently influencing students in a wide range of disciplines.

This paper deals with tokens recovered in archaeological sites of the ancient Middle East.[1] The first part summarizes the factual evidence available on the artifacts. The second part discusses what can be extrapolated from these facts for reconstructing what the tokens stood for and their significance. The interpretation focuses, in particular, on the way the objects were manufactured, their function as a counting device, the mode of reckoning they illustrate, and finally, the socio-political role they play in pre- and protoliterate communities. In the conclusion it will be proposed that tokens led ultimately to writing as a consequence of interrelated economic, social, and conceptual changes.

The factual evidence on tokens includes their physical aspect, geographic distribution, number and findspots at given sites. Gathering this data involved visiting all possible collections of tokens in major museums of North America, Europe and the Middle East where they have been stored since excavation, counting the number of specimens, making a sketch of their shape and eventual markings, measuring their size and making note of all particular features. In the best instances, tokens identified by a field or museum number could be traced to the corresponding entry in field notes, excavation catalogue or site report in order to identify the level and location where they were found in excavation.

THE PHYSICAL EVIDENCE

Tokens are small artifacts modelled into standard forms either geometric or naturalistic. The shapes are as follows: spheres, disks, cones, tetrahedrons, biconoids, ovoids, cylinders, triangles, paraboloids, rectangles, cubes, rhomboids and hyperboloids (see page 16). Others are miniature representations of tools, containers, pieces of furniture, fruit, animals and parts thereof. Tokens can be classified according to types and subtypes. The types refer to the shapes as described above whereas the subtypes refer to the intentional variations of size within the types or the addition of markings. Spheres, cones and tetrahedrons, for example, occur consistently in two sizes. Spheres also occur as fractions such as hemispheres and ¾ spheres. The markings consist of incised lines, notches, punches, pinched appendices or appliqué pellets. These are applied clearly on the face of tokens but with no particular concern for composition or esthetics. The lines and punctuations are displayed on a single face of the disks, triangles, paraboloids and other flat tokens, but cover the entire surface of spheres, ovoids, cones and other globular forms. The practice of applying markings on tokens is attested in the earliest assemblages of the VIIIth millennium B.C.[2] Tokens bearing markings remain rare, however, during the entire duration of the system, except between 3400–3100 B.C., when they become widely used at selected sites such as Uruk and Tello in Mesopotamia; Susa and Chogha Mish in Iran; and Habuba Kabira and Tell Kannas in Syria.[3] These assemblages of tokens characterized by a proliferation of markings are referred to as "complex tokens." Some complex tokens are also perforated. In the case of Uruk, for instance, 35.4% of the collection of 647 tokens bear markings and 15.6% are perforated.[4] The various assemblages of complex tokens are strikingly similar.

Tokens from Seh Gabi, Iran. *Courtesy of Royal Ontario Museum.*

They share, in particular, a same fine clay of buff-pink color and the markings they bear are identical in pattern and manufacture.

The size of tokens ranges, usually, between 1–3 cm across, with some examples measuring between 3–5 cm and rare specimens being less than 1 cm. There are sites, like Tepe Asiab, where tokens are consistently smaller than usual, with series of spheres, measuring less than 1 cm. On the other hand, sites like Tepe Yahya produced tokens larger than the norm.

The choice of material used to manufacture tokens is limited to four. As a rule, tokens are made of fine untempered clay. There are also examples made of stone, bitumen or plaster. The stone specimens are found, mostly, in north Mesopotamia and those of bitumen, which are exceedingly rare, seem restricted to the Susiana plain of Western Iran. There are occasional tokens made of plaster, for example, at Suberde in Turkey.

There can be great differences in the care given to the manufacture of tokens even among specimens from a same assemblage. Most clay tokens are modelled into a well defined shape with precise and crisp edges but others are sloppily done. The stone tokens which required far greater skills to manufacture and a time consuming polishing process usually show excellent craftsmanship.

The color of clay tokens varies from buff to black with grey, red, and pink specimens. To-

kens of the neolithic period often show a black core whereas complex tokens of the IVth millennium B.C. are buff-pink throughout their thickness. Stone tokens are often made of colorful stones such as pink, green or black marble or white alabaster.

A number of logical inferences can be drawn from the facts summarized above concerning the manufacture, function and significance of the tokens. These interpretations, in turn, give new insights into the technology, economy, cognitive skills and social organization of the cultures that used the artifacts.

THE MANUFACTURE

The fact that tokens exhibit variations in size and form indicates that they were not produced in molds but handmade. Consequently, it can be assumed that each token was separately modelled by pinching a small lump of clay between the fingers and that markings were added, individually, with a pointed instrument or stylus. Furthermore, the striking resemblance between the various assemblages of complex tokens from distant sites such as Uruk, Susa and Habuba Kabira suggests that in the IVth millennium B.C. tokens may have been mass produced in central workshops.

The various tests, such as DTA and electron microscopy establish that tokens were among the earliest clay artifacts to be subjected to fir-ing—if not the earliest. It is probable that, dur-ing the Neolithic period, tokens were baked in an open fire. This is suggested by the low tem-perature of combustion and the black core showing an incomplete firing. Moreover, the range of colors represented among the tokens probably derived from the position the artifacts occupied in the hearth during the firing process. The black and grey specimens can be explained by the reducing atmosphere prevalent in the cen-ter of an open fire, whereas the red and buff specimens could result from the oxidizing at-mosphere of the periphery. The tokens of the IVth millennium B.C., on the other hand, which were buff pink throughout their thickness, were baked, possibly, in an oven where temperature and ventilation were fully controlled.

A SYSTEM

The fact that groups of different types of tokens are found together, recurrently, either in hoards, such as those of Uruk, or enclosed in envelopes (see below), indicate that all the to-kens, including plain and complex specimens, belonged to a single system. Furthermore, be-cause tokens of the same type, manufactured in

the same way in similar sizes and bearing identi-cal markings, are recovered, without any dis-continuity, in most archaeological sites of the Middle East, there can be no doubt that the to-ken system was widely used in the region during five millennia.

Concerning the size of token assemblages, it is interesting to note that Uruk and Susa, the main centers of Mesopotamia and Elam in the IVth millennium B.C., produced an almost iden-tical number of tokens amounting to some 700 specimens. Otherwise, the number of tokens at each site is not always meaningful because it de-pends on such variables as the volume of dirt examined, the methods of excavation and luck. On the one hand, the fact that Jarmo produced 2000 tokens demonstrates that the artifacts could be plentiful in a typical Neolithic village. On the other hand, the single paraboloid de-scribed at the site of Ubaid should not be inter-preted as indicating that Ubaid used only one type of token. It merely acknowledges that only one token has been found, identified or re-ported upon at Ubaid. In fact, this particular specimen was included and illustrated in the re-port not because it was identified as a counter but only because it was misinterpreted as the part of a monumental sculpture, namely, the tongue of a lion.

Envelope from Susa, Iran, show-ing markings cor-responding to the tokens enclosed. *Musée du Louvre.*

THE PRECURSOR OF WRITING

Two pieces of evidence support the argument that tokens are the precursor of writing: chronology and the similarities between tokens and the first signs of writing. Assyriologists have established that the evolution of the cuneiform script, written on clay tablets, can be divided into three main phases:

1. IIIrd millennium B.C.: archaic script.
2. 2900–3100 B.C.: pictography.
3. ca. 3100–3150 B.C.: impressed signs.

A still earlier stage can now be added:

4. ca. 3200 B.C. impressed signs on envelopes holding tokens.

Carbon[14] dates available for Mureybet III, Tepe Asiab, Hajji Firuz, Arpachiyah, Seh Gabi, etc. . . . and the relative chronology of Uruk, indicate that the token system evolved as follows:

1. 8000–3100 B.C. Token assemblages include many shapes (page 16).
2. ca. 3400–3200 B.C. Groups of tokens are enclosed in envelopes (page 17).
3. 3100–3000 B.C. The token system dwindles.

In this perspective, the envelopes emerge as a link between tokens and writing, establishing a continuity between the two systems. Accordingly, the evolution of record keeping in the ancient Middle East can be summarized as follows:

1. 8000–3200 B.C. Accounting is performed with tokens.
2. 3200–3000 B.C. The token system and writing overlap.
3. 3100–3000 B.C. The advent of pictography which marks the true take off of writing coincides with the decline of the token system.

It should be emphasized here that the steps that led from tokens to writing cannot be precisely dated. There is no Carbon[14] date available, in particular, for the chronology of envelopes, marked envelopes and the first tablets bearing impressed signs. The artifacts are presently dated only according to the relative chronology of Uruk. This is due to the fact that the events leading from tokens to scripts occurred in rapid succession between 3400–3150 B.C. making it difficult to pinpoint exactly each stage of the sequence.

The problem is aggravated by the fact that envelopes are not found in a stratigraphic context but among trash accumulated at unknown times in antiquity. Even the envelopes of Susa recovered on the floor of buildings cannot be considered *in situ*. The artifacts were discarded, probably, by the occupants of the buildings seemingly because they were not worth saving when the rooms had to be cleared for repairs or rebuilding. The fact that we are dealing with trash is shown by the pattern of distribution of the artifacts on the floors. They were not clustered together along a wall as is the case of archives found *in situ*. Instead they were scattered randomly on large surfaces of the rooms. This also explains the heterogeneous nature of some groups of artifacts such as, for example, the jar holding one envelope together with a spindle whorl, a flint blade, a shell and pierced stone roundels.

The envelopes are also the crucial link between the shape of tokens and that of the first signs of writing. The method of storing tokens in clay envelopes where they were no longer visible, made it necessary to indicate the token contents on the surface. Consequently, the marks shown on the face of the envelopes duplicate, unambiguously, the shape of the tokens enclosed. In fact, at Habuba Kabira, the marks consisted visibly of the negative impression of the incised ovoids the envelope obtained. The complete metamorphosis of tokens into graphic signs was realized on the so-called impressed tablets when the token images were separated, definitively, from the actual tokens. Finally, when pictography was introduced the most refined incised signs featured also token prototypes, either plain or with markings. Writing thus perpetuated the repertory of symbols used for millennia for accounting with tokens.

SYMBOLS FOR ECONOMIC UNITS

Sumerian pictographs are held to be the key to cracking the code of the token system. This hypothesis is founded on the fact that signs may change form without altering their meaning. Most letters of our Latin script, for example, have preserved the value they had in the former Greek and Phoenician alphabets of 2500 and 3500 years ago. Egyptian and Chinese writing systems are other notorious examples of the preservation of symbols through the ages. Egyptian signs, for instance, can be identified at various stages of their 4000 years evolution in demotic, hieratic and hieroglyphic scripts and, in some cases, with predynastic prototypes as three dimensional amulets.[5]

Some cuneiform signs evolved from three dimensional artifacts. The sign for "sheep" for example, can be followed backwards in time through its 3000-year evolution, starting with the Assyrian cuneiform of 500 B.C. to the Sumerian pictograph of 3000 B.C. In turn, because the Sumerian pictograph is the exact rendition of a token—namely a disc with an incised cross—it seems logical to assume that the disc with an incised cross also stood for "sheep."

The symbols for *ban* and *bariga* (two measures of grain) probably equivalent to our "peck" and "bushel" may have a record longevity of about 8000 years. These signs can be traced without discontinuity in the following stages of their evolution:

1. I–IIIrd millennium B.C.: cuneiform sign.
2. III–late IVth millennium B.C.: impressed sign.
3. ca. 3200 B.C.: impressed sign on envelope cones and spheres in envelopes (page 16).
4. 3200–8000 B.C.: cones and spheres (page 17).

Unfortunately, most pictographs are presently undeciphered; so, consequently, the meaning of most tokens remains enigmatic.

It is noteworthy that all the tokens identified so far stand for units of merchandise,[6] leading to the conclusion that during its entire existence the token system was an accounting system restricted to keeping track of goods. Furthermore, the plain tokens typical of the neolithic and chalcolithic assemblages, such as spheres, cones, cylinder and lenticular disks, can be matched to the symbols of staples, such as measures of grain and number of animals. On the other hand, the complex tokens familiar in the large centers of the IVth millennium B.C. are parallel to series of signs standing for manufactured goods. Among them feature, for instance, products such as bread, oil, perfume, wool, various types of cloth and garments, rope mats, pieces of furniture, tools and a variety of stone and pottery vessels. It thus appears that mostly staples were accounted for during the Neolithic and Chalcolithic periods. On the other hand, the quantum jump in the token and subtypes which occurred in large cities such as Uruk and Susa about 3400 B.C. reflected a profound change in the economy indicating the addition of manufactured goods among the commodities accounted for in the emerging state bureaucracy.

A TOOL OF THE MIND

The tokens were counters and thus belong to the category of items considered by Jack Goody as "tools of the mind."[7] It is reasonable to assume, therefore, that the artifacts may shed light on the cognitive skills of the people who used them.

Tokens expressed plurality in a way fundamentally different from the way our 20th-century writing system expresses it. For example, when we write "3 sheep," we separate the concept of number from the concept of the item counted, showing each of these concepts by different symbols, numerals or letters. Tokens, on the other hand, expressed plurality in one-to-one correspondence.[8] The counters, in other words, were repeated as many times as the number of the items counted. "1 sheep" was shown by one token standing for "sheep"; "2 sheep" by two tokens; "3 sheep" by three tokens; and so on. Such a group of three tokens indicated, literally "sheep, sheep, sheep" instead of the modern Western usage, "3 sheep" (or "three sheep").

Tokens also expressed plurality in a way fundamentally different from a 20th-century counting device such as the abacus. Because the abacus is based on abstract numbers which can be applied to any and everything to be counted, the beads are uniform and are used to compute any possible item under the sun. The beads of the abacus can be used, for example, to count either sheep, measures of grain or jars of oil. On the other hand, the token system is characterized by counters of different shapes to count different items. Sheep were counted with disks, small and large measures of grain with cones and spheres and ovoids served to compute jars of oil. Reciprocally, jars of oil could be counted with ovoids, small and large measures of grain with cones and spheres and sheep with disks. There were no tokens standing for 1, 2, 3, etc. applicable to any possible item. Each token, in other words, fused together the concept of the number "1" and the concept of the item counted. The lack of counters to express abstract numbers is well illustrated by the groups of tokens enclosed in envelopes. At Habuba Kabira, for example, an envelope yielded eight identical ovoids in order to indicate "8 jars of oil."

The token system seems to correspond to the stage of "concrete counting" which preceded the acquisition of abstract numbers. Concrete counting is characterized by different numerations, or sets of numbers to count different categories of items. This mode of reckoning is illustrated by the Gilyaks on the River Amur, who use as many as 24 different classes of numbers. They express "two" by different numerical expressions in each of the following connotations: 2 spears "mex," 2 arrows "mik," 2 houses "meqr," 2 hands "merax," 2 boards "met," 2 boots "min," 2 sledges "mir" etc. . . .[9] The many shapes of the tokens seem particularly well suited to concrete counting. Put differently, if we had to imagine what kind of counters would best suit concrete counting, we would have to come up with a sys-

tem, similar to that of the tokens, with different counters to count different things.

The archaeological evidence is also supported by linguistics. Igor Diakonoff proposes that the many different numerical signs to express quantities, capacity, area measures etc. . . ., and the presence of at least six different numeration systems in Sumerian suggest the use of concrete counting in prehistoric Mesopotamia.[10] Starting from different sets of evidence, archaeology and linguistics arrive at the same hypothesis, namely, the existence of an archaic method of reckoning, prior to abstract counting.

THE EARLIEST PRECURSOR OF NUMERALS

Sumerian numerals—i.e., ideograms expressing number concepts—can be traced back to token prototypes. This is shown by the way numerosity is featured on the pictographic tablets of the IVth millennium B.C. With the advent of pictography, about 3100 B.C., the concepts of numerosity and of the items counted are no longer fused in a single sign. As a result, pictographs are never repeated in a one-to-one correspondence to indicate the number of units, as was the case with the signs impressed on envelopes and tablets. Instead, pictographs, such as those standing for "jar of oil" or "sheep," for example, are preceded by numerals. Furthermore, the same numerals are used to express the numerosity of all possible units of goods, showing that they stood for abstract numbers, universally applicable.

The signs indicating numerals derive from the signs for grain measures. The sign for "1" was a short wedge, identical to the sign for *ban,* a small measure of grain; the sign of "6" was a circular sign, identical to *bariga,* a large measure of grain. It appears, therefore, that the signs, while retaining their primary meaning as grain measures, acquired a secondary abstract meaning as numerals. This phenomenon of bifurcation is shown, explicitly, on particular tablets where, in the same text, the signs are used alternately to express grain measures or numerals. Tablets recording the rations allotted to workers, for example, feature the same signs to indicate the number of workers paid and the units of grain they received.[11] The same is true in the Proto Elamite system of writing.[12]

The choice of the signs for grain units to express abstract numbers can be explained by the two following reasons. First, grain being the staple of the Middle East, it was the commodity most widely exchanged. Consequently, the signs for grain measures were most familiar to accountants. Second, the multiple grain measures could be easily converted into a sequence of numerical units.

In sum, cones and spheres indicating measures of grain in the prehistoric token system led to graphic signs expressing: 1. measures of grain, and 2. numerals.

AN INSTRUMENT OF CONTROL

According to Claude Levi-Strauss, writing was invented for the exploitation of man by man.[13] The context in which tokens are found suggests that tokens were, also, a means of power in the hands of a few. The fact that the earliest tokens occur in the Fertile Crescent about 8000 B.C. (i.e., in the region and at the time when agriculture came about) leaves little doubt that the need for record keeping was related to particular aspects of human adaptation to food production. This is particularly evident at the site of Mureybet where tokens appear in level III, coinciding with the first cultivation of cereals indicated by a quantum jump in the yield of cereal pollen. Tokens, on the other hand, were not present in the earlier levels, Mureybet I and II, when the occupants of the sites relied on an economy based on hunting and gathering.

It is unlikely, however, that the mere fact of harvesting crops and tending herds brought about the need for record keeping. According to ethnographic parallels, staples accumulated in communal storage, as was probably the case in early farming communities, are redistributed among members of the community without involving any reckoning.[14] Also, herding societies do not count their flocks. They know each animal by its particular characteristics.[15] Trade, which was based on barter, probably also did not rely on accounting. It consisted in face to face transactions which, as noted by Goody, would not necessitate any record keeping.[16] It should be considered, therefore, that the primary role of the tokens may have been more than a memory aid.

The information available on record keeping in the ancient Middle East, and in particular, on the accounting devices closest to the token system in form or time, such as the Nuzi envelope or the Uruk tablets, suggest that they were used as a means of control. According to the inscription it bears, the Nuzi envelope was a legal document listing animals entrusted to a shepherd.[17] As far as we know, the pictographic tablets of Uruk kept precise records of entries and expenditures of goods in temple granaries. The seals of the various stewards demonstrate that the function of the pictographic tablets was to control the movement of goods in the temple.[18]

It is likely that the complex tokens of 3200 B.C. served the same function as the tablets that replaced them about 3100 B.C. Both of them kept records of lists of goods using related symbols; at Uruk, both tablets and tokens were recovered in the same area of the temple precinct; the seals covering envelopes and tablets were identical. It is, therefore, probable that, like pictographic tablets, complex tokens served the temple administration to control the amounts of goods delivered to the temple and their redistribution.

The notion that the tokens had a connotation of power is supported by the fact that they were deposited in the burials of prestigious individuals at Tepe Gawra. This suggests that, together with seals and maceheads, the tokens served as status symbols for the administrators who used them in daily life.

Further back in prehistory, tokens included in the infant burials of Tepe Gawra and Telles-Sawwan may suggest that, in these communities, the authority associated with handling tokens was a hereditary function. Lastly, the fact that, at Hajji Firuz, tokens were recovered in a non-residential building, indicates that, even at this early date, they were not mere household items but were handled in a particular place, probably by a particular individual.

On the basis of these interences it is presumable that the development of the token system reflects the development of authority. The emergence of tokens probably marks the transition from simple household-based political systems to village-level organization. They served as a bureaucratic tool to control the production of goods and their pooling for the benefit of the community. It was the first step towards the administrative complexity of chiefdom and the state.

Tokens and writing are considered in this paper to be two increments in the development of record keeping in the ancient Middle East. The increasing complexity of the device was due to interrelated economic, social and conceptual changes. Plain tokens merely kept track of staples; complex tokens served for the inventorying of manufactured goods; and writing fulfilled the needs of a temple economy. The three steps of evolution of the system can also be correlated to the stages of village organization, cities and the state. Finally, the tokens were suitable for an archaic method of reckoning, called concrete counting, whereas writing was based on abstract counting.

REFERENCES

UVB Vol. II & III.

Vorläufiger Bericht über die von der Deutschen Forschungsgemeinschaft in Uruk-Warka unter nommenen Ausgrabungen. Abhandlungen der Preüssichen Akademie der Wissenschaften. Phil.-hist. Klasse, Berlin.

UVB Vol. XXI & XXV.

Vorläufiger Bericht über die von dem Deutschen Archäologischen Institut und der Deutschen Orientgesellschaft aus Mitteln der Deutschen Forschungsgemeinschaft unternommenen Ausgrabungen in Uruk-Warka, Berlin.

NOTES

1. Denise Schmandt-Besserat, "The Earliest Precursor of Writing," *Scientific American,* vol. 283, no. 6, 1978, pp. 50–59.
2. Denise Schmandt-Besserat, "The Emergence of Recording," *American Anthropologist,* vol. 84, no. 4, 1982, pp. 872.
3. Denise Schmandt-Besserat, "An Archaic Recording System in the Uruk-Jemdet Nasr Period," *American Journal of Archaeology,* vol. 83, no. 1, 1979, pp. 19–48.
4. Denise Schmandt-Besserat and Liane Jacob-Rost, "Tokens from the Sanctuary of Eanna at Uruk," *Forschungen und Berichte,* (forthcoming).
5. W. A. Arnett, *The Predynastic Origin of Egyptian Hieroglyphs.* Washington, 1982, pp. 23–24.
6. Denise Schmandt-Besserat, *op. cit.,* 1979, pp. 41–49.
7. Jack Goody, *The Domestication of the Savage Mind,* Cambridge University Press, 1977.
8. Denise Schmandt-Besserat, "Before Numerals," *Visible Language,* vol. 18, no. 1, 1984, pp. 48–60.
9. Igor M. Diakonoff, "Some Reflections on Numerals in Sumerian Towards a History of Mathematical Speculations," *Journal of the American Oriental Society,* vol. 103, no. 1, 1983, p. 88.
10. Ignor M. Diakonoff, *ibid.*
11. Joran Friberg, "Numbers and Measures in the Earliest Written Records," *Scientific American,* vol. 250, no. 2, 1984, p. 111.
12. Joran Friberg, *ibid.,* p. 118.
13. Georges Charbonnier, "Entretiens avec Claude Levi-Strauss," *Les Lettres Nouvelles,* vol. 10, 1961, p. 33.
14. Kent V. Flannery, "The Origins of the Village as a Settlement Type in Mesoamerica and the Near East: A Comparative Study," in Peter J. Ucko, Ruth Tringham and G. W. Dimbleby, eds. *Man, Settlement and Urbanism.* Cambridge, Mass. 1972, p. 31.

15. E. E. Evans-Pritchard, *The Nuer*. Oxford University Press, London, 1969, p. 20.
16. Jack Goody, *op. cit.,* 1977, p. 15.
17. Tzvi Abusch, "Notes on a Pair of Matching Texts: A Shepherd's Bulla and an Owner's Receipt," in Martha A. Morrison and David I.

Owen, eds. *Studies in the Civilization and Culture of Nuzi and the Hurrians*. Eisenbrauns, Winona Lake, Indiana, 1981, pp. 1–9.
18. Erica Fiandra, "The Connection between Clay Sealings and Tablets in Administration," *South Asian Archaeology*, 1979, pp. 29–43.

3 MEDIA IN ANCIENT EMPIRES
Harold Innis

Harold Innis (1894–1952) was a Canadian scholar of world renown. He was trained in economics at the University of Chicago and, toward the close of his life, extensively explored the field of communication history. Two of his books on the subject have become classics, Empire and Communications *and* The Bias of Communication.

FROM STONE TO PAPYRUS

The profound disturbances in Egyptian civilization involved in the shift from absolute monarchy to a more democratic organization coincided with a shift in emphasis on stone as a medium of communication or as a basis of prestige, as shown in the pyramids, to an emphasis on papyrus.[1] Papyrus sheets dated from the first dynasty and inscribed sheets dated from the fifth dynasty (2680–2540 B.C. or 2750–2625 B.C.).

Papyrus Technology

In contrast with stone, papyrus as a writing medium was extremely light. It was made from a plant *(Cyperus papyrus)* that was restricted in its habitat to the Nile delta, and was manufactured into writing material near the marshes where it was found. Fresh green stems of the plant were cut into suitable lengths and the green rind stripped off. They were then cut into thick strips and laid parallel to each other and slightly overlapping on absorbent cloth. A similar layer was laid above and across them, and the whole covered by another cloth. This was hammered with a mallet for about two hours and the sheets welded into a single mass which was finally pressed and dried. Sheets were fastened to each other to make rolls, in some cases of great length. As a light commodity it could be transported over wide areas.[2]

Hieroglyphic inscription on a fragment of limestone, Egypt, Third Dynasty, 2686–2613 B.C. *Royal Ontario Museum.*

Brushes made from a kind of rush *(Funcus maritimus)* were used for writing. Lengths ranged from 6 to 16 inches and diameters from 1/16 to 1/10 of an inch. The rushes were cut slantingly at one end and bruised to separate the fibres.[3] The scribe's palette had two cups for black and red ink, and a water-pot. He wrote in hieratic characters from right to left, arranging the text in vertical columns or horizontal lines of equal size which formed pages. The rest of the papyrus was kept rolled up in his left hand.[4]

Thought Gained Lightness

Writing on stone was characterized by straightness or circularity of line, rectangularity of form, and an upright position, whereas writing on papyrus permitted cursive forms suited to rapid writing. "When hieroglyphs were chiselled on stone monuments they were very carefully formed and decorative in character. When written on wood or papyrus they became simpler and more rounded in form . . . The cursive or hieratic style was still more hastily written, slurring over or abbreviating and running together . . . they ceased to resemble pictures and became script."[5]

"By escaping from the heavy medium of stone" thought gained lightness. "All the circumstances arouse interest, observation, reflection."[6] A marked increase in writing by hand was accompanied by secularization of writing, thought, and activity. The social revolution between the Old and the New Kingdom was marked by a flow of eloquence and a displacement of religious by secular literature.

The Organization of Scribes

Writing had been restricted to governmental, fiscal, magical, and religious purposes. With the increased use of papyrus and the simplification of hieroglyphic script into hieratic characters— in response to the demands of a quicker, cursive hand and the growth of writing and reading—

administration became more efficient. Scribes and officials charged with the collection and administration of revenues, rents, and tributes from the peasants became members of an organized civil service, and prepared accounts intelligible to their colleagues and to an earthly god, their supreme master.

After 2000 B.C. the central administration employed an army of scribes, and literacy was valued as a stepping-stone to prosperity and social rank. Scribes became a restricted class and writing a privileged profession. "The scribe comes to sit among the members of the assemblies . . . no scribe fails to eat the victuals of the king's house."[7] "Put writing in your heart that you may protect yourself from hard labour of any kind and be a magistrate of high repute. The scribe is released from manual tasks."[8] "But the scribe, he directeth the work of all men. For him there are no taxes, for he payeth tribute in writing, and there are no dues for him."[9]

EFFECTS OF WRITING AND EQUALITY

New Religions

The spread of writing after the democratic revolution was accompanied by the emergence of new religions in the immortality cult of Horus and Osiris. Ra worship had become too purely political, and individuals found a final meaning and a fulfilment of life beyond the vicissitudes of the political arbitrator.[10] Osiris, the god of the Nile, became the Good Being slain for the salvation of men, the ancestral king and model for his son Horus. As an agricultural god, he had faced death and conquered it. His wife Isis, the magician, made codes of law and ruled when Osiris was conquering the world. She persuaded the Sun-god Ra to disclose his name, and since knowledge of a person's name[11] gave to him who possessed it magical power over the person himself, she acquired power over Ra and other gods. In the twelfth dynasty, Osiris became the soul of Ra, the great hidden name which resided

A detail from an Egyptian painted papyrus, known as the Papyrus of Nany. The complete illustration is 17 feet in length and 2.5 inches wide, ca. 1039–991 B.C. *The Metropolitan Museum of Art, Museum Excavations, 1928–1929 and Rogers Fund, 1930.*

in him. With Ra, he shared supremacy in religion and reflected the twofold influence of the Nile and the Sun. Night and day were joined as complementary—Osiris, yesterday and death; Ra, tomorrow and life. Funerary rites invented by Isis were first applied to Osiris. Conferring immortality, they have been described by Moret as "the most precious revelation which any Egyptian god had ever made to the world."[12]

Magic and Writing

Osiris was served by Thoth as vizier, sacred scribe, and administrator. As the inventory of speech and writing, "Lord of the creative voice, master of words and books,"[13] he became the inventor of magic writings. Osiris became the centre of a popular and priestly literature to instruct people in the divine rights and duties. Words were imbued with power. The names of gods were part of the essence of being, and the influence of the scribe was reflected in the deities. Since religion and magic alike were sacred, they became independent. The priest used prayers and offerings to the gods, whereas the magician circumvented them by force or trickery. Family worship survived in the Osirian cult, and because of a practical interest, magic was used by the people. Since to know the name of a being was to have the means of mastering him; to pronounce the name was to fashion the spiritual image by the voice; and to write it, especially with hieroglyphics, was to draw a material image. In the manifold activity of the creative word, magic permeated metaphysics. Polytheism persisted, and names were among the spiritual manifestations of the gods. Magical literature and popular tales preserved the traditions of the great gods of the universe.

Redistribution of Power

The king gained from the revolution as the incarnation of the king gods: Falcon; Horus-Seth; Ra; Ra-Harakhti; Osiris; Horus, son of Isis; and Amon-Ra, who ruled Egypt. The king's devotion created a great wave of faith among the people. Ritual enabled him to appoint a proxy to act as prophet. Power was delegated to professional priests, who first incarnated themselves in the king and performed the ceremonies in every temple every day. The worship of Ra and the celestial gods was confined to priests and temples. The priests of Atum condensed revelation in the rituals of divine worship, and a cult supplied the needs of living images in statues in the temple.

EFFECTS OF CHANGE

Invasion

The shift from dependence on stone to dependence on papyrus and the changes in political and religious institutions imposed an enormous strain on Egyptian civilization. Egypt quickly succumbed to invasion from peoples equipped with new instruments of attack. Invaders with the sword and the bow and long-range weapons broke through Egyptian defence which was dependent on the battle-axe and dagger. With the use of bronze and, possibly, iron weapons, horses, and chariots, Syrian Semitic peoples under the Hyksos or Shepherd kings captured and held Egypt from 1660 to 1580 B.C.

Cultural Resistance

Egyptian cultural elements resisted alien encroachments and facilitated reorganization and the launching of a counterattack. The conquerors adopted hieroglyphic writing and Egyptian customs, but the complexity of these enabled the Egyptians to resist and expel the invaders. They probably acquired horses[14] and light four-spoked chariots from the Libyans to the west, and after 1580 B.C. the Nile valley was liberated. In a great victory at Megiddo in 1478 B.C.,[15] Thutmose III gave a final blow to Hyksos' power. Under rulers of the eighteenth dynasty (1580–1345 B.C.), the New Theban Kingdom was established.

Priests, Property, and Power

In the New Kingdom, the Pharaohs at Thebes (the capital and metropolis of the civilized east) had resumed their sovereign rights, taken possession of the goods of the temples, and brought clerical vassalage to an end. Monarchical centralization was accompanied by religious centralization. The gods were "solarized," and Amon, the God of the Theban family, reigned over all the gods of Egypt as Amon-Ra after

1600 B.C. As a result of the success of war in imperial expansion, the priests became securely established in territorial property and assumed increasing influence. Problems of dynastic right in the royal family gave them additional power.

Magic and Medicine

The use of papyrus rapidly increased after the expulsion of the Hyksos. The cult of Thoth had played an important role in the New Kingdom and in the expulsion of the Hyksos. Thoth became the god of magic. His epithets had great power and strength, and certain formulae were regarded as potent in the resistance to, or in the expulsion of, malicious spirits. To about 2200 B.C., medicine and surgery had advanced, since mummification had familiarized the popular mind with dissection of the human body, and had overcome an almost universal prejudice. But after the Hyksos invasion, medicine became a matter of rites and formulae[16] and opened the way to Greek physicians and anatomists in Alexandria. . . .

THE CITY-STATES OF SUMER

In Egypt, ability to measure time and to predict the dates of floods of the Nile became the basis of power. In the Tigris and Euphrates valleys in southern Mesopotamia, the rivers[17] were adapted to irrigation and organized control, and less exacting demands were made on the capacity to predict time. Sumer was a land of small city-states in which the chief priest of the temple was the direct representative of the god. The god of the city was king, and the human ruler was a tenant farmer with the position and powers of a civil governor.

It has been suggested that writing was invented in Sumer to keep tallies and to make lists and, hence, was an outgrowth of mathematics. The earliest clay tablets include large numbers of legal contracts, deeds of sale, and land transfers, and reflect a secular and utilitarian interest.

Old Babylonian period cylinder seal and its impression. *Royal Ontario Museum.*

Lists, inventories, records, and accounts of temples and small city-states suggest the concerns of the god as capitalist, landlord, and bank. Increased revenues necessitated complex systems of accounting and writing intelligible to colleagues and successors. Temple offices became continuing and permanent corporations. Growth of temple organizations and increase in land ownership were accompanied by accumulation of resources and differentiation of functions. Specialization and increased wealth brought rivalry and conflict.

CLAY AND CUNEIFORM

Alluvial clay found in Babylonia and Assyria was used for the making of brick and as a medium in writing. Modern discoveries of large numbers of records facilitate a description of important characteristics of Sumerian and later civilizations, but they may reflect a bias incidental to the character of the material used for communication. On the other hand, such a bias points to salient features in the civilization.

In preparation for writing, fine clay was well kneaded and made into biscuits or tablets. Since moist clay was necessary and since the tablet dried quickly, it was important to write with speed and accuracy.[18] Pictographs of fine lines made by an almost knife-sharp reed were probably followed by linear writing such as might be easily cut on stone records. But the making of straight lines tended to pull up the clay, and a cylindrical reed stylus was stamped perpendicularly or obliquely on the tablet. A triangular stylus of about the size of a small pencil with four flat sides and one bevelled end was introduced, probably in the second half of the third millennium. It was laid on a sharp edge, and if the tip was pressed deeply, a true wedge or cuneiform appeared on the tablet. If the stylus was pressed lightly, a large number of short strokes was necessary to make a single sign.

Economy of effort demanded a reduction in the number of strokes, and the remnants of pictorial writing disappeared. As a medium, clay demanded a shift from the pictograph to formal patterns. "The gap between picture and word is bridged."[19] Cuneiform writing was characterized by triangles and the massing of parallel lines. The complexity of a group of wedges of different sizes and thicknesses, and an increase in the size of the tablets, which changed the angle at which they were held in the writer's hand, hastened the tendency towards conventionalization. A change in the direction of the angle[20] meant a change in the direction of the strokes or wedges and hastened the transition from pictographs to signs.[21] Conventionalization of pictographs began with signs most frequently used and advanced rapidly with the replacement of strokes by wedges. Pictographic expression became inadequate for the writing of connected religious or historical texts, and many signs were taken to represent syllables.

By 2900 B.C. the form of the script and the use of signs had been fully developed, and by 2825 B.C. the direction of writing and the arrangement of words according to their logical position in the sentence had been established. Signs were arranged in compartments on large tablets. The writing ran from left to right, and the lines followed horizontally. Cylinders could be rolled on wet clay to give a continuous impression, and cylinder seals of hard stone were introduced. Engraved with various designs, they served as personal symbols and were used as marks of identification of ownership in a community in which large numbers were unable to read and write. Seals were carried around the neck and served to stamp signatures on contracts concerning property and ownership.

Concrete pictographs involved an elaborate vocabulary with large numbers of items. To show modifications of the original meaning, signs were added to the pictures. As many as 2,000 signs were used. By 2900 B.C. the introduction of syllabic signs in a vocabulary which was largely monosyllabic had reduced the number of signs to about 600. Of these signs, about 100 represented vowels, but no system was devised for representing single consonantal sounds or creating an alphabet. Cuneiform writing was partly syllabic and partly ideographic, or representative of single words. Many of the signs were polyphonic or had more than one meaning. Sumerian had no distinctions of gender and often omitted those of number, persons, and tenses. An idea had not fully developed to the symbol of a word or syllable. Pictographs and ideograms took on abstract phonetic values, and the study of script became linked to the study of language.

Sun-dried tablets could be altered easily; this danger was overcome by baking in fire. Indestructibility assured inviolability for commercial and personal correspondence. Though admirably adapted by its durability to use over a long period of time, clay as a heavy material was less suited as a medium of communication over large areas. Its general character favoured the collection of permanent records in widely scattered communities.

CLAY AND SOCIAL ORGANIZATION

Religious Power

Adaptability to communication over long distances emphasized uniformity in writing and the development of an established and authorized canon of signs. Extensive commercial activity required a large number of professional scribes or those who could read and write. In turn, the difficulties of writing a complex language implied a long period of training and the development of schools. Temple accounts and sign lists with the names of priests inventing the signs were made into school texts. In order to train scribes and administrators, schools and centres of learning were built up in connection with temples, and special emphasis was given to grammar and mathematics.

Since the art of writing as the basis of education was controlled by priests, scribes, teachers, and judges, the religious point of view in general knowledge and in legal decisions was assumed. Scribes kept the voluminous accounts of the temples and recorded the details of regulations in priestly courts. Practically every act of civil life was a matter of law which was recorded and confirmed by the seals of contracting parties and witnesses. In each city, decisions of the courts became the basis of civil law. The growth of temples and extension in power of the cult enhanced the power and authority of priests. The characteristics of clay favoured the conventionalization of writing, decentralization of cities, the growth of continuing organization in the temples, and religious control. Abstraction was furthered by the necessity of keeping accounts and the use of mathematics, particularly in trade between communities.

Clay tablet and
envelope, later
Persian period.
*Royal Ontario
Museum.*

The accumulation of wealth and power in the hands of the priests and the temple organization, which accompanied the development of mathematics and writing, was probably followed by ruthless warfare between city-states and the emergence of military specialization and mercenary service. It has been suggested that the control of religion over writing and education entailed a neglect of technological change and military strength. Temple government or committees of priests were unable to direct organized warfare, and temporal potentates appeared beside the priest. The latter enjoyed a prerogative and led the prince into the presence of the deity.

NOTES

1. In particular heavy emphasis on papyrus as a basis of feudalism in contrast with alphabet and bureaucray of Roman Empire.
2. Napthali Lewis, *L'industrie du papyrus dans L'Egypte Gréco-Romain* (Paris, 1834), p. 117. See F. G. Kenyon, *Ancient Books and Modern Discoveries* (Chicago, 1927).
3. Alfred Lucas, *Ancient Egyptian Materials and Industries* (London, 1934), pp. 133 *ff.*
4. Alexander Moret, *The Nile and Egyptian Civilization* (London, 1927), p. 457 n.
5. Lynn Thorndike, *A Short History of Civilization* (New York, 1927), pp. 37–8.
6. Moret, *The Nile and Egyptian Civilization,* p. 457.

   > *Till to astonish'd realms PAPYRA taught*
   > *To paint in mystic colours Sound and Thought.*
   > *With Wisdom's voice to print the page sublime.*
   > *And mark in adamant the steps of Time.*
   > (Erasmus Darwin, The Loves of the Plants, 1789.)

7. Cited Moret, *The Nile and Egyptian Civilization,* p. 270.
8. Cited V. Gordon Childe, *Man Makes Himself* (London, 1936), p. 211.
9. Cited V. Eric Peet, *A Comparative Study of the Literature of Egypt, Palestine, and Mesopotamia* (London, 1931), pp. 105–6.
10. Reinhold Niebuhr, *The Children of Light and the Children of Darkness* (New York, 1945), p. 80.
11. Cassirer had described language and myth as in original and indissoluble correlation with one another and as emerging as independent elements. Mythology reflected the power exercised by language on thought. The word became a pri-

mary force in which all being and doing originate. Verbal structures appeared as mythical entities endowed with mythical powers. The word in language revealed to man that world that was closer to him than any world of material objects. Mind passed from a belief in the physio-magical power comprised in the word to a realization of its spiritual power. Through language the concept of the deity received its first concrete development. The cult of mysticism grappled with the task of comprehending the Divine in its totality and highest inward reality, and yet avoided any name or sign. It was directed to the world of silence beyond language. But the spiritual depth and power of language was shown in the fact that speech itself prepared the way for the last step by which it was transcended. The demand for unity of the Deity took its stand on the linguistic expression of Being, and found its surest support in the word. The Divine excluded from itself all particular attributes and could be predicated only of itself.

12. Moret, *The Nile and Egyptian Civilization,* p. 383.
13. Ibid., p. 403.
14. Sir William Ridgeway, *The Origin and Influence of the Thoroughbred Horse* (Cambridge, 1903). On the significance of the Hyksos invasion in introducing the horse and chariot, see H. E. Wenlock, *The Rise and Fall of the Middle Kingdom in Thebes* (New York, 1947), ch. 8.
15. h 1479 (?) Breasted.
16. See Herman Ranke, "Medicine and Surgery in Ancient Egypt," *Studies in the History of Science* (Philadelphia, 1941), pp. 31–42.
17. Flooding irregular and incalculable.
18. Administrators wrote on ledgers all at one time.
19. *Studies in the History of Science* (Philadelphia, 1941).
20. Angle changed 90 degrees and perpendicular columns turned so that characters on their sides and scribe reading left to right—shift from space to time arrangement.
21. S. H. Hooke, "The Early History of Writing" (*Antiquity,* XI, 1937, p. 275).

4 CIVILIZATION WITHOUT WRITING— THE INCAS AND THE QUIPU

Marcia Ascher and Robert Ascher

Marcia Ascher is a mathematician and Robert Ascher is an anthropologist with an interest in how a major New World culture, the Incas, developed "civilization" without writing— using the quipu described in the excerpt to follow. Their book, Mathematics of the Incas: Code of the Quipu, *should be of interest to all students of communication media.*

A quipu is a collection of cords with knots tied in them. The cords were usually made of cotton, and they were often dyed one or more colors. When held in the hands, a quipu is unimpressive; surely, in our culture, it might be mistaken for a tangled old mop [see photo on opposite page]. For the Spanish, the Inca quipu was the equivalent of the Western airplane for native Australians.

In earlier times, when the Incas moved in upon an area, a census was taken and the results were put on quipus. The output of gold mines, the composition of work forces, the amount and kinds of tribute, the contents of storehouses— down to the last sandal—were all recorded on quipus. At the time of the transfer of power from one Sapa Inca to the next, information stored on quipus was called upon to recount the accomplishments of the new leader's predecessors. Quipus probably predate the coming to power of the Incas. But under the Incas, they became a part of state-craft. Cieza, who attributed much to the action of kings, concluded his chapter on quipus this way: "Their orderly system in Peru is the work of the Lord-Incas who rule it and in every way brought it so high, as those of us here see from this and other greater things. With this, let us proceed."

There are several extremely important properties of quipus. . . . First of all, *quipus can be assigned horizontal direction.* When seeing a film, there usually are credits at one end and the word END at the other. Even if the meaning of these were not understood, they could still be used when faced with a jumble of film strips. With them, all the film strips could be oriented in the same direction. All viewing and analysis would be based on the same running direction. Therefore, terms like *before* and *after* could be applied. Similarly, a main cord has direction. Quipumakers knew which end was which; we will assume that they start at the looped ends and proceed to the knotted ends. *Quipus also can be assigned vertical direction.* Pendant cords and top cords are vertically opposite to each other with pendant cords considered to go downward and top cords upward. Terms like *above* and *below,* therefore, also become applicable. Quipus *have levels.* Cords attached to the main cord are on one level; their subsidiaries form a second level. Subsidiaries to these subsidiaries form a third level, and so on. Quipus are made up of cords and spaces between cords. Cords can easily be moved until the last step in their attachment when they are fixed into position. Therefore, larger or smaller spaces between cords are an intentional part of the overall construction.

The importance of these properties is that cords can be associated with different meanings depending on their vertical direction, on their level, on their relative positions along the main cord, and, if they are subsidiaries, on their rela-

An example of the Quipu, the early communication medium used by the ancient Incan empire throughout the Andean region of the South America. *The Peabody Museum of Archeology and Ethnology, Harvard University. Reprinted by permission of the authors.*

tive positions within the same level. And, just as one suspects having missed the beginning of a film when walking in on action rather than credits, quipu readers can doubt a specimen complete if the main cord doesn't have both a looped and a knotted end and can surmise that suspended cords are incomplete if they lack knotted tapered ends.

As well as having a particular placement, each cord has a color. Color is fundamental to the symbolic system of the quipu. Color coding, that is, using colors, to represent something other than themselves, is a familiar idea. But color systems are used in different ways.

The colors red and green used in traffic signals have a universal meaning in Western culture. It is generally understood that red is stop

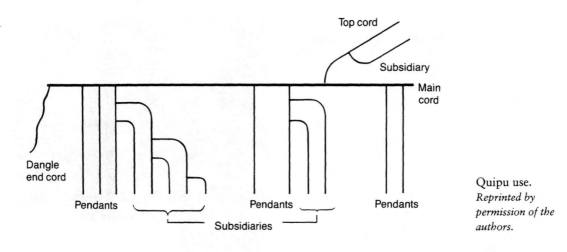

Quipu use.
Reprinted by permission of the authors.

and green is go. Moreover, this common understanding is incorporated into the traffic regulations of Western governments. The color system is simple and specific, and certainly no driver is free to assign his or her own meanings to these colors.

Several more elaborate color systems are used elsewhere in Western culture, for example in the electronics field. The color system for resistors, espoused by the International Electrotechnical Commission, has been adopted as standard practice in many countries. Resistors are ubiquitous in electrical equipment because the amount of electrical current in different parts of the circuitry can be regulated by their placement. In this international system, four bands of color appear on each resistor. Each of twelve colors is associated with a specific numerical value and each of the bands is associated with a particular meaning. The first two bands are read as digits (for example, violet = 7 and white = 9 so /violet/white/ = 79); the next band tells how many times to multiply by 10 (for example, red = 2) so /violet/white/red = 79 × 10 × 10); and the last describes the accuracy (for example, silver = 10 percent, so /violet/white/red/ silver = 7,900 ohms plus or minus 10 percent). By combining meanings for colors with meanings for the positions, the information that can be represented has been greatly increased.

Clearly, lettered signs for traffic messages and printed words on resistors would be less effective than colors. In the case of traffic messages, visibility from a distance and eliciting a rapid response are the important criteria. Locating and reading letters small enough to fit on a resistor when these components are intermingled with others in compact spaces would be difficult. Directing one's fingers to the right component is what is important, and with color coding this can be more readily done. As useful as they are, these systems are inflexible. Some group, not the individual users, defines the system and, therefore, sets its limits.

Consider another form of representation, the use of letters in physics formulas:

$$V=\frac{RT}{P}; \qquad V=IR; \qquad V=\frac{ds}{dt}.$$

In these formulas, the letter V is shorthand for volume, or voltage, or velocity because the formulas come from three different contexts within physics. Their contexts are a discussion of gases, electricity, and motion respectively. What V stands for or what each formula means, of course, depends on a knowledge of context. We are, however, free to change the shorthand. In the first formula, which represents Boyle's Law, instead of V, T, P, R, we could use, say a = volume,

b = temperature, c = pressure, and d = universal gas constant. But, because of the behavior of gases, we are not free to change the relationship between a, b, c, d to, say,

$$a = \frac{dc}{b}.$$

So, too, a color system increases in complexity as the number of contexts it describes increase and as statements of relationship become involved.

In the context of the traffic and resistor color systems, there is *an* answer to the question, What does red mean? But V has no fixed meaning in physics and red is associated with no specific lobsterman in Maine. However, in their local context, be it a discussion of gases or a particular port, and in association with other letters or colors, the meaning is sufficiently clear. The quipu color system, like the latter systems, is rich and flexible and of the type for which there is no one answer to such questions. Basically, the quipumaker designed each quipu using color coding to relate some cords together and to distinguish them from other cords. The number of colors on a particular quipu depends on the number of distinctions that are being made. The overall patterning of the colors exhibits the relationships that are being represented. The color coding of cords that are compactly connected together and likely to become intertwined, shares with the resistor color system the function of uniting the visual with the tactile. Also, recall that quipu cords can be on different levels, have different directions, and have relative positions. Another feature shared with the resistor color system is that meanings for color and meanings for positions are used in combination with each other.

Yarns dyed different colors were available to the quipumaker. Additional cord colors were created by spinning the colored yarns together. Two solid colors twisted together gives a candy cane effect, two of these twisted together using the opposite twist direction gives a mottled effect, and the two solid colors can be joined so that part of the cord is one color and the rest of it is another color. And the cord colors thus created can then be spun together creating new cord colors. With just three yarn colors, say red, yellow, and blue, and the three operations of candy striping, mottling, and joining, consider the distinctly different cord colors that are possible. There is red alone, yellow alone, blue alone; red and yellow striped, red and blue striped, yellow and blue striped; red and yellow mottled, red and blue mottled, yellow and blue mottled; red above yellow, yellow above red, red above blue, blue above red, yellow above blue, and blue above yellow. Selecting from these fifteen and using the same operations on them, there are many more.

In some cases, the quipumaker extended the subtlety of the color coding by having a two-color combination on one cord retain the significance of both colors rather than taking on a significance of its own. In these cases, a cord made of one color yarn had a small portion striped or mottled with a second color. Thus the overall cord color had one significance while the inserted color had another significance.

For the most part, cords had knots tied along them and the knots represented numbers. But we are certain that before knots were tied in the cords, the entire blank quipu was prepared. The overall planning and construction of the quipu was done first, including the types of cord connections, the relative placement of cords, the selection of cord colors, and even individual decorative finishings. In a few cases, quipus were found in groups mingled with other cords. Some of these quipu groups contain quipus in different stages of preparation from bundles of prepared blank quipu cords, to completely constructed blank quipus, to completely constructed quipus with some or all cords knotted. Cords with knots tied in them are only found detached when they are evidently broken.

What particular abilities did a person need to be a quipumaker? What was his position in the Inca bureaucracy? In what ways did one quipumaker differ from another? And what did the quipumaker have to know? These are interesting questions, and they are going to be answered. The route to the answers will often appear to be a thin line of scant information, or a dotted line—information with many gaps—or a broken line as when, for example, information from another culture is introduced. At the end, all questions having been answered, there will emerge a still too darkly shaded picture of the quipumaker.

His material—colored strings of cotton and sometimes wool—will give us some notion of the abilities the quipumaker needed. They become apparent when we contrast his material with those of his counterparts in other civilizations.

Many different substances have been used for recording. Stone, animal skin, clay, silk, and various parts of plants including slips of wood, bark, leaves, and pulp are some of them. The material used for a medium in a civilization is often derived from a substance that is common and abundant in its environment. (The simultaneous use of several mediums in one area is a recent development. Even if two were used, one tended to dominate the other and gradually replaced it.) Each kind of material calls forth a somewhat different set of abilities. For contrast with the quipumaker's cotton and wool, we choose to detail the clay of the Sumerian scribe and the papyrus of the Egyptian record keeper.

The Sumerian scribe lived in the southern part of what today is called Iraq, between, say 2700 and 1700 B.C.E. The clay he used came from the banks of rivers. He kneaded it into a tablet that varied in size from a postage stamp to a pillow. (For special purposes, the clay was shaped into a tag, a prism, or a barrel.) Pulling a piece of thread across the clay, he made rulings on the tablet. He was then prepared to record. This he did with a stylus, a piece of reed about the size of a small pencil shaped at one end so that it made wedgelike impressions in the soft, damp clay. If he lived toward the early part of the thousand-year time interval, he made impressions vertically, from top to bottom. Later on, they were made from left to right across the tablet. Having finished one side, he turned the tablet over by bringing the lower edge to the top, continuing the record on the observe side. He had to work fast: the clay dried out and hardened quickly; when that happened, erasures, additions, and other changes were no longer possible. If he ran short of space on the tablet, or if the tablet dried out before he was done, he started a second one. When he was finished recording, the tablet or tablets were dried in the sun or baked in a kiln, permanently fixing the impressions. . . .

In Egypt, at about the same time, the scribe used papyrus. Its source was the interior of the stem of a tall sedge that flourished in swampy depressions. Fresh stems were cut, the rinds were removed, and the soft interiors were laid out and beaten until they were formed into sheets. The natural gum of the pith was the adhesive. A papyrus sheet was about six inches wide and nine inches high. It was white or faintly colored, the surface was shiny and smooth, and it was flexible. Dry sheets could be joined with a prepared adhesive; twenty of them, for example, made a surface six feet long. The Egyptian scribe used brush and ink. To make a brush, he cut a rush about one foot in length; then, he cut one end at an angle and bruised it to separate the fibers. His inks were actually small cakes resembling modern water colors and they were used in much the same way. Black cakes were made with soot scraped from cooking vessels; red cakes, from ocher. Moving from right to left, the Egyptian scribe brushed his record onto the papyrus.

An obvious contrast between the quipumaker and his Sumerian and Egyptian counterparts is that the former used no instruments to record. The quipumaker composed his recording by tracing fingers in space as when, for example, he turned a string in an ever changing direction in the process of tying a knot. All of this was not preparatory to making a record; it was part of the very process of recording. The stylus and the brush were held in the hand, their use had to be learned, and the learning involved a sense of touch. But the quipumaker's way of recording—direct construction—required tactile sensitivity to a much greater degree. In fact, the overall aesthetic of the quipu is related to the tactile: the manner of recording and the recording itself are decidedly rhythmic; the first in the activity, the second in the effect. We seldom realize the potential of our sense of touch, and we are usually unaware of its association with rhythm. Yet anyone familiar with the activity of caressing will immediately see the connection between touch and rhythm. In fact, tactile sensitivity begins in the rhythmic pulsating environment of the unborn child far in advance of the development of other senses.

Color is another point of contrast: the Sumerian used none, the Egyptians two (black and red), and the quipumakers used hundreds. All three needed keen vision; the quipumaker alone had to recognize and recall color differences and use them to his advantage. His color vocabulary was large; it was not simply red, green, white, and so on, but various reds, greens, and whites. Drawing upon this color vocabulary, his task was to choose, combine, and arrange colors in varied patterns to express the relationships in whatever it was that he was recording. Confronted with a quipu, it is not easy to grasp immediately, if at all, the complex use of colors. The quipumaker, and the people of the Andean world who were a part of his everyday experience, understood complex color usage because they were accustomed to it in the textiles they saw, just as we comprehend polyphonic music because we hear it often enough. This appeal to musical imagery comes from an art historian; others in our culture have also turned to musical composition to translate their understanding of Andean color composition. At the base of their musical imagery is the formal patterning and structure which can also be translated into mathematical language.

The third contrast is perhaps the most important. Both the Sumerian and the Egyptian recorded on planar surfaces. In this regard, papyrus had certain advantages over clay. For example, sheets could be added or deleted, thus changing the dimensions of the surface; the dimensions of the clay surface were fixed once the tablet was formed. By contrast to both papyrus and clay, the quipumaker's strings present no surface at all. Recording in papyrus or clay involved filling the space in a more or less continuous process either up or down, or from right to left, or from left to right. This is linear composition. By contrast, the quipumaker's recording was nonlinear. The nonlinearity is a consequence of the soft material he used. A group of strings occupy a space that has no definite orientation; as the quipumaker connected strings to each other, the space became defined by the points where the strings were attached. The establishment of these points did not have to follow any set left-to-right or right-to-left sequence. The relative positions of the strings are set by their points of attachment, and it is the relative position, along with the colors and the knots, that renders the recording meaningful. Essentially then, the quipumaker had to have the ability to conceive and execute a recording in three dimensions with color.

The quipumaker fits somewhere in the bureaucracy that developed in the Inca state: the question is, Where? In theory, his position was one of privilege. As for the facts in the case, the one good piece of evidence that exists supports what one would expect from theory.

Hand in hand with massive construction, standing armies, and all the other attributes of the state, there is always a bureaucracy to administer its affairs. And bureaucratic administration, in the words of Max Weber "... means fundamentally the exercise of control on the basis of knowledge." The knowledge is stored in records. These, together with people who have "official functions," form the "office" that carries on the state's affairs. The bureaucracy keeps records of everything that can be recorded, but especially things that are quantifiable: the number of people living at a certain place, the tribute that was collected in a village, the day the river flooded. The bureaucracy believes in its rationality; its records give assurance to those who wield power. The more records there are, and the more the bureaucracy has experience with them, the more power to the state. A bureaucracy's records are peculiar to itself, and bureaucrats try very hard to keep it that way.

In the Inca state, the quipumaker composed the records for the bureaucracy. He might know, for example, how many men in a group of villages were suitable for army service, how many could work in the mines, and much else of interest. He worked with privileged information, so he was privileged. We expect that he was more important than an ordinary man, yet he was not as important as the really important men who held authority in the community where he lived, or the Incas who watched over them.

5 THE ORIGINS OF WRITING
Andrew Robinson

Andrew Robinson is a King's Scholar at Eton College and Literary Editor of The Times Higher Education Supplement. His books include, The Shape of the World: The Mapping and Discovery of the Earth *and* The Story of Writing, *from which the present excerpt is taken.*

Writing is among the greatest inventions in human history, perhaps *the* greatest invention, since it made history possible. Yet it is a skill most writers take for granted. We learn it at school, building on the alphabet, or (if we live in China or Japan) the Chinese characters. As adults we seldom stop to think about the mental-cum-physical process that turns our thoughts into symbols on a piece of paper or on a video screen, or bytes of information in a computer disc. Few of us have any clear recollection of how we learnt to write.

A page of text in a foreign script, totally incomprehensible to us, reminds us forcibly of the nature of our achievement. An extinct script, such as Egyptian hieroglyphs or cuneiform from the ancient Near East, strikes us as little short of miraculous. By what means did these pioneering writers of 4000–5000 years ago learn to write? How did their symbols encode their speech and

thought? How do we decipher (or attempt to decipher) the symbols after centuries of silence? Do today's writing systems work in a completely different way from the ancient scripts? What about the Chinese and Japanese scripts—are they like ancient hieroglyphs? Do hieroglyphs have any advantages over alphabets? Finally, what kind of people were the early writers—and what kind of information, ideas and feelings did they make permanent?

THE FUNCTION OF WRITING

Writing and literacy are generally seen as forces for good. It hardly needs saying that a person who can read and write has greater opportunities for fulfilment than one who is illiterate. But there is also a dark side to the spread of writing that is present throughout its history, if somewhat less obvious. Writing has been used to tell lies as well as truth, to bamboozle and exploit as well as to educate, to make minds lazy as well as to stretch them.

Socrates pinpointed our ambivalence towards writing in his story of the Egyptian god Thoth, the inventor of writing, who came to see the king seeking royal blessing on his enlightening invention. The king told Thoth: "You, who are the father of letters, have been led by your affection to ascribe to them a power the opposite of that which they really possess ... You have invented an elixir not of memory, but of reminding; and you offer your pupils the appearance of wisdom, not true wisdom, for they will read many things without instruction and will therefore seem to know many things, when they are for the most part ignorant." In a late 20th-century world drenched with written information and surrounded by information technologies of astonishing speed, convenience and power, these words spoken in antiquity have a distinctly contemporary ring.

Political leaders have always used writing for propaganda purposes. Nearly 4000 years and a totally different script separate the famous black basalt law code of Hammurabi of Babylon from the slogans and billboards of 1990s Iraq—but the message is similar. Hammurabi called himself "mighty King, King of Babylon, King of the whole country of Amurru, King of Sumer and Akkad, King of the Four Quarters of the World"; and he promised that if his laws were obeyed, then all his people would benefit. "Writing," wrote H. G. Wells in his *Short History of the World,* "put agreements, laws, commandments on record. It made the growth of states larger than the old city states possible. The command of the priest or king and his seal could go far beyond his sight and voice and could survive his death."

Yes, regrettably, Babylonian and Assyrian cuneiform, Egyptian hieroglyphs and the Mayan glyphs of Central America, carved on palace and temple walls, were used much as

Stalin used posters about Lenin in the Soviet Union: to remind the people who was the boss, how great were his triumphs, how firmly based in the most high was his authority. At Karnak, in Egypt, on the outer wall of a temple, there are carved representations of the battle at Kadesh fought by Ramesses II against the Hittites, around 1285 BC. Hieroglyphs recount a peace treaty between the pharaoh and the Hittite king, and celebrate a great Egyptian victory. But another version of the same treaty found at the Hittite capital Boghazköy turns the battle into a win for the Hittites!

The urge for immortality has always been of the first importance to writers. Most of the thousands of known fragments written by the Etruscans, for instance, are funerary inscriptions. We can read the name, date and place of death because they are written in an adaptation of the Greek alphabet; but that is about all we know of the enigmatic language of this important people, who borrowed the alphabet from Greece, handed it on to the Romans, who in turn gave it to the rest of Europe. Decipherment of the Etruscan language is like trying to learn English by reading nothing but gravestones.

Another purpose for writing was to predict the future. All ancient societies were obsessed with what was to come. Writing allowed them to codify their worries. Among the Maya it took the form of bark-paper books elaborately painted in colour and bound in jaguar skin; the prognostications were based on a written calendrical system so sophisticated it extended as far back as 5 billion years ago, more than our present scientifically estimated age for the earth. In China, on the other hand, during the Bronze Age Shang dynasty, questions about the future were written on turtle shells and ox bones, so-called "oracle bones." The bone was heated with a brand until it cracked, the meaning of the shape of the crack was divined, and the answer to the question was inscribed. Later, what actually transpired might be added to the bone.

But of course most writing was comparatively mundane. It provided, for instance, the equivalent of an ancient identity card or a property marker. The cartouche enclosing the name of Tutankhamun was found on objects throughout his tomb, from the grandest of thrones to the smallest of boxes. Anyone who was anyone among ancient rulers required a personal seal for signing clay tablets and other inscriptions. So did any merchant or other person of substance. (Today in Japan, a seal, rather than a western-style signature, is standard practice for signing business and legal documents.) Such name-tagging has been found as far apart as Mesopotamia, China and Central America. The stone seals from the Indus Valley civilization, which flourished around 2000 BC, are especially interesting: not only are they exquisitely carved—depicting, among other motifs, a mysterious unicorn—the symbols written on them are undeciphered. Unlike the script of Babylonia, the Indus Valley writing does not appear on walls as public inscriptions. Instead the seals have been found scattered around the houses and streets of the "capital" city. They were probably worn on a cord or thong and used as a personal "signature" or to indicate a person's office or the social or professional group to which he or she belonged.

Writing used for accountancy was much commoner than that on seals and tags. The earliest writing of all, on Sumerian clay tablets from Mesopotamia, concerns lists of raw materials and products, such as barley and beer, lists of labourers and their tasks, lists of field areas and their owners, the income and outgoings of temples, and so forth—all with calculations concerning production levels, delivery dates, locations and debts. And the same is true, generally speaking, of the earliest deciphered European writing, tablets from pre-Homeric Greece and Crete written in Linear B script. The tablet that clinched the decipherment of Linear B in 1953 was simply an inventory of tripod cauldrons (one of them with its legs burnt off), and of goblets of varying sizes and numbers of handles.

THE ORIGIN(S) OF WRITING

Most scholars now accept that writing began with accountancy, even though accountancy is little in evidence in the surviving writing of ancient Egypt, China and Central America. To quote an expert on early Sumerian tablets, writing developed "as a direct consequence of the compelling demands of an expanding economy". In other words, some time in the late 4th millennium BC, the complexity of trade and administration in the early cities of Mesopotamia reached a point at which it outstripped the power of memory of the governing élite. To record transactions in a dependable, permanent form became essential. Administrators and merchants could then say the Sumerian equivalents of "I shall put it in writing" and "Can I have this in writing?"

But this does not explain how writing actually emerged out of no-writing. Divine origin, in favour until the Enlightenment in the 18th century, has given way to the theory of a pictographic origin. The first written symbols are generally thought to have been pictograms, pictorial representations of concrete objects. Some scholars believe that writing was the result of a conscious search by an unknown Sumerian individual in the city of Uruk (biblical Erech), in about 3300 BC. Others believe it was the work of a group, presumably of clever administrators and merchants. Still others think it was not an invention at all, but an accidental discovery. Many regard it as the result of evolution over a long period, rather than a flash of inspiration. One particularly well-aired theory holds that writing grew out of a long-standing counting system of clay "tokens" (such "tokens," exact purpose unknown, have been found in many Middle Eastern archaeological sites): the substitution of two-dimensional signs for these tokens, with the signs resembling the shapes of the tokens, was a first step towards writing, according to this theory.

In any case, essential to the development of full writing, as opposed to the limited, purely pictographic writing of North American Indians and others, was the discovery of the rebus principle. This was the radical idea that a pictographic symbol could be used for its phonetic value. Thus a drawing of an owl in Egyptian hieroglyphs could represent a consonantal sound with an inherent *m;* and in English a picture of a bee with a picture of a leaf might (if one were so minded) represent the word belief.

THE DEVELOPMENT OF WRITING

Once invented, accidentally discovered or evolved—take your pick—did writing then diffuse throughout the globe from Mesopotamia? The earliest Egyptian writing dates from 3100 BC, that of the Indus Valley from 2500 BC, that of Crete from 1900 BC, that of China from 1200 BC, that of Central America from 600 BC (all dates are approximate). On this basis, it seems reasonable that the idea of writing, but not the particular symbols of a script, did spread gradually from culture to distant culture. It took 600 or 700 years for the idea of printing to reach Europe from China, and even longer for the idea of paper: why should writing not have reached China from Mesopotamia over an even longer period?

Nevertheless, in the absence of solid evidence for transmission of the idea (even in the case of the much nearer civilizations of Mesopotamia and Egypt), a majority of scholars prefer to think that writing developed independently in the major civilizations of the ancient world. The optimist, or at any rate the anti-imperialist, will prefer to emphasize the intelligence and inventiveness of human societies; the pessimist, who takes a more conservative view of history, will tend to assume that humans prefer to copy what already exists, as faithfully as they can, restricting their innovations to cases of absolute necessity. The latter is the preferred explanation for how the Greeks borrowed the alphabet from the Phoenicians, adding in the process the vowels not expressed in the Phoenician script.

There can be no doubt about certain script borrowings, such as the Romans taking the Etruscan script, the Japanese taking the Chinese characters and, in our own time, the Turks (under Kemal Atatürk) abandoning the Arabic script in favour of the Latin script. Changes are made to a borrowed script because the new language has sounds in it that are not found in the language for which the script was being used (hence the umlaut on the "u" of Atatürk). This idea is easy enough to grasp when the two languages are similar, but it can be extremely awkward to follow when the two languages differ vastly, as Japanese does from Chinese. In order to cope with the differences, the Japanese script has *two* entirely distinct sets of symbols: Chinese characters (thousands), and Japanese syllabic signs (about 50) that symbolize the basic sounds of Japanese speech. A Japanese sentence therefore mixes Chinese characters and Japanese syllabic signs in what is generally regarded as the most complicated system of writing in the world.

SCRIPT, SPEECH AND LANGUAGE

Europeans and Americans of ordinary literacy must recognize and write around 52 alphabetic signs, and sundry other symbols, such as numerals, punctuation marks and "whole-word" semantic symbols, for example +, &, £, $, 2, which are sometimes called logograms. Their Japanese counterparts, by contrast, are supposed to know and be able to write some 2000 symbols, and, if they are highly educated, must recognize 5000 symbols or more. The two situations, in Europe/America and in Japan, appear to be poles apart. But in fact, the positions resemble each other more than appears.

All scripts that are full writing—that is, a "system of graphic symbols that can be used to

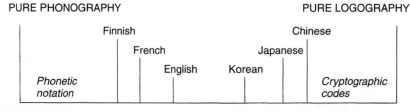

Phonography to logography. Written versus spoken language (after DeFrancis and Unger). Writing systems are shown on a theoretical continuum of writing between pure phonography and pure logography, with Finnish script as the most phonetically efficient and Japanese script the least efficient.

convey any and all thought" (to quote John DeFrancis, a distinguished American student of Chinese)—operate on one basic principle, contrary to what most people think, some scholars included. Both alphabets and the Chinese and Japanese scripts use symbols to represent sounds (i.e. phonetic signs); and all writing systems use a mixture of phonetic and semantic signs. What differs—apart from the outward forms of the symbols, of course—is the *proportion* of phonetic to semantic signs. The higher the proportion, the easier it is to guess the pronunciation of a word. In English the proportion is high, in Chinese it is low. Thus English spelling represents English speech sound by sound more accurately than Chinese characters represent Mandarin speech; but Finnish spelling represents the Finnish language better than either of them. The Finnish script is highly efficient phonetically, while the Chinese (and Japanese) script is phonetically seriously deficient.

The difficulty of learning the Chinese and Japanese scripts cannot be denied. In Japan, in the mid-1950s, a peak in teenage suicides seems to have been connected with the expansion of mass education post-war, using the full-blown Japanese script with its several thousand characters. It takes a Chinese or Japanese person several years longer than a western counterpart to achieve fluency in reading.

That said, there are many millions of westerners who have failed to learn to read and

write. The level of literacy in Japan is higher than in the West (though probably not as high as is claimed). The intricacy of the Japanese script has not stopped the Japanese from becoming a great economic power; nor has it caused them to abandon their use of Chinese characters in favour of a much smaller set of signs based on their already-existing syllabic signs—a theoretically feasible move.

MODERN "HIEROGLYPHS"

Are the huge claims made for the efficiency of the alphabet then perhaps misguided? Maybe writing and reading would work best if alphabetic scripts contained more logograms standing for whole words, as in Chinese and Japanese writing and (less so) in Egyptian hieroglyphs? Why is it necessarily desirable to have a *sound*-based script? What, after all, has sound got to do with the actual process of writing and reading?

We have only to look around us to see that "hieroglyphs" are striking back—beside highways, at airports, on maps, in weather forecasts, on clothes labels, on computer screens and on electronic goods including the keyboard of one's word processor. Instead of "move cursor to right," there is a simple ⇨. The hieroglyphs tell us where we must not overtake, where the nearest telephone is, which road is a motorway, whether it is likely to rain tomorrow, how we should (and should not) clean a garment, and how we should rewind a tape. Some people, beginning with the philosopher and mathematician Leibniz in the 17th century, even like to imagine that we can invent an entire written language for universal communication. It would aim to be independent of any of the spoken languages of the world, dependent only upon the concepts essential to high-level philosophical, political and scientific communication. If music and mathematics can achieve it, so the thought goes—why not more generally?

Modern hieroglyphs.

Writing: A Chronicle

Ice Ages (after 25,000 BC)	Proto-writing, i.e., pictographic communication, in use
8000 BC onwards	Clay "tokens" in use as counters, Middle East
3300 BC	Sumerian clay tablets with writing, Uruk, Iraq
3100 BC	Cuneiform inscriptions begin, Mesopotamia
3100–3000 BC	Hieroglyphic inscriptions begin, Egypt
2500 BC	Indus script begins, Pakistan/N.W. India
18th cent. BC	Cretan Linear A inscriptions begin
1792–1750 BC	Hammurabi, king of Babylon, reigns; inscribes law code on stela
17th–16th cent. BC	First known alphabet, Palestine
1450 BC	Cretan Linear B inscriptions begin
14th cent. BC	Alphabetic cuneiform inscriptions, Ugarit, Syria
1361–1352 BC	Tutankhamun reigns, Egypt
c. 1285 BC	Battle of Kadesh celebrated by both Ramesses II and Hittites
1200 BC	Oracle bone inscriptions in Chinese characters begin
1000 BC	Phoenician alphabetic inscriptions begin, Mediterranean area
730 BC	Greek alphabetic inscriptions begin
c. 8th cent. BC	Etruscan alphabet appears, northern Italy
650 BC	Demotic inscriptions, derived from hieroglyphs, begin, Egypt
600 BC	Glyphic inscriptions begin, Mesoamerica
521–486 BC	Darius, king of the Persians, reigns; creates Behistun inscription (key to decipherment of cuneiform)
400 BC	Ionian alphabet becomes standard Greek alphabet

(continued)

c. 270–*c.* 232 BC	Ashoka creates rock edicts in Brahmi and Kharosthi script, northern India
221 BC	Qin dynasty reforms Chinese character spelling
c. 2nd cent. BC	Paper invented, China
1st cent. AD	Dead Sea Scrolls written in Aramaic/Hebrew script
75 AD	Last inscription written in cuneiform
2nd cent.	Runic inscriptions begin, northern Europe
394	Last inscription written in Egyptian hieroglyphs
615–683	Pacal, Classic Maya ruler of Palenque, Mexico
712	*Kojiki,* earliest work of Japanese literature (in Chinese characters)
Before 800	Printing invented, China
9th cent.	Cyrillic alphabet invented, Russia
1418–1450	Sejong, king of Korea, reigns; invents Hangul alphabet
15th cent.	Movable type invented, Europe
1560s	Diego de Landa records Mayan "alphabet," Yucatán
1799	Rosetta stone discovered, Egypt
1821	Cherokee "alphabet" invented by Sequoya, USA
1823	Egyptian hieroglyphs deciphered by Champollion
1840s onwards	Mesopotamian cuneiform deciphered by Rawlinson, Hincks and others
1867	Typewriter invented
1899	Oracle bone inscriptions discovered, China
1900	Knossos discovered by Evans, who identifies Cretan Linear A and B
1905	Proto-Sinaitic inscriptions discovered by Petrie, Serabit el-Khadim, Sinai
1908	Phaistos Disc discovered, Crete
1920s	Indus civilization discovered
1940s	Electronic computers invented
1948	Hebrew becomes a national language in Israel
1953	Linear B deciphered by Ventris
1950s onwards	Mayan glyphs deciphered
1958	Pinyin spelling introduced in China
1980s	Wordprocessors invented; writing becomes electronic
23 Dec. 2012	Current Maya Great Cycle of time due to end

PART II

The Tradition of Western Literacy

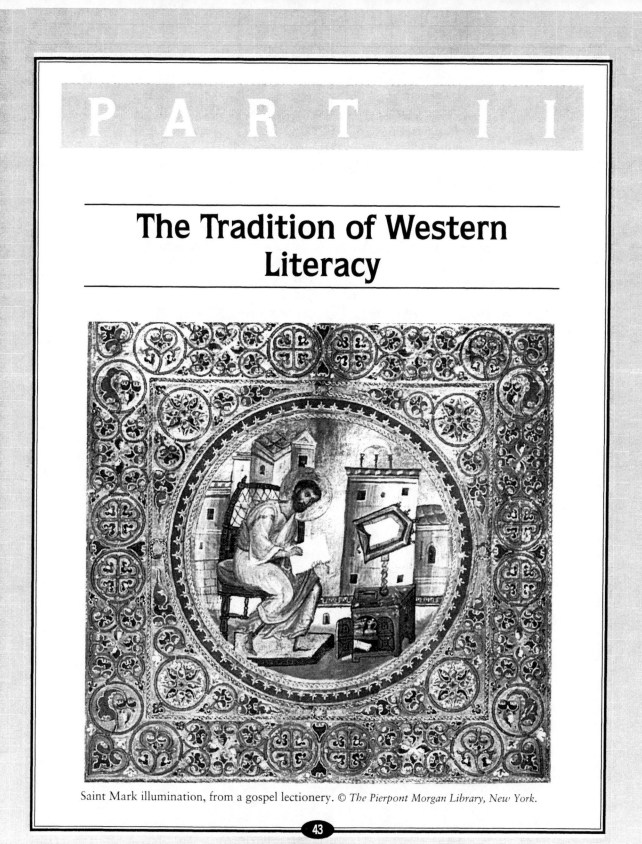

Saint Mark illumination, from a gospel lectionery. © *The Pierpont Morgan Library, New York.*

As we have just seen, the first writing systems initiated a major communications revolution. Writing made possible the storage and retrieval of vast amounts of information. It enabled the civilizations employing it to achieve a size and complexity that was previously unparalleled. These early scripts were used primarily for economic and political purposes. Their individual signs represented ideas, objects, and actions, not speech. Eventually, however, in places such as Egypt and Babylonia, writing developed an acoustic dimension. For example, a picture in hieroglyphics or a cuneiform character came to indicate not the object represented, but the sound (usually the main syllable) uttered when the object was spoken.

The use of these sound signs, known as phonograms, added to the possibilities of writing. Myths and histories began to be transcribed. Nevertheless, the scripts remained complex and difficult; an elite group of full-time scribes was still necessary. This situation was challenged by the emergence of the twenty-two-character Phoenician alphabet around 1500 B.C. Unlike the Egyptians and Babylonians, the Phoenicians did not build an empire. They were a seafaring trading people based in the western Mediterranean. Each character in their alphabet represented a consonant linked to several possible syllables. The proper one to "read" was deduced through the context of the adjacent "letters." This is a slow process compared to the way we read today, and one that makes it difficult for us to read a Phoenician text in a manner that is faithful to the spoken language on which it was based.

The Phoenician alphabet was economical and provided a rough approximation of speech. When introduced to the Greek-speaking peoples of Asia Minor, it underwent significant modifications. Vowels were added. This converted the former consonant syllables into pure consonants—abstract bits of sound—that, when combined with vowel letters, produced an immediately recognizable range of syllables and words. This new way of writing, although not a perfect representation of speech, was a rich approximation, and the ancestor of all the subsequent scripts of the West.

The extraordinary vistas opened up by the Greek alphabet are dealt with in our first two selections. In "The Consequences of Literacy," Jack Goody and Ian Watt present an anthropologically informed look at this achievement and how it provided the unsuspected foundations for much of Western thought and culture. They work with an interesting concept: the *mode of communication*. In so doing, Goody and Watt contrast societies that are "oral"—societies without any type of writing—with "protoliterate" societies such as Egypt and Babylonia. Their approach may at times seem somewhat deterministic, since they so strongly emphasize the often overlooked factor of communications. Yet it is always tendencies that they discuss, not causes.

Our next selection is by Eric Havelock, who spent a major part of his life studying the culture and communication of ancient Greece. He argues that the new literacy, born of the Greek experience, challenged the "craft literacy" of the ancient empires. It created the common reader: large numbers of literate people who were not part of an elite scribal tradition. Havelock also comments on the psychological implications of the alphabet, how it affected memory and cognition. Finally, he assesses specific media, such as wax tablets and papyrus, which the Greeks used to produce written texts. An important point to keep in mind, as he reminds us, is that Greek literacy is still not modern literacy as we know it. Texts such as those by Plato were in part transcribed from an earlier oral tradition. At the same time, such texts provide a glimpse of the conceptual directions that would become dominant after the advent of movable type printing.

The essays of both Havelock and Goody and Watt allude to a preliterate oral tradition. Elsewhere they write—as do Innis, McLuhan, Ong, and a host of other communication scholars—with considerable respect regarding the intelligence of people who live in such societies. Therefore, readers should not assume that literate is superior to oral in terms of some absolute measure of intelligence. As Harold Innis, Marshall Netwhein, and Walter Ong argues in our next selection, the differences are cultural, not hierarchical. We gain new insight with the acquisition of literacy, but we also lose. The world of primary oral cultures is rich in metaphor, nonlineal creative thought, and memory stepped in a multisensory apprehension of the world. Genius is a legacy of both the oral and literate worlds. After all, Homer could not write. His epics were transcribed by others. Yet for generations it was assumed that such artistry was possible only in a literate mind.

Our next selection, by Umberto Eco, takes us into Europe during the Middle Ages. During this period the great literate/philosophical traditions of Greece and Rome went into eclipse. Europe became a countryside of feudal estates based on agriculture. Literacy was almost solely the preserve of the Catholic Church. Using Latin on parchment (treated animal skins), the Church functioned as a spiritually oriented bureaucracy, linking together diverse cultural and linguistic regions. Church-sanctioned texts were primarily scriptural or moral. Often, they were intended for total or partial memorization. By the thirteenth century, secular writing in the vernacular (the local languages) began to appear. The new, less costly medium of paper facilitated this process. Both the religious and secular writings of the Middles Ages were stylistically different from what would come after print, in that a firm grounding in the oral tradition was still present.

The selection by Eco is somewhat unusual in that it comes from a best-selling novel, *The Name of the Rose*. The excerpt presents us with an imaginative portrait of manuscript production in a medieval monastery. We encounter the scriptorium, complete with the raw materials used for writing, and overhear several discussions about the nature of knowledge and the way books were classified before the age of print. We hope that this brief glimpse of a world so different from our own will inspire some of you to read the novel itself, which uses the monastery as the setting for an exciting detective story in the Sherlock Holmes tradition.

James Burke concludes this section with a lively look at the social life and communication of the Middle Ages. Some readers might already be familiar with Burke from his innovative television series dealing with the history of technology: *"Connections," "The Day the Universe Changed,"* and *"Connections2."* Here, he works in the print medium to draw us into awareness of the oral nature of everyday communication in the Middle Ages, and a consideration of the implications of the literacy of the time. Note the importance he places on memory and memory devices. This was of concern to both the nonliterate peasant and literate scribe. It would greatly diminish in importance under the impact of one of the most powerful all technological revolutions: the invention of movable type printing.

6 THE CONSEQUENCES OF LITERACY

Jack Goody and Ian Watt

Jack Goody and Ian Watt are anthropologists who have done pioneering work on the cultural and psychological implications of literacy. In recent years, Goody has published several books in this area, among them The Logic of Writing and the Organization of Society, *which have garnered a wide, interdisciplinary following.*

It is hardly possible, in this brief survey, to determine what importance must be attributed to the alphabet as the cause or as the necessary condition of the seminal intellectual innovations that occurred in the Greek world during the centuries that followed the diffusion of writing; nor, indeed, does the nature of the evidence give much ground for believing that the problem can ever be fully resolved. The present argument must, therefore, confine itself to suggesting that some crucial features of Western culture came into being in Greece soon after the existence, for the first time, of a rich urban society in which a substantial portion of the population was able to read and write; and that, consequently, the overwhelming debt of the whole of contemporary civilization to classical Greece must be regarded as in some measure the result, not so much of the Greek genius, as of the intrinsic differences between non-literate (or protoliterate) and literate societies—the latter being mainly represented by those societies using the Greek alphabet and its derivatives. If this is so, it may help us to take our contrast between the transmission of the cultural heritage in non-literate and alphabetically literate societies a little further.

To begin with, the ease of alphabetic reading and writing was probably an important consideration in the development of political democracy in Greece; in the fifth century a majority of the free citizens could apparently read the laws, and take an active part in elections and legislation. Democracy as we know it, then, is from the beginning associated with widespread literacy; and so to a large extent is the notion of the world of knowledge as transcending political units; in the Hellenic world diverse people and countries were given a common administrative system and a unifying cultural heritage through the written word. Greece is therefore considerably closer to being a model for the world-wide intellectual tradition of the contemporary literate world than those earlier civilizations of the Orient which each had its own localized traditions of knowledge: as Oswald Spengler put it, *"Writing is the grand symbol of the Far"* (1934:11, 150).

Yet although the idea of intellectual, and to some extent political, universalism is historically and substantively linked with literate culture, we too easily forget that this brings with it other features which have quite different implications, and which go some way to explain why the long-cherished and theoretically feasible dream of an "educated democracy" and a truly egalitarian society has never been realized in practice. One of the basic premises of liberal reform over the last century and a half has been that of James Mill, as it is described in the *Autobiography* of his son, John Stuart Mill:

> So complete was my father's reliance on the influence of reason over the minds of mankind, whenever it is allowed to reach them, that he felt as if all would be gained if the whole population were taught to read, if all sorts of opinions were allowed to be addressed to them by word and in writing, and if, by means of the suffrage, they could nominate a legislature to give effect to the opinions they adopted [p. 74].

All these things have been accomplished since the days of the Mills, but nevertheless "all" has not been "gained"; and some causes of this shortfall may be found in the intrinsic effects of literacy on the transmission of the cultural heritage, effects which can be seen most clearly by contrasting them with their analogues in non-literate society.

The writing down of some of the main elements in the cultural tradition in Greece, we say, brought about an awareness of two things: of the past as different from the present; and of the inherent inconsistencies in the picture of life as it was inherited by the individual from the cultural tradition in its recorded form. These two effects of widespread alphabetic writing, it may be surmised, have continued and multiplied themselves ever since, and at an increasing pace since the development of printing. "The printers," Jefferson remarked, "can never leave us in a state of perfect rest and union of opinion,"[1] and as book follows book and newspaper newspaper, the notion of rational agreement and democratic coherence among men has receded further and further away, while Plato's attacks on the venal purveyors of knowledge in the market-place have gained increased relevance.

But the inconsistency of the totality of written expression is perhaps less striking than its enormous bulk and its vast historical depth. Both of these have always seemed insuperable obstacles to those seeking to reconstruct society on a more unified and disciplined model: we find the objection in the book-burners of all periods; and it appears in many more respectable thinkers. In Jonathan Swift, for example, whose perfectly rational Houyhnhnms "have no letters," and whose knowledge "consequently . . . is all traditional."[2] These oral traditions were of a scale, Swift tells us, that enabled "the historical part" to be "easily preserved without burthening their memories." Not so with the literate tradition, for, lacking the resources of unconscious adaptation and omission which exist in the oral transmission, the cultural repertoire can only grow; there are more words than anybody knows the meaning of—some 142,000 vocabulary entries in a college dictionary like the *Webster's New World*. This unlimited proliferation also characterizes the written tradition

in general: the mere size of the literate repertoire means that the proportion of the whole which any one individual knows must be infinitesimal in comparison with what obtains in oral culture. Literate society, merely by having no system of elimination, no "structural amnesia," prevents the individual from participating fully in the total cultural tradition to anything like the extent possible in non-literate society.

One way of looking at this lack of any literate equivalent to the homeostatic organization of the cultural tradition in non-literate society is to see literate society as inevitably committed to an ever-increasing series of culture lags. The content of the cultural tradition grows continually, and in so far as it affects any particular individual he becomes a palimpsest composed of layers of beliefs and attitudes belonging to different stages in historical time. So too, eventually, does society at large, since there is a tendency for each social group to be particularly influenced by systems of ideas belonging to different periods in the nation's development; both to the individual, and to the groups constituting society, the past may mean very different things.

From the standpoint of the individual intellectual, of the literate specialist, the vista of endless choices and discoveries offered by so extensive a past can be a source of great stimulation and interest; but when we consider the social effects of such an orientation, it becomes apparent that the situation fosters the alienation that has characterized so many writers and philosophers of the West since the last century. It was surely, for example, this lack of social amnesia in alphabetic cultures which led Nietzsche to describe "we moderns" as "wandering encyclopaedias," unable to live and act in the present and obsessed by a "'historical sense' that injures and finally destroys the living thing, be it a man or a people or a system of culture" (1909:9, 33). Even if we dismiss Nietzsche's views as extreme, it is still evident that the literate individual has in practice so large a field of personal selection from the total cultural repertoire that the odds are strongly against his experiencing the cultural tradition as any sort of patterned whole.

From the point of view of society at large, the enormous complexity and variety of the cultural repertoire obviously create problems of an unprecedented order of magnitude. It means, for example, that since Western literate societies are characterized by these always increasing layers of cultural tradition, they are incessantly exposed to a more complex version of the kind of culture conflict that has been held to produce *anomie* in oral societies when they come into contact with European civilization, changes which, for example, have been illustrated with a wealth of absorbing detail by Robert Redfield in his studies of Central America.[3]

Another important consequence of alphabetic culture relates to social stratification. In the protoliterate cultures, with their relatively difficult non-alphabetic systems of writing, there existed a strong barrier between the writers and non-writers; but although the "democratic" scripts made it possible to break down this particular barrier, they led eventually to a vast proliferation of more or less tangible distinctions based on what people had read. Achievement in handling the tools of reading and writing is obviously one of the most important axes of social differentiation in modern societies; and this differentiation extends on to more minute differences between professional specializations so that even members of the same socio-economic groups of literate specialists may hold little intellectual ground in common.

Nor, of course, are these variations in the degree of participation in the literate tradition, together with their effects on social structure, the only causes of tension. For, even within a literate culture, the oral tradition—the transmission of values and attitudes in face-to-face contact—nevertheless remains the primary mode of cultural orientation, and, to varying degrees, it is out of step with the various literate traditions. In some respects, perhaps, this is fortunate. The tendency of the modern mass-communications

industries, for example, to promote ideals of conspicuous consumption which cannot be realized by more than a limited proportion of society might well have much more radical consequences but for the fact that each individual exposed to such pressures is also a member of one or more primary groups whose oral converse is probably much more realistic and conservative in its ideological tendency; the mass media are not the only, and they are probably not even the main, social influences on the contemporary cultural tradition as a whole.

Primary group values are probably even further removed from those of the "high" literate culture, except in the case of the literate specialists. This introduces another kind of culture conflict, and one which is of cardinal significance for Western civilization. If, for example, we return to the reasons for the relative failure of universal compulsory education to bring about the intellectual, social and political results that James Mill expected, we may well lay a major part of the blame on the gap between the public literate tradition of the school and the very different and indeed often directly contradictory private oral traditions of the pupil's family and peer group. The high degree of differentiation in exposure to the literate tradition sets up a basic division which cannot exist in non-literate society: the division between the various shades of literacy and illiteracy. This conflict, of course, is most dramatically focused in the school, the key institution of society. As Margaret Mead (1943:637) has pointed out: "Primitive education was a process by which continuity was maintained between parents and children ... Modern education includes a heavy emphasis upon the function of education to create discontinuities—to turn the child ... of the illiterate into the literate." A similar and probably even more acute stress develops in many cases between the school and the peer group; and, quite apart from the difficulties arising from the substantive differences between the two orientations, there seem to be factors in the very nature of literate methods which make them ill suited to bridge the gap between the street-corner society and the blackboard jungle.

First, because although the alphabet, printing, and universal free education have combined to make the literate culture freely available to all on a scale never previously approached, the literate mode of communication is such that it does not impose itself as forcefully or as uniformly as is the case with the oral transmission of the cultural tradition. In non-literate society every social situation cannot but bring the individual into contact with the group's patterns of thought, feeling and action: the choice is between the cultural tradition—or solitude. In a literate society, however, and quite apart from the difficulties arising from the scale and complexity of the "high" literate tradition, the mere fact that reading and writing are normally solitary activities means that in so far as the dominant cultural tradition is a literate one, it is very easy to avoid; as Bertha Phillpotts (1931:162–3) wrote in her study of Icelandic literature:

> Printing so obviously makes knowledge accessible to all that we are inclined to forget that it also makes knowledge very easy to avoid . . . A shepherd in an Icelandic homestead, on the other hand, could not avoid spending his evenings in listening to the kind of literature which interested the farmer. The result was a degree of really national culture such as no nation of today has been able to achieve.

The literate culture, then, is much more easily avoided than the oral one; and even when it is not avoided its actual effects may be relatively shallow. Not only because, as Plato argued, the effects of reading are intrinsically less deep and permanent than those of oral converse; but also because the abstractness of the syllogism and of the Aristotelian categorizations of knowledge do not correspond very directly with common experience. The abstractness of the syllogism, for example, of its very nature disregards the individual's social experience and immediate personal context; and the compartmentalization of

knowledge similarly restricts the kind of connections which the individual can establish and ratify with the natural and social world. The essential way of thinking of the specialist in literate culture is fundamentally at odds with that of daily life and common experience; and the conflict is embodied in the long tradition of jokes about absent-minded professors.

It is, of course, true that contemporary education does not present problems exactly in the forms of Aristotelian logic and taxonomy; but all our literate modes of thought have been profoundly influenced by them. In this, perhaps, we can see a major difference, not only from the transmission of the cultural heritage of oral societies, but from those of proto-literate ones. Thus Marcel Granet relates the nature of the Chinese writing system to the "concreteness" of Chinese thought, and his picture of its primary concentration on social action and traditional norms suggests that the cultural effect of the writing system was in the direction of intensifying the sort of homeostatic conservation found in non-literate cultures; it was indeed conceptualized in the Confucian *tao-'tung*, or "orthodox transmission of the way." In this connection it may be noted that the Chinese attitude to formal logic, and to the categorization of knowledge in general, is an articulate expression of what happens in an oral culture (Granet 1934: vii–xi, 8–55; Hu Shih 1922). Mencius, for example, speaks for the non-literate approach in general when he comments: "Why I dislike holding to one point is that it injures the *tao*. It takes up one point and disregards a hundred others" (Richards 1932:35).

The social tension between the oral and literate orientations in Western society is, of course, complemented by an intellectual one. In recent times the Enlightenment's attack on myth as irrational superstition has often been replaced by a regressive yearning for some modern equivalent of the unifying function of myth: "Have not," W. B. Yeats asked, "all races had their first unity from a mythology that marries them to rock and hill?" (1955:194).

In this nostalgia for the world of myths Plato has had a long line of successors. The Rousseauist cult of the Noble Savage, for instance, paid unwitting tribute to the strength of the homogeneity of oral culture, to the yearning admiration of the educated for the peasant's simple but cohesive view of life, the timelessness of his living in the present, the unanalytic spontaneity that comes with an attitude to the world that is one of absorbed and uncritical participation, a participation in which the contradictions between history and legend for example, or between experience and imagination, are not felt as problems. Such, for example, is the literary tradition of the European peasant from Cervantes' Sancho Panza to Tolstoy's Platon Karataev. Both are illiterate; both are rich in proverbial lore; both are untroubled by intellectual consistency; and both represent many of the values which, it was suggested above, are characteristic of oral culture. In these two works, *Don Quixote* and *War and Peace,* which might well be considered two of the supreme achievements of modern Western literature, an explicit contrast is made between the oral and literate elements of the cultural tradition. Don Quixote himself goes mad by reading books; while, opposed to the peasant Karataev, stands the figure of Pierre, an urban cosmopolitan, and a great reader. Tolstoy writes of Karataev that—in this like Mencius or like Malinowski's Trobrianders—he

> did not, and could not, understand the meaning of words apart from their context. Every word and every action of his was the manifestation of an activity unknown to him, which was his life. But his life, as he regarded it, had no meaning as a separate thing. It has a meaning only as part of a whole of which he was always conscious [*War and Peace*].

Tolstoy, of course, idealizes; but, conversely, even in his idealization he suggests one major emphasis of literate culture and one which we immediately associate with the Greeks—the stress upon the individual; Karataev does not re-

gard "his life . . . as a separate thing." There are, of course, marked differences in the life histories of individual members of non-literate societies: the story of Crashing Thunder differs from that of other Winnebago (Radin 1926, 1927); that of Baba of Karo from other Hausa women (Smith 1954); and these differences are often given public recognition by ascribing to individuals a personal tutelary or guardian spirit. But on the whole there is less individualization of personal experience in oral cultures, which tend, in Durkheim's phrase, to be characterized by "mechanical solidarity"[4]—by the ties between like persons, rather than by a more complicated set of complementary relationships between individuals in a variety of roles. Like Durkheim, many sociologists would relate this greater individualization of personal experience in literate societies to the effects of a more extensive division of labour. There is no single explanation; but the techniques of reading and writing are undoubtedly of very great importance. There is, first of all, the formal distinction which alphabetic culture has emphasized between the divine, the natural, and the human orders; secondly, there is the social differentiation to which the institutions of literate culture give rise; third, there is the effect of professional intellectual specialization on an unprecedented scale; lastly, there is the immense variety of choice offered by the whole corpus of recorded literature; and from these four factors there ensues, in any individual case, the highly complex totality deriving from the selection of these literate orientations and from the series of primary groups in which the individual has also been involved.

As for personal awareness of this individualization, other factors doubtless contributed, but writing itself (especially in its simpler, more cursive forms) was of great importance. For writing, by objectifying words, and by making them and their meaning available for much more prolonged and intensive scrutiny than is possible orally, encourages private thought; the diary or the confession enables the individual to objectify his own experience, and gives him some check upon the transmutations of memory under the influences of subsequent events. And then, if the diary is later published, a wider audience can have concrete experience of the differences that exist in the histories of their fellow men from a record of a life which has been partially insulated from the assimilative process of oral transmission.

The diary is, of course, an extreme case; but Plato's dialogues themselves are evidence of the general tendency of writing to increase the awareness of individual differences in behavior, and in the personality which lies behind them;[5] while the novel, which participates in the autobiographical and confessional direction of such writers as St. Augustine, Pepys and Rousseau, and purports to portray the inner as well as the outer life of individuals in the real world, has replaced the collective representations of myth and epic.

From the point of view of the general contrast between oral and alphabetically literate culture, then, there is a certain identity between the spirit of the Platonic dialogues and of the novel:[6] both kinds of writing express what is a characteristic intellectual effort of literate culture, and present the process whereby the individual makes his own more or less conscious, more or less personal selection, rejection and accommodation among the conflicting ideas and attitudes in his culture. This general kinship between Plato and the characteristic art form of literate culture, the novel, suggests a further contrast between oral and literate societies: in contrast to the homeostatic transmission of the cultural tradition among non-literate peoples, literate society leaves more to its members; less homogeneous in its cultural tradition, it gives more free play to the individual, and particularly to the intellectual, the literate specialist himself; it does so by sacrificing a single, ready-made orientation to life. And, in so far as an individual participates in the literate, as distinct from the oral, culture, such coherence as a person

achieves is very largely the result of his personal selection, adjustment and elimination of items from a highly differentiated cultural repertoire; he is, of course, influenced by all the various social pressures, but they are so numerous that the pattern finally comes out as an individual one.

Much could be added by way of development and qualification on this point, as on much else that has been said above. The contrast could be extended, for example, by bringing it up to date and considering later developments in communication, from the invention of printing and of the power press to that of radio, cinema and television. All these latter, it may be surmised, derive much of their effectiveness as agencies of social orientation from the fact that their media do not have the abstract and solitary quality of reading and writing, but on the contrary share something of the nature and impact of the direct personal interaction which obtains in oral cultures. It may even be that these new modes of communicating sight and sound without any limit of time or place will lead to a new kind of culture: less inward and individualistic than literate culture, probably, and sharing some of the relative homogeneity, though not the mutuality, of oral society.

To speculate further on such lines would be to go far beyond the purposes of this essay; and it only remains to consider briefly the consequences of the general course of the argument for the problem as it was posed at the outset in terms of the distinction between the disciplines primarily (though not exclusively) concerned in the analysis of non-literate and literate societies, that is, anthropology and sociology.

One aspect of the contrast drawn between non-literate and alphabetic culture would seem to help explain one of the main modern trends in the development of anthropology: for part of the progress which anthropology has made beyond the ethnocentrism of the nineteenth century surely derives from a growing awareness of the implications of one of the matters discussed above: an awareness, that is, of the extent to which, in the culture of oral societies, non-Aristotelian models[7] are implicit in the language, the reasoning, and the kinds of connection established between the various spheres of knowledge. The problem has been approached in many ways; particularly illuminating, perhaps, is Dorothy D. Lee's contrast between the "lineal" codifications of reality in Western culture and the "non-lineal" codifications of the Trobriand Islanders; and there, incidentally, although Aristotle is not mentioned, his characteristically analytic, teleological and relational thinking is recognizable in the governing attitudes that Dorothy Lee presents as the typical literate mode of thought in contrast to that of the Trobrianders.[8] Benjamin Lee Whorf makes a similar point in his contrast of Hopi with SAE (standard average European). He sees the "mechanistic way of thinking" of Europeans as closely related to the syntax of the languages they speak, "rigidified and intensified by Aristotle and the latter's medieval and modern followers" (Whorf 1956:238). The segmentation of nature is functionally related to grammar; Newtonian space, time and matter, for example, are directly derived from SAE culture and language (1956:153). He goes on to argue that "our objectified view of time is . . . favourable to historicity and to everything connected with the keeping of records, while the Hopi view is unfavourable thereto." And to this fact he links the presence of:

1. Records, diaries, bookkeeping, accounting, mathematics stimulated by accounting.
2. Interest in exact sequences, dating, calendars, chronology, clocks, time wages, time graphs, time as used in physics.
3. Annals, histories, the historical attitude, interest in the past, archeology, attitudes of introjection towards past periods, e.g., classicism, romanticism (Whorf, 1956:153).

Many of these features are precisely those which we have mentioned as characteristic of societies with easy and widespread systems of writing.

But while Whorf and other anthropological linguists have noted these differences between European institutions and categories on the one hand and those of societies like the Trobriands and the Hopi on the other, they have tended to relate these variations to the languages themselves, giving little weight to the influence of the mode of communications as such, to the intrinsic social consequences of literacy.[9]

On the other hand, what has been said about literacy and the consequent developments of Greek thought leading to the logical methods, and the categories, of Aristotle may seem to attribute to one individual, and to the civilization to which he belonged, a kind of absolute claim to intellectual validity to which neither the philosopher, the anthropologist, nor the historian of ancient civilization is likely to assent. The currency of such diffuse assumptions in general long ago moved John Locke to an unwonted burst of wintry humour: "God has not been so sparing to men to make them barely two-legged creatures, and left it to Aristotle to make them rational" (*Essay Concerning Human Understanding,* bk. IV, chap. 17, 84). Nevertheless, Locke's own treatment of the "forms of argumentation" and of "the division of the sciences" is itself recognizably within the tradition that derives from Aristotle and his time; and so, in some important ways, is the literate culture, not only of the West, but of the civilized world today. There is obviously some more or less absolute efficacy in the organization of human knowledge which appears in the thoughtways of the first substantially literate culture, although its definition (which could hardly be more difficult) is well beyond the scope of this paper. Max Weber saw as the essential differentiating factor of Western civilization the "formal rationality" of its institutions; and this, in turn, he regarded as a more fully developed and more exclusively practised version of the ordinary human tendency to act reasonably—to behave with "substantive rationality." For Weber "formal rationality" was merely an institutionalized form of this general tendency working through "rationally established norms, by enactment, decrees, and regulations"[10] rather than through personal, religious, traditional or charismatic allegiances. Weber's differentiation in some respects parallels the differentiation made above between oral and alphabetic culture, and in various places he anticipates part of the argument advanced in this paper.[11]

The present study, then, is an attempt to approach a very general problem from one particular point of view. In that perspective it suggests one reason for what has been widely remarked upon in the comparison between anthropology and sociology: the relative incompleteness of sociological analyses as compared with those of anthropology, and the tendency for anthropologists studying European societies to limit their observations to village communities or family groups. For, quite apart from differences of scale and complexity of social structure, there are two other dimensions of analysis which can in practice be largely disregarded by the anthropologist but not by the student of literate societies.

First, the reifying of the past in written record means that sociology must inevitably be the more deeply concerned with history. The kinds of practical and theoretical issues involved here are numerous, for the great importance of the historical dimension, with its very different kind of impact on various social groups, obviously poses acute methodological problems. At the most general level, the analytic model of the sociologist must take into account the fact that from one point of view his data include materials accumulated from earlier cultures and periods, and that the existence of these records greatly increases the possible alternative ways of thinking and behaving for the members of the society he is studying, as well as influencing their action in other ways. This added complexity means that certain aspects of the past continue to be relevant (or at least potentially so) for the contemporary scene; and it also means that when functional theoretical models are used, the interconnections can hardly be as direct or immediate as those the anthropologist might expect in nonliterate societies.

Secondly, the sociologist must in any case recognize that, since in alphabetic society much of the homeostatic function of the oral tradition works at the inward and individual rather than at the overt and public level, sociological descriptions, which inevitably deal primarily with collective life, are considerably less complete than those of anthropology, and consequently provide a less certain guide to understanding the behavior of the particular individuals of whom the society is composed.

Notes

1. *Cit.* Harold A. Innis, "Minerva's Owl," *The Bias of Communication* (Toronto, 1951), p. 24. Harold Innis was much occupied with the larger effects of modes of communication, as appears also in his *Empire and Communications* (Oxford, 1950). This direction of investigation has been taken up by the University of Toronto review *Explorations;* and the present authors are also indebted to the then unpublished work of Professor E. A. Havelock on the alphabetic revolution in Greece. Among the many previous writers who have been concerned with the Greek aspect of the problem, Nietzsche (*Beyond Good and Evil,* Edinburgh, 1909, p. 247), and José Ortega y Gasset ("The Difficulty of Reading," *Diogenes,* XXVIII (1959), pp. 1–17) may be mentioned. Among those who have treated the differences between oral and literate modes of communication in general, David Reisman ("The Oral and Written Traditions," *Explorations,* VI, 1956, pp. 22–8, and *The Oral Tradition, the Written Word and the Screen Image* (Yellow Springs, Ohio, 1956)) and Robert Park ("Reflections on Communication and Culture," *American J. of Sociology,* XLIV, 1938, pp. 187–205) are especially relevant here.
2. *Gulliver's Travels,* part IV, chap. 9, ed. Arthur E. Case (New York, 1938), p. 296.

3. *Chan Kam, a Maya Village* (Washington, D.C., 1934); *The Folk Culture of Yucatan* (Chicago, 1941); *A Village that Chose Progress: Chan Kam Revisited* (Chicago, 1950); and for a more general treatment, *The Primitive World and its Transformations* (Ithaca, New York, 1953), pp. 73, 108. See also Peter Worsley, *The Trumpet Shall Sound* (London, 1957). For the concept of *anomie,* see Emile Durkheim, *Le Suicide* (Paris, 1897), book II, chap. 5.

4. Emile Durkheim, *The Division of Labor in Society,* trans. G. Simpson (New York, 1933), p. 130.

5. In the *Theaetetus,* for example, emphasis is placed on the inner dialogue of the soul in which it perceives ethical ideas "by comparing within herself things past and present with the future" (186b).

6. Jaeger, *Paiedeia* (Oxford, 1939), II, p. 18, speaks of the dialogues and the memoirs by many members of the circle of Socrates as "new literary forms invented by the Socratic circle . . . to re-create the incomparable personality of the master."

7. Just as it has been argued that a proper understanding of Homer depends upon a non-Aristotelian literary criticism which is appropriate to oral literature: James A. Notopoulos, "Parataxis in Homer: a New Approach to Homeric Literary Criticism," *Transactions of the American Philological Association,* LXXX (1949), pp. 1, 6.

8. "Codifications of Reality: Lineal and Nonlineal," in *Freedom and Culture* (Englewood Cliffs, New Jersey, 1959), pp. 105–20; see also her "Conceptual Implications of an Indian Language," *Philosophy of Science,* V (1938), pp. 89–102.

9. For example, in his paper "A linguistic consideration of thinking in primitive communities" (*Language, Thought and Reality,* pp. 65–86), Whorf discusses Lévy-Bruhl's account of the thinking of primitive man as characterized by *participation mystique,* and suggests that the differences are related to the structure of language. No mention is made of the role of writing and he seems to see language itself as the independent variable, although in his later paper on "Habitual thought" he does make a passing reference to writing, as well as to the *interdépendence* of language and culture (p. 153). Lévi-Strauss, who is much concerned with the linguistic aspects of the problem, makes no mention of the role of literacy in his analysis of the differences between *la pensée sauvage* and *la pensée domestiquée,* but again the actual process of domestication is peripheral to his study (1962).

10. From *Max Weber: Essays in Sociology,* trans. H. H. Gerth and C. Wright Mills (New York, 1946), pp. 298–9. See also *The Theory of Social and Economic Organization,* trans. A. M. Henderson and Talcott Parsons (New York, 1947), pp. 184–6.

11. Especially in the "Author's Introduction" to *The Protestant Ethic,* trans. Talcott Parsons (London, 1930), pp. 13–31, where Weber gives a rapid but comprehensive survey of the problem.

THE GREEK LEGACY
Eric Havelock

Eric Havelock (1903–1989) was professor of classics at Yale University. A one-time colleague of Harold Innis, Havelock wrote extensively on the impact of literacy on the history of the West, especially with reference to the legacy of Greek alphabetization.

The introduction of the Greek letters into inscription somewhere about 700 B.C. was to alter the character of human culture, placing a gulf between all alphabetic societies and their precursors. The Greeks did not just invent an alphabet, they invented literacy and the literate basis of modern thought. Under modern conditions there seems to be only a short time lag between the invention of a device and its full social or industrial application, and we have got used to this idea as a fact of technology. This was not true of the alphabet. The letter shapes and values had to pass through a period of localization before being standardized throughout Greece. Even after the technology was standardized or relatively so—there were always two competing versions, the Eastern and the Western—its effects were registered slowly in Greece, were then partly cancelled during the European Middle Ages, and have been fully realized only since the further invention of the printing press. But it is useful here and now to set forth the full theoretic possibilities that would accrue from the use of the Greek alphabet, supposing that all human impediments to their realization could be removed, in order to place the invention in its proper historical perspective.

It democratized literacy, or rather made democratization possible. This point is often made, but in simplistic terms, as though it were merely a matter of learning a limited number of letters, that is, learning to write them. Hence even the Semitic system has often been erroneously credited with this advantage. If Semitic societies in antiquity showed democratic tendencies, this was not because they were literate. On the contrary, to the extent that their democracy was modified by theocracy, with considerable prestige and power vested in priesthoods, they exhibited all the symptoms of craft literacy. The Greek system by its superior analysis of sound placed the skill of reading theoretically within the reach of children at the stage where they are still learning the sounds of their oral vocabulary. If acquired in childhood, the skill was convertible into an automatic reflex and thus distributable over a majority of a given population provided it was applied to the spoken vernacular. But this meant that democratization would depend not only upon the invention but also upon the organization and maintenance of school instruction in reading at the elementary level. This second requirement is social rather

than technological. It was not met in Greece for perhaps three hundred years after the technological problem was solved, and was abandoned again in Europe for a long period after the fall of Rome. When operative, it rendered the role of the scribe or the clerk obsolete, and removed the elitist status of literacy characteristic of craft-literate epochs.

Have the outward social and political effects of full literacy really been as important and profound as is sometimes claimed? Our later examination of oral cultures and the way they function may throw some doubt on this. What the new script may have done in the long run was to change somewhat the content of the human mind. This is a conclusion which will not be argued fully here. But this much should be said at once. The acoustic efficiency of the script had a result which was psychological: once it was learned you did not have to think about it. Though a visible thing, a series of marks, it created to interpose itself as an object of thought between the reader and his recollection of the spoken tongue. The script therefore came to resemble an electric current communicating a recollection of the sounds of the spoken word directly to the brain so that the meaning resounded as it were in the consciousness without reference to the properties of the letters used. The script was reduced to a gimmick; it had no intrinsic value in itself as a script and this marked it off from all previous systems. It was characteristic of the alphabet that the names of the Greek letters, borrowed from the Phoenician, for the first time became meaningless: *alpha*, *beta*, *gamma*, etc. constitutes simply a nursery chant designed to imprint the mechanical sounds of the letters, by using what is called the acrophonic principle, in a fixed series on the child's brain, while simultaneously tightly correlating them with his vision of a fixed series of shapes which he looks at as he pronounces the acoustic values. These names in the original Semitic were names of common objects like "house" and "camel" and so on. Uncritical students of the history of writing will even make it a reproach against the Greek system that the names became "meaningless" in Greek. The reproach is very foolish. A true alphabet, the sole basis of future literacy, could only become operative when its components were robbed of any independent meaning whatever, in order to become convertible into a mechanical mnemonic device.

The fluency of reading that could result depended upon fluency of recognition and this in turn as we have seen upon the removal so far as possible of all choices upon the part of the reader, all ambiguities. Such an automatic system brought within reach the capacity to transcribe the complete vernacular of any given language, anything whatever that could be said in the language, with a guarantee that the reader would recognize the unique acoustic values of the signs, and so the unique statements conveyed thereby, whatever they happened to be. The need for authorized versions restricted to statements of a familiar and accepted nature was removed. Moreover the new system could identify the phonemes of any language with accuracy. Thus the possibility arose of placing two or several languages within the same type of script and so greatly accelerating the process of cross-translation between them. This is the technological secret which made possible the construction of a Roman literature upon Greek models—the first such enterprise in the history of mankind. For the most part, however, this advantage of interchange between written communications has accrued to the later alphabetic cultures of Europe. By way of contrast, the historian Thucydides in the Greek period records an episode where the documents of a captured Persian emissary had to be "translated" into Greek. That is how the word is interpreted by the commentators who explain this passage. But Thucydides does not say "translated." What the would-be translators had first to do was to "change the letters" of the original syllabic script into the Greek alphabet. How could they have done this? I suggest that it

was done only with the previous assistance of the spoken tongue, not the written. That is, an orally bilingual Persian who was also craft-literate in the Persian sense, that is, knew his cuneiform, would read aloud what the document said, translating as he went into spoken Greek. His opposite number would then transcribe from his dictation into the Greek alphabet, unless there was a Persian available who could use both cuneiform and alphabet. Then the Persian dispatch, now in Greek alphabetic form, could be carried to Athens and read there. In the United Nations today some such procedure is still required for cross-communication between the alphabetic cultures and the non-alphabetic ones like the Arabic, Chinese, and Japanese, leading as it often does to ambiguities and even misunderstandings of a special sort that do not arise between the alphabetic cultures, misunderstandings which can even have political consequences.

These effects, to repeat, were theoretically attainable. For reasons to be explained later, the full vernacular was not in fact the first thing to be transcribed. The alphabet was not originally put at the service of ordinary human conversation. Rather it was first used to record a progressively complete version of the "oral literature" of Greece, if the paradox may be permitted, which had been nourished in the non-literate period and which indeed had sustained the identity of the previous oral culture of Greece. Although today we "read" our Homer, our Pindar, or our Euripides, a great deal of what we are "listening to" is a fairly accurate acoustic transcription of all the contrived forms in which oral speech had hitherto been preserved. This phenomenon as it occurs in the formation of what we call Greek literature has been imperfectly understood and will be explored in depth when the Greeks are at last allowed, as they will be, to take over the course and direction of this history.

And yet, though fluent transcription of the oral record became the primary use to which the alphabet was put, the secondary purpose which it came to serve was historically more important. I could say that it made possible the invention of fluent prose, but this would be misleading, since obviously the larger component of oral discourse even in an oral culture is prosaic. What is effectively brought into being was prose recorded and preserved in quantity. To interpret this innovation as merely stylistic would be to miss the point of a profound change occurring in the character of the content of what could be preserved. A revolution was underway both psychological and epistemological. The important and influential statement in any culture is the one that is preserved. Under conditions of non-literacy in Greece, and of craft literacy in pre-Greek cultures, the conditions for preservation were mnemonic, and this involved the use of verbal and musical rhythm, for any statement that was to be remembered and repeated. The alphabet, making available a visualized record which was complete, in place of an acoustic one, abolished the need for memorization and hence for rhythm. Rhythm had hitherto placed severe limitations upon the verbal arrangement of what might be said, or thought. More than that, the need to remember had used up a degree of brain-power—of psychic energy—which now was no longer needed. The statement need not be memorized. It could lie around as an artifact, to be read when needed; no penalty for forgetting—that is, so far as preservation was concerned. The mental energies thus released, by this economy of memory, have probably been extensive, contributing to an immense expansion of knowledge available to the human mind.

These theoretic possibilities were exploited only cautiously in Graeco-Roman antiquity, and are being fully realized only today. If I stress them here in their twofold significance, namely, that all possible discourse became translatable into script, and that simultaneously the burden of memorization was lifted from the mind, it is to bring out the further fact that the alphabet therewith made possible the production of novel or unexpected statement, previously unfamiliar

and even "unthought." The advance of knowledge, both humane and scientific, depends upon the human ability to think about something unexpected—a "new idea," as we loosely but conveniently say. Such novel thought only achieves completed existence when it becomes novel statement, and a novel statement cannot realize its potential until it can be preserved for further use. Previous transcription, because of the ambiguities of the script, discouraged attempts to record novel statements. This indirectly discouraged the attempt to frame them even orally, for what use were they likely to be, or what influence were they likely to have, if confined within the ephemeral range of casual vernacular conversation? The alphabet, by encouraging the production of unfamiliar statement, stimulated the thinking of novel thought, which could lie around in inscribed form, be recognized, be read and re-read, and so spread its influence among readers. It is no accident that the pre-alphabetic cultures of the world were also in a large sense the pre-scientific cultures, pre-philosophical and pre-literary. The power of novel statement is not restricted to the arrangement of scientific observation. It covers the gamut of the human experience. There were new inventible ways of speaking about human life, and therefore of thinking about it, which became slowly possible for man only when they became inscribed and preservable and extendable in the alphabetic literatures of Europe. . . .

READERSHIP BEFORE THE PRINTING PRESS

There were limits set to classical literacy by the character of the materials and the methods employed to manufacture the written word. The alphabet did not fully come into its own until Western Europe had learned to copy the letter shapes in movable type and until progress in industrial technique made possible the manufacture of cheap paper. So-called book production in antiquity and the various styles of writing employed have received substantial scholarly attention, the results of which need not be recapitulated here except as they throw light on the material difficulties which any extension of popular literacy was bound to encounter. For literacy is not built upon a fund of inscriptions. In Greece, where stone and baked clay initially provide our earliest testimony to the use of the alphabet, what we would like to know more about is the availability of those perishable surfaces which could perform the casual and copious services now supplied by the paper which we moderns so thoughtlessly consume and throw away. Herodotus reports that the earliest material of this nature in use was parchment, that is, animal skins, obviously a very limited resource, quantitatively speaking, though qualitatively superior as later antiquity was to realize. The other basic surface was that of the papyrus sheet available in Egypt. How soon did Greece import papyrus in quantity? The texts of Homer, so we were told by late tradition, received a recension of some sort in the period when Pisistratus ruled Athens about the middle of the sixth century. In what form were these texts available? Were they inscribed on papyrus? Certainly the first half of the fifth century saw the increasing use of papyrus in Athens, and also of the waxed tablet for making notes on. References in the plays of Aeschylus make this certain. But it is possible to deduce that the references are there because the use of such items was novel rather than familiar. The words "biblos" or "byblos" are translatable as either "papyrus" the material, or as the object consisting of papyrus on which writing is placed. The common translation "book" is misleading. Individual sheets of papyrus, as is well known, could be gummed together at the edges in series, thus forming a continuously extended surface which could be rolled up. To find the place you had to unroll until you came to it. "Biblion," the diminutive, meant neither book nor roll but a simple folded sheet or conceivably two or three

such, folded once over together. Such details as these, coupled with the certain scarcity of material when judged by modern standards, serve to remind us that the would-be reader in ancient Athens encountered certain obstacles to his reading which we would regard as constricting. In estimating the degree of literacy and the rate of its spread, how far should such material limitations be taken into account? Should they not make us more cautious in this matter than Hellenists usually are? To give just one example: Plato in his *Apology* makes Socrates refer to the *biblia* of Anaxagoras the philosopher, "purchasable for a drachma at most," which he says "are chockfull" (*gemei*) of such statements (*logoi*) as the prosecution has referred to. Are these books? Of course not. The reference is to those summary pronouncements of the philosopher's doctrine which still survive in quotation from later antiquity and which we now call the "fragments" of the philosopher. They are compressed in style and even oracular and, we suggest, were published as a guide to the philosopher's system to be used as a supplement to oral teaching. Such summaries could be inscribed in installments upon separate sheets of papyrus purchasable for a drachma per sheet. But a good deal has been made of his reference in describing the supposed Athenian book trade of the period and also in affirming a sophisticated literacy which is presupposed by the misleading translation "book."

This is not to discount the degree of literacy achieved in Athens in the last third of the fifth century before Christ but to emphasize that however general the management of the alphabet became, the habit of rapid reading which we are accustomed to identify as the hallmark of a verbally competent person would be very difficult to implement. There was no large volume of documentation to practice on. If Plato's Academy in the fourth century B.C. had a library, how many shelves were filled? The very term "library" is almost a mistranslation, considering the modern connotation, as when we are told that Euripides possessed the first library. This tradition appears to base itself upon an inference drawn from a piece of burlesque concocted by Aristophanes in his play *The Frogs* at the poet's expense. Euripides and his poetry, in a contest with Aeschylus in Hades, have to be "weighed," so he is told to get into the scale pan, after "picking up his papyri," indicating that the poet could be expected to carry a parcel with him. He is satirized as a composer who had turned himself into a reader and who made poetry out of what he had read, in supposed contrast to his antagonist who is orally oriented.

On what materials did Athenian children in elementary school learn their letters? Probably sand and slate, rather than papyrus, both being media quantitatively copious, since they admit of continual reuse through erasure. A "school scene" which predates the age of social literacy in Athens portrays an older man using a waxed tablet. Such waxed tablets but not paper are actually featured in the plots of a few plays of Euripides produced in the last third of the century when the delivery of a message or letter is called for. Aeschylus is aware only of their use for memoranda. In either case the material used would favor brevity of composition. It also could of course be reused, which again implies continual erasure of the written word. Documents can be flourished in a comedy of Aristophanes to back up an oral statement with the implication that only shysters would use this resource; the written word is still under some suspicion or is a little ridiculous. All in all, one concludes that the reading of the literate Athenian was confined within limits that we would think narrow, but what he did read he read deliberately and carefully. Speed of recognition, the secret of the alphabetic invention, was still likely to be slow relative to modern practice, and thus likelihood bears on the acknowledged attention which writers and readers of the high classical period gave to words and their weighing. Inscribed language was not being manufactured at a rate great enough to dull the attention or impair verbal taste. The written word carried the value of a commodity in limited supply. The literature of the period bears the hallmark of a verbal nicety never excelled and rarely equalled in European practice.

As a corollary to this verbal sophistication (which was reinforced by residual habits of oral composition), the writers of the classical period consulted each other's works and wrote what they had to say out of what others had written before them to a degree difficult for a modern author to appreciate. The world of literature, because quantitatively so restricted, could constitute itself a sort of large club, the members of which were familiar with each other's words even though separated by spans of historic time. A good deal of what was written therefore called upon the reader to recognize echoes from other works in circulation. If the modern scholar thinks he is able to trace influences and interconnections which seem excessive by modern standards of free composition, he is not necessarily deluding himself. The world of the alphabet in antiquity was like that.

Books and documentation multiplied in the Hellenistic and Roman periods. Papyrological discoveries indicate that papyrus was in ready supply in Hellenistic Egypt, where indeed one would expect to find it. But up to the end of antiquity and beyond that through the medieval centuries, extending through the invention of the codex or book proper, so much easier to handle and consult, the distinction between our modern paper literacy, if I may call it, and the literacy of our ancestors still holds. It is a distinction determined in part by the sheer quantitative limitations placed in antiquity upon the materials available for inscription. The use of the palimpsest—the document hoarded and then erased and reused, sometimes twice over—is eloquent testimony to the scarcity and the preciousness of the material surfaces upon which alphabetic script could be written.

But scarcity of materials aside, the production of script and hence the resources available for readership were bound to remain restricted beyond the imagination of any modern reader as long as such production remained a handicraft. This set a second quantitative limitation upon the creation of all documentation, whether for literary or business purposes, as is obvious. A decree or law could not be promulgated in a newspaper; copies of accounts could not be distributed to shareholders; an author could not commit his manuscript to a publisher for mass manufacture and sale.

But the qualitative restrictions thus imposed were if anything more drastic. Strict uniformity of letter shapes was rendered impossible by the vagaries of personal handwriting. A degree of standardization was theoretically possible and certainly aimed at in the Graeco-Roman period. It quickly broke up thereafter. A handicraft may and does produce a custom-made product of fine quality, and in the case of those artifacts that we use and consume in daily living such competitive excellence becomes esteemed and valuable. But the production of custom-built products on the same lines when the goal is the manufacture of communication becomes self-defeating. To the extent that the scribes formed schools or guilds, formal or otherwise, to foster the elaboration of local hands and embellish competing styles of writing,

readership of that sort which alone furnishes the basis of a literate culture was bound to be impaired. Calligraphy, as already noted above, becomes the enemy of literacy and hence also of literature and of science.

Alphabetic literacy, in order to overcome these limitations of method and so achieve its full potential, had to await the invention of the printing press. The original achievement, the Greek one, had solved an empirical problem by applying abstract analysis. But the material means for maximizing the result required the assistance of further inventions and had to await a long time for it. Such necessary combination of technologies is characteristic of scientific advance. To realize that there is energy available when water is converted into steam was one thing. To harness the energy successfully was another, requiring the parallel construction of machine tools capable of producing fine tolerances to fit piston to cylinder, the manufacture of lubricants capable of sealing the fit, the parallel invention of slide-rod mechanisms to control the periods of steam pressure, and of crank and connecting rod to convert the thrust into rotation. The energy of the alphabet likewise had to await the assistance provided by the dawning age of scientific advance in Europe in order to be fully released.

8 ORALITY, LITERACY, AND MODERN MEDIA
Walter Ong

Walter Ong was, until his recent retirement, professor of humanities at Saint Louis University. He has written extensively on the orality/literacy question, as well as the communications dimension of the shift from the medieval to the modern era.

Fully literate persons can only with great difficulty imagine what a primary oral culture is like, that is, a culture with no knowledge whatsoever of writing or even of the possibility of writing. Try to imagine a culture where no one has even "looked up" anything. In a primary oral culture, the expression "to look up something" is an empty phrase: it would have no conceivable meaning. Without writing, words as such have no visual presence, even when the objects they represent are visual. They are sounds. You might "call" them back—"recall" them. But there is nowhere to "look" for them. They have no focus and no trace (a visual metaphor, showing dependency on writing), not even a trajectory. They are occurrences, events.

To learn what a primary oral culture is and what the nature of our problem is regarding such a culture, it helps first to reflect on the nature of sound itself as sound (Ong 1967b, pp. 111–38). All sensation takes place in time, but sound has a special relationship to time unlike that of the other fields that register in human sensation. Sound exists only when it is going out of existence. It is not simply perishable but essentially evanescent, and it is sensed as evanescent. When I pronounce the word "permanence," by the time I get to the "-nence," the "perma-" is gone, and has to be gone.

There is no way to stop sound and have sound. I can stop a moving picture camera and hold one frame fixed on the screen. If I stop the movement of sound, I have nothing—only silence, no sound at all. All sensation takes place in time, but no other sensory field totally resists a holding action, stabilization, in quite this way. Vision can register motion, but it can also register immobility. Indeed, it favors immobility, for to examine something closely by vision, we prefer to have it quiet. We often reduce motion to a series of still shots the better to see what motion is. There is no equivalent of a still shot for sound. An oscillogram is silent. It lies outside the sound world.

For anyone who has a sense of what words are in a primary oral culture, or a culture not far removed from primary orality, it is not surprising that the Hebrew term *dabar* means "word" and "event." Malinowski (1923, pp. 451, 470–81) has made the point that among "primitive" (oral) peoples generally language is a mode of action and not simply a countersign of thought, though he had trouble explaining what he was getting at . . . , since understanding of the psychodynamics of orality was virtually nonexistent in 1923. Neither is it surprising that oral peoples commonly, and probably universally, consider words to have great power. Sound cannot be sounding without the use of power. A hunter can see a buffalo, smell, taste, and touch a buffalo when the buffalo is completely inert, even dead, but if he hears a buffalo, he had better watch out: something is going on. In this sense, all sound, and especially oral utterance, which comes from inside living organisms, is "dynamic."

The fact that oral peoples commonly and in all likelihood universally consider words to have magical potency is clearly tied in, at least unconsciously, with their sense of the word as necessarily spoken, sounded, and hence power-driven. Deeply typographic folk forget to think of words as primarily oral, as events, and hence as necessarily powered: for them, words tend rather to be assimilated to things, "out there" on a flat surface. Such "things" are not so readily associated with magic, for they are not actions, but are in a radical sense dead, though subject to dynamic resurrection (Ong 1977, pp. 230–71).

Oral peoples commonly think of names (one kind of words) as conveying power over things. Explanations of Adam's naming of the animals in Genesis 2:20 usually call condescending attention to this presumably quaint archaic belief. Such a belief is in fact far less quaint than it seems to unreflective chirographic and typographic folk. First of all, names do give human beings power over what they name: without learning a vast store of names, one is simply powerless to understand, for example, chemistry and to practice chemical engineering. And so with all other intellectual knowledge. Secondly, chirographic and typographic folk tend to think of names as labels, written or printed tags imaginatively affixed to an object named. Oral folk have no sense of a name as a tag, for they have no idea of a name as something that can be seen. Written or printed representations of words can be labels; real, spoken words cannot be.

You Know What You Can Recall: Mnemonics and Formulas

In an oral culture, restriction of words to sound determines not only modes of expression but also thought processes.

You know what you can recall. When we say we know Euclidean geometry, we mean not that we have in mind at the moment every one of its propositions and proofs but rather that we can bring them to mind readily. We can recall them. The theorem "You know what you can recall" applies also to an oral culture. But how do persons in an oral culture recall? The organized knowledge that literates today study so that they "know" it, that is, can recall it, has, with very few if any exceptions, been assembled and made available to them in writing. This is the case not only with Euclidean geometry but also with American Revolutionary history, or even baseball batting averages or traffic regulations.

An oral culture has no texts. How does it get together organized material for recall? This is the same as asking, "What does it or can it know in an organized fashion?"

Suppose a person in an oral culture would undertake to think through a particular complex problem and would finally manage to articulate a solution which itself is relatively complex, consisting, let us say, of a few hundred words. How does he or she retain for later recall the verbalization so painstakingly elaborated? In the total absence of any writing, there is nothing outside the thinker, no text, to enable him or her to produce the same line of thought again or even to verify whether he or she has done so or not. *Aides-mémoire* such as notched sticks or a series of carefully arranged objects will not of themselves retrieve a complicated series of assertions. How, in fact, could a lengthy, analytic solution

ever be assembled in the first place? An interlocutor is virtually essential: it is hard to talk to yourself for hours on end. Sustained thought in an oral culture is tied to communication.

But even with a listener to stimulate and ground your thought, the bits and pieces of your thought cannot be preserved in jotted notes. How could you ever call back to mind what you had so laboriously worked out? The only answer is: Think memorable thoughts. In a primary oral culture, to solve effectively the problem of retaining and retrieving carefully articulated thought, you have to do your thinking in mnemonic patterns, shaped for ready oral recurrence. Your thought must come into being in heavily rhythmic, balanced patterns, in repetitions or antitheses, in alliterations and assonances, in epithetic and other formulary expressions, in standard thematic settings (the assembly, the meal, the duel, the hero's "helper," and so on), in proverbs which are constantly heard by everyone so that they come to mind readily and which themselves are patterned for retention and ready recall, or in other mnemonic form. Serious thought is intertwined with memory systems. Mnemonic needs determine even syntax (Havelock 1963, pp. 87–96, 131–2, 294–6).

Protracted orally based thought, even when not in formal verse, tends to be highly rhythmic, for rhythm aids recall, even physiologically. Jousse (1978) has shown the intimate linkage between rhythmic oral patterns, the breathing process, gesture, and the bilateral symmetry of the human body in ancient Aramaic and Hellenic targums, and thus also in ancient Hebrew. Among the ancient Greeks, Hesiod, who was intermediate between oral Homeric Greece and fully developed Greek literacy, delivered quasi-philosophic material in the formulaic verse forms that structured it into the oral culture from which he had emerged (Havelock 1963, pp. 97–8, 294–301).

Formulas help implement rhythmic discourse and also act as mnemonic aids in their own right, as set expressions circulating through the mouths and ears of all. "Red in the morning, the sailor's warning; red in the night, the sailor's delight." "Divide and conquer." "To err is human, to forgive is divine." "Sorrow is better than laughter, because when the face is sad the heart grows wiser" (Ecclesiastes 7:3). "The clinging vine." "The sturdy oak." "Chase off nature and she returns at a gallop." Fixed, often rhythmically balanced, expressions of this sort and of other sorts can be found occasionally in print, indeed can be "looked up" in books of sayings, but in oral cultures they are not occasional. They are incessant. They form the substance of thought itself. Thought in any extended form is impossible without them, for it consists in them.

The more sophisticated orally patterned thought is, the more it is likely to be marked by set expressions skillfully used. This is true of oral cultures generally from those of Homeric Greece to those of the present day across the globe. Havelock's *Preface to Plato* (1963) and fictional works such as Chinua Achebe's novel *No Longer at Ease* (1961), which draws directly on Ibo oral tradition in West Africa, alike provide abundant instances of thought patterns of orally educated characters who move in these oral, mnemonically tooled grooves, as the speakers reflect, with high intelligence and sophistication, on the situations in which they find themselves involved. The law itself in oral cultures is enshrined in formulaic sayings, proverbs, which are not mere jurisprudential decorations, but themselves constitute the law. A judge in an oral culture is often called on to articulate sets of relevant proverbs out of which he can produce equitable decisions in the cases under formal litigation before him . . .

In an oral culture, to think through something in non-formulaic, non-patterned, non-mnemonic terms, even if it were possible, would be a waste of time, for such thought, once worked through, could never be recovered with any effectiveness, as it could be with the aid of writing. It would not be abiding knowledge but

simply a passing thought, however complex. Heavy patterning and communal fixed formulas in oral cultures serve some of the purposes of writing in chirographic cultures, but in doing so they of course determine the kind of thinking that can be done, the way experience is intellectually organized. In an oral culture, experience is intellectualized mnemonically. This is one reason why, for a St Augustine of Hippo (A.D. 354–430), as for other savants living in a culture that knew some literacy but still carried an overwhelmingly massive oral residue, memory bulks so large when he treats of the powers of the mind.

Of course, all expression and all thought is to a degree formulaic in the sense that every word and every concept conveyed in a word is a kind of formula, a fixed way of processing the data of experience, determining the way experience and reflection are intellectually organized, and acting as a mnemonic device of sorts. Putting experience into any words (which means transforming it at least a little bit—not the same as falsifying it) can implement its recall. The formulas characterizing orality are more elaborate, however, than are individual words, though some may be relatively simple: the *Beowulf*-poet's "whale-road" is a formula (metaphorical) for the sea in a sense in which the term "sea" is not.

THE INTERIORITY OF SOUND

In treating some psychodynamics of orality, we have thus far attended chiefly to one characteristic of sound itself, its evanescence, its relationship to time. Sound exists only when it is going out of existence. Other characteristics of sound also determine or influence oral psychodynamics. The principal one of these other characteristics is the unique relationship of sound to interiority when sound is compared to the rest of the senses. This relationship is important because of the interiority of human consciousness and of human communication itself. It can be discussed only summarily here. I have treated the matter in greater fullness and depth in *The Presence of the Word,* to which the interested reader is referred (1967, Index).

To test the physical interior of an object as interior, no sense works so directly as sound. The human sense of sight is adapted best to light diffusely reflected from surfaces. (Diffuse reflection, as from a printed page or a landscape, contrasts with specular reflection, as from a mirror.) A source of light, such as a fire, may be intriguing but it is optically baffling: the eye cannot get a "fix" on anything within the fire. Similarly, a translucent object, such as alabaster, is intriguing because, although it is not a source of light, the eye cannot get a "fix" on it either. Depth can be perceived by the eye, but most satisfactorily as a series of surfaces: the trunks of trees in a grove, for example, or chairs in an auditorium. The eye does not perceive an interior strictly as an interior: inside a room, the walls it perceives are still surfaces, outsides.

Taste and smell are not much help in registering interiority or exteriority. Touch is. But touch partially destroys interiority in the process of perceiving it. If I wish to discover by touch whether a box is empty or full, I have to make a hole in the box to insert a hand or finger: this means that the box is to that extent open, to that extent less an interior.

Hearing can register interiority without violating it. I can rap a box to find whether it is empty or full or a wall to find whether it is hollow or solid inside. Or I can ring a coin to learn whether it is silver or lead.

Sounds all register the interior structures of whatever it is that produces them. A violin filled with concrete will not sound like a normal violin. A saxophone sounds differently from a flute: it is structured differently inside. And above all, the human voice comes from inside the human organism which provides the voice's resonances.

Sight isolates, sound incorporates. Whereas sight situates the observer outside what he views, at a distance, sound pours into the hearer. Vision dissects, as Merleau-Ponty has observed (1961). Vision comes to a human being from one direction at a time: to look at a room or a landscape, I must move my eyes around from one part to another. When I hear, however, I gather sound simultaneously from every direction at once: I am at the center of my auditory world, which envelops me, establishing me at a kind of core of sensation and existence. This centering effect of sound is what high-fidelity sound reproduction exploits with intense sophistication. You can immerse yourself in hearing, in sound. There is no way to immerse yourself similarly in sight.

By contrast with vision, the dissecting sense, sound is thus a unifying sense. A typical visual ideal is clarity and distinctness, a taking apart (Descartes' campaigning for clarity and distinctness registered an intensification of vision in the human sensorium—Ong 1967, pp. 63, 221). The auditory ideal, by contrast, is harmony, a putting together.

Interiority and harmony are characteristics of human consciousness. The consciousness of each human person is totally interiorized, known to the person from the inside and inaccessible to any other person directly from the inside. Everyone who says "I" means something different by it from what every other person means. What is "I" to me is only "you" to you. And this "I" incorporates experience into itself by "getting it all together." Knowledge is ultimately not a fractioning but a unifying phenomenon, a striving for harmony. Without harmony, an interior condition, the psyche is in bad health.

It should be noted that the concepts interior and exterior are not mathematical concepts and cannot be differentiated mathematically. They are existentially grounded concepts, based on experience of one's own body, which is both inside me (I do not ask you to stop kicking my body but to stop kicking *me*) and outside me (I feel myself as in some sense inside my body). The body is a frontier between myself and everything else. What we mean by "interior" and "exterior" can be conveyed only by reference to experience of bodiliness. Attempted definitions of "interior" and "exterior" are inevitably tautological: "interior" is defined by "in," which is defined by "between," which is defined by "inside," and so on round and round the tautological circle. The same is true with "exterior." When we speak of interior and exterior, even in the case of physical objects, we are referring to our own sense of ourselves: I am *inside* here and everything else is *outside*. By interior and exterior we point to our own experience of bodiliness (Ong 1967, pp. 117–22, 176–9, 228, 231) and analyze other objects by reference to this experience.

In a primary oral culture, where the word has its existence only in sound, with no reference whatsoever to any visually perceptible text, and no awareness of even the possibility of such a text, the phenomenology of sound enters deeply into human beings' feel for existence, as processed by the spoken word. For the way in which the word is experienced is always momentous in psychic life. The centering action of sound (the field of sound is not spread out before me but is all around me) affects man's sense of the cosmos. For oral cultures, the cosmos is an ongoing event with man at its center. Man is the *umbilicus mundi*, the navel of the world (Eliade 1958, pp. 231–5, etc.). Only after print and the extensive experience with maps that print implemented would human beings, when they thought about the cosmos or universe or "world," think primarily of something laid out before their eyes, as in a modern printed atlas, a vast surface or assemblage of surfaces (vision presents surfaces) ready to be "explored." The ancient oral world knew few "explorers," though it did know many itinerants, travelers, voyagers, adventurers, and pilgrims.

It will be seen that most of the characteristics of orally based thought and expression discussed earlier in this chapter relate intimately to the unifying, centralizing, interiorizing economy of sound as perceived by human beings. A sound-dominated verbal economy is consonant with aggregative (harmonizing) tendencies rather than with analytic, dissecting tendencies (which would come with the inscribed, visualized word: vision is a dissecting sense). It is consonant also with the conservative holism (the homeostatic present that must be kept intact, the formulary expressions that must be kept intact), with situational thinking (again holistic, with human action at the center) rather than abstract thinking, with a certain humanistic organization of knowledge around the actions of human and anthromorphic beings, interiorized persons, rather than around impersonal things.

The denominators used here to describe the primary oral world will be useful again later to describe what happened to human consciousness when writing and print reduced the oral–aural world to a world of visualized pages.

SECONDARY ORALITY

. . . With telephone, radio, television and various kinds of sound tape, electronic technology has brought us into the age of "secondary orality." This new orality has striking resemblances to the old in its participatory mystique, its fostering of a communal sense, its concentration on the present moment, and even its use of formulas (Ong 1971, pp. 284–303; 1977, pp. 16–49, 305–41). But it is essentially a more deliberate and self-conscious orality, based permanently on the use of writing and print, which are essential for the manufacture and operation of the equipment and for its use as well.

Secondary orality is both remarkably like and remarkably unlike primary orality. Like primary orality, secondary orality has generated a strong group sense, for listening to spoken words forms hearers into a group, a true audience, just as reading written or printed texts turns individuals in on themselves. But secondary orality generates a sense for groups immeasurably larger than those of primary oral culture—McLuhan's "global village." Moreover, before writing, oral folk were group-minded because no feasible alternative had presented itself. In our age of secondary orality, we are group-minded self-consciously and programmatically. The individual feels that he or she, as an individual, must be socially sensitive. Unlike members of a primary oral culture, who are turned outward because they have had little occasion to turn inward, we are turned outward because we have turned inward. In a like vein, where primary orality promotes spontaneity because the analytic reflectiveness implemented by writing is unavailable, secondary orality promotes spontaneity because through analytic reflection we have decided that spontaneity is a good thing. We plan our happenings carefully to be sure that they are thoroughly spontaneous.

The contrast between oratory in the past and in today's world well highlights the contrast between primary and secondary orality. Radio and television have brought major political figures as public speakers to a larger public than was ever possible before modern electronic developments. Thus in a sense orality has come into its own more than ever before. But it is not the old orality. The old-style oratory coming from primary orality is gone forever. In the Lincoln–Douglas debates of 1858, the combatants—for that is what they clearly and truly were—faced one another often in the scorching Illinois summer sun outdoors, before wildly responsive audiences of as many as 12,000 or 15,000 persons (at Ottawa and Freeport, Illinois, respectively—Sparks 1908, pp. 137–8, 189–90), speaking for an hour and a half each. The first speaker had one hour, the second an hour and a half, and the first another half hour

of rebuttal—all this with no amplifying equipment. Primary orality made itself felt in the additive, redundant, carefully balanced, highly agonistic style, and the intense interplay between speaker and audience. The debaters were hoarse and physically exhausted at the end of each bout. Presidential debates on television today are completely out of this older oral world. The audience is absent, invisible, inaudible. The candidates are ensconced in tight little booths, make short presentations, and engage in crisp little conversations with each other in which any agonistic edge is deliberately kept dull. Electronic media do not tolerate a show of open antagonism. Despite their cultivated air of spontaneity, these media are totally dominated by a sense of closure which is the heritage of print: a show of hostility might break open the closure, the tight control. Candidates accommodate themselves to the psychology of the media. Genteel, literate domesticity is rampant. Only quite elderly persons today can remember what oratory was like when it was still in living contact with its primary oral roots. Others perhaps hear more oratory, or at least more talk, from major public figures than people commonly heard a century ago. But what they hear will give them very little idea of the old oratory reaching back from pre-electronic times through two millennia and far beyond, or of the oral lifestyle and oral thought structures out of which such oratory grew.

BIBLIOGRAPHY

Achebe, Chinva (1961) *No Longer at Ease* (New York: Ivan Obolensky).

Eliade, Mircea (1958) *Patterns in Comparative Religion,* trans. by Willard R. Trask (New York: Sheed & Ward).

Havelock, Eric A. (1963) *Preface to Plato* (Cambridge, MA: Belknap Press of Harvard University Press).

Jousse, Marcel (1925) *Le Style oval rhythmique et mnemotechnique chez les Verbomoteurs* (Paris: G. Beauchesne).

Malinowski, Bronislaw (1923) "The Problem of Meaning in Primitive Languages," in C. K. Ogden and I. A. Richards (eds.), *The Meaning of Meaning* (New York: Harcourt Brace; London: Kegan Paul, Trench, Trubner).

Merleau-Ponty, Maurice (1961) "L'Oeil et l'esprit," *Les Temps modernes*, 18, 184–5. Numéro spécial: "Maurice Merleau-Ponty," 193–227.

Ong, Walter (1967) *The Presence of the Word* (New Haven and London: Yale University Press).

—— (1971) *Rhetoric, Romance, and Technology* (Ithaca and London: Cornell University Press).

—— (1977) *Interface of the Word* (Ithaca and London: Cornell University Press).

Sparks, Edwin Erle (ed.) (1908) *The Lincoln-Douglas Debates of 1858*, Collections of the Illinois State Historical Library, Vol. III, Lincoln Series, vol. 1 (Springfield, IL: Illinois State Historical Library).

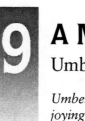

9 A MEDIEVAL LIBRARY
Umberto Eco

Umberto Eco, author of The Name of the Rose *and* Foucault's Pendulum, *is currently enjoying a reputation as a best-selling novelist. He is also a medieval scholar and prolific writer in the field of communication studies and popular culture.*

In which there is a visit to the scriptorium, and a meeting with many scholars, copyists, and rubricators, as well as an old blind man who is expecting the Antichrist.

. . .

When we reached the top of the stairs, we went through the east tower into the scriptorium, and there I could not suppress a cry of wonder. This floor was not divided in two like the one below, and therefore it appeared to my eyes in all its spacious immensity. The ceilings, curved and not too high (lower than in a church, but still higher than in any chapter house I ever saw), supported by sturdy pillars, enclosed a space suffused with the most beautiful light, because three enormous windows opened on each of the longer sides, whereas a smaller window pierced each of the five external sides of each tower; eight high, narrow windows, finally, allowed light to enter from the octagonal central well.

The abundance of windows meant that the great room was cheered by a constant diffused light, even on a winter afternoon. The panes were not colored like church windows, and the lead-framed squares of clear glass allowed the light to enter in the purest possible fashion, not modulated by human art, and thus to serve its purpose, which was to illuminate the work of reading and writing. I have seen at other times and in other places many scriptoria, but none where there shone so luminously, in the outpouring of physical light which made the room glow, the spiritual principle that light incarnates, radiance, source of all beauty and learning, inseparable attribute of that proportion the room embodied. For three things concur in creating beauty: first of all integrity or perfection, and for this reason we consider ugly all incomplete things; then proper proportion or consonance; and finally clarity and light, and in fact we call beautiful those things of definite color. And since the sight of the beautiful implies peace, and since our appetite is calmed similarly by peacefulness, by the good, and by the beautiful, I felt myself filled with a great consolation and I thought how pleasant it must be to work in that place.

As it appeared to my eyes, at that afternoon hour, it seemed to me a joyous workshop of learning. I saw later at St. Gall a scriptorium of similar proportions, also separated from the library (in other convents the monks worked in the same place where the books were kept), but

Illuminated manuscript: The miraculous draught of fishes. *The British Library.*

not so beautifully arranged as this one. Antiquarians, librarians, rubricators, and scholars were seated, each at his own desk, and there was a desk under each of the windows. And since there were forty windows (a number truly perfect, derived from the decupling of the quadragon, as if the Ten Commandments had been multiplied by the four cardinal virtues), forty monks could work at the same time, though at that moment there were perhaps thirty. Severinus explained to us that monks working in the scriptorium were exempted from the offices of terce, sext, and nones so they would not have to leave their work during the hours of daylight, and they stopped their activity only at sunset, for vespers.

The brightest places were reserved for the antiquarians, the most expert illuminators, the rubricators, and the copyists. Each desk had everything required for illuminating and copying: inkhorns, fine quills which some monks were sharpening with a thin knife, pumice stone for smoothing the parchment, rulers for drawing the lines that the writing would follow. Next to each scribe, or at the top of the sloping desk, there was a lectern, on which the codex to be copied was placed, the page covered by a sheet with a cut-out window which framed the line being copied at that moment. And some had inks of gold and various colors. Other monks were simply reading books, and they wrote down their annotations in their personal notebooks or on tablets.

I did not have time, however, to observe their work, because the librarian came to us. We already knew he was Malachi of Hildesheim. His face was trying to assume an expression of welcome, but I could not help shuddering at the sight of such a singular countenance. . . .

My master began speaking with Malachi, praising the beauty and the industry of the scriptorium and asking him for information about the procedure for the work done there, because, he said very acutely, he had heard this library spoken of everywhere and would like to examine many of the books. Malachi explained to him what the abbot had already said: the monk asked the librarian for the work he wished to consult and the librarian then went to fetch it from the library above, if the request was justified and devout. William asked how he could find out the names of the books kept in the cases upstairs, and Malachi showed him, fixed by a little gold chain to his own desk, a voluminous codex covered with very thickly written lists.

William slipped his hands inside his habit, at the point where it billowed over his chest to make a kind of sack, and he drew from it an object that I had already seen in his hands, and on his face, in the course of our journey. It was a forked pin, so constructed that it could stay on a man's nose (or at least on his, so prominent and aquiline) as a rider remains astride his horse or as a bird clings to its perch. And, one on either side of the fork, before the eyes, there were two ovals of metal, which held two almonds of glass, thick as the bottom of a tumbler. William preferred to read with these before his eyes, and he said they made his vision better than what nature had endowed him with or than his advanced age, especially as the daylight failed, would permit. They did not serve him to see from a distance, for then his eyes were, on the contrary, quite sharp, but to see close up. With these lenses he could read manuscripts penned in very faint letters, which even I had some trouble deciphering. He explained to me that, when a man had passed the middle point of his life, even if his sight had always been excellent, the eye hardened and the pupil became recalcitrant, so that many learned men had virtually died, as far as reading and writing were concerned, after their fiftieth summer. A grave misfortune for men who could have given the best fruits of their intellect for many more years. So the Lord was to be praised since someone had devised and constructed this instrument. And he told me this in support of the ideas of his Roger Bacon, who had said that the aim of learning was also to prolong human life.

The other monks looked at William with great curiosity but did not dare ask him questions. And I noticed that, even in a place so zealously and proudly dedicated to reading and writing, that wondrous instrument had not yet arrived. I felt proud to be at the side of a man who had something with which to dumbfound other men famous in the world for their wisdom.

With those objects on his eyes William bent over the lists inscribed in the codex. I looked, too, and we found titles of books we had never before heard of, and others most famous, that the library possessed.

"*De pentagono Salomonis, Ars loquendi et intelligendi in lingua hebraica, De rebus metallicis* by Roger of Hereford, *Algebra* by Al-Kuwarizimi, translated into Latin by Robertus Anglicus, the *Punica* of Silius Italicus, the *Gesta francorum, De laudibus sanctae crucis,* by Rabanus Maurus, and *Flavii Claudii Giordani de aetate mundi et hominis reservatis singulis litteris per singulos libros ab A usque ad Z,*" my master read. "Splendid works. But in what order are they listed?" He quoted from a text I did not know but which was certainly familiar to Malachi: "'The librarian must have a list of all books, carefully ordered by subjects and authors, and they must be classified on the shelves with numerical indications.' How do you know the collocation of each book?"

Malachi showed him some annotations beside each title. I read: "iii, IV gradus, V in prima graecorum"; "ii, V gradus, VII in tertia anglorum," and so on. I understood that the first number indicated the position of the book on the shelf or gradus, which was in turn indicated

by the second number, while the case was indicated by the third number; and I understood also that the other phrases designated a room or a corridor of the library, and I made bold to ask further information about these last distinctions. Malachi looked at me sternly: "Perhaps you do not know, or have forgotten, that only the librarian is allowed access to the library. It is therefore right and sufficient that only the librarian know how to decipher these things."

"But in what order are the books recorded in this list?" William asked. "Not by subject, it seems to me." He did not suggest an order by author, following the same sequence as the letters of the alphabet, for this is a system I have seen adopted only in recent years, and at that time it was rarely used.

"The library dates back to the earliest times," Malachi said, "and the books are registered in order of their acquisition, donation, or entrance within our walls."

"They are difficult to find, then," William observed.

"It is enough for the librarian to know them by heart and know when each book came here. As for the other monks, they can rely on his memory." He spoke as if discussing someone other than himself, and I realized he was speaking of the office that at that moment he unworthily held, but which had been held by a hundred others, now deceased, who had handed down their knowledge from one to the other. . . .

10   Communication in the Middle Ages
James Burke

James Burke is well known for his two award-winning television series, Connections *and* The Day the Universe Changed. *He has also written other series and books upon which those series are based.*

The medieval adult was in no way less intelligent than his modern counterpart. He merely lived in a different world, which made different demands on him. His was a world without facts. Indeed, the modern concept of a fact would have been an incomprehensible one. Medieval people relied for day to day information solely on what they themselves, or someone they knew, had observed or experienced in the world immediately around them. Their lives were regular, repetitive and unchanging.

There was almost no part of this life-without-fact that could be other than local. Virtually no information reached the vast majority of people from the world outside the villages in which they lived. When all information was passed by word of mouth, rumour ruled. Everything other than personal experience was the subject of hearsay, a word which carried little of the pejorative sense it does today. Reputation was jealously guarded because it was easily ruined by loose talk. Denial of a rumour was difficult, if not impossible, and credulity was the stock in trade of the illiterate.

What medieval man called "fact" we would call opinion, and there were few people who travelled enough to know the difference. The average daily journey was seven miles, which was the distance most riders could cover and be sure of return before dark.

There was much intermarriage in these isolated communities, and each had its share of idiots. In an age when experience was what counted most, power was in the hands of the elders. They approved local customs and practice, and in matters of legal dispute they were the judges. They resisted change: things were done because the elders confirmed that they had always been done so.

The dialect spoken in one community was all but incomprehensible fifty miles away. As Chaucer relates, a group of fourteenth-century London merchants shipwrecked on the north coast of England were jailed as foreign spies. Without frequent social or economic exchange between communities, the language remained fragmented in local forms.

For the illiterate dialect-speaking villager, the church was the main source of information. The scriptures illustrated holy themes, recalled the work of the seasons and pointed morals. Biblical tales glowed from the stained-glass windows. Gothic cathedrals have been called "encyclopedias in stone and glass." The news of the world, both ecclesiastical and civil, came from the pulpit.

In communities that had for centuries been isolated and self-sufficient, the social structure was feudal. There were three classes: noble, priest and peasant. The noble fought for all. The peasant worked for all. The priest prayed for all.

On the very rare occasions when news arrived from outside, it was shouted through the community by a crier. For this reason few villages were bigger than the range of the human voice, and towns were administratively subdivided on the same scale. Village laws and customs were passed on by word of mouth. Living memory was the ultimate judge. It was a legal commonplace, even in town courts, that a live witness deserved more credence than words on parchment.

Manuscripts were rare. They were, after all, little more than marks of doubtful significance on dead animal skins. To the illiterate, documents were worthless as proof because they were easy to forge. A living witness told the truth because he wanted to go on living. Legal proceedings were conducted orally, a practice that continues to this day. Parties were summoned by word of mouth, sometimes with the aid of a bell. Charges were read aloud to the defendant. In the late Middle Ages the litigant was obliged to speak for himself, so there was little justice for the deaf and dumb. The court "heard" the evidence. Guilt or innocence was a matter for debate.

Without calendars and clocks or written records, the passage of time was marked by memorable events. In villages it was, of course, identified by seasonal activity: "When the woodcock fly," "At harvest time," and so on. Country people were intensely aware of the passage of the year. But between these seasonal cues, time, in the modern sense, did not exist. Even in rich villages which could afford a water clock or a sun dial, a watchman would call out the passing hours, shouting them from the church tower. The hours would echo through the surrounding countryside, shouted along by the workers in the fields. Units of time smaller than an hour were rarely used. They would have had no purpose in a world that moved at the pace of nature.

Months were measured only approximately, since major divisions of the calendar such as the spring equinox happened at different times each year. Easter was a source of considerable confusion because its date depended on the positional relationship of the sun and moon, and this conjunction often occurred when the moon was not visible. Important events in life were recalled by more reliable markers, such as a particularly hard frost, an abnormal harvest or a death. Saints' days were unreliable. Even the great Erasmus was not sure whether he had been born on St. Jude's or St. Simon's Day.

Such temporal markers were important as they would often be needed to determine birthdays, of vital concern during the Middle Ages in regard to inheritance. In an oral life the acts of giving and taking were complicated by the need to have witnesses present. In 1153, for example, the gift of a salt-pan was made to the Priory of St. Peter at Sele, in Sussex, "Many people seeing and hearing." The use of the oath to reinforce the legality of the event was, and still is, a means of reinforcing the testimony of an oral witness.

Even when, in late medieval times, documentation began to be introduced on a wide scale, the old habits died hard. Symbolic objects were still exchanged to represent a transaction. Knives were favourite symbols. The transaction would often be recorded on the knife haft, as in the case of a gift made in the middle of the twelfth century to the monks of Lindisfarne in northern England. The monks had been given the Chapelry of Lowick and the tithes due to it. On the knife haft is written *sygnum de capella*

de lowic ("to represent the Chapel of Lowick"). But it was the knife, not the inscription, that symbolised the event and that served to jog the memory. The same reasoning lay behind the use of the personal seal on letters, and the wearing of a wedding ring.

Documents were often forged. In the Middle Ages, it was common to write undated texts. One out of three was false. Canterbury monks, concerned that the Primacy in England should not pass to their rivals in York, "found" papal bulls dating from between the seventh and tenth centuries which supported their cause. The manuscripts had "turned up inside other books." The monks admitted that they were "only copies, but nonetheless valid . . ."

The general laxity in the transmission of information affected many aspects of medieval life. Travel was more hazardous because of it. For the majority of those who were obliged to move about, journeys consisted of brief periods of security in the communities along the route, interspersed with hours or days of fear and danger in the forests. This was not primarily due to the presence of outlaws or wild animals lurking in the trackless woods that covered most of Europe at the time, but because the majority of travellers had only the haziest notion of where their destination lay.

There were no maps, and few roads. Travellers had a keen sense of direction which took account of the position of the sun and the stars, the flight of birds, the flow of water, the nature of the terrain, and so on. But even information gleaned from another traveller who had previously taken the same route was of limited value if he had travelled in a different season or under different conditions. Rivers changed course. Fords deepened. Bridges fell.

The safe way, indeed the only way, to travel was in groups. In the Middle Ages, a lone traveller was a rare figure. He was usually a courtier on the king's business, trained to repeat long messages word for word. Such a message could

One Burgundian merchant, Jacques Coeur, used his own pigeon post. The Medici bankers kept in regular contact with their branch managers and their forty-odd representatives all over Europe by using posting messengers. These went very much faster than the average traveller, who could not afford to change horses when they became exhausted. With fresh horses the couriers could average ninety miles a day, more than twice as much as an ordinary rider.

Nonetheless, rumour coloured the reception of news even in the cities, when it arrived often after lengthy delays. In the fifteenth century it took eighteen months for the news of Joan of Arc's death to reach Constantinople. The news of that city's fall in 1453 took a month to get to Venice, twice as long to Rome, and three months to reach the rest of Europe. Later, the perception of the distance travelled by Columbus was coloured by the fact that the news of his landfall across the Atlantic had taken as long to reach the streets of Portugal as did news from Poland.

For the villager or household not connected with trade, news came for the most part with the travelling entertainers, small parties of musicians and poets called jongleurs, or troubadours. The former was usually the performer, the latter the writer or composer. Their acts might also include juggling, magic, performing animals and even circus acts. Principally, their entertainment took the form of recitals of poems and songs written about real events.

Since the audience would hear the story only once, the performance was histrionic, repetitive, easily memorised, and often reworked from the original into local dialect for the benefit of the audience. The portrayal of emotion was simple and exaggerated. The entire performance was in rhyme, so that both performer and audience could more easily remember it. The performer took all the parts, changing voice and gesture to suit. The more enjoyable the act, the

Great seal of Richard the Lionheart of England. The symbol, rather than a signature, served to assure the illiterate of the authority and source of what was contained in the document. *Permission of Little Brown.*

not be forged or lost. By the fifteenth century there were regular courier services working for the Roman Curia and the royal houses of England, Aragon, the republic of Venice and the university of Paris. In some places, such as Ulm, Regensburg and Augsburg, three mining towns of southern Germany, there were regular local postal services.

more money he made. If a poem were particularly successful, other jongleurs would try to hear it several times in order to memorise and later perform it themselves.

The travelling poets were often used by a patron to spread a particular piece of propaganda. Poems of this nature were called *sirventes*. Ostensibly on a romantic theme, they often concealed political or personal messages. In rare cases the object of the satire was openly named. In 1285 Pedro III of Aragon attacked Philip III of Spain in a sirvente. The most famous thirteenth-century propaganda writer of this type of material was Guillaume de Berjuedin. The performances of these kinds of poems must have had the desired effect, because in an oral world where the strongest bond was loyalty, reputation was of cardinal importance and rumour therefore an effective weapon.

The jongleurs would often meet and exchange parts of their repertoire. These meetings, called *puys*, were held all over France and took the form of a kind of poetry competition at which the jongleurs would display their phenomenal memories. A good jongleur needed to hear several hundred lines of poetry only three times to commit them all to memory. This was a common enough ability at the time: university teachers were known to be able to repeat a hundred lines of text shouted to them only once by their pupils.

In a world where few could read or write, a good memory was essential. It is for this reason that rhyme, a useful *aide-mémoire,* was the prevalent form of literature at the time. Up to the fourteenth century almost everything except legal documents was written in rhyme. French merchants used a poem made up of 137 rhyming couplets which contained all the rules of commercial arithmetic.

Given the cost of writing materials, a trained memory was a necessity for the scholar as much as for the merchant. For more specific tasks than day to day recall, medieval professionals used a learning aid which had originally

been composed in late classical times. Its use was limited to scholars, who learned how to apply it as part of their training in the seven liberal arts, where memorising was taught under the rubric of rhetoric. The text they learned from was called *Ad Herennium,* the major mnemonic reference work of the Middle Ages. It provided a technique for recalling vast quantities of material by means of the use of "memory theatres."

The material to be memorised was supposed to be conceived of as a familiar location. This could take the form of all or part of a building: an arch, a corner, an entrance hall, and so on. The location was also supposed to satisfy certain criteria. The interior was to be made up of different elements, easily recognised one from the other. If the building were too big, accuracy of recall would suffer. If it were too small, the separate parts of what was to be recalled would be too close to each other for individual recall. If it were too bright it would blind the memory. Too dark, it would obscure the material to be remembered.

Each separate part of the location was to be thought of as being about thirty feet apart, so as to keep each major segment of the material isolated from the others. Once the memory theatre was prepared in this way, the process of memorising would involve the memoriser in a mental walk through the building. The route should be one which was logical and habitual, so that it might be easily and naturally recalled. The theatre was now ready to be filled with the material to be memorised.

This material took the form of mental images representing the different elements to be recalled. *Ad Herennium* advised that strong images were the best, so reasons should be found to make the data stand out. The images should be funny, or bloody, or gaudy, ornamented, unusual, and so on.

These images were to act as "agents" of memory and each image would trigger recall of several components of the material. The individual elements to be recalled should be imaged according to the kind of material. If a legal argument were being memorised, a dramatic scene might be appropriate. At the relevant point in the journey through the memory theatre, this scene would be triggered and played out, reminding the memoriser of the points to be recalled. The stored images could also relate to individual words, strings of words or entire arguments. Onomatopoeia, the use of words that sound like the action they describe, was particularly helpful in this regard.

The great medieval theologian St. Thomas Aquinas particularly recommended the theatrical use of imagery for the recall of religious matters. "All knowledge has its origins in sensation," he said. The truth was accessible through visual aids. Especially in the twelfth and thirteenth centuries the influx of new Greek and Arab knowledge, both scientific and general, made memorisation by scholars and professionals more necessary than ever.

As painting and sculpture began to appear in churches the same techniques for recall were applied. Church imagery took on the form of memory agent. In Giotto's paintings of 1306 on the interior of the Arena Chapel in Padua the entire series of images is structured as a memory theatre. Each Bible story illustrated is told through the medium of a figure or group in a separate place, made more memorable by the use of the recently developed artistic illusion of depth. Each image is separated by about thirty feet, and all are carefully painted to achieve maximum clarity and simplicity. The chapel is a mnemonic path to salvation.

In the frescoes of St. Maria Novella in Florence the order of seven arts, seven virtues, seven sins, is depicted. In the painting of the four cardinal virtues, additional memory cues are provided. The figure of Prudence holds a circle (representing time) in which are written the eight parts of the virtue. Putting together the images, the layout, and the use of lettering, it was thus possible to derive an entire system of knowledge from one mnemonic fresco. Cathedrals became enormous memory theatres built to aid the worshippers to recall the details of heaven and hell.

Mnemonics were also used by the growing university population. All lectures were read from a set text to which teachers added their glosses, or comments. Many of the instructions to students took the form of mnemonic lists and abbreviations for use when the time came for examinations.

For those who were rich enough to be familiar with written manuscripts, there was a difference between reading and writing which has since disappeared. A member of a noble family would have in his household at least one person who could read and another who could write. Letters were almost never read by the recipient, but by these servants. Moreover, a servant who could read would not necessarily be able to write. As will be seen, writing was a separate art requiring much more than simple knowledge of the shape of letters.

Our modern word "auditing" comes from this practice of hearing, for accounts would be read aloud to those concerned. Abbot Samson of Bury St. Edmunds heard his accounts once a week. Pope Innocent III could read, but always had letters read aloud to him. It was this habit which explains the presence in the text of warnings such as, "Do not read this in the presence of others as it is secret." In fact, those who could read silently were regarded with some awe. St. Augustine, speaking in the fifth century about St. Ambrose, said: ". . . a remarkable thing . . . when he was reading his eye glided over the pages and his heart sensed out the sense, but his voice and tongue were at rest."

It was for this reason that writing fell under the discipline of rhetoric in the schools, since writing was meant to be read aloud. Early charters, or land grants, would therefore often end with the word *valete* (goodbye), as if the donor had finished speaking to his listeners. Even today, wills are still read aloud.

It was this oral habit which separated reading from writing. The former used the voice, the latter the hand and eye. But even writing was not a silent occupation. In the thirteenth century, with the influx of new knowledge and with the general economic improvement, the demand for manuscripts grew. Monasteries began to partition off one wall of their cloisters, dividing it into small cubicles, some no wider than 2 feet 9 inches, to accommodate monks whose duty it was to copy manuscripts. These cubicles were called "carols." They usually had window spaces facing the garden or cloister of the church, and in bad weather oiled paper, rush matting or glass and wood partitions could be erected to fill these spaces.

In England there were carols at Bury St. Edmunds, Evesham, Abingdon, St. Augustine's in Canterbury, and at Durham, where there were eleven windows along the north wall, each accommodating three carols.

As they copied, the monks would whisper the words to themselves, and knowledge would sound in the cold, vaulted air. The technique was painstakingly slow. Each monk prepared his sheet of animal skin. The finest was calf skin, or vellum. First the skin was smoothed with a pumice stone and a scraper (*plana*). It was then softened with a crayon, folded four times, and placed on the vertical desk in front of the copyist. To write, he used black ink and a bird-feather quill pen, which he sharpened when blunt with a penknife.

Each monk sat on a stool, copying from the original manuscript placed on a reading frame above his desk. Horizontal lines of tiny holes were pricked across the page with an awl or a small spiked wheel. There were no page numbers as we know them, but at the bottom right-hand corner of the "quaternion," as the folded page was called, was the number of the quaternion and of its folded page: 9i, 9ii, etc. Monks seldom completed more than one text each year, the process was immensely slow and fatiguing.

The act of copying also had liturgical significance. A twelfth-century sermon on the subject, delivered to the copyists of Durham Cathedral, stated:

> You write with the pen of memory on the parchment of pure conscience, scraped by the knife of divine fear, smoothed by the pumice of heavenly desires, and whitened by the chalk of holy

Illuminated manuscript: From The Sforza Hours, later fifteenth century. *The British Library.*

thoughts. The ruler is the will of God. The split nib is the joint love of God and our neighbour. Coloured inks are heavenly grace. The exemplar is the life of Christ.

The copyist would try to reproduce on the parchment exactly what he saw on the original. This was often extremely difficult to decipher, particularly if, as was often the case, it had been penned during times of disturbance or famine, when standards of writing and scholarship were low. Also, if the writer of the original had been in a hurry he would have used abbreviations, which might take much time and effort to decipher. Above all, if the original had been written to dictation there would often be errors of transmission.

The copyist usually identified a word by its sound. The carols would be filled with monks mouthing and mumbling, often getting the spelling of a word wrong—writing "er" for "ar," for instance—because of the difference between their pronunciation and that of the original writer. Spelling was a matter for the individual, while punctuation consisted only of a dash or a dot.

The oral "chewing" of the words had a dual purpose. The act of prayer was closely associated with reading aloud. The words written in a prayer would therefore take on added significance through being spoken. The reading of holy text was a more a matter of savouring divine wisdom than of seeking information. Reading was almost an act of meditation. It was said of Peter the Venerable of Cluny, that "without resting, his mouth ruminated the sacred words." And in the 1090s St. Anselm wrote about the act of reading: "taste the goodness of your Redeemer . . . chew the honeycomb of his words, suck their flavour which is sweeter than honey, swallow their wholesome sweetness; chew by thinking, suck by understanding, swallow by loving and rejoicing."

All writing held a kind of magic quality for the reader, most of all that of the holy texts. The feeling was that the light of God shone on the reader through "the letters' veil." Reading was a physical act of spiritual exhilaration, in which the meaning of the words came like an illumination, much as light came through stained glass.

Books were, in a sense, miraculous objects. After the growth of the European economy in the early fifteenth century, demand grew steadily for these wonder-working texts: Books of Hours, Psalters and Scriptures. Of course the great books, like the Psalter of Eadwine of Canterbury and the Book of Kells in Ireland, were relics in their own right. Bound in leather and encrusted with precious jewels, embellished with magnificently illuminated letters to help the reader to find his place, these masterpieces were kept in cathedral treasuries along with the plate and the holy vessels. Such writing was for God's eyes, not for communicating everyday things to common men.

The problem with these great works, whose creation involved immense, time-consuming acts of worship, was that not only were they filled with errors, but very often the entire texts were irretrievably lost because there was no way of finding them once they had been written and placed in the monastery or church. There was no filing system.

First of all it was very hard to tell what the name of the author might be, or indeed what the subject of the work was. For example, a manuscript entitled *Sermones Bonaventurae* could be any one of the following:

Sermons composed by St. Bonaventure of Fidenza
Sermons composed by somebody called Bonaventure
Sermons copied by a Bonaventure
Sermons copied by somebody from a church of St. Bonaventure
Sermons preached by a Bonaventure
Sermons that belonged to a Bonaventure
Sermons that belonged to a church of St. Bonaventure
Sermons by various people of whom the first or most important was somebody called Bonaventure.

Where would such a book be filed?

In spite of this rather haphazard attitude to placement, the book itself was an extremely rare and valuable object. Warnings such as this were often added to the text: "Whoever steals this book let him die the death; let him be frizzled in a pan; may the falling sickness rage within him; may be he broken on a wheel and be hanged."

Even if it were known in which church or monastery a text was, retrieval might involve a long and risky journey, which might even then end in failure because the book was lost within the library through lack of cataloguing. Reference material of all kinds was therefore at a premium. In spite of the scarcity of information, however, it was still not considered necessary to corroborate the accuracy of information contained in a text by comparison with another.

For this reason there was no concept of history; there were only chivalrous romances and chronicles based on widely differing monastic views of what had happened in the world beyond the community's walls. There was no geography, no natural history and no science, because there could be no sure confirmation of the data upon which such subjects would rely. This absence of proven fact bothered few people. Life was depicted by the medieval Christian Church as ephemeral and irrelevant to salvation. The only true reality lay in the mind of God, who knew all that needed to be known and whose reasons were inscrutable.

Into this alien world of memorising, hearsay and fantasy, the pressure for rational, factual information began to come first from the traders. For centuries they had travelled the roads, keeping their accounts by the use of tally sticks. The word "tally" comes from the Latin for "to cut." The sticks had a complicated series of notches in them and were used by all accountants, including the Exchequer of England, until well into the late Middle Ages. Tally sticks may have sufficed for the travelling salesman, but they were not good enough for the early fifteenth-century merchant with international bank accounts and complex transactions to handle in various currencies.

Pressure for access to information also came from the growing number of universities and grammar and church schools, whose students were entering an increasingly commercial world. The kings and princes of Europe also needed ever-larger bureaucracies to handle the increasing responsibilities devolving on them as the feudal system gave way to centralised, tax-collecting monarchies. In fairs all over Europe, from the fourteenth century on, international trade had been stimulated by the use of Arab mathematics which made documenting easier than with the old-fashioned abacus and the Roman numerals of earlier times.

The greatest pressure of all for literacy, however, was caused by the sudden availability of paper. Originally a Chinese invention, paper had been discovered by the Arabs when they overran Samarkand in the eighth century. Captured workmen had been sent to Samarkand from China to set up a papermaking factory. By the fourteenth century new water-powered technology was pounding linen rags as fast as they could be collected by the rag and bone man and turning them into cheap, durable paper. In

Bologna at the end of the fourteenth century the price of paper had dropped by 400 per cent. It was much cheaper than parchment, though there was still some opposition to its use. "Parchment lasts a thousand years," they said. "How long will paper exist?"

As the paper mills spread, so too did the spirit of religious reform. The Church had long been criticised for simony and equivocal practices, and in the late Middle Ages came the birth of a reforming movement led by the Brothers of the Common Life who preached a simpler, purer form of Christianity. Their *devotio moderna* attracted many of the scholars of the day, including eminent men such as Erasmus. Above all their schools and others like them began to turn out relatively large numbers of literate clerics. These men rapidly found employment in the *scriptoria*, or writing shops, which were springing up all over the Continent to meet the demand for documentation from traders and governments, as well as from the lawyers and notaries who formed the single largest and fastest-growing professional body in Europe.

The best known *scriptorium* was in Florence. It was run by a man called Vespasiano da Bisticci, one of the new breed of "stationers," so called because they had stopped being itinerant paper-sellers and had set up shop. At one time Bisticci may have employed as many as fifty copyists who were paid piece-rates for copying at home. He commissioned translators to bring in new texts, sent out his book list, lent texts on approval, and encouraged aspiring writers to have their finished works copied.

As the price of paper continued to fall, the development of eye-glasses intensified the pressure for literacy. Glasses had first appeared in the early fourteenth century, and a hundred years later they were generally available. Their use lengthened the working life of copyist and reader alike. Demand for texts increased.

But the apparently insoluble problem which bedevilled Europe was that there were far too few scribes to handle the business being gener-

The greatest pressure of all for literacy, however, was caused by the sudden

Early paper-making used the power of a waterwheel to trip hammers which pounded linen rag to pulp (*bottom right*). The pulp was shaped into squares in trays while wet, and then pressed and hung to dry in sheets. *Permission of Little Brown.*

ated and their fees were, in consequence, astronomically high. Economic development appeared to be blocked.

At some time in the 1450s came the answer to the problem, and with it a turning-point in Western civilisation. The event occurred in a mining area of southern Germany, where precious metal was plentiful. Major silver finds had been made there, and the most powerful family in Europe, the Fuggers, operated a vast financial empire with its headquarters at Augsburg, the chief city of the region. The nearby towns of Regensburg, Ulm and Nuremberg had for long been the heart of the European metal-working industry.

These cities were also centres for the manufacture of astronomical and navigational instruments, the source of the first engraving techniques, and the home of some of the best watch- and clock-makers on the Continent. Expert jewellers and goldsmiths inlaid precious metal on ceremonial armour and made complicated toys that were operated by wire. The region held many men highly experienced in the working of soft metals.

It was probably one of these metal-workers who recognised that the goldsmith's hallmark punch could be used to strike the shape of a letter in a soft metal mould. This would be filled with a hot tin–antimony alloy which, when cooled, formed the first interchangeable typeface which could be used in a printing press. The press itself was a modified linen-press that had been in use for centuries; it was now adapted to push paper down on to an inked matrix of upturned letters, each one of which was close enough in dimension to its neighbour to fit into standard holes in the matrix base. The technique would not have worked with parchment because it was not porous enough to take the ink.

The man who is credited with inventing the process was Johannes Gansfleisch zur Laden zum Gutenberg. His new press destroyed the oral society. Printing was to bring about the most radical alteration ever made in Western intellectual history, and its effects were to be felt in every area of human activity.

PART III

The Print Revolution

Dutch Printing office

A Dutch printing office from the 16th Century. On the right, paper arrives, the type is inked, the pages are printed, and then stacked by the office boy. On the left, compositors prepare new texts and the proofreader checks a page. *Barnaby's Picture Library, London.*

In closing the previous section, James Burke took us to the mid-fifteenth century and the beginnings of the print revolution. His belief that print was the major cultural/technological transformation in the history of the West is shared by several of our contributors. Traditionally, the view has been that printing, along with numerous other developments, marked the transition between the end of the Middle Ages and the dawn of the modern era. However, the more we study this remarkable invention, the more we realize that it was not just one factor among many. Although we hesitate to argue for historical "prime movers," certainly the printing press comes close to what is meant by this term. It was a technology that influenced other technologies—and a prototype for mass production—one that directly affected the world of ideas by making knowledge widely available and creating a space in which new forms of expression could flourish.

The repercussions of the printing press in early modern Europe did not come about in an inherently deterministic manner. Rather, they resulted from the existence of conditions whereby print could enhance a context receptive to its potential. We must not forget that there *was* change in the Middle Ages, although slower than in subsequent centuries, and that several earlier shifts in communications prepared the way for and accelerated the influence of print: vernacular literacy, the use of paper, and the adoption of Arabic numbers.

Vernacular literacy, as was noted in the previous section, emerged during the twelfth and thirteenth centuries. It challenged the church's monopoly on written communication. The acquisition of literacy now became a one-step process, whereas with Latin it entailed the learning of a second language. Vernacular writings instilled in its audiences, both those that were literate and nonliterates who were read to aloud, a sense of cultural tradition and regional place. This was facilitated through the use of a new medium, paper, which was less costly than parchment.

Paper was invented in China perhaps as early as the first century A.D. It entered Western Europe in the twelfth century and began to be manufactured there in the thirteenth. By 1500, every major European city had a paper mill, without which the growing demand for printed books in the vernacular could not have been met. Paper also helped to spread a new language, mathematics, using Arabic numbers. This system was superior for doing calculations. It had entered Europe in the twelfth century. Yet for the next four hundred years its potential was infrequently realized. Since the scribal/manuscript tradition failed to standardize the form of the numbers or produce adequate instructional texts explaining their use. The printing press did both. Science and commercialism directly benefited.

Europe owed China a debt not only as regards the gift of paper. Printing from carved wooden blocks, an essential precursor to the movable type press, was likewise Chinese in origin. China was not only a literate civilization (using ideograms), but one that was capable of research and development as well. Paper was created to offset the inadequacies of other media, notably silk and bamboo, and subsequently improved upon. Block printing began in the eighth century. Thus, when Europe was in the so-called Dark Ages, China was producing large numbers of printed paper books. Europe started to use block printing in the fourteenth century, acquiring the idea via the trade routes set up in the wake of the Mongol conquests.

One final point on printing in China: Chinese printing sometimes employed movable type and thus anticipated Gutenberg by over five centuries. However, baked clay rather than metal characters were used to replicated a nonalphabetic script composed of thousands of characters. In such circumstances a Chinese print shop could be a complex facility! For most purposes, however, carving a page of text on a wooden block remained both more expedient and aesthetically pleasing.

With the coming of the printing press to Europe, as Lewis Mumford points out in our first selection, the reproduction of written texts became mechanized. At first, printers tried to reproduce writing as it appeared in earlier manuscripts. However, in time it was realized that a less ornate and more standarized style was desirable. As the art and craft of calligraphy declined, a new world of mass produced knowledge based on typography replaced it. This loss of the scribe was, for Mumford, "a reasonable price to pay" for the increased access to books made possible by print.

As Elizabeth Eisenstein points out in our next selection, the reproduction of written materials moved the copyist's desk to the printer's workshop. She begins by setting the stage for a concerted examination of this problem. What was the world of the scribe, before print, like? How can we access such an understanding, when to do so we must use standardized texts, charts, and maps that were alien to the period we are trying to fathom? To use the same historical strategy for different epochs may obscure more than it reveals. Take nothing for granted, she suggests, and the enormity of the transformation will become apparent.

Eisenstein goes on to show us how printing brought forth a new class of intellectuals, "men of letters." Previously, those who produced knowledge worked under the auspices of the church or acquired a patron from the nobility or wealthy merchant class. The printer became a new kind of patron, one linked to a growing market economy. As a result, the nature of texts changed.

An important point to keep in mind in considering the print revolution is that it did not occur in one generation. Two hundred years were necessary for most of the definitive changes to knowledge and society produced by print to fall into place. This illustrates a tendency that we examined in the previous part: how new media, before they exert their distinctive influence, often do what was done by older forms. In the case of printed books, the first wave, known as *incunabula*, included many of the older manuscript titles. However, texts on the new science and philosophy would soon become a major aspect of the printing industry.

The next selection, by Walter Ong, directs our examination of the print revolution toward the nature of the textual changes it brought about and the way readers appropriated them. A fundamental aspect of Ong's argument is that print made the transformation from aural to visual more complete than writing alone. Rapid silent reading, a rarity in the Middle Ages, became widespread. This was accompanied and facilitated by marked changes in books, which we frequently take for granted. The index is a case in point. Indexes were rare in manuscripts, in which auditory recall helped to orient readers to texts. In the printer era, as Ong shows, indexes helped to give rise to the book as a work of reference, that could be consulted periodically without having to be mastered in its entirety. The quintessential expression of this trend was the rise of dictionaries, encyclopedias, and grammatical texts. All contributed to standardizing the language in ways that were alien to the Middle Ages.

One of the most significant consequences of printing was its influence on the Protestant Reformation. Harvey Graff explores this relationship in our next excerpt.

Print allowed for the rapid dissemination of the ideas of Martin Luther as well as their easy entry into the vernacular. Graff is quick to point out that the new medium did not cause, in a deterministic sense, the Reformation's many changes. However, it did facilitate them in profound ways. He concludes with a look at how the legacy of the Reformation, and the new culture of the printed book, affected literacy, education, and religion in colonial North America.

Print also made possible the widespread dissemination of news. In our next selection, John Thompson traces the early history of printed newspapers, from the first weeklies to the dailies that are still with us. News, of course, especially foreign news, circulated before print, mainly through word of mouth, troubadour performances, and hand-written news sheets that could be read aloud to the illiterate. However, with the advent of printed news, individual citizens had rapid and widespread access to information, especially economic and political information, upon which they could act.

Three centuries after its inception, the printed book gave rise to authors who were secular and often heretical. The philosophes of the eighteenth-century French Enlightenment are a case in point. Surveillance of them, and what they wrote, is dealt with in our concluding essay by Robert Darnton. He shows us how the culture of the book and the new literacy it brought about were visible in the work of both dissident writers and police bureaucrats assigned to observe their activities. We gain a sense of writing as a career during the Enlightenment and the way dossiers and files were set up as a form of sustained observation. The latter recalls Walter Ong's earlier observations on the new forms of textual representation created by print. Finally, Darnton seems to subtly suggest that the Enlightenment was the most literate of all periods. After all, even the police inspector made critical stylistic comments on the work he was assigned to monitor.

11 THE INVENTION OF PRINTING

Lewis Mumford

Lewis Mumford is among the most respected of twentieth-century humanist scholars who have addressed the issues of communication history. His many works all deal in some manner with the link between culture and technology.

The invention of printing from movable types is second only to the clock in its critical effect upon our civilization; and in its own right exemplifies the much broader passage, constantly going on in our own day, from the tool to the handworked machine, and from the machine to the completely automatic self-regulating device from which, at the end, almost every intervention of the human person is eliminated, except at the very beginning, in the arrangement of the works, and at the very end, in the consumption of the product. Finally, and not least, I have chosen printing because it shows, in the course of its own development, how art and technics may be brought together, and how necessary it is, even for technical development, to have the person that presides over the process refresh himself constantly at those sources in life from which the symbol, in its purest forms, comes forth.

Probably many people in this audience know, at least in outline, the story of printing, so admirably put together by Thomas Carter, the veritable unraveling of a mystery from which only the very last link in the chain seems still to be absent. For one thing, though it is in the nature of mechanical inventions to spread widely from their original center, the spread of printing and the accessory arts upon which it depends, like that of papermaking, is one that wove into a single web the cultures of the East and West, with each part contributing its share to the final product. In a special sense, therefore, printing is a universal art, prophetic of that One World which our technical instruments make it possible for man now to achieve—though we do not yet know whether it will be one world blasted and ruined by atomic bombs or one world

pushed to a higher plane of development through the abundant practice of mutual aid. At all events, printing swept across the world, from China and Korea, where movable types were first invented, into Europe, in the course of a century. We can trace its progress in a series of steps, by way of Persia and Turkey and Russia, till we find the first printed book in Holland and the first European book printed from movable types in Germany. This art had many beginnings in earlier civilizations, from signet rings to coins. It *might* have been applied to the printing of books at almost any moment for the last 2500 years. But before the method was applied to books a new social medium was necessary: a community that had abandoned slavery and was ready, indeed eager, to equalize cultural advantages once reserved for a ruling caste; so that the rise of free cities, of urban democracy, of an increasingly literature group of citizens gave an incentive to a method for manifolding and cheapening the process of producing books.

And here again—you must forgive me if I drive this point home a little insistently, to compensate for the more dominant opposite view— here again the esthetic symbol preceded the practical use. For the first application of printing was in the domain of art, the printing of woodcuts: it was only at a later stage that the interest in the word led to that consummate invention, so advanced, so modern at every point—the invention of movable type. For note what was involved in the concept of setting up a line of type by using separate letters cast on a uniform pattern in a mold: the movable type is the original model of the standardized, replaceable part, which some forgetful historians are inclined to attribute to a much later inventor, Eli Whitney, in his perfection of the standardized gun. Finally, the printing press itself, first hand-operated, then, in the nineteenth century power-driven, became one of the earliest pieces of standardized, increasingly automatic, machinery. Within a century of the invention of printing, the calligrapher, the hand-copyist, had been driven out the field of book production over which he had long presided; and yet, so far from this being a serious loss, it was in its initial stages a mighty gain, since all that was good in the handwork was preserved, while some part of what was bad, the inevitable monotony and tedium, was eliminated. Within a generation of Gutenberg's invention, the book in fact reached a perfection in type, impression, and general form that has not in fact been surpassed by any later efforts.

To understand what was involved in this change-over from writing to printing, we must compare the difference visible at an earlier stage between cursive handwriting, longhand, and the more highly formed hand-printed letter. Though there is a typical element in all handwriting—so that one can identify the clerical hand or the humanist hand, the civil service hand or the Palmer method hand or the boarding school hand—there is no form of art that tells one so much, at every stroke, about the individuality of the writer, about his tone and his temper and his general habits of life. So truly is handwriting a key to the human personality that when one wants to refer to the highest type of individuation in art, we refer to the artist's signature. As you know, Chinese calligraphy usually accompanies a picture, done in the same style—visually a part of it. But this very individuality of handwriting is itself a handicap to the widest kind of communication. Reading would be a most laborious art if, on every page, one had to struggle with a new personality and master his vagaries of written expression as well as his thought. For the sake of general legibility and universality it was important that the human being who copied a book should achieve

a certain kind of neutrality and impersonality, that he should sacrifice expressiveness to order, subduing his idiosyncrasies, making each letter conform to a common type, rigorously standardizing the product. The typical and the repeatable—what is that but the province of the machine? After a copyist repeated the same letter a thousand times, his letters would achieve that impersonal quality. And by habit and repetition, by restraint and humility, he brought the manuscript to a point of mechanical perfection at which the letters themselves could readily be transferred into movable types.

But note how perverse art itself can be when divorced from other equally central human purposes. From the standpoint of effective communication, the handwrought manuscript tended by its very elaboration to lose sight of its essential reason for existence. In this respect, its development was very similar to that we often find in other arts, a tendency on the part of human fantasy, once it is emancipated from the restraint of practical needs, to run riot, to seek to prolong the esthetic moment beyond any reasonable duration. In medieval cathedrals this sometimes went so far that Ruskin even discovered carving in places where no human eye but his own—if we except the original worker—had probably ever beheld it. Quite evidently this desire to prolong a pleasurable occupation, while it makes for a good life, has its own kind of shortcoming; and in the case of the book, the very esthetic excellence of the illuminators and illustrators served also to retard the process of copying and so limit the circulation of books. Even if the hand labor had been rough and quick, it would have produced too few; but since it was actually measured and meticulous, it served as a further brake on the spread of learning. How unique and precious books were, how well respected they were as works of art, we know from the state they come down to us in: no scrawls in the margins! no dirty fingerprints! no dog ears! But as long as art held production in check, there were never enough books, even in an illiterate age, to go

12 THE RISE OF THE READING PUBLIC

Elizabeth Eisenstein

Elizabeth Eisenstein is a historian whose book The Printing Press as an Agent of Change *has been hailed by people in many disciplines as a landmark study of how a particular technology has influenced history.*

In the late fifteenth century, the reproduction of written materials began to move from the copyist's desk to the printer's workshop. This shift, which revolutionized all forms of learning, was particularly important for historical scholarship. Ever since then historians have been indebted to Gutenberg's invention; print enters their work from start to finish, from consulting card files to reading page proofs. Because historians are usually eager to investigate major changes and this change transformed the conditions of their own craft, one would expect the shift to attract some attention from the profession as a whole. Yet any historiographical survey will show the contrary to be true. It is symbolic that Clio has retained her handwritten scroll. So little has been made of the move into the new workshops that after five hundred years, the muse of history still remains outside. "History bears witness," writes a sociologist, "to the cataclysmic effect on society of inventions of new media for the transmission of information among persons. The development of writing, and later the development of printing, are examples." Insofar as flesh-and-blood historians who turn out articles and books actually bear witness to what happened in the past, the effect on society of the development of printing, far from appearing cataclysmic, is remarkably inconspicuous. Many studies of developments during the last five centuries say nothing about it at all.

There is, to be sure, a large, ever-growing literature on the history of printing and related topics. Several works that synthesize and summarize parts of this large literature have appeared. Thus Rudolf Hirsch surveys problems associated with "printing, selling, reading," during the first century after Gutenberg. A more extensive, well-organized volume by Febvre and Martin, which skillfully covers the first three centuries of printing and was first published in a French series devoted to "the evolution of humanity," has recently been translated into English. An even broader coverage, embracing "five hundred years," is provided by Steinberg's remarkably succinct semi-popular survey. All three of these books summarize data drawn from many scattered studies. But although the broader historical implications of these data are occasionally hinted at, they are never really spelled out. Like the section on printing in the *New Cambridge Modern History,* the contents of these surveys rarely enter into treatments of other aspects of the evolution of humanity.

According to Steinberg: "The history of printing is an integral part of the general history of civilization." Unfortunately, the statement is not applicable to written history as it stands, although it is probably true enough of the actual course of human affairs. Far from being integrated into other works, studies dealing with the history of printing are isolated and artificially sealed off from the rest of historical literature. In theory, these studies center on a topic that impinges on many other fields. In fact, they are seldom consulted by scholars who work in any other field, perhaps because their relevance to other fields is still not clear. "The exact nature of the impact which the invention and spread of printing had on Western civilization remains subject to interpretation even today." This seems to understate the case. There are few interpretations even of an inexact or approximate nature upon which scholars may draw when pursuing other inquiries. The effects produced by printing have aroused little controversy, not because views on the topic coincide, but because almost none has been set forth in an explicit and systematic form. Indeed, those who seem to agree that momentous changes were entailed always seem to stop short of telling us just what they were.

"Neither political, constitutional, ecclesiastical, and economic events, nor sociological, philosophical, and literary movements can be fully understood," writes Steinberg, "without taking into account the influence the printing press has exerted upon them." All these events and movements have been subjected to close scrutiny by generations of scholars with the aim of understanding them more fully. If the printing press exerted some influence upon them, why is this influence so often unnoted, so rarely even hinted at, let alone discussed? The question is worth posing if only to suggest that the effects produced by printing are by no means self-evident. Insofar as they may be encountered by scholars exploring different fields, they are apt to pass unrecognized at present. To track them down and set them forth—in an outline or some other form—is much easier said than done.

When authors such as Steinberg refer to the impact of printing on every field of human enterprise—political, economic, philosophical, and so forth—it is by no means clear just what they have in mind. In part at least they seem to be pointing to indirect consequences which have to be inferred and which are associated with the consumption of printed products or with changed mental habits. Such consequences are, of course, of major historical significance and impinge on most forms of human enterprise. Nevertheless, it is difficult to describe them precisely or even to determine exactly what they are. It is one thing to describe how methods of book production changed after the mid-fifteenth century or to estimate rates of increased output. It is another thing to describe how access to a greater abundance or variety of written records affected ways of learning, thinking, and perceiving among literate elites. Similarly, it is one thing to show that standardiza-

tion was a consequence of printing. It is another to decide how laws, languages, or mental constructs were affected by more uniform texts. Even at present, despite all the data being obtained from living responsive subjects; despite all the efforts being made by public opinion analysts, pollsters, or behavioral scientists; we still know very little about how access to printed materials affected human behavior. (A glance at recent controversies on the desirability of censoring pornography shows how ignorant we are.) Historians who have to reach out beyond the grave to reconstruct past forms of consciousness are especially disadvantaged in dealing with such issues. Theories about unevenly phased changes affecting learning processes, attitudes, and expectations do not lend themselves, in any event, to simple, clear-cut formulations that can be easily tested or integrated into conventional historical narratives.

Problems posed by some of the more indirect effects produced by the shift from script to print probably can never be overcome entirely. But such problems could be confronted more squarely if other impediments did not lie in the way. Among the far-reaching effects that need to be noted are many that still affect present observations and that operate with particularly great force upon every professional scholar. Thus constant access to printed materials is a prerequisite for the practice of the historian's own craft. It is difficult to observe processes that enter so intimately into our own observations. In order to access changes ushered in by printing, for example, we need to survey the conditions that prevailed before its advent. Yet the conditions of scribal culture can only be observed through a veil of print.

Even a cursory acquaintance with the findings of anthropologists or casual observations of preschool-age children may help to remind us of the gulf that exists between oral and literate cultures. Several studies, accordingly, have illuminated the difference between mentalities shaped by reliance on the spoken as opposed to the written word. The gulf that separates our experience from that of literate elites who relied exclusively on hand-copied texts is much more difficult to fathom. There is nothing analogous in our experience or in that of any living creature within the Western world at present. The conditions of scribal culture thus have to be artificially reconstructed by recourse to history books and reference guides. Yet for the most part, these works are more likely to conceal than to reveal the object of such a search. Scribal themes are carried forward, postprint trends are traced backward, in a manner that makes it difficult to envisage the existence of a distinctive literary culture based on hand copying. There is not even an agreed-upon term in common use which designates the system of written communications that prevailed before print.

Schoolchildren who are asked to trace early overseas voyages on identical outline maps are likely to become absent-minded about the fact that there were no uniform world maps in the era when the voyages were made. A similar absent-mindedness on a more sophisticated level is encouraged by increasingly refined techniques for collating manuscripts and producing authoritative editions of them. Each successive edition tells us more than was previously known about how a given manuscript was composed and copied. By the same token, each makes it more difficult to envisage how a given manuscript appeared to a scribal scholar who had only one hand-copied version to consult and no certain guidance as to its place or date of composition, its title or author. Historians are trained to discriminate between manuscript sources and printed texts; but they are not trained to think with equal care about how manuscripts appeared when this sort of discrimination was inconceivable. Similarly, the more thoroughly we are trained to master the events and dates contained in modern history books, the less likely we are to appreciate the difficulties confronting scribal scholars who had access to assorted written records, but lacked uniform chronologies, maps, and all the other reference guides which are now in common use.

Efforts to reconstruct the circumstances that preceded printing thus lead to a scholarly predicament. Reconstruction requires recourse

to printed materials, thereby blurring clear perception of the conditions that prevailed before these materials were available. Even when the predicament is partly resolved by sensitive scholars who manage to develop a genuine "feel" for the times after handling countless documents, efforts at reconstruction are still bound to be frustratingly incomplete.

For the very texture of scribal culture was so fluctuating, uneven, and multiform that few long-range trends can be traced. Conditions that prevailed near the bookshops of ancient Rome, in the Alexandrian Library, or in certain medieval monasteries and university towns, made it possible for literate elites to develop a relatively sophisticated "bookish" culture. Yet all library collections were subject to contraction, and all texts in manuscript were liable to get corrupted after being copied over the course of time. Outside certain transitory special centers, moreover, the texture of scribal culture was so thin that heavy reliance was placed on oral transmission even by literate elites. Insofar as dictation governed copying in scriptoria and literary compositions were "published" by being read aloud, even "book" learning was governed by reliance on the spoken word—producing a hybrid half-oral, half-literate culture that has no precise counterpart today. Just what publication meant before printing or just how messages got transmitted in the age of scribes are questions that cannot be answered in general. Findings are bound to vary enormously depending on date and place. Contradictory verdicts are especially likely to proliferate with regard to the last century before printing—an interval when paper had become available and the literate man was more likely to become his own scribe.

Specialists in the field of incunabula, who are confronted by ragged evidence, are likely to insist that a similar lack of uniformity characterizes procedures used by early printers. To generalize about early printing is undoubtedly hazardous, and one should be on guard against projecting the output of modern standard editions too far back into the past. Yet one must also be on guard against blurring a major difference between the last century of scribal culture and the first century after Gutenberg. Early print culture is sufficiently uniform to permit us to measure its diversity. We can estimate output, arrive at averages, trace trends. For example, we have rough estimates of the total output of all printed materials during the so-called age of incunabula (that is, the interval between the 1450s and 1500). Similarly, we can say that the "average" early edition ranged between two hundred and one thousand copies. There are no comparable figures for the last fifty years of scribal culture. Indeed, we have no figures at all. What is the "average edition" turned out between 1400 and 1450? The question verges on nonsense. The term "edition" comes close to being an anachronism when applied to copies of a manuscript book.

As the difficulties of trying to estimate scribal output suggest, quantification is not suited to the conditions of scribal culture. The production figures which are most often cited, on the basis of the memoirs of a Florentine manuscript bookdealer, turn out to be entirely untrustworthy. Quattrocento Florence, in any case, is scarcely typical of other Italian centers (such as Bologna), let alone of regions beyond the Alps. But then *no* region is typical. There is no "typical" bookdealer, scribe, or even manuscript. Even if we set aside problems presented by secular book producers and markets as hopelessly complex and consider only the needs of churchmen on the eve of printing, we are still faced by a remarkable diversity of procedures. Book provisions for diverse monastic orders varied; mendicant friars had different arrangements from monks. Popes and cardinals often turned to the "multifarious activities" of the Italian *cartolai;* preachers made their own anthologies of sermons; semi-lay orders attempted to provide primers and catechisms for everyman.

The absence of an average output or a typical procedure poses a stumbling block when we try to set the stage for the advent of print. Let us take, for example, a deceptively simple summary statement which I made when first trying to describe the printing revolution. Fifteenth-century book production, I asserted, moved from scriptoria to printing shops. The assertion was criticized for leaving out of account a previous move from scriptoria to stationers' shops. In the course of the twelfth century, lay stationers began to replace monastic scribes. Books needed by university faculties and the mendicant orders were supplied by a "putting-out" system. Copyists were no longer assembled in a single room, but worked on different portions of a given text, receiving payment from the stationer for each piece (the so-called pecia system). Book production, according to my critic, had thus moved out of scriptoria three centuries *before* the advent of print.

The objection seems worth further thought. Certainly one ought to pay attention to the rise of the lay stationer in university towns and other urban centers during the twelfth and thirteenth centuries. The contrast between the free labor of monks working for remission of sins and the wage labor of lay copyists is an important one. Recent research has stressed the use of a putting-out system and has also called into question long-lived assumptions about the existence of lay scriptoria attached to stationers' shops. Thus one must be especially cautious about using the term scriptoria to apply to conditions in the later Middle Ages—more cautious than I was in my preliminary version.

Yet, on the other hand, one must also be wary about placing too much emphasis on trends launched in twelfth-century Paris, Oxford, Bologna, and other university towns where copies were multiplied rapidly to serve special institutional needs. Caution is needed when extending university regulations designed to control copyists to the actual practices of university stationers—let alone to bookdealers serving nonuniversity clientele. That relatively clear thirteenth-century patterns get smudged by the late fourteenth century must also be kept in mind. During the interval between 1350 and 1450— the crucial century when setting our stage—conditions were unusually anarchic, and some presumably obsolete habits were revived. Monastic scriptoria, for example, were beginning to experience their "last golden age."

The existence of monastic scriptoria right down to and even beyond the days of early printing is most intriguingly demonstrated by a treatise which is often cited as a curiosity in books on early printing: Johannes Trithemius's *De laude scriptorum*. In this treatise, the Abbot of Sponheim not only exhorted his monks to copy books, but also explained why "monks should not stop copying because of the invention of printing." Among other arguments (the usefulness of keeping idle hands busy, encouraging diligence, devotion, knowledge of Scripture, and so on), Trithemius somewhat illogically compared the written word on parchment which would last one thousand years with the printed word on paper which would have a shorter life span. The possible use of paper (and scraped parchment) by copyists, or of skin for a special printed version, went unmentioned. As a Christian scholar, the abbot was clearly familiar with earlier writings which had set durable parchment against perishable papyrus. His arguments show his concern about preserving a form of manual labor which seemed especially suitable for monks. Whether he was genuinely worried about an increased use of paper—as an ardent bibliophile and in the light of ancient warnings—is an open question. But his activities show clearly that as an author he did not favor handwork over presswork. He had his *Praise of Scribes* promptly printed, as he did his weightier works. Indeed, he used one Mainz print shop so frequently that "it could almost be called the Sponheim Abbey Press."

Even before 1494, when the Abbot of Sponheim made his trip from scriptorium to printing shop, the Carthusians of Saint Barbara's Charterhouse in Cologne were turning to local printers to extend their efforts, as a cloistered order bound by vows of silence, to preach "with their hands." As many accounts note, the same thing happened outside Cologne and not just among the Carthusians. A variety of reformed Benedictine orders also kept local printers busy, and in some cases monks and nuns ran monastic presses themselves. The possible significance of this intrusion of a capitalist enterprise into consecrated space is surely worth further consideration. Thus, to rule out the formula "scriptorium to printing shop" completely seems almost as unwise as to attempt to apply it in a blanket form. Even while acknowledging the significance of changes affecting twelfth-century book production, we should not equate them with the sort of "book revolution" that occurred in the fifteenth century. The latter, unlike the former, assumed a cumulative and irreversible form. The revival of monastic scriptoria during the century before Gutenberg was the last revival of its kind. . . .

Given the religious, linguistic, and socioeconomic diversity of European readers, it is difficult to imagine just what figure Marshall McLuhan had in mind when he wrote about the "making of typographical man." By making us more alert to the possibility that the advent of printing had social and psychological consequences, McLuhan performed, in my view at least, a valuable service. But he also glossed over multiple interactions that occurred under widely varying circumstances. Granted that the replacement of discourse by silent scanning, of face-to-face contacts by more impersonal interactions, probably did have important consequences, it follows that we need to think less metaphorically and abstractly, more historically and concretely, about the sorts of effects that were entailed and how different groups were affected. Even at first glance both issues appear to be very complex.

We will not pause for long over one complication that has recently attracted attention: namely, Paul Saenger's demonstration that habits of silent reading developed during the Middle Ages. It is now clear that McLuhan and the scholars upon whom he relied overstated the oral character of medieval interchanges and mistakenly assigned to printing responsibility for introducing habits of silent scanning which had already developed among some literate groups in the age of scribes. But although printing did not introduce silent reading, it did encourage an increasing recourse to "silent instructors, which nowadays carry farther than do public lectures" (in the words of a sixteenth-century professor of medicine). To show that the habit predated Gutenberg does not diminish the significance of its becoming increasingly more pervasive and ever more elaborately institutionalized after the shift from script to print.

Even while insisting on this point, we shall need to be cautious about assuming, as did McLuhan and other authorities, that the spread of habits of silent scanning invariably diminished recourse to the spoken word. Although the textbook industry flourished, classroom lectures never died. Printed sermons and orations did not remove preachers from their pulpits or speakers from their podiums. To the contrary, priests and orators both benefited from the way their personal charisma could be augmented and amplified by the printed word.

The increased recourse to silent publication undoubtedly altered the character of some spoken words. Exchanges between members of parliament, for example, were probably affected by the printing of parliamentary debates. The printing of poems, plays, and songs altered the way "lines" were recited, composed, and sung. On the one hand, some "dying speeches" were fabricated for printing and never did get delivered; on the other, printed publicity enabled evangelists and demagogues to practice traditional arts outdoors before an expanded hearing public. A literary culture created by typography was conveyed to the ear, not the eye, by repertory companies and poetry readings. No simple formula will cover the changes these new activities reflect.

The same is true of how different groups were affected. Most rural villagers, for example, probably belonged to an exclusively hearing public down to the nineteenth century. Yet what they heard had, in many instances, been transformed by printing two centuries earlier. For the storyteller was replaced by the exceptional literate villager who read out loud from a stack of cheap books and ballad sheets turned out anonymously for distribution by peddlers. A fairly sleazy "popular" culture, based on the

mass production of antiquated vernacular medieval romances, was thus produced well before the steam press and mass literacy movements of the nineteenth century. Yet the bulk of this output was consumed by a hearing public, separated by a psychological gulf from their contemporaries who belonged to a reading one.

The disjunction between the new mode of production and older modes of consumption is only one of many complications that need further study. Members of the same reading public, who confronted the same innovation in the same region at the same time, were nonetheless affected by it in markedly different ways. Trends pointing both to modernism and to fundamentalism, for example, were launched by Bible printing—as later discussion suggests. Pornography as well as piety assumed new forms. Book reading did not stop short with guides to godly living or practical manuals and texts, any more than printers stopped short at producing them. The same silence, solitude, and contemplative attitudes associated formerly with spiritual devotion also accompanied the perusal of scandal sheets, "lewd Ballads," "merry books of Italie," and other "corrupted tales in Inke and Paper." Not a desire to withdraw from a worldly society or the city of man, but a gregarious curiosity about them, could be satisfied by silent perusal of journals, gazettes, or newsletters. Complaints about the "sullen silence" of newspaper readers in seventeenth-century coffeehouses point to the intrusive effects of printed materials on some forms of sociability.

As communion with the Sunday paper has replaced church-going, there is a tendency to forget that sermons had at one time been coupled with news about local and foreign affairs, real estate transactions, and other mundane matters. After printing, however, news gathering and circulation were handled more efficiently under lay auspices. As contemporaries observed, there were resemblances between coffeehouse and conventicle. But the pipe-smoking habitues of the former gave otherworldly concerns low priority. Such considerations might be noted when thinking about the "secularization" or "desacralization" of Western Christendom. For in all regions (to go beyond the eighteenth century for a moment) the pulpit was ultimately displaced by the periodical press, and the dictum "nothing sacred" came to characterize the journalist's career. Pitted against "the furious itch of novelty" and the "general thirst after news," efforts by Catholic moralists and Protestant evangelicals, even Sunday schools and other Sabbatarian measures proved of little avail. The monthly gazette was succeeded by the weekly and finally by the daily paper. More and more provincial newspapers were founded. By the last century, gossiping churchgoers could often learn about local affairs by scanning columns of newsprint in silence at home.

The displacement of pulpit by press is significant not only in connection with secularization but also because it points to an explanation for the weakening of local community ties. To hear an address delivered, people have to come together; to read a printed report encourages individuals to draw apart. "What the orators of Rome and Athens were in the midst of a people

Jakob Bornitz's *emlematum sacrorum et civilum miscellaneorum*, Heidelberg, 1659. *Emblem book collection of the Newberry Library.*

assembled," said Malesherbes in an address of 1775, "men of letters are in the midst of a *dispersed* people." His observation suggests how the shift in communications may have changed the sense of what it meant to participate in public affairs. The wide distribution of identical bits of information provided an impersonal link between people who were unknown to each other.

By its very nature, a reading public was not only more dispersed; it was also more atomistic and individualistic than a hearing one. To catch the contrast, Walter Ong suggests that we imagine a speaker addressing an audience equipped with texts and stopping at one point with the request that a textual passage be read silently. When the readers look up again, the fragmented audience has to be reassembled into a collectivity. Insofar as a traditional sense of community entailed frequent gathering together to receive a given message, this sense was probably weakened by the duplication of identical messages which brought the solitary reader to the fore. To be sure, bookshops, coffeehouses, reading rooms provided new kinds of communal gathering places. Yet subscription lists and corresponding societies represented relatively impersonal group formations, while the reception of printed messages in any place still required temporary isolation—just as it does in a library now. The notion that society may be regarded as a bundle of discrete units or that the individual is prior to the social group seems to be more compatible with a reading public than with a hearing one. The nature of man as a political animal was less likely to conform to classical models after tribunes of the people were transmuted from orators in public squares to editors of news sheets and gazettes.

Even while communal solidarity was diminished, vicarious participation in more distant events was also enhanced; and even while local ties were loosened, links to larger collective units were being forged. Printed materials encouraged silent adherence to causes whose advocates could not be found in any one parish and who addressed an invisible public from afar. New forms of group identity began to compete with an older, more localized nexus of loyalties. Urban populations were not only pulled apart, they were also linked in new ways by the more impersonal channels of communication. The exchange of goods and services, real estate transactions, the provision of charity were all eventually affected. Personal attendance was increasingly supplemented by vicarious participation in civic functions and municipal affairs. Cheap versions of the magnificent prints which commemorated civic ceremonies, such as royal entries, enabled some stay-at-homes to experience "public" festivals.

The features of individual rulers and of members of their entourage came into sharper focus for scattered subjects in a given realm. The circulation of prints and engravings made it possible for a reigning dynasty to impress a personal presence on mass consciousness in a new way. The effect of duplicating images and portraits of rulers—which were eventually framed and hung in peasant hovels throughout Catholic Europe, along with saints and icons—has yet to be assessed by political scientists. The mass following of a single leader and the nationwide extension of his or her charismatic appeal, at all events, are possible by-products of the new communications systems which ought to be further explored. Joseph Klaits's study of Louis XIV's propaganda efforts describes how early modern rulers deliberately set out to exploit the new presses:

> Princes who had employed the cumbersome methods of manuscript to communicate with their subjects switched quickly to print to announce declarations of war, publish battle accounts, promulgate treaties or argue disputed points in pamphlet form. Theirs was an effort . . . "to win the psychological war which prepared and accompanied the military operations" of rulers . . . The English crown under Henry VIII and Thomas Cromwell made systematic use of both Parliament and press to win public support for the Reformation . . .
>
> In France the regency of Louis XIII saw the last meeting of the Estates General before 1789; it also saw the founding of the first royally sponsored newspaper in Europe. The replacement of

the volatile assembly by the controlled weekly *Gazette* is a concurrence symptomatic of the importance Cardinal Richelieu attached to print in his state-building objectives.

As these references to Richelieu and Thomas Cromwell suggest, even while making room for the heightened visibility of individual rulers, we also need to note how the powers of officials and bureaucrats were extended once government regulations became subject to the duplicative powers of print. The expansion of leviathan states, as might be expected, provoked countermeasures from parliaments and assemblies. Traditional tensions between court and country, crown and estates, were exacerbated by propaganda wars. A greater uniformity began to characterize provincial demands, with the circulation of model petitions and lists of grievances.

Recently some historians have begun to abandon, as fruitless, older debates about the "rise" of a new class to political power in early modern times. They seek to focus attention instead on the reeducation and regroupment of older governing elites—and have, thereby, precipitated new debates. Both lines of inquiry might be reconciled and fruitfully pursued if the consequences of printing received more attention.

SELECTED READINGS

Febvre, Lucien, and Martin, H-J. *The Coming of the Book*, trans. David Gerard (London, 1976). First ed.: *L'Apparition du livre* (Paris, 1958). Readers competent in French should get the original 1958 French version, which is superior in every way (including its bibliography and index) to this recent English translation. The book (which was written almost entirely by Martin) is a masterful survey and has more comprehensive coverage than any other title on this list.

Hirsch, Rudolf. *Printing, Selling, and Reading 1450–1550* (Wiesbaden, 1967; rev. ed. 1974). Crammed with facts; emphasis on German developments. By a rare-book librarian who is especially knowledgeable about European book-selling and printing.

McLuhan, Marshall. *The Gutenberg Galaxy: The Making of Typographical Man* (Toronto, 1962). Deliberately departs from conventional book format. Bizarre "mosaic" of citations drawn from diverse texts designed to stimulate thought about effects of printing. By a recently deceased Canadian literary scholar turned media analyst. Careless handling of historical data may mislead uninformed readers. Surprisingly useful bibliography.

Saenger, Paul. "Silent Reading: Its Impact on Late Medieval Script and Society." *Viator* 13 (1982), 367–414. Presents evidence showing that silent reading occurred before advent of printing. Overstates novelty of practice in late Middle Ages and ignores the extent to which silent reading was reinforced and institutionalized after printing.

Steinberg, S. H. *Five Hundred Years of Printing*, rev. ed. (Bristol, 1961). Remarkably succinct survey. Better coverage of first century of printing than of later ones.

PRINT, SPACE, AND CLOSURE
Walter Ong

Walter Ong was, until his recent retirement, professor of humanities at Saint Louis University. He has written extensively on the orality/literacy question, as well as the communications dimension of the shift from the medieval to the modern era.

In a work of this scope there is no way even to enumerate all the effects of print. Even a cursory glance at Elizabeth Eisenstein's two volumes, *The Printing Press as an Agent of Change* (1979), makes abundantly evident how diversified and vast the particular effects of print have been. Eisenstein spells out in detail how print made the Italian Renaissance a permanent European Renaissance, how it implemented the Protestant Reformation and reoriented Catholic religious practice, how it affected the development of modern capitalism, implemented western European exploration of the globe, changed family life and politics, diffused knowledge as never before, made universal literacy a serious objective, made possible the rise of modern sciences, and otherwise altered social and intellectual life. In *The Gutenberg Galaxy* (1962) and *Understanding Media* (1964) Marshall McLuhan has called attention to many of the subtler ways print has affected consciousness, as

George Steiner has also done in *Language and Silence* (1967) and as I have undertaken to do elsewhere (Ong 1958b; 1967b; 1971; 1977). These subtler effects of print on consciousness, rather than readily observable social effects, concern us particularly here.

For thousands of years human beings have been printing designs from variously carved surfaces, and since the seventh or eighth century Chinese, Koreans and Japanese have been printing verbal texts, at first from wood blocks engraved in relief (Carter 1955). But the crucial development in the global history of printing was the invention of alphabetic letterpress print in fifteenth-century Europe. Alphabetic writing had broken the word up into spatial equivalents of phonemic units (in principle, though the letters never quite worked out as totally phonemic indicators). But the letters used in writing do not exist before the text in which they occur. With alphabetic letterpress print it is otherwise.

Words are made out of units (types) which pre-exist as units before the words which they will constitute. Print suggests that words are things far more than writing ever did.

Like the alphabet, alphabetic letterpress print was a nonce invention (Ong 1967b, and references there cited). The Chinese had had movable type, but no alphabet, only characters, basically pictographic. Before the mid-1400s the Koreans and Uigur Turks had both the alphabet and movable type, but the movable types bore not separate letters but whole words. Alphabet letterpress printing, in which each letter was cast on a separate piece of metal, or type, marked a psychological breakthrough of the first order. It embedded the word itself deeply in the manufacturing process and made it into a kind of commodity. The first assembly line, a technique of manufacture which in a series of set steps produces identical complex objects made up of replaceable parts, was not one which produced stoves or shoes or weaponry but one which produced the printed book. In the late 1700s, the industrial revolution applied to other manufacturing the replaceable-part techniques which printers had worked with for three hundred years. Despite the assumptions of many semiotic structuralists, it was print, not writing, that effectively reified the word, and, with it, noetic activity (Ong 1958b, pp. 306–18).

Hearing rather than sight had dominated the older noetic world in significant ways, even long after writing was deeply interiorized. Manuscript culture in the west remained always marginally oral. Ambrose of Milan caught the earlier mood in his *Commentary on Luke* (iv. 5): "Sight is often deceived, hearing serves as guarantee." In the west through the Renaissance, the oration was the most taught of all verbal productions and remained implicitly the basic paradigm for all discourse, written as well as oral. Written material was subsidiary to hearing in ways which strike us today as bizarre. Writing served largely to recycle knowledge back into the oral world, as in medieval university dispu-

tations, in the reading of literary and other texts to groups (Crosby 1936; Ahern 1981; Nelson 1976–7), and in reading aloud even when reading to oneself. At least as late as the twelfth century in England, checking even written financial accounts was still done aurally, by having them read aloud. Clanchy (1979, pp. 215, 183) describes the practice and draws attention to the fact that it still registers in our vocabulary: even today, we speak of "auditing," that is, "hearing" account books, though what an accountant actually does today is examine them by sight. Earlier, residually oral folk could understand even figures better by listening than by looking.

Manuscript cultures remained largely oral-aural even in retrieval of material preserved in texts. Manuscripts were not easy to read, by later typographic standards, and what readers found in manuscripts they tended to commit at least somewhat to memory. Relocating material in a manuscript was not always easy. Memorization was encouraged and facilitated also by the fact that in highly oral manuscript cultures, the verbalization one encountered even in written texts often continued the oral mnemonic patterning that made for ready recall. Moreover, readers commonly vocalized, read slowly aloud or *sotto voce*, even when reading alone, and this also helped fix matter in the memory.

Well after printing was developed, auditory processing continued for some time to dominate the visible, printed text, though it was eventually eroded away by print. Auditory dominance can be seen strikingly in such things as early printed title pages, which often seem to us crazily erratic in their inattention to visual word units. Sixteenth-century title pages very commonly divide even major words, including the author's name, with hyphens, presenting the first part of a word in one line in large type and the latter part in smaller type, as in the edition of Sir Thomas Elyot's *The Boke Named the Gouernour* published in London by Thomas Berthelet in 1534. Inconsequential words may be set in huge type faces: on the title page the initial "THE" is by far the most prominent word of all. The result is often aesthetically pleasing as a visual design, but it plays havoc with our present sense of textuality. Yet this practice, not our practice, is the original practice from which our present practice has deviated. Our attitudes are the ones that have changed, and thus that need to be explained. Why does the original, presumably more "natural" procedure seem wrong to us? Because we feel the printed words before us as visual units (even though we sound them at least in the imagination when we read). Eventually, in processing text for meaning, the sixteenth century was concentrating less on the sight of the word and more on its sound than we do. All text involves sight and sound. But whereas we feel reading as a visual activity cueing in sounds for us, the early age of print still felt it as primarily a listening process, simply set in motion by sight. If you felt yourself as readers to be listening to words, what difference did it make if the visible text went its own visually aesthetic way? It will be recalled that preprint manuscripts commonly ran words together or kept spaces between them minimal.

Eventually, however, print replaced the lingering hearing-dominance in the world of thought and expression with the sight-dominance which had its beginnings with writing but could not flourish with the support of writing alone. Print situates words in space more relentlessly than writing ever did. Writing moves words from the sound world to a world of visual space, but print locks words into position in this space. Control of position is everything in print. "Composing" type by hand (the original form of typesetting) consists in positioning by hand preformed letter types, which, after use, are carefully repositioned, redistributed for future use into their proper compartments in the case (capitals or "upper case" letters in the upper compartments, small or "lower case" letters in the lower compartments). Composing on the Linotype consists in using a machine to position the separate matrices for individual lines so that a line of type can be cast from the properly positioned

matrices. Composing on a computer terminal or word-processor positions electronic patterns (letters) previously programmed into the computer. Printing from "hot metal" type (that is, from cast type—the older and still widely used process) calls for locking up the type in an absolutely rigid position in the chase, locking the chase firmly onto a press, affixing and clamping down the makeready, and squeezing the forme of type with great pressure onto the paper printing surface in contrast with the platen.

Most readers are of course not consciously aware of all this locomotion that has produced the printed text confronting them. Nevertheless, from the appearance of the printed text they pick up a sense of the word-in-space quite different from that conveyed by writing. Printed texts look machine-made, as they are. Chirographic control of space tends to be ornamental, ornate, as in calligraphy. Typographic control typically impresses more by its tidiness and inevitability: the lines perfectly regular, all justified on the right side, everything coming out even visually, and without the aid of the guidelines or ruled borders that often occur in manuscripts. This is an insistent world of cold, non-human, facts. "That's the way it is"—Walter Cronkite's television signature comes from the world of print that underlies the secondary orality of television (Ong 1971, pp. 284–303).

By and large, printed texts are far easier to read than manuscript texts. The effects of the greater legibility of print are massive. The greater legibility ultimately makes for rapid, silent reading. Such reading in turn makes for a different relationship between the reader and the authorial voice in the text and calls for different styles of writing. Print involves many persons besides the author in the production of a work—publishers, literary agents, publishers' readers, copy editors and others. Before as well as after scrutiny by such persons, writing for print often calls for painstaking revisions by the author of an order of magnitude virtually unknown in a manuscript culture. Few lengthy prose works from manuscript cultures could pass editorial scrutiny as original works today: they are not organized for rapid assimilation from a printed page. Manuscript culture is producer-oriented, since every individual copy of a work represents great expenditure of an individual copyist's time. Medieval manuscripts are turgid with abbreviations, which favor the copyist although they inconvenience the reader. Print is consumer-oriented, since the individual copies of a work represent a much smaller investment of time: a few hours spent in producing a more readable text will immediately improve thousands upon thousands of copies. The effects of print on thought and style have yet to be assessed fully. The journal *Visible Language* (formerly called the *Journal of Typographic Research*) publishes many articles contributory to such an assessment.

SPACE AND MEANING

Writing had reconstituted the originally oral, spoken word in visual space. Print embedded the word in space more definitely. This can be seen in such developments as lists, especially alphabetic indexes, in the use of words (instead of iconographic signs) for labels, in the use of printed drawings of all sorts to convey information, and in the use of abstract typographic space to interact geometrically with printed words in a line of development that runs from Ramism to concrete poetry and to Derrida's logomachy with the (printed, typically, not simply written) text.

Indexes

Lists begin with writing. Goody has discussed (1977, pp. 74–111) the use of lists in the Ugaritic script of around 1300 B.C. and in other early scripts. He notes (1977, pp. 87–8) that the information in the lists is abstracted from the social situation in which it had been embedded ("fattened kids," "pastured ewes," etc., with no

further specifications) and also from linguistic context (normally in oral utterance nouns are not free-floating as in lists, but are embedded in sentences: rarely do we hear an oral recitation of simply a string of nouns—unless they are being read off a written or printed list). In this sense, lists as such have "no oral equivalent" (1977, pp. 86–7) though of course the individual written words sound in the inner ear to yield their meanings. Goody also notes the initially awkward, *ad hoc* way in which space was utilized in making these lists, with word-dividers to separate items from numbers, ruled lines, wedged lines, and elongated lines. Besides administrative lists, he discusses also event lists, lexical lists (words are listed in various orders, often hierarchically by meaning—gods, then kin of the gods, next gods' servants), and Egyptian onomastica or name-lists, which were often memorized for oral recitation. Still highly oral manuscript culture felt that having written series of things readied for oral recall was of itself intellectually improving. (Educators in the west until recently had the same feeling, and across the world most educators probably still do.) Writing is here once more at the service of orality.

Goody's examples show the relatively sophisticated processing of verbalized material in chirographic cultures so as to make the material more immediately retrievable through its spatial organization. Lists range names of related items in the same physical, visual space. Print develops far more sophisticated use of space for visual organization and for effective retrieval.

Indexes are a prime development here. Alphabetic indexes show strikingly the disengagement of words from discourse and their embedding in typographic space. Manuscripts can be alphabetically indexed. They rarely are (Daly 1967, pp. 81–90; Clanchy 1979, pp. 28–9, 85). Since two manuscripts of a given work, even if copied from the same dictation, almost never correspond page for page, each manuscript of a given work would normally require a separate index. Indexing was not worth the effort. Auditory recall through memorization was more economical, though not thoroughgoing. For visual location of materials in a manuscript text, pictorial signs were often preferred to alphabetic indexes. A favorite sign was the "paragraph," which originally meant this mark ¶, not a unit of discourse at all. When alphabetic indexes occurred, they were rare, often crude, and commonly not understood, even in thirteenth-century Europe, when sometimes an index made for one manuscript was appended without change of page numbers to another manuscript with a different pagination (Clanchy 1979, p. 144). Indexes seem to have been valued at times for their beauty and mystery rather than for their utility. In 1286, a Genoese compiler could marvel at the alphabetical catalog he had devised as due not to his own prowess but "the grace of God working in me" (Daly 1967, p. 73). Indexing was long by first letter only—or, rather, by first sound: for example, in a Latin work published as late as 1506 in Rome, since in Italian and Latin as spoken by Italian-speakers the letter *h* is not pronounced, "Halyzones" is listed under *a* (discussed in Ong, 1977, pp. 169–72). Here even visual retrieval functions aurally. Ioannes Ravisius Textor's *Specimen epithetorum* (Paris, 1518) alphabetizes "Apollo" before all other entries under *a,* because Textor considers it fitting that in a work concerned with poetry, the god of poetry should get top billing. Clearly, even in a printed alphabetic index, visual retrieval was given low priority. The personalized, oral world still could overrule processing words as things.

The alphabetic index is actually a crossroads between auditory and visualist cultures. "Index" is a shortened form of the original *index locorum* or *index locorum communium,* "index of places" or "index of commonplaces." Rhetoric had provided the various *loci* or "places"—headings, we would style them—under which various "arguments" could be found, headings such as cause, effect, related things, unlike things, and so on. Coming with this orally based, formulary equipment to the text, the indexer of 400 years ago simply noted on what pages in the text one or another *locus* was exploited, listing there the locus and the corresponding pages in the *index locorum*. The *loci* had originally been thought of as, vaguely, "places" in the mind where ideas were stored. In the printed book, these vague psychic "places" became quite physically and visibly localized. A new noetic world was shaping up, spatially organized.

In this new world, the book was less like an utterance, and more like a thing. Manuscript culture had preserved a feeling for a book as a kind of utterance, an occurrence in the course of conversation, rather than as an object. Lacking title pages and often titles, a book from pre-print, manuscript culture is normally catalogued by its "incipit" (a Latin verb meaning "it begins"), or the first words of this text (referring to the Lord's Prayer as the "Our Father" is referring to it by its incipit and evinces a certain residual orality). With print, as has been seen, come title pages. Title pages are labels. They attest a feeling for the book as a kind of thing or object. Often in medieval western manuscripts, instead of a title page the text proper might be introduced by an observation to the reader, just as a conversation might start with a remark of one person to another: "Hic habes, carissime lector, librum quem scripset quidam de. . . ." (Here you have, dear reader, a book which so-and-so wrote about. . . .) The oral heritage is at work here, for, although oral cultures of course have ways of referring to stories or other traditional recitations (the stories of the Wars of Troy, the Mwindo stories, and so on), label-like titles as such are not very operational in oral cultures: Homer would hardly have begun a recitation of episodes from the *Iliad* by announcing "The Iliad."

Books, Contents, and Labels

Once print had been fairly well interiorized, a book was sensed as a kind of object which "contained" information, scientific, fictional or other, rather than, as earlier, a recorded utterance (Ong

1958b, p. 313). Each individual book in a printed edition was physically the same as another, an identical object, as manuscript books were not, even when they presented the same text. Now, with print, two copies of a given work did not merely say the same thing, they were duplicates of one another as objects. The situation invited the use of labels, and the printed book, being a letter object, naturally took a lettered label, the title page (new with print—Steinberg 1974, pp. 145–8). At the same time the iconographic drive was still strong, as is seen in the highly emblematic engraved title pages that persisted through the 1660s, filled with allegorical figures and other nonverbal designs.

Meaningful Surface

Ivins (1953, p. 31) has pointed out that, although the art of printing designs from various carved surfaces had been known for centuries, only after the development of movable letterpress type in the mid-1400s were prints used systematically to convey information. Hand-done technical drawings, as Ivins has shown (1953, pp. 14–16, 40–5) soon deteriorated in manuscripts because even skilled artists miss the point of an illustration they are copying unless they are supervised by an expert in the field the illustrations refer to. Otherwise, a sprig of white clover copied by a succession of artists unfamiliar with real white clover can end up looking like asparagus. Prints might have solved the problem in a manuscript culture, since printmaking had been practiced for centuries for decorative purposes. Cutting an accurate printing block for white clover would have been quite feasible long before the invention of letterpress printing and would have provided just what was needed, an "exactly repeatable visual statement." But manuscript production was not congenial to such manufacture. Manuscripts were produced by handwriting, not from pre-existing parts. Print was congenial. The verbal text was reproduced from pre-existing parts, and so

could prints be. A press could print an "exactly repeatable visual statement" as easily as a forme set up from type.

One consequence of the new exactly repeatable visual statement was modern science. Exact observation does not begin with modern science. For ages, it has always been essential for survival among, for example, hunters and craftsmen of many sorts. What is distinctive of modern science is the conjuncture of exact observation and exact verbalization: exactly worded descriptions of carefully observed complex objects and processes. The availability of carefully made, technical prints (first woodcuts, and later even more exactly detailed metal engravings) implemented such exactly worded descriptions. Technical prints and technical verbalization reinforced and improved each other. The resulting hypervisualized noetic world was brand new. Ancient and medieval writers are simply unable to produce exactly worded descriptions that appear after print and, indeed, that mature chiefly with the Age of Romanticism, that is, the age of the Industrial Revolution. Oral and residually oral verbalization directs its attention to action, not to the visual appearance of objects or scenes or persons (Fritschi 1981, pp. 65–6; cf. Havelock 1963, pp. 61–96). Vitruvius' treatise on architecture is notoriously vague. The kinds of exactitude aimed at by the long-standing rhetorical tradition were not of a visual–vocal sort. Eisenstein (1979, p. 64) suggests how difficult it is today to imagine earlier cultures where relatively few persons had ever seen a physically accurate picture of anything.

The new noetic world opened by exactly repeatable visual statement and correspondingly exact verbal description of physical reality affected not just science but literature as well. No pre-romantic prose provides the circumstantial description of landscape found in Gerard Manley Hopkins's notebooks (1937) and no pre-romantic poetry proceeds with the close, meticulous, clinical attention to natural phenomena found, for example, in Hopkins's description of a plunging brook in *Inversnaid*. As much as Darwin's evolutionary biology or Michelson's physics this kind of poetry grows out of the world of print.

Typographic Space

Because visual surface had become charged with imposed meaning and because print controlled not only what words were put down to form a text but also the exact situation of the words on the page and their spatial relationship to one another, the space itself on a printed sheet—"white space" as it is called—took on high significance that leads directly into the modern and post-modern world. Manuscript lists and charts, discussed by Goody (1977, pp. 74–111), can situate words in specific spatial relationships to one another, but if the spatial relationships are extremely complicated, the complications will not survive the vagaries of successive copiers. Print can reproduce with complete accuracy and in any quantity indefinitely complex lists and charts. Early in the age of print, extremely complex charts appear in the teaching of academic subjects (Ong 1958b, pp. 80, 81, 202, etc.).

Typographic space works not only on the scientific and philosophic imagination, but also on the literary imagination, which shows some of the complicated ways in which typographic space is present to the psyche. George Herbert exploits typographic space to provide meaning in his "Easter Wings" and "The Altar," where the lines, of varying lengths, give the poems a visualized shape suggesting wings and an altar respectively. In manuscripts, this kind of visual structure would be only marginally viable. In *Tristram Shandy* (1760–7), Laurence Sterne uses typographic space with calculated whimsy, including in his book blank pages, to indicate his unwillingness to treat a subject and to invite the reader to fill in. Space here is the equivalent of silence. Much later, and with greater sophistication, Stéphane Mallarmé designs his poem "Un Coup de dés" to be set in varying fonts and sizes

of type with the lines scattered calculatingly across the pages in a kind of typographical free-fall suggesting the chance that rules a throw of dice (the poem is reproduced and discussed in Bruns 1974, pp. 115–38). Mallarmeé's declared objective is to "avoid narrative" and "space out" the reading of the poem so that the page, with its typographic spaces, not the line, is the unit of verse. E. E. Cummings's untitled Poem No. 276 (1968) about the grasshopper disintegrates the words of its text and scatters them unevenly about the page until at last letters come together in the final word "grasshopper"—all this to suggest the erratic and optically dizzying flight of a grasshopper until he finally reassembles himself straightforwardly on the blade of grass before us. White space is so integral to Cummings's poem that it is utterly impossible to read the poem aloud. The sounds cued in by the letters have to be present in the imagination but their presence is not simply auditory: it interacts with the visually and kinesthetically perceived space around them.

Concrete poetry (Solt 1970) climaxes in a certain way the interaction of sounded words and typographic space. It presents exquisitely complicated or exquisitely uncomplicated visual display of letters and/or words some of which can be viewed but not read aloud at all, but none of which can be appropriated without some awareness of verbal sound. Even when concrete poetry cannot be read at all, it is still not merely a picture. Concrete poetry is a minor genre, often merely gimmicky—a fact which makes it all the more necessary to explain the drive to produce it.

Hartman (1981, p. 35) has suggested a connection between concrete poetry and Jacques Derrida's on-going logomachy with the text. The connection is certainly real and deserves more attention. Concrete poetry plays with the dialectic of the word locked into space as opposed to the sounded, oral word which can never be locked into space (every text is pretext), that is, it plays with the absolute limitations of textuality which paradoxically reveal the built-in limitations of the spoken word, too. This is Derrida's terrain, though he moves over it at his own calculated gait. Concrete poetry is not the product of writing but of typography, as has been seen. Deconstruction is tied to typography rather than, as its advocates seem often to assume, merely to writing.

MORE DIFFUSE EFFECTS

One can list without end additional effects, more or less direct, which print had on the noetic economy or the "mentality" of the west. Print eventually removed the ancient art of (orally based) rhetoric from the center of academic education. It encouraged and made possible on a large scale the quantification of knowledge, both through the use of mathematical analysis and through the use of diagrams and charts. Print eventually reduced the appeal of iconography in the management of knowledge, despite the fact that the early ages of print put iconographic illustration into circulation as they had never been before. Iconographic figures are akin to the "heavy" or type characters of oral discourse and they are associated with rhetoric and with the arts of memory that oral management of knowledge needs (Yates 1966).

Print produced exhaustive dictionaries and fostered the desire to legislate for "correctness" in language. This desire in great part grew out of a sense of language based on the study of Learned Latin. Learned tongues textualize the idea of language, making it seem at root something written. Print reinforces the sense of language as essentially textual. The printed text, not the written text, is the text in its fullest, paradigmatic form.

Print established the climate in which dictionaries grew. From their origins in the eighteenth century until the past few decades, dictionaries of English have commonly taken as their norm for language only the usage of writers producing text for print (and not quite all of them). The usage of all others, if it deviates from this typographic usage, has been regarded as "corrupt." *Webster's Third New International Dictionary* (1961) was the first major lexicographical work to break cleanly with this old typographical convention and to cite as sources for usage persons not writing for print—and of course many persons, formed in the old ideology, immediately wrote off this impressive lexicographical achievement (Dykema 1963) as a betrayal of the "true" or "pure" language.

Print was also a major factor in the development of the sense of personal privacy that marks modern society. It produced books smaller and more portable than those common in a manuscript culture, setting the stage psychologically for solo reading in a quiet corner, and eventually for completely silent reading. In manuscript culture and hence in early print culture, reading had tended to be a social activity, one person reading to others in a group. As Steiner (1967, p. 383) has suggested, private reading demands a home spacious enough to provide for individual isolation and quiet. (Teachers of children from poverty areas today are acutely aware that often the major reason for poor performance is that there is nowhere in a crowded house where a boy or girl can study effectively.)

Print created a new sense of the private ownership of words. Persons in a primary oral culture can entertain some sense of proprietary rights to a poem, but such a sense is rare and ordinarily enfeebled by the common share of lore, formulas, and themes on which everyone draws. With writing, resentment at plagiarism begins to develop. The ancient Latin poet Martial (i.53.9) uses the word *plagiarius,* a torturer, plunderer, oppressor, for someone who appropriates another's writing. But there is no special Latin word with the exclusive meaning of plagiarist or plagiarism. The oral commonplace tradition was still strong. In the very early days of print, however, a royal decree or *privilegium* was often secured forbidding the reprinting of a printed book by others than the original publisher. Richard Pynson secured such a *privilegium* in 1518 from Henry VIII. In 1557 the Stationers' Company was incorporated in London to oversee authors' and printers' or printer-publishers' rights, and by the eighteenth century modern copyright laws were shaping up over western Europe. Typography had made the word into a commodity. The old communal oral world had split up into privately claimed freeholdings. The drift in human consciousness toward greater individualism had been served well by print. Of course, words were not quite private property. They were still shared property to a degree. Printed books did echo one another, willy-nilly. At the onset of the electronic age, Joyce faced up to the anxieties of influence squarely and in *Ulysses* and *Finnegans Wake* undertook to echo everybody on purpose.

By removing words from the world of sound where they had first had their origin in active human interchange and relegating them definitely to visual surface, and by otherwise exploiting visual space for the management of knowledge, print encouraged human beings to think of their own interior conscious and unconscious resources as more and more thinglike, impersonal and religiously neutral. Print encouraged the mind to sense that its possessions were held in some sort of inert mental space.

PRINT AND CLOSURE: INTERTEXTUALITY

Print encourages a sense of closure, a sense that what is found in a text has been finalized, has reached a state of completion. This sense affects literary creations and it affects analytic philosophical or scientific work.

Before print, writing itself encouraged some sense of noetic closure. By isolating thought on a written surface, detached from any interlocutor, making utterance in this sense autonomous and indifferent to attack, writing presents utterance and thought as uninvolved with all else, some-

how self-contained, complete. Print in the same way situates utterance and thought on a surface disengaged from everything else, but it also goes farther in suggesting self-containment. Print encloses thought in thousands of copies of a work of exactly the same visual and physical consistency. Verbal correspondence of copies of the same printing can be checked with no resort to sound at all but simply by sight: a Hinman collator will superimpose corresponding pages of two copies of a text and signal variations to the viewer with a blinking light.

The printed text is supposed to represent the words of an author in definitive or "final" form. For print is comfortable only with finality. Once a letterpress forme is closed, locked up, or a photolithographic plate is made, and the sheet printed, the text does not accommodate changes (erasures, insertions) so readily as do written texts. By contrast, manuscripts, with their glosses or marginal comments (which often got worked into the text in subsequent copies) were in dialogue with the world outside their own borders. They remained closer to the give-and-take of oral expression. The readers of manuscripts are less closed off from the author, less absent, than are the readers of those writing for print. The sense of closure or completeness enforced by print is at times grossly physical. A newspaper's pages are normally all filled—certain kinds of printed material are called "fillers"—just as its lines of type are normally all justified (i.e., all exactly the same width). Print is curiously intolerant of physical incompleteness. It can convey the impression, unintentionally and subtly, but very really, that the material the text deals with is similarly complete or self-consistent.

Print makes for more tightly closed verbal art forms, especially in narrative. Until print, the only linearly plotted lengthy story line was that of the drama, which from antiquity had been controlled by writing. Euripides' tragedies were texts composed in writing and then memorized verbatim to be presented orally. With print, tight plotting is extended to the lengthy narrative, in the novel from Jane Austen's time on, and reaches its peak in the detective story. . . .

In literary theory, print gives rise ultimately to Formalism and the New Criticism, with their deep conviction that each work of verbal art is closed off in a world of its own, a "verbal icon." Significantly, an icon is something seen, [but] not heard. Manuscript culture felt works of verbal art to be more in touch with the oral plenum, and never very effectively distinguished between poetry and rhetoric. . . .

Print ultimately gives rise to the modern issue of intertextuality, which is so central a concern in phenomenological and critical circles today (Hawkes 1977, p. 144). Intertextuality refers to a literary and psychological commonplace: a text cannot be created simply out of lived experience. A novelist writes a novel because he or she is familiar with this kind of textual organization of experience.

Manuscript culture had taken intertextuality for granted. Still tied to the commonplace tradition of the oral world, it deliberately created texts out of other texts, borrowing, adapting, sharing the common, originally oral, formulas and themes, even though it worked them up into fresh literary forms impossible without writing. Print culture of itself has a different mind-set. It tends to feel a work as "closed," set off from other works, a unit in itself. Print culture gave birth to the romantic notions of "originality" and "creativity," which set part an individual work from other works even more, seeing its origins and meaning as independent of outside influence, at least ideally. When in the past few decades doctrines of intertextuality arose to counteract the isolationist aesthetics of a romantic print culture, they came as a kind of shock. They were all the more disquieting because modern writers, agonizingly aware of literary history and of the *de facto* intertextuality of their own works, are concerned that they may be producing nothing really new or fresh at all, that they may be totally under the "influence" of others' texts. Harold Bloom's

work *The Anxiety of Influence* (1973) treats this modern writer's anguish. Manuscript cultures had few if any anxieties about influence to plague them, and oral cultures had virtually none.

Print creates a sense of closure not only in literary works but also in analytic philosophical and scientific works. With print came the catechism and the "textbook," less discursive and less disputatious than most previous presentations of a given academic subject. Catechisms and textbooks presented "facts" or their equivalents: memorizable, flat statements that told straight-forwardly and inclusively how matters stood in a given field. By contrast, the memorable statements of oral cultures and of residually oral manuscript cultures tended to be of a proverbial sort, presenting not "facts" but rather reflections, often of a gnomic kind, inviting further reflection by the paradoxes they involved.

Peter Ramus (1515–72) produced the paradigms of the textbook genre: textbooks for virtually all arts subjects (dialectic or logic, rhetoric, grammar, arithmetic, etc.) that proceeded by cold-blooded definitions and divisions leading to still further definitions and more divisions, until every last particle of the subject had been dissected and disposed of. A Ramist textbook on a given subject had no acknowledged interchange with anything outside itself. Not even any difficulties or "adversaries" appeared. A curriculum subject or "art," if presented properly according to Ramist method, involved no difficulties at all (so Ramists maintained): if you defined and divided in the proper way, everything in the art was completely self-evident and the art itself was complete and self-contained. Ramus relegated difficulties and refutations of adversaries to separate "lectures" (*scholae*) on dialectic, rhetoric, grammar, arithmetic, and all the rest. These lectures lay outside the self-enclosed "art." Moreover, the material in each of the Ramist textbooks could be presented in printed dichotomized outlines or charts that showed exactly how the material was organized spatially in itself and in the mind. Every art was in itself completely separate from every other, as houses with intervening open spaces are separate from one another, though the arts were mingled in "use"—that is to say, in working up a given passage of discourse, one used simultaneously logic, grammar, rhetoric, and possibly other arts as well (Ong 1958b, pp. 30–1, 225–69, 280).

A correlative of the sense of closure fostered by print was the fixed point of view, which as Marshall McLuhan has pointed out (1962, pp. 126–7, 135–6), came into being with print. With the fixed point of view, a fixed tone could now be preserved through the whole of a lengthy prose composition. The fixed point of view and fixed tone showed in one way a greater distance between writer and reader and in another way a greater tacit understanding. The writer could go his or her own way confidently (greater distance, lack of concern). There is no need to make everything a kind of Menippean satire, a mixture of various points of view and tone for various sensibilities. The writer could be confident that the reader would adjust (greater understanding). At this point, the "reading public" came into existence—a sizable clientele of readers unknown personally to the author but able to deal with certain more or less established points of view.

SELECTED BIBLIOGRAPHY

Ahern, John (1982) "Sing the book: orality in the reception of Dante's *Comedy*." *Annals of Scholarship* (in press).

Bloom, Harold (1973) *The Anxiety of Influence* (New York: Oxford University Press).

Bruns, Gerald L. (1974) *Modern Poetry and the Idea of Language: A Critical and Historical Study* (New Haven and London: Yale University Press).

Carter, Thomas Francis (1955) *The Invention of Printing in China and Its Spread Westward*, rev. by L. Carrington Goodrich, 2nd edn (New York: Ronald Press).

Clanchy, M. T. (1979) *From Memory to Written Record: England, 1066–1307* (Cambridge, Mass.: Harvard University Press).

Crosby, Ruth (1936) "Oral delivery in the Middle Ages," *Speculum*, II, 88–110.

Daly, Lloyd S. (1967) *Contributions to a History of Alphabetization in Antiquity and the Middle Ages*, Collection Latomus, vol. xc (Bruxelles: Latomus, Revue d'études latines).

Derrida, Jacques (1976) *Of Grammatology,* trans. by Gayatri Chakravortry Spivak (Baltimore and London: Johns Hopkins University Press).

———. (1978) *Writing and Difference,* trans., with an introduction and additional notes, by Alan Bass (Chicago: University of Chicago Press).

Dykema, Karl (1963) "Cultural lag and reviewers of Webster III," *AAUP Bulletin* 49, 364–69.

Eisenstein, Elizabeth (1979) *The Printing Press as an Agent of Change: Communications and Cultural Transformations in Early-Modern Europe*, 2 vols (New York: Cambridge University Press).

Elyot, Sir Thomas (1534) *The Boke Named the Gouernour* (London: Thomas Berthelet).

Fritschi, Gerhard (1981) "Oral experience in some modern African novels," typescript, 282 pp. received from the author.

Goody, Jack (John Rankin) (1977) *The Domestication of the Savage Mind* (Cambridge, England: Cambridge University Press).

Hartman, Geoffrey (1981) *Saving the Text: Literature/Derrida/Philosophy* (Baltimore, Md.: Johns Hopkins University Press).

Havelock, Eric A. (1963) *Preface to Plato* (Cambridge, Mass.: Belknap Press of Harvard University Press).

Hawkes, Terence (1977) *Structuralism and Semiotics* (Berkeley and Los Angeles: University of California Press; London: Methuen).

Hopkins, Gerard Manley (1937) *Note-Books and Papers of Gerard Manley Hopkins*, ed. Humphrey House (London: Oxford University Press).

Ivins, William M., Jr. (1953) *Prints and Visual Communication* (Cambridge, Mass.: Harvard University Press).

McLuhan, Marshall (1962) *The Gutenberg Galaxy: The Making of Typographic Man* (Toronto: University of Toronto Press).

———. (1964) *Understanding Media: The Extensions of Man* (New York: McGraw-Hill).

Nelson, William (1976–7) "From 'Listen, Lordings' to 'Dear Reader'," *University of Toronto Quarterly*, 46, 111–24.

Ong, Walter J. (1958a) *Ramus and Talon Inventory* (Cambridge, Mass.: Harvard University Press).

———. (1958b) *Ramus, Method, and the Decay of Dialogue* (Cambridge, Mass.: Harvard University Press).

———. (1962) *The Barbarian Within* (New York: Macmillan).

———. (1967a) *In the Human Grain* (New York: Macmillan; London: Collier-Macmillan).

———. (1967b) *The Presence of the Word* (New Haven and London: Yale University Press).

———. (1971) *Rhetoric, Romance, and Technology* (Ithaca and London: Cornell University Press).

———. (1977) *Interfaces of the Word* (Ithaca and London: Cornell University Press).

———. (1978) "Literacy and orality in our times," *ADE Bulletin*, 58 (September), 1–7.

———. (1981) *Fighting for Life: Contest, Sexuality, and Consciousness* (Ithaca and London: Cornell University Press).

Solt, Mary Ellen (ed.) (1970) *Concrete Poetry: A World View* (Bloomington: Indiana University Press).

Steinberg, S. H. (1974) *Five Hundred Years of Printing*, 3rd edn rev. by James Moran (Harmondsworth, England: Penguin Books).

Steiner, George (1967) *Language and Silence: Essays on Language, Literature, and the Inhuman* (New York: Athenaeum).

Visible Language (formerly *Journal of Typographic Research*). Publishes many valuable articles about typography, its constitution and development, its psychological and cultural effects, etc.

Yates, Frances A. (1966) *The Art of Memory* (Chicago: University of Chicago Press).

14 EARLY MODERN LITERACIES

Harvey J. Graff

Harvey J. Graff is professor of history and humanities at the University of Texas at Dallas and author of several acclaimed books on literacy, including The Literacy Myth *and* Literacy in History.

PRINT, REFORM, AND REFORMATION

In the history of the West, the Protestant Reformation is said to be one of the greatest positive forces toward the spread of literacy and schooling. It can easily be viewed as an educational reform movement: "The basic assumptions of the reformers were that one must start with the young, that indoctrination is necessary for religious and moral improvement . . . , that this indoctrination must be done in public schools. . . ."[1] The Reformation involved factors far beyond the religious and theological. Its roots lay in the Middle Ages; economic, political, cultural, and social issues inextricably intertwined to give rise to a deep and bitterly divi-

sive mass movement. Its conflicts lasted through much of the sixteenth and seventeenth centuries; the reformation of social life was a long-term endeavor in Western society and culture, to which literacy was often central.

Ecclesiastical reform movements were the central cause of the Reformation, which was triggered by the "publication" of Martin Luther's ninety-five theses in 1518. Increasing dissatisfaction with the church and papacy resulted in a slow, but steady, development of active dissent in the first half of the sixteenth century.

The major reform movements that helped to shape the context for the Reformation shared a common concern with moral criteria and a common approach: except for the "Devotio Moderna," the movements all looked to secular authorities for aid, took arguments and inspiration from the Bible, and appealed to the early church. They sought the reaffirmation of community, the reorganization of lay piety and religion, and the reintegration of the outer and inner self. The Northern Renaissance, with its central current of humanism, was probably the most important. Humanism benefited from such new factors as the role of printing, the urban and articulate commercial classes, and the increasingly literate laity; it offered an optimistic, progressive reform program.[2]

Early-sixteenth-century humanism appealed to the educated laity in their search for more religion and a more active piety. But the impact of the doctrines of the religious reformers went beyond theology alone; in addition, political changes in the territorial states necessitated major social and economic adjustments. Some turned to the new Protestiantism, others toward Catholicism and the church. Townspeople, nobility, and even the peasants responded to the calls for reform or counter reform.

Martin Luther's own reform began as a university-based effort to transform the curriculum, replacing Aristotle and scholasticism with the Bible and St. Augustine. He was aware of the sensitive nature of his theses and made his challenge patiently through official channels. When no response arrived, he sent handwritten copies of the theses to some friends for clarification. Those copies were reproduced and circulated, and were even translated into German. They spread widely, and soon all of Germany, and then all of Christendom, had been aroused by Luther's theses.[3]

Two of the most significant developments of the Reformation were the contribution of the printing press and the use of the vernacular. These seminal currents were especially relevant to the history of literacy, yet their contributions were not always direct or immediately recognized. Neither Luther and his theses, the church's hierarchy, the social context, the printing press, nor any single factor or development *caused* the events that permanently split the world of Western Christendom and firmly ended the Middle Ages.

The contribution of movable typography to the religious revolution of the sixteenth century is easily exaggerated. At the beginning of the century, traditional moral and religious books were popular, but newly developing literary forms were also being published before the Reformation, including collections of sermons and the works of the church fathers. A large number of religious works were being published, but they constituted a smaller percentage of the total production. They may not have reached a larger public after the turn of the century than before.

The situation changed rapidly in Germany by 1517. Religious issues quickly took on the utmost importance. The first propaganda campaign with the help of the printing press was conducted, as the power of the press to influence public thought and opinion was realized. An attempt was made "to place within the reach of everyone and in the vernacular the Holy Writ which provided the basis of the reformed and restored religion."

The printing press did not determine the Reformation, for it had been technologically prepared for some time. Pious materials had been printed for many years—Bibles, books of simple piety, posters, handbills, and broadsheets. The press, rather, prepared the coming of the Reformation, providing a tried and tested vehicle for both reformers and their opposition to spread their ideas.

Leaflets and, especially, posters helped to keep the public informed. Illiterates could receive the message by having a poster read to them. The availability of printed matter did not cause an increase in literacy; it increased the flow of communications and raised the probability of more and more persons' receiving information. The use of printing insured that Luther's theses and later writings were rapidly and widely circulated.[4]

The contribution of print was dramatic. Notices posted on walls, church doors, and gateways were read with interest. Luther's own writings were in demand, and he and his colleagues produced more and more literature in the vernacular, hoping to reach the widest audience possible. In support and response came pamphlets caricaturing the church fathers and monks. More important, the number of books printed in Germany rose quickly. The presses of Germany were kept busy with the business of the Reformation until well past mid-century.

Colporteurs and book peddlers carried Reformation propaganda into the countryside. In this way, printing was a direct influence in the Peasants' Revolt of 1524–1525. That revolt marked a watershed in the Lutheran Reformation, as reform leaders recognized dangers to social order and drew back in their calls for mass participation. A greater effort at formal, more cautious institutional and religious change was made—more directed and controlled. The number of pamphlets and polemical works declined as printing became a more controlled measure of propaganda. Reform-related printing became more narrowly religious and theological, but publishing in the vernacular remained a major preoccupation.[5]

Luther continued his translation of the Bible into German, and it was a great success. Some buyers were probably unable to read or comprehend it for themselves; to many it was more a symbol of faith, piety, and, perhaps, status. Despite a relatively high rate of literacy in urban areas, the ensuing educational campaign of the Reformation indicates that popular reading habits and skills were far from satisfactory.

Recognizing that rising lay literacy was one of the preconditions for the reform and that the struggles for reform depended upon print, and hence reading, requires no determin-

ism about their roles. They were vehicles among many others; their larger importance was realized through the interactive potentials of print and literacy. Some readers could "enlighten" many others; high levels of literacy were hardly a requirement for embracing the Scriptures and making faith real. The roles of literacy and print, in a popular rather than an intellectual or theological sense, must be placed in sixteenth-century sociocultural settings.

The ideas of the Reformation were spread through various channels. One way was through personal contact. Luther and his supporters were responsible for some of the diffusion, but more significant were itinerant middlemen—preachers, salesmen, and journeymen. Print and literacy surely contributed here.

The message was also disseminated through print and writing—the distribution of books, manuscripts, pictures, personal letters, and songs. More was involved than literacy alone; sales of Reformation literature could yield high profits, and as this literature was bought in one place and reprinted and sold to other towns and cities, Lutheran ideas were spread without direct personal contact. Illiterates were attracted to Luther's ideas through visual devices (woodcuts and copperplates) and oral communications.

Institutions, including universities and political administrations, also helped to circulate evangelical ideas, supplementing and reinforcing personal contacts. Professors and students frequently returned to their home areas after their university studies and spread the new gospel through preaching, official service, or active citizenship. Other institutional contributions came from servants in imperial and territorial city administrations and similar agencies. Literacy and print acted in concert with personal and institutional contacts and exchanges to spread the Reformation. The sermon movement and preachers played an important role. From this basis, we begin to grasp the fuller nature of communications linkages and the mixture of media in sixteenth-century society. Print and literacy, while important, were parts of a larger whole. Personal relations, printing and writing, oral communications, institutions: each played a part, separately and interactively. The meaning of literacy to the reform effort, and its opposition, lies precisely in the nature of these relationships.[6]

The roles played by print and other media and channels were not exceptional to Germany. Similar processes within the international reform movement occurred in France, Switzerland, England, the Low Countries, and Scandinavia. The Reformation was brought to the New World by colonists.[7]

On a different level, among intellectuals and churchmen, the advent of printing had an important, contradictory impact. The use of printing assisted the movement for reform within the church, advanced the standardization of texts and observances within liturgical practices, influenced habits of sermonizing, and duplicated all sorts of literature, new and old. While changed by print, none of that was new. On the other hand, these uses of the press were not determined in advance; virtually all of them worked toward the efforts of the church or its critics. Printed texts could standardize church practices and improve them; or they could reveal, to literates at least, the gap between official doctrine and clerical practice. "With typographical fixity, moreover, positions once taken were more difficult to reverse. Battles of books prolonged polarization, and pamphlet wars quickened the press."

Despite the many claims advanced for the powers of "typographical fixity," the force has stopped few writers from changing their minds or positions in print, revising their work, or even, knowingly or unknowingly, contradicting themselves. Many of the reformers, from Luther on, did so. The battles of words, on printed pages, had a force that earlier, manuscript debates did not. Reducing face-to-face debates and disputations, they carried the issues, the divisions, the vehemence far beyond that possible in the age of script. Printing made propaganda, in a modern sense, possible; the Reformation was an early example, although perhaps not the first. Humanists and the church had engaged in such pursuits before the first international age of reform erupted.

One of the principal eruptions centered on the vernacular Bible, which the church was unwilling to countenance. One of the most important innovations furthered by the Reformers, it was a principal use of print. A tremendous incentive for literacy and a great boost to the vernacular followed. Yet, it is necessary to distinguish Bible study as scholarly exegesis from Bible study as lay Bible reading. Protestantism supported both; Catholicism promoted only the former.

Thus, Protestant doctrines stressing Bible reading for salvation generated special incentives toward literacy. That is a stereotypical view now, almost a myth, and *almost* true. Protestantism *was* a vital force toward the propagation of literacy among the populace in the West. But Catholicism has suffered a too negative, too unilaterally condemnatory press on this issue.[8] The written texts of the Bible had been a sacred and extraordinarily highly valued part of Christianity from its earliest days. It was Christianity more generally, long before Protestantism, that stressed the need to circulate *written* versions of the Bible despite the fact that severely restricted educational opportunities and literacy prevented the overwhelming number of adherents from confronting the great book for themselves. For this reason—and the fact that the Bible was not withheld from adherents who mastered Latin—comparisons with the Koran, on one hand, and strict Protestant-Catholic dichotomies, on the other, misrepresent realities that are more complex and interesting. The Bible was never restricted to a set of holy priests who recited it in the ways of the Koran and Islam; the Catholic church did not forbid the learned lay person from access to the Scriptures. Other issues were more central.

Post-Tridentine (Council of Trent, 1546) policies differed from those of the medieval church. A dramatic hardening of policy occurred, with vernacular Bibles prohibited, removing the Holy Scriptures from the direct access of virtually all adherents—an access marked by ability to read and perhaps even understand it. The Scriptures long assumed the qualities of sacred untouchable symbols to the Catholic laity. Trent curiously endorsed some forms of educational advancement and lay learning, but proscribed direct access to the Bible through the vernacular languages. The consequences were many. Not only were lay congregations further removed from clergy and texts, but an end was put to serious translations by Catholics for almost two centuries. Venetian printers were severely hit by the loss of some of their most salable products. Only in countries in which the Roman Catholic church was threatened by Protestant traditions was publication of vernacular Bibles permitted.[9]

In contrast, vernacular Bibles, prayer books, and catechisms were adopted by all the reformed and reforming churches. These materials, more traditional than innovative, served as a basis for schooling and literacy instruction, now in the native tongue. Educational and religious promotion were combined and reciprocally reinforced. Linguistic uniformity, as a part of nation building, was also advanced.[10]

The difference in support for public or popular schooling and promotion of literacy between lands Catholic and Protestant is often exaggerated, and the peculiar mix of local factors unexplored. Protestant promotion of literacy had social morality and secularized religious concerns at its core, rather than in-dividualized, liberating, independent, self-advancement goals. The individual applications of literacy, of course, could not always be controlled, although the promoted ones were often dominant. Contrary to many generalizations, neither printing *alone* nor Protestantism *alone* shaped outcomes during the sixteenth century or the early modern period. Just as one should not be divorced from the other, neither should either by removed from its context or special mix of factors, local and national, that gave it meaning and shaped its use.

In this respect, it is important to note that by the second half of the sixteenth century, the post-Tridentine Catholic church had successfully and consciously mobilized printers for its counter-reform offensive. They, too, used print for proselytizing, produced devotional materials for clerics and laity, and contributed to printers' profits. In England, "Catholic printers proved as skillful as their Puritan counterparts in handling problems posed by the surreptitious printing and the clandestine marketing of books." Although their limits differed and their enthusiasm was restrained by a greater ambivalence, Catholic reformers had to promote lay literacy to combat the Protestants and struggle for their place in the new religious pluralism.[11] Printing comprised issues religious, economic, *and* political; so did literacy and its provision. . . .

LITERACY IN COLONIAL NORTH AMERICA

Contrary to historical stereotype, North American colonial settlers were born neither modern nor universally literate. Their origins were European, primarily English.[12] American students of American history, in stressing the exceptionality and uniqueness of these "plantations" of the Old World, have distorted the transatlantic connection that the colonists themselves held so dearly. A new, more contextually accurate and sophisticated understanding has recently developed, seeing the colonists as linked to the world in which the first generation was born and socialized and to a culture that shaped not only their lives but the lives of their children. Attitudes toward education, values of literacy, and notions about institutions, as well as the larger cultural universe, were brought from one side of the Atlantic to the other with the immigrants, but changes also occurred in the process of founding and developing a society in the wilderness of the North Atlantic coastal regions.[13]

The literacy levels of seventeenth-century colonists were relatively high. The rate of male literacy in New England was around 60 percent, as compared to a rate in contemporary England of no higher than 40 percent.[14] Puritanism was one reason. A religion of the Word and of the Book, it had a dynamic propelling its adherents toward literacy. This impetus was complex; in some ways it played a direct, almost linear, role in increasing rates and uses of literacy.[15] But more than Puritanism was responsible for the level of literacy among the first generation. Migratory selectivity was most important; persons more likely to be literate for religious, familial, occupational, demographic, geographic, or economic reasons, and/or from places with higher-than-average rates of literacy, were more likely to migrate over the long transatlantic distance. Both kinds of selectivity joined to constitute a population of movers whose ability to sign was perhaps (among males) one and one-half times the level at home—and possibly even higher.[16]

The situation of early French settlers in Quebec was similar. During the second half of the seventeenth century, migrants from the old country had relatively high levels of literacy. Marriage registers show that of those born in France and marrying between 1657 and 1715, 38 percent of men and 32 percent of women were able to sign. In contrast to British North American colonies, formal parish schooling was satisfactorily initiated. Of marriage partners born in the colony, 46 percent of grooms and 43 percent of brides signed, higher rates but also less differentiated by gender. The second generation progressed in this urban place in a way that was far more difficult in more rural, agrarian areas, whether in Quebec or in the English colonies. Here, too, schooling was traditional, and it was distinguished by class, gender, and geographic locale.[17]

For many English persons, especially Puritans, education, schooling, and literacy were acquiring a new importance by the early seventeenth century. That this value was transported with the colonists should be expected. English Protestant concern with schooling intersected with the Puritan stress on the importance of individual access to the Book and the Word among the New England settlers. Within a relatively few years of settlement in the Massachusetts colonies, the famous school laws were enacted requiring schooling for all children. An expression of piety, not a fearful reaction to the colonial wilderness, the laws derived from traditional Puritan motives, which were instrumental in raising literacy rates in England and which, when compulsory, seemed a powerful force for education. Literacy was a universal prerequisite to spiritual preparation, the central duty of the covenant about which Puritans were deeply concerned.[18]

Colonial New England witnessed a rise in literacy from little more than one-half of males to almost all men between the mid-seventeenth century and the end of the eighteenth. In the seventeenth century, literacy's progress was slow and uneven. Overall, levels of literacy barely moved during the lifetime of the second generation, those dying around the year 1710 and educated during the 1660s. The rise of high levels of literacy, part of a trend in much of the West, came only after a slow start. The success of New England's literacy campaign, largely through local, town, or parish schools (the English model), came mainly in the eighteenth century.[19]

Women's literacy was also relatively high in colonial New England. About one-third of the women who died prior to 1670, and who left wills, could sign their names. This rate, about one-half that of males, may have been about one and one-half times that of women in England, the same proportional advantage as among the men. However, the seventeenth century was not a time of opportunities for schooling; not until the eighteenth century does it seem that the teaching of literacy to girls as well as boys was frequently attempted. The literacy of a woman's parents had no effect on her own literacy. Church membership was the only variable significantly related to women's literacy. A traditional Puritan concern with religion was felt on the individual as well as the societal level. The only families in which daughters were literate in most cases had two parents who were full members of the church. Familiar wealth was not related to daughters' literacy, as it was for sons. For women, not even elite status was a guarantee of literacy.[20]

The desired rise in literacy, a skill not practically useful to most settlers, took place primarily after the turn of the eighteenth century. The increasing level of signatures most likely resulted from a rising inclination *and* ability of families to send their children, especially sons, to schools, and from the increasing availability of schools, due in large part to population density and the processes of social development. With rising levels of commercialization and urbanization came for more men a need for and advantages from reading and writing. In this way, social development intersected with original intentions to drive the rates of literacy from about two-thirds of men to almost all men. This progress was more conservative than revolutionary or "liberating," and was essentially a movement among previously less literate peoples and regions that began to negate the traditional association of literacy with social status but not with economic standing.

In the seventeenth century, the social and geographic distribution of literacy was much more "traditional" than it would become. The more urban residents and higher-ranking persons, as in the Old World, were much more likely to be literate than lower-ranking and rural persons. As in England, literacy was linked directly to social standing. Social status, in wealth, occupation, deference, and the like, was brought with the settlers; it shaped literacy levels.

A number of historians have implied that literacy was instrumental to the formation of modern personality characteristics in the new colonies: activism, participation, optimism, awareness, cosmopolitanism, and larger loyalties. The presumed result was a more rational, planning, and calculating sort of person.[21] With regard to charitable behavior, however, studies have shown no modernization of attitudes occurring in colonial New England. Rather than literate men showing an increasing tendency to give to the needs of society, especially outside their families; to give to abstract causes and institutions rather than to persons; to give beyond their home villages and towns; or to give to rehabilitate rather than to alleviate, the analysis of charitable gifts revealed no such pattern, either for all givers or as a distinction between literate and illiterate givers. Literates, with their greater wealth, tended to give more often than illiterates, but when wealth is controlled, virtually no distinction existed.

The reason for charitable giving was usually traditional, to aid the poor or to further religion. Very few gifts were meant to rehabilitate the poor or turn religion to constructive secular needs; hardly any went to educate men or improve society. Literacy, it seems, did not press mightily upon men's beliefs or attitudes.[22]

Literacy did equip men with a skill that could be useful. But the quality of literacy and the environment limited and restrained its uses. In the seventeenth century many persons were not literate, but a high level of universal literacy was not required. Most transactions were localized and personal contacts; Puritans had a strong oral culture that shaped and received their value of the importance of individual access to the Book and the Word. Reading and writing were not often required in daily affairs outside the needs of devotion and piety. Land was obtained from towns by grant, and deeds were usually registered locally by clerks. "The gap between the literacy of the population and the functional demands of the society was not great."[23] High levels of literacy did not assist colonial New Englanders in dealing with the confusion that regularly plagued their social and cultural maturation and road to revolution.

As in England, the oral and the literate culture intertwined. The oral medium was employed to disseminate much of print culture. Illustrations in books helped to carry ideas to illiterates, as did books designed to be read aloud. The substance of the world of print was transmitted and broadcast well beyond the relatively narrow boundaries of the individual, silent reader.[24]

Printing existed in New England from 1630, a year after the first press arrived. The establishment of this press, in Cambridge, Massachusetts, probably was influenced by events at home, especially the extension of control over the press from censorship within England to pressure over publishing of Puritan works in the Netherlands. The presses started

out slowly; most production was religious or administrative. Booksellers peddled their wares gradually. Their books were primarily religious; they also sold popular almanacs, medical manuals, and some literature—classics, histories, and other practical books. Other books were brought directly by the wealthiest or most educated settlers, who had the most important private libraries in seventeenth-century New England.[25] Primarily, only college graduates had collections that justified the label of library. The print culture of the early settlers, the limited evidence suggests, was not a vibrant, lively, and enlivening secular culture. Most print material related to religion.

The history of schooling in New England belongs more to the end of the seventeenth and the eighteenth centuries than to this period. The evidence of literacy and the limited reconstruction of educational activities join in suggesting that schooling, in a fairly systematic, regularized, and institutional way, came *after* initial plantation founding and society building. The social structure of literacy, for the seventeenth century, tended to vary mainly with the literacy levels of the founders themselves; levels of population concentration, wealth, commercialization, and "institutional maturity" related more closely to the presence of schools than did the facts of settlement per se. That English men and women brought English and Puritan motives, values, and plans for schooling with them is clear; it is also likely that they were not able to erect many schools at first. The compulsory schools required by the laws do not seem to have been established.[26] More developed areas and towns were able to sustain schools, but many simply were not.

The schooling that took place was traditional and religiously oriented. Children learned much as they had in England, from hornbooks and/or primers, either in school-houses under a schoolmaster or from their pastors. Catechisms were central to the curriculum. Primers, such as the famous *New England Primer,* were filled with religious material. Moral and religious training and knowledge were the most prized accomplishments of schooling.

Education was to begin as soon as the child was able to absorb it. The very young were to be prepared by oral instruction and moral comments on their actions. The household's piety and morality were to condition the child from the earliest moments of awareness. As the child grew, more formal instruction was to replace informal socialization. Other teaching took place in the church, and when possible in a school. At school, training was more intellectual, to provide the pupil with the tools, such as literacy, for acquiring religious knowledge. By the age of five, boys might be attending reading or dame schools. These elementary schools of colonial New England supplemented the lessons of the church.[27] As soon as they were old enough, children were taken regularly to church, to learn their religious knowledge from the pulpit. In theory, all aspects of education and literacy aimed at one central lesson.

In the Southern colonies of Virginia and Maryland, the male literacy rate in the seventeenth century was around 50 percent, again indicating the literacy selectivity of the generation migrating to the North American colonies. The rich were almost all literate, but only about half of the farmers and a third of the poor could sign. The level rose to about two-thirds by the middle of the eighteenth century, then stopped, at the same time that New England was achieving near-universal rates of male literacy.

A lack of intense Protestantism and the resulting school laws contributed to this stagnation, but other factors were equally important. The Puritan connection between individual literacy and reading the Scriptures was absent here. Piety and devotion were of interest, but education was viewed as academic and practical, as a means of teaching trades to boys and of giving domestic training to girls. An academic education was based on an ability "to read distinctly in the Bible"; pupils learned how to make a living and gained firsthand knowledge of the Bible at the same time. Schooling was also clearly class-biased. The paucity of formal education in the Colonial South was also due partly to the low population density, but more to the short life expectancy of the settlers. Parents often did not live long enough to see to their children's education.

Education of children in this area had little bearing on their success as adults. Literacy was not necessary for economic prosperity; occupation and age were more important. "The wealth differences between literates and illiterates among those engaged in agriculture and common laboring pursuits indicate that society did not provide much economic incentive for literacy for those people."

Although there were persistent desires for schools, and the early laws of each colony called for schooling of all children, few institutions followed. Literacy rose slightly through the period, but mainly through selective migration streams; the progress of educational development was slow.

One problem in places such as Virginia and Maryland was that the dispersed nature of geographic settlement required for the land- and labor-intensive plantation system greatly reduced the possibilities of formal schools' being founded and maintained. In huge parishes, some as large as a hundred square miles, churches reached only a portion of the population. "And, with residences scattered across the countryside, schools became uneconomical, for lack of both funds and scholars. Indeed, even the formal education of communal life was missing. . . ." Some Virginians hoped that towns, concentrating settlement and resources, would solve some of the problems, but for all their administrative, economic, and cultural importance, towns never played this role on a level sufficient for mass schooling.

Despite conviction, interest, and intention, schools remained restricted in the Southern colonies. That is as true for free and charity schooling for the poor as for other formal educational foundation. Little institutional progress took place until the second century of development. Education for the elite and wealthy was more successful before 1700 than were plans and desires for more inclusive schooling, with the exception of a handful of bequests for free and charity schools. Apprenticeship apparently developed on the English model, but fulfillment of its educational requirements proved a constant source of complaints and litigation.[28] The systematic program that came with time in the Puritan areas never developed in the Southern colonies.

Books and other elements of print culture were imported with the Southern colonists. Tastes were largely traditional, with major interests in religious literature, followed by a diversity of other materials. Indigenous printing developed more slowly than in New England; English products were even more pervasive. Book ownership and libraries were limited overwhelmingly to elites. . . .

NOTES

1. Gerald Strauss, *Luther's House of Learning* (Baltimore: Johns Hopkins Press, 1978).
2. John Headley, "The Continental Reformation," in Richard L. DeMolen, ed., *The Meaning of the Renaissance and Reformation* (Boston: Houghton Mifflin, 1974). . . .
3. Headley, "Continental," pp. 150–51; . . . Richard Crofts, "Books, Reform, and the Reformation," *Archives for Reformation History* 7 (1980):21–36.
4. Louise Holborn, "Printing and the Growth of a Protestant Movement in Germany," *Church History* 11 (1942):123. . . .
5. Lucien Febvre and H-J Martin, *The Coming of the Book* (London: NLB, 1976), pp. 287–88, 288, 289, 289–95, 290, 291, 291–92, 292–93, 292–95; A. G. Dickens, *Reformation and Society in Sixteenth-Century Europe* (London: Thames and Hudson, 1966), p. 51. . . .
6. Manfred Hanneman, *The Diffusion of the Reformation in Southwestern Germany*, Department of Geography, Research Paper no. 167 (Chicago: University of Chicago, 1975), pp. 9, 7–9, chaps. 5–7, pp. 12, 9–13, 12–13, 13, 212. Conclusion. . . .
7. Febvre and Martin, *Coming*, pp. 295ff. . . .
8. Elizabeth Eisenstein, *The Printing Press as an Agent of Change* (Cambridge: Cambridge University Press, 1979), chap. 4, pp. 310, 326, chap. 4, sec. 2, p. 333. . . .
9. Eisenstein, *Printing Press*, pp. 344, 348; see also Febvre and Martin, *Coming*. . . .
10. Eisenstein, *Printing Press*, p. 349, passim. . . .
11. Eisenstein, *Printing Press*, p. 354. . . .
12. On the equation of modernity with literacy for this period, see Bernard Bailyn, *Education in the Forming of American Society* (Chapel Hill: University of North Carolina Press, 1960); Lawrence Cremin, *American Education: The Colonial Experience* (New York: Harper and Row, 1970); Richard D. Brown, "Modernization and the Formation of the Modern Personality in Early America, 1600–1865: A Sketch of a Synthesis," *Journal of Interdisciplinary History* 2 (1972): 201–228. . . .
13. For useful introductions and evidence, see Bailyn, *Education*; Cremin, *American Education*; Kenneth A. Lockridge, *Literacy in Colonial New England* (New York: Norton, 1974). . . . On schooling, see R. R. Reeder, *The Historical Development of School Readers and of Method in Teaching Reading*, Columbia University Contributions to Philosophy, Psychology, and Education, vol. 8 (New York: Macmillan, 1900); Sanford Fleming; *Children and Puritanism* (New Haven: Yale University Press, 1933); Herbert Baxter Adams, *The Church and Popular Education*, Johns Hopkins University Studies in Histori-

cal and Political Science, vol. 28 (Baltimore, 1900)....

14. See, in particular, the work of Lockridge....

15. Lockridge, *Literacy*, pp. 43, 99....

16. Kenneth A. Lockridge, "L'alphabétisation en Amérique," *Annales: e, s, c* 32 (1977); p. 509.... For example, see Alex Inkeles and David H. Smith, *Becoming Modern* (Cambridge, Mass.: Harvard University Press, 1974); Goody and Watt, "Consequences."...

17. Louise Dechêne, *Habitants et Marchants de Montreal au XVIIIe siècle* (Paris and Montreal: Plon, 1974), pp. 465–67.

18. Lockridge, *Literacy*, pp. 49–50 (his quotation is from Bailyn, *Education*, p. 27)....

19. Lockridge, *Literacy*, p. 15....

20. Lockridge, *Literacy*, p. 38, passim....

21. Lockridge, *Literacy*, pp. 15, 17, 22, 29; Bailyn, *Education*, pp. 48–49; Cremin, *American Education*, pp. 546–50....

22. Lockridge, *Literacy*, pp. 33, 35–36. More recently, John Frye ("Class, Generation, and Social Change: A Case in Salem, Massachusetts, 1636–1656," *Journal of Popular Culture* 11 [1977]:743–51) argues that a deviant subculture

existed in New England communities, which included literates as well as illiterates.

23. Jon Butler, "Magic, Astrology, and the Early American Religious Heritage, 1600–1760," *American Historical Review* 84 (1979):317–46; Lockridge, *Literacy*, p. 37; John Frye, "Class, Generation, and Social Change: A Case in Salem, Massachusetts, 1636–1656," *Journal of Popular Culture* II (1977):743–51.

24. David D. Hall, "The World of Print and Collective Mentality in Seventeenth Century New England," in *New Directions in American Intellectual History,* ed. John Higham and Paul Contein (Baltimore: Johns Hopkins University Press, 1979), pp. 167, 169....

25. Samuel Blist Morison, *The Intellectual Life of Colonial New England* (Ithaca: Cornell University Press, 1956), pp. 113, 115, 115–27, 127–32, chap. 6.

26. Morison, *Intellectual*, p. 71.

27. Edmund Morgan, *The Puritan Family* (New York: Harper and Row, 1965), pp. 88, 98, ... 101....

28. Cremin, *American Education*, pp. 240–41, bk. 1, pt. 2, passim....

THE TRADE IN NEWS

John B. Thompson

John B. Thomspon is a Lecturer at the University of Cambridge and the author of several works on social theory, including The Media and Modernity, *from which the present excerpt is taken. He is also an editor and a founding member of Polity Press.*

There is another way in which the development of printing transformed the patterns of communication in early modern Europe: it gave rise to a variety of periodical publications which reported events and conveyed information of a political and commercial character. Prior to the advent of printing, a number of regularized networks of communication had been established

throughout Europe. We can distinguish at least four distinct types of pre-print communication network. First, there was an extensive network of communication established and controlled by the Catholic Church. This network enabled the papacy in Rome to maintain contact with the clergy and political elites dispersed throughout the loosely knit realm of Christendom. Second, there were networks of communication established by the political authorities of states and principalities; these networks operated both within the territories of particular states, facilitating administration and pacification, and between states which maintained some form of diplomatic communication with one another. A third type of network was linked to the expansion of commercial activity. As trade and manufacturing increased, new networks of communication were established within the business community and between the major trading centres. Commercial and banking houses—like the Fugger family of Augsburg and the great merchant houses of Florence—built up extensive systems of communication and began to supply information to clients on a commercial basis. Finally, information was also transmitted to towns and villages via networks of merchants, pedlars and travelling entertainers, such as storytellers and ballad singers. As individuals gathered in market-places or taverns and interacted with merchants and travellers, they picked up news about events which took place in distant locales.

In the course of the fifteenth, sixteenth and seventeenth centuries, these networks of communication were affected by two key developments. In the first place, some states began to establish regular postal services which became increasingly available for general use. In France Louis XI established a royal post in 1464; private individuals could use the post by special permission and payment of a fee.[1] In central Europe Maximilian I developed an extensive postal network which linked the heartland of the Habsburg empire with cities throughout Europe. In 1490 he appointed Franz and Johann von Taxis as chief postmasters, thus establishing an imperial postal system that remained under the control of the von Taxis family for several centuries.[2] In England a royal post was established early in the reign of Henry VIII, and a postmaster was appointed around 1516, although the development of regular postal services for general public use did not occur until

the early seventeenth century.[3] Gradually in the course of the seventeenth and eighteenth centuries, an integrated network of public postal communication emerged, providing common carrier services for both domestic and foreign post. Of course, by twentieth-century standards, postal communication in early modern Europe was very slow. Messages were transported by horse and carriage at a time when the roads in many parts of Europe were of poor quality. Mail rarely travelled at more than 10 miles per hour over extended distances. In the late eighteenth century, Edinburgh was still a journey of 60 hours from London, and it took 24 hours to travel from London to Manchester. It was not until the early nineteenth century, with the development of the railways, that the time required to transmit messages through the post was sharply reduced.

The second development which profoundly affected the established networks of communication in early modern Europe was the application of printing to the production and dissemination of news. Soon after the advent of printing in the mid-fifteenth century, a variety of printed information leaflets, posters and broadsheets began to appear. These were a mixture of official or semi-official statements of government decrees; polemical tracts; descriptions of particular events, such as military encounters or natural disasters; and sensationalized accounts of extraordinary or supernatural phenomena, like giants, comets and apparitions. These leaflets and news sheets were generally one-off or irregular publications. They were printed by the thousands and sold in the streets by hawkers and pedlars. They provided individuals with a valuable source of information about current and distant events.

Periodical publications of news and information began to appear in the second half of the sixteenth century, but the origins of the modern newspaper are usually traced to the first two decades of the seventeenth century, when regular journals of news began to appear on a weekly basis with some degree of reliability.[4] In 1609 weekly journals were published in several German cities, including Augsburg, Strasbourg and Wolfenbüttel, and there is some evidence to suggest that a weekly paper may have appeared somewhat earlier (1607) in Amsterdam. Printed weeklies—or 'corantos', as these early compilations of news were called at the time—soon appeared in other cities and languages. The cities located along the major European trading routes, such as Cologne, Frankfurt, Antwerp and Berlin, became early centres of newspaper production. The news which made up the corantos was often supplied by postmasters, who collected the news in their regions and then forwarded it to the major cities. A single individual could then assemble and edit the postmasters' reports, printing them in the form of a series of short paragraphs with details of the date and place of origin of the information. The weeklies could also be translated into other languages and sold in different cities and countries.

By 1620 Amsterdam had become the centre of a rapidly expanding trade in news. There was a growing public interest in the Thirty Years' War and this provided a major stimulus to the development of the fledgling newspaper industry. The first newspaper to appear in English was probably produced in Amsterdam in 1620 by the Dutch printer and map engraver Pieter van den Keere and exported to London.[5] Between 2 December 1620 and 18 September 1621, 15 issues of van den Keere's coranto appeared. Although it was not published weekly, it did appear fairly frequently and it provided regular coverage of the Thirty Years' War. The first coranto printed in England was probably produced by the London stationer Thomas Archer in 1621. Archer was subsequently imprisoned for publishing an unlicensed news sheet on the war in the Palatinate, but other English corantos and news pamphlets soon appeared.

Most of these early forms of newspaper were concerned primarily with foreign news,

that is, with events which were taking place (or had taken place) in distant locales. The individuals who read these papers, or listened to them being read aloud by others, would learn of events taking place in distant parts of Europe—events they could not witness directly, in places they would never, in all likelihood, visit. Hence the circulation of the early forms of newspaper helped to create a sense of a world of events which lay beyond the individual's immediate milieu, but which had some relevance to, and potentially some bearing on, his or her life. Of course, the geographical scope of this world remained quite limited in the early seventeenth century: it rarely extended beyond the major cities and countries of Europe. Moreover, the circulation of the early newspapers was very low by present-day standards (one estimate puts the minimum print run of the early newspapers at 400 copies,[6] and in many cases it was probably not much more than that), although papers were no doubt read by more than one individual, and were commonly read aloud. But the importance of this new mode of information diffusion, through which printed reports of distant events were made available on a regular basis to an unlimited number of recipients, should not be underestimated.

While the early corantos were concerned mainly with foreign news, it was not long before newspapers began to devote more attention to domestic events. In England this development had to wait until 1640, when the government's strict control of the press began to weaken. Since 1586 a Star Chamber decree had established a comprehensive system of licensing and censorship (supplemented by a further decree of 1637), which limited the number of printers in England and subjected them to specific censors for each type of publication. But as the crisis between Charles I and Parliament deepened, it became increasingly difficult for the Crown to enforce its control of the press, and in July 1641 the Star Chamber was abolished. The crisis also stimulated a public demand for up-to-date news of domestic political affairs. Between mid-November 1641 and the end of December 1641 three domestic weekly newspapers appeared, each providing summaries of the proceedings of Parliament; and in the first three months of 1642 another eight newspapers appeared, though some did not last for long.[7] This was the beginning of a period of relatively uncontrolled and intensive publication of newspapers, newsbooks and pamphlets dealing with the events of the Civil War and the issues surrounding it. During most weeks of 1645, 14 newspapers were on sale in the streets of London, as well as a multitude of other pamphlets and political tracts. While strict controls were reimposed by Charles II after the restoration of the monarchy in 1660, the period between 1641 and the restoration was an important one in the history of the press. For it was during this time that periodical publications emerged as key players in the affairs of state, providing a continuous flow of information on current events and expressing a range of differing views—sometimes sharply conflicting views—on matters of public concern.

The development of a commercially based periodical press which was independent of state power, and yet was capable of providing information and critical commentary on issues of general concern, entered a new phase in eighteenth-century England. The system of licensing, which had been re-established by Charles II in 1662, fell into abeyance at the end of the seventeenth century and was followed by a spate of new periodical publications. The first daily newspaper in England, Samuel Buckley's *Daily Courant,* appeared in 1702 and was soon joined by others. A variety of more specialized periodicals appeared, some concentrating on entertainment and cultural events, some on financial and commercial news, and others on social and political commentary. The latter included a number of journals which popularized the genre of the political essay, like the *Tatler,* the *Spectator,* Nicholas Amhurst's *Craftsman,* Daniel Defoe's

Review and Jonathan Swift's *Examiner.* By 1750 London had five well-established daily papers, six thrice-weeklies, five weeklies and several other cut-price periodicals, with a total circulation between them of around 100,000 copies per week.[8] The papers were distributed in the city by networks of hawkers and agents, as well as by a loose federation of coffee houses which acquired the major papers and made them available for their customers to read. Since many papers were read in public places like taverns and coffee houses, their readership was almost certainly much higher than their circulation—perhaps as much as ten times higher. London papers were also distributed to the provinces by rapidly improving stage-coach and postal services.

The political authorities sought to exercise some control over the proliferation of newspapers and periodicals by imposing special taxes, which would, it was thought, serve to restrict production and force the more marginal periodicals out of business, while at the same time raising additional revenue for the Crown. The Stamp Act of 1712 required newspaper proprietors to pay one penny for every printed sheet and one shilling for every advertisement. Subsequent Acts increased the amounts and broadened the basis for the application of the law. The Stamp Acts were bitterly opposed and became a rallying point in the struggle for the freedom of the press. It was not until the 1830s that the taxes were progressively reduced, and in the 1860s they were eventually abolished. Elsewhere in Europe the periodical press of the eighteenth century was controlled and censored with varying degrees of severity.[9] In the United Provinces the press remained relatively free, although it was discouraged from discussing local politics and was occasionally subjected to bouts of intensive censorship. In France a centralized and highly restrictive system of licensing, supervision and censorship existed until the Revolution; a brief post-revolutionary period of press freedom was finally brought to an end by

Napoleon, who instituted a strict system of censorship and control. In the states and principalities of Germany and Italy the degree of official control varied from one state to another, but newspapers were generally allowed more leeway in reporting foreign news than in discussing domestic politics.

There is considerable force in the argument that the struggle for an independent press, capable of reporting and commenting on events with a minimum of state interference and control, played a key role in the development of the modern constitutional state. Some of the early liberal and liberal democratic thinkers, such as Jeremy Bentham, James Mill and John Stuart Mill, were fervent advocates of the liberty of the press. They saw the free expression of opinion through the organs of an independent press as a vital safeguard against the despotic use of state power.[10] It is significant that, following their successful war of independence against the British Crown, the American colonists incorporated the right of press freedom in the First Amendment to the Constitution. Similarly, the post-revolutionary French constitutions of 1791 and 1793, building on the Declaration des Droits de l'Homme of 1789, explicitly protected the freedom of expression (even if this freedom was subsequently abolished by Napoleon). Statutory guarantees of freedom of expression were eventually adopted by various European governments so that by the end of the nineteenth century the freedom of the press had become a constitutional feature of many Western states.

NOTES

1. See Howard Robinson, *The British Post Office: A History* (Princeton: Princeton University Press, 1948), p. 4.
2. For an account of the 'Thurn und Taxis' postal service, as it became known, see Martin Dallmeier, *Quellen zur Geschichte des Europäischen Postwesens, 1501–1806*, Part 1: *Quellen-Literatur Einleitung* (Kallmünz: Michael Lassleben, 1977), pp. 49–220.
3. Robinson, *The British Post Office*, chs 1–3; J. Crofts, *Packhorse, Waggon and Post: Land Carriage and Communications under the Tudors and Stuarts* (London: Routledge and Kegan Paul, 1967), chs 8–17.
4. The identification of what could be called 'the first newspaper' is a matter of dispute, though most historians would agree that something resembling the modern newspaper first appeared around 1610. See Eric W. Allen, 'International Origins of the Newspapers: The Establishment of Periodicity in Print', *Journalism Quarterly*, 7 (1930), pp. 307–19; Joseph Frank, *The Beginnings of the English Newspaper, 1620–1660* (Cambridge, Mass.: Harvard University Press, 1961), ch. 1.
5. Frank, *The Beginnings of the English Newspaper*, p. 3.
6. Folke Dahl, *A Bibliography of English Corantos and Periodical Newsbooks, 1620–1642* (London: Bibliographical Society, 1952), p. 22.
7. Frank, *The Beginnings of the English Newspaper*, pp. 21–2.
8. Anthony Smith, *The Newspaper: An International History* (London: Thames and Hudson, 1979), pp. 56–7.
9. For more detailed discussions of the history of political control and censorship of the press, see F. S. Siebert, *Freedom of the Press in England, 1476–1776* (Urbana: University of Illinois Press, 1952); A. Aspinall, *Politics and the Press, c.1780–1850* (Brighton: Harvester, 1973); Smith, *The Newspaper*, chs 3–5.
10. See especially James Mill, 'Liberty of the Press', in his *Essays on Government, Jurisprudence, Liberty of the Press and Law of Nations* (New York: Kelly, 1967); John Stuart Mill, 'On Liberty', in his *Utilitarianism, On Liberty and Considerations on Representative Government*, ed. H. B. Acton (London: Dent, 1972).

16 FILES, BUREAUCRATS, AND INTELLECTUALS

Robert Darnton

Robert Darnton is professor of history at Princeton University. He is best known as a cultural historian whose work on France has been much cited and praised, especially by those interested in the implications of literacy and the culture of the book.

While the bourgeois from Montpellier tried to sort out his fellow citizens, a police officer in Paris was sifting and filing information on another species of urban animal: the intellectual. Although the word for them had not yet been coined, intellectuals were already multiplying in garrets and cafés; and the police were keeping them under surveillance. Our policeman, Joseph d'Hémery, was an inspector of the book trade; so he also inspected the men who wrote books. In fact, he investigated so many of them that his files constitute a virtual census of the literary population of Paris, from the most famous *philosophes* to the most obscure hacks. The files make it possible for one to trace a profile of the intellectual at the height of the Enlightenment, just when he was beginning to emerge as a social type. And they reveal the way a fairly enlightened official of the Old Regime attempted to make sense of this new phenomenon—a matter of imposing a framework on the world as it appeared on a particular police beat.[1]

To be sure, d'Hémery did not present his survey as a sociology of culture and did not question its epistemological basis. He merely went about his work, inspecting. In five years, from 1748 to 1753, he wrote five hundred reports on authors, which now lie unpublished in the Bibliothèque Nationale. Just why he undertook such a task is difficult to say. The reports appear in three huge registers under the title "Historique des auteurs," without any introduction, explanation, or textual evidence about the way they were used. D'Hémery, who took up his office in June, 1748, may

simply have wanted to build up his files so that he could do an effective job of policing his new administrative territory. But he had some extraordinary books to police during those first five years: *L'Esprit des lois,* the *Encyclopédie.* Rousseau's *Discours sur les sciences et les arts,* Diderot's *Lettre sur les aveugles,* Buffon's *Histoire naturelle,* Toussaint's *Les Moeurs,* and the scandalous thesis by the abbé de Prades. The whole Enlightenment seemed to burst out all at once in print. And at the same time, the tax reforms of Machault d'Arnouville, the Jansenist-Jesuit controversy, the agitation over the billets de *confession,* the struggle between the crown and the *parlements,* and the *frondeur* spirit following France's humiliation in the Peace of Aix-la-Chapelle produced a general heating up of the ideological atmosphere. However absolute the monarchy claimed to be, it had to take account of public opinion and of the men who directed it with their pens.

The new inspector of the book trade clearly had his work cut out for him, and he went about it systematically. He built up dossiers from all kinds of sources: journals, spies, concièrges, café gossips, and interrogations in the Bastille. Then he selected information from the dossiers and transcribed it on standard forms with printed headings, which he filed in alphabetical order and brought up to date as the occasion arose. The procedure was more thorough than anything done before, but it looks primitive in the light of the subsequent history of ideological police work. Instead of adapting data to a computerized program, d'Hémery recounted anecdotes.

In the report on Crébillon fils, for example, he noted: "His father said, 'There are only two things that I regret having done, *Semiramis* and my son.' 'Oh, don't worry,' the son replied. 'No one attributes either of them to you.'" Not only did d'Hémery go about information retrieval with an unscientific sense of humor, he also exercised literary judgment. La Barre wrote passable prose but could not manage verse, he observed. And Robbé de Beauveset sinned in the opposite way: "There is some genius in his poetry, but he writes harshly and has very little taste." D'Hémery would not have gone down well with the Deuxième Bureau or the F.B.I.

It would be a mistake, therefore, to treat d'Hemery's reports as hard data of the kind one can find in a modern census; but it would be a greater mistake to dismiss them for excessive subjectivity. D'Hémery had a more intimate knowledge of the eighteenth-century world of letters than any historian can hope to acquire. His reports provide the earliest known survey of writers as a social group, and they do so at a critical moment of literary history. Moreover, they can be checked against a vast array of biographical and bibliographical sources. Once one has worked through all this material and compiled the statistics, one can enjoy the first clear view of the republic of letters in early modern Europe.

D'Hémery actually reported on 501 persons, but 67 of them never published anything, or anything beyond a few lines in the *Mercure.* So the reports cover 434 active writers. Of them, the date of birth can be established in 359 cases, the place of birth in 312, and the socio-occupational position in 333. The statistical basis of the survey therefore seems wide enough to support some firm conclusions.

But how widely did d'Hémery cast his net in the first place? The only source against which to compare his survey is *La France littéraire,* a literary almanac that purported to list every living French author in 1756. As the list ran to 1,187 names, it seems likely that d'Hémery covered about a third of the total population of French writers. But which third? That question raises the problem of defining a writer. D'Hémery used the term "auteur" without explaining it, and *La France littéraire* claimed to include everyone who had ever published a book. But the "books" it listed were mainly ephemeral works—sermons by village curés, orations by provincial dignitaries, medical pamphlets by small-town doctors, in fact anything that anyone wanted mentioned—for the authors of the almanac had offered to include in their own lists the names of any books and authors that the general public could supply. As a result, *La France littéraire* favored the minor provincial literati. D'Hémery dealt with a broad range of writers, but he restricted himself almost entirely to Paris. It seems reasonable to conclude that his files covered a major proportion of the active literary population and that the statistics drawn from them give a fairly accurate picture of literary life in the capital of the Enlightenment.[2]

In 1750, the writers ranged in age from ninety-three (Fontenelle) to sixteen (Rulhière), but most of them were relatively young. Rousseau, at thirty-eight, represented the median age exactly. The inner circle of Encyclopedists was composed mainly of men in their thirties, beginning with Diderot, thirty-seven, and d'Alembert, thirty-three. Thus the bulge in the bar graph suggests something akin to a literary generation. With exceptions like Montesquieu and Voltaire, who had one foot in the France of Louis XIV, the philosophes belonged to cohorts that reached their prime at mid-century.[3]

The geographical origins of the writers fall into a familiar pattern. The south looks backward, except in urban areas scattered around the Rhône delta and the Garonne. Three-quarters of the writers were born above the celebrated Saint Malo-Geneva line, in northern and northeastern France, where literacy and schools were densest. Paris supplied a third (113) of the writers. So the map does not bear out another cliché of cultural history—namely, that Paris has always dominated the country by soaking up talent from the provinces. There were more home-grown authors than one might expect in the Paris of 1750.[4]

Any attempt to analyze the social composition of a group of Frenchmen who lived two centuries ago is liable to flounder in faulty data and ambiguous classification schemes. But three-quarters of d'Hémery's writers can be identified and classified unambiguously according to the categories in Table 1. The remaining quarter of "unidentified" writers contains a large number of *gens sans état*—who drifted from job to job, as Diderot and Rousseau did for many years. Although a good deal of information exists about many of them, they defy classification and statistical analysis. But if one makes allowances for their existence in the unfathomable floating population of the Old Regime, one can (make certain observations about) the social dimensions to the republic of letters in Paris.

The privileged orders occupied a far more important place in d'Hémery's files than they did within the population at large. Seventeen percent of the identified authors were noblemen. Although they included some serious writers, like Montesquieu, they tended to be gentleman amateurs and to write incidental verse or light comedies. As in the case of the marquis de Paulmy, who published novelettes under the name of his secretary, Nicolas Fromaget, they did not often want to be identified with such frothy stuff. Nor did they write for the marketplace. D'Hémery noted that the comte de Saint-Foix "works as a gentleman author and never takes any money for his plays." The aristocratic writers generally appear in the reports as power brokers, channeling patronage toward more lowly *littérateurs*.

Writing also tended to be a secondary activity for the clergymen in the reports, and there were a great many of them: 12 percent of the authors who can be identified. Only four belonged to the upper clergy in contrast to dozens of abbés, among them Condillac, Mably, Raynal, and the threesome of the *Encyclopédie*, Yvon, Pestré, and de Prades. A few priests, like J.-B.-C.-M. de Beauvais and Michel Desjardins, continued to produce court sermons and funeral eulogies in the style of Bossuet. But in general the courtier-cleric had given way to the omnipresent abbé of the Enlightenment.

Although 70 percent of the writers came from the third estate, few of them can be considered "bourgeois" in the narrow sense of the term—that is, capitalists living from trade and industry. They included only one merchant, J. H. Oursel, the son of a printer, and no manufacturers. There was a certain business element—eleven merchants—among their fathers, 156 of whom can be identified. But literature flourished less in the marketplace than in the professions and the royal administration. Ten percent of the writers were doctors or lawyers; 9 percent held minor administrative offices; and 16 percent belonged to the apparatus of the state, if magistrates from the parlements and lower courts are included in the count. The largest group of fathers, twenty-two, came from the lower administration; the next largest, nineteen, were lawyers. After sifting through the statistics and reading hundreds of biographical sketches, one gets the impression that behind many literary careers stood an ambitious, sharp-witted, royal bureaucrat. French literature owes an incalculable debt to the *commis* and the law clerk as well as to the abbé. Prévost epitomized this species. The son of a lawyer turned court official in the bailliage of Hesdin, he was an abbé many times over. "He has been a member of every religious order," d'Hémery observed.

When it came to earning a living, however, the largest group of writers depended upon what may be called the intellectual trades. Thirty-six percent of them worked as journalists, tutors, librarians, secretaries, and actors, or else relied on the income from a sinecure procured for them by a protector. This was the bread-and-butter element in the republic of letters; and as it was dispensed by patronage, the writers knew which side their bread was buttered on. According to d'Hemery, François-Augustin Paradis de Moncrif certainly did:

TABLE 1   AUTHORS' SOCIO-OCCUPATIONAL POSITIONS

	Authors in 1750	Authors at Unspecified Date	Authors Total	Percent	Fathers of Authors	Percent of Total
Upper clergy, secular	3		3	1		
Upper clergy, regular	1		1			
Lower clergy, secular	31		31	9		
Lower clergy, regular	4	1	5	2		
Titled nobility, no office	11		11	3	16	10
Officer, high administration	4		4	1	1	1
Officer, military	20	7	27	8	12	8
Officer, sovereign courts	10	2	12	4	12	8
Officer, high finance	2		2	1	6	4
Officer, lower courts	4	2	6	2	8	5
Lower administration	20	10	30	9	22	14
Lawyer, attorney	26	2	28	8	19	12
Law personnel	3		3	1	1	1
Doctor	6		6	2	1	1
Apothecary		1	1		4	3
Professor	10		10	3		
Lower finance	2	1	3	1	2	1
Merchant	1		1		11	7
Manufacturer						
Rentier	10		10	3		
Journalist	9	11	20	6		
Private teacher	27	8	35	11	4	3
Librarian	6		6	2		
Secretary	15	10	25	8	1	1
Sinecure	10	1	11	3		
Actor	8	1	9	3	1	1
Musician	1		1		1	1
Student	3		3	1		
Employee	5	1	6	2	8	5
Shopkeeper	2		2	1	6	4
Artisan	6	1	7	2	14	9
Servant	1	1	2	1	1	1
Wives, widows	9		9	3		
Other	1	2	3	1	5	3
TOTAL	271	62	333		156	

TABLE 1 (continued)

Total Number of Writers	
Identified authors, 1750	271
Identified authors, unspecified date	62
Excluded (nonauthors)	67
Unidentified	101
	501 (434 "writers")

Alternate Breakdown	
Probable nobility	60
Tonsured clerics	69
Women	16
Imprisoned	45

He was a tax inspector in the provinces when M. d'Argenson was intendant. The pretty songs he composed made him noticed by d'Argenson, who brought him to Paris and gave him a position. From that time on, he [Moncrif] has always been attached to him.... He is also secretary general of the French postal service, a position that brings him in 6,000 livres a year and that M. d'Argenson gave to him as a present.

At a lower level, the literary population contained a surprising proportion, 6 percent, of shopkeepers, artisans, and minor employees. They included both master craftsmen—a printer, an engraver, a painter-enameler—and relatively humble workers—a harness maker, a binder, a gatekeeper, and two lackeys. D'Hémery noted that one of the lackeys, Viollet de Wagnon, published his L'Auteur laquais with the help of a valet and a grocer. Charles-Simon Favart reputedly acquired his facility with verse by listening to his father improvise songs while kneading dough in the family's pastry shop.[5] Thus the lower classes played some part in the literary life of the Old Regime—a substantial part, if one considers the writers' fathers. Nineteen percent of them belonged to the *petites gens:* they were ordinary artisans for the most part—cobblers, bakers, and tailors. So the careers of their sons,

who became lawyers, teachers, and journalists, showed that exceptional possibilities of social advancement sometimes opened up for young men who could wield a pen. The literary world remained closed, however, to one social group: the peasantry. Of course, d'Hémery did not look for writers in the countryside, but he did not find the slightest peasant element in the background of writers who came to Paris from the provinces. Restif de la Bretonne notwithstanding, literary France seems to have been primarily urban.

It was also mainly male. Women presided over the famous salons and therefore won a few places in the police files. But only sixteen of them ever published anything. Like Mme de Graffigny, the most famous of their number, the female authors often turned to writing after being widowed or separated from their husbands. Most of them were independently wealthy. Two were teachers. One, Charlotte Bourette, *la muse limonadière,* ran a soft-drink shop; and one was a courtesan. The report on the courtesan, Mlle de Saint Phalier, reads like the précis of a novel. After leaving her father, a horse dealer in Paris, she became a chambermaid in the house of a wealthy financier. The son of the house seduced and abducted her, only to be arrested by the father, who then forced him to marry a more suitable woman, leaving Mlle de Saint Phalier in the streets. By the time the police ran across her, she had become a kept woman, consorted with actresses, and was about to publish her first book, *Le Portefeuille rendu,* dedicated to Mme de Pompadour.

D'Hémery had sadder stories to tell when he filled in the entries under the rubric *histoire,* for many careers followed trajectories that led from the garret to the gutter, with stopovers in the Bastille. L.-J.-C. Soulas d'Allainval illustrates the pattern. Unable to support himself by the farces he wrote for the Comédie Italienne, he took up political *libelles* and clandestine journalism, which brought him straight to the Bastille. After his release, he sank deeper into debt. Ultimately, he was unable even to get paper from his stationer, who cut off the pittance he received from the box office of the Comédie Italienne in order to collect an unpaid bill of sixty livres. D'Allainval began to sleep *à la belle étoile* (in the streets). His health gave out. D'Hémery recounted the rest:

> He was struck down by an attack of apoplexy in September, 1752, while a dinner guest of M. Bertin of the parties casuelles, who put two louis in his pocket, and sent him off. As there was no means of nursing him at his place, he was brought to the Hôtel-Dieu [paupers' hospital], where he vegetated for a long while. He finally remained paralyzed and now is reduced to looking for a place at Bicêtre or at the Incurables. What a sad end for a talented man.

D'Hémery expressed less sympathy for François-Antoine Chevrier, "a bad subject, an audacious liar, trenchant, critical, and unbearably pretentious." After failing as a lawyer, soldier, playwright, and poet, Chevrier turned to pamphleteering, underground journalism, and espionage. The police chased him with a *lettre de cachet* through Germany and the Low Countries; but just as they were closing in on him, he died down and out in Rotterdam. The police got their man in the case of Emmanuel-Jean de La Coste, a fifty-nine-year-old defrocked monk, who was condemned to a whipping and the galleys for the rest of his life. He had run off to Liège with a young girl and had supported himself by peddling anti-French pamphlets, counterfeit lottery tickets, and, it seems, the girl herself. These characters belonged to Grub Street, an important ingredient in the republic of letters. To be sure, most writers did not sink so low as d'Allainval, Chevrier, and La Coste; but many shared an experience that marked the men of Grub Street: *embastillement.* Forty-five writers, 10 percent of those in the survey, were locked up at least once in a state prison, usually the Bastille. If the Bastille was almost empty on July 14, 1789, it was full of meaning for the men who made it into the central symbol of radical propaganda before the French Revolution.[6]

Of course, no one could foresee 1789 in 1750. At mid-century the literary population may have been restive, but it was not revolutionary. Most of its members were struggling to get a review in the *Mercure,* an *entrée* in the Comédie Française, or a seat in the Academy. They supported themselves in dozens of ways, some from *rentes,* some from offices, some from professions, and a great many from the jobs that were open to men of the pen: journalism, teaching, secretaryships, and, for the fortunate, sinecures. They came from all sectors of society except the peasantry and from all corners of the kingdom except the backward areas of the south. They included a small number of women and a large number of bright young men, sons of minor officials and artisans, who won scholarships, published poems, and ended up as lawyers and civil servants—or, in a few cases, full-time writers, living like Diderot, *aux gages des libraires* (in the pay of the booksellers).

It would be satisfying to end on that note, with a pattern firmly established and the *philosophes* located within it. Unfortunately, however, literary theorists have taught historians to beware of texts, which can be dissolved into "discourse" by critical reading, no matter how solid they may seem. So the historian should hesitate before treating police reports as hard nuggets of irreducible reality, which he has only to mine out of the archives, sift, and piece together in order to create a solid reconstruction of the past. The reports are constructions of their own, built on implicit assumptions about the nature of writers and writing at a time when literature had not yet been recognized as a vocation.

In drafting his reports, d'Hémery acted as a kind of writer himself. He, too, played a role in the republic of letters while at the same time remaining subordinate to the Lieutenant-Général de Police and other officials in the French state. The reports show a combination of literary sensitivity and bureaucratic orderliness that would be unthinkable in most police headquarters today. They contain as many remarks about the quality of the authors' style as about the character of their religious and political opinions. In the report on the marquise de Créquy, for example, d'Hémery included a three-page excerpt of a dialogue she had written, not because it had any relevance to the ideological issues of the day but because it demonstrated her perfect mastery of prose. He praised "taste," "wit," and "talent" wherever he found it, even among "bad subjects" like Voltaire. *Esprit* (cleverness) was his favorite term. It seems to have been the first thing that he looked for in a writer, and it compensated for a good deal of straying from the straight and narrow. The abbé Paul-François Velly was "a very clever man" and a skirt chaser, but so were "almost all monks when they leave the monastery." The same went for Jean-Pierre Bernard, a "clever" priest with a special talent for funeral sermons: "He is a jolly old boy who enjoys pleasure and spends an evening with the girls whenever he gets a chance."

D'Hémery understood the ways of the world. He did not take offense at a little bawdiness or anticlericalism, especially when it was offset by "genius," as in the work of Alexis Piron: "His biting wit and reputation for impiety means that he is not a member of the Académie Française. M. de Crébillon advised him never to think of being elected. But *Les fils ingrats, Gustave,* and *La métromanie* bear sufficient testimony to his genius. He can succeed in anything he undertakes." D'Hémery admired the *philosophes,* at least the moderate ones, like Fontenelle, Duclos, and d'Alembert. But he was horrified at atheism, and he seems to have sincerely believed in the official orthodoxies. His values show through clearly in all the reports, but especially in off-hand remarks on ordinary writers, like Jean-Baptiste Le Mascrier:

> He was a Jesuit for a long time. He edited *Télliamed* and various other publications for the booksellers. He contributed to the *Cérémonies religieuses* and worked over the *Mémoires de M. de Maillet sur la description de l'Egypte,* which does great honor to him by its style. He turns poems very nicely, as is clear from a prologue to a play that was performed some years ago.
>
> The Benedictines, where he had worked, agree that he is a man of talent. Too bad that he isn't more creative. He has published an excellent work of piety, a book that is useful for every true Christian, but the people who know him most intimately think that the need to produce copy is making him gradually shift to different sentiments.

In short, d'Hémery took stock of the literary world with sympathy, humor, and an appreciation of literature itself. He shared some of the values held by the people under his surveillance, but he did not waver in his loyalty to church and state. Nothing could be more anachronistic than to picture him as a modern cop or to interpret his police work as witch-hunting. It really represents something less familiar and more interesting: information gathering in the age of absolutism. No one expected to uncover revolutionary conspiracies in the mid-eighteenth century, when the Revolution was unthinkable; but many bureaucrats in the Bourbon monarchy wanted to learn as much as possible about the kingdom—about the number of its inhabitants, the volume of its trade, and the output of its presses. D'Hémery belonged to a line of rationalizing officials that extended from Colbert and Vauban to Turgot and Necker. But he operated at a modest level—an inspector of the book trade belonged a notch or two below an inspector of manufactures—and he built up his files on a smaller scale than some of the surveys undertaken by ministers and intendants.[7]

NOTES

1. This study is based on the manuscript reports of Joseph d'Hémery in the Bibliothèque Nationale of Paris, nouv. acq. fr. 10781–10783. All quotations come from that source and can be identified easily in the manuscript, because the reports are arranged alphabetically according to the names of the authors under investigation. I plan to publish the full texts of the reports in a volume to be edited in collaboration with Robert Shackleton and eventually to use them for a book on the rise of the intellectual in France. Although they have never been studied as a whole, the reports have been consulted for a few biographical works, notably *Jeunesse de Diderot* 1713–1753 (Paris, 1939) by Franco Venturi, which quotes most of the report on Diderot (p. 379).

2. Jacques Hébrail and Joseph de La Porte, *La France littéraire* (Paris, 1756). The authors explained the character and purpose of their work in an *avertissement,* which contained a general appeal for bibliographical information to be sent in by anyone, and especially by unknown writers. The new information appeared in the form of *additions* in the edition of 1756, and *supplements* were published in 1760, 1762, 1764, and 1784. In the edition of 1762, p. v, the authors estimated that somewhat more than 1,800 auteurs were then alive in France. Allowing for the growth in the population, in the prestige of authorship, and in book production, it seems likely that about 1,500 Frenchmen had published a book or pamphlet in 1750.

3. On the much-debated questions concerning generations, cohorts, and other age groups, see Clifton Cherpack, "The Literary Periodization of Eighteenth-Century France," *Publications of the Modern Language Association of America,* LXXXIV (1969), 321–28 and Alan B. Spitzer, "The Historical Problem of Generations," *The American Historical Review,* LXXVIII (1973), 1353–83.

4. On the Saint Malo-Geneva line as a demarcation of socio-cultural history, see Roger Chartier, "Les Deux France: Histoire d'une géographie," *Cahiers d'histoire,* XXIV (1979), 393–415. For a discussion of the Paris-province question, see Robert Escarpit, *Sociologie de la litterature* (Paris, 1968), 41–44. Of course, as Paris is located in the north, one might expect a map of the birthplaces of authors living in Paris to underrepresent the south. It also seems unreasonable to expect a close correlation between the birthplaces of authors and crude indicators of literacy such as those discussed in François Furet and Jacques Ozouf, *Lire et écrire: L'Alphabétisation des Français de Calvin à Jules Ferry* (Paris, 1977), 2 vols.

5. See the article on Favart in J.-F. and L.-G. Michaud, eds., *Biographie universelle* (Paris, 1811–52), XIII, 440–42; as well as the more scholarly studies of Georges Desnoireterres, *Epicuriens et lettrés* (Paris, 1879); and Auguste Font, *Favart, l'Opéra-Comique et la comédie-vaudeville aux XVIIe et XVIIIe siècles* (Paris, 1894).

6. In almost half the cases, the *embastillement* came after the completion of d'Hémery's report. Despite their vigilance concerning suspicious characters, the police did not orient their surveillance toward the criminal element in the republic of letters but rather attempted to do a general survey of all the writers they could find.

7. The attempts of officials to increase the power of the state by systematic study of its resources goes back to Machiavelli and the development of "reason of state" as a principle of government. Although this tendency has usually been treated as an aspect of political theory it also belongs to the history of bureaucracy and to the spread of "rationalization" (rather than Enlightenment), as Max Weber understood it. For a recent study of the literature on the intellectual history side of the question, see Michael Stolleis, *"Arcana imperii* und *Ratio status:* Bemerkungen zur politischen Theorie des frühen 17, Jahrhunderts," *Veröffentlichung der Joachim-Jungius-Gesellschaft der Wissenschaften,* no. 39 (Göttingen, 1980), 5–34.

Electricity Creates the Wired World

Promoting the telephone to businesses for local and long distance calls. *New York Telephone Archives.*

Up to this point we have looked at the history of communications in terms of a variety of media that physically carried certain kinds of information. To move the information, one moved the medium. The book and manuscript passed from place to place in much the same fashion as did clay tablets, tokens, and the quipu. With the advent of harnessable electricity, a major shift occurred: The telegraph and telephone became the first wave of a new communications revolution. To paraphrase Marshall McLuhan, beginning with the telegraph, messages could travel faster than messengers. Communication over distance was no longer tied to the available means of transportation. The effects of this breakthrough are still occurring. Through the use of a fax machine, for example, a handwritten letter can now be freed from a dependency on the mails for speedy delivery.

This leap, from what is called a "transportation" model of communication to a "transmission one," was not without precursors. Talking drums, smoke signals, and the use of polished metal to direct sunlight (heliograph) were early ways of sending messages without messengers. The ancient Greeks developed a system of torch signals between towers several miles apart that could relay the letters of the alphabet. In Europe, just before the invention of the telegraph, ship-to-ship and ship-to-shore semaphore inspired the construction of a land-base system—towers that used mechanical arms to signal alphabet letters—that in one case could send a message of several sentences from the south of France to Paris in four hours. There were even plans in the United States during the 1830s (when Samuel Morse was working on his telegraph) to establish a similar "optical telegraph" from Washington to New Orleans. The need for more rapid communication was gaining wider recognition, along with such an unusual delivery system. Electricity and the telegraph provided an effective alternative.

With the coming of the telegraph in the 1840s, words were transformed into electrical impulses—the dots and dashes of Morse code—which passed through a network that eventually wired the continent. With this development, communication was, in theory, separable from modes of transportation. In reality, the two worked hand-in-hand. Almost everywhere that the railroad went, the telegraph followed. Initially, it was mutual benefit that made partners of the railroad and the telegraph. Telegraph companies found it convenient to use an already established right-of-way. The railroads benefited as well through the telegraph's ability to monitor rail traffic and warn of breakdowns. Paralleling these specific services, the telegraph also functioned as a background director of commerce. It forwarded orders, coordinated shipments, and reported transactions.

The telegraph's role in bringing about what we call the "wired world," is explored by James Carey in our first selection. Beginning in the 1840s, the telegraph emerged as a powerful instrument of continental communication in the United States and, thanks in part to the development of transoceanic cable technology, became a global system before the end of the century. An important point to note in the development of telegraphy is how the U.S. government, over the objections of the postal service, chose not to own and operate the telegraph—the opposite of what would occur in Europe. This gave rise to one of the first corporate monopolies in the United States, Western Union, and set the stage for a future of private media ownership.

Carey charts the telegraph's influence on a range of business practices. His perspective is influenced by the concepts of Harold Innis, whom we encountered in Part I. Carey applies Innis's emphasis on space and time to an analysis of the way the telegraph brought diverse regional centers of buying and selling under a unified price and market system and to a consideration of the implications of the creation of standard time zones. He stresses the way it initiated, or foreshadowed, cultural technological changes that we frequently take for granted.

Carey is concerned with a theme that has been discussed in previous selections: the impact of new media on old. He mentions the influence that the telegraph had on the newspaper and journalistic practices. However, it is the next excerpt, by Michael Schudson, which concentrates most fully on the new forms of news that emerged in the second half of the nineteenth century. Schudson sketches out two kinds of journalism that prevailed: the information press and the entertainment press. The former was oriented to political and economic news and the business community, the latter to the dramatic, scandalous, and everyday life world of a growing urban working class. Both were tied to a new system of reportage: feeding stories into major centers, where they could be pooled and forwarded elsewhere through the growing influence of the telegraph-based wire services, such as the Associated Press. Schudson shows us how newspapers created new forms of meaning in response to social and technological changes that yielded a new reading public, one that would eventually lead to the rise of mass society in the twentieth century.

After the telegraph, the next major electric communications medium to develop was the telephone. It emerged in the third quarter of the nineteenth century. Based on voice transmission, it overcame several limitations of the telegraph. The most notable one was that, unlike the telegraph, the telephone was not restricted to transmitting mostly written documents. Also, since the telegraph required skilled mastery of Morse code, as well as literacy, its potential spread into the home did not seem viable.

The prevalent early use of the telephone was in the urban context of business and government, the same areas in which telegraphy got its start. This illustrates a recurring theme in the history of communications. A new medium often tries to do what was already the preserve of earlier one but in ways that *bypass* some of the problems and complexities of its predecessor. The telephone in this case could be described as bypassing the telegraph because voice transmission eliminated the need for literate telegraphers who were skilled in Morse code.

It should also be noted that in its early operation the telephone was as much complementary to the telegraph as competitive. The telephone allowed for rapid two-way exchange, which could speed up business decisions. The telegraph facilitated the sending of detailed and often quantitative information that could be collected at specific points for later action. The telegraph favored a linear logic of one thing at a time. The telephone was an immediately interactive medium. By the late 1880s the ease and efficiency of the telephone led to its use in wealthy private homes. As the cost of units dropped around the turn of the century, the telephone began to spread throughout society, creating new dimensions of interpersonal interaction.

In our next excerpt, Claude Fischer gives us the story of Alexander Graham Bell and the Bell companies as they tried to build a viable business around early telephone technology. Fischer notes how in the 1870s the telephone had been more a novelty than a practical tool—It was easier to draw a Sunday audience for an exhibition of the "singing telephone" than to attract business users. There was, of course, the telegraph, with local offices, messenger boys, and the beginnings of reliable service nationally and internationally. Fischer also makes the interesting point that the earliest users of the telephone were concerned with simple two-point communications, between two buildings of the same firm or between the home and office of an executive.

The installation of switchboards on a large scale made the telephone competitive with the telegraph. From the 1880s onward the telephone grew as rapidly as exchanges could be installed. The base of customers expanded among business and professional users. By the 1890s, significant growth in residential services had occurred. The Bell companies in these decades succeeded both in promoting the adoption of the telephone and in policing the system they built against rivals. Fischer's essay is especially useful in alerting us to the emerging role of the customer, who influenced the development of telephony by demanding new and innovative applications of the medium.

The telephone was revolutionary in other ways, which Carolyn Marvin discusses in our next entry. She looks at several experiments in what is known as "proto-broadcasting." This entailed transmitting information to multiple subscribers who listened "on-line" simultaneously. It started with church services and sporting events. The remarkable Telefon Hirmondó system in Budapest "proto-broadcast" concerts, plays, children's fare, and stock market reports in this way. Telefon Hirmondó spawned several less successful imitators in North America, where the telephone "broadcasts" consciously attempted to compete with the newspapers for more rapid reportage of current events, especially election results. Thus, several decades before broadcast radio became widespread, its potential was anticipated by another medium.

The transition from the nineteenth-century wired world to its apparent realization in the omnipresent technology and new patterns of consumption of the twentieth century is the subject of our final selection, "Dream Worlds of Consumption," by Rosalynd Williams. She begins with a discussion of universal expositions, what we now call World's Fairs. The one held at the Crystal Palace in London in 1851 is cited as the first of an initial series that culminated with the turn-of-the-century extravaganza in Paris in 1900. During the Paris celebration, notions of abstract technological progress, a central theme of previous exhibitions, were overshadowed by the possibilities of consumer goods—a new world of things that challenged art and religion as focal points of human aspiration. Underwriting this shift was the development of department stores. As disposable income increased in an expanding industrial economy, these giant commercial sites enabled at least part of the "dream world" to be experienced by the public at large.

The 1900 Paris exhibition also affected the imagination of its visitors in other ways. It dramatized the power of the motion picture. The emergence of movies as a mass medium took place between this time and World War I. Building on the reproductive powers of the photograph, the cinematic experience is one that we still struggle to explain. Williams discusses some early reactions to it.

17 TIME, SPACE, AND THE TELEGRAPH

James Carey

James Carey is professor at the Columbia School of Journalism and a leading figure in advancing the study of communications history. His book, Communication as Culture, *source of the present excerpt, develops a model for examining the implications of early media development in the United States.*

The simplest and most important point about the telegraph is that it marked the decisive separation of "transportation" and "communication." Until the telegraph these words were synonymous. The telegraph ended that identity and allowed symbols to move independently of geography and independently of and faster than transport. I say decisive separation because there were premonitions earlier of what was to come, and there was, after all, pre-electric telegraphy—line-of-sight signaling devices.

Virtually any American city of any vintage has a telegraph hill or a beacon hill reminding us of such devices. They relied on shutters, flaps, disks, or arms operating as for semaphoric signaling at sea. They were optical rather than "writing at a distance" systems and the forerunners of microwave networks, which rely on relay stations on geographic high points for aerial transmissions.

Line-of-sight telegraphy came into practical use at the end of the eighteenth century. Its principal architect was a Frenchman, Claud-Chappe, who persuaded the Committee of Public Instruction in post-Revolutionary France to approve a trial. Joseph Lakanal, one of its members, reported back to the committee on the outcome: "What brilliant destiny do science and the arts not reserve for a republic which by its immense population and the genius of its inhabitants, is called to become the nation to instruct Europe" (Wilson, 1976: 122).

The National Convention approved the adoption of the telegraph as a national utility and instructed the Committee of Public Safety to map routes. The major impetus to its development in France was the same as the one that led to the wave of canal and railroad building in America. The pre-electric telegraph would provide an answer to Montesquieu and other political theorists who thought France or the United States too big to be a republic. But even more, it provided a means whereby the departments that had replaced the provinces after the Revolution could be tied to and coordinated with the central authority (Wilson, 1976: 123).

The pre-electric telegraph was also a subject of experimentation in America. In 1800, a line-of-sight system was opened between Martha's Vineyard and Boston (Wilson, 1976: 210). Between 1807 and 1812, plans were laid for a telegraph to stretch from Maine to New Orleans. The first practical use of line-of-sight telegraphy was for the transmission of news of arriving ships, a practice begun long before 1837 (Thompson, 1947: 11). But even before line-of-sight devices had been developed, alterations in shipping patterns had led to the separation of information from cargo, and that had important consequences for international trade. . . .

Despite these reservations and qualifications, the telegraph provided the decisive and cumulative break of the identity of communication and transportation. The great theoretical significance of the technology lay not merely in the separation but also in the use of the telegraph as both a model of and a mechanism for control of the physical movement of things, specifically for the railroad. That is the fundamental discovery: not only can information move independently of and faster than physical entities, but it also can be a simulation of and control mechanism for what has been left behind. The discovery was first exploited in railroad dispatching in England in 1844 and in the United States in 1849. It was of particular use on the long stretches of single-track road in the American West, where accidents were a serious problem. Before the use of the telegraph to control switching, the Boston and Worcester Railroad, for one example, kept horses every five miles along the line, and they raced up and down the track so that their riders could warn engineers of impending collisions (Thompson, 1947: 205–206). By moving information faster than the rolling stock, the telegraph allowed for centralized control along many miles of track. Indeed, the operation of the telegraph in conjunction with the railroad allowed for an integrated system of transport and communication. The same principle realized in these mundane circumstances governs the development of all modern processes in electrical transmission and control from guided gun sights to simple servo mechanisms that open doors. The relationship of the telegraph and the railroad illustrates the basic notion of systems theory and the catch phrase that the "system is the solution," in that the integrated switched system is more important than any of its components.

The telegraph permitted the development, in the favorite metaphor of the day, of a thoroughly encephalated social nervous system in which signaling was divorced from musculature. It was the telegraph and the railroad—the actual, painful construction of an integrated system—that provided the entrance gate for the organic metaphors that dominated nineteenth-century thought. Although German romanticism and idealism had their place, it is less to the world of ideas and more to the world of actual practice that we need to look when trying to figure out why the nineteenth century was obsessed with organicism.

The effect of the telegraph on ideology, on ordinary ideas, can be shown more graphically with two other examples drawn from the commodities markets and the development of standard time. The telegraph, like most innovations in communication down through the computer, had its first and most profound impact on the conduct of commerce, government, and the military. It was, in short, a producer good before it was a consumer good. The telegraph . . . was used in its early months for the long-distance playing of chess. Its commercial significance was slow to be realized. But once that significance was determined, it was used to reorganize commerce; and from the patterns of usage in commerce came many of the telegraph's most profound consequences for ordinary thought. Among its first effects was the reorganization of commodity markets.

It was the normal expectation of early nineteenth century Americans that the price of a commodity would diverge from city to city so that the cost of wheat, corn, or whatever would be radically different in, say, Pittsburgh, Cincinnati, and St. Louis. This belief reflected the fact that before the telegraph, markets were independent of one another, or, more accurately, that the effect of one market on another was so gradually manifested as to be virtually unnoticed. In short, the prices of commodities were largely determined by local conditions of supply and demand. One of the leading historians of the markets has commented, "To be sure in all articles of trade the conditions at all sources of supply had their ultimate effect on distant values and yet even in these the communication was so slow that the conditions might change entirely before their effect could be felt" (Emery, 1896: 106).

Under such circumstances, the principal method of trading is called arbitrage: buying cheap and selling dear by moving goods around in space. That is, if prices are higher in St. Louis than in Cincinnati, it makes sense to buy in Cincinnati and resell in St. Louis, as long as the

The telegraph moved west with the railways, utilizing the railroad right of way and quickly becoming an essential information system both for coordinating rail traffic and for managing the flow of goods and services. *National Archives of Canada.*

the options available in all relevant markets—a situation rarely approached in practice before the telegraph.

Throughout the United States, price divergence between markets declined during the nineteenth century. Arthur H. Cole computed the average annual and monthly price disparity for uniform groups of commodities during the period 1816–1842, that is, up to the eve of the telegraph. Over that period the average annual price disparity fell from 9.3 to 4.8; and the average monthly disparity, from 15.4 to 4.8 (Cole, 1938: 94–96, 103). The decline itself is testimony to improvements in communication brought about by canal and turnpike building. The steepness of the decline is probably masked somewhat because Cole grouped the prices for the periods 1816–1830 and 1830–1842, whereas it was late in the canal era and the beginnings of large-scale railroad building that the sharpest declines were felt.

Looked at from one side, the decline represents the gradual increase in the effective size of the market. Looked at from the other side, it represents a decline in spatially based speculative opportunities—opportunities, that is, to turn trade into profit by moving goods between distinct markets. In a sense the railroad and canal regionalized markets; the telegraph nationalized them.

The effect of the telegraph is a simple one: it evens out markets in space. The telegraph puts everyone in the same place for purposes of trade; it makes geography irrelevant. The telegraph brings the conditions of supply and demand in all markets to bear on the determination of a price. Except for the marginal exception here and there, it eliminates opportunities for arbitrage by realizing the classical assumption of perfect information.

But the significance of the telegraph does not lie solely in the decline of arbitrage; rather, the telegraph shifts speculation into another dimension. It shifts speculation from space to time, from arbitrage to futures. After the telegraph, commodity trading moved from trading

price differential is greater than the cost of transportation between the two cities. If arbitrage is widely practiced between cities, prices should settle into an equilibrium whereby the difference in price is held to the difference in transportation cost. This result is, in turn, based on the assumption of classical economics of perfect information—that all buyers and sellers are aware of between places to trading between times. The arbitrager trades Cincinnati for St. Louis; the futures trader sells August against October, this year against next. To put the matter somewhat differently, as the telegraph closed down spatial uncertainty in prices, it opened up, because of improvements in communication, the uncertainty of time. It was not, then, mere historic accident that the Chicago Commodity Exchange, to this day the principal American futures market, opened in 1848, the same year the telegraph reached that city. In a certain sense the telegraph invented the future as a new zone of uncertainty and a new region of practical action.

Let me make a retreat from that conclusion about the effects of the telegraph on time because I have overdrawn the case. First, the opportunities for arbitrage are never completely eliminated. There are always imperfections in market information, even on the floor of a stock exchange: buyers and sellers who do not know of one another and the prices at which the others are willing to trade. We know this as well from ordinary experience at auctions, where someone always knows a buyer who will pay more than the auctioned price. Second, there was a hiatus between arbitrage and the futures market when time contracts dominated, and this was a development of some importance. An approximation of futures trading occurred as early as 1733, when the East India Company initiated the practice of trading warrants. The function of a warrant was to transfer ownership of goods without consummating their physical transfer. The warrant did not represent, as such, particular warehoused goods; they were merely endorsed from person to person. The use of warrants or time contracts evolved rapidly in the United States in the trading of agricultural staples. They evolved there to meet new conditions of effective market size, and as importantly, their evolution was unrestrained by historic practice.

The critical condition governing the development of time contracts was also the separation of communication from transport. Increasingly, news of crop conditions reached the market before the commodity itself. For example, warrant trading advanced when cotton was shipped to England by sail while passengers and information moved by steamer. Based on news of the crop and on samples of the commodity, time contracts or "to-arrive" contracts were executed. These were used principally for transatlantic sales, but after the Mississippi Valley opened up to agricultural trade, they were widely used in Chicago in the 1840s (Baer and Woodruff, 1935: 3–5).

The telegraph started to change the use of time contracts, as well as arbitrage. By widely transmitting knowledge of prices and crop conditions, it drew markets and prices together. We do not have good before-and-after measures, but we do have evidence, cited earlier, for the long-run decline in price disparities among markets. Moreover, we have measures from Cincinnati in particular. In the 1820s Cincinnati lagged two years behind Eastern markets. That meant that it took two years for disturbances in the Eastern market structure to affect Cincinnati prices. By 1840 the lag was down to four months; and by 1857—and probably much earlier—the effect of Eastern markets on Cincinnati was instantaneous. But once space was, in the phrase of the day, annihilated, once everyone was in the same place for purposes of trade, time as a new region of experience, uncertainty, speculation, and exploration was opened up to the forces of commerce.

A back-door example of this inversion of space and time can be drawn from a later episode involving the effect of the telephone on the New York Stock Exchange. By 1894 the telephone had made information time identical in major cities. Buyers and sellers, wherever they were, knew current prices as quickly as traders did on the floor of the exchange. The information gap, then, between New York and Boston had been eliminated and business gravitated from New York to Boston brokerage firms. The New York exchange countered this movement by creating a thirty-second time advantage that ensured New York's superiority to Boston. The exchange ruled that telephones would not be allowed on the floor. Price information had to be relayed by messenger to an area off the floor of the exchange that had been set aside for telephones. This move destroyed the temporal identity of markets, and a thirty-second monopoly of knowledge was created that drew business back to New York (Emery, 1896: 139).

This movement of commodities out of space and into time had three other consequences of great importance in examining the effect of the telegraph. First, futures trading required the decontexualization of markets; or, to put it in a slightly different way, markets were made relatively unresponsive to local conditions of supply and demand. The telegraph removed markets from the particular context in which they were historically located and concentrated on them forces emanating from any place and any time. This was a redefinition from physical or geographic markets to spiritual ones. In a sense they were made more mysterious; they became everywhere markets and everytime markets and thus less apprehensible at the very moment they became more powerful.

Second, not only were distant and amorphous forces brought to bear on markets, but the commodity was sundered from its representations; that is, the development of futures trading depended on the ability to trade or circulate negotiable instruments independently of the actual physical movement of goods. The representation of the commodity became the warehouse receipts from grain elevators along the railroad line. These instruments were then traded independently of any movement of the actual goods. The buyer of such receipts never expected to take delivery; the seller of such receipts never expected to make delivery. There is the old joke, which is also a cautionary tale, of the futures trader who forgot what he was up to and ended up with forty tons of wheat on his suburban lawn; but it is merely a joke and a tale. The futures trader often sells before he buys, or buys and sells simultaneously. But the buying and selling is not of goods but of receipts. What is being traded is not money for commodities but time against price. In short, the warehouse receipt, which stands as a representation of the product, has no intrinsic relation to the real product.

But in order to trade receipts rather than goods, a third change was necessary. In futures trading products are not bought or sold by inspection of the actual product or a sample thereof. Rather, they are sold through a grading system. In order to lend itself to futures trading, a product has to be mixed, standardized, diluted in order to be reduced to a specific, though abstract, grade. With the coming of the telegraph, products could no longer be shipped in separate units as numerous as there were owners of grain. "The high volume sales required impersonalized standards. Buyers were no longer able personally to check every lot" (Chandler, 1977: 211). Consequently, not all products are traded on the futures market because some resist the attempt to reduce them to standardized categories of quality.

The development of the futures markets, in summary, depended on a number of specific changes in markets and the commodity system. It required that information move independently of and faster than products. It required that prices be made uniform in space and that markets be decontextualized. It required, as well, that commodities be separated from the receipts that represent them and that commodities be reduced to uniform grades.

These were, it should be quickly added, the conditions that underlay Marx's analysis of the commodity fetish. That concept, now used widely and often indiscriminately, was developed in the *Grundrisse* and *Das Kapital* during the late 1850s, when futures trading became the dominant arena for the establishment of agricultural values. In particular, Marx made the key elements in the commodity fetish the decontextualization of markets, the separation of use value from exchange value brought about by the decline in the representative function of the warehouse receipt, and the abstraction of the

The original bicycle courier. In urban areas, telegrams had to be collected and delivered by squadrons of young messengers. *National Archives of Canada*

product out of real conditions of production by a grading system. In the *Grundrisse* he comments, "This locational movement—the bringing of the product to market which is a necessary condition of its circulation, except when the point of production is itself a market—could more precisely be regarded as the transformation of the product into a commodity" (Marx, 1973: 534).

Marx's reference is to what Walter Benjamin (1968) would later call the "loss of aura" in his parallel analysis of the effect of mechanical reproduction on the work of art. After the object is abstracted out of the real conditions of its production and use and is transported to distant markets, standardized and graded, and represented by fully contingent symbols, it is made available as a commodity. Its status as a commodity represents the sundering of a real, direct relationship between buyer and seller, separates use value from exchange value, deprives objects of any uniqueness (which must then be returned to the object via advertising), and, most important, masks to the buyer the real conditions of

production. Further, the process of divorcing the receipt from the product can be thought of as part of a general social process initiated by the use of money and widely written about in contemporary semiotics; the progressive divorce of the signifier from the signified, a process in which the world of signifiers progressively overwhelms and moves independently of real material objects.

To summarize, the growth of communications in the nineteenth century had the practical effect of diminishing space as a differentiating criterion in human affairs. What Harold Innis called the "penetrative powers of the price system" was, in effect, the spread of a uniform price system throughout space so that for purposes of trade everyone was in the same place. The telegraph was the critical instrument in this spread. In commerce this meant the decontextualization of markets so that prices no longer depended on local factors of supply and demand but responded to national and international forces. The spread of the price system was part of the attempt to colonize space. The correlative to the penetration of the price system was what the composer Igor Stravinsky called the "statistical-ization of mind": the transformation of the entire mental world into quantity, and the distribution of quantities in space so that the relationship between things and people becomes solely one of numbers. Statistics widens the market for everything and makes it more uniform and interdependent. The telegraph worked this same effect on the practical consciousness of time through the construction of standard time zones.

BIBLIOGRAPHY

Baer, Julius B., and George P. Woodruff (1935). *Commodity Exchanges*. New York: Harper & Bros.

Benjamin, Walter (1968). *Illuminations*. New York: Harcourt, Brace and World.

Chandler, Alfred D. (1977). *The Visible Hand: The Managerial Revolution in American Business*. Cambridge, MA: Harvard University Press.

Cole, Arthur H. (1938). *Wholesale Commodity Prices in the United States, 1700–1861*. Cambridge, MA: Harvard University Press.

Emery, Henry Crosby (1896). *Speculation on the Stock and Produce Exchanges of the United States, Studies in History, Economics and Public Law* (332.6EM3STX.AGX). New York: Columbia University Press.

Marx, Karl (1973). *Grundrisse: Foundations of the Critique of Political Economy*. New York: Vintage.

Thompson, Robert L. (1947). *Wiring a Continent*. Princeton, NJ: Princeton University Press.

Wilson, Geoffrey (1976). *The Old Telegraph*. London: Phillimore.

18 · THE NEW JOURNALISM
Michael Schudson

Michael Schudson is a professor of communications and a historian of the development of the institutions of mass communication in the United States. In this excerpt from his book Discovering the News, *he demonstrates how the familiar models of news as information and news as entertainment grew significantly out of the organizational struggles of the New York press for readership in the late nineteenth century.*

Reporting was an invention of the end of the nineteenth century, but it was a two-part invention: the emergence of the new occupation played off against the industrialization of the newspaper. And while there was much that united the ideology of reporters, there was much that divided the identities of the newspapers for which they worked. In New York, most of the major papers were direct descendants of the penny press: the *Sun*, the *Herald*, the *Tribune*, and the *Times*. Of papers that antedated the penny press, only the *Evening Post* still had an important following. The two largest papers were the *World*, begun in 1859 and revived by Joseph Pulitzer in 1883, and the *Journal*, begun in 1882 by Pulitzer's brother but escorted to the stage of history when William Randolph Hearst bought it in 1895. Both of these papers were sharply distinguished from the others; they represented what contemporaries generally referred to as "the new journalism." The established papers found their competition and their manners deeply disturbing and wrote of them with the same moral horror that had greeted their own arrival in New York journalism fifty years before.

While reporters subscribed concurrently to the ideals of factuality and of entertainment in writing the news, some of the papers they worked for chose identities that strongly emphasized one ideal or the other. The *World* and the *Journal* chose to be entertaining; the old penny press, especially the *Times* after Adolph Ochs rejuvenated it in 1896, took the path of factuality. I shall refer to these two models of journalism as the ideal of the "story" and the ideal of "information." When telling stories is taken to be the role of the newspaper, journalism is said to fulfill what George Herbert Mead described as an "aesthetic" function. Mead wrote that some parts of the news—the election results or stock market reports—emphasize exclusively "the truth value of news," but for most of the news in a paper, the "enjoyability" or "consummatory value" is more important. The news serves primarily to create, for readers, satisfying aesthetic experiences which help them to interpret their own lives and to relate them to the nation, town, or class to which they belong. Mead took this to be the actual, and the proper, function of a newspaper and observed that it is manifest in the fact that "the reporter is generally sent out to get a story, not the facts."[1] In this view, the newspaper acts as a guide to living not so much by providing facts as by selecting them and framing them.

An alternative model of the newspaper's role proposes that the newspaper is uniquely defined as a genre of literature precisely to the extent that the facts it provides are unframed, that it purveys pure "information." Walter Benjamin suggested that "information" is a novel form of communication, a product of fully developed capitalism, whose distinguishing characteristic is that it "lays claim to prompt verifiability." Its aim, above all, is to be "understandable in itself." While it may actually be no more exact than varieties of "intelligence" of the past, unlike earlier intelligence, which might be justified by reference to the miraculous, "it is indispensable for information to sound plausible." For

this reason, in Benjamin's analysis, information "proves incompatible with the spirit of story-telling."[2] This view of the newspaper is echoed in the recent work of Alvin Gouldner, who refers to news as "decontextualized" communication. It is a form of what Basil Bernstein, on whose work Gouldner relies, calls an "elaborated code," in which all is spelled out, nothing left to implicit or tacit understanding.[3]

Rightly or wrongly, the informational ideal in journalism is associated with fairness, objectivity, scrupulous dispassion. Newspapers which stress information tend to be seen as more reliable than "story" papers. But who makes this judgment and on what grounds? Who regards the information model as more trustworthy than the story ideal, and what is meant, after all, by "reliable" or "trustworthy"? If journalists on the whole give credit to both ideas at once, how is it that different newspaper institutions come to stand for one or the other? And how is it that those which stand for the information model come to be regarded as the more responsible?

It is the unexceptional theme of this chapter that, in the most general terms, there is a connection between the educated middle class and information and a connection between the middle and working classes and the story ideal. The puzzle here, as in most other discussions of popular culture, is why this should be the case. What is it about information that seems to appeal to the educated middle class? What is it about the story that seems to attract the working-class reader? Is it right to associate the information model with the notion of objectivity? Should we regard it as a "higher" form of journalism than the story model? In the critical decades from 1883 to the first years of this century, when at the same moment yellow journalism was at its height and the *New York Times* established itself as the most reliable and respected newspaper in the country, why did wealthier people in New York read the *Times* and less wealthy people read the *World*? What is the meaning of the two journalisms of the 1890s?

JOURNALISM AS ENTERTAINMENT: JOSEPH PULITZER AND THE *NEW YORK WORLD*

Joseph Pulitzer began his newspaper career in St. Louis. Party papers prevailed there until the 1870s when "independent journalism" gained a foothold. A turning point for St. Louis journalism came in 1871 when the *Morning Globe* hired Chicago's Joseph McCullagh as editor. McCullagh stressed news, rather than opinion, and, on what was by then the increasingly familiar model of James Gordon Bennett, concentrated on local police, court, society, and street reporting.

Pulitzer was an Austrian Jewish immigrant who arrived in the United States in 1864, at the age of seventeen, to fight in the Civil War. In St. Louis, after the war, he studied law and was admitted to the bar, but, in part because of his limited facility in English, he did not practice law. Instead, he became a reporter for the city's German-language newspaper, the *Westliche Post*. Active and successful in journalism and in politics—first Republican, then Democratic—Pulitzer was able to buy the *St. Louis Post and Dispatch* in 1878. He served as its publisher, editor, and business manager. Under his guidance, the paper became more audacious in promoting the Democratic Party and turned much brighter in its style. It began to carry statistics of trade from the Merchants' Exchange, the produce markets, and the waterfront. In 1879 it became the first St. Louis paper to publish quotations on stocks issued by local firms. Pulitzer repeatedly appealed to "the people," by which he meant, it seems, "the stable householder, of whatever class."[4] The *Post and Dispatch* was antagonistic to labor, and it held to the high price of five cents an issue. According to Julian Rammelkamp, historian of Pulitzer's years as St. Louis editor, "The fundamental aims of the paper were middle class—to foster the development of St. Louis as a business center and as an attractive place of residence for the average citizen."[5] Pulitzer's great

innovation in his years in St. Louis was the development of the newspaper crusade. The crusade was by no means unknown elsewhere, especially in New York, but Pulitzer made startling headlines and political exposes a constant feature of his paper, stimulating circulation and presumably changing the city for the better.

In 1883 Pulitzer plugged his Western voice into the amplifier of the East, New York City. He bought the *New York World,* a paper of some reputation during the 1860s and 1870s which had fallen on hard times. When Pulitzer bought it, its circulation was about fifteen thousand. A year later it was sixty thousand. In another year it was one hundred thousand, and by the fall of 1886 it passed a quarter million. Pulitzer attributed this astonishingly rapid success to his editorial position. "We can conscientiously say," he wrote in an 1884 editorial, "that we believe the success of THE WORLD is largely due to the sound principles of the paper rather than to its news features or its price."[6]

There was a measure of truth in this. It is not an accident that the *World* and Hearst's *Journal,* the city's two most widely read papers at the turn of the century, were both Democratic. But this was not the mainspring, or mainstay, of Pulitzer's (or Hearst's) success. Pulitzer's energy and innovation in business practice played a larger role. Publishing the *World* at a penny a copy, he forced the *Times* to drop its price from four cents to two, the *Herald,* from three to two, and the *Tribune,* from four to three (the two-cent *Sun* stayed the same). He initiated the practice of selling advertising space on the basis of actual circulation and selling it at fixed prices; at the same time, he abandoned the traditional penalties for advertisers who used illustrations or broke column-rules.[7] Pulitzer thus helped rationalize newspapers business practice and the relations between newspapers and advertisers. . . .

Pulitzer's rationalization of the *World*'s advertising policies helped the *World* adapt to general changes in the social organization of business, but the innovation most responsible for the paper's rapidly growing circulation was, in a word, sensationalism. The sensationalism Pulitzer brought to New York was not altogether revolutionary. Its attention to local news, especially crime and scandal and high society, continued in the tradition of the penny press. Indeed, this subject-matter focus, which had scandalized the established press of the 1830s, was typical of most major papers by the 1880s in New York—with some variation, of course, and with the lagging and Olympian exception of the *Evening Post*. But what defined sensationalism in the 1880s was less substance than style: how extravagantly should the news be displayed? Sensationalism meant self-advertisement. If, as James Gordon Bennett recognized in the 1840s, everything, including advertising, could and should be news, the sensational papers of the 1880s and 1890s discovered that everything, including news, could and should be advertising for the newspapers. For instance, the *World* in the 1890s regularly took a column or two on the front page to boast of its high circulation. It regularly headlined the fact, in its advertising pages, that it printed more advertisements than any other paper in the country and included the facts and figures to prove it.

Self-advertisement, as I use the term, is anything about newspaper layout and newspaper policy, outside of basic news gathering, which is designed to attract the eye and small change of readers. One of the most important developments of self-advertising in this sense was the use of illustrations. Pulitzer, perhaps feeling that illustrations lowered the dignity of a newspaper, intended at first to eliminate them from the *World*, but he found, as *The Journalist* wrote, that "the circulation of the paper went with the cuts."[8] Pulitzer reversed field and, within the first year of his *World* management, hired Valerian Gribayedoff, a portrait artist, and Walt McDougall, a cartoonist. Their efforts, according to Robert Taft's history of American photography, "mark the beginning of the modern era of newspaper illustration."[9] The *New York Daily Graphic*, in 1873, became the first Ameri-can daily to regularly use illustrations—and it offered little except illustrations. At first, Pulitzer did not regard the *World* as competing with the *Daily Graphic*. By the summer of 1884, however, Pulitzer classified both papers as "illustrated daily journals"; by 1889, the *World*'s extravagant use of both political cartoons and, especially in the Sunday editions, "cuts whose only justification was the fun of looking at pictures" drove the *Daily Graphic* out of business.[10]

Another major development in self-advertisement was larger and darker headlines. Here Pulitzer remained conservative for years. Rather than introduce headlines spanning several columns, he emphasized important stories simply by adding more banks of headlines within the same column. Headlines, like advertisements, abided by column-rules. Not until 1889 did the *World* run a two-column headline, but by the late 1890s, especially through the competition with Hearst, large, screaming headlines were frequently a part of the *World*'s make-up.[11] . . .

Hearst proudly proclaimed: "It is the *Journal*'s policy to engage brains as well as to get the news, for the public is even more fond of entertainment than it is of information."[12] Melville Stone, of the *Chicago Morning News* and *Daily News,* maintained that the newspaper had three functions: to inform, to interpret, and to entertain.[13]

Pulitzer did not talk up the idea of entertainment, but the *World* came to embody it. The importance of the entertaining function of the paper was marked especially by the growth of the Sunday *World* which, like Sunday newspapers still, was as close to an illustrated magazine as to a daily newspaper in style and content. Sunday papers had been rare early in the century. In 1842 only one New Yorker in twenty-six bought a Sunday paper, while one in seven bought a daily. In 1850, after heavy Irish immigration, one in nine New Yorkers bought a Sunday paper. The Irish and other later immigrants came to the country without the American conservatism about Sabbath observance. This, plus the practice newspapers developed during the Civil War of printing special Sunday editions with war news, made it easier for papers to take the plunge into Sunday journalism and to appeal directly to the interests of readers for diversion on the day of rest. By 1889, one New Yorker in two bought a Sunday paper, making more Sunday newspapers readers than daily readers that year.[14] Charles Dana, editor of the *Sun,* estimated in 1894 that a paper with a daily edition of 50,000, at two or three cents, would have a Sunday edition of 100,000 to 150,000, at five cents.[15] What readers found and liked in the Sunday papers, they began to find in the daily press, too. Pulitzer used the Sunday *World* "as a laboratory to test ideas that finally proved to be applicable throughout the week."[16] Illustrations and comic strips (the first color comic strips appeared in the Sunday *World* in 1894) spread from the Sunday paper to the daily editions. . . .

Newspapers, like the *World,* which sought a wide and general readership, responded to the changing experience, perceptions, and aspirations of urban dwellers. This meant, indeed, an enlargement of the "entertainment" function of the newspaper, but it also meant the expansion of what has recently been called the "use-paper" rather than the newspaper, the daily journal as a compendium of tips for urban survival. City living, by the 1880s, had become very different from what it had been in the 1830s. It was much more a mosaic of races and social types; it was much more a maelstrom of social and geographic movement. Geographic mobility for a growing middle class was something it had never been before—it was a daily round of movement from home to work and back again. Improved urban transportation and the movement of the middle class into the suburbs meant that this daily movement could be considerable in terms of miles and time consumed. Horse-drawn omnibuses helped urban expansion away from a port-based locus beginning in the 1830s, but the growth of intracity transportation was even more dramatic in the last half of the century. The walking city of 1850 had become a riding city by 1900. The expansion of horse-drawn buses and railways (horse manure and urine had become a serious pollution problem in New York by 1890), and later cable lines and electric surface lines, elevated rapid transit and subways, made mass suburban living possible by 1900 and created a new segregation in the city: the poor lived near the city's center, while the middle class moved farther out.[17]

This had several consequences for the newspaper. Riding an omnibus or street railway was a novel experience. For the first time in human history, people other than the very wealthy could, as a part of their daily life, ride in vehicles they were not responsible for driving. Their eyes and their hands were free; they could read on the bus. George Juergens has suggested that the *World*'s change to a sensational style and layout was adapted to the needs of commuters: reading on the bus was difficult with the small print and large-sized pages of most papers. So the *World* reduced the size of the page, increased the size of headlines and the use of pictures, and developed the "lead" paragraph, in which all of the most vital information of a story would be concentrated.[18] From the 1840s, the "lead" had been pushed by the high cost of telegraphic transmission of news; now it was pulled by the abbreviated moments in which newspapers were being read. It is likely, then, that the growing use of illustration and large headlines in newspapers was as much an adaptation to the new habits of the middle class as to the new character of the immigrant working class. . . .

JOURNALISM AS INFORMATION: THE RISE OF THE *NEW YORK TIMES*

The *World* may have set the pace for modern mass-circulation journalism, but after 1896 the *New York Times* established the standard. *The Journalist,* in a 1902 editorial on "Standards in

American Journalism," recalled Charles Dudley Warner's claim in 1881 that the successful newspaper of the future would be the best newspaper: ". . . only that type of newspaper can live which represents something, accurately and sufficiently, to command a growing and attached clientele." *The Journalist* took this to be a prophecy of the success of the *New York Times:* ". . . there is a clear recognition as the road to substantial success in the newspaper business of the course which the *New York Times* has aimed to follow. . . ."[19] Reporter and newspaper critic Will Irwin wrote in 1911 that the *Times* came "the nearest of any newspaper to presenting a truthful picture of life in New York and the world at large."[20] Melville Stone, writing in the *Times'* seventy-fifth anniversary issue (1926), praised publisher Adolph Ochs for having defied the view that only the sensational newspaper could be a successful newspaper: "He in the end taught them [his competitors] that decency meant dollars."[21] There would probably have been little dissent from Frank Presbrey's estimation of the *Times,* in his 1929 *History and Development of Advertising,* as "the world's most influential newspaper. . . ."[22]

George Jones, who had edited the *Times* from 1869 until his death in 1891, had boasted that no man had ever been asked to subscribe to, or advertise in, the *Times.*[23] Ochs had no such contempt for solicitation. He became the first publisher, in 1898, to solicit circulation by telephone. He offered a bicycle tour of France and England to the one hundred persons bringing in the most new subscribers. The former campaign, of course, reached only the relatively well-to-do who had telephones. The latter scheme focused on school and college teachers and stressed, in the contest advertising, that "To be seen reading *The New York Times* is a stamp of respectability."[24]

Two months after Ochs took over the paper, the famous motto, "All the News That's Fit to Print," first appeared on the editorial page. At the same time, Ochs started a circulation-building contest offering $100 for a better slogan. The winning entry was "All the World's News, but Not a School for Scandal." Still, the editors preferred their own invention, and by February, 1897, "All the News That's Fit to Print" was moved permanently to the front page.

The *Times'* slogan, like its general statement of policy, emphasized decency as much as accuracy. The *Times* could not, and did not, compete with the *World* and the *Journal* for circulation; advertising in *The Journalist* in 1902, the *Times* claimed the highest circulation of any newspaper in the city—and then, in smaller print, excepted the *World* and the *Journal,* as if they were in another category of publication altogether.[25] In a sense, they were, and the *Times* used them as a foil in promoting itself. The *Times* joined the *Sun* and *Press* and other papers in a new "moral war" in journalism. It pointedly advertised itself with the slogan, "It does not soil the breakfast cloth," as opposed to the "yellow" journals.[26] Some items from the *Times,* in the winter of 1897, are probably representative of its attitude toward the yellow press. In a story headed "The Modern Newspaper" on February 12, the *Times* covered a speech at the Press Club of Colgate University given by the city editor of the *Utica Observer* in which editor W. W. Canfield attacked papers which padded news, printed private matters, spread indecent literature, and proved themselves unreliable. He pleaded for more newspapers like the *Times.* "A newspaper," he said, "was declared to be a companion, and surely the intelligent would not accept as a companion the vicious and the depraved." On the same day, the *Times* editorialized on "Freak Journalism and the Ball." It attacked the *World*'s extravagant coverage of the Bradley Martin ball at the Waldorf, suggesting that the *World*'s artists made their drawings of the festivities before the ball took place. (It should be observed that the *Times* did not skimp on its own coverage of the ball. It reported the gala affair in a page-one, column-one story on February 12 and devoted all of page two to detailing who the guests were, what they wore, and where they dined before the great event.) . . .

There is, then, a moral dimension to the reading of different kinds of newspapers; there is pride and shame in reading. This helps establish the plausibility of the hypothesis that the *Times'* readership was not won simply by the utility of the articles it printed for businessmen and lawyers or the resonance of its political outlook with the politics of affluent readers. The *Times* attracted readers among the wealthy and among those aspiring to wealth and status, in part, because it was socially approved. It was itself a badge of respectability.

But this only poses the question in a different way: what made the *Times* respectable? What made it seem morally superior? Was it deemed respectable because it appealed to the affluent? Or did it appeal to the affluent because it was respectable? And if the latter, is "respectability" to be understood as a moral ideal emerging from the life experience of a particular social group at a particular time or as a moral ideal with legitimate claims to wider allegiance or, perhaps, both?

This repeats, within the field of journalism, perennial questions about high culture and popular culture. What distinguishes them? Can we find any grounds for asserting that "art" is superior to popular culture? The question is of sociological interest because the taste for high culture is so regularly associated with educated and wealthy classes, the taste for popular culture, with lower classes. And yet, while the tastes of different classes remain different from one another in a given period, they change over time. Up until about the Civil War in the United States, the most sophisticated elements in the population preferred their literature, and even their journalism, flowery rather than plain, magniloquent rather than straightforward.[27] By

1900, when "information" journalism was sponsored by an economic and social elite, it was prized, but in 1835, when the first steps toward an information model were taken by the penny press in challenge of the elite of the day, it was reviled. The moral war between information journalism and story journalism in New York in the 1890s was, like the moral wars of the 1830s, a cover for class conflict. . . .

The readers of the *World* were relatively dependent and nonparticipant. The experience engendered by affluence and education makes one comfortable with a certain journalistic orientation, one which may indeed be, in some respects, more mature, more encompassing, more differentiated, more integrated. It may also be, in its own ways, more limited; refinement in newspapers, people, and sugar, is bleaching. If the *World*'s readers might have longed for more control of their lives, the readers of the *Times* may have wished for more nutrients in theirs.

At the turn of the century and even as late as the 1920s, "objectivity" was not a term journalists or critics of journalism used. Newspapers were criticized for failing to stick to the facts, and the *Times* boasted that it printed "all the news"—by which it meant information. But this was not objectivity; the attachment to information did not betray much anxiety about the subjectivity of personal perspective. The *Times* in 1900 trusted to information, that body of knowledge understandable in itself without context (or with a context taken for granted). That was not to last. By the 1920s, journalists no longer believed that facts could be understood in themselves; they no longer held to the sufficiency of information; they no longer shared in the vanity of neutrality that had characterized the educated middle class of the Progressive era. In the twentieth century, the skepticism and suspicion which thinkers of the late nineteenth century, like Nietzsche, taught, became part of general education. People came to see even the findings of facts as interested, even memory and dreams as selective, even rationality itself a front for interest or will or prejudice. This influenced journalism in the 1920s and 1930s and gave rise to the ideal of objectivity as we know it.

Notes

1. George Herbert Mead, "The Nature of Aesthetic Experience," *International Journal of Ethics* 36 (July 1926): 390. John Dewey made a similar point: "...the newspaper is the only genuinely popular form of literature we have achieved. The newspaper hasn't been ashamed of localism, it has revelled in it, perhaps wallowed is the word. I am not arguing that it is high-class literature, or for the most part good literature, even from its own standpoint. But it is permanently successful romance and drama; and that much can hardly be said for anything else in our literary lines." ("Americanism and Localism," *The Dial* 68 [June 1920]: 686).

2. Walter Benjamin, *Illuminations* (New York: Schocken Books, 1969), pp. 88–89.

3. Alvin Gouldner, *The Dialectic of Ideology and Technology* (New York: Seabury Press, 1976); and Basil Bernstein, "Elaborated and Restricted Codes" in "The Ethnography of Communication," ed. John Gumperz and Dell Hymes, *American Anthropologist* 66, (1964), pt. 2: 55–69. See also Basil Bernstein, *Class, Codes, and Control* (New York: Schocken Books, 1974).

4. Julian S. Rammelkamp, *Pulitzer's* Post-Dispatch *1878–1883* (Princeton: Princeton University Press, 1967), p. 109.

5. Ibid., p. 239.

6. *New York World,* September 30, 1884, quoted in Willard G. Bleyer, *Main Currents in the History of American Journalism* (Boston: Houghton Mifflin, 1927), p. 333.

7. Frank Presbrey, *The History and Development of Advertising* (Garden City, N.Y.: Doubleday, Doran, 1929), p. 356.

8. *The Journalist* (August 22, 1885); quoted in George Juergens, *Joseph Pulitzer and the New York World* (Princeton: Princeton University Press, 1966), p. 95.

9. Robert Taft, *Photography and the American Scene* (New York: Macmillan, 1942), p. 428.

10. Juergens, *Joseph Pulitzer,* pp. 98–105.

11. Ibid., p. 27. Juergens stresses the conservatism of *World* typography in Pulitzer's first years.

12. Quoted in W. A. Swanberg, *Citizen Hearst* (New York: Charles Scribner's, 1961), p. 90. The statement appeared in a *Journal* editorial on November 8, 1896.

13. Melville Stone, *Fifty Years a Journalist* (Garden City, N.Y.: Doubleday, Page, 1921), pp. 53, 107.

14. Juergens, *Joseph Pulitzer,* pp. 56–57.

15. Charles Dana, *The Art of Newspaper Making* (New York: D. Appleton, 1900), p. 84. From a lecture delivered at Cornell University, January 11, 1894.

16. Juergens, *Joseph Pulitzer,* p. 57.

17. See Theodore Hershberg et al., "The 'Journey-to-Work': An Empirical Investigation of Work, Residence and Transportation, Philadelphia, 1850 and 1880" in *Toward an Interdisciplinary History of the City: Work, Space, Family and Group Experience in Nineteenth-Century Philadelphia,* ed. Theodore Hershberg (New York: Oxford University Press, forthcoming).

18. Juergens, *Joseph Pulitzer,* pp. 39, 47.

19. *The Journalist* 32 (December 27, 1902).

20. Will Irwin, "The American Newspaper. VI: The Editor and the News," *Colliers* 47 (April 1, 1911).

21. *New York Times,* September 19, 1926.

22. Presbrey, *History and Development of Advertising,* p. 354.

23. Elmer Davis, *History of the* New York Times: *1851–1921* (New York: The New York Times, 1921), p. 218.

24. Meyer Berger, *The Story of the* New York Times *1851–1951* (New York: Simon and Schuster, 1951; reprint ed., New York: Arno Press, 1970), p. 124.

25. *The Journalist* 32 (December 20, 1902).

26. Davis, *History of the New York Times,* pp. 223–224.

27. Edmund Wilson, *Patriotic Gore* (London: Oxford University Press, 1962), pp. 635–669, discusses the shift in American tastes in prose and in oratory from the well-embroidered to the efficient and plain-spoken in the mid-nineteenth century.

19 THE TELEPHONE TAKES COMMAND

Claude S. Fischer

Claude S. Fischer is professor of sociology at the University of California at Berkeley. He is the author of America Calling: A Social History of the Telephone to 1940.

FOUNDING THE TELEPHONE INDUSTRY

. . . Alexander Graham Bell had been trying to improve the telegraph when he constructed the first telephone in March of 1876. That month he filed his patent claim, later to be a matter of legal dispute, and in May he showed the primitive device at the Centennial Exposition in Philadelphia. Alexander Graham Bell and his associates spent much of the next year or so giving demonstrations around the country of this "wonder," sometimes borrowing telegraph wires for long-distance calls (and sometimes failing). Watson would, for example, sing over the telephone to an audience gathered elsewhere in town. In 1877 a New York poster announced "An Entertainment of the Sunday School of Old John St. M. E. Church," including recitations, singing, and an exhibition of "Prof. Bell's Speaking and Singing Telephone." Admission was 25 cents.[1] These stunts garnered considerable publicity and awe as journalists relayed the news around the world.

Making a business of what was a novelty was more difficult. The backers of Alexander Graham Bell's telegraph work were his father-in-law, Gardiner Hubbard, and the father of one of his speech students, Thomas Sanders. In July 1877 the three men reorganized as the Bell Telephone Company, with Hubbard as trustee, and began seriously marketing the device. Initially, they leased pairs of telephones for simple two-point communications, commonly between two buildings of a business or between a businessman's home and office. The opening of the first

telephone exchange, or switchboard, in New Haven in January 1878 was a profound step. Any subscriber could now be connected to any other.

The key financial decision, one of great long-term import, was Hubbard's determination that the company, as the exclusive builder of telephones, would lease the instruments and license local providers of telephone service. Bell thus controlled both the service and the consumers' equipment. (It is as if gas companies exclusively leased stoves and furnaces or electric utilities were the sole lessors of lamps.[2]) In this way Hubbard attracted franchisees around the country who used their own capital to rent telephones, string wires, build switchboards, and sell interconnections. Bell provided the instruments and technical advice and, in turn, collected rental fees. Over the years the company used its leverage on license renewals to set rates and to dictate technical and other features of the service. This close supervision allowed the company to convert a confederation of local franchisees into a "system" of local "Bell Operating Companies" acting in concert. Eventually, AT&T replaced the rents it charged with stock ownership in the local companies and, using this leverage, set common nationwide policies. But in the earliest years perhaps dozens of entrepreneurs in towns across America—some rounded up by Watson himself on marketing trips—made individual licensing agreements with Hubbard.[3]

By mid-1878 the telephone business was in ferment. About 10,000 Bell instruments were in use throughout the nation, but Bell now had serious competition. Western Union, already located in telegraph offices almost everywhere, adopted telephones designed by Thomas Edison and Elisha Gray to offer a competing service. Bell sued Western Union for patent infringement and hurriedly founded exchanges around the country to preempt markets. At the end of 1879 the contestants settled: Western Union conceded Bell all patent rights and instruments. In return, Bell agreed to renounce telegraph service, to pay Western Union 20 percent of gross receipts for a time, and to grant the telegraph company partial interest in a few local Bell companies. The resolution left Bell in early 1880 with about 60,000 subscribers in exchanges scattered about the country and a monopoly on the telephone business. (About 30 years later, Bell briefly absorbed Western Union until pressured by the federal government to sell it off.)

THE ERA OF MONOPOLY: 1880–1893

The typical telephone system of the 1880s was a cumbersome affair.... The instrument itself was a set of three boxes. The top box held a magneto generator, a crank, and a bell. The middle box had a speaker tube protruding forward and a receiver tube hanging from the side. The third box contained a wet-cell battery that needed to be refilled periodically and occasionally leaked. A caller turned the crank to signal the switchboard operator; the signal mechanically released a shutter on the switchboard in the central office, showing the origin of the call. The operator plugged her headset into the designated socket and asked the caller whom he or she was seeking. Then the operator rang the desired party and connected the two by wires and plugs in the switchboard. The two parties talked, usually loudly and with accompanying static, and then hung up. In some systems the caller cranked again to signal the end of the conversation. In others the operator listened in periodically to find out when the conversation was over so that she could disconnect the plugs.

The race to build exchanges, rapid adoption by businessmen, and other changes raised some technical problems in the 1880s. Edward J. Hall, considered "the most far-seeing, all around competent and efficient telephone man of his day," complained from his franchise in Buffalo as early as February 1880 of too much business and too many calls to provide subscribers adequate service.[4] One consequence of growth was increasing congestion at the switchboards. Spaghetti-like masses of wires crisscrossed the boards, which in turn grew in number, size, and complexity beyond the capacities of the operators struggling to reach around one another. Temporary solutions did not solve the problem, especially in the large urban centers, until the late 1890s.[5] In some places new electric and streetcar power lines created intolerable interference on the adjacent telephone lines. Some observers believe that this problem stunted telephone development in the late 1880s. (This nuisance recurred in rural America with the construction of power lines by the Rural Electrification Administration in the 1930s.)

Bell responded to the challenges by rebuilding its hardware. It eventually replaced single iron or steel wires (a system in which the electrical circuit was completed through the ground) with pairs of copper wires that returned the current. Bell also replaced wet batteries with a common-system battery; the power for all telephones on a line now came from the central exchange. In addition, Bell eventually developed new switchboards and procedures to alleviate switchboard congestion. These and other technical developments completely revamped much of Bell's telephone system by the early 1900s. Company leaders sought to develop high-quality service—clear sound, instant access, and the like—for the urban business customers they courted. To this end they rounded up as many telephone patents as possible, sponsored further research, and pooled the practical experience of their franchisees. Theodore N. Vail, as general manager and then president until 1887, used

The early telephone call boxes were artful mixtures of wood, metal, and electrical components.
National Archives of Canada.

Bell's temporary patent monopoly to secure a technical and organizational edge over all future competitors, especially by developing long-distance service.

Although not favored, like Alexander Graham Bell, by a Hollywood biography, Theodore N. Vail is a figure of mythic stature in the telephone industry and in American corporate history. Beginning as a lowly telegrapher, Vail deployed his organizational skills and modern methods to rise to superintendent of the federal Railway Mail Service. Hubbard lured Vail, then 33, away to manage the fledgling Bell company in 1878. For several years Vail pressed aggressive expansion, patent protection, and business reorganization. In 1887, by then president, Vail resigned after conflicts with a more cautious board

of financial officers. He succeeded in several business ventures around the world, but kept abreast of the telephone industry. Vail would come back.[6]

Vail's policy of establishing high-quality service meant that costs were high, especially in the larger cities where the complexities of switching were most difficult. The minimum flat rate in central Los Angeles in 1888, for example, was $4 per month plus two cents a connection after the fortieth call. This rate equaled about 10 percent of the average nonfarm employee's wages. That same year Boston subscribers paid a minimum flat rate of $6 a month.[7] In addition, Bell's affiliates took every advantage of their monopoly to levy what the market could bear. For example, when the competing telephone exchange closed in San Francisco in 1880, the Bell local raised its charges from $40 to $60 a year. The local manager justified the move: "The increase was made because the public always expects to be 'cinched' when opposing corporations consolidate and it was too good an opportunity to lose. (Moreover, it would have been wrong to disappoint the confiding public.)"[8] Conflicts with irate customers arose, the most famous of which was an 18-month boycott of telephones organized in Rochester, New York, in 1886.[9] Bell's rates began to drop as 1894 approached, probably because of the competition it anticipated when its patents expired, although Bell claimed that improved technology explained the drop in charges. By 1895 the Los Angeles rate was down by 38 percent to $2.50 a month—7 percent of wages—plus two cents a call. Even then, telephone service remained expensive.[10]

The common practice during this era and beyond was to charge customers a flat-rate for the telephone service, allowing unlimited calls. During the 1880s local Bell companies repeatedly debated and experimented with a message-rate formula, charging by the call. One argument in favor of this approach was that it would permit the basic rental fee to be lowered and thereby encourage small users, such as families, to subscribe. Edward J. Hall was a leading proponent, labeled by some the "father of the message-rate system." Another reason for a pricing change, more favored by Vail and others, was that ending flat-rate service would discourage use, and thus "cut off all the superfluous business that tends to make the operation of the business so unremunerative." Existing customers, however, resisted the change by complaining, by petitioning the town officials who issued permits for telephone poles, or, as in Rochester, by boycotting the telephone service. Not until after the era of monopoly did message-rate service become common, although still not universal, in Bell's largest exchanges.[11]

Vail's agenda went beyond securing a technical monopoly. Through various devices he centralized control of the Bell System and its affiliates. Doing so was complex, since local situations varied widely. Each regional operating company had to deal with many governments to secure permits, to fend off complaints about the unsightliness of the wires, and sometimes to negotiate rates. Still, standardized policies, as well as a superior technology, helped brace the Bell system against challenge. Vail's successors after 1887 were, in retrospect, more interested in extracting monopoly profits from the system than in securing its future. That shift in priorities would become evident when the patents expired.

Strategic disagreements about pricing policy arose inside Bell, in part from different visions of the telephone's potential. It was not at all obvious whom the telephone would serve and how. As Sidney Aronson has noted, "[T]he inventor and his backers . . . faced the formidable task of inventing uses for the telephone and impressing them on others."[12] During the first few decades of telephony, industry marketers devised a variety of applications, including transmitting sermons, broadcasting news, providing wake-up calls, and many other experiments. As late as the 1910s, the trade journal *Telephony* had an index entry under

"Telephone, novel uses of."* The industry spent considerable time, especially in the nineteenth century, simply introducing the public to the instrument and dispelling suspicions about it. . . .

Industry leaders approached telephony from their experiences with telegraphy. Alexander Graham Bell and his backers were initially trying to improve the telegraph. Theodore Vail came from a family involved in telegraphy and had been a telegrapher. Many local telephone entrepreneurs had started out selling telegraph service. An important exception was Edward J. Hall, the message-rate enthusiast, who started in his family's brick business after earning a degree in metallurgy. Hall established the first Buffalo telephone exchange, left the telephone business a few years later, and was lured back by Vail to manage long-distance development in 1885 and then Southern Bell for over 10 years.[13] Because telegraphy defined the background of most executives,[14] and because Americans in the nineteenth century used the telegraph almost exclusively as a business tool, it was logical that Bell used the telegraphy model to define the telephone as a device for business as well.

Who were the first telephone subscribers? Physicians were notable among the early users. The telephone allowed them to hear of emergencies quickly and to check in at their offices when they were away. Druggists typically had telephones, as well.[15] But businessmen formed the primary market.

Bell found some businessmen hesitant to replace the telegraph with the telephone because they valued a written record. Nevertheless, some manufacturers, lawyers, bankers, and the like—and later small shopkeepers—adopted the technology. In 1891 the New York and New Jersey Telephone Company served 937 physicians and hospitals, 401 drug stores, 363 liquor stores,

---

*Included under that entry in volume 71, for example, are "degree conferred by telephone, dispatching tugs in harbor service, gauging water by telephone, telephoning in an aeroplane."

315 livery stables, 162 metalworking plants, 146 lawyers, 126 contractors, 100 printing shops—7322 commercial customers all told—but only 1442 residences. Residences with telephones were typically those of doctors or of business owners or managers.[16]

One issue for Bell was whether it could fruitfully expand into the general residential market (that is, beyond the households of the business elite). In late 1883, noting that "the Telephone business has passed its experimental stage," Vail surveyed affiliates around the country, asking, among other questions: "Is it desirable and what would be the most practical way, to provide a service which would be in the reach of families, etc.?" His aide summarized the responses:

> There would seem to be but one opinion on this query and that is, that it is *most desirable*. The difficulty which presents itself is the manner in which the desired end should be reached. It is admitted that a great increase in the business would occur by the introduction of a rate and system, whereby the Telephone would be made universal so to speak, amongst families, and several modes [are] suggested . . . [including more pay-telephone stations, party lines, and lower residential rates]. It would appear from many of the answers to this query, "that a reduction in royalty" would be a necessity. . . .[17]

There was the rub: Locals would have to reduce their rates, and to ease that reduction Bell would have to lower its charges on the locals. Except for a handful of populists in this era—notably Edward Hall of Buffalo; John I. Sabin, later president of Pacific Telephone; and Angus Hibbard of Chicago—the consensus was that any increased business would not make up for the profits lost by reducing rates, even in a measured-rate system. At the time many also believed that operating costs per subscriber increased as the number of customers increased because of the technical complications of interconnection.[18] Only later did industry analysts appreciate that, as a network, telephones became more attractive as more people subscribed

and that there might be economies of scale. George Ladd, president of Pacific Telephone in 1883, expressed the conservative position. He wrote to Vail that he opposed the reduction of residential rates because it could not pay and customers would not be grateful: "I am opposed to low rates unless made necessary by competition. . . . Cheaper service will simply multiply the nuisance of wires and poles and excite [political pressure to put wires underground], without materially improving profits or permanently improving relations with the public."[19] Residential service was therefore a stepchild in the system.

This attitude, later described even by Bell's friends as arrogant, predominated in the company. In 1906, for example, New England Bell commissioned an attorney to study telephone service in the Midwest. In its earlier history, he reported, "the public interest received scant attention" from Bell companies. They "were almost, if not quite, inexcusably slow in coming to an intelligent apprehension of the public need and desire for increased and improved telephone service."[20]

Bell managers were also skeptical about providing service in smaller communities. Businessmen in several small California towns, for example, appealed to Pacific Telephone for service but were turned away. In a few cases local entrepreneurs built bootleg systems, risking lawsuits.[21] AT&T focused on providing big-city businesses with high-quality service, including long-distance calling, at high prices. Its representatives later explained that the pressures of escalating demand and technical renovations prevented the company from pursuing wider markets until the mid-1890s.[22] Still, most Bell managers saw few possibilities for expansion, and nearly none for greater profit, in the general residential market or even the business market outside the major centers.

Between 1880 and 1893 the number of telephones in the United States grew from about 60,000—roughly one per thousand people—to about 260,000—or one per 250 people. The vast

The early urban telephone system required large numbers of telephone operators whose job was to connect the sender and receiver of a call through exchanges like this one. *National Archives of Canada.*

majority, more than two-thirds, were located in businesses.[23] This expansion, while dramatic in the early years, slowed after 1883, perhaps because of the technical problems or, just as likely, because of predatory monopoly pricing.

NOTES

1. Reproduced in AT&T, *A Capsule History of the Bell System* (New York: AT&T, 1979), 11.
2. Crandall, "Has the AT&T Break-up Raised Telephone Rates?" *The Brookings Review* 5 (Winter), 40–41.
3. On the early evolution of the Bell System, see especially Robert Garnett, *The Telephone Enterprise* (Baltimore: Johns Hopkins Press, 1985); Kenneth Lipartito, *The Bell System and Regional Business* (Baltimore: Johns Hopkins Press, 1989).
4. Letter of 2 February 1880, in "Measured Rate Service," Box 1127, AT&THA [American Tele-

phone and Telegraph Historical Archives]. In 1884 Hall recalled the situation in 1879: "In Buffalo we had so many subscribers that the service became demoralized. Our switchboards were not equipped to handle the necessary amount of business . . . growing under the high pressure of competition" (Hall, "Notes on History of the Bell Telephone Co. of Buffalo, New York," [1884], 9). . . .
5. See Robert J. Chapius, *100 Years of Telephone Switching* (New York: Elsevier, 1982); Morton Mueller, "The Switchboard Problem," *Technology and Culture* 30 (July) 534–60.
6. See Albert Paine, *Theodore N. Vail* (New York: Harper, 1929). Accounts of Vail appear in most telephone histories.
7. Los Angeles: "Telephone on the Pacific Coast, 1878–1923," Box 1045, AT&THA; Boston: Moyer, "Urban Growth," 352.
8. Letter (no. 75968) to Vail, 13 February 1884, in "San Francisco Exchange," Box 1141, AT&THA.

9. Bell had planned to switch from flat-rate to measured-rate (per-call) charges. With the support of city hall, subscribers organized a boycott. Eventually, Bell agreed to delay measured service for five years, place its wires underground, and pay the legal costs. See H. B. MacMeal, *The Story of Independent Telephony* (Chicago: Independent Pioneer Telephony Assoc., 1934), 111.

10. Los Angeles rates: "Telephone on the Pacific Coast, 1878–1923," Box 1045, AT&THA. Wage data come from the United States Bureau of the Census, *Historical Statistics of the United States,* tables D735–38.

11. On the debate over rates, see "Measured Rate Service" and other files in Box 1127, AT&THA. The quotation about "superfluous business" is from a Vail letter to Hall dated 7 February 1880.

12. Sidney Aronson, "Bell's Electrical Toy," in *The Social Impact of the Telephone,* ed. Ithiel de Sola Paul (Cambridge, MA: MIT, 1977), 19.

13. Biographical notes on Hall were culled from press releases and clippings provided by Mildred Ettlinger at AT&THA. See also Lipartito, *The Bell System,* for an account of Hall's work in the South.

14. William Patten, *Pioneering the Telephone in Canada* (Montreal: Telephone Pioneers, 1926), 1ff, points out that Canadian telephone executives also had backgrounds in telegraphy.

15. On doctors and telephony, see Sidney Aronson, "*Lancet* on the Telephone," *Medical History* 21 (January): 69–87, and S. Aronson and R. Greenbaum, "Take Two Aspirin and Call Me in the Morning," Queens College, N.Y. Typescript courtesy of Sidney Aronson, 1985. Histories of telephony often note the early role of doctors....

16. Letter to Thomas Sherwin, 11 July 1891, in "Classification of Subscribers," Box 1247, AT&THA.

17. Circular by Vail, 28 December 1883, and attachments, in Box 1080, AT&THA.

18. Mueller, "The Switchboard Problem."

19. Responses to 28 December 1883, circular by Vail, Box 1080, AT&THA.

20. G. W. Anderson, *Telephone Competition in the Middle West and Its Lesson in New England* (Boston: New England Telephone & Telegraph, 1906), 13–14.

21. The California cases are in "PT&T News Bureau Files," Telephone Pioneer Communications Museum of San Francisco, Archives and Historical Research Center....

22. See, e.g., the rationale for not pursuing wider markets as expressed in the United States Bureau of the Census, *Special Reports: Telephones and Telegraphs 1902* (1906), chap. 10. The stress on high quality was indeed important. In the South, for example, local managers were discouraged from building simple, low-cost systems, because of the national company's insistence on maintaining quality levels needed for the long-distance network (Lipartito, *The Bell System*)....

23. In the New York–New Jersey data over 80 percent of telephones were located in businesses. In the same year, in Kingston, Ontario, about 70 percent of telephones were located in businesses, although many officially listed as residential were really used for business by people such as physicians [Robert M. Pike, "Kingston Adopts the Telephone," *Urban History Review* 18 (June): 32–47; Robert M. Pike and Vincent Mosco, "Canadian Consumers and Telephone Pricing," *Telecommunications Policy* 10 (March): 17–32].

20 EARLY USES OF THE TELEPHONE

Carolyn Marvin

Carolyn Marvin is professor of communications at the University of Pennsylvania. Her recent book, When the Old Technologies Were New, *provides a richly detailed social history of electric communication in the latter part of the nineteenth century.*

In the late nineteenth century, single events such as a declaration of war, a baseball game, a church service, or a concert were transmitted by new technologies with unprecedented immediacy to scattered audiences *on occasion.* Although modern media transmit content of a similar kind, late-nineteenth-century telephone occasions otherwise bear little resemblance to twentieth-century mass media programming. Nineteenth-century telephone occasions were derived transmissions of independently occurring events and were intended to extend the primary audiences of the pulpit, stage, concert hall, and playing field. Wholly invented programming, by contrast, is a distinctive social feature of electronic mass media.

Commercial efforts to enlarge audiences electrically for some regularly repeated occasions in the late nineteenth century were generally of short duration; the audiences they attracted were small. Electrophone parties in Britain were said to be a pastime of the idle rich, not the humble poor.[1] Electrophone Ltd., one of the sturdier British companies to take up regular telephone transmission, piped sermons from the most prestigious pulpits and plays from the most prestigious theatres to London's leading hospitals for the edification of affluent patients, and to occasional private residences as well. Nevertheless, twelve years after its incorporation, Electrophone had a regular subscriber audience of barely six hundred.[2]

But from 1893 until after World War I, when a number of private companies and national states began to create radio broadcasting systems, an organization in Budapest was a remarkable exception to the usual pattern. This was the Telefon Hirmondó, which for almost a generation transmitted daily programming over telephone wires to supplement the regular telephone service of more than six thousand subscribers. *Hirmondó* was a Magyar term for the crier who shouted the news from the center of the medieval village for all to hear. Today it denotes a radio announcer. Its semantic transformation followed a path directly through the career of the Telefon Hirmondó. For twenty years the Hirmondó's audience received a full daily schedule of political, economic, and sporting news, lectures, plays, concerts, and recitations. The language of the Telefon Hirmondó was Magyar, the language of Hungarian nationalism. In operation, the Telefon Hirmondó was a closed and exclusive system of cultural communication among the Hungarian elite during the last decades of Magyar power before World War I, a fact that appears to account for both its economic and its cultural staying power.

The Telefon Hirmondó was the brainchild of Tivadar Puskás, a Hungarian engineer who had worked on Thomas Edison's staff of inventors and researchers at Menlo Park. To Puskás, according to Edison, belonged the original credit for suggesting the concept of the telephone switchboard that made the telephone a powerful and practical means of communication. Accounts of the Telefon Hirmondó were followed with interest in the British and American press, and a short-lived imitation of it appeared in the United States. It provided perhaps the only example of sustained and systematic programming in the nineteenth century that truly prefigures twentieth-century broadcasting systems.

The origins of the Telefon Hirmondó lay in the novel and popular theatrophone exhibition that Puskás helped mount at the Paris Exposition Internationale d'Electricité in 1881. The following year he staged his own theatrophone demonstration in Budapest by transmitting a National Theatre opera performance to a nearby grand ball.[3] In the meantime, Puskás's brother, Ferenc, acquired the first telephone concession in Budapest, and the Puskás family hired Nikola Tesla, a longtime friend, to engineer its construction.[4] The Budapest telephone system prospered under Ferenc Puskás, and in 1892 Tivadar Puskás, who had played a minor role in some of the more exciting electrical developments of the age and knew many of its foremost inventors and engineers personally, returned to Budapest to implement his own remarkable idea of a Telefon Hirmondó. The first program was transmitted from the central telephone exchange to one thousand regular telephone subscribers in 1893. Within weeks of the inception of the Telefon Hirmondó, Tivadar Puskás was dead. His creation outlived him by almost a quarter of a century.

At first the Telefon Hirmondó's programming consisted of news summaries read at the beginning of each hour and immediately repeated. Silence reigned until the next hour's transmission. Five months into the new experiment, *Science Siftings* reported:

> The news collector does his work in the night, and having his budget filled he takes his place in the central office at nine in the morning and begins to tell his story, which is given in a telegraphic style, clear, condensed, and precise. In five minutes after the first delivery the budget of news is repeated, in case some of the subscribers may not have heard. It consists for the most part of home events and news of Hungary. At ten o'clock the foreign news is given, and after eleven the doings of the Hungarian Parliament. Various items of city news are given during the day.[5]

News in the daytime was balanced by cultural programs in the evening—perhaps a report of a lecture at the Hungarian Academy, or the recitation "with all due emphasis" of a new poem.

Efforts to transmit music met with poor success and provided the first indications of a problem that increased with the listening audience. Simply stated, the addition of subscriber outlets diminished the volume of sound for every subscriber. When control of the Hirmondó passed out of the hands of the Puskás family in 1894, a new distribution system that bypassed the regular telephone network eliminated this and other technical problems.[6] The new company was granted the same right to place its wires as the telephone and telegraph companies. By 1900 the Telefon Hirmondó employed over 150 people in its offices at 22 Megrendelhetö Ráköczi, on one of the "finest avenues" in Budapest.[7]

The news operation was like that of any newspaper. News from abroad came by telegraph. Local news was assigned to a staff of twelve reporters. A special staff assigned to the galleries of the Hungarian and Austrian Houses of Parliament forwarded half-hourly reports of the latest developments.[8] Galley proofs of every story were printed by hand roller presses in parallel columns on sheets of paper two feet by six inches. Several sheets constituted the daily program. The work of the "stentors" who read the news was thought to be so exhausting that they were rotated at ten-minute intervals in groups of four.[9]

By 1896 the daily program of the Telefon Hirmondó had achieved virtually its final form. This version is translated from a German publication, which published it in full:

"Telefon Hirmondó" Order of the Day

9.30–10.00	Daily calendar, Vienna news (telephone report), latest telegrams (arrived during the night), train departures listed in the railway gazette
10.00–10.30	Report of the stock exchange
10.30–11.00	Review and summary of the day's newspapers, telegrams
11.00–11.15	Report of the stock exchange
11.15–11.30	Theatre news, sport and local news
11.30–11.45	Report of the stock exchange
11.45–12.00	Parliamentary, foreign and provincial news
12.00–12.30	Parliamentary, military, political and court news
12.30–1.30	Report of the stock exchange
1.30–2.00	Repeat of the most interesting news read so far
2.00–2.30	Parliamentary and municipal news, telegrams
2.30–3.00	Parliamentary, telegraphic and local news
3.00–3.30	Report of the stock exchange

3.30–4.00	Parliamentary news, exact zone time, weather report, medley
4.00–4.30	Report of the stock exchange
4.30–5.00	Vienna news (telephone report), political economy
5.00–5.30	Report on theatre, art, literature, sport and fashion, theatre and amusement notices, calendar for the next day
5.30–6.00	Legal, local and telegraphic news
6.00–6.30	Repeat of the most interesting news read so far
about 6.00	Presentation of the Royal Hungarian Opera House, or performance of the Folk Theatre

If nothing is heard at this time, this is because of a scheduled:

7.00–8.15	Pause
8.15–8.25	Report of the stock exchange
8.25–9.00	Concert of the *Telefon Hirmondó*
9.00–10.00	Latest telegraphic, local and market report
10.00–10.30	The above news will be presented here at the conclusion of the performance of the Folk Theatre

Thursday evening

6.00–6.45   Children's concert

Program for Sundays and holidays

11.00–11.15	Daily calendar, report of the stock exchange
11.15–12.00	Review and summary of the day's newspapers, telegrams, gazette
12.00–12.30	Municipal news, sport and theatre news
12.30–1.00	Local and Vienna news (telephone report)
4.00	Grand concert of the *Telefon Hirmondó*[10]

Beginning about 1896, nationally known authors read serial installments of their novels, to the delight, it was said, of the female audience. A popular innovation the following year was a special time signal, a powerful oscillator that buzzed for precisely fifteen seconds before each hour.[11]

Photographs and illustrated advertising posters show that subscribers listened to the Hirmondó through two small round earpieces hanging from a diamond-shaped board mounted on the wall.[12] The audience for which the service was intended apparently possessed wealth, education, and leisure. Its cultural relaxations were those of the opera and the theatre. Its attachment to sport was aristocratic. The latest intelligence from the principal Hungarian and Austrian racetracks, the cycling and automobile track, and the rugby field and billiard table was "flashed over the wires the moment the results are known."[13] Its children received proper cultural exposure in a weekly children's program of short stories, songs, recitations, and instrumental music.[14]

The Hirmondó devoted the largest share of its programming to the conditions and exigencies of the financial world. Even on Sundays and during evening programs with an artistic and performing emphasis, due attention was given to the stock exchange. Subscribers were kept posted about developments in the Hungarian and Austrian exchanges and the foreign exchanges, including Wall Street and London.[15] News was also communicated directly from the agriculture districts of the country for speculators in corn and wheat.

Our hypothesis that the audience of the Telefon Hirmondó was composed of elite and influential Budapest citizens is confirmed for the few subscribers whose names we have—the prime minister and all the members of the Hungarian cabinet, the mayor of Budapest, and Moric Jokai, a Magyar author and celebrity whose work was often featured by the Hirmondó.[16] A partial street-wiring diagram published in an 1897 Hungarian encyclopedia shows

Telefon Hirmondó connections to what was then and is still a wealthy section of the city, an area of elegant avenues, fine hotels, government buildings, and luxurious private residences within a famous half-circle of boulevards on the Pest bank of the Danube River.[17] The Telefon Hirmondó was also connected with doctors' waiting rooms, large coffeehouses and cafés, hospitals and hotels, merchants' and lawyers' offices, babershops and dentists' parlors.[18] By 1896 the Hirmondó boasted six thousand subscribers, but this figure represented barely one percent of the population of Budapest.[19] The number of subscribers remained almost constant until 1917, after which reports of the Telefon Hirmondó dropped out of the foreign press. The audience of the Hirmondó was probably larger, since each household may have represented several listeners, and semipublic installations seemed to attract many different listeners. A traveler's account from 1908 explained how this worked:

> You may be seated as I was in the reading-room of one of the hotels or in a large coffee-house, when suddenly a rush is made for a telephone-looking instrument [the Telefon Hirmondó] which hangs from the wall. In time perhaps you will become one of these "rushers."[20]

Nevertheless, subscription figures were small, a fact that cannot be accounted for by price, since the installation of the Hirmondó apparatus was free, and subscriber fees were only a penny a day. Not even the fact that the Hirmondó transmitted exclusively in Magyar, a minority language, explains the size of its subscribing audience, since Magyar was also the official language of Parliament, the universities, and the high courts. (Foreign-language lessons were regularly featured in Hirmondó programming, but not instruction in Croatian or Slovak, the languages of peasant peoples within Hungarian boundaries. Subscribers learned French, English, or Italian—useful languages to the cosmopolitan leisured, to merchants and diplomats.[21]) The most likely hypothesis is that Hirmondó connections were officially limited, since no citizen received regular telephone service without government permission.[22] The Hirmondó was authorized to offer its services by an exclusive government license; its programming was identified with the ruling Magyar elite.

Articles on the Telefon Hirmondó appeared frequently in European and American journals during the 1890s and early twentieth century. It was featured in the expert press, in penny weeklies with mass appeal, and in sober middle-class monthlies. Popular comment about the Hirmondó associated it with leisurely Continental lifestyles, since British and American observers often remarked with disapproval that the length of the connecting wires made it possible for subscribers to recline while listening to its programs.[23] Little is known of the Telefon Hirmondó following World War I, during which most of its exterior installations were destroyed. In 1925 the Telefon Hirmondó and Hungarian Radio Broadcasting were combined into a single organization, and the Hirmondó became merely a wire-diffusion agency for studio-broadcast programs.[24]

In the United States at least one brief experiment was directly inspired by the Hirmondó. This was the Telephone Herald of Newark, New Jersey. After sampling the Telefon Hirmondó on vacation in Budapest, a former *New York Herald* advertising manager, M. M. Gillam, set about organizing a similar enterprise in the United States.[25] Gillam and William E. Gun, builder of the battleship *Oregon,* organized the New Jersey Telephone Herald Company with promises of financial backing from a wealthy New York coal magnate. Just as the service was scheduled to begin operating, in March 1911, the New York Telephone Company reneged on its contract to lease wires to the Telephone Herald, which it regarded as a competing public utility.[26] After six months of legal wrangling, the New Jersey Public Utilities Commission held the telephone company to its original agreement. The Telephone Herald inaugurated service on October 23, 1911, with the following daily program:

Daily Program of the "Telephone Herald"

8.00	Exact astronomical time
8.00–9.00	Weather, late telegrams, London exchange quotations, chief items of interest from the morning papers
9.00–9.45	Special sales at the various stores; social program for the day
9.45–10.00	Local personals and small items
10.00–11.30	New York Stock Exchange quotations and market letter
11.30–12.00	New York miscellaneous items
Noon	Exact astronomical time
12.00–12.30	Latest general news; naval, military, and Congressional notes
12.30–1.00	Midday New York Stock Exchange quotations
1.00–2.00	Repetition of the half-day's most interesting news
2.00–2.15	Foreign cable dispatches
2.15–2.30	Trenton and Washington items
2.30–2.45	Fashion notes and household hints
2.45–3.15	Sporting news; theatrical news
3.15–3.30	New York Stock Exchange closing quotations
3.30–5.00	Music, readings, lectures
5.00–6.00	Stories and talks for the children
8.00–10.30	Vaudeville, concert, opera[27]

The schedule of items presented by the Telephone Herald was faithfully modeled on the Telefon Hirmondó's "order of the day." The style of program presentation was also familiar:

> With his mouth between the [two] transmitters the stentor reads an item, says "change," then immediately begins upon another. As the stentors have had special courses in distinct enunciation every word can be clearly heard. The work is so exhausting that one man reads only fifteen minutes, then rests for forty-five minutes while others take his place.[28]

No programming was originated by the Herald itself, besides occasional concerts performed in a room set aside for that purpose. The Telephone Herald also had no reporters of its own. Its newsroom was entirely devoted to editorial functions:

> There is the usual barn-like room meagerly furnished, with dirty windows guiltless of shades, the floor littered with waste paper and the regulation paste pot that has not been cleaned since the year one. In these familiar surroundings a couple of editors smoke cigarets and clip the morning papers, go through press reports, proofs from a local evening paper, and correspondents' manuscripts, receive telephone messages, condensing everything to the uttermost, two hundred and fifty words being the maximum limit for the most important items.[29]

Within a month of its beginning, the Telephone Herald had acquired more than a thousand subscribers, each of whom paid a nickel a day for its services. Among them were not only individuals, but a Newark department store, whose use of the Telephone Herald as a promotional draw anticipated efforts by Gimbel's and other stores several years later to attract patrons with wireless hookups.[30] The success of the department store encouraged a local restaurant to make connection. Reportedly, its customers were so interested in the news that they ceased to find fault with their food.[31] Several clubs also subscribed.

The capital reserves of the Telephone Herald proved to be unequal to the popular demand for it, and the legal contest with the telephone company had frightened off investors. With depleted financial resources, the Herald was unable to install equipment fast enough to meet its subscription orders. After three months, twenty-five hundred subscriber contracts had been drawn up, but the number of installations was not much over a thousand.[32] Soon the financial strain began to show. Employees were irregularly paid. The musical service ended abruptly one afternoon when the musicians refused to play any longer without salary. The newsroom staff of two editors and four stentors departed a month later. Lacking capital funds, the service was suspended, and then entirely disbanded.[33]

The history of the Telefon Hirmondó and its admiring imitator, the Telephone Herald, demonstrates that the notion of transmitting regular news and entertainment programming to large audiences existed well before the advent of twentieth-century wireless broadcasting. The existence of these two precursors did not generate any popular shock of recognition, however, or nurture any expert consensus that their efforts marked an inevitable path to the future. While the public was generally confident that something fantastic and all-embracing was germinating among the many remarkable contraptions of electrical communication, the boundaries of immediate possibility appeared much narrower to those closest to the technologies involved.

The historical development of mass broadcasting ahead of cable programming, which the Hirmondó more closely resembled, might have been reversed if radio had not been invented at a time when wire diffusion was still largely experimental. It was not immediately realized how significant a departure from telephony and telegraphy radio would be, however. As late as 1921, Walter Gifford, then four years away from assuming the presidency of AT&T, had difficulty visualizing separate roles for wired and wireless media in the twentieth century. He recalled in 1944:

> Nobody knew early in 1921 where radio was really headed. Everything about broadcasting was uncertain. For my own part I expected that since it was a form of telephony, and since we were in the business of furnishing wires for telephony, we were sure to be involved in broadcasting somehow. Our first vague idea, as broadcasting appeared, was that perhaps people would expect to be able to pick up a telephone and call some radio station, so that they could give radio talks to other people equipped to listen.[34]

Late in 1921 an internal Bell Telephone memorandum had projected the future of broadcasting simply as the transmission of important occasions, such as Armistice Day ceremonies or presidential inaugurations:

> We can imagine the President or other official speaking in Washington . . . and that his voice is then carried out over a network of wires extending to all the important centers of the country. . . . In each city and larger town there are halls equipped with loud speaking apparatus at which the people in the neighborhood are gathered.[35]

If historical events had occurred in a different order and wire diffusion had been left unchallenged to develop at its own pace, that pace might have been a slow one. Through a combination of technical and economic constraints, wire diffusion might have evolved to suit the needs and interests of privileged minorities, filtering down only gradually to a wider population. By making the delivery of content cheaper and more democratic, wireless communication made mass audiences possible for electric media, and accelerated the development of programming of all kinds.

The Telefon Hirmondó was a hybrid of newspaper practices, conventional modes of oral address, and telephone capabilities that anticipated twentieth-century radio. In operation it was a transitional form using conservative techniques that looked backward to newspaper methods for gathering information, which it presented as spoken newspaper items. In its time it was seen as a novel newspaper form, but it was radically forward-looking in its continuous and regularly scheduled programming, the origination of some programs from its own studios, and the combination of news and entertainment in the same service. No other telephone diffusion experiments embraced a system of regular, timely programming like that of the Hirmondó. Most were limited simply to the reproduction of full-length "occasions."

NOTES

1. *Lightning* (London), Jan. 5, 1893, p. 1.
2. Paul Adorian, "Wire-Broadcasting," *Journal of the Society of Arts* (London), Aug. 31, 1945, p. 514. See also *Electrical Engineer* (London), July 19, 1895, p. 57, and *Electrician* (London), June 9, 1899, p. 243.
3. "The Telephone in Hungary," *Scientific American,* July 2, 1881, p. 5.
4. John J. O'Neill, *Prodigal Genius, The Life of Nikola Tesla* (New York: Ives Washburn, 1944), pp. 45–46.
5. "The Telephone Journal," *Science Siftings* (London), July 15, 1893, p. 362.
6. Ferenc Erdei, ed., "Radio and Television," *Information Hungary* (New York: Pergamon Press, 1968), p. 645; "Telephone-Zeitung," *Zeitschrift für Elektrotechnik* (Vienna), Dec. 1, 1896, p. 741.
7. Thomas S. Denison, "The Telephone Newspaper," *World's Work,* Apr. 1901, p. 641.
8. W. G. Fitzgerald, "A Telephone Newspaper," *Scientific American,* June 22, 1907, p. 507; Frederick A. Talbot, "A Telephone Newspaper," *Littell's Living Age* (Boston), Aug. 8, 1903, pp. 374–75.
9. Denison, "The Telephone Newspaper," p. 642.
10. "Telephon-Zeitung," *Zeitschrift für Elektrotechnik* (Vienna), p. 741.
11. "The Telephone Newspaper," *Electrical Engineer* (London), Sept. 6, 1895, p. 257.
12. Toth Endréné, ed., *Budapest Enciklopédia* (Budapest: Corvina Kiadó, 1970), p. 313.
13. Fitzgerald, "A Telephone Newspaper," p. 507; Talbot, "A Telephone Newspaper," p. 375.
14. "Telephon-Zeitung," *Zeitschrift für Elektrotechnik* (Vienna), pp. 740–41.
15. Talbot, "A Telephone Newspaper," p. 507. By 1907 the list of foreign exchanges included New York, Frankfurt, Paris, Berlin, and London.
16. Denison, "The Telephone Newspaper," p. 642.
17. *A Pallas Nagy Lexicon* (Budapest: Pallas Irodalmi, 1897), 16:20–21.
18. "The Telephone Newspaper," *Electrical Engineer* (London), p. 257; Fitzgerald, "A Telephone Newspaper," p. 507.
19. Jules Erdoess, "Le Journal Téléphonique de Budapest: L'Ancêtre de la Radio," *Radiodiffusion* (Geneva), Oct. 1936, p. 37.
20. W. B. Forster Bovill, *Hungary and the Hungarians* (London: Methuen, 1908), p. 111.
21. "A Talking Newspaper," *Invention* (London), Mar. 26, 1898, p. 203; Talbot, "A Telephone Newspaper," p. 375.
22. Denison, "The Telephone Newspaper," p. 642.
23. See, for example, *Lightning* (London), Feb. 23, 1893, p. 115; "A Telephone Newspaper," *Newspaper Owner and Manager,* May 4, 1898, p. 22; "The Telephone Newspaper," *Scientific American,* Oct. 26, 1895, p. 26, reprinted from the *New York Sun.*
24. Erdoess, "Le Journal Téléphonique de Budapest," p. 39.
25. Arthur F. Colton, "Telephone Newspaper—A New Marvel," *Technical World Magazine* (Chicago), Feb. 1912, p. 668.
26. "Order in the Matter of the Petition of the New Jersey Herald Telephone Company," *Second Annual Report of the Board of Public Utility Commissioners for the State of New Jersey* (Trenton: MacCrellish and Quigley, 1912), pp. 147–50.
27. Colton, "Telephone Newspaper," p. 669.
28. Ibid.
29. Ibid.
30. Erik Barnouw, *A History of Broadcasting in the United States,* 3 vols. *A Tower in Babel,* vol. 1 (New York: Oxford University Press, 1969), p. 100.
31. Colton, "Telephone Newspaper," p. 669.
32. "An American Telephone Newspaper," *Literary Digest,* Mar. 16, 1912, p. 529, quoting *Editor & Publisher.*
33. "Phone Herald's Short Life," *Fourth Estate,* Mar. 2, 1912, p. 23.
34. William Peck Banning, *Commercial Broadcasting Pioneer, The WEAF Experiment, 1922–1926* (Cambridge: Harvard University Press, 1946), p. 59.
35. Ibid., p. 60.

DREAM WORLDS OF CONSUMPTION

Rosalynd Williams

Rosalynd Williams is a cultural historian and professor at the Massachusetts Institute of Technology. In her books Dream Worlds, *from which this excerpt is taken, and* Notes on the Underground: An Essay on Technology, Society, and the Imagination, *she explores the relationship between the rapidly changing character of industrial production in the late nineteenth century and the rise of consumer culture.*

THE SCHOOL OF TROCADÉRO

The arrival of the twentieth century was celebrated in Paris by a universal exposition spread over 550 acres and visited by 50 million people from around the world. The 1900 exposition was the climax of a series of similar events that began with the Crystal Palace exposition in London in 1851 and continued to be held at regular intervals during the second half of the century (in 1855, 1867, 1878, and 1889) in Paris, the undisputed if unofficial capital of European civilization. The purpose of all expositions was, in the popular phrase of the time, to teach a "lesson of things." "Things" meant for the most part, the recent products of scientific knowledge and technical innovation that were revolutionizing daily life; the "lesson" was the social benefit of this unprecedented material and intellectual progress. The 1855 exposition featured a Palace of Industry filled with tools, machinery, and sequential exhibits of products in various stages of manufacture. The 1867 fair had an even more elaborately organized Palace of Industry (including the first displays of aluminum and of petroleum distillation), and a History of Labor exhibit showing tools from all eras. At the 1878 exposition the wonders of scientific discovery, especially electricity and photography, were stressed. In 1889, at the exposition commemorating the outbreak of the French Revolution, the "lesson of things" was taught on a grand

scale. The two focal points of the 1889 fair were the Gallery of Machines, a lone hall with a vault nearly 400 feet across where sightseers could gaze from a suspended walkway at a sea of spinning wheels, clanking hammers, and whirring gears, and the Eiffel Tower, a monument at once scientific, technological, and aesthetic, the architecture of which was derived from that of iron railroad bridges; at its summit was an assortment of apparatus for meteorological, aeronautical, and communications research.

Over the decades, the dominant tone of these expositions altered. The emphasis gradually changed from instructing the visitor in the wonders of modern science and technology to entertaining him. In 1889, for all their serious didactic intent, the Eiffel Tower and Gallery of Machines were popular above all because they provided such thrilling vistas. More and more, consumer merchandise rather than productive tools was displayed. The Crystal Palace exposition had been so innocent of commercial purpose that no selling prices were posted there, but at the Paris exposition in 1855 began the tradition of placing price tags on all objects, as well as of charging admission.[1] From then on the emphasis on selling, prizes, and advertising grew until one booster of the 1900 exposition enthused:

> Expositions secure for the manufacturer, for the businessman, the most striking publicity. In one day they bring before his machine, his display, his shop windows, more people than he would

see in a lifetime in his factory or store. They seek out clients in all parts of the world, bring them at a set time, so that everything is ready to receive them and seduce them. That is why the number of exhibitors increases steadily.[2]

At the 1900 exposition the sensual pleasures of consumption clearly triumphed over the abstract intellectual enjoyment of contemplating the progress of knowledge. This emphasis was evident the moment a visitor entered the grounds through the Monumental Gateway, which, according to one bemused contemporary, consisted of "two pale-blue, pierced minarets and polychrome statues surmounted by oriflammes and adorned with cabochons," terminating in "an immense flamboyant arch" above which, perched on a golden ball, "stood the flying figure of a siren in a tight skirt, the symbolic ship of the City of Paris on her head, throwing back an evening coat of imitation ermine—La Parisienne."[3] Whatever this chic madonna represented, it was certainly not science nor technology. Inside this gateway the sprawling exposition had no orderly arrangement or focal points such as previous ones had possessed. Machines were scattered throughout the grounds next to their products, an indication that tools of production now seemed hopelessly boring apart from the things they made. The vault of the Gallery of Machines had been cut up—desecrated like a "secularized temple," complained one admirer of the 1889 version[4]— and overrun by a display of food products:

> [Instead of] a universal workshop . . . a festival hall has invaded the center of the structure. The extremities are abandoned to the rustic charms of agriculture and to the fattening joys of eating. No more sharp whistles, trembling, clacking transmission belts; nothing being released except champagne corks.[5]

Despite this confusion or, rather, because of it, thoughtful observers sensed that the 1900 exposition was particularly prophetic, that it was a microcosm of emerging France, a scale model of future Paris, that something rich and strange was happening there which broke decisively with the past and prefigured twentieth-century society. In 1889 and even more in 1900, the expositions attracted a host of journalists of a philosophical bent who provided not only descriptions of the various exhibits but also reflections on their significance. For the most part their sense of the exposition's prophetic value remained poorly articulated. While convinced that the fair revealed the shape of things to come, they were unsure of the contours and were vaguely apprehensive without knowing quite why. One exception was Maurice Talmeyr (1850–1933), a journalist who reported regularly on the 1900 exposition in a Catholic periodical. No less apprehensive than many of his colleagues, he was unusual in being able to explain why he found the fair so disturbing. He summarized his conclusions in his article "L'École du Trocadéro" ("The School of Trocadéro"), published in November, 1900, just as the exposition was drawing to a close, in the *Revue des deux mondes,* the most prestigious biweekly in France at that time.[6]

The Trocadéro was the section of the exposition on the Right Bank of the Seine, directly across the river from the Eiffel Tower, where all the colonial exhibits were gathered. It was in this "school," Talmeyr contended, that the true lesson of the exposition could be discerned. Exhibits of exotic places were not a new feature. As far back as 1867 expositions had included reproductions of an Egyptian temple and a Moroccan tent, and in 1889 one of the most popular attractions had been the notorious Rue du Caire ("Street of Cairo") where dark-eyed belly dancers performed seductive dances before patrons in "Oriental" cafés. In 1900, when imperial adventurism was at its height, the number of colonial exhibits expanded accordingly to become, in Talmeyr's words, a gaudy and incoherent jumble of "Hindu temples, savage huts, pagodas, souks, Algerian alleys, Chineses, Japanese, Sudanese, Senegalese, Siamese, Cam-

The Place of Electricity at the Paris Exposition of 1900. Expositions became important sites for introducing the populace of the "wonders" of technology and important sites for the emerging consumer culture of industrial countries. *Archiv fur Kunst und Geschichte.*

bodian quarters . . . a bazaar of climates, architectural styles, smells, colors, cuisine, music." Reproductions of the most disparate places were heaped together to "settle down together, as a Lap and a Moroccan, a Malgache and a Peruvian go to bed in the same sleeping car . . . the universe in a garden!" . . .

THE SIGNIFICANCE OF THE EXPOSITION

The exposition of 1900 provides a scale model of the consumer revolution. The cultural changes working gradually and diffusely throughout society were there made visible in a concrete and concentrated way. One change was the sheer emphasis on merchandising. Even more striking and disturbing, at least to observers like Talmeyr, was the change in how this merchandising was accomplished—by appealing to the fantasies of the consumer. The conjunction of banking and dreaming, of sales pitch and seduction, of publicity and pleasure, is far more unsettling than when each element is taken separately. As Talmeyr appreciates, the conjunction is inherently deceptive.

Fantasy which openly presents itself as such keeps its integrity and may claim to point to truth beyond everyday experience, what the poet Keats called the "truth of the imagination." At the Trocadéro, on the contrary, reveries were passed off as reality, thereby losing their independent status to become the alluring handmaidens of commerce. When they assume concrete form and masquerade as objective fact, dreams lose their liberating possibilities as alternatives to daylight reality. What is involved here is not a casual level of fantasy, a kind of mild and transient wishful thinking, but a far more thoroughgoing substitution of subjective images for external reality. Talmeyr stresses the inevitable corruption that results when business exploits dreams. To him all advertising is false advertising. Blatant lies and subtle ones, lies of omission and of commission, lies in detail and in the ensemble, the exhibits claiming to represent the "real Java" or the "real China" or the real anything are not real at all. People are duped. Seeking a pleasurable escape from the workaday world, they find it in a deceptive dream world which is no dream at all but a sales pitch in disguise.

The 1900 exposition incarnates this new and decisive conjunction between imaginative desires and material ones, between dreams and commerce, between events of collective consciousness and of economic fact. It is obvious how economic goods satisfy physical needs such as those for food and shelter; less evident, but of overwhelming significance in understanding modern society, is how merchandise can fill needs of the imagination. The expression "the dream world of the consumer" refers to this non-material dimension. From earliest history we find indications that the human mind has transcended concerns of physical survival to imagine a finer, richer, more satisfying life. Through most of history, however, only a very few people ever thought of trying to approximate such dreams in daily life. Instead, art and religion provided ways to express these desires. But in the late nineteenth century, commodities that provided an approximation of these age-old longings began to be widely available. Consumer goods, rather than other facets of culture, became focal points for desire. The seemingly contrary activities of hard-headed accounting and dreamy-eyed fantasizing merged as business appealed to consumers by inviting them into a fabulous world of pleasure, comfort, and amusement. This was not at all the future that a conservative nationalist like Talmeyr wished; it was not the vision of a workers' society that socialists wanted; nor did it conform to traditional bourgeois virtues of sobriety and rationality. But welcome or not, the "lesson of things" taught by the make-believe city of the 1900 exposition was that a dream world of the consumer was emerging in real cities outside its gates.

EXOTICISM IN DEPARTMENT STORES

One obvious confirmation of this lesson was the emergence of department stores (in French *grands magasins,* "big" or "great" stores) in Paris. The emergence of these stores in late nine-teenth-century France depended on the same growth of prosperity and transformation of merchandising techniques that lay behind the international expositions. Talmeyr was on the mark when he observed that the Indian exhibit at the Trocadéro reminded him of an Oriental Louvre or Bon Marché. The Bon Marché was the first department store, opening in Paris in 1852, the year after the Crystal Palace exposition, and the Louvre appeared just three years later. The objective advantages of somewhat lower prices and larger selection which these stores offered over traditional retail outlets were not the only reasons for their success. Even more significant factors were their practices of marking each item with a fixed price and of encouraging customers to inspect merchandise even if they did not make a purchase. Until then very different customs had prevailed in retail establishments. Prices had generally been subject to negotiation, and the buyer, once haggling began, was more or less obligated to buy.

The department store introduced an entirely new set of social interactions to shopping. In exchange for the freedom to browse, meaning the liberty to indulge in dreams without being obligated to buy in fact, the buyer gave up the freedom to participate actively in establishing prices and instead had to accept the price set by the seller.[7] Active verbal interchange between customer and retailer was replaced by the passive, mute response of consumer to things—a striking example of how "the civilizing process" tames aggressions and feelings toward people while encouraging desires and feelings directed toward things. Department stores were organized to inflame these material desires and feelings. Even if the consumer was free not to buy at that time, techniques of merchandising pushed him to want to buy *sometime.* As environments of mass consumption, department stores were, and still are, places where consumers are an audience to be entertained by commodities, where selling is mingled with amusement, where arousal of free-floating desire is as important as immediate pur-

Department stores become important sites for consumer culture, using electricity to extend hours into the night and popularizing the idea of browsing. *La Lumière électrique 1881.*

chase of particular items. Other examples of such environments are expositions, trade fairs, amusement parks, and (to cite more contemporary examples) shopping malls and large new airports or even subway stations. The numbed hypnosis induced by these places is a form of sociability as typical of modern mass consumption as the sociability of the salon was typical of pre-revolutionary upper-class consumption. . . .

THE ELECTRICAL FAIRYLAND

By now it is becoming clear how momentous were the effects of nineteenth-century technological progress in altering the social universe of consumption. Besides being responsible for an increase in productivity which made possible a rise in real income; besides creating many new products and lowering the prices of traditional ones; besides all this, technology made possible the material realization of fantasies which had hitherto existed only in the realm of imagina-

tion. More than any other technological innovation of the late nineteenth century, even more than the development of cinematography, the advent of electrical power invested everyday life with fabulous qualities. The importance of an electrical power grid in transforming and diversifying production is obvious, as is its eventual effect in putting a whole new range of goods on the market. What is less appreciated, but what amounts to a cultural revolution, is the way electricity created a fairyland environment, the sense of being, not in a distant place, but in a make-believe place where obedient genies leap to their master's command, where miracles of speed and motion are wrought by the slightest gesture, where a landscape of glowing pleasure domes and twinkling lights stretches into infinity.

Above all, the advent of large-scale city lighting by electrical power nurtured a collective sense of life in a dream world. In the 1890s nocturnal lighting in urban areas was by no means novel, since gas had been used for this purpose for decades; however, gas illumination was pale and flickering compared to the powerful incandescent and are lights which began to brighten the night sky in that decade. The expositions provided a preview of the transformation of nighttime Paris from somber semidarkness to a celestial landscape. At the 1878 exposition an electric light at a café near but not actually on the fairgrounds caused a sensation. In 1889 a nightly show of illuminated fountains entranced crowds with a spectacle of falling rainbows, cascading jewels, and flaming liquids, while spotlights placed on the top of the Eiffel Tower swept the darkening sky as the lights of the city were being turned on. At the 1900 exposition electrical lighting was used for the first time on a massive scale, to keep the fair open well into the night. Furthermore, the special lighting effects were stunning. In one of his articles for the *Revue de Paris,* Corday describes the nightly performance:

> A simple touch of the finger on a lever, and a wire as thick as a pencil throws upon the Monumental Gateway . . . the brilliance of three thousand incandescent lights which, under uncut gems of colored glass, become the sparkling soul of enormous jewels.
>
> Another touch of the finger: The banks of the Seine and the bridges are lighted with fires whose reflection prolongs the splendor. . . . The façade of the Palace of Electricity is embraced, a stained-glass window of light, where all these diverse splendors are assembled in apotheosis.[8]

Like the technological marvels already mentioned, this one was at once exploited for commercial purposes. As early as 1873 the writer Villiers de l'Isle-Adam (1838–1889) predicted in a short story, "L'Affichage céleste" (which might be loosely translated as "The Heavenly Billboard"), that the "seeming miracles" of electrical lights could be used to generate "an absolute Publicity" when advertising messages were projected upward to shine among the stars:

> Wouldn't it be something to surprise the Great Bear himself if, suddenly, between his sublime paws, this disturbing message were to appear:

> *Are corsets necessary, yes or no?* . . . What emotion concerning dessert liqueurs . . . if one were to perceive, in the south of Regulus, this heart of the Lion, on the very tip of the ear of corn of the Virgin, an Angel holding a flask in hand, while from his mouth comes a small paper on which could be read these words: *My, it's good!*[9]

Thanks to this wonderful invention, concluded Villiers, the "sterile spaces" of heaven could be converted "into truly and fruitfully instructive spectacles. . . . It is not a question here of feelings. Business is business. . . . Heaven will finally make something of itself and acquire an intrinsic value." As with so many other writers of that era, Villiers's admiration of technological wonders is tempered by the ironic consideration of the banal commercial ends to which the marvelous means were directed. Unlike the wonders of nature, the wonders of technology could not give rise to unambiguous enthusiasm or unmixed awe, for they were obviously manipulated to arouse consumers' enthusiasm and awe.

The prophetic value of Villiers's story lies less in his descriptions of the physical appearance of the nocturnal sky with its stars obscured by neon lights, than in his forebodings of the moral consequences when commerce seizes all visions, even heavenly ones, to hawk its wares. Villiers's prophecies were borne out by the rapid application of electrical lighting to advertising. As he foresaw, electricity was used to spell out trade names, slogans, and movie titles. Even without being shaped into words, the unrelenting glare of the lights elevated ordinary merchandise to the level of the marvelous. Department-store windows were illuminated with spotlights bounced off mirrors. At the 1900 exposition, wax figurines modeling the latest fashions were displayed in glass cages under brilliant lights, a sight which attracted hordes of female spectators.

When electrical lighting was used to publicize another technical novelty, the automobile, the conjunction attracted mammoth crowds of both sexes. Beginning in 1898, an annual Salon de l'Automobile was held in Paris to introduce the latest models to the public. It was one of the first trade shows; the French were pioneers in advertising the automobiles as well as in developing the product itself. This innovation in merchandising—like the universal expositions the Salon de l'Automobile resembles so closely—claimed the educational function of acquainting the public with recent technological advances, a goal, however, which was strictly subordinate to that of attracting present and future customers. The opening of the 1904 Salon de l'Automobile was attended by 40,000 people (compared to 10,000 who went to the opening of the annual painting salon), and 30,000 came each day for the first week. Each afternoon during the Salon de l'Automobile, the Champs-Elysées was thronged with crowds making their way to the show, which was held in the Grand Palais, an imposing building constructed for the 1900 universal exposition. During the Salon the glass and steel domes of the Grand Palais were illuminated at dusk with 200,000 lights; the top of the building glowed in the gathering darkness like a stupendous lantern. People were enchanted: "a radiant jewel," they raved, "a colossal industrial fairyland," "a fairytale spectacle."[10]

Notes

1. Many of these details are from Richard D. Mandell, *Paris 1900: The Great World's Fair* (n.p.: University of Toronto Press, 1967), chapter 1. For an excellent short summary of the French universal expositions, see Raymond Isay, *Panorama des expositions universelles* (3rd ed., Paris: Gallimard, 1937).
2. Henri Chardon, "L'Exposition de 1900," *Revue de Paris* 1 (February 1, 1896): 644. Chardon was participating in a debate as to whether another

exposition should be held in 1900. Because of the commercialism of the 1889 event, there was strong opposition to the proposal. On the debate see Mandell, *Paris 1900,* pp. 25–51.
3. This description is from Paul Morand, *1900 A.D.,* trans. Mrs. Romilly Fedden (New York: William Farquhar Payson, 1931), p. 66. See also pp. 65–66 and the photograph facing p. 67.
4. Eugene-Melchior de Vogüé, "La Défunte Exposition," *Revue des deux mondes,* 4th per., 162 (November 15, 1900): 384–85.
5. Michel Corday (Louis-Léonard Pollet), "La Force à l'Exposition," *Revue de Paris* 1 (January 15, 1900): 439.
6. Maurice Talmeyr, "L'École du Trocadéro," *Revue des deux mondes.* All quotations from Talmeyr are from this article unless otherwise noted. He also wrote a series "Notes sur l'Exposition" that appeared in *Le Correspondant* between April 10, 1899, and April 25, 1900. Altogether the series included thirteen articles.
7. Richard D. Sennett, *The Fall of Public Man* (New York: Alfred A. Knopf, 1976), pp. 141–49.
8. Michel Corday, "A l'Exposition.—La Force a l'Exposition," *Revue de Paris* 1 (January 15, 1900): 438–39. See his note at the bottom of p. 438 regarding the number of kilowatts involved in this display.
9. In Villiers de l'Isle-Adam, *Oeuvres,* ed. Jacques-Henry Bornecque (n.p.: Le Club Français du Livre, 1957), p. 57. The short story was first republished in *La Renaissance littéraire et artistique* (November 30, 1873) and was republished in 1883 as part of Villiers's *Contes cruels.*
10. Robert de La Sizeranne, "La Beauté des machines, a propos du Salon de l'Automobile," *Revue des deux mondes,* 5th per., 42 (December 1, 1907): 657; Camille Mauclair, "La Decoration lumineuse," *Revue bleue* 8 (November 23, 1907): 656; and Emile Berr, "Une Exposition parisienne.—Le 'Salon' des chauffeurs," *Revue bleu* 11 (December 24, 1904): 829.

Image Technologies and the Emergence of Mass Society

Front page picture from *The Washington Post* the day following the Hindenburg disaster, May 7, 1937. *Copyright The Washington Post, Bettmann Photo Archives.*

By the end of the nineteenth century the "wired world," chiefly through the telephone and telegraph, had extended the scope of previous communication by distributing messages farther, faster, and with less effort. As a result, news was packaged differently and had a new emphasis, as did popular entertainment. Ways of reading also changed, along with the constitution of reading publics. These developments were paralleled and influenced by a century-long transition to a predominantly industrial economy, with its accompanying urbanization. One result was the emergence of "mass society." The local and regional lost their hold as new ideas, images, and patterns of consumption ushered in the twentieth century.

The decades that marked the end of the nineteenth century and beginning of the twentieth century were characterized by many developments in addition to those we have already considered and those to be taken up in the essays that follow. As background it might be useful to mention that this period saw the bicycle, automobile, and airplane emerge as significant modes of transportation. The sense of space they fostered, coupled with the increased speed of railway and steamship travel, led to World Standard Time via the creation of time zones. This further shifted cultural identification away from the immediate and local. In the sphere of art, Cubism and Futurism also responded to and celebrated changes in space and time. Cubism broke up and repositioned space by simultaneously putting several perspectives onto one plane. Futurism celebrated the accelerated pace of life propelled by the new technologies.

This was also a time of major public works, such as bridges, canals, and tunnels. Urban electrification integrated rail transportation into the city, as streetcar and subway lines took hold in major cities of the world. This in turn promoted further urban growth, permitting workers to live at increasing distances from their workplace, creating thereby a commuter as well as consumer society.

One of the key elements prefacing the transition to twentieth-century mass society and culture was a new awareness of people, places, and things fostered by photography. Several implications of this medium are discussed by Susan Sontag in our first selection. Photography began in 1839, and during its first decades it influenced illustrators working in a variety of disciplines, thereby creating a new standard for the quality of information in pictures. It would also go on to change forever the way we view and relate to the world. Sontag explores several facets of this power, citing examples from recent times as well as the nineteenth century.

What unleashed this influence was not the photograph per se, but its wide circulation as a mass medium. This occurred in the final decades of the nineteenth century, when new techniques of lithography enabled photographic reproductions to be used in newspapers, books, and magazines. In our next excerpt, Ulrich Keller examines this development by looking at some well-known and not so well-known images from the early history of photojournalism.

In the next selection, Daniel Czitrom considers the cinematic experience by looking at the early history of movie theaters and their publics. Moviegoing as a collective public experience began, as he notes, with the nickelodeons that sprang up shortly after the turn of the century. These small, makeshift venues can be compared physically to the boxlike multiplexes we sometimes frequent today. Their appeal was mainly to working-class audiences, many of them immigrants whose lack of fluency in English posed no problem during the silent screen era—the occasional intertitles were often read aloud and translated by other members of the audience. The period following the one discussed by Czitrom, saw the emergence of grandiose movie palaces, especially during the 1920s. By that time, all social classes had become enthralled by the moviegoing experience, which had dire consequences for vaudeville. This old and established form of live variety entertainment came to a virtual end by the late 1920s. However, as we shall see in the next section, some of its performers were able to make the leap to radio.

In the early years of moviegoing, the novelty of seeing action on screen was sufficient to satisfy audiences. After 1910, however, certain genres of film and identifiable actors were preferred. The star system was born. In our next selection, Jib Fowles looks at this phenomenon. He links it to the changing social patterns that gave rise to less-rooted working- and middle-class populations, who saw entertainment and sports personalities as the embodiment of many of their aspirations. As he notes, this transformation did not occur overnight; it had been building during the post–Civil War decades, as the telegraph, photograph, and improved transportation helped to make entertainers and athletes more widely known. With the establishment of motion pictures, this tendency escalated tremendously. Actors became recognizable personalities who were often associated with particular roles.

During the early decades of the twentieth century, photojournalism entered a period of spectacular prominence, a rise that is the subject of Vicki Goldberg's essay. Beginning her analysis with events that occurred during the 1920s, she discusses the way in which photojournalism changed the nature of the newspaper, giving rise to formats that have continued to the present day. The visibility of a disaster—her well-chosen example is the explosion of the Hindenberg—in the next day's newspaper increased peoples' desire to see as well as read about such events. This trend dominates today's electronic journalism, but the primary medium has changed from still photography to film and video.

We close this section with what has arguably become *the* major link between images and mass society: advertising. William Leiss, Stephen Kline, and Sut Jhally explore this arena using the concept of "consumption communities." They comment on the immediate preconditions that made possible the emergence of advertising: increasing income and leisure time, along with the proliferation of a variety of commodities. The dominant advertising medium early in this century was the newspaper, and it, along with the growing number of popular magazines, began to increasingly rely on the resulting revenues.

Leiss, Kline, and Jhally do not consider electronic media in their discussion of advertising. However, as a bridge to the next part, we can note that by the late 1920s, radio programs began to mention their sponsors. At first, announcements to this effect were made at the beginning and end of broadcasts. These seemingly mild and inoffensive statements nonetheless annoyed many listeners. Yet the desirability of the programming that sponsorship could provide outweighed other options. Eventually, commercials punctuated the programs at increasingly frequent intervals. In 1934 the U.S. government passed legislation to limit their number and orientation.

22 ON PHOTOGRAPHY
Susan Sontag

Susan Sontag is an essayist and novelist. She has studied at Berkeley, Harvard, Oxford, and the Sorbonne and considers herself a writer without specialization. Among her books are several works of criticism, Against Interpretation, On Photography, AIDS and Its Metaphors, *as well as a novel,* The Volcano, *and a play,* Alice in Bed.

To collect photographs is to collect the world. Movies and television programs light up walls, flicker, and go out; but with still photographs the image is also an object, lightweight, cheap to produce, easy to carry about, accumulate, store. In Godard's *Les Carabiniers* (1963), two sluggish lumpen-peasants are lured into joining the King's Army by the promise that they will be able to loot, rape, kill, or do whatever else they please to the enemy, and get rich. But the suitcase of booty that Michel-Ange and Ulysse triumphantly bring home, years later, to their wives turns out to contain only picture postcards, hundreds of them, of Monuments, Department Stores, Mammals, Wonders of Nature, Methods of Transport, Works of Art, and other classified treasures from around the globe. Godard's gag vividly parodies the equivocal magic of the photographic image. Photographs are perhaps the most mysterious of all the objects that make up, and thicken, the environment we recognize as modern. Photographs really are experience captured, and the camera is the ideal arm of consciousness in its acquisitive mood.

To photograph is to appropriate the thing photographed. It means putting oneself into a certain relation to the world that feels like knowledge—and, therefore, like power. A now notorious first fall into alienation, habituating people to abstract the world into printed words, is supposed to have engendered that surplus of Faustian energy and psychic damage needed to build modern, inorganic societies. But print seems a less treacherous form of leaching out the world, of turning it into a mental object, than photographic images, which now provide most of the knowledge people have about the look of the past and the reach of the present. What is written about a person or an event is frankly an interpretation, as are handmade visual statements, like paintings and drawings. Photographed images do not seem to be statements about the world so much as pieces of it, miniatures of reality that anyone can make or acquire.

Photographs, which fiddle with the scale of the world, themselves get reduced, blown up, cropped, retouched, doctored, tricked out. They age, plagued by the usual ills of paper objects; they disappear; they become valuable, and get bought and sold; they are reproduced. Photographs, which package the world, seem to invite packaging. They are stuck in albums, framed and set on tables, tacked on walls, projected as slides. Newspapers and magazines feature them; cops alphabetize them; museums exhibit them; publishers compile them.

For many decades the book has been the most influential way of arranging (and usually miniaturizing) photographs, thereby guaranteeing them longevity, if not immortality—photographs are fragile objects, easily torn or mislaid—and a wider public. The photograph in a book is, obviously, the image of an image. But since it is, to begin with, a printed, smooth object, a photograph loses much less of its essential quality when reproduced in a book than a painting does. Still, the book is not a wholly satisfactory scheme for putting groups of photographs into general circulation. The sequence in which the photographs are to be looked at is proposed by the order of pages, but nothing holds readers to the recommended order or indicates the amount of time to be spent on each photograph. Chris Marker's film, *Si j'avais quatre dromadaires* (1966), a brilliantly orchestrated meditation on photographs of all sorts and themes, suggests a subtler and more rigorous way of packaging (and enlarging) still photographs. Both the order and the exact time for looking at each photograph are imposed; and there is a gain in visual legibility and emotional impact. But photographs transcribed in a film cease to be collectible objects, as they still are when served up in books.

Photographs furnish evidence. Something we hear about, but doubt, seems proven when we're shown a photograph of it. In one version of its utility, the camera record incriminates. Starting with their use by the Paris police in the murderous roundup of Communards in June 1871, photographs became a useful tool of modern states in the surveillance and control of their increasingly mobile populations. In another version of its utility, the camera record justifies. A photograph passes for incontrovertible proof that a given thing happened. The picture may distort; but there is always a presumption that something exists, or did exist, which is like what's in the picture. Whatever the limitations (through amateurism) or pretensions (through artistry) of the individual photographer, a photograph—any photograph—seems to have a more innocent, and therefore more accurate, relation to visible reality than do other mimetic objects. Virtuosi of the noble image like Alfred Stieglitz and Paul Strand, composing mighty, unforgettable photographs decade after decade, still want, first of all, to show something "out there," just like the Polaroid owner for whom photographs are a handy, fast form of note-taking, or the shutterbug with a Brownie who takes snapshots as souvenirs of daily life.

While a painting or a prose description can never be other than a narrowly selective interpretation, a photograph can be treated as a narrowly selective transparency. But despite the presumption of veracity that gives all photographs authority, interest, seductiveness, the work that photographers do is no generic exception to the usually shady commerce between art and truth. Even when photographers are most concerned with mirroring reality, they are still haunted by tacit imperatives of taste and conscience. The immensely gifted members of the Farm Security Administration photographic project of the late 1930s (among them Walker Evans, Dorothea Lange, Ben Shahn, Russell Lee) would take dozens of frontal pictures of one of their sharecropper subjects until satisfied that they had gotten just the right look on film—the precise expression on the subject's face that supported their own notions about poverty, light, dignity, texture, exploitation, and geometry. In deciding how a picture should look, in preferring one exposure to another, photographers are always imposing standards on their subjects. Although there is a sense in which the camera does indeed capture reality, not just interpret it, photographs are as much an interpretation of the world as paintings and drawings are. Those occasions when the taking of photographs is relatively undiscriminating, promiscuous, or self-effacing do not lessen the didacticism of the whole enterprise. This very passivity—and ubiquity—of the photographic record is photography's "message," its aggression.

Images which idealize (like most fashion and animal photography) are no less aggressive than work which makes a virtue of plainness (like class pictures, still lifes of the bleaker sort, and mug shots). There is an aggression implicit in every use of the camera. This is as evident in the 1840s and 1850s, photography's glorious first two decades, as in all the succeeding decades, during which technology made possible an ever increasing spread of that mentality which looks at the world as a set of potential photographs. Even for such early masters as David Octavius Hill and Julia Margaret Cameron who used the camera as a means of getting painterly images, the point of taking photographs was a vast departure from the aims of painters. From its start, photography implied the capture of the largest possible number of subjects. Painting never had so imperial a scope. The subsequent industrialization of camera technology only carried out a promise inherent in photography from its very beginning: to democratize all experiences by translating them into images.

That age when taking photographs required a cumbersome and expensive contraption—the toy of the clever, the wealthy, and the obsessed—seems remote indeed from the era of sleek pocket cameras that invite anyone to take pictures. The first cameras, made in France and England in the early 1840s, had only inventors and buffs to operate them. Since there were then no professional photographers, there could not be amateurs either, and taking photographs had no clear social use; it was a gratuitous, that is, an artistic activity, though with few pretensions to being an art. It was only with its industrialization that photography came into its own as art. As industrialization provided social uses for the operations of the photographer, so the reaction against these uses reinforced the self-consciousness of photography-as-art.

Recently, photography has become almost as widely practiced an amusement as sex and dancing—which means that, like every mass art form, photography is not practiced by most people as an art. It is mainly a social rite, a defense against anxiety, and a tool of power.

Memorializing the achievements of individuals considered as members of families (as well as of other groups) is the earliest popular use of photography. For at least a century, the wedding photograph has been as much a part of the ceremony as the prescribed verbal formulas. Cameras go with family life. According to a sociological study done in France, most households have

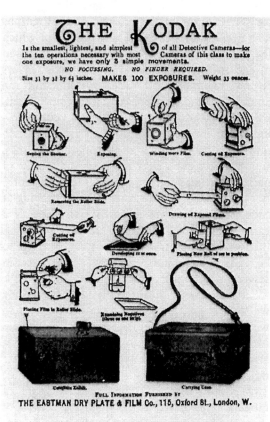

267. *Advertisement of the first Kodak camera, 1888*

The Kodak. Early efforts to popularize the camera used the instructional forms in magazine and newspaper advertising. *National Archives of Canada.*

a camera, but a household with children is twice as likely to have at least one camera as a household in which there are no children. Not to take pictures of one's children, particularly when they are small, is a sign of parental indifference, just as not turning up for one's graduation picture is a gesture of adolescent rebellion.

Through photographs, each family constructs a portrait-chronicle of itself—a portable kit of images that bears witness to its connectedness. It hardly matters what activities are photographed so long as photographs get taken and are cherished. Photography becomes a rite of family life just when, in the industrializing countries of Europe and America, the very institution of the family starts undergoing radical surgery. As that claustrophobic unit, the nuclear family, was being carved out of a much larger family aggregate, photography came along to memorialize, to restate symbolically, the imperiled continuity and vanishing extendedness of family life. Those ghostly traces, photographs, supply the token presence of the dispersed relatives. A family's photograph album is generally about the extended family—and, often, is all that remains of it.

As photographs give people an imaginary possession of a past that is unreal, they also help people to take possession of space in which they are insecure. Thus, photography develops in tandem with one of the most characteristic of modern activities: tourism. For the first time in history, large numbers of people regularly travel out of their habitual environments for short periods of time. It seems positively unnatural to travel for pleasure without taking a camera along. Photographs will offer indisputable evidence that the trip was made, that the program was carried out, that fun was had. Photographs document sequences of consumption carried on outside the view of family, friends, neighbors. But dependence on the camera, as the device that makes real what one is experiencing, doesn't fade when people travel more. Taking photographs fills the same need for the cosmopolitans accumulating photograph-trophies of their boat trip up the Albert Nile or their fourteen days in China as it does for lower-middle-class vacationers taking snapshots of the Eiffel Tower or Niagara Falls.

A way of certifying experience, taking photographs is also a way of refusing it—by limiting experience to a search for the photogenic, by converting experience into an image, a souvenir. Travel becomes a strategy for accumulating photographs. The very activity of taking pictures is soothing, and assuages general feelings of disorientation that are likely to be exacerbated by travel. Most tourists feel compelled to put the camera between themselves and whatever is remarkable that they encounter. Unsure of other responses, they take a picture. This gives shape to experience: stop, take a photograph, and move on. The method especially appeals to people handicapped by a ruthless work ethic—Germans, Japanese, and Americans. Using a camera appeases the anxiety which the work-driven feel about not working when they are on vacation and supposed to be having fun. They have something to do that is like a friendly imitation of work: they can take pictures.

People robbed of their past seem to make the most fervent picture takers, at home and abroad. Everyone who lives in an industrialized society is obliged gradually to give up the past, but in certain countries, such as the United States and Japan, the break with the past has been particularly traumatic. In the early 1970s, the fable of the brash American tourist of the 1950s and 1960s, rich with dollars and Babbittry, was replaced by the mystery of the group-minded Japanese tourist, newly released from his island prison by the miracle of overvalued yen, who is generally armed with two cameras, one on each hip.

Photography has become one of the principal devices for experiencing something, for giving an appearance of participation. One full-page ad shows a small group of people standing pressed together, peering out of the photograph, all but one looking stunned, excited, upset. The one who wears a different expression holds a camera to his eye; he seems self-possessed, is almost smiling. While the others are passive, clearly alarmed spectators, having a camera has transformed one person into something active, a voyeur: only he has mastered the situation. What do these people see? We don't know. And it doesn't matter. It is an Event: something worth seeing—and therefore worth photographing. The ad copy, white letters across the dark lower third of the photograph like news coming over a teletype machine, consists of just six words: ". . . Prague . . . Woodstock . . . Vietnam . . . Sapporo . . . Londonderry . . . LEICA." Crushed hopes, youth antics, colonial wars, and winter sports are alike—are equalized by the camera. Taking photographs has set up a chronic voyeuristic relation to the world which levels the meaning of all events.

A photograph is not just the result of an encounter between an event and a photographer; picture-taking is an event in itself, and one with ever more peremptory rights—to interfere with, to invade, or to ignore whatever is going on. Our very sense of situation is now articulated by the camera's interventions. The omnipresence of cameras persuasively suggests that time consists of interesting events, events worth photographing. This, in turn, makes it easy to feel that any event, once underway, and whatever its moral character, should be allowed to complete itself—so that something else can be brought into the world, the photograph. After the event has ended, the picture will still exist, conferring on the event a kind of immortality (and importance) it would never otherwise have enjoyed. While real people are out there killing themselves or other real people, the photographer stays behind his or her camera, creating a tiny element of another world: the image-world that bids to outlast us all.

Photographing is essentially an act of nonintervention. Part of the horror of such memorable coups of contemporary photojournalism as the pictures of a Vietnamese bonze reaching for the gasoline can, of a Bengali guerrilla in the act of bayoneting a trussed-up collaborator, comes from the awareness of how plausible it has become, in situations where the photographer has the choice between a photograph and a life, to choose the photograph. The person who intervenes cannot record; the person who is recording cannot intervene. Dziga Vertov's great film, *Man with a Movie Camera* (1929), gives the ideal image of the photographer as someone in perpetual movement, someone moving through a panorama of disparate events with such agility and speed that any intervention is out of the question. Hitchcock's *Rear Window* (1954) gives the complementary image: the photographer played by James Stewart has an intensified relation to one event, through his camera, precisely because he has a broken leg and is confined to a wheelchair; being temporarily immobilized prevents him from acting on what he sees, and makes it even more important to take pictures. Even if incompatible with intervention in a physical sense, using a camera is still a form of participation. Although the camera is an observation station, the act of photographing is more than passive observing. Like sexual voyeurism, it is a way of at least tacitly, often explicitly, encouraging whatever is going on to keep on happening. To take a picture is to have an interest in things as they are, in the status quo remaining unchanged (at least for as long as it takes to get a "good" picture), to be in complicity with whatever makes a subject interesting, worth photographing—including, when that is the interest, another person's pain or misfortune.

EARLY PHOTOJOURNALISM
Ulrich Keller

Ulrich Keller is a professor in the department of art history at the University of California at Santa Barbara and an adjunct curator of photography at the University of California at Santa Barbara Art Museum.

More than half a century elapsed between Daguerre's epochal invention and the early 1890s when it finally became commercially feasible to reproduce photographs as photographs in large newspaper editions. Prior to this point, the continuous tones of the camera image had to be transcribed into line engraving—which meant that there was little incentive for newspapers to employ photographers on a regular or even just intermittent basis. The picture reporters on the payroll of *Harper's, L'Illustration, The Illustrated London News,* etc., were all draughtsmen whose sketches were produced at considerably lower cost than wet collodion glass negatives in big view cameras. Invariably representing battles, accidents, and ceremonial events at the peak moment—whether or not the artist had been there—the sketches also were more exciting than images out of the camera, which usually arrived too late and could not record fast action anyway. And while the drawings of the Special Artists were usually imprecise, if not altogether fictitious in character, this did not give an edge to the photographic images, because the latter lost their specific mark of authenticity when transferred to woodblocks.[1]

Thus it is no wonder that until ca. 1885 the history of photography does not know of a single photographer who specialized exclusively in news reporting, or worked solely for press organs for any length of time. Limited and instructive exceptions to the rule were prompted only by major wars, which held sufficient incentive to a few enterprising men such as Brady, Beato, and Fenton to embark on extended news photo campaigns. Even the longest of these, [Mathew] Brady's two-year campaign covering the Civil War with dozens of cameramen, was just that: a temporary effort, not a permanent news gathering machinery. Moreover, with his galleries in Washington and New York continuing to turn out a large volume of *cartes de visite,* portraiture still seems to have been Brady's mainstay product. And if his grand war reportage eventually ended in bankruptcy, it was precisely because no commercially viable link could be forged to the existing pictorial mass media. As it seems, Brady derived only publicity but no revenues from the publication of his images by *Leslie's* and *Harper's.* For profits he had to rely on the marketing of original prints through his galleries and perhaps a few book and stationery stores. The large potential audience of Brady's war documentation could not be reached in this haphazard way, and retail sales proved altogether inadequate to cover the enormous production costs of ca. \$100,000.[2]

If the prehistory of photojournalism is therefore the story of an ideally indicated but practically unfeasible alliance between camera and printing press, we encounter a fundamentally different situation around the turn of the century. . . . The cameraman, while anonymous, can be identified as one of several photographers on the staff of the news agency Underwood & Underwood, which regularly furnished pictures to *Harper's Weekly.* He must have used a light, fast, hand-held camera fitted with a telephoto lens; most likely he operated from a privileged, cordoned-off press location, and it is entirely possible that Teddy Roosevelt's expressive performance was directly addressed to the press. We need not stress that the resulting photographs were reproduced *as* photographs on the magazine page. Furthermore, since the photographer submitted a whole series of images, an editor had to think about an effective layout strategy. He found an intelligent, witty solution, indeed, foreshadowing the fact that photojournalism was going to be a matter of teamwork, with editors and art directors destined to add an important creative dimension to the photographer's basic camera work. The contrast to Lincoln's campaign photograph of 1860 is certainly striking. Under the pressure of corporate employers catering to mass audiences, news photography has developed a captivating, dynamic style. Instead of a posed portrait we are presented with exciting closeups of a statesman in action. . . .

Mathew Brady's *carte-de-visite* portrait of President Abraham Lincoln, 1860. Lincoln was the first president to be photographed in office. *Courtesy Library of Congress.*

There can be no doubt, then, that the much-debated "birth" of photojournalism *pre*dates, rather than *post*dates, Theodore Roosevelt's presidency. The years from 1890 to the beginning of the First World War can indeed be identified as the formative period, one which was inaugurated but not wholly defined by the halftone innovation. It was at this time that photojournalism established itself technically and aesthetically, as a professional career and a social institution. The complexity of the phenomenon warrants a detailed analysis.

THE CONSTITUTIVE ELEMENTS OF PHOTOJOURNALISM

Somewhat crudely, and leaving aside for the moment all practical and ideological ramifications, it is possible to distinguish three basic ingredients in the organizational infrastructure of early photojournalism: a new brand of newspapers using halftone illustrations based on photographs in lieu of woodcuts based on drawings; a new type of news agency distributing photographs rather than texts; and a new generation of photographers equipped with small, fast, hand-held cameras instead of slow and big ones mounted on tripods. To begin with the first and most important (even if somewhat overrated) element, it was the advent of the halftone printing block that prompted the transition from pictorial to photographic journalism.

Halftone Pictures

On an experimental basis, halftone reproductions were used since 1867 in weekly magazines and since 1880 in daily papers. But only after substantial improvements had been made by American inventors in 1889–1890 did it become feasible for large-circulation newspapers to print photographic halftone illustrations regularly in large quantities. The development was significant and amounted to a radical redefinition if not a second "invention" of picture journalism.[3] True, fifty years earlier the use of the illustrated weeklies had produced the eminent cultural phenomenon of a *permanent, institutionalized supply of news pictures to mass audiences.* The shockwaves of the event had been registered in Wordsworth's notorious attack on "Illustrated Books and Newspapers":

Discourse was deemed Man's noblest attitude,
And written words the glory of his hand. . . .
Now prose and verse sunk into disrepute.
Must laquey a dumb Art that best can suit
The taste of this once-intellectual Land.

A backward movement surely have we here.
From manhood,—back to childhood....
Avaunt this vile abuse of pictured page!
Must eyes be all in all, the tongue and ear
Nothing? Heaven keep us from a lower stage![4]

In spite of the anxieties it spawned in some quarters, early picture journalism was a relatively modest affair in terms of the quantity of reproductions involved. Until 1873 not a single daily newspaper carried images regularly, and the illustrated weeklies devoted to the publication of news for the general public were few in number, perhaps less than two dozen in all of Europe and America. It can be estimated that the total volume of news pictures to which a given country's public was exposed rarely exceeded 100 per week. By 1910, after the fast, efficient halftone block had all but eliminated the older reproduction technologies, the statistics reveal a dramatic increase. Hundreds of illustrated dailies and weeklies were now published in every industrialized nation, and the total number of pictures published reached staggering proportions, at least by contemporary standards. Fourteen daily newspapers in New York City *alone,* for example, inundated their readers with an average of 903 pictures per week in 1910.[5] While the steep rise is attributable to a variety of factors, few experts will deny that the halftone block was the single most important of these. The permanent supply of news pictures to the urban mass audiences, at any rate, had established itself on a markedly higher level than in the woodcut era.

Significantly, it was no longer possible to launch a wholesale attack on the legitimacy of the pictorial press, as Wordsworth had done half a century earlier. Instead, the danger was now seen in the excessive quantity of reproductions. As *Harper's Weekly* declared in a 1911 editorial on "Over-Illustration," "We can't see the ideas for the illustration. Our world is simply flooded with them."[6] Popular picture consumption had become a fact of life; only its extent and pervasiveness remained subject to debate.

Apart from quantities, there is a qualitative side to the halftone revolution. In a justly acclaimed analytical investigation of countless manual and photomechanical printing techniques of the late nineteenth century, Estelle Jussim claimed that the halftone picture creates "an optical illusion with surrogate power" where line engravings had rendered more subjective, less reliable images. While Jussim is only thinking of art reproductions, the intellectual historian Neil Harris has broadened her claim of the halftone's "illusionary" and at the same time "objective" powers to include all kinds of photomechanical imagery, especially in newspapers and magazines.[7] According to this view, the halftone process reproduces a given "reality" more "realistically" than ever; in a somewhat tautological manner, it is seen to simply repeat and confirm what exists already. However, if we take the position that is nowadays perhaps more tenable—that reality is not given but rather socially constructed through competing representations—a different conclusion suggests itself. The power of the halftone technology then arises precisely from the fact that it bestows the quality of authentic "reality" on constructed, in many cases biased and contrived scenes. Under this assumption our interest shifts automatically from the technical intricacies of line engravings and dot screens to the institutional framework behind and around them. It is this social instance that formulates the meanings and messages that photomechanical printing encodes "realistically" for mass consumption in a merely secondary operation. It is this social instance that must be analyzed.

Press Photographers

If the halftone block had made the newspapers accessible to photography around 1890, it was substantial improvements in emulsions and camera design that made photography attractive to the papers. The fast gelatin dry plates and roll films of the 1880s, coupled with the hand-held

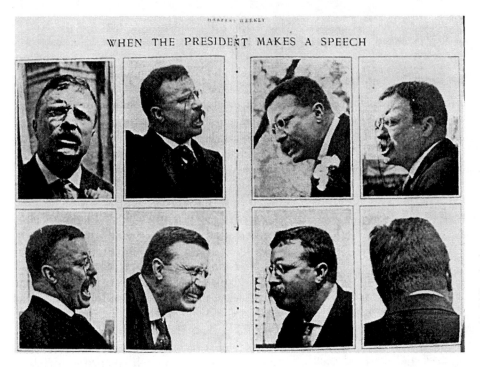

WHEN THE PRESIDENT MAKES A SPEECH

Underwood & Underwood, President Theodore Roosevelt speaking. *From Harper's Weekly, January 26, 1907.*

snapshot cameras made possible by them, opened up the realm of movement and action to photography.[8] Previously, the newspaper had relied on the camera for a very limited subject range, especially portraits and sites. Even with the halftone innovation the newspapers would have continued to make very broad use of hand art, had it not been for the new emulsions, which ensured that instead of a few selected subjects photography could now be used to cover practically the whole range of newsworthy subjects. Combined, the halftone block and the gelatin emulsion represented an irresistible force which proceeded with breathtaking speed to ban graphic imagery from the illustrated press. Within fifteen years, many daily and weekly newspapers replaced their draughtsmen with cameramen. By 1900 a large corps of press photographers existed in America, and with the steady increase in the volume of news imagery published, this corps kept growing until it spanned the world in an every more finely woven capillary network.

Inevitably, the subject range covered by this press corps became almost limitless. From a war in Asia to a railway accident in Brazil, a presidential campaign stop in Little Rock, Arkansas, and the little girl feeding a pigeon in Central Park, everything could take the form of a news photograph. Especially the trivial phase of the expanding spectrum of news imagery deserves to be emphasized here. Important events had always been illustrated. Trivial incidents made an appearance in force only around 1900 and they have stayed with us ever since, underscoring once more that this is the period from which modern photojournalism should be dated.

In press archives, one can occasionally find visual evidence of the newly won importance of photojournalism. An Underwood & Underwood stereograph of president McKinley's funeral procession, to cite just one instance, features a wooden platform populated by a whole battalion of press photographers. . . . It is not a sensational picture, but it confirms that in a matter of a few years photojournalism had become a built-in feature of public life. A point is reached where no important event can take place without extensive photographic coverage. More than that, it is obvious that these newspaper representatives are highly privileged witnesses of the event in progress. Forty years earlier, only one photographer is known to have been present at the no-less-important event of Lincoln's inauguration, and he had to be content with a peripheral, impractical vantage point. In 1901, however, a large platform is expressly built to give the press photographers an optimal viewpoint: they now act as lieutenants of powerful news organizations and millions of readers. Clearly, the alliance of the press and photography has produced an institution of consequence.

The Spanish-American War appears to have been the first major armed conflict in history to be depicted primarily by photographers, as opposed to draughtsmen. It came too soon, however, to lead to any highly organized form of coverage. This distinction belongs to the Russo-Japanese War, which took place half a world away from the United States but nonetheless became subject to more massive photographic documentation than all previous wars together. *Collier's* alone employed six photographers on both sides of the front, not to mention a host of correspondents.[9] Again, no principal difference sets this monumental effort apart from the superbly organized photo campaigns of foreign wars and domestic pomp and circumstance that *Life* magazine was to stage a few decades later.

While the bulk of the growing army of press photographers consisted of lowly staffers careening about town on motorcycles in pursuit of accident victims and police interviews, a few specially talented photojournalists soon obtained high status as chroniclers of "big-time" news events. The heyday of star-photographers on the order of Erich Salomon and Margaret Bourke-White was to come later, but already in the early 1900s some press photographers began to circle the globe, accumulating large expense

accounts and representing big-time publishers and millions of readers at the major events of the day. The days of intermittent, entrepreneurial news photography by men such as Fenton, Brady, and Gardner with their limited resources and distribution networks had definitely come to an end.

One man deserves to be singled out in the present context as the epitome of the species of the "big-time" news photographer, if not the emerging profession of photojournalism in general. Born in 1856 in England, Jimmy Hare became a photojournalist of the first hour when, after years of freelancing for illustrated magazines, he was hired as a full-time staff photographer by the *Illustrated American* in 1895. Three years later he switched to *Collier's,* a newly founded weekly destined to play a leading role in the early phase of photojournalism. Hare's first major assignment was the Spanish-American War; a few years later he was back in the camps and trenches as the most productive member of *Collier's* camera team covering the Russo-Japanese conflict. In the following years, Hare continued to document major domestic news stories, such as the sensational exploits of pioneer aviators from the Wright brothers to Bleriot. A last challenge was provided by the First World War, which Hare covered in the service of *Leslie's* magazine. When he retired he was a celebrity of sorts. Newspapers and press associations frequently paid homage to him with articles and honorary memberships, and shortly before he died, a colorful biography was published about "the man who never faked a picture nor ran from danger." True, the star photojournalists of the *Berliner Illustrierte Zeitung* and *Life* were to reap greater fame, but Jimmy came first.

All this said, the fact remains that, as a class, early photojournalists were still relatively unsophisticated in their use of aesthetic and discursive strategies. Even the best Hare photographs look plain and unexciting next to those of Felix Man, Henri Cartier-Bresson, and Margaret

Bourke-White, who managed to impress recognizable "authorial," if not artistic, signatures on their work. Early photojournalism was marked by a clear aesthetic deficit, and the as yet very rudimentary editorial planning and processing procedures alone cannot account for this deficit. An additional factor comes into view when we remember that the pay scale and social prestige of any incipient profession tends to be too low to attract eminent talents. More importantly, it seems that in looking for inspiration from other branches of photography and the arts in general, early press photographers were not likely to be richly rewarded. Most of contemporary painting and all of "Art" or "Pictorial" photography were entrenched in elitist social rituals, lofty ideologies, and romantic to symbolist styles. A photojournalist could find precious little stimulation for his daily work here, which thus never escaped the narrow confines of a cut-and-dried routine operation. Only the 1920s brought a dramatic narrowing of the gap between art and industry, technology, mass communication. Formerly despised contexts of picture-making in science, industry, advertising, and press now came to be accepted as legitimate fields of aesthetic productivity, and steeply rising earnings lent these fields an additional lure. To put it in the form of a speculative example, if around 1900 someone wanted to build an oeuvre and a reputation by means of camera work at all, he or she had hardly any choice but to join the Photo-Secession and to produce dream-like gum prints of languid females in symbolic guises. Only the functionalistic reorientation of the arts in the 1920s provided the context in which photojournalism could become a challenging aesthetic practice likely to attract individuals of talent and ambition.[10]

Photo Agencies

In addition to newspapers using halftone illustrations and a corps of press photographers using snapshot cameras, a third factor contributed essentially to the institutionalization of photojournalism: the emergence of agencies disseminating photographic news pictures. At the root of this latter development was the fact that not even the greatest newspapers with the most versatile staff photographers could cover every important news event, especially if it happened in an unpredictable moment and place. Therefore, a mechanism was needed which could supply a newspaper with pictures of noteworthy occurrences beyond the reach of its own investigative apparatus. This intermediary function was assumed by picture agencies, which made it their business to secure photographs of worthwhile subjects for sale to subscribing newspapers.

. . . It goes without saying that the sinking of the *Titanic* represented the type of unforeseeable and inaccessible event that must always elude planned, systematic news coverage. However, an anonymous amateur photographer was at hand on one of the rescue ships, and he found the opportunity for a snapshot as some survivors of the catastrophe approached the *Carpathia*. The resulting picture was aesthetically poor, but the subject matter made it sensational. The New York–based photo agency, Bain's News Picture Service, somehow got hold of the snapshot and distributed it to many newspapers that otherwise would have gone without illustration of the *Titanic* episode.

Photo agencies not only bought pictures from outside sources, they also employed their own staff photographers, some of whom generated unprecedented in-depth reportages of the political scene. In 1899 George Grantham Bain, director and photographer of a fledgling picture agency, decided to attach himself to the office of the American president. Over an extended period of time, Bain accompanied McKinley on every trip and also gained frequent access to the White House for formal portrait sessions. The product of this sustained effort was a voluminous reference album containing hundreds of news pictures, meticulously numbered and captioned for commercial

Bain News Picture Service, *Titanic's* lifeboats on the way to the Carpathia, April 15, 1912. *Courtesy Library of Congress.*

distribution.[11] . . . Naturally, an individual newspaper never could have afforded to devote so much attention to a single political figure. For picture agencies, on the other hand, which catered to the American press as a whole, a profitable line of business opened up here.

As far as I can see, no similar undertaking had ever been carried out under earlier presidents. The Bain album marks the historically significant transition from the intermittent pictorial news recording method of the nineteenth century to the permanent, institutionalized mode of coverage made possible by the increasingly complex machinery of photojournalism at the beginning of our own century. It is a mode of operation that has been perfected ever since. When President Lyndon B. Johnson woke up at 6:30 A.M. in his White House living quarters, he pressed two buttons: that of his body guard and that of Yoichi Okamoto, his personal photographer. Okamoto

was one of two persons permitted to enter the Oval Office without knocking, and within the first three months of Johnson's term he took 11,000 pictures.[12] Bain was more conservative in his use of film, but he set the basic pattern for a long line of White House photographers.

Historically, it is worth pointing out that *verbal* news reportages became subject to distribution by commercial agencies already during the 1830s, i.e., as soon as a host of mass circulation newspapers emerged in Paris and other metropolitan centers. Given the fact that the big picture magazines made their appearance soon thereafter, one might expect to see the establishment of *pictorial* news agencies during the 1850s and 1860s, but no such development occurred. For one thing, there was only a small number of news-oriented illustrated weeklies, just one or two per country, and since each of these pursued limited national interests, few picture topics would have been in sufficiently broad demand to warrant commercial distribution. Furthermore, as long as most news images took the form of drawings, quick forwarding to a multitude of subscribing papers would have been difficult because of duplication problems. Photographic copying of drawings, for example, would have involved a considerable loss of time and graphic quality. . . .

NOTES

1. For pre-photographic picture journalism see: M. Jackson, *The Pictorial Press: Its Origins and Progress* (London: Hurst & Blackett, 1885); C. Thomas, "Illustrated Journalism," in *Journal of the Society of Arts,* vol. 39 (30 January 1891), pp. 173ff.; and P. Hodgson, *The War Illustrators* (New York: Macmillan, 1977).

2. D. M. Kunhardt and P. B. Kunhardt, *Mathew Brady and His World* (Alexandria, VA: Time-Life, 1977), pp. 56ff; J. D. Horan, *Mathew Brady, Historian with a Camera* (New York: Bonanza, 1955), pp. 35ff; R. Meredith, *Mr. Lincoln's Cameraman, Mathew B. Brady,* 2nd rev. ed. (New York: Dover, 1974), pp. 88ff.

3. . . . See H. and A. Gernsheim, *The History of Photography From the Camera Obscura to the Beginning of the Modern Era* (New York: McGraw-Hill, 1969), pp. 539ff.; E. Ostroff, "Etching, Engraving and Photography: History of Photomechanical Reproduction," and "Photography and Photogravure: History of Photomechanical Reproduction," in *Journal of Photographic Science,* vol. 27 (1969), pp. 65ff. and 101ff.

4. W. Knight, ed., *The Poetical Works by William Wordsworth,* vol. 8 (Edinburgh: Paterson, 1886), p. 172.

5. R. S. Schunemann, *The Photograph in Print: An Examination of New York Daily Newspapers, 1890–1937* (University of Minnesota, 1966), pp. 102ff. In the picture magazines, halftone photographs outnumbered engravings by the late 1890s. (C. K. Shorter, "Illustrated Journalism: Its Past and Its Future," *The Contemporary Review,* vol. 75, 1899, pp. 481 ff.)

6. *Harper's Weekly,* vol. 55 (29 July 1911), p. 6.

7. E. Jussim, *Visual Communication and the Graphic Arts: Photographic Technologies in the Nineteenth Century* (New York: Bowker, 1974, 1983), p. 288; Neil Harris, "Iconography and Intellectual History: The Half-Tone Effect," in J. Higham and P. K. Conklin, eds., *New Directions in American Intellectual History* (Baltimore: Johns Hopkins University Press, 1979) pp. 198ff. Jussim clearly states that she is primarily interested in the modalities of transmission. "The meanings transmitted do not concern us here" (p. 12); that's exactly the problem.

8. Compare Gernsheim (1969), pp. 397ff.

9. L. L. Gould, R. Greffe, *Photojournalist: The Career of Jimmy Hare* (Austin: Univ. of Texas, 1977), pp. 31 ff.; C. Carnes, *Jimmy Hare, News Photographer: Half a Century with a Camera* (New York: Macmillan, 1940), pp. 152ff.; *The Russo-Japanese War: A Photographic and Descriptive Review* . . . (New York: Collier, 1905).

10. For Art Photography, see U. Keller, "The Myth of Art Photography: A Sociological Analysis," and "The Myth of Art Photography: An Iconographic Analysis," in *History of Photography,* vol. 8 (October–December 1984), pp. 249ff.; and vol. 9 (January–March 1985), pp. 1ff. For the changing concerns of the 1920s, especially in Germany, see D. Mellor, ed., *Germany: The New Photography,* 1927–33 (London: Arts Council of Great Britain, 1978).

11. The anonymous album is part of the legacy of Underwood & Underwood. Since this firm did not enter the field of news photography until 1901 and Bain is the only photographer known to have accompanied President McKinley in 1899, it seems likely, though not certain, that the anonymous album is Bain's. J. Price, "Press Pictures Have Come Far in Half a Century," in *Editor and Publisher,* vol. 71 (February 19, 1938), p. 7.

12. Y. Okamoto, "Photographing President LBJ," in R. S. Schunemann, ed., *Photographic Communication: Principles, Problems and Challenges of Photojournalism* (New York: Hastings, 1972), pp. 194ff.

24 EARLY MOTION PICTURES

Daniel Czitrom

Daniel Czitrom is a professor of history at Mount Holyoke College. His recent interest has been in American communications history and its theorists.

Projected motion picture photography became a reality in the 1890s, but the dream of throwing moving pictures on a screen stretched back at least three centuries. Various European inventors described and created "magic lanterns" (primitive slide projectors) as early as the mid-seventeenth century. But not until the early nineteenth century did Peter Mark Roget and others seriously consider the principle of persistence of vision, a concept fundamental to all moving pictures, drawn or photographed.

In the 1870s and 1880s several scientists engaged in the investigation of animal and human movement turned to photography as a research tool. The most important of these, Etienne Jules Marey of France and Eadweard Muybridge, an Englishman living in America, created varieties of protocinema that greatly advanced visual time-and-motion study. They also inspired inventors around the world to try their hand at constructing devices capable of producing the illusion of motion photography. Most of these inventors, including Thomas Edison, took up motion picture work for quite a different reason than Marey and Muybridge: the lure of a profit-making commercial amusement.[1]

Early film historians and journalists chose to perpetuate and embellish the legend of Edison's preeminence in the development of motion pictures. In fact, as the painstaking and voluminous research of Gordon Hendricks has shown, the true credit for the creation of the first motion picture camera (*kinetograph*) and viewing machine (*kinetoscope*) belongs to Edison's employee, W. K. L. Dickson. Between 1888 and 1896, Dickson was "the center of all Edison's

motion picture work during the crucial period of its technical perfection, and when others were led to the commercial use of the new medium, he was the instrument by which the others brought it into function." Edison himself admitted in 1895 that his reason for toying with motion pictures was "to devise an instrument which should do for the eye what the phonograph does for the ear"; however, his interest in motion pictures always remained subordinate to his passion for the phonograph.[2]

With the perfection of a moving picture camera in 1892, and the subsequent invention of the peep hole kinetoscope in 1893, the stage was set for the modern film industry. Previewed at the Columbian Exposition in Chicago during the summer of 1893, the kinetoscope could handle only one customer at a time. For a penny or a nickel in the slot, one could watch brief, unenlarged 35-mm black-and-white motion pictures. The kinetoscope provided a source of inspiration to other inventors; and, more importantly, its successful commercial exploitation convinced investors that motion pictures had a solid financial future. Kinetoscope parlors had opened in New York, Chicago, San Francisco, and scores of other cities all over the country by the end of 1894. The kinetoscope spread quickly to Europe as well, where Edison, revealing his minimal commitment to motion pictures, never even bothered to take out patents.[3]

At this time the Dickson-Edison kinetograph was the sole source of film subjects for the kinetoscopes. These early films were only fifty feet long, lasting only fifteen seconds or so. Beginning in 1893 dozens of dancers, acrobats, animal acts, lasso throwers, prize fighters, and assorted vaudevillians traveled to the Edison compound in West Orange, New Jersey. There they posed for the kinetograph, an immobile camera housed in a tarpaper shack dubbed the "Black Maria," the world's first studio built specifically for making movies.[4]

Although it virtually disappeared by 1900, the kinetoscope provided a critical catalyst to further invention and investment. With its diffusion all over America and Europe, the competitive pressure to create a viable motion picture projector, as well as other cameras, intensified. During the middle 1890s various people worked furiously at the task. By 1895, in Washington, D.C., C. Francis Jenkins and Thomas Armat had discovered the basic principle of the projector: intermittent motion for the film with a period of rest and illumination in excess of the period of movement from frame to frame. In New York, Major Woodville Latham and his two sons, along with Enoch Rector and Eugene Lauste, contributed the famous *Latham loop,* which allowed the use of longer lengths of film. William Paul successfully demonstrated his *animatograph* projector in London in early 1896. The Frenchmen Auguste and Louis Lumiere opened a commercial showing of their *cinematograph* in Paris in late 1895—a remarkable combination of camera, projector, and developer all in one. W. K. L. Dickson and Herman Casler perfected their *biograph* in 1896, clearly the superior projector of its day and the foundation for the American Mutoscope and Biograph Company.[5]

Once again, the name of Edison is most closely associated in the popular mind with the invention of the first projection machine. Actually, the basis of the *Edison Vitascope,* first publicly displayed in New York on 24 April 1896, was essentially the projector created by Thomas Armat. The Edison interests persuaded Armat "that in order to secure the largest profit in the shortest time it is necessary that we attach Mr. Edison's name in some prominent capacity to this new machine. . . . We should not of course

misrepresent the facts to any inquirer, but we think we can use Mr. Edison's name in such a manner as to keep with the actual truth and yet get the benefit of his prestige."[6]

With the technology for the projection of motion pictures a reality, where were they to be shown? Between 1895 and 1905, prior to the nickelodeon boom, films were presented mainly in vaudeville performances, traveling shows, and penny arcades. Movies fit naturally into vaudeville; at first they were merely another novelty act. Audiences literally cheered the first exhibitions of the vitascope, biograph, and cinematograph in the years 1895 to 1897. But the triteness and poor quality of these early films soon dimmed the novelty and by 1900 or so vaudeville shows used films mainly as chasers that were calculated to clear the house for the next performance. Itinerant film exhibitors also became active in these years, as different inventors leased the territorial rights to projectors or sold them outright to enterprising showmen. From rural New England and upstate New York to Louisiana and Alaska, numerous visitors made movies a profitable attraction in theaters and tent shows. Finally, the penny arcades provided the third means of exposure for the infant cinema. Aside from their use of kinetoscopes, arcade owners quickly seized on other possibilities. Arcade patrons included a hard core of devoted movie fans, who wandered from place to place in search of films they had not seen yet. Some arcade owners bought, rented, or built their own projectors; they then partitioned off part of the arcade for screening movies. They acquired films from vaudeville managers who discarded them.[7]

The combination of the new audience and a growing class of profit-minded small entrepreneurs resulted in the explosion of store theaters (nickelodeons) after 1905. A supply of film subjects and equipment was necessary to meet the demand, and the first of several periods of wildcat development ran from 1896 to 1909. The three pioneer companies of Edison, Vitagraph, and Biograph in effect controlled the production of motion picture equipment, but a black market quickly developed. Each company that sprang up in these years became a manufacturer of instruments in addition to producing films. Many firms had long lists of patent claims, each arguing that it had a legal right to do business. Aside from the few real inventors and holders of legitimate patents, a good deal of stealing and copying of equipment took place. Lawsuits ran a close second to movies in production priorities. In 1909 the ten major manufacturers finally achieved a temporary peace with the formation of the Motion Picture Patents Company, a patent pooling and licensing organization. In addition to granting only ten licenses to use equipment and produce films, the Patents Company created the General Film Exchange to distribute films only to licensed exhibitors, who were forced to pay a two dollar weekly fee. The immediate impetus for this agreement, aside from the desire to rationalize profits, offers one clue as to how early motion pictures became a big business. Edison and Biograph had been the main rivals in the patents struggle, and the Empire Trust Company, holder of two hundred thousand dollars in Biograph mortgage bonds, sent J. J. Kennedy (an executive and efficiency expert) to hammer out an agreement and save their investment.[8]

By 1909 motion pictures had clearly become a large industry, with three distinct phases of production, exhibition, and distribution; in addition, directing, acting, photography, writing, and lab work emerged as separate crafts. The agreement of 1909, however, rather than establishing peace, touched off another round of intense speculative development, because numerous independent producers and exhibitors openly and vigorously challenged the licensing of the Patent Company. In 1914, after five years of guerrilla warfare with the independents, the trust lay dormant; the courts declared it legally dead in 1917. Several momentous results accrued from the intense battle won by the innovative and adventurous independents. They pro-

duced a higher quality of pictures and pioneered the multireel feature film. Under their leadership Hollywood replaced New York as the center of production, and the star system was born. At the close of the world war, they controlled the movie industry not only in America, but all over the globe.[9]

Of all the facets of motion picture history, none is so stunning as the extraordinarily rapid growth in the audience during the brief period between 1905 and 1918. Two key factors, closely connected, made this boom possible. First, the introduction and refinement of the story film liberated the moving picture from its previous length of a minute or two, allowing exhibitors to present a longer program of films. One-reel westerns, comedies, melodramas, and travelogues, lasting ten to fifteen minutes each, became the staple of film programs until they were replaced by feature pictures around World War I. George Melies, Edwin S. Porter (*The Great Train Robbery*, 1903), and D. W. Griffith, in his early work with Biograph (1908 to 1913), all set the pace for transforming the motion picture from a novelty into an art.

Secondly, the emergence of the nickelodeon as a place devoted to screening motion pictures meant that movies could now stand on their own as an entertainment. These store theaters, presenting a continuous show of moving pictures, may have begun as early as 1896 in New Orleans and Chicago. In 1902 Thomas Tally closed down his penny arcade in Los Angeles and opened the Electric Theater, charging ten cents for "Up to Date High Class Moving Picture Entertainment, Especially for Ladies and Children." But the first to use the term *nickelodeon* were John P. Harris and Harry Davis, who converted a vacant store front in Pittsburgh in late 1905.[10]

News of their success spread quickly and spawned imitators everywhere. All over America adventurous exhibitors converted penny arcades, empty store rooms, tenement lofts, and almost any available space into movie theaters. Because no official statistics remain from those years, we must rely on contemporary estimates. By 1907 between three and five thousand nickelodeons had been established, with over two million admissions a day. In 1911 the Patents Company reported 11,500 theaters across America devoted solely to showing motion pictures, with hundreds more showing them occasionally; daily attendance that year probably reached five million. By 1914 the figures reached about 18,000 theaters, with more than seven million daily admissions totaling about $300 million.[11]

All of the surveys of motion picture popularity, and indeed a large fraction of all discussions of the new medium, placed movies in a larger context of urban commercial amusements. Movies represented "the most spectacular single feature of the amusement situation in recent years," a situation that included penny arcades, dance academies and dance halls, vaudeville and burlesque theaters, pool rooms, amusement parks, and even saloons. Motion pictures inhabited the physical and psychic space of the urban street life. Standing opposite these commercial amusements, in the minds of the cultural traditionalists, were municipal parks, playgrounds, libraries, museums, school recreation centers, YMCAs, and church-sponsored recreation. The competition between the two sides, noted sociologist Edward A. Ross, was nothing less than a battle between "warring sides of human nature—appetite and will, impulse and reason, inclination and ideal." The mushrooming growth of movies and other commercial amusements thus signaled a weakness and perhaps a fundamental shift in the values of American civilization. "Why has the love of spontaneous play," wondered Reverend Richard H. Edwards, "given way so largely to the love of merely being amused?"

For those who spoke about "the moral significance of play" and preferred the literal meaning of the term *recreation*, the flood of commercial amusements posed a grave cultural threat. Most identified the amusement situation as inseparable from the expansion of the city and factory labor. Referring to the enormous vogue of the movies in Providence, Rhode Island before World War I, Francis R. North noted the "great alluring power in an amusement which for a few cents . . . can make a humdrum mill hand become an absorbed witness of stirring scenes otherwise unattainable, a quick transference from the real to the unreal."

Commercial amusements tempted rural folk as well, and some writers argued that "the young people coming from the country form the mainstay of the amusement resorts." Frederick C. Howe warned in 1914 that "commercialized leisure is moulding our civilization—not as it should be moulded but as commerce dictates. . . . And leisure must be controlled by the community, if it is to become an agency of civilization rather than the reverse."

A scientific assessment of the situation, as attempted by the myriad of recreation and amusement surveys of the early twentieth century, seemed a logical first step. Beyond this, the drive for municipal supervision of public recreation and commercial amusements fit comfortably into the Progressive ethos of philanthropists, social workers, and urban reformers all over America. "In a word," asserted Michael M. Davis of the Russell Sage Foundation in 1912, "recreation within the modern city has become a matter of public concern; laissez faire, in recreation as in industry, can no longer be the policy of the state."[12]

What actually transpired in and around the early nickelodeons varied from theater to theater and city to city. On the whole they do not seem to have been an especially pleasant place to watch a show. A 1911 report made on moving picture shows by New York City authorities disclosed that "the conditions found to exist are such as to attach to cheap and impermanent places of amusement, to wit: poor sanitation, dangerous overcrowding, and inadequate protection from fire or panic." Despite the foul smells, poor ventilation, and frequent breakdowns in projection, investigators found overflow crowds in a majority of theaters. Managers scurried around their halls, halfheartedly spraying the fetid air with deodorizers and vainly trying to calm the quarrels and shoving matches that commonly broke out over attempts to better one's view. The overall atmosphere was perhaps no more rowdy or squalid than the tenement home life endured by much of the audience; but the nickelodeons offered a place of escape for its eager patrons.[13]

The darkness of the nickelodeon theater, argued some doctors and social workers, caused eye strain and related disorders: "Intense ocular and cerebral weariness, a sort of dazed 'good-for-nothing' feeling, lack of energy, or appetite, etc.," as one physician put it. The health problem melted into a moral one, as critics condemned the darkness. Declared John Collier at a child welfare conference, "It is an evil pure and simple, destructive of social interchange, and of artistic effect." Jane Addams observed that "the very darkness of the theater is an added attraction to many young people, for whom the space is filled with the glamour of love-making." Darkness in the nickelodeon reinforced old fears of theaters as havens for prostitutes and places where innocent girls could be taken advantage of. John Collier asked: "Must moving picture shows be given in a dark auditorium, with all the lack of social spirit and the tendency to careless conduct which a dark auditorium leads to?"[14]

If the inside of the theaters was seamy, the immediate space outside could be severely jolting. Gaudy architecture and lurid, exaggerated posters were literally "a psychological blow in the face," as one writer put it. Sensational handbills, passed out among school children, vividly described movies such as *Temptations of a Great City:* "Wine women and gayety encompass his downfall. Sowing wild oats. See the great cafe scene, trap infested road to youth, and the gilded spider webs that are set in a great city after dark." Phonographs or live barkers would often be placed just outside the theater, exhorting passers-by to come in. Inside, the nick-

elodeon program varied from theater to theater. An hour-long show might include illustrated song slides accompanying a singer, one or more vaudeville acts, and an illustrated lecture, in addition to several one-reelers. But movies were the prime attraction.[15]

In the summer of 1909, while strolling in a provincial New England town, economist Simon Patten found the library, church, and schools, "the conserving moral agencies of a respectable town," all closed. In contrast to this literally dark side of town, Patten described the brighter side where all the people were. Alongside candy shops, fruit and nut stands, and ice cream parlors, Patten noted the throngs at the nickel theater:

> Opposite the barren school yard was the arcaded entrance to the Nickelodeon, finished in white stucco, with the ticket seller throned in a chariot drawn by an elephant trimmed with red, white and blue lights. A phonograph was going over and over its lingo, and a few machines were free to the absorbed crowd which circulated through the arcade as through the street. Here were groups of working girls—now happy "summer girls"—because they had left the grime, ugliness, and dejection of their factories behind them, and were freshened and revived by doing what they liked to do.[16]

Here the contrast was more than symbolic. Like many others, Patten warned that the traditional cultural institutions needed to adapt quickly in the face of movies and other commercial amusements. They could compete only by transforming themselves into active and "concrete expressions of happiness, security, and pleasure in life."[17]

As for the nickelodeon program itself, everyone concurred that vaudeville was "by far the most pernicious element in the whole motion picture situation." Early projected motion pictures had found their first home in vaudeville houses during the 1890s. But with the rise of theaters devoted to motion pictures, the situation reversed itself. Exhibitors across the nation added vaudeville acts to their film shows as a novelty for attracting patronage in a highly competitive business. Not all movie houses included vaudeville acts on the bill; local demand, availability of talent, and other conditions dictated the exact format of the show. But vaudeville became enough of a commonplace in American nickelodeons for observers to agree that it was the most objectionable feature of them. Particularly in immigrant ghettos, where ethnic vaudeville remained popular until the 1920s, reformers feared the uncontrolled (and uncensorable) quality of the live performance. The singers, dancers, and dialect comics of vaudeville appalled and frustrated those who were struggling to regulate the burgeoning nickelodeon movement.

The mayor's committee in Portland, Oregon complained in 1914, for example, about the numerous shows "where decent and altogether harmless films are combined with the rankest sort of vaudeville. There is a censorship upon the films, but none at all on male and female performers, who in dialog, joke, and song give out as much filth as the audience will stand for." In 1910 an Indianapolis civic committee denounced the vaudeville performances in local movie theaters as unfit for any stage: "Almost without exception the songs were silly and sentimental and often sung suggestively." Robert O. Bartholomew, the Cleveland censor of motion pictures, could not believe some of the things he witnessed in that city's nickelodeons in 1913:

> Many verses of different songs have been gathered which would not bear printing in this report. Dancers were often seen who endeavored to arouse interest and applause by going through vulgar movements of the body. . . . A young woman after dancing in such a manner as to set off all the young men and boys in the audience in a state of pandemonium brought onto the stage a large python snake about ten feet long. The snake was first wrapped about the body, then caressed and finally kissed in its mouth.[18]

Nickelodeon vaudeville was usually cheap, almost impossible to regulate, and socially ob-

jectionable—to the authorities, if not to the audience. As a result, police harassment and stricter theater regulations were employed all over the country to exclude vaudeville from movie houses. By 1918 nearly all movie exhibitors had responded to external pressure and internal trade opinion by eliminating vaudeville. They were forced to concede what one exhibitor had written in a trade paper in 1909, that "a properly managed exclusive picture show is in a higher class than a show comprised partly of vaudeville."[19]

In every town and city the place of exhibition proved the most vulnerable point of the industry, a soft underbelly for critics to attack. New York's experience between 1908 and 1913 provides a rough historical model for what transpired all over the country as cultural traditionalists sought to control the sphere of exhibition. By 1908 over five hundred nickelodeons had appeared in New York, a large proportion of them in tenement districts. A city ordinance required only a twenty-five dollar license for theaters with common shows (movies were so designated) that had a capacity below three hundred; the regular theater license of five hundred dollars was well above the means of average exhibitors, so they made certain that their number of seats remained below three hundred. At a stormy public meeting on 23 December 1908, prominent clergymen and laymen urged Mayor George McClellan to close the nickelodeons for a variety of reasons. These included violation of Sunday blue laws (the busiest day for the nickelodeon trade), safety hazards, and degradation of community morals. "Is a man at liberty," demanded Reverend J. M. Foster, "to make money from the morals of people? Is he to profit from the corruption of the minds of children?" The next day Mayor McClellan revoked the licenses of every movie show in the city, some 550 in all.

On Christmas day exhibitors, film producers, and distributors responded by meeting and forming the Moving Picture Exhibitors Association, with William Fox as their leader. The movie men successfully fought the order with injunctions, but the message was clear: some form of regulation was necessary. Marcus Loew began to ask various civic bodies for names of potential inspectors to investigate the theaters. It took several years, however, for New York to enact the first comprehensive law in the United States regulating movie theaters. The 1913 legislation included provisions for fire protection, ventilation, sanitation, exits, and structural requirements. Seating limits increased from three hundred to six hundred to provide exhibitors more funds for making improvements. Significantly, all vaudeville acts were banned from movie houses unless they met the stiffer requirements of regular stage theaters.[20]

Notes

1. The best account of the prehistory of the motion picture is in Kenneth MacGowan, *Behind the Screen: The History and Techniques of the Motion Picture* (New York: Delacorte Press, 1965), pp. 25–84. Also useful are Kurt W. Marek, *Archaeology of the Cinema* (London: Thames and Hudson, 1965); and Frederick A. Talbot, *Moving Pictures: How They are Made and Worked* (Philadelphia: J. B. Lippincott, 1912), pp. 1–29. On the specific contributions of Marey, Muybridge, and others, see Robert Sklar, *Movie-Made America* (New York: Random House, 1975), pp. 5–9; MacGowan, *Behind the Screen*, pp. 45–64.

2. Gordon Hendricks, *The Edison Motion Picture Myth* (Berkeley: University of California Press, 1961), p. 142. The Edison quotation is taken from his preface to W. K. L. Dickson and Antonia Dickson, *History of the Kinetograph, Kinetoscope, and Kinetophonograph* (New York: n.p., 1895), the Dicksons' own history of the inventions.

3. On the success and wide geographical dispersion of kinetoscopes, see Gordon Hendricks, *The Kinetoscope* (New York: Beginnings of the American Film, 1966), pp. 64–69. These parlors often contained phonographs and other machine novelties. On the kinetoscope at the Chicago fair, see Robert Grau, *The Theater of Science: A Volume of Progress and Achievement in the Motion Picture Industry* (New York: Broadway Publishing Co., 1914), pp. 3–4; and Hendricks, *Kinetoscope*, pp. 40–45.

4. For descriptions of these early films and how they were made, see Dickson and Dickson, *History*, pp. 23–40; Hendricks, *Kinetoscope*, pp. 21–28, 70–97; Joseph H. North, *The Early Development of the Motion Picture, 1887–1900* (New York: Arno Press, 1973), pp. 1–26.

5. Gordon Hendricks, *Beginnings of the Biograph* (New York: Beginnings of the American Film, 1964); MacGowan, *Behind the Screen*, pp. 75–84; North, *Early Development*, pp. 23–33; Terry Ramsaye, "The Motion Picture," *Annals of the American Academy of Political and Social Science* 128 (November 1926): 1–19.

6. Norman C. Raff and Frank R. Gammon, two of Edison's business partners, to Thomas Armat, 5 March 1896, in Terry Ramsaye, *A Million and One Nights: A History of the Motion Picture* (New York: Simon and Schuster, 1926), p. 224.

7. FILMS IN VAUDEVILLE: "Edison Vitascope Cheered," *New York Times*, 24 April 1896; Grau, *Theater of Science*, pp. 11–12; Benjamin B. Hampton, *History of the American Film Industry* (1931; reprint ed., New York: Dover Publications, 1971), pp. 12–14. ITINERANT EXHIBITORS: Grau, *Theater of Science*, pp. 28–33; North, *Early Development*, pp. 55–56; George Pratt, "No Magic, No Mystery, No Sleight of Hand," *Image* 8 (December 1959): 192–211. PENNY ARCADES: Lewis Jacobs, *The Rise of the American Film* (New York: Harcourt, Brace and Co., 1939), pp. 5–8; Grau, *Theater of Science*, pp. 11–16; Hampton, *History*, pp. 12–14.

8. Jacobs, *Rise*, pp. 52–66, 81–85; Hampton, *History*, pp. 64–82; Ramsaye, *Million and One Nights*, pp. 59–72. An important review of the activities of the Motion Picture Patents Company is Ralph Cassady, Jr., "Monopoly in Motion Picture Production and Distribution: 1908–1915," *Southern California Law Review* 32 (Summer 1959): 325–90.

9. The rise of the independents and their contributions to both film industry and film art is a whole story in itself. See Jacobs, *Rise*, pp. 51–94; Hampton, *History*, pp. 83–145; Anthony Slide, *Early American Cinema* (New York: A. S. Barnes, 1970), pp. 102–35.

10. Tally's advertisement reproduced in MacGowan, *Behind the Screen,* p. 128; Hampton, *History,* pp. 44–46; Jacobs, *Rise,* pp. 52–63.

11. I have compiled these figures from several sources, using the more conservative estimates where there is conflict. 1907: Joseph M. Patterson, "The Nickelodeon," *Saturday Evening Post* 180 (23 November 1907): 10; "The Nickelodeon," *Moving Picture World* 1 (4 May 1907): 140. 1911: Patents Company figures are in Cassady, "Monopoly in Motion Picture Production and Distribution," p. 363 (a little over half of these were licensed by the trust, paying the weekly two-dollar fee); William Inglis, "Morals and Moving Pictures," *Harper's Weekly* 54 (30 July 1910): 12–13. 1914: Frederic C. Howe, "What to do With the Motion Picture Show," *Outlook* 107 (20 June 1914): 412–16. Howe, chairman of the National Board of Censorship of Moving Pictures, estimated a daily attendance of between seven and twelve million; W. P. Lawson, "The Miracle of the Movie," *Harper's Weekly* 60 (2 January 1915): 7–9.

12. Statistics gathered from the following sources: U.S. Department of Commerce, *Thirty-eighth Statistical Abstract of the United States* (Washington, D.C.: Government Printing Office, 1915). NEW YORK: Michael M. Davis, *The Exploitation of Pleasure: A Study of Commercial Recreation in New York* (New York: Russell Sage Foundation, 1911). Davis's careful study of the attendance at New York City theaters estimated 900,000 for Manhattan movie houses alone. Three years later the National Board of Censorship placed the New York daily attendance between 850,000 and 900,000, so the 1.5 million weekly figure for 1911 is probably low. CLEVELAND: Robert O. Bartholomew, *Report of Censorship of Motion Pictures* (Cleveland: n.p., 1913). DETROIT: Rowland Haynes, "Detroit Recreation Survey" (1912), cited in Richard H. Edwards, *Popular Amusements* (New York: Association Press, 1915), pp. 50–51. SAN FRANCISCO: "Public Recreation," *Transactions of the Commonwealth Club of California* (1913), cited in Edwards, *Popular Amusements,* pp. 16, 51. MILWAUKEE: Rowland Haynes, "Recreation Survey, Milwaukee, Wisconsin," *Playground* 6 (May 1912): 38–66. KANSAS CITY: Rowland Haynes and Fred F. Mc-

Clure, *Second Annual Report of the Recreation Department of the Board of Public Welfare* (Kansas City: n.p., 1912). INDIANAPOLIS: F. R. North, "Indianapolis Recreation Survey" (1914), cited in Edwards, *Popular Amusements,* p. 33. TOLEDO: J. J. Phelan, *Motion Pictures as a Phase of Commercialized Amusements in Toledo, Ohio* (Toledo: Little Book Press, 1919).

13. Edward A. Ross, Introduction to Richard H. Edwards, *Popular Amusements* (New York: Associated Press, 1915), p. 5; Edwards, *Popular Amusements,* pp. 20–21, 133; Francis R. North, *A Recreation Survey of the City of Providence* (Providence: Providence Playground Association, 1912), p. 58; Belle L. Israels, "Recreation in Rural Communities," *Proceedings of the International Conference of Charities and Correction* (Fort Wayne: n.p., 1911), p. 105; Frederic C. Howe, "Leisure," *Survey* 31 (3 January 1914): 415–16; Davis, *Exploitation of Pleasure,* p. 4.

14. Raymond Fosdick, *A Report on the Condition of Moving Picture Shows in New York* (New York: n.p., 1911), p. 11. See also Charles de Young Elkus, "Report on Motion Pictures," *Transactions of the Commonwealth Club of California* 8 (1914): 251–72, a report on fifty-eight motion picture houses in San Francisco.

15. Dr. George M. Gould in the *Journal of the American Medical Association,* quoted in "Health," *Survey* 29 (15 February 1913): 677; John Collier, *The Problem of Motion Pictures* (New York: National Board of Censorship, 1910), p. 5; Jane Addams, *The Spirit of Youth and the City Streets* (New York: Macmillan Co., 1910), p. 86; John Collier, "Light on Moving Pictures," *Survey* 25 (1 October 1910): 801. See also Vice Commission of Chicago, *The Social Evil in Chicago* (Chicago: Gunthrop Warner, 1911), p. 247, for claims that "children have been influenced for evil by the conditions surrounding some of these shows."

16. Davis, *Exploitation of Pleasure,* p. 54; Haynes and McClure, *Recreation Survey of Kansas City,* p. 78, quotes examples of the handbills. For further descriptions of what went on inside the nickelodeons, as well as the reasons for their rapid spread across the country, see the trade papers, for example: "Trade Notes," *Moving Picture World* 1 (30 March 1907): 57–58; Melville C. Rice, "The Penny Arcade as a Side Show," *The*

Nickelodeon 1 (January 1909): 23; "Vaudeville in Picture Theaters," *The Nickelodeon* 1 (March 1909): 85–86. See also Edward Wagenknecht, *Movies in the Age of Innocence* (Norman: University of Oklahoma Press, 1962), Introduction.

17. Ibid., p. 28.

18. Collier, *The Problem of Motion Pictures*, p. 5; Grau, *Theater of Science*, pp. 19–20; Marcus Loew, "The Motion Picture and Vaudeville," in Joseph P. Kennedy, ed., *The Story of the Films* (Chicago: A. W. Shaw, 1927), pp. 285–300; William T. Foster, *Vaudeville and Motion Picture Shows: A Study of Theaters in Portland, Oregon* (Portland: Reed College, 1914), pp. 12–13; "Moving Pictures in Indianapolis," *Survey* 24 (23 July 1910): 614; Bartholomew, *Report of Censorship of Motion Pictures*, p. 14.

19. "Vaudeville or Not?" *The Nickelodeon* 1 (November 1909): 134. For an example of provaude-villian sentiment in the trade, see "The Elevation of Vaudeville," *Moving Picture World* 1 (18 May 1907): 164. See also Boyd Fisher, "The Regulation of Motion Picture Theaters," *American City* 7 (September 1912): 520–22; John Collier, "'Movies' and the Law," *Survey* 27 (20 January 1912): 1628–29.

20. "Say Picture Shows Corrupt Children," *New York Times,* 24 December 1908; "Picture Shows All Put Out of Business," *New York Times,* 25 December 1908; "Picture Show Men Organize to Fight," *New York Times,* 26 December 1908; "Mayor Makes War on Sunday Vaudeville," *New York Times,* 29 December 1908; Sonya Levien, "New York's Motion Picture Law," *American City* 9 (October 1913): 319–21. See also Sklar, *Movie-Made America,* pp. 30–31.

25 MASS MEDIA AND THE STAR SYSTEM
Jib Fowles

Jib Fowles is professor of media studies at the University of Houston–Clear Lake. His articles have appeared in numerous popular as well as scholarly journals. The most recent of his several books is Advertising and a Popular Culture.

. . . In the period between 1870 and 1920, first slowly and then with quickening ardor, Americans had become fascinated with entertainers. This fascination grew so intense that a group of performers obtained a historically unique degree of conspicuousness. Why did it happen? What was going on in the United States that can account for the phenomenal birth of the star role?

The social changes that followed the Civil War can be encapsulated in a word: cities. According to the Bureau of the Census, the U.S. population was 20 percent urban and 80 percent rural in 1860; by 1880 it was 28 percent urban, and by 1900 40 percent urban.[1] The pace of urbanization continued steadily in the twentieth century, and in the second decade the United States crossed the line separating a chiefly rural society from a chiefly urban one. This decade can be seen as the hinge of U.S. history; it is no coincidence that the star role materialized then.

There were two wellsprings of the large numbers congregating in towns and cities. Many were Americans who had been raised on small farms or in villages only to turn their backs on that way of life. Other millions were migrants from Europe and elsewhere. In 1862 less than 100,000 immigrants were counted, but over 400,000 arrived in 1872, and 800,000 in 1882.

Immigration peaked in 1914 when 1,218,000 new citizens entered, the majority taking up residence in urban settings. Whether their previous experiences had been rural or not, once they reached this country they tended to stay in metropolitan areas.

What these droves of new arrivals sought and found in the exploding cities and towns was employment. The fertility of the newly opened Great Plains, together with the increasing mechanization of farming, meant that less labor was required to feed the nation efficiently. Correspondingly, after the Civil War the manufacturing sector of the economy began to grow by leaps and bounds. Individuals found that their best employment opportunities lay in the new urban factories, foundries, plants, and mills. Situated at these transportation hubs, other business enterprises grew in size and complexity, creating more jobs. This was the period when the large business organization became increasingly prevalent, eventually dominating the economic landscape. Over several decades of pell-mell change, America was transformed from a nation of self-sufficient small farmers to a nation of urbanized wage earners.

Although these changes were uneven and at times bitterly conflictful, it is clear from the present vantage point that in the long haul the people caught up in the transformation materially benefited and had steadily more wealth at their disposal, at least up to the onslaught of the Great Depression. Census Bureau data reveal that in constant (1914) dollars the average annual income for a non-farm employee was $375 in 1870, $395 in 1880, $519 in 1890, and $573 in 1900.[2] This climb continued, reaching $607 in 1910, $672 in 1920, and $834 in 1930. As wages rose, the average hours of weekly work in manufacturing industries dropped slowly but steadily: in 1890, the first year for which government data on this topic were reported, the average was sixty hours; this figure fell to fifty-one in 1920 and forty-two in 1930.

Increasingly, then, city dwellers were people with coins in their pockets and time on their hands. The majority of the population enjoyed a modicum of leisure. James A. Garfield, in his 1880 presidential campaign, declaimed, "We may divide the whole struggle of the human race into two chapters: first the fight to get leisure; and then the second fight of civilization—what shall we do with our leisure when we get it?"

Some of the development of leisure activities occurred in the public domain, such as city parks and libraries. But much of it beckoned entrepreneurs. Entertainment and amusements of every sort and for every price sprang up. Much free time and loose change were absorbed by the budding saloon industry. Besides the combination companies, vaudeville shows, and eventually moving pictures, there were also circuses and Wild West extravaganzas, "museums" (collections of oddities) and minstrel shows, amusement parks, and horse races. In contrast to the austerity of the preceding two centuries of American history, the variety of diversions was astounding.

Baseball as a spectator sport also came into its own after the Civil War. Originally a village pastime, baseball was brought to urban centers by the new arrivals. As cities prospered and began to rival each other, they started to contest on the baseball diamond. At first the teams were composed of amateurs, but when the Cincinnati Red Stockings were humiliated by the touring Washington Nationals in 1867, local partisans resolved it would not happen again. The Red Stockings were reconstituted the following year as the first team with salaried players. In the 1869 season they competed without defeat, winning fifty-six games and tying one. Other municipalities began to follow suit, and soon interurban leagues were forming. In cities nationwide an increasing number of enthusiasts began to troop out to the ballpark in fair weather to cheer their local team.

If this growing urban population was gaining more per capita wealth, more free time, and more engaging diversions, then what might it have been losing? This, it turns out, is the key question.

In moving from farms and small villages to towns and cities, individuals were undertaking a radical shift from one kind of social existence to another. The lower the human density had been in rural areas, the stronger the social emphasis had been upon conventionality, fellow feeling, and cohesion. But in cities, the higher the density became, the greater was the extent of impersonality and normlessness. The social sanctions prevailing in rural areas or back in home countries may have imposed uncomfortable strictures upon the individual, but they had also brought personal definition. Religious and community pressures had lent sure guidelines to beliefs and behavior. But once individuals had joined the urban throng, they were stripped of these supporting prescriptions and left to their own devices. For the new urbanites the abiding question became one of self-definition.

City folk were alone in ways more profound than country folk had ever experienced. Urban individuals had to determine their own economic locus; no longer did one follow in the footsteps of a parent, or search through just a handful of potential occupations. Employment options proliferated. One's private life was also increasingly of one's own making, rather than being handed to a person. If marriages had previously been arranged or at least guided, now everyone was on his or her own. Gone were the rigid behavioral precepts of rural Protestant creeds. Gone was any single, uncontested set of standards. As people flowed into metropolises from all walks of life and all corners of the globe, the chances of any one ethos prevailing could only decline.

Previous to this period, a premium upon the individual had received much philosophical endorsement in Western civilization, especially in the United States and particularly at the time of the American Revolution. In those feisty days, the Founding Fathers advocated a faith in the stalwart independent figure who bowed to no external authority. Visiting the country early in the nineteenth century, the French nobleman Alexis de Tocqueville observed that "'individualism' is a word recently coined to express a new idea." That new idea took on a hard edge in Ralph

Waldo Emerson's 1841 essay "Self-Reliance": "Society everywhere is in conspiracy against the manhood of every one of its members," he wrote, and "Who so would be a man, must be a nonconformist." When the poet Walt Whitman later published his famous volume *Leaves of Grass,* the first line was "I celebrate myself."

It was one thing for social philosophers and poets to uphold the ideal of the autonomous individual, but it was quite another for that ideal to become an actuality in the lives of numerous disconnected city dwellers in the last third of the nineteenth and first third of the twentieth centuries. The reality was not half so pleasant as the concept. A new peril had emerged: to be lost in the crowd, to forfeit emotional grounding. One outcome of the transformation from the close-knit human fabric of the countryside to the loose-knit one of the city was a general manifestation of anxiety and mental distress. This development had been foreseen by James Bruce, a British lord and historian who visited the United States in 1876. He noted that "the urban type of mind and life" was coming to predominate, and predicted that "it will tend to increase that nervous strain, that sense of tension, which Americans are already doomed to show as compared with the more sluggish races of Europe."[3]

As individuals left behind the highly prescriptive Protestant ideology of rural America, historian Jackson Lears relates, they left behind a sturdy framework of purpose, sliding into anomie and psychic discomfort. He traces the rise of what was variously called the "American nervousness," "nervous prostration," and "neurasthenia," and observes, "By the early twentieth century, the problem seemed general; references to 'our neurasthenia epidemic' proliferated in the established press."[4]

Among the many antidotes for the widespread malaise of anxiety and depression was a growing number of self-help manuals and behavioral guides. Until the turn of the century, the majority of these exhorted individuals to strengthen their "character"—to bolster their resoluteness and inner strength. Devoid of meaningful support, individuals had to tighten the screws on their resolve. At a certain point, however, this kind of self-help book began to lose favor, and a second brand with a different emphasis started to catch on. According to Warren Susman's scholarly scrutiny of these manuals, instead of emphasizing "character" the replacements explained how to develop "personality."[5] The individual, in the face of a strident and traceless urban environment, had temporized. Rather than forcing his or her will upon this new world, and perhaps battering oneself senseless in the process, a person was now to take a more accommodating path, one that emphasized personal charm. Honey was to be used instead of vinegar as the social lubricant; the goal was to attract. In order to endure and find purpose, the individual needed to develop his personality and get others to like him.

Personality was never an issue until the sense of identity was called into question. Previous to the urban explosion, Americans had little difficulty in knowing who they were; the very dilemma would have seemed absurd to most of them. Within the confines of cultural heritage, family tradition, community, church, political persuasion, and profession, they were sharply defined. But shorn of these supports and isolated in the new urban milieu, their identities had to derive from inside, not outside. To establish the self called for establishing one's personality.

The stream of humans leaving old modes of existence and pouring into a new one needed models of personality—models of worldly, successful, attractive people free of "neurasthenia." Where were such models who could help in defining the individual against the backdrop of urban anonymity?

They were—it was increasingly if unreflectingly felt—on stage, on screen, and on the playing fields. Stars seemed to exude the perfected, confident behavior that unanchored city dwellers coveted. As performers acted and reacted in emotionally charged dramas, as they be-

came decisive or adorable, their performances seemed to reveal purified feelings within, and to issue from harmonious personalities. How to be a whole and resolved person, what the peerless male or ideal female was like: this is what spectators thought they were viewing. Performers offered various models of the well-integrated self, at a time of excruciating need, and when other well-wrought exemplars were not forthcoming. In a most revealing word choice, celebrated actors came to be called "personalities."

Chaplin once tried to describe why his early comedies had so decisively surpassed the Keystone reels in popularity. He explained that the Keystone films always built to an extended chase scene, and that "personally I hated a chase. It dissipates one's personality; little as I knew about the movies, I knew that nothing transcended personality."

Chaplin, Pickford, and Fairbanks were the particular personalities most generally appreciated, for good reason. Despite their differences, there was much they had in common. All three were slight of stature and brimming with a compacted, radiant energy. Their slightness emphasized their youthfulness—an important empathetic feature for an audience of newcomers to a new culture. The stars' small bodies, moving with practiced grace, suggested uncorrupted souls. All three demonstrated tenacity and pluck in their roles; they were never undone for long. They would overcome the forces of evil, authority, and tedium, and would venture forward as intact, happy individuals. They were resolute but never stiff; a liberal dose of comedy made their roles delectable—more so in the case of Chaplin, but humor was never absent for Fairbanks or for Pickford, who once commented, "I always tried to get laughter into my pictures." As well as beating the opposition, these idols pursued love and were sure to end up in exalting unions. For a moment, unsure urban viewers could experience exaltation, too. Here, in these three protostars, they found their inspiration for coping with a strange new world.

The star role thus arrived at the time when ancient institutions—ones that had helped lend each individual a sense of personal identity—were slackening. While the changing nature of social organization after the Civil War accounts in a general way for the unprecedented interest in performing artists, the actual delivery of stars to the American public has to be seen as a technological achievement, or a series of such achievements. Without these technologies the star role would never have taken shape. Technologies fulfilled the culture's mandate for stars.

What this sequence of technical advances accomplished was the circulation of performers' images to an ever-widening audience. By allowing a large number of people to focus on a small number of performers, these technologies fashioned the crucible of extensive public attention from which issued the star role.

The technological side to the story of the star role actually began before images could be easily circulated. Immediately after the Civil War it was the performers themselves who were circulated; the technologies responsible were the newly developed railroad and telegraph systems. Absent these transportation and communication lines, organized baseball with its star players would never have come into existence. To set up a season's schedule, make travel arrangements, keep in touch with touring teams, and relay messages back to the home stand, the telegraph was indispensable. (The telephone was largely restricted to local calls until the turn of the century.) The telegraph was also an important implement of the growing clan of sportswriters, who were spinning out column after column of baseball stories for a fascinated readership. "Box scores, betting odds, and all kinds of messages were relayed from one city to another; and by 1870 daily reports were published in many metropolitan newspapers," states historian John Betts. "Sport had emerged into such a popular topic of conversation that newspapers rapidly expanded their coverage in the 1880s and 1890s, relying in great part on messages sent over the lines from distant points."[6]

What the readers of the sports pages principally wanted to learn about were the achievements of the starring players. Conveyed to a national audience by the railroad and the telegraph, certain players began to stand out from the rest. One of those was Cap Anson, who played for eight years before becoming manager of the Chicago White Sox in 1880, and then continued both to play and manage for another nineteen. Writing about Anson's long career, baseball historian Harold Seymour states, "During that time, his name became a household word—better known, it was said, than that of any statesman or soldier of his time. The fans in Chicago flocked to cheer him. On the road they came out in equally large numbers to jeer."[7]

Just as the railroad and telegraph helped to create a following for baseball players, they also built a national audience for certain actors and actresses. Without these technologies the combination companies could not have toured so readily, and vaudeville acts could not have been booked and been transported so efficiently. Events would have proceeded at the horse-and-buggy pace of earlier times; schedules would not have been half so tight; and the extent of the players' exposure would never have been sufficient to create celebrities. With the railroad and telegraph systems in place, performers could be rotated rapidly through the populace, and some of them would catch and hold the regard of a large audience. Telegraphed accounts of new performers, which appeared in journals and newspapers, produced initial familiarity, and publicity wired ahead brought out ticket-buying customers.

Although the railroad and telegraph initiated the closer relationship of player and public, they were quickly proven less than adequate. The audience's need for stars was deeper than the ability of these technologies to satisfy. The stars could not be in all places at all times, but suddenly their images could. As the technologies of photography and photographic reproduction advanced, they were swiftly put to the purpose of disseminating stars' pictures, particularly of their faces. Photographs of baseball players and other sports figures were circulated widely in the 1880s and 1890s. Pictures of stage performers, especially actresses like Maude Adams and Ethel Barrymore, came into vogue at the same time. The public wanted to get closer to the players they had seen in the theater or on the playing field; they wanted to hold their likenesses in their hands.

Then something cataclysmic happened: the pace of the technologized distribution of star images turned furious with the advent of motion pictures. It was this technology, above all others, that ushered in the age of the star. When Thomas Edison combined several existing and arriving inventions to construct the system of movie camera, film stock, and projector, it was an epochal advance. Photography's advantage for the wide and rapid distribution of the star's image was combined with the theater's advantage at presenting the star in performance.

The ability to provide people across the nation with virtually simultaneous exposure to a star was an important feature of the movies. No longer did years have to pass before a performer and a sizable audience got to know each other. Because many prints would be made and distributed, the star could be seen by millions of people within months or even weeks. When Americans left farm and village life, they had sacrificed a commonality of experience; now here was something new to be shared by all: the celebrity performer whose image was flushed through the culture upon a movie's release.

Beyond distribution, the other star-creating feature of film technology was that audiences could now see not a static image of a performer, as in a photograph, but the performer in motion. The star's behavior could now be observed. Behavior defines a social entity and reveals the person within, and it was the person within that Americans were most curious about and most receptive to.

Above all, the technology of the cinema permitted audiences to concentrate on the faces of the performers. The close-up shot, conveying

visages and excluding all else, eradicated the distance between viewer and actor, and so represented a great improvement over traditional proscenium theater. It was even an improvement over real life: moviegoers could stare at those famous faces unabashedly and study every feature, every tic of feeling.

The close-up shot, so simple in its execution and so profound in its consequences, was the greatest gift of the new entertainment form. There is no exaggerating the importance of this cinematic technique in providing the audience with what it desired. Although probably apocryphal, the tale goes that when early directors like D. W. Griffith were first experimenting with the close-up, some theater-trained producers scoffed, arguing that patrons expected to see the entire performer top to bottom, not just the head. In any case, it quickly became clear that a camera shot tightly framed around the face had majestic properties and captured attention as nothing else. It was not long before leading performers were fighting for close-ups and demanding the camera operators, lighting specialists, and makeup experts who were gifted at them. These masters could create closeups of bewitching brilliance and appeal.

Of all portions of the human body, the face is the primary one to go unclothed, unshielded. It is via the face that privacy is broached and humans enter into contact with each other. Behavioral science research has demonstrated that in face-to-face communication, words count for less than 10 percent of what is exchanged. The real messages are carried in the tone of voice (38 percent) and in facial expressions (55 percent).[8] The face discloses the fundamentals of affect; the close-up enthrones this primal language and prohibits irrelevant clues.

The face in a close-up may be emoting or it may be responding. But whether it is acting or reacting, it is still the avenue to the soul, the inner personality of the star. Everything else about the movies of the early twentieth century—the plots, the dialogue, the direction, the cinematography, the supporting characters—existed to highlight these luminous personalities. While closeness to others was diminishing in urbanized life, here was first-rate intimacy. If identity was in question, here were personalities to try on.

The proximity of star and spectator was further narrowed by the advent of sound reproduction, coming to movies late in the 1920s. Now the audience knew leading performers through their voices as well as their images. Studios responded to the new familiarity by providing publicity of a less fantastic nature; stars were now represented as being similar to other mortals. They were shown as domesticated, with spouses and children. Kitchens cropped up in publicity stills.

The arrival of sound precipitated pronounced changes in the movie industry and in the way stars were delivered to Americans. Sound movies cost over twice as much to produce as silent films, so the industry was required to recapitalize. Financial resources did come to Hollywood's aid, but with them arrived a new breed of movie executives who realized that the likelihood of a proper return on investment could be improved only by controlling what everyone recognized was the central element of movie production: the stars. Stars could no longer be permitted to ride roughshod, their inflated egos wrecking production schedules. The need to exert control was hastened by the onset of the Great Depression. As the economic straits worsened, the volume of ticket sales entered its first major reversal. When unemployment climbed to one-third of the labor force, many Americans had to forgo their weekly visits with their star friends. At home a competing new medium was waiting to take up some of the slack. Radio might not have had pictures, but it offered everything else: it delivered comedy and sports stars for free, at a click of the knob. All these factors increased the pressure for the close corporate rule of the movie business.

The upshot was the "star system," by which a degree of orderliness and predictability was brought to the rambunctious film industry. Since stars were what the movies were selling, stars would have to be carefully cultivated and regulated. Only in this way could the eight major studios meet their annual combined production quota of three to four hundred films. The development of stars was systematized to the extent possible: each studio would present a crop of new aspirants to the public, largely in B movies; the less successful would be weeded out, and the more successful would be put to work on a regular basis. Seven-year contracts became standard throughout the industry. By regularizing the process of star selection and use, studios diligently worked to stabilize themselves in turbulent times.

From the celebrity actor's point of view, the star system brought both advantages and disadvantages. The pressures for regularity steered most stars into stereotyped molds. There was little leeway for experimentation in roles. Some, like Bette Davis, chafed against this restrictiveness, but most accepted it without comment, if not willingly. The standardizing of their image brought them steady work, and indeed longer careers than stars had previously enjoyed. Once a studio had gone to the expense of developing a star, it had every inclination to employ the person as long as possible. The average star career in the silent movie period has been estimated at three to five years; under the star system it could be six to eight times longer.

As the 1930s wore on and movie attendance continued to drop, cost-cutting measures became prevalent in Hollywood. Popular but expensive performers were released by studios like Paramount and Universal in an attempt to reduce burdensome financial commitments. As Leo Rosten explains the results of this maneuver, "The 'sensible' businessmen did cut their movie costs by letting high-priced stars go—but they cut their profits (or increased their lack of profits) even more. And the stars which Paramount and Universal dropped—or who were lured away by Warner Brothers or MGM—kept bringing the big money into the coffers of the studios for which they worked."[9] Again it was demonstrated that, above all, stars were what the public wanted. Even in times of extreme exigency, when studios cut stars they hurt themselves.

It was not until the Depression and World War II were over that the 1929 high of 90 million tickets sold weekly was again reached. But even though attendance had slumped, Americans had not been losing their commitment to stars. Other indicators suggest that fan devotion remained high over the 1930s. People who could not afford ticket prices were buying postage stamps and mailing in their pledges of adoration. It has been estimated that at the beginning of the 1930s more than 30 million letters were sent to stars each year. The studios were in danger of being swamped by this outpouring. Moviegoers organized themselves into fan clubs to more powerfully display their affection. In 1934 there were 535 recognized clubs, with a combined membership of 750,000—a horde of devotees. According to Alexander Walker's tally, Joan Crawford and Jean Harlow each had about fifty clubs, and Clark Gable had over seventy.[10] The burden on the studios to handle this star worship became onerous, and new clubs had to be discouraged.

Matters continued in this vein until mid-century, when a new technology arrived that did yet better at distributing star images. This was accomplished by delivering the imagery directly into homes.

NOTES

1. U.S. Department of Commerce, Bureau of the Census, *Historical Statistics of the United States: Colonial Times to 1970* (Washington, D.C.: U.S. Government Printing Office, 1975), 11–12.
2. Ibid., 165.
3. Quoted in Russell Lynes, *The Lively Audience: A Social History of the Visual and Performing Arts in America, 1890–1950* (New York: Harper and Row, 1985), 2.
4. T. J. Jackson Lears, *No Place of Grace: Antimodernism and the Transformation of American Culture, 1880–1920* (New York: Pantheon, 1984), 280.
5. Warren I. Susman, *Culture as History: The Transformation of American Society in the Twentieth Century* (New York: Pantheon, 1984), 280.
6. John Richards Betts, "The Technological Revolution and the Rise of Sport, 1850–1900," *Mississippi Valley Historical Review* 40 (1953): 240.
7. Harold Seymour, *Baseball: The Early Years* (New York: Oxford University Press, 1960), 173.
8. Albert Mehrabian, *Silent Messages* (Belmont, Calif.: Wadsworth, 1971), 44.
9. Leo C. Rosten, *Hollywood: The Movie Colony, The Movie Makers* (New York: Harcourt Brace, 1941), 143.
10. Alexander Walker, *Stardom* (New York: Stein and Day, 1970), 251.

26 THE NEWS PHOTOGRAPH
Vicki Goldberg

Vicki Goldberg is a New York curator and historian of photography. Her most recent book is The Power of Photography, *a comprehensive history of the medium.*

In the late 1920s the news photograph spread out to claim yet more territory as its own. Photojournalism reached the acme of its influence during the great era of the photo magazine and the picture paper, lasting roughly from the late 1920s to the late 1960s. As improvements to the printing press made possible cheaper and better reproduction, hundreds of thousands of copies of stories illustrated by photographs hit the newsstands. The 35mm camera, first marketed in the mid-1920s and popular among photographers from the early 1930s, combined with faster film and flashbulbs to introduce new subjects and a cheeky familiarity with people from all walks of life, who now could be easily caught off-guard.

As technical factors made the picture press possible, cultural change made it desirable. In the first two decades after World War I, shorter work weeks, better transportation, and work-saving devices added hours to people's leisure just at the moment they began to feel pressured by a lack of time and intent upon shortcuts. Lunch counters, plane travel, the *Reader's Digest,* and the tabloids all promised to streamline daily existence. When the *New York Daily News* was founded in 1919 as the *Illustrated Daily News,* the editors assured readers that to save them trouble no story would be continued to another page.[1] In terms of information the biggest time-saver of all was the photograph, which told the story far faster and more efficiently than words.

Tabloid papers quickly put people in the habit of taking their news with a dose of pictures, and by now photographs took up so much space that text shriveled in response. After a while more traditional newspapers felt obliged to add some photographic coverage in order to compete. At the end of the 1920s German papers like the *Berliner Illustrierte Zeitung* and the *Münchener Illustrierte Presse,* followed soon by magazines like the French *Vu,* changed the terms, putting more of the world on display at one time than the press had done before. They printed groups of photographs on a single subject, pictures that told stories and illuminated events from a variety of angles. Thus the picture essay and the picture magazine were born.

They grew to giant proportions in no time at all. In the 1930s *Picture Post* in England,

Paris-Match in France, and *Life* and *Look* in America marked the weeks off for millions. People hung on these magazines, anticipating that the news they had glimpsed in the papers or heard on the radio would be amplified and explained in detail before their very eyes. When they finished looking at the pictures they flocked en masse to the movies, where newsreels sent more picture stories flashing by.

It was already becoming clear that news consisted principally of what could be shown—a foretaste of the world we know today. The privilege of vicariously experiencing events came to be accepted as everyone's natural right. Henry Luce put it rather grandly in the 1936 prospectus for *Life:* "To see life; to see the world; to eyewitness great events; to see strange things . . . to see and to take pleasure in seeing; to see and be amazed; to see and be instructed; Thus to see, and to be shown, is now the will and new expectancy of half mankind."[2] People had long since become addicted to photographs; now the general dependency was rationalized by the idea that seeing the news was one of the prerogatives of modern life.

With the growth of the picture magazines the picture culture triumphantly took over, without so much as a battle. Society, long since infiltrated, happily surrendered. In 1948 Wilson Hicks, *Life's* director of photography, proclaimed the new kingdom: "World War II was a Photographer's War," he said. "This is a Photographer's World."[3]

All I could think of was that the ship [*Hindenburg*] had fallen out of the sky. They were not supposed to touch land, they were tethered to tall towers, they were sky creatures; and this one had fallen in flames to the ground. I could not get the picture of that out of my mind.

E. L. Doctorow, *World's Fair,* 1985

There were real pictures, too, that were hard to get out of the mind. When the ship docked at its mooring mast in Lakehurst, New Jersey, on May 6, 1937, it was almost twelve hours late because of bad weather. The flight was routine, the eleventh North Atlantic round-trip for the big German dirigible. It was the first landing of the year, and twenty-two photographers, several reporters and newsreel men, plus a radio announcer were on hand. Moments after it landed, the great airship exploded with a burst of brilliant flame. The tail, hovering in air and burning fast, broke apart and sank to earth. Bodies fell from the air like cinders. One newsreel man, who had been photographing the ground crew hauling on the land ropes, was so stupefied he never shifted his camera until his crew chief shouted at him, "For God's sake! Turn it up!" One of the still photographers cried "Oh my God! Oh my God!" over and over as he loaded and shot his camera like an automaton. There were ninety-seven passengers and crew aboard that flight; thirty-five of them died.[4]

The day the *Hindenburg* went down was one of the first times a mass audience achieved the immediate shared experience of the news and the proximity to disaster that have since become components of contemporary life. The camera made people direct spectators of the *Hindenburg* explosion no matter where they were when it happened, and technology put them on the scene within hours of the event. By 1937 there were numerous picture newspapers eager to tell a story in photographs: the *New York World Telegram* printed twenty-one pictures of the dirigible; the *New York Post*, seven pages of pictures; the *New York Daily Mirror*, nine. New York had theaters that played nothing but newsreels, and theaters everywhere included them on their programs. Film of the explosion was being shown on Broadway by noon the following day, and late that afternoon prints were rushed to theaters across the country. Audiences were not accustomed to witnessing horror and death as they happened: screams frequently rang out across the theater.[5]

Radio, which had just become a truly mass medium earlier in the 1930s, brought the stunning news of the dirigible's crash directly into millions of homes. Herbert Morrison, an announcer for a Chicago station, had gone to record the landing for his regular program. He intoned, in true radio reporter fashion, "The vast motors are just holding it, just enough to keep it from . . ." Suddenly he broke off, then came in quickly in an anguished voice: "It's broken into flames! It's flashing—flashing! It's flashing terrible!" He continued his report but at length burst out sobbing. "I'm going to have to stop for a moment because I've lost my voice. This is the worst thing I've ever witnessed!"[6] The recording was nationally broadcast the next day at 4:30; by then, most people had seen photographs and had an image in their minds. (The on-the-spot immediacy of this account, broadcast so soon after the explosion, was eclipsed a year later when Edward R. Murrow began broadcasting directly from Europe about the lengthening shadows of war.)

What the reporting of the *Hindenburg* disaster did was to change the nature of the news and the public's expectations of it. Previously, firsthand reports of disaster had depended on verbal accounts by survivors; now it was possible to see the catastrophe itself, to hear about it as it unfolded. Occasional events of great magnitude had been photographed ever since the camera became fast enough: burning mills in Oswego, New York, in 1855; the attempted assassination of Mayor Gaynor in New York in 1910; the execution of Ruth Synder in 1928, photographed with a concealed camera and printed on the front page of the *Daily News*. But disaster usually doesn't wait around for a photographer, who seldom has a chance to depict anything but the aftermath. Even Arnold Genthe, who lived through the San Francisco earthquake, took pictures of the city burning afterward.

Now the nation and the world were witnesses to an accident in a small town in New Jersey. The picture magazine, the wire service, and the newsreel had widened the dominion of photographs over the mind, and, with the collaboration of radio, established the reign of instant news that addressed both the eye and the ear. The way was prepared for the entry of television.

The immediate reports in three media on the *Hindenburg* explosion depended first on a fluke and second on technology. The fluke was that representatives of all the media were present at the disaster because they expected to cover the landing. Had the explosion occurred a mile away, the event would have taken on an entirely different character. News was becoming not only whatever could be photographed, but more specifically, what could be photographed dramatically.

Technological advances moved the accounts across the nation and the world with unprecedented speed. Photographs had begun to travel by wire in the first decade of the century and had a limited national distribution by the mid-1920s; in January 1935 the Associated Press Wirephoto network was inaugurated. (The first photograph sent by wire across the Atlantic, in 1935, was a view of a plane crash.) Not only did the pictures move faster, but tabloid papers made them available to enormous audiences. Most news photographs before the 1930s had a fairly limited circulation. The advent of the picture magazine in mid-decade provided huge numbers of people with the same visual experiences but made them wait a couple of weeks: the *World Telegram* gave the *Hindenburg* extensive coverage on May 7, the day after the explosion; *Life*'s appeared ten days later.

Between photographs, newsreels, and radio, a far-flung public was *there*, and everyone received just about the same account. At least since the 1920s—with syndicated news articles, wide-circulation magazines, and nationwide broadcasting—the media had been in the process of homogenizing experience within nations and to some extent across the world. The reporting of the *Hindenburg* explosion unified the culture in a nearly simultaneous observation of disaster. The world was rapidly filling in the outlines of Marshall McLuhan's global village.

It is often assumed that the explosion of the *Hindenburg*, and the photographs that fixed it so starkly and irrevocably in memory, spelled the end of commercial dirigible travel. There is some truth to this, but less than first appears. Dirigible crashes in the 1920s and early 1930s had already made the public wary. After a British airship crashed in 1930—killing the secretary of state for air, the director of airship development, and six officials of the Royal Airship Works—Britain gave up developing rigid dirigibles. Americans had their own crashes, but Dr. Hugo Eckener, head of the German Zeppelin Transport Company, wooed American industrialists with demonstrations of his crafts' brilliant performance. By 1935 the luxurious, relatively inexpensive crossings of the *Hindenburg* and the *Graf Zeppelin* had quieted the world's doubts about the dirigible. The *Hindenburg* flew so smoothly that the pope, convinced there was no risk of spilling the consecrated wine, permitted a priest to celebrate the first mass ever said in the sky. Not even the hurricane of 1936 roiled the ship's calm progress.[7]

When it went down in flames, a hard-won sense of safe travel went with it, and no rigid dirigible ever again carried a paying passenger. In some respects this was a great setback to aerial transportation. Heavier-than-air craft did not even attempt the North Atlantic crossing until 1939, and commercial nonstop transatlantic service, which the *Hindenburg* had offered from 1937 and the *Graf Zeppelin* from 1931 (between Germany and Brazil), was not available again until 1957.[8]

The extensive and terrifying photographic coverage of the *Hindenburg* catastrophe was all too persuasive. But dirigible travel ceased for more complex reasons. After the explosion Dr. Eckener decided that passengers would never again fly in craft inflated by highly flammable hydrogen. He lobbied the U.S. for heavier, safer helium and America agreed, but the secretary of the interior held out, fearing that the Germans might convert their airships into bombers. By early 1938, when Hitler seized Austria, refusing assistance to the Germans became the politically correct decision.[9] The *Hindenburg* lived on, but only in photographs—forever burning, forever in the throes of death.

NOTES

1. Simon Michael Bessie, *Jazz Journalism: The Story of Tabloid Newspapers* (New York: E. P. Dutton, 1938), pp. 238, 84.
2. Luce, in Vicki Goldberg, *Margaret Bourke-White: A Biography* (New York: Harper and Row, 1986), pp. 174–75.
3. Wilson Hicks, "The News Photographer," January 14, 1948; ibid., p. 269.
4. Twenty-two photographers: Beaumont Newhall, *The History of Photography from 1839 to the Present* (New York: Museum of Modern Art, 1982), p. 258. Bad weather, newsreels: John

Toland, *The Great Dirigibles: Their Triumphs and Disasters* (New York: Dover, 1972), pp. 313, 323.
5. Picture newspapers: Newhall, *History of Photography,* p. 258. By noon: Toland, *Great Dirigibles,* p. 336.
6. Toland, *Great Dirigibles,* pp. 319–22.
7. Ibid., pp. 23, 9, 10.
8. Harold G. Dick with Douglas H. Robinson, *The Golden Age of the Great Passenger Airships* (Washington, D.C.: Smithsonian Institution Press, 1985), p. 166.
9. Ibid., pp. 151–64. During World War I, a Zeppelin had dropped bombs on London. Eventually, the remains of the *Hindenburg* were melted down and used in Nazi planes. (Michael MacDonald Mooney, *The Hindenburg* [New York: Dodd, Mead, 1972], pp. 38, 262.)

27 ADVERTISING, CONSUMERS, AND CULTURE
William Leiss, Stephen Kline, and Sut Jhally

William Leiss is professor at Queens University; Stephen Kline is professor of communication at Simon Fraser University; and Sut Jhally is professor of communication at the University of Massachusetts at Amherst. Their collaborative book, Social Communication in Advertising, *has become a definitive text.*

The coming of a market-industry society introduced a radical change. For the first time, the majority of the population was surrounded by goods produced in settings that were no longer familiar, although initially most goods and the materials they were made from resembled those that had been used at home and in local shops. But gradually the consumer marketplace became flooded with items whose purposes and benefits could not be ascertained by the shopper's unaided senses and intellect alone. . . .

The developed phase of the market industrial society is the consumer society, where a truly enormous assortment of goods confronts the individual—and where the characteristics of those goods changes constantly. The dramatic rise in real incomes, discretionary spending, and leisure time also meant that a far higher proportion of the marketing effort could be devoted to human wants not directly tied to basic necessities. More precisely, messages about necessities (such as food) could be incorporated within broader "transformational" message formats, which culminated in the present "lifestyle" image. Just as most individuals in the consumer society had been freed from concentrating on the bare necessities of existence, so marketers and advertisers could now for the most part safely ignore life's humdrum aspects and play freely, and apparently endlessly, with structures of imagery for the consumption process.

What marketers had realized was that, with the population as a whole having far greater discretionary income, leisure time, and employment security than ever before, work was no longer the focus of everyday life. The sphere of consumption could take its place. By linking consumption through electronic media to popular entertainment and sports, marketers and advertisers eventually fashioned a richly decorated setting for an elaborate play of messages, increasingly in imagistic or iconic form, about the ways to happiness and social success.

Marketing practices had realized that the market-industrial society was becoming a consumer society long before most social commentators did. Until quite recently our thinking about consumption was almost primitive. Reinforced by economists, a powerful cultural tradition lauded the moral benefits of hard work and obedience to authority and concentrated its attention on increasing production; the process of consuming the things so assiduously produced was regarded as a less worthy enterprise, which in any case would take care of itself. Indeed, as the economic historian A. O. Hirschman has noted, attacks on "consumerism" are as old as the literature on economic development itself: The new productive possibilities, which began to be glimpsed in the eighteenth century, have always led to fears that the availability of new types of goods would corrupt society and individuals alike (Hirschman 1982, ch. 3).

Around the turn of this century the realization dawned that a satisfactory end use for the industrial system's vast productive capacities could be found in unfettered mass consumption. (Later it was discovered that protracted warfare on a global scale, and even more protracted preparation for a war that must never be allowed to happen, would also occasion reinvestment and help to absorb the output.) This caused concern because commentators believed that ordinary folk could not handle more than a rude array of goods without becoming dissolute, a diagnosis that reflected the dominant social interests in the earlier phases of industrialism.

Factory owners and shopkeepers seeking to teach the new discipline of market relations— regular hours and days of work, punctuality, subordination to the machine, wage income as the sole means of subsistence—to a workforce steeped in peasant rhythms had encountered a recalcitrant and often hostile audience who had little reason to be grateful to its teachers. Employers lamented their employees' love of cheap but debilitating spirits and the "Blue Mondays" that shortened the working week; the frequent absences for long celebrations of traditional festive occasions or just for going hunting or attending to domestic business; and the stubborn resistance in general to the new work discipline that offended customary practices and the profound sense of personal dignity rooted in them.

These themes are nicely illustrated in a splendid essay by the historian Herbert Gutman, who also shows how European immigrants to North America constructed defenses against oppression out of their popular cultures: "Peasant parades and rituals, religious oaths and food riots, and much else in the culture and behavior of early twentieth-century immigrant American factory workers were . . . natural and effective forms of self-assertion and self-protection" (Gutman 1977, 66). Both secular and religious elements in transplanted ethnic communities were called upon to sustain labor solidarity, especially in the bitter and all-too-frequent strikes. Group traditions supplied not only the means to struggle against degradation and injustice, but also to retain a foothold in a remembered world having an elemental coherence fashioned out of custom, venerated objects, ancient loyalties, and intergenerational memory.

Gradually, however, the older patterns of life and culture fell apart. The unity and continuity of daily life in village settlements could not

Advertising made wide use of picture magazines in the early 20th century. Eastman utilized such magazines to promote the "home" movie as a way of strengthening ties with one's personal past. *National Archives of Canada.*

be sustained amid increasing urbanization, especially when workplace, domicile, and commerce were separated. Linked intimately with craft labor, the old ways of life could not stamp their accumulated meanings on the anonymous products that were beginning to pour off the assembly lines. And the highly restrictive codes of personal behavior shaped by the closed worlds of religious values and distinct ethnic communities could not survive the more subtle blows of industrialism: the cultural relativism resulting from the quick amalgamation of so many different groups, the erosion of the economic function of the extended family, and the dawning of a new type of leisure time highly individualized in nature and no longer bound to the traditional collective forms of popular entertainment or domestic routine.

These diverse but interconnected changes affected the principal channels of public intercourse and also the smallest details of everyday life. For example, they are represented both in the character formation and values of individuals. David Riesman summarizes these changes in

The Lonely Crowd (1950) by contrasting "inner-directed" and "other-directed" characters: The former's goals are set early in life and remain largely unaffected by later events; the latter are influenced continuously by what is happening around them, and their goals shift with circumstances. Inner-directed characters emphasize production, and other-directed characters, consumption. Riesman contends that there has been a shift from the former to the latter as the predominant character type in modern society.

The recognition that the progress of industrialism itself would require society to change its emphasis from a "production ethic" to a "consumption ethic" began to dawn at the close of the nineteenth century. Rosalynd Williams has spotted in French thought of the period the evocation of what she calls "dream worlds of the consumer." At this time the large urban department stores were established, and the great expositions that had started with the Crystal Palace in 1851, where the wonders of science, technology, and machinery were at the forefront, completed the transition from production to consumption with the Paris Exposition of 1900: "At the 1900 exposition the sensual pleasures of consumption clearly triumphed over the abstract intellectual enjoyment of contemplating the progress of knowledge" (Williams 1982, 59–60). As soon as cheap consumer goods began to appear in large quantities, commentators started to fret about the "levelling of tastes," that is, the collapse of the distinction, formerly so clear, between items of refined design possessed by the rich and the rough possessions of the poor. Industry's cleverness was beginning to devise passable mass-produced imitations of objects that the poor had only dreamed of owning in the past.

Once again we have to make an effort to think back in time to visualize an epoch vastly different from our own. At the turn of the twentieth century, many of those in more fortunate circumstances felt two sensations when they surveyed the common run of humanity: first, terror that the police and army might one day be unable to stifle the upwellings of violence against property and order; and second, dread that this teeming mass might some day discard the shackles of moral restraint so carefully fashioned by religion and traditional culture. Curiously enough, few among the scions of the propertied classes, wrapped so thoroughly in the finely spun cocoon of conservatism, imagined that even a paltry share of nature's bounty and humanity's skill, along with a modicum of dignity and self-respect, would cause the same conservatism to take root among the general population as well.

But that world view was slipping away irretrievably in the industrializing nations. The restraint on worldly desires preached to the poor for so long made less and less sense as the factory system's astonishing productive capacities became apparent. For the only arena capable of absorbing the system's output was the one occupied by those who had been poor for so long. The American writer Simon N. Patten (1852–1922) was one of the first to see this clearly. In *The New Basis of Civilization* (1907)

he argued that society should preach not renunciation of desire but expansion of consumption and should accept as its goal the attainment of a general state of abundance (Horowitz 1980, 303–304).

This point is the origin of what has been called "the culture of consumption." The foundation stone for everything that was to emerge from it was a new type of personality and "social self" based on individuality, which has the qualities ascribed by David Riesman to the other-directed character. Gradually set loose from restrictive behavioral codes by the crumbling of older cultures that measured persons against fixed standards of achievement and moral worth, persons became oriented instead to the ever fuller consumer marketplace—a marketplace *that had begun to address them as individuals*. The new social self was set against an open-ended scale of success—a scale set to whatever criteria happen to be applicable at the time. It is no accident that income eventually emerged as the single most important status indicator in the United States, where the culture of consumption is most fully developed: "Income is of overwhelming importance in how Americans think about social standing" (Coleman and Rainwater 1978, 220). Income provides access to whatever visible and tangible tokens of success happen to be most prized at any moment.

For Riesman, the other-directed character is open to ever-shifting environmental influences, especially peer-group pressures. Given the predominant features of the new social environment of the early twentieth century, it is hardly surprising that a tendency towards other-directedness should arise. Older extended family and ethnic community bonds were unravelling, urbanization and the personal anonymity it confers were proceeding apace, and individuals were being confronted more and more with the fact of incessant change in everyday life, as industrial technologies and design were applied to proliferating consumer products.

Judging from the great popularity of the "anxiety format" in advertising during the period between the two world wars, the new social self was tormented by anxiety as it looked for a safe niche in largely uncharted domains of social approval. Jackson Lears quotes a classic example from a Brunswick toilet seat ad of 1930. Beneath a scene of well-dressed women drinking coffee the text runs as follows:

> "And . . . did you notice the bathroom?" At that moment the hostess reentered the room. She had just barely overheard. But it was more than enough. She began talking about Junior, about bridge, anything—but like chain lightning her mind reviewed the bathroom. She saw it suddenly as a guest must see it, saw the one offending detail that positively clamored for criticism. (Fox and Lears 1983, 25)

The detail in question was a wooden toilet seat! The charming aspect of this tale is that two generations later the descendants of these anxiety-striken women, responding to the beat of a different peer-group drummer, scoured junkyards and used furniture stores for the surviving population of old wooden toilet seats, carefully refinished them, and reinstalled them proudly in their bathrooms. This recent practice, it should be noted, ran counter to prevailing contemporary industry advertising.

Jackson Lears suggests that in the social environment we have just sketched, the new social self experienced a feeling of "unreality," in response to which a "therapeutic ethos" flourished. With the erosion of social group supports for personal identity sustained by older cultures, the generation and maintenance of selfhood became a lifetime task for individuals: an endless series of exercises in self-improvement, personal development, self-expression, mental and physical tone, "selling oneself," cultivating approval, "winning friends and influencing people," continuing down to the present outpouring of manuals on such subjects as "power lunching" for teaching aggressive (and by now somewhat hysterical) self-assertion.

Lears sees the therapeutic ethos as a cultural response to the uncertainties introduced into the social environment by urbanization, industrial technology, and market relations. He also suggests that it prepared fertile ground for the rising prominence of national consumer product advertising, for the "longings for reintegrated selfhood and intense experience" could be employed by advertisers "to arouse consumer demand by associating products with imaginary states of well-being." The erosion of older cultures created a void in personal life. For all practical purposes there was an empty slate on which to write, and advertisers seized the pen: "The decline of symbolic structures outside the self has been a central process in the development of a consumer culture, joining advertising strategies and the therapeutic ethos" (Fox and Lears 1983, 17–21).

There is, of course, another side to the story. Business and industry had awakened at the same time to the need for a greatly intensified selling effort in order to "move the goods" cascading off their assembly lines. Daniel Pope, discussing "industry's need for advertising" around the turn of this century, mentions exactly the same key factors, looked at from the business angle, as Lears does in examining the culture of consumption: industrialization, urbanization, and new forms of communication. Marketing emerged as a recognized professional activity, and corporations established marketing departments in their organizational structures.

During this period advertising came to constitute the largest share of print media revenues, and by 1920 it accounted for about two-thirds of all newspaper and magazine income. More important than the volume of advertising was the fact that "the lead in advertising had passed to manufacturers of nationally distributed, brand-named goods" (Pope 1983, 30), for it was in the formation of a national consumer market that the advertising industry as we know it today was born and nurtured.

Selected Bibliography

Coleman, R., and L. Rainwater, 1978. *Social Standing in America.* New York: Basic Books.

Fox, Richard Wrightman, and T. J. Jackson Lears, eds. 1983. *The Culture of Consumption.* New York: Pantheon.

Gutman, Herbert. 1977. *Work, Culture and Society in Industrializing America.* New York: Vintage.

Hirschman, A. O. 1982. *Shifting Involvements.* Princeton: Princeton University Press.

Horowitz, D. 1980. "Consumption and Its Discontents." *Journal of American History* 67.

Pope, Daniel. 1983. *The Making of Modern Advertising.* New York: Basic Books.

Riesman, David. 1950. *The Lonely Crowd.* New Haven, Conn.: Yale University Press.

PART VI

Radio Days

Front page of *The New York Times* the day following the *Titanic* tragedy, based largely on wireless reports from the North Atlantic, 1912. *Reprinted by permission of The New York Times Company.*

The transition to "mass society," discussed in the previous selection, was further accelerated by the birth of broadcast radio during the 1920s. It was an outgrowth of the "wireless," sometimes referred to as "radiotelegraphy," invented by Marconi shortly before the turn of the century. Marconi's goal was to successfully transmit Morse-coded messages from point to point without the use of wires. Transatlantic communication in this manner was regarded as a major achievement by almost everyone—except the cable companies! Marconi, however, had little interest in the wireless as a medium for voice transmission. Others, most notably the Canadian Reginald Fessenden, worked on this problem. Considerable strides were made until World War I impeded further research.

After the end of the war a number of amateur stations began "broadcasting" voice, together with live and recorded music. Enthusiastic hobbyists listened in on earphones using inexpensive crystal sets. Initially, they were students of the new technology, versed in Morse code and keen to decipher military, civilian, and maritime messages. But as voice and music broadcasts increased, other family members donned the earphones. They created a scenario reminiscent of "proto-broadcasting" over the telephone. What began as a hobby became an entertainment experience, greatly facilitated in the early 1920s by the emergence of an increasing number of corporate stations that broadcast on a regular basis. The end of this decade saw the creation of the vacuum tube radio with loudspeakers. Within a half dozen years, despite economic hard times during the Depression, many families owned a set. Radio had become a true mass medium. The glow of the dial in the dark of the evening, as voices from afar entered the living room, recalled storytelling around a primeval campfire.

Radio, no matter how it developed as a mass medium, through private ownership in the United States, through government sponsorship in Europe, or in both ways as in Canada, captivated a generation. Looking back at the 1930s, we can see several parallels between attitudes toward, and the influence of, radio and what would occur in the 1950s during the "Golden Age" of television. Woody Allen gives us a vivid commentary on this in his excellent film *Radio Days*, from which we have drawn the title of this part. It is well worth considering in conjunction with the chapters that follow, as are recently available tapes and records of broadcasts from radio's "Golden Age".

In the decade before World War I, as wireless use expanded, most people thought radio telegraphy was novel and useful. The attitude changed to indispensable following the sinking of the *Titanic* in 1912. The communications implications of this disaster are discussed by Stephen Kern in our first essay. He argues that the wireless and a number other electric technologies deriving from what we have called the "wired world" expanded the way the present was regarded. It enabled people to experience distant events as they occurred. He shows how this capacity was foreshadowed in a more limited way, from station-to-station by the telegraph and at the interpersonal level (as well as through "proto-broadcasting") by the telephone. We should add that disasters such as the *Titanic*'s sinking, which highlighted the potential of wireless, are sometimes vivid illustrations of how the dominant medium of a period operates. In the early years of radio broadcasting, the crash of the *Hindenburg* and Orson Welles's broadcast of H.G. Wells's *War of the Worlds* attest to this. During the television era the Kennedy assassination and the NASA *Challenger* explosion are further examples.

One of the issues we think readers should consider in conjunction with early radio is the coming of sound to motion pictures. That this occurred in the late 1920s, at the same time network broadcasting began, was no accident. As Scott Eyman notes in our next excerpt, hearing performers on radio made people want to hear the voices of actors in the movies. He goes on to chronicle the enormous changes brought about by the coming of sound, arguing that it was the most far-reaching transformation in motion picture history since the advent of film projection itself.

The remarkable, though often overlooked, transition that radio underwent during the 1920s, from popular hobby to major mass medium, is discussed by Susan J. Douglas in our next selection. She presents a range of perceptions that existed toward the new medium on the eve of its "Golden Age"—from the belief that it could be a way to communicate with extraterrestrials to its use as a promotor of national unity. Also commented on, and an issue today with television and the use of VCRs, was the convenience of radio in accessing entertainment. Often, people preferred to stay at home and listen, rather than go to hear live music or a play. As a result certain forms of popular culture began a shift to broadcasting to maintain and eventually increase their audiences. Debates about programming resulted. They are still with us, as is an ongoing critique of the way the medium—radio then, television now—has presented politics and religion.

Radio in the 1930s created enormous interest in various forms of popular entertainment: dramas, comedies, sports, and the music of the big band era. But as William Stott argues in our next selection, its effect on news documentation was no less profound. Radio gave the listener a greater sense of immediacy with what was happening than the newspaper. This was accomplished through reporting via the direct voice and, on occasion, "live" from an event in progress. President Franklin Roosevelt's "fireside chats" riveted a generation. Radio provided an immediacy and a link with the public that allowed political leaders a way around the newspapers for reaching the public. It gave us, as well, yet another version of the "star" system. Stott skillfully documents the impact that these political uses of broadcasting had on the credibility and popularity of newspapers. He concludes with a look at radio's role in reporting international news and its ability to influence public attitudes. Both would be crucial during the unfolding drama of World War II.

No look at radio's "Golden Age" would be complete without a sample of the various programs that filled the airwaves. The excerpt by Christopher Sterling and John M. Kitross provides us with a representative glimpse of what was available. Their survey includes musical variety, comedy, drama, sports, and political programming. How many of these formats are still on radio? What changes have taken place in those that remain? Which types of programming made a successful shift to television, and why?

Our last contributor to this section, Marshall McLuhan (1911–1980), would not have needed introduction a generation ago. A wide public would inevitably think of his name whenever the subject of communications media was mentioned. McLuhan was a Canadian literary critic who turned his attention to communication studies during the 1950s and 1960s. He was influenced by the ideas of his University of Toronto colleague, Harold Innis, whom we introduced in Part I. Like Innis, McLuhan believed that media have a powerful influence on the world around us, that they are not neutral carriers of information but contain inherent biases that profoundly affect their content. He looked at these biases in terms of the way in which media influence psychological organization and thought, whereas Innis had focused on consequences of new communications for social and institutional organization.

McLuhan also popularized his work in ways that offended many scholars and critics. This entailed the cultivation of an outrageous and sometimes bewildering style, which frequently incorporates the very language of the medium under examination! The excerpt that we have included, "Understanding Radio," demonstrates this. McLuhan argues that the auditory power of radio has an almost tribal effect by appealing to primal emotions. During its "Golden Age", the 1930s and 1940s, this was evidenced in diverse ways—through Hitler's emotional speeches broadcast to the German public as well as in curious incidents such as the minor panic created in New Jersey in 1937 when listeners mistook Orson Welles's dramatic broadcast of *War of the Worlds* for a news report of the real thing. At the time of his writing in the 1960s, McLuhan saw the tribal effect of radio shifting to youth via radio's embrace of rock music.

Readers should note that what McLuhan claims to do is to explore—or "probe," as he calls it—our sense of media's role in daily reality. His observations are not intended to provide factual support for specific theories, but to draw our attention to key questions and to provoke further thinking about the role of media in society.

28 WIRELESS WORLD

Stephen Kern

Stephen Kern is Presidential Research Professor at Northern Illinois University. He is the author of a major and widely influential work in cultural history, The Culture of Time and Space: 1880–1918.

On the night of April 14, 1912, the largest moving structure ever built, the *Titanic,* steamed at a recklessly high speed into an ice field in the North Atlantic. The first officer recalled that the sea was especially calm and so that night there were no "ice blinks"—flashes of light given off when waves splash against icebergs and illuminate their crystallized surfaces. Visibility was further reduced by fog. At 11:40 P.M. a lookout suddenly spotted an iceberg dead ahead. The ship turned sharply and, as it scraped by, was opened up like a tin can with a gash below the water line three hundred feet long. The captain determined that they were going to sink fast and at 12:15 A.M. ordered his wireless operator to send the distress call. Within a few minutes the airwaves were rippling with signals as over a dozen ships became aware of the disaster. This was simultaneous drama on the high seas, driven by steam power and choreographed by the magic of wireless telegraphy.

Ten ships heard the call from over a hundred miles away and remained in contact but were too distant to help, as were also the *Hellig Olav* at 90 miles and the *Niagara* at 75 miles. The *Mount Temple* was 50 miles away but had to move slowly through ice fields. The *Carpathia* at 58 miles was the first to arrive, but not until almost two hours after the *Titanic* went down with 1,522 passengers. Another ship, close enough to have saved all the passengers, was not in wireless contact. The *Californian* was approximately 19 miles away, but its wireless operator had hung up his earphones for the night about ten minutes before the *Titanic* sent out its first CQD. Two watchmen on the deck of the *Californian* saw the rockets that the *Titanic* fired but could not figure out what they meant or convince their captain to pull anchor and find out. What the eyes and ears of man could not perceive the wireless could receive over vast distances and through darkness and fog.

The operator on the *Carpathia* got the call for help when he put on his earphones to verify a "time rush" (an exchange of time signals with a neighboring ship to see if their clocks agree). At 1:06 A.M. he heard the *Titanic* tell another ship coming to help, "Get your boats ready; going down fast on the head." The world began to get news of the disaster at 1:20 A.M., when a wireless station in Newfoundland picked up the message that the *Titanic* was sinking and was putting women off in boats. Shortly after that hundreds of wireless instruments along the Atlantic coast began to transmit and the airways became jumbled in confusion. The *Titanic's* wireless had a range of only 1,500 miles, so signals to Europe had to go first to New York and then across the ocean by cable; still, by early morning the entire world was privy to news of the disaster.[1]

To one of the survivors in a life boat it seemed as if the stars above saw the ship in distress and "had awakened to flash messages across the black dome of the sky to each other."[2] The communication that he imagined between stars was accomplished on a lesser scale between the ships at sea by wireless. On April 21, the *New York Times* commented on its magical power.

Night and day all the year round the millions upon the earth and the thousands upon the sea now reach out and grasp the thin air and use it as a thing more potent for human aid than any strand of wire or cable that was ever spun or woven. Last week 745 [*sic*] human lives were saved from perishing by the wireless. But for the almost magic use of the air the *Titanic* tragedy would have been shrouded in the secrecy that not so long ago was the power of the sea. . . . Few New Yorkers realize that all through the roar of the big city there are constantly speeding messages between people separated by vast distances, and that over housetops and even through the walls of buildings and in the very air one breathes are words written by electricity.

An editorial in the *London Times* of April 16 noted the expanded range of experience made possible by the wireless. "The wounded monster's distress sounded through the latitudes and longitudes of the Atlantic, and from all sides her sisters great and small hastened to her succor . . . We recognize with a sense near to awe that we have been almost witness of a great ship in her death agonies." An officer of the American Telephone and Telegraph Company praised the communication that made it possible to follow the rescue. The telephone and wireless, he wrote, "enabled the peoples of many lands to stand together in sympathetic union, to share a common grief." William Alden Smith, the Michigan senator who chaired an exhaustive inquiry into the sinking, as part of his summary of those hearings before the United States Senate on May 18, 1912, referred to the new sense of world unity that required worldwide safety regulations. "When the world weeps together over a common loss," he said, "when nature moves in the same directions in all spheres, why should not the nations clear the sea of its conflicting idioms and wisely regulate this new servant of humanity?"[3] Although the wireless had been used before to save lives at sea, this rescue effort was particularly highlighted because so many were aware of the tragedy: the survivors watching from life boats, the wireless operators in distant places, and the frustrated seamen in the rescue ships.

The ability to experience many distant events at the same time, made possible by the wireless and dramatized by the sinking of the *Titanic*, was part of a major change in the experience of the present. Thinking on the subject was

divided over two basic issues: whether the present is a sequence of single local events or a simultaneity of multiple distant events, and whether the present is an infinitesimal slice of time between past and future or of more extended duration. The latter debate was limited largely to philosophers, but the issue of sequence versus simultaneity was expressed by numerous artists, poets, and novelists and was concretely manifested in some new technology in addition to the wireless—the telephone, the high-speed rotary press, and the cinema.

Already in 1889 Lord Salisbury commented on the simultaneity of experience made possible by the telegraph, which had "combined together almost at one moment . . . the opinions of the whole intelligent world with respect to everything that is passing at that time upon the face of the globe."[4] The telegraph had been in operation since the 1830s, but its use was limited to trained operators and confined to transmitting stations. The wireless proliferated source points of electronic communication, and the telephone brought it to the masses.

The history of wireless telegraphy begins with a paper by James Clerk Maxwell in 1864, which argued that electromagnetic waves must exist and should be able to be propagated through space. In 1887 Heinrich Hertz produced those waves in a laboratory, and in 1894 Guglielmo Marconi devised an apparatus to transmit and receive them. In 1897 Marconi went to England and established the first coast station on the Isle of Wight for communication with ships at sea. In 1901 a message was sent across the Atlantic from a special high-power transmitter in England, and two years later King Edward VII and President Theodore Roosevelt exchanged messages over it. As wireless instruments proliferated, an International Congress on Wireless Telegraphy was held at Berlin in 1903 to regulate their use. The Marconi Company established the first wireless news service in 1904 with nightly transmissions from Cornwall and Cape Cod. The first distress signal from a ship at sea was sent in 1899, and in 1909, following a collision between two ships, a wireless call saved 1700 lives. The technology got some sensational publicity in 1910 when a wireless message led to the arrest of an American physician in London, who murdered and buried his wife and attempted to escape aboard a ship with his secretary dressed as a boy. The captain became suspicious of the two, wired Scotland Yard, and arranged to have a detective arrest the couple at sea before they arrived in port. By 1912 the wireless was an essential part of international communication linking land stations and ships at sea in an instantaneous, worldwide network.[5]

The telephone had an even broader impact and made it possible, in a sense, to be in two places at the same time. It allowed people to talk to one another across great distances, to think about what others were feeling and to respond at once without the time to reflect afforded by written communication. Business and personal exchanges suddenly became instantaneous instead of protracted and sequential. Party lines created another kind of simultaneous experience, because in the early systems bells rang along the entire line and everyone who was interested could listen in. One imaginative journalist envisioned the simultaneity of telephone communication as a fabric made from the fibers of telephone lines, switchboard cables, and speech: "Before the great switchboard the girls seem like weavers at some gigantic loom, the numerous cords crossing and recrossing as if in the execution of some wondrous fabric. Indeed, a wondrous fabric of speech is here woven into the record of each day."[6]

Within a few years of its invention in 1876 the telephone was used for public "broadcasts." In 1879 sermons were broadcast over telephone lines in the United States, and in 1880 a concert in Zurich was sent over telephone lines fifty miles to Basel. The following year an opera in Berlin and a strong quartet in Manchester were transmitted to neighboring cities. The Belgians began such transmissions in 1884: the telephone company of Charleroi gave a concert which could be heard by all of the subscribers, an opera in Monnaie was heard 250 kilometers

away at the royal palace at Ostend, and the North Railroad Station in Brussels piped in music from the Vaux-Hall in what was perhaps the first experiment with Muzak.[7]

Jules Verne envisioned "telephonic journalism" in a science fiction story of 1888.[8] Five years later it became a reality when a Hungarian engineer started such a news service in Budapest and expanded it into a comprehensive entertainment service with outlets in the homes of its 6000 subscribers, each of whom had a timetable of programs including concerts, lectures, dramatic readings, newspaper reviews, stock market reports, and direct transmissions of speeches by members of Parliament. It focused the attention of the inhabitants of an entire city on a single experience, regulated their lives according to the program schedules, and invaded their privacy with an emergency signal that enabled the station to ring every subscriber when special news broke. An English journalist imagined that this service, if introduced in England, would "democratize" many luxuries of the rich as the "humblest cottage would be in immediate contact with the city, and the 'private wire' would make all classes kin."[9] At the same time it would diminish the isolation of individuals in cities and make it possible for one voice to be heard simultaneously by the six million people of London. In the United States in 1896, telephones were used to report presidential election returns, and, according to a contemporary report, "thousands sat with their ear glued to the receiver the whole night long, hypnotized by the possibilities unfolded to them for the first time."[10]

There was diverse critical response to the simultaneity of experience created by modern journalism. Already in 1892 the indefatigable alarmist Max Nordau complained that the simplest village inhabitant has a wider geographical horizon than the prime minister of a century ago. If the villager reads a paper he "interests himself simultaneously in the issue of a revolution in Chile, a bush-war in East Africa, a massacre in North China, a famine in Russia."[11] Nordau anticipated that it would take a century for people to be able "to read a dozen square yards of newspapers daily, to be constantly called to the telephone, to be thinking simultaneously of the five continents of the world" without injury to the nerves. Paul Claudel reacted more positively in 1904 when he wrote that the morning newspaper gives us a sense of "the present in its totality,"[12] and an editorial in *Paris-Midi* of February 23, 1914, characterized the headlines of one daily paper as "simultaneous poetry."

NOTES

1. Walter Lord, *A Night to Remember* (New York, 1955); Richard O'Connor, *Down to Eternity* (New York, 1956); Peter Padfield, *The Titanic and the Californian* (London, 1965); Geoffrey Marcus, *The Maiden Voyage* (New York, 1969).

2. Lawrence Beesley, *The Loss of the SS Titanic* (New York, 1912), 101.

3. U. N. Bethell, *The Transmission of Intelligence by Electricity* (New York, 1912), 6; Smith quote cited by Wyn Craig Wade, *The Titanic: End of a Dream* (New York, 1979), 399–400.

4. Lord Salisbury's speech was printed in *The Electrician,* November 8, 1889, and cited by Asa Briggs, "The Pleasure Telephone: A Chapter in the Prehistory of the Media," in *The Social Impact of the Telephone,* ed. Ithiel Pool (Cambridge, 1977), 41.

5. G. E. C. Wedlake, *SOS: The Story of Radio-Communication* (London, 1973), 18–74.

6. Sylvester Baxter, "The Telephone Girl," *The Outlook* (May 26, 1906): 235.

7. Julien Brault, *Histoire du téléphone* (Paris, 1888), 90–95.

8. Jules Verne, "In the Year 2889," *The Forum,* 6 (1888): 664.

9. "The Telephone Newspaper," *Scientific American* (October 26, 1896); Arthur Mee, "The Pleasure Telephone," *The Strand Magazine,* 16 (1898): 34; and Asa Briggs, "The Pleasure Telephone," 41.

10. "The Telephone and Election Returns," *Electrical Review* (December 16, 1896): 298.

11. Max Nordau, *Degeneration* (1892; rpt. New York, 1968), 39.

12. Paul Claudel, "Connaissance du temps," in *Fou-Tcheou* (1904), quoted in Pär Bergman, *"Moder-nolatria" et "Simultaneità": Recherches sur deux tendances dans l'avant-garde littéraire en Italie et en France à la veille de la première guerre mondiale* (Uppsala, Sweden, 1962), 23.

29 MOVIES TALK
Scott Eyman

Scott Eyman is the book editor of the Palm Beach Post *and the author of five books of film scholarship, including biographies of Mary Pickford and Ernest Lubitsch. His most recent work is* The Speed of Sound: Hollywood and the Talkie Revolution, 1926–1930, *from which the present excerpt is taken.*

It is the muggy afternoon of August 30, 1927. On the newly constructed soundstage of the Warner Bros. Studio on Sunset Boulevard, Al Jolson is industriously, unwittingly, engaged in the destruction of one great art and the creation of another.

The scene: a son's homecoming. The man universally recognized as the greatest entertainer of his day is singing Irving Berlin's "Blue Skies" to Eugénie Besserer, playing his mother. After an initial chorus sung with Jolson's usual nervy bravura, he suddenly stops. He asks his mother if she likes the song, tells her he'd rather please her than anybody. The floodgates open and the hilarious babbling begins:

"Mama, darlin', if I'm a success in this show, well, we're gonna move from here. Oh yes, we're gonna move up in the Bronx. A lot of nice green grass up there and a whole lot of people you know. There's the Ginsbergs, the Guttenbergs, and the Goldbergs. Oh, a whole lotta Bergs, I don't know 'em all.

"And I'm gonna buy you a nice black silk dress, Mama. You see Mrs. Friedman, the butcher's wife, she'll be jealous of you . . . Yes, she will. You see if she isn't. And I'm gonna get you a nice pink dress that'll go with your brown eyes . . ."

While the crew stands transfixed, Jolson keeps talking, a torrent of unaccustomed words in the midst of a predominantly silent film, a medium that has proudly subsisted on pantomime or, at the most, synchronized underscoring, sound effects, and a laconic word or two. But now every word that Jolson says is being recorded by a single large, black, cylindrical microphone a foot above his head, which transmits the sound to a 16-inch wax disc spinning at 33 $\frac{1}{3}$ revolutions a minute.

Singing has never been a trial for Al Jolson; it is life that is difficult, and carrying a picture, a family drama mixed with a rough approximation of a backstage musical before backstage musicals are invented, has been causing him enormous anxiety. Only four years before, he walked out on a silent film for D. W. Griffith because of nerves, and the desperate volubility with which Jolson is haranguing Besserer may well be the result of an adrenaline rush of pure fear.

Certainly, costar May McAvoy has observed a much quieter, needier man than will ever be on public view in later years. "Act like he knew it all?" asked McAvoy. "Oh no. Never! He was the most cooperative person, and just darling." Jolson leans on McAvoy, an experienced actress who has worked for leading directors such as Ernst Lubitsch. After most scenes, he asks "How'd I do? Was I all right? Please tell me. Let me know. Let's do it over again if it wasn't good."

Production of *The Jazz Singer* had actually begun two months earlier. While Jolson is out of town fulfilling a nightclub engagement, Warners begins production with location scenes in New York that don't require his presence. Meanwhile, the Warner studio on Sunset Boulevard gears up for sound with difficulty, for the studio is stretched thin financially.

"I ordered $40 worth of parts to build a sound-mixing panel," Warner Bros. technician William Mueller will remember years later, "but the man wouldn't leave [the parts] until he got his money. I paid him out of my own pocket only to be told by the studio purchasing agent, Jack Warner's brother-in-law, that I probably wouldn't get my money back. They also demanded that I return what I had left from a $500 cash advance so they could meet the payroll that week."

Likewise, Mueller and Nathan Levinson, Western Electric's man in Hollywood, knew they needed $10,000 to build proper sound facilities and had taken an entire morning to convince Jack Warner to spend the money. He finally agreed, then left for lunch. Knowing their man, Levinson and Mueller got the studio superintendent to clear the necessary area and began construction. "When Jack came back two hours later, he told us he'd changed his mind, but by that time it was too late."

The "Blue Skies" sequence is business as usual for *The Jazz Singer*. All the sound scenes are being made as separate little films, after the surrounding silent footage has been shot. With one exception, the sound sequences are shot within nine consecutive days beginning August 17, and each of them is given its own production code number on the schedule sheets. (Warners might be thinking about eventually releasing them separately as short subjects should Sam Warner's crazy advocacy of feature-length sound films not work out. It is also possible that this is simply because Vitaphone, the name of their sound system, is a separate production entity.)

The sound scenes are usually shot in the afternoon, from 1 to 5 P.M., with three cameras. Work throughout the rest of the studio is suspended while the production staff gathers to listen to Jolson give what amounts to free concerts.

Shooting of the sound sequences begins with "It All Depends on You," completed in seven takes; "Mother of Mine," shot on August

18, in only two; "Mammy," shot that same day in three takes; and so on. The last number is "Blue Skies," which replaces "It All Depends on You." It is the only scene with any meaningful dialogue beyond Jolson's catchphrase "You ain't heard nothin' yet!" Aside from its comfortable position in the arsenal of Jolson hits, "Blue Skies" is a favorite of the Warners; it has already been performed twice in their Vitaphone sound shorts within the last year.

In later years, sound engineer George Groves asserts that Jolson's cheerful speech to his movie mother is "*purely* ad-lib . . . without any rehearsal. Everybody just held their breath." Likewise, head engineer Stanley Watkins says that "Jolson was to sing, but there was to be no dialogue . . . when the picture was being made he insisted on ad-libbing in a couple of places. Sam Warner managed to persuade his brothers to leave the scenes in. 'It won't do any harm,' [Sam said.] In my opinion it was a put-up job between Sam Warner and Jolson."

Yet, technician William Mueller will have a diametrically opposed recollection and spins a remarkably involved conspiratorial tale: "When the songs went well, someone—I don't remember who—decided to have a talking sequence as well. Jolson absolutely would not do it. He said he was a singer and not an actor. He thought it would ruin his career and even offered to pay Warners the money they had already spent to get out of it.

"Finally, they got him to make a test. Then they framed him. While the director and assistant director went to his house to tell him how wonderful it was, they had the prop man view the dailies . . . He rushed out to Jolson's house, burst in, and raved about the films. Then he said that [George] Jessel had sneaked in to watch and was very excited about it. He said that Jessel, knowing that Jolson wanted out, also had gone to Jack Warner and offered to do the film for nothing. That did it. Jolson couldn't stand that, so he agreed to do [the scene] himself."

The Jazz Singer offers not just music but an effervescent personality projecting itself in words, bursting through the screen to wrap the audience in an exuberant embrace. The picture is a gamble, of course—the brothers have spent $500,000 on a film that can be shown in precisely two theaters in the United States—but, as Sam, Jack, and Harry Warner look at it for the first time, it must seem like the gamble has paid off: the first feature starring the world's most popular entertainer—and in synchronized sound. Surely, triumph is only a month away.

Within three weeks, Sam Warner, who has ramrodded sound past his obstinate brothers, will be suddenly, incomprehensibly dead. *The Jazz Singer*, his best testament, will be acclaimed and settle in for long, successful runs everywhere in the world. Warner Bros. will begin a sudden ascent from a position in the lower third of the industry to highly competitive jostling with MGM and Paramount.

Because of this single scene, made as a flier on a hot summer afternoon, a modest story about a cantor's son who would rather sing Irving Berlin than "Kol Nidre" fires the starting pistol for an unparalleled industrial and aesthetic revolution.

Hollywood, 1927.

Silent films—an art impassioned by music, focused by darkness, pure emotion transmitted through light—were at the height of their aesthetic and commercial success.

In the late summer of that last tranquil year, *Beau Geste* and *Seventh Heaven* were finishing up their successful roadshow engagements. *Wings,* William Wellman's World War I epic, was opening, as was Josef von Sternberg's *Underworld.* Paramount announced that they were going to take the mass of footage Erich von Stroheim had shot for *The Wedding March* and make two separate movies out of it. *Variety*'s headline for Dorothy Arzner's new assignment WAS GIRL DIRECTING CLARA BOW. Mary Pickford was thinking of playing Joan of Arc, and 2,000 girls were vying for the part of Lorelei Lee in *Gentlemen Prefer Blondes.* New York's Cameo Theater was advertising "Emil Jannings in *Passion.* Cooled by Refrigeration."

On La Brea Avenue, the Chaplin studio was ust days away from resuming production on *The Circus,* a tortured film that had been on hia-:us since December 1926, when Chaplin's wife ;erved him with divorce papers and attached the ;tudio. In Culver City, Ramon Novarro an-1ounced that he was quitting movies and enter-ing a monastery. MGM didn't renew Lillian Gish's contract; but, in a not entirely unrelated event, the studio signed Louis B. Mayer to a new five-year deal that could bring him as much as $800,000 annually, making him the highest-paid production head in Hollywood.

And, in a small item, *Variety* reported that Warner Bros. might have as many as eleven theaters equipped to show Vitaphone in an-other month.

Eight hundred feature films a year were being turned out for an audience of 100 million people who attended 25,000 movie theaters every week. Three-quarters of those theaters were located in small towns, but they took in less than a quarter of the box-office receipts, which amounted to be-tween $1 billion and $1.2 billion a year.

Some 42,000 people were employed in Hol-lywood. The American film industry accounted for 82 percent of the world's movies, while the foreign market accounted for 40 percent of Hol-lywood's total business. The American studios, exclusive of their attached theater chains, were valued at about $65 million.

Despite the presence of big money, Holly-wood had retained its alfresco, bucolic atmos-phere. Sets for silent films were constructed next to each other, and the photographing of a scene would be punctuated by hammering and sawing going on just out of camera range. The atmos-phere tended strongly toward the informal. "When I first came out to Hollywood in 1919," said the cameraman Karl Struss, "I was walking down Hollywood Boulevard and here come Doug [Fairbanks] and Charlie Chaplin, one rid-ing a donkey, the other a horse. They stopped near Highland Avenue—this is around eleven at night—got off the horses and went in. They

were having a good time; nothing alcoholic, just fooling around."

Stars and directors were well-paid and well-treated, but otherwise the men who ran the stu-dios could do what they pleased with their em-ployees. While the American Federation of Labor had tried to unionize the studio crafts as early as 1916, and there had been a labor strike in 1918, Hollywood would remain a nonunion town until the Depression.

Within the studios, there was an element of personal pride in making pictures that relied on the visuals rather than the titles. SAY IT WITH PROPS—SAY IT WITH ACTION were signs that hung over scenario writers' desks. Speech was indicated by printed titles that interrupted the picture itself, always an irritant to creative directors. The ideal, of course, was the picture without titles, which was accomplished a few times, once by a director named Joseph De Grasse in a film called *The Old Swimming Hole,* and once by the great F. W. Murnau in his fabled *The Last Laugh.* Further than that, they could not go. Or so they thought.

Even though there were no microphones, actors were not free to mouth any clownish thing that came to mind. "In the silent days, you did learn the lines that you were supposed to speak," said the actor William Bakewell. "But technique-wise, before you spoke an important line, it was important that you register the ex-pression, the thought . . . because the cutter then could have a clean cut there in which to inject the subtitle. In other words, you had to time it, to register enough ahead before you spoke, so that [the title] would fit."

Some actors were less painstaking than oth-ers. The child star Frank "Junior" Coghlan re-membered making a silent film called *Rubber Tires,* which had a scene where the leading man [Harrison Ford, emphatically not the Harrison Ford of the present day] stops his car and runs across the road to see if he can be of any help to a car that's broken down. Ford walked up to the other actors and said, "Geef geef geef. Geef geef geef. Geef geef geef." Since it was a long shot, not even the director, let alone the audience, could tell the difference, but Ford's lack of participatory spirit startled the other actors.

Even modestly budgeted films provided musical ensembles of two or three pieces on the set—a typical grouping would be organ, violin, and cello. The mood music helped the actors express the emotion of a given scene . . . and helped them block out the construction sounds from nearby sets. For heavily emotional moments, actors would request their favorite lachrymose ballads or tragic arias from opera; for comedies, sprightly, up-tempo jazz numbers.

"I used to have the little orchestra play from *Samson and Delilah,*" remembered the MGM star Anita Page. "The music was one of the reasons that I loved silent pictures much better than talkies. You acted better in silents—talkies had so many more things to worry about. But in silents, you could just float. You moved to the music and you lived the part. You just did it!"

How the director talked the actors through the scene varied with the personality. Madge Bellamy, the star of John Ford's *The Iron Horse,* recalled that "[Allan] Dwan used sarcasm. He would say, for instance, 'To the left, you see your love approaching. You believe that he doesn't love you anymore. He comes up and kisses you tenderly. You burst into tears of happiness and relief—if you can manage it.'

"[Thomas] Ince would have yelled, 'You see him coming. You love him. God, how you love him! What pain you feel—you are in an agony of suspense! He kisses you! What happiness! Cut! Let's do it again!'

"[Frank] Borzage was just as emotional, but quieter. He would weep as he directed. He would say, 'You see him. He means everything to you. He may not love you anymore! He is your whole life! Doesn't he care for you now?' By this time, Borzage would be in tears. 'He kisses you! Oh, what joy!' Frank would be too choked up to go on."

On Tuesday nights around town, the place to be seen was The Coconut Grove, the nightclub at the Ambassador Hotel. The promenading of the stars was the main attraction, despite the ostensible presence of Gus Arnheim's orchestra. Another popular nightspot was The Biltmore Hotel in downtown Los Angeles, where the second Saturday of the month was the occasion for The Mayfair Club. It was a dinner dance, with speakers. "Jack Warner would get up and make his usual wisecracks," recalled Evelyn Brent. "It was a small industry . . . (and) everybody in the business was at those Mayfair dances."

For kicks, people would pile into their cars and head down to Venice to ride the roller coaster. The entertainment at parties was usually a buffet supper, unless it was at Pickfair, in which case it was a formal sit-down dinner. For after-dinner, there was often a screening of a movie, or a new game called charades that swept through the community. Paramount's leading lady Esther Ralston traditionally gave a New Year's Eve party for about 100 people. One year, there was a prize for whoever dressed the youngest. Director Frank Tuttle won the prize when he arrived dressed as an unborn child, complete with umbilical cord.

In Hollywood itself, the Montmartre was the favorite place for lunch, while Musso & Frank's was already in place on Hollywood Boulevard, one door north of where it is now (it would relocate in 1936). Musso's had stiff competition from Henry's, also on Hollywood Boulevard, five doors east of Vine Street. Although the restaurant was named after and run by Henry Bergman, a rotund member of Charlie Chaplin's repertory company, it was common knowledge that Chaplin had financed the establishment. The great comedian would eat there at least one night a week. In keeping with his own culinary tastes, the bill of fare was basic, steaks and chops, immaculately prepared. And, Henry's delivered.

Although the factory town that turned out the movies was largely unpretentious in matters of style, the theaters in which the movies were shown were palaces, baroque fantasies on Moorish/Byzantine/Oriental themes. The carpeting was plush, the orchestra in the pit superb. The audience walked to their seats through air scented with incense to worship at the cathedral of light, part of a congregation composed of all members of society, in all parts of the world. Silent movies were more than an accomplished popular art; as Lillian Gish often insisted, they were a universal language.

Because of the immensely seductive atmospherics of the overall experience, the silent film had an unparalleled capacity to draw an audience inside it, probably because it demanded the audience use its imagination. Viewers had to supply the voices and sound effects; in so doing, they made the final creative contribution to the film-making process. Silent film was about more than a movie; it was about an experience.

The joining together of a movie with live music and the audience's participation created something that was more than the sum of its parts; in Kevin Brownlow's metaphor, the effect was that of cultural carbons joined in an arc lamp, creating light of extraordinary intensity.

Sound changed *everything*.

It changed how movies were made, of course, but more importantly, it changed what movies *were*.

To take just one example, sound permanently altered the nature of screen comedy: the fizzy surrealism of Mack Sennett, the incredibly expressive pantomime of Chaplin, gave way to the racy cross-talk of Ben Hecht and his confreres. The primarily visual was supplanted by the primarily verbal.

Sound standardized movies, made them less malleable, less open to individual interpretation. Allusion and metaphor were the bedrocks of the silent medium, but dialogue literalized every moment, converted it from subjective to objective.

Sound also changed the character of the men and women who made the movies. Sound demanded writers of dialogue, and it seemed as if anyone with the most modest theatrical or journalistic credentials was imported to Hollywood. Paramount went in so heavily for journalists that their hiring strategy was informally but widely known as the Paramount Fresh Air Fund for New York Newspapermen. Lightweight New York literati became West Coast wage slaves and hated themselves for abandoning what they

imagined would have been glorious literary careers. While $50-a-week journalists became grudgingly affluent, veteran actors, writers, and directors used to making $100,000 a year suddenly had their credentials called into question.

And, sound brought the unions to Hollywood, for, along with New York journalists, it brought a mass importation of New York actors and playwrights, all of them members of one union or another who saw no reason why Hollywood should be exempt from the same nominal bargaining agents as New York.

And all of it happened within four short years.

There is no aspect of film history that has been so slighted. After noting the extermination of an art form at the height of its power—something unprecedented in history—the conventional volume gives us a nudge of Jolson, a touch of Lubitsch and Mamoulian, a mention of *All Quiet on the Western Front,* a sorrowing comment on Chaplin's Luddite tendencies, and suddenly it's 1935 and Victor McLaglen is staggering through the fog-shrouded streets of *The Informer.* As a result, most people assume the delightful, if broadly exaggerated, satire of *Singin' in the Rain* is more or less the whole story.

To examine this period of unparalleled industrial change, it is necessary to reverse the perspective, to give a fair, detailed idea of what silents were like to the people who made and watched them, and how talkies permanently changed the creative and personal equations.

As if the art form had an independent consciousness and was determined to flaunt its attributes in the face of imminent extinction, in 1927 and 1928 silent movies exploded in a riot of style, dramatic intensity, and thematic complexity. There were accomplished works of art such as King Vidor's *The Crowd* and von Sternberg's *The Last Command,* eye-popping entertainments like *The Beloved Rogue* and *The Gaucho,* the intense lyrical romanticism of Borzage's *Seventh Heaven* and *Street Angel.*

In most respects, late silent pictures seem more complete than early talkies, so painfully landlocked, so eerily styleless. With few exceptions, we see early talkies as grotesque curios; beginning in 1926, with the first Vitaphone films, audiences saw them as miracles. It is impossible to re-create the sense of wonder that made the public eager to abandon the visual and gestural dynamism of silent film, made them so eager to overlook the crudity of the technology and the stiffness of the first wave of sound films. For audiences of 1926–1930, talkies were what the Lumière films had been for audiences of 1895—the recording function was paramount; that what was being recorded was of no real dramatic interest was irrelevant.

The conventional wisdom has always been that talkies evolved out of silent films, but sound actually grew up alongside silents. The initially half-witted hybrid thrived in spite of itself, expanding voraciously and choking off the more fragile strain. Talkies were not an evolution, but a mutation, a different art form entirely; as a result, an art form was eliminated and hundreds of careers were extinguished. Major directors were ruined, great stars plummeted.

It is an epic story, full of bewildered losers who exceeded the abilities of their primitive technology and ran out of capital, counter-pointed by the triumph of the flamboyant Warner Bros. and of William Fox, whose tremendous commercial success was purchased with full shares of the hubris that eventually destroyed him.

So Hollywood was nudged, however unwillingly, into its corporate and creative future. Victims retired, victors took their place. In the early 1930s, the deco designs of Hans Dreier and Van Nest Polglase replaced the stuffy English furniture that was *de rigueur* at most studios in the silent days; short, stylish hair was adopted by women stars. The industry had been turned upside down, but had righted itself with considerable dispatch.

The fact that sound wasn't accepted until thirty years after it was first (roughly) devised was due in great part to factors both sociological and human: the immaculate presentation of silent films, and the reactionary attitudes of producers and exhibitors. Then there were two secondary technical factors: amplification (had that been available, talkies might have arrived in the 1900s) and electrical recording (acoustic recording lacked the necessary clarity).

Sound gave us the artistry of Astaire, the shattering screech of Kane's cockatoo, the wrenching anguish of Brando's "I coulda been a contender." It gave movies a more comprehensive form and smoothed out their dramatic flow. But the transition to sound was no gentle grafting, but a brutal, crude transplantation. As a result, many of cinema's roots withered and died, and much native strength was lost. The culture of Hollywood itself grew harsher, more Darwinian.

"The fun, easy, relaxed days of the motion picture were over the minute dialogue came in," asserted Charles "Buddy" Rogers. "Not only did the director want the dialogue his way, but the dialogue director, the soundman—we had to cope with about six or seven different technicians, and it was quite different."

BROADCASTING BEGINS
Susan J. Douglas

Susan J. Douglas is professor of history at Hampshire College. Her book Inventing American Broadcasting: 1912–1922 *deserves serious attention from students of communication for its close reading of the early, formative period of broadcasting in the United States.*

In the winter and spring of 1922, magazines and newspapers rediscovered radio. To the press, the fad seemed to come from nowhere. "Little more than a year ago," observed a writer in *Current Opinion,* "the public regarded radiotelephony as a great mystery."[1] Now, millions were "listening in." Official announcement of the boom came from Herbert Hoover, then secretary of commerce, who described the "wireless fever" as "one of the most astounding things that [has] come under my observation of American life."[2] This proclamation from an official of Hoover's stature alerted the press that it had better take note of a pastime quickly assuming major cultural and economic significance. "The rapidity with which the thing has spread has possibly not been equalled in all the centuries of human progress," noted the *Review of Reviews.* "Never in the history of electricity has an invention so gripped the popular fancy."[3] Radio emerged "with almost stunning suddenness," becoming "within a few weeks . . . a force in public opinion and public taste fitly comparable to the press."[4] In March of 1922, the *New York Times* observed, "In twelve months radio phoning has become the most popular amusement in America. If every boy does not possess a receiving outfit, it is because he lacks either imagination or money. . . . In every neighborhood people are stringing wires to catch the ether wave currents."[5] The public demand for receiving apparatus seemed insatiable, and RCA, Westinghouse, and many smaller firms went into overdrive to supply customers. The first issue of *Radio Broadcast,* in May 1922, described people standing "in the fourth or fifth row at the radio counter waiting their turn only to be told when they finally reached the counter that they might place an order and it would be filled when possible."[6] In 1922, sales of radio sets and parts totaled $60 million; in 1923, $136 million; by 1924, $358 million.[7]

Now the press, responding to the "tidal wave of interest in the subject," overflowed with interpretive articles on the social destiny of radio. Magazines such as *Collier's* and *Literary Digest* inaugurated radio sections in 1922, and new magazines such as *Radio Broadcast* were devoted entirely to the new craze. How would radio change America? What did the spread of broadcasting mean for Americans? These were the questions the popular magazines addressed.

The radio boom seemed all the more sudden because radio had been badly neglected by newspapers and magazines between 1915 and 1922. The press, through the content and tone of its articles, constantly emphasized the newness of the phenomenon. Little attention was paid to broadcasting's twenty-year gestation period. In this way, in its coverage of radio, the press helped to reinforce the media's tendency to ignore and thus deny their own history. This ahistorical stance made radio seem an autonomous force, so grand, complex, and potentially unwieldy that only large corporations with their vast resources and experience in efficiency and management could possibly tame it.

The sense of awe that had permeated the early articles on wireless telegraphy also colored the early articles on radio. To many writers, it was as if a fantastic dimension that people had suspected and hoped existed had finally been penetrated. People responded as if radio put them in touch with primordial forces. In "Broadcasting to Millions," A. Leonard Smith described hearing the sounds of static through his headphones: "You are fascinated, though a trifle awestruck, to realize that you are listening to sounds that, surely, were never intended to be heard by a human being. The delicate mechanism of the radio has caught and brought to the ears of us earth dwellers the noises that roar in the space between the worlds."[8] Joseph K. Hart wrote in the *Survey:* "We are playing on the shores of the infinite." He found this probing of the cosmos thrilling; he also sensed that the hubris that had made such exploration possible had a potentially dangerous underside: "The most occult goings-on are about us. Man has his fingers on the triggers of the universe.

Magazines helped promote early forms of radio, initially to those with technical curiosity. In promoting radio in the 1920s, magazines were helping to put in place what would for a time become their greatest source of competition. *The Orion Publishing Group.*

He doesn't understand all he is doing. He can turn strange energies loose. He may turn loose more than he figured on; more than he can control."[9] Grappling with the concept that something seemingly dark, quiet, and empty actually contained invisible life, another writer observed, "You look at the cold stars overhead, at the infinite void around you. It is almost incredible that all this emptiness is vibrant with human thought and emotion."[10] The air had been cracked open, revealing a realm in which the human voice and the sounds of the cosmos commingled.

Could this great void be filled not just with our voices, but with the voices of others, farther out in the cosmos? What were the sounds we called static, anyway? And could those in other spheres be listening in on us? Such questions were irresistible, especially when provoked by legitimate scientific observation. In the spring of 1919, Marconi announced that several of his wireless stations were picking up very strong signals "seeming to come from beyond the earth."[11] Nikola Tesla, another prominent inventor, believed these signals were coming from Mars. Marconi, too, considered Mars a not unlikely possibility. While *Scientific American* urged skepticism, *Current Opinion* quoted Tesla extensively in support of the Mars hypothesis. *Illustrated World,* a magazine that popularized recent technical developments, ardently embraced the prospect of interplanetary communication. In its article "Can We Radio a Message to Mars?" the magazine urged Americans to try to respond to the signals from beyond. This would no doubt require scientists to mobilize "all the electrical energy of the nation" to transmit signals of sufficient power. But the effort had to be made, for only then would the Martians know that "their signals were being responded to, and that intelligent beings actually inhabit the earth." The article enthused: "We can imagine what excitement this would cause on Mars." The most important reason for trying to contact Mars was to learn what the magazine assumed the Martians must know about improving, even perfecting, the quality of earthlings' lives. "It is not unreasonable to believe," predicted *Illustrated World,* "that the whole trend of our thoughts and civilization might change for the better."[12] These Martians could not only view our civilization with considerable detachment, they could also, presumably, give us all the secret answers, at last.

Illustrated World was a publication in which the distinctions between science and science fiction were minimized; its articles were written with an unsophisticated or credulous audience in mind. Its predictions about signaling to Mars would not have been taken seriously by some sectors of American society. Yet the underlying longings this article exposed are revealing, and they could hardly have been confined to readers of science fiction. In fact, the article contained themes that would be embellished in less fantastic, more earthbound articles about radio's potential. There was a hunger for contact over great distances and with beings who presumably knew more, and were wiser, than most contemporary Americans. Such contact would temper our deep and long held fears about being alone in the universe. Such contact would bring wisdom; it would be reassuring; it would be religious. Thus did the rhetoric surrounding radio draw from the past while it looked to the future.

The aspect of radio most universally praised in the press was its ability to promote cultural unity in the United States. "The day of universal culture has dawned," proclaimed the *Survey*.[13] The author of an article titled "The Social Destiny of Radio" maintained that prior to broadcasting, a sense of nationhood, a conception that Americans were all part of one country, was only an abstract idea, often without much force. The millions of towns and houses across America were unrelated and disconnected. But now that atomized state of affairs was changing: "If these little towns and villages so remote from one another, so nationally related and yet physically so unrelated, could be made to acquire a sense of intimacy, if they could be brought into direct contact with one another! This is exactly what radio is bringing about. . . . How fine is the texture of the web that radio is even now spinning! It is achieving the task of making us feel together, think together, live together."[14]

Stanley Frost, in his *Collier's* article "Radio Dreams That Can Come True," saw radio "spreading mutual understanding to all sections of the country, unifying our thoughts, ideals, and purposes, making us a strong and well-knit people."[15] Those isolated from the mainstream of American culture would now be brought into the fold. Farmers, the poor, the housebound, and the uneducated were repeatedly mentioned as the main beneficiaries of the culture surrounding people "in the flexible, tenuous ether."[16] Frost reprinted in his article two letters

of thanks written to Newark station WJZ by culturally dispossessed listeners. To set the stage for the first letter, Frost wrote, "There is a dingy house in a dreary street in a little factory town, where the miracle is working. A worried mother frets through the day to achieve a passable cleanliness for her flock, without power to give them the 'better start' and wider happiness she had dreamed. [A] little flurry of prosperity" allowed her to get a radio. The letter followed: "My husban and I thanks yous all fore the gratiss programas we received every night and day from WJZ. . . . The Broklin teachers was grand the lecturs was so intresing . . . [the] annonnser must be One grand man the way he tell the stores to the chilren." Frost stated: "There are others, hundreds of letters a day of appreciation and delight from illiterate or broken people who are for the first time in touch with the world about them."[17]

A writer predicted in *Century Magazine* that radio would "do much to create a sense of national solidarity in all parts of the country, and particularly in remote settlements and on the farm."[18] The farmer's loneliness would be abolished, radio making him a real "member of the community." The writer continued, "If I am right, the 'backwoods,' and all that the word connotes, will undoubtedly dwindle if it does not entirely disappear as an element in our civilization."[19] Repeatedly, the achievement of cultural unity and homogeneity was held up, implicitly and explicitly, as a goal of the highest importance. One writer went so far as to complain, "At present, broadcasting stations are far too eclectic." The ultimate ethnocentric extension of the impulse toward cultural unity was the prediction that English would become the universal language. Argued one writer, "It so happens that the United States and Great Britain have taken the lead in broadcasting. If that lead is maintained it follows that English must become the dominant tongue."[20]

Yet, this desire for unity, for sameness, was not without its opposite, the pleasure taken in discovering cultural diversity. In the first years of the broadcasting boom, listeners delighted in picking up as many stations as possible. Dedicated enthusiasts posted a special map of the United States on a wall near the radio. Red dots on the map designated the location of operating broadcast stations across the country; the call letters of each station were also listed. Listeners would spend the evening tuning their radios in the hopes of hearing stations thousands of miles away. One self-described radio maniac referred to the actual radio programs as "the tedium between call letters." He maintained, "It is not the *substance* of communication without wires, but the *fact* of it that enthralls. . . . To me no sounds are sweeter than 'this is station soandso.' "[21] He described his delight in hearing "the soft Southern voice of Atlanta," while another enthusiast relished picking up the Spanish emanating from the station in Havana. Many of these stations adopted slogans that highlighted their special regionalism. Atlanta was "The Voice of the South," Minneapolis "The Call of the North," Davenport "Where the West Begins."[22] Radio allowed people to skip across the country, to go to neverseen and exotic places, all by turning a dial. Like the movies, radio blended the urge for adventure with the love of sanctuary in an ideal suspension. The difference with radio, at least in these early years, was the greater sense of control the listener enjoyed.

This feeling of mastery, coupled with the sense of adventure, kept radio enthusiasts at their sets night after night. Picking up faraway stations was frequently likened to other sports, especially fishing. "There are times when it is as difficult to land a given station—making the same demands upon patience, ingenuity, and even skill—as to bring to boat that elusive creature, the sailfish."[23] Another writer used the same metaphor: "This fishing in the far away with the radio hook and line is rare sport. The line is long, the fishing is getting better all the time, and it usually does not take many minutes to find out what you have on the hook."[24] As such a metaphor suggests, this active type of listening, which involved some technical expertise

in adjusting the apparatus and bringing it to its maximum efficiency, was confined almost entirely to men and boys. Those who wrote about their ethereal adventures celebrated the manly challenges radio posed: "Your wits, learning and resourcefulness are matched against the endless perversity of the elements."[25] Within the safety of one's home, and out of public view, one's masculinity could be tested and reaffirmed.

Even after the desired station was reeled in the essentially passive act of listening to radio programming was imbued in magazine articles with a sense of empowerment. Listeners had a choice: they could turn the dial until they got exactly what they wanted to listen to; if they didn't like what they heard, they could shut the radio off. More people, whatever their circumstances, had access to cultural events than ever before. "We have all free tickets to the greatest radio show on earth," noted one writer. As Stanley Frost put it, "With radio we, the listeners, will have an advantage we have never had before. We do not even have to get up and leave the place. All we have to do is press a button, and the speaker is silenced." Therefore, predicted Frost, "We will get what we want."[26] This sense of control over cultural content, combined with increased access to cultural events, cultivated a sense of cushioned privilege. One "music loving gentleman" decided to turn in his ticket to hear the Philharmonic Orchestra and to listen to the performance on radio instead. "I can only afford a top gallery ticket," the man explained, "but the radio microphone always gets a good seat downstairs. I enjoy the music just as well here by my fireside and I save a lot of climbing."[27]

Another writer hinted at how monetary and class differences had, in the past, determined who got the good seats at a concert. Those with the cheapest seats usually could not hear the music very well. With radio, though, everyone hears the music "as plainly as if he had the best seat in the auditorium."[28] Everyone who previously could not attend such concerts now could. Thus was radio seen as democratizing some of the advantages previously enjoyed by the well-to-do, and bringing all the benefits of high culture to the masses. At the same time, radio helped insulate its listeners from heterogeneous crowds of unknown, different, and potentially unrestrained individuals. One writer absolutely reveled in the marriage between entertainment and solitude: "This vast company of listeners . . . do not sit packed closely, row on row, in stuffy discomfort endured for the delight of the music. The good wife and I sat there quietly and comfortably alone in the little back room of our own home that Sunday night and drank in the harmony coming three hundred miles to us through the air." He imagined other listeners in their back rooms, garages, dining rooms, attics, or cabins, "each and all sitting and hearing with the same comfort just where they happen to be."[29] The listeners sat suspended, in delicious tension, between their hunger for contact with the outside world and their craving for the comforts of home. With radio, both appetites were satisfied at once.

Although radio had indeed become embedded within the larger network of commercial entertainment in America, for those who wrote about radio and its role in American life, radio represented an antidote to what critics considered the more debasing effects of mass culture. Reformers who fancied themselves the true custodians of American culture believed that leisure activities should be educational and morally uplifting, and should not overly stimulate the senses. These reformers were witness to the rise of public amusements and commercialized leisure activities that often deliberately flouted such genteel precepts. Dime novels relied on hackneyed writing and action-packed stories, and at times they even glorified their criminal protagonists. Comic strips told their stories with pictures. The dark, crowded nickelodeons in working-class neighborhoods seemed to reformers to be dens of iniquity. Amusement parks were specifically designed to overstimulate the senses. Leisure had not taken the course many reformers had hoped. Radio seemed to hold out a remedy, or at least an alluring alternative, to

all this. Like the first press coverage of wireless in 1899, the new hopes invested in radio were shaped by a faith in technological determinism, a belief that certain machines could make history. The educated bourgeoisie who believed their conception of culture to be at risk became newly optimistic with the advent of broadcasting. Here, at last, was a mass medium that could instill the right values in people.

The educational possibilities seemed unlimited. *Collier's* "radio maniac" claimed that radio provided "an education both precise and varied." Through the radio hobby, his son had become more technically informed and manually dexterous while mastering American geography. In listening to the programs, he had learned about politics, music, agriculture, and sports.[30] Magazines also offered grander visions. Radio could "give everyone the chance and the impulse to learn to use his brains." In doing so, radio would "tend strongly to level the class distinctions, which depend so largely on the difference in opportunity for information and culture."[31] "Who can help conjuring up a vision of a super radio university educating the world?" asked one writer. With radio, minds could "be detonated like explosives."[32] In his essay "Radiating Culture," Joseph Hart envisioned previously bored students now being instructed "by a single, inspiring teacher who speaks to the thousands of revived students through a central radio-phone. A whole nation of students might thus come under the stimulating touch of some great teacher."[33] Colleges and universities set up radio extension schools, and anyone could listen in. As one writer stated, every home had "the potentiality of becoming an extension of . . . Harvard University."[34]

Anxieties about musical tastes surfaced in these articles, although there was optimism that as radio matured, the quality of music played would improve. Several writers made explicit distinctions between "good music" and jazz, which was made popular and more frequently played. One complained, "Most of the musical talent that is now attracted by the broadcasting

Early broadcasters began to piggy-back on the STAR System. Here touring heavy-weight boxing champion Jack Demsey does a studio interview at a local station in 1922. *National Archives of Canada.*

stations is of mediocre nature." He also contended, however, that there were "thousands upon thousands of people whose musical tastes [ran] high above the average received from the air." To prove that people preferred a "higher class of talent," he cited the popularity of AT&T's WEAF, which could afford to recruit such talent because it accepted advertising.[35] Thus might radio, by bringing opera and other "good music" to the millions, upgrade American musical standards.

Another area of American life radio might improve was politics. "We may even become more thoughtful about the selection of our presidents," noted one observer sarcastically, "If we have to run the risk of hearing them speaking directly to us, however far from them we may try to keep ourselves."[36] Another commentator believed radio would make politicians more sensible and accountable to their constituencies: "Let a legislator now commit himself to some policy that is obviously senseless, and the editorial writers must first proclaim his imbecility to the community. But let the radiophone in the legislative halls of the future flash his absurdities into space and a whole state hears them at once." Citizens would be better able to judge a president who was "a real personality" instead of "a political abstraction."[37]

Bruce Bliven, writing for *Century Magazine,* gave voice to a progressive hope for radio's salubrious effects on politics. Crowds listening to a politician's speech in a large public setting were subject to "the mob spirit, with its factitious enthusiasm." The astute politician sought to take advantage of such mob psychology, and thus would cater more to the emotions than to the intellect. But with radio, argued Bliven, people would listen to the speech not as members of a crowd, but as individuals. The politician's ideas therefore would "have a better chance of being weighed for what they are really worth." Thus, radio might even produce a new kind of politician, a "man without the ordinary tricks of delivery, but possessed of a quiet, logical persuasiveness." Bliven allowed that such a man would have to have a "deep resonant voice such as will carry well in the microphone."[38] A major benefit was that more people than ever before would be able to hear their political leaders simultaneously. Political speeches reprinted in the newspapers often went unread, according to Bliven. With radio, more people could become politically informed than ever before, and they would have a sense of immediacy about the information they received. Politicians would seem less remote, more accountable, while the audience would gain a new sense of cohesiveness, even political empowerment, through the knowledge that everyone in a city, state, or region, or even everyone in the country, had heard the same speech at the same time without the distorting effects of mob response. This knowledge would further the sense of cultural unity: millions of people across the country, hearing together, reacting together, thinking together, as informed, politically aware citizens.

Religion was another area of life destined for change through radio. Sermons were an early staple of broadcasting; by 1921 KDKA transmitted the complete church service of the Calvary Episcopal Church of Pittsburgh every Sunday night. "Think of what this means to many people," urged the reporter for *Scientific American*.[39] He, too mentioned the farmer, the invalid, the housebound who, prior to radio, had been cut off from religious services. All of these people could now "almost imagine being in church." "The preacher who has a little black box mounted on the pulpit," wrote another commentator, "comes very soon to know that the congregation seated before him is to the great invisible listening throng but as the sprinkle of a few drops over the baptismal font to the pouring rain outside."[40] The preacher came to know this because preachers who broadcast their services received thousands of letters and telephone calls expressing thanks and requesting copies of the sermons. That radio seemed to be bringing more Americans into the religious fold was significant indeed. Since the late nineteenth century, religious authority had been undermined by Darwinism, the ethics of industrial

capitalism, and a reverence for science and technology. Radio, however, promised a reconciliation between religion and the corporate-industrial secular world, for it was the first technology that could bring religion into people's homes. Radio, the product of monopolistic capitalism, would help reassert precapitalist, Christian values in America.

Contemporary writers, whatever their hopes or biases, were all aware that they were witnessing a social transformation of monumental importance. Radio listeners constituted "the greatest audience ever assembled by any means for any purpose in the history of the world." This audience was "remarkable" and "totally different in several ways from anything before known."[41] First of all, it was huge; conceiving of an audience as hundreds of thousands or millions of people required a major imaginative leap. Second, the audience was invisible and unknown. The speaker or performer could not see facial responses or hear laughter, booing, or silence; nor was there applause. At the same time that the size of the speaker's audience had multiplied beyond anyone's calculation, his visual relationship with that audience was severed. Bruce Bliven thought that "so much listening without seeing" had "upset one of nature's subtle biological balances" and had created "what might be called 'a hunger of the eyes.'"[42]

Because this audience was invisible, scattered, and unknown, commentators were unsure about its character. Was this audience just like a mob, only dispersed, but equally capable of being excited and manipulated by an ambitious speaker who was newly empowered by radio? Or was the audience comprised more of people like the magazine writers themselves: discriminating, thoughtful, with values and ideas of their own, certainly impervious to the wiles of a disembodied voice? The answers to these questions were critical, for they were directly related to radio's potential as a tool for social control. The magazine articles on the topic revealed an uneasy ambivalence about the audience. What did these invisible listeners want? How pliant were they? Would radio be a "tremendous civilizer," increasing public demand for "the daily news of events, the opinions of leaders, the counsel of the wise, the comments of observers, [and] the hopes of the prophets," as one magazine suggested?[43] If so, how would such broadcasts be received? Might one of these leaders or prophets be able to "tell men what to think and say and how to act"? Would he be able to "shape them to a common, uniform, subservient mediocrity"?[44] Would this audience be content to hear primarily "outrageous rubbish, verbal and musical," and would it be swayed by the "appalling mass of solemn bunk and some really vicious propaganda" that was already flowing through the ether?[45]

Implicit in virtually all of the magazine articles written in the early 1920s about radio's promise was a set of basic, class-bound assumptions about who should be allowed to exert cultural authority in the ether. The *New Republic* stated the position baldly. Radio, asserted the editors, "is mainly under control of men unfitted by training and personality for posts of such importance." These were businessmen, ignorant of radio's "proper use" and "indifferent as to whether it is used properly or not." Such men were not unlike those who first controlled motion pictures: "fly-by-nights, adventurers and reformed pushcart peddlers, not one in a hundred of whom had reached the social level where one takes one's hat off indoors." The proper use of radio, according to the *New Republic,* was educational: radio should be "an intellectual force." Radio could never fulfill this mission as long as it was managed by those whose interest was music or entertainment. Such men, the magazine asserted, "are admirably fitted to assemble orchestras, pianists and singers; but when it comes to lectures and addresses they are about as competent as Florenz Ziegfeld is to run Columbia University."[46]

It was not that members of the educated bourgeoisie objected to radio being used to influence those millions of invisible listeners; the bourgeoisie's major concern was that those exerting the influence embrace genteel values about what culture should be. The subtext of these magazine articles maintained that radio should be edifying—should appeal to the intellect rather than the emotions—should elevate musical tastes, and should promote contemplation and the ability to discriminate between the worthy and the base. Radio, by providing the perfect instrument for delivering high culture to the masses, could produce a new midculture that combined the content of high culture with the techniques of commercialized entertainment. As one writer put it, "The man who directs a broadcasting station must combine the astuteness of P. T. Barnum and the good taste of a Gatti Cassaza."[47]

NOTES

1. "The Long Arm of Radio Is Reaching Everywhere," *Current Opinion* 72 (May 1922): 684.
2. "Astonishing Growth of the Radiotelephone," *Literary Digest,* April 15, 1922, 28.
3. "'Listening In,' Our New National Pastime," *Review of Reviews* 67 (Jan. 1923): 52; Waldemar Kaempffert, "Radio Broadcasting," *Review of Reviews* 65 (Apr. 1922): 399.
4. "Radio: The New Social Force," *Outlook,* Mar. 19, 1924, 465.
5. *New York Times,* Mar. 2, 1922, 20.
6. Gleason Archer, *The History of Radio to 1926* (New York: American Historical Society, 1938), 241.
7. Erik Barnouw, *A Tower In Babel* (New York: Oxford University Press, 1966), 125.
8. A. Leonard Smith, Jr., "Broadcasting to Millions," *New York Times,* Feb. 19, 1922, sec. 7, 6.
9. Joseph K. Hart, "Radiating Culture," *Survey,* Mar. 18, 1922, 949.
10. Waldemar Kaempffert, "The Social Destiny of Radio," *Forum* 71 (June 1924): 772.
11. "That Prospective Communication with Another Planet," *Current Opinion* 66 (Mar. 1919): 170; "Those Martian Radio Signals," *Scientific American* 122 (Feb. 14, 1920): 156.
12. Thomas Walker, "Can We Radio a Message to Mars?" *Illustrated World* 33 (Apr. 1920); 242.

13. Hart, "Radiating Culture," 948.

14. Kaempffert, "Social Destiny of Radio," 771–72.

15. Stanley Frost, "Radio Dreams That Can Come True," *Collier's* 69 (June 10, 1922): 18.

16. Hart, "Radiating Culture," 949.

17. Frost, "Radio Dreams," 9.

18. Bruce Bliven, "How Radio Is Remaking Our World," *Century Magazine* 108 (June 1924): 149.

19. Ibid., 152.

20. Waldemar Kaempffert, "Social Destiny of Radio," 771.

21. Howard Vincent O'Brien, "It's Great to Be a Radio Maniac," *Collier's* 74 (Sept. 13, 1924): 16.

22. Orange Edward McMeans, "The Great Audience Invisible," *Scribner's Magazine* 73 (Apr. 1923): 413.

23. O'Brien, "It's Great to Be a Radio Maniac," 16.

24. McMeans, "Great Audience Invisible," 412.

25. O'Brien, "It's Great to Be a Radio Maniac," 16.

26. Frost, "Radio Dreams," 18.

27. Bliven, "Radio Is Remaking Our World," 148.

28. McMeans, "Great Audience Invisible," 411.

29. Ibid.

30. O'Brien, "It's Great to Be a Radio Maniac," 16.

31. Frost, "Radio Dreams," 18.

32. Kaempffert, "Social Destiny of Radio," 768.

33. Hart, "Radiating Culture," 949.

34. Kaempffert, "Social Destiny of Radio," 768.

35. Raymond Francis Yates, "What Will Happen to Broadcasting?" *Outlook* 136 (Apr. 9, 1924): 604.

36. Hart, "Radiating Culture," 949.

37. Kaempffert, "Social Destiny of Radio," 768, 772.

38. Bliven, "Radio Is Remaking Our World," 153.

39. L. H. Rosenberg, "A New Era in Wireless," *Scientific American* 124 (June 4, 1921): 449.

40. McMeans, "Great Audience Invisible," 415.

41. Ibid., 411.

42. Bliven, "Radio Is Remaking Our World," 147.

43. Frost, "Radio Dreams," 18.

44. Hart, "Radiating Culture," 949.

45. Bliven, "Radio Is Remaking Our World," 151, 154.

46. "The Future of Radio," *New Republic* 40 (Oct. 8, 1924): 136.

47. Waldemar Kaempffert, "The Progress of Radio Broadcasting," *Review of Reviews* 66 (Sept. 1922): 305.

DOCUMENTING MEDIA

William Stott

William Stott is a cultural historian. His book Documentary Expression and Thirties America *provides a detailed analysis of the styles of communication that resulted from the major media of the 1930s and 1940s. This book is regarded as a classic of its kind and deserves to be studied by communication students as a model of how communication media can be treated as cultural history.*

Unlike movies and radio, newspapers were hard hit by the Depression. Many folded or were merged; many more fought back with their only easy weapons, exaggeration and sensationalism. Furthermore, as George Seldes demonstrated in *Freedom of the Press* (1935) and *Lords of the Press* (1938), newspapers of the day, with a handful of exceptions, colored, suppressed, and even concocted facts to fit their editorial bias. In his conference with the editors, Roosevelt gave an example which he said he could multiply a thousand times. The Sunday before there had been a radio debate on WOR between a Republican senator, Arthur Vandenberg, and a Democrat, Lister Hill. Each talked for fifteen minutes on the New Deal's program for economic recovery. Monday's New York *Sun,* an anti-Roosevelt paper, put the story on page one, right-hand column. Its headline read: "Huge Recovery Plan Attacked by Republicans; Vandenberg Denounces Roosevelt Relief Program; Says Pump Priming Means Bigger Deficits." The dispatch ran down the column, was continued inside, reported similar remarks made that Sunday on a C.B.S. program by the Republican National Committee chairman— and never once mentioned Senator Hill. Because Hill spoke on behalf of policies abhorrent to the *Sun*'s publishers, the paper's editors had cropped every reference to him and what he said from an AP dispatch. Roosevelt deplored the *Sun*'s leaving out "half the truth" and said there were hundreds of papers that did the same.[1]

There were. In no other decade was the American press so out of step with its audience. At no other time did it impress millions of Americans as "a rich man's property, conducted to curry to the rich man's favor, to spread the rich man's prejudices, to impose the rich man's will on the nation," as the liberal Protestant *Christian Century* said in 1936. *Time*'s head editor confided in Henry Luce in the mid-thirties that the magazine's news would be more responsible were it not based on the U.S. press: "The U.S. press," he said, "is stupid and reactionary." Throughout the early thirties the press generally managed to ignore or belittle the evidence of a depression. In the 1936 Presidential campaign, more than 80 per cent of the press opposed Roosevelt, and he won by the highest percentage ever. During the campaign and for years after, many newspapers, including major syndicates, went beyond all legitimate bounds in an effort to disparage the President and the New Deal. And as Roosevelt warned the editors, the press lost by it. Public opinion polls in the late thirties suggested that 30 million Americans, nearly one adult in three, doubted the honesty of the American press.[2]

Unquestionably the crucial event in this "repudiation of the press by the public," as George Seldes thought it, was the 1936 election. When Roosevelt motored through Chicago at the height of the campaign, a reporter in the press car noticed that the enormous crowd was making "menacing cries of anger against the Chicago *Tribune* and the Hearst papers in Chicago which were fighting Roosevelt so bitterly. These people no longer had any respect for the press or confidence in it. The press had finally overreached itself . . . and was losing influence." After the election the *Christian Century* wrote the newspaper publishers of America a scathing open letter to tell them that "in the minds of hosts of your fellow Americans, you stand today indicted" for arrogance, tyranny, greed, and scorn of fair play. "Election day 1936 was judgement day for America's daily press," the letter said; "when the people voted, they voted against *you*." The *Century* tried to maintain a tone free of gloating and vituperation, but it could not. It assured the publishers that those who voted for Roosevelt

> obtained a deep emotional satisfaction from the fact that you had not merely been defeated, but that you had been smashed. A vendor selling election extras at a stand across the street from the building of a great city newspaper, cried to the crowd in a transport of ecstasy, "We showed the ———!" While he shook his fist at the newspaper office, the crowd cheered. Didn't you hear him, gentlemen? Then truly you have become isolated from the American public.

So low had the press fallen in public esteem that well-bred Christians would leave no doubt that they felt newspaper publishers sons-of-bitches.[3]

The press had lost credibility and influence, but the press was no longer all of journalism. By the late thirties, radio journalism, though only in its teens (the first scheduled newscast was in 1920), had come of age. In 1939 *Fortune* sponsored an Elmo Roper survey* on what the

---

*Public opinion polling began in the 1930s and is an example of another way in which the nation then tried to discover itself and its people. Roper's was far the most accurate poll of the time, predicting the treacherous 1936 Presidential election to within a percentage point and the 1940 election to three-fifths of a point.

American people thought of the press; the people, it turned out, didn't think much and preferred radio. If presented with conflicting versions of the same story in two media, the respondents believed the radio (40.3 per cent) rather than the newspaper (26.9 per cent). When asked "Which of the two—radio or newspaper—give you news freer from prejudice?" 49.7 per cent answered radio, only 17.1 per cent answered newspaper (18.3 per cent said both were the same, 14.9 per cent said they didn't know). This stunning confidence in radio's credibility and impartiality made it already the "preferred source of news interpretation." Commentators like Lowell Thomas, H. V. Kaltenborn, Boake Carter, and Edwin C. Hill were more respected than editorials and columnists combined.[4]

Why was radio trusted and the newspaper not? *Fortune* suggested several reasons. The public doubted a newspaper's disinterestedness—and the doubt focused on "the publisher's office, where policy is made." The people interviewed believed, 65.8 per cent to 14.8 per cent, that the publisher managed news to his own benefit.* Radio didn't excite this suspicion, and with some reason, *Fortune* argued. The magazine pointed out that there were three kinds of news on radio: on-the-spot news, bulletins, and commentary. "Spot-news coverage," instantaneous reporting of an event, was impossible in the written press. Bulletins were simply abbreviated versions of the wire-service dispatches the newspapers print. Though radio got them to the public quicker, it gave fewer facts; but actually this may have been to its benefit, *Fortune* implied, since radio confined itself to "the naked, irrefutable highlights of the news" and shunned interpretation. Radio commentaries, unlike newspaper editorials, expressed no opinion on issues that might stir controversy and get the station in trouble with the FCC. In short, ac-

cording to *Fortune*, the radio's news might then have seemed more credible than the newspaper's because it did less; it said less, pled less, had fewer opinions and almost none that would upset anybody.[5]

Paul Lazarsfeld's *Radio and the Printed Page* (1940), which reported the media preferences of 5528 "representative" Americans, came to the same conclusions as the *Fortune* poll. It found radio preferred to the press as a source of news and overwhelmingly favored by people of lower income, by women, and by those in rural areas. Lazarsfeld and *Fortune* implied that radio was more trusted because it was less untrustworthy. While this may have been true, the media preference can be looked at from another angle. If in the late thirties and early forties radio was more readily accepted than the press, the content of each may have been only part of the reason; the *medium* of radio may then have seemed more credible.[6]

The difference between the two media is plain. Radio is people talking to us (or apparently us). Newspapers are articles in uniform typeface. Radio is direct: Vandenberg and Hill each has his say. Newspapers are unimaginably indirect: they are writing, to begin with—writing by someone the name of whom is rarely given, someone usually at great distance from where the article was, with such obvious labor, set in type, printed, and distributed. In a newspaper all the talking of Vandenberg and Hill gets flattened into 500 words by persons unknown; drastic simplification and subordination of one fact, one man, to another turns an event into copy. Yet this "copy" exists in a wholly different form from the original: it is report of experience, not the experience. Radio provides experience; "coming instantaneously from the very scenes of events and entering directly into the home," it gives listeners, Lazarsfeld suggested, "a feeling of personal touch with the world." Direct, on-the-spot coverage, impossible in a newspaper, is in a sense perpetual on radio. We hear Vandenberg and Hill for ourselves, but we

*Consider how the films of the period portray the newspaper publisher as sneaky villain (*Mr. Smith Goes to Washington*, 1939), as egomaniac (*Citizen Kane*, 1941), as prototascist (*Meet John Doe*, 1941).

hear also newscasters, announcers, Mary Margaret McBrides, men in the street. The people on radio all have names (except those in the ads, whom we don't believe), and speak to us, without apparent intermediary, in voices of our kind.* However trivial and dull, radio offers human experience—the experience of another human. "People who weren't around in the twenties when radio exploded can't know what it meant," the sportscaster Red Barber has written. "Suddenly, with radio, there was instant human communication."[7]

Human communication is the lifeblood of the medium. Historians agree that Franklin Roosevelt's use of radio in his Fireside Chats made him, though President, a living human, an acquaintance, to millions in America. Roosevelt used the medium more as it should be used than other public men had dared to. He was personal, friendly, even a bit casual. He ad-libbed in the days before ad-libbing was allowed. During a 1933 broadcast he interrupted his talk to ask for a glass of water, paused while it was brought, took a swallow audible in living rooms across the country, and then told the listeners: "My friends, it's very hot here in Washington tonight." His simple gesture drew thousands of sympathetic letters.[8]

For many people in the thirties the newspaper form itself was apparently compromised, while the radio was not. The newspaper's indirectness—the gap between an event and the published report—left too much room for tampering. People didn't suspect the radio of tampering in part because it used direct and human communication. There was always, at the least, an announcer explaining things to them; and

"the announcer," many people felt, "would not say something if it was not true." This sentence was the rationale of a listener misled into panic by Orson Welles' 1938 radio production "The War of the Worlds." The listener, like thousands in the audience of the day, accepted without reservation the news announcer's veracity. Said another: "I always feel the commentators bring the best possible news. Even after this I still will believe what I hear on the radio." Archibald MacLeish tried to coax poets to write for the radio because the medium's credibility was so high. "Only the ear is engaged," he said, "and the ear is already half poet. It believes at once; creates and believes." Chief cause of belief was "the commentator," an "integral part of radio technique" and the "most useful dramatic personage since the Greek Chorus." The commentator (or announcer) was the listener's surrogate—an eyewitness often, but at any rate one closer to the facts than he. In radio drama, where experimentation centered on the narrator and his possible uses, a commentator might prove a liar or, more frequently, a madman. But in general he was there to be trusted: his reactions vocalized the audience's own and influenced them. What he said was probably trite; it was also undeniable. Robert Warshow, writing in 1949, jeered at the American media's use of the commentator, yet had to admit that he couldn't finally dissociate himself from what the commentator said:

> A typical figure in our culture is the "commentator," whose accepted function is to make some "appropriate" statement about whatever is presented to his attention. "Grim evidence of man's inhumanity to man," he remarks of the corpses of Buchenwald. "The end of the road," he says as we stare at dead Mussolini on the newsreel screen. (And what can one do but agree?) Even in its most solemn and pessimistic statements, this voice is still a form of "affirmation" (its healthy tone betrays it); at bottom, it is always saying the same thing: that one need never be entirely passive, that for every experience there is some adequate response.

---

*Voice matters. Lazarsfeld remarked that "again and again in our case studies, respondents mentioned the human voice as if it were of especial importance." Respondents said, typically, "I like the voice. It is *nearer* to you"; "A voice to me has always been more *real* than words to be read." C.B.S.'s Paul Kesten claimed in a 1935 brochure promoting radio advertising that voices of affection and authority make people do what they are told seven times out of ten or better, even when the voice is on radio. A wild exaggeration, Kesten's argument was taken seriously at the time.

President Franklin Delano Roosevelt looking over the array of microphones set up for
one of his "fireside chats." What the audience experienced was the capacity of radio for
direct appeal, one that effectively allowed the U.S. president to bypass both the apparatus
of party politics and the press corps. Executive use of electronic media for "live" broadcasts has continued to be an important instrument of politics in most countries. *By permission of the Bettmann Archives.*

Which response it thrusts upon its audience.[9]

Radio convinced people in the thirties, then, both directly and by example. Indeed, it synthe-sized two methods of persuasion: it presented the audience the facts firsthand—on the spot or nearer the spot—yet did so usually through an observer or commentator (and always framed by an announcer). The facts and the observer re-inforced each other's credibility: if one was be-lieved, it was hard not to believe the other; if lis-teners accepted a report, they probably took over its tone as well and echoed its observer's re-sponse. Radio was influential in the thirties be-cause it was believed; it was believed because, as much as film or photograph, it was then a docu-mentary medium.

The "golden age" of radio reporting in the late thirties and early forties added two phrases to the language. The two, significantly, are ex-pressive of the time's documentary bent. The first was Edward Murrow's grim "This ... is London," the salutation with which he began his London broadcasts from September 1938 till the end of the war. "This is London": the direct method could not be put more plainly. This is London: here it is, talking right to you. The second phrase had a variety of forms: "We take you now to Nuremberg, Germany"; "We take you to Paris"; "I return you now to America"; "We return you to the studio." It was the spoken signal announcers used to cue in and cue out live remotes, and became an established technique during C.B.S.'s coverage of the three-week Munich crisis of 1938, the event that proved the value of radio journalism. Again we notice the direct method. "You," the listener, are apparently hustled from place to place in order to be an on-the-spot witness in each.[10]

Radio technology was still primitive in the late thirties, and the role of the broadcast correspondent somewhat undefined. Yet these shortcomings oddly enhanced the medium's credibility. A listener would believe he heard Prague, Czechoslovakia, direct when it took luck to do so, and when exchanges such as the following occurred:

CBS ANNOUNCER: At this time . . . Maurice Hindus, prominent authority on central European affairs, will speak to you from Prague, Czechoslovakia. This is America calling. We take you now to Prague.
A long pause. Static. Silence.
CBS ANNOUNCER: Prague apparently is not prepared to transmit the voice of Maurice Hindus at this moment. We shall be in constant contact with Prague, however, and when the moment comes we shall switch to that capital. May we ask you to stand by.

Then, nearly six hours later:

CBS ANNOUNCER: That was London speaking. And now Maurice Hindus in Prague, Czechoslovakia, is to be interviewed by H. V. Kaltenborn. And here is Mr. Kaltenborn.
KALTENBORN: Hello is this Prague? Who is talking please?
HINDUS: Is this Columbia?
KALTENBORN: Maurice Hindus is that you?
HINDUS: Speaking.
KALTENBORN: Oh fine. See here, this is H. V. Kaltenborn. I am speaking from the Columbia office and I want to ask you a few questions about the situation in Prague. This is going to be an interview and I don't know whether they have it on the air. I know they intended to have it on. In any case, I'm going to fire ahead, and ask you whether Prague had any report of Litvinoff's speech at Geneva today. . . .
HINDUS: I haven't seen any of it in any of the papers.
KALTENBORN: I see. Have you had all of the evening papers?
HINDUS: I have all the evening papers.
KALTENBORN: And there is nothing about Litvinoff's speech?
HINDUS: Not a word that I have read.
KALTENBORN: I see. Well, he made a very important address in which he stated . . .

And the conversation, though carried on across thousands of miles of oceans, was unmistakably spontaneous.[11]

The spontaneity of radio remotes in the thirties encouraged audience participation: as the technicians sweated to get Prague on the line, the listener labored too, in his imagination. Frederick Lewis Allen remembered turning the dial to find

a voice swelling forth in the midst of a sentence: . . . "attempt first to receive a broadcast direct from Prague, the capital of Czechoslovakia, where Maurice Hindus, well-known authority on Central European affairs, has been observing the day's happenings. We take you now to Prague." A pause, while the mind leapt the Atlantic in anticipation; then another voice: "Hello, America, this is Prague speaking."

The listener felt close to Europe because he put himself there.[12]

World War II helped establish the role of the radio correspondent as equivalent to that of the newspaper correspondent. Scanning the airwaves gave radio reporters access to shortwave broadcasts from around the world, often providing them with a jump on newspapers. *National Archives of Canada.*

This was the object of documentary radio: to make the listener believe he was there. Ed Murrow, the most influential radio journalist, seems to have understood this instinctively. Even at the beginning of his career, during the Munich crisis, while experimenting with formats (debate, guest commentary) he later discarded, he told his audience: "Now, we're trying in these talks from London to really hold a mirror behind these very fast-moving events. We're trying to recite what you would see and hear if you were in London." During the Battle of Britain, he confided to his listeners that he spent hours collecting news and impressions, and "more hours wondering what you'd like to hear," what detail would make an event real to you because it was the sort of thing you would have noticed. Nothing was beneath regard.

> Perhaps you'd like to know what's being advertised in London's newspapers after forty days and forty nights of air raids. Here's a random selection taken from today's papers. On the front page is the old favorite—hair tonic, under the title "Why be gray? Gray hair makes you look old before your time."

His concern was not so much with relating the news to the listener as with relating the listener and the news. "You will want to know how the British took last night's announcement of the creation of a new French government"; because you want to know, he tells. Always he spoke to what he thought the audience was thinking, often to qualify and sometimes to contradict:

> During the last week you have heard much of the bombing of Buckingham Palace and probably seen pictures of the damage. You have been told by certain editors and commentators who sit in New York that the bombing of the Palace, which has one of the best air-raid shelters in England, caused a great surge of determination—a feeling of unity—to sweep this island. The bombing was

World War II was "radio's war," helping to establish the credibility of radio news organizations as more people turned to the media to monitor the course of events. *National Archives of Canada.*

called a great psychological blunder. I do not find much support for that point of view amongst Londoners with whom I've talked. . . . It didn't require a bombing of Buckingham Palace to convince these people that they are all in this thing together.[13]

The quality of Murrow's broadcasts surprised veteran journalists; some were scandalized, Elmer Davis said in 1941, that such good reporting could be done by someone without any newspaper experience. But in fact Murrow was so good on radio exactly because he had never been a newspaperman and didn't approach the medium from this perspective. He hadn't trained as a writer. In college he majored in Speech, was an actor, campus politician, and debater; then and later, as Alexander Kendrick has observed, Murrow wasn't interested in the written word but in the spoken. Before joining C.B.S. he worked as lecturer and advance-man for the National Student Federation and the Institute of International Education. His forte was direct persuasion. In consequence, he put things more personally, less abstractly than the press.

Unlike a newspaper reporter (and most radio commentators of the thirties), he constantly referred to himself, the "I" who spoke, and to the "you" who listened. Moreover, he was unremittingly particularistic. Kendrick has said that the Murrow style of broadcasting, which became the model for a generation of commentators, might be called "subjectively objective." It dealt with public fact in concrete and human terms. Murrow concentrated on what he called "the little picture," "the little incidents, the things the mind retains"; and these he captured with a poet's eye:

> One night last week I stood in front of a smashed grocery store and heard a dripping inside. It was the only sound in all London. Two cans of peaches had been drilled clean through by flying glass and the juice was dripping down onto the floor.[14]

To make the war vivid to his listeners, to bring them what he called "the real thing," Murrow made ad-lib reports from bombers over Germany; from C-47s dropping paratroops in the Lowlands; from a London air-raid shelter;

from the street outside where he lay on the side-walk to capture the sound of the English walking, not running, to safety; and, most memorably, from a rooftop over-looking London in the Blitz. His first rooftop broadcast was drowned out by the sound of planes and antiaircraft fire. The second broadcast was on September 21, 1940, two weeks after the terror bombing began:

> I'm standing on a roof top looking out over London. At the moment everything is quiet. For reasons of national as well as personal security,* I'm unable to tell you the exact location from which I'm speaking. Off to my left, far away in the distance, I can see just the faint red angry snap of antiaircraft bursts against the steel-blue sky.... You may be able to hear the sound of guns off in the distance very faintly, like someone kicking a tub....
>
> The lights are swinging over in this general direction now. You'll hear two explosions. There they are! That was the explosion overhead, not the guns.... Earlier this evening we could hear occasional—again, those were explosions overhead. Earlier this evening we heard a number of bombs go sliding and slithering across, to fall several blocks away. Just overhead now the burst of the antiaircraft fire. The searchlights now are feeling almost directly overhead. Now you'll hear two bursts a little nearer in a moment.
>
> There they are! That hard, stony sound.[15]

The one precept Murrow gave the staff of correspondents he recruited for C.B.S. was "Never sound excited," because an impassioned observer isn't trusted. But during this rooftop broadcast, far from being dispassionate, he spoke in a trembling voice that once broke into sobs. His emotion was genuine, but during the Blitz—and indeed until America entered the war—Murrow consciously let it come out. He thought conditions demanded no less. As he explained in a note to his wife written shortly after he began the rooftop broadcasts:

*Note how completely Murrow identified with the British cause: the "national" security sounds like *his* nation's.

> Have been doing some fair talking last few nights. Pulled out all the stops and let them [the listeners] have it. Now I think is the time. A thousand years of history and civilization are being smashed. Maybe the stuff I am doing is falling flat. Would be better if you could look at it, but have spent three years trying to make people believe me and am now using that for all it's worth.

By careful attention to his audience, Murrow had built up credibility; he now tried to use it to persuade America, as movingly as he could, of the evil of Fascism and the decency of the British. He told his wife in a later note that he had broken network rules and run the transcribed sound of a bomb falling nearly on mike, because he wanted "pretty strong meat" to "take the heart out of a few people" listening; he wanted to shake his audience, wake them up. He wished that his reportage were visual—it "would be better if you could look at it"—but actually he was more effective than any camera. For he communicated not only fact but emotion—and not only these but values. As Eric Barnouw has said, "Murrow and his colleagues offered something akin to drama: vicarious experience of what they were living and observing. It put the listener in another man's shoes. No better way to influence opinion has ever been found."[16]

None has. That Murrow's broadcasts during the Battle of Britain stirred the heart and conscience of America, all witnesses agree. Whether or not one calls this Murrow a propagandist depends on whether one thinks the word inherently disreputable. Beyond question, though, he was a practitioner of social documentary, which, in John Grierson's words, "is an instrument of human observation and judgement" concerned "with 'bringing alive' everyday affairs, evidently with a view of altering old loyalties or . . . crystallizing new loyalties." Beyond question, too, Murrow helped crystallize new loyalties toward Great Britain, a nation many Americans hated in the thirties. Archibald MacLeish considered Murrow's persuading the American people that Britain's fight was their fight "one of the miracles of the world"; he wondered in passing, though, as he praised Murrow to his face, "how much of it was you and how much of it was the medium you used."[17]

It was both, and circumstance more than either. Murrow had the eye to describe the passing moment and a voice for final things. But perhaps the miracle belonged even more to radio. Radio was the ideal medium for putting the audience in another man's shoes. Unlike the written word, it offered a sense of intimate participation, the immediacy of the human voice and of spot-coverage. Such coverage had direct elements—the bombs bursting on mike—but background noise did not overwhelm the commentary as the video overwhelms the audio in a TV report. Furthermore, a remote reporter on radio could take more liberties than one on TV, because his audience had to rely on his word. Murrow's listeners accepted the fact that Londoners were "magnificent" with no more tangible proof than his saying, "I've seen them, talked with them, and I know." On TV, one would expect to see some magnificence face to face.

Radio was such an effective documentary medium, a central medium in the 1930s, because it inextricably joined the two methods of persuasion, direct and vicarious. The listener witnessed firsthand, yet through another's eyes. The relation of listener and speaker was paradoxical, and like all paradoxes instable and unresolvable. The listener never could get from the speaker just the information he wanted as he wanted it, because to believe entirely he needed it firsthand. The speaker never could give the information he wanted as he wanted to. Always an insuperable limitation remained: "It's one of language," Murrow said, "there are no words to describe the thing that is happening." To know it one had to be there: "These things must be experienced to be understood." The speaker really couldn't take the listener there via radio.[18]

And yet, paradoxically, not being able to, he could. Radio's limitation became its strength. For as the speaker acknowledged his limits, the listener grew less observant of them. As the speaker disclaimed the transparency of the camera, as he intruded between the experience and the listener, selecting what had to be said but telling what he had left out and why, the listener came to believe in the experience. He felt the pressure of reality on the speaker, endless and incommunicable. All that the speaker left unspoken—found unspeakable—testified to the reality of his experience. And though the listener did not have the experience firsthand, he had another: his experience of the speaker. Listener and speaker engaged in "something akin to drama." The report of one voice was a dialogue; the commentary itself had a commentary, in the listener's mind. And when the listener believed, it was because he had convinced himself through his own imaginative trial of the facts.

BIBLIOGRAPHY

Barnouw, Eric, *A History of Broadcasting in the United States.* 3 vols. New York: Oxford University Press, 1966–70.

Kendrick, Alexander, *Prime Time: The Life of Edward R. Murrow.* Boston: 1969.

Stryker, Roy, Arthur Rothstein, and John Grierson, *The Complete Photographer,* ed. Willard D. Morgan. 10 vols. New York: 1942–43.

Warshow, Robert, *The Immediate Experience.* Garden City, NY: 1962.

NOTES

1. Roosevelt, *Public Papers,* VII, 278–80.
2. Editorial, CC, Nov. 18, 1936, p. 1519. Robert T. Elson, *Time Inc.* (New York, 1968), p. 322. George Seldes, statement of purpose on beginning his newsletter *In Fact,* May 20, 1940; reprinted in his *Never Tire of Protesting* (New York, 1968), p. 21.
3. George Seldes, *Lords of the Press* (New York, 1938), p. 331. Stokes, pp. 449–50. Editorial, CC, Nov. 18, 1936, pp. 1518, 1519.
4. Elson, pp. 224, 443. "The Press and the People—A Survey," *Fortune,* Aug. 1939, pp. 70, 65, 70.

5. "The Press and the People," pp. 70, 72, 65, 70.

6. Paul F. Lazarsfeld, *Radio and the Printed Page* (New York, 1940), pp. 232, 218, 141–43.

7. Lazarsfeld, pp. 201, 181. Barnouw. II, 62. Jonathan Yardley, review, *NR*, Feb. 6, 1971, p. 33.

8. Barnouw, II, 8.

9. Hadley Cantril and others, *The Invasion from Mars* (Princeton, 1940), p. 70. Archibald MacLeish, Foreword to *The Fall of the City* (New York, 1937), pp. x, xi; see Ruth Lechlitner, "The 1930's: A Symposium," *Carleton Miscellany*, winter 1965, p. 81. Barnouw, II, 69, Warshow, p. 255.

10. Edward R. Murrow, *This Is London,* ed. Elmer Davis (New York, 1941), p. 13; see Kendrick, p. 103. Columbia Broadcasting System, "Crisis: September 1938: A Complete and Verbatim Transcript of What America Heard over the Columbia Broadcasting System during the 20 Days of the Czechoslovakian Crisis" (10 vols., mimeographed, n.p., C.B.S., 1938), I, Sept. 12, p. 4; IV, Sept. 19, p. 26; IV, Sept. 21, p. 36.

11. C.B.S., "Crisis," IV, Sept. 21, pp. 27, 44–45 (Maxim Litvinoff was Stalin's foreign minister).

12. Frederick Lewis Allen, *Since Yesterday* (New York, 1940), p. 316.

13. C.B.S., "Crisis," IV, Sept. 20, p. 47. Murrow, *This Is London,* pp. 172, 204–5, 129, 174–75.

14. Murrow, *This Is London,* p. vii, 172, 173. Kendrick, pp. 107, 246, 247. Edward R. Murrow and Fred W. Friendly, *See It Now* (New York, 1955), p. 55.

15. Kendrick, p. 207. Murrow, *This Is London,* pp. 179–80; part of this broadcast is reprinted in Kendrick, pp. 207–8, and I have adopted some of his punctuation.

16. Kendrick, pp. 246, 208, 221. Barnouw, I, 151.

17. Irving Settel, *A Pictorial History of Radio* (New York, 1967), p. 122; for furthering Anglo-American friendship, Murrow was twice decorated by the British: see Kendrick, p. 512. To avoid the term "propagandist," Murrow has been called a "reporter-preacher": see Robert Lewis Shayon, "The Two Men Who Were Murrow," *Columbia Journalism Review,* fall 1969, p. 51. Grierson, *Complete Photographer,* IV, 1380. MacLeish, *A Time to Act,* p. 159.

18. Murrow, *This Is London,* p. 150, 151, 177, 178.

THE GOLDEN AGE OF PROGRAMMING
Christopher Sterling and John M. Kittross

Christopher Sterling is a professor at George Washington University in Washington, D.C. John M. Kittross is a professor at Emerson College, Boston.

THE GOLDEN AGE OF PROGRAMMING

In the last half of the 1930s, most full-time radio stations broadcast at least 12 hours a day, and many for 18 hours or more. Generally stations filled the expanded air time with variations of program types already developed. Three departures from this pattern were news and commentary, the daytime serial drama, and quiz and audience-participation programs.

The FCC's March 1938 survey of programming showed that 53 percent was devoted to music, 11 percent to talks and dialogues, 9 percent to drama, 9 percent to variety, 9 percent to news (which would not have been measurable a few years earlier), 5 percent to religion and devotion, 2 percent to special events, and 2 percent to miscellaneous. While network affiliates got from 50 percent to 70 percent of programming from their network, they also increased the time devoted to local and live programming. Of all radio programming in the survey period, 64 percent was live—roughly half network and half local—while 21 percent was from electrical transcriptions and 12 percent was from phonograph records—a definite increase in nonlive programming on the typical station. . . .

Music remained the staple of most radio schedules. Several transcription companies, operated both by networks and some independents, offered local stations prerecorded music, sometimes assembled into programs. By early 1939 more than 575 stations subscribed to at least one transcription service, and nearly half of them used two or more. RCA's transcription operation probably accounted for 35 percent of the industry's business, although 25 or 30 companies had combined annual revenues of $5 million in the late 1930s.

A station usually signed a contract with a transcription firm to deliver several hundred recorded musical selections—usually on 16-inch discs, running at $33\frac{1}{3}$ rpm, with approximately 15 minutes per side—to start, and then perhaps 50 additional selections a month. The transcription firm usually dealt with only one station in a particular market to avoid program duplication, and payment by the station was either a percentage of its gross revenues or a flat sum. While such material averaged only 10–15 percent of time on network-affiliated stations, nonaffiliated local stations used it much more, some for 80 percent of their schedules. Popular songs and instrumentals predominated, but all kinds of music were offered.

Although the use of music increased locally, classical musical programs declined in importance on the networks after the early 1930s. A notable exception was the NBC Symphony Orchestra, one of the outstanding cultural creations of radio in America. The orchestra was founded when David Sarnoff helped persuade Arturo Toscanini, the just retired conductor of the New York Philharmonic, to return from Italy to conduct ten concerts, the first one on

Christmas night 1937. NBC hired the best musicians possible to work in the new symphony orchestra. Three months later the network announced that Toscanini would lead the orchestra for another three years; but, as it turned out, the NBC Symphony continued for nearly 17 years until Toscanini's final retirement, well into his eighties, in 1954. The broadcasts normally originated from specially built Studio 8H, then the largest in the world, in the RCA Building in Rockefeller Center, and were broadcast on NBC-Blue on a sustaining basis, at the conductor's insistence. From 1948 the NBC Symphony was seen on television as well. After the NBC Symphony formally disbanded, the orchestra continued to play independently as the "Symphony of the Air."

Large dance bands were increasingly heard on both national and local programs. The 1930s were the "big band era," and many famous orchestras were heard first locally and then on the networks. Both industries benefited from such broadcasts, since the publicity of a major radio appearance attracted more people to the band's concerts. By 1937 the bands of Benny Goodman, Ozzie Nelson, Russ Morgan, Sammy Kaye, and Tommy Dorsey had played on network radio. *Your Hit Parade,* one of the top long-running radio programs, presented the most popular songs of the previous week, as determined by a national "survey" of record and sheet music sales, performed live by major singers and orchestras. The show began in fall 1935 and was sponsored on radio until 1953, and from 1951 until 1959 on television, by the American Tobacco Company's Lucky Strike (and, toward the very end, Hit Parade) cigarettes.

Local stations presented a wide range of live music, some stations supporting a full orchestra, and an increasing amount of recorded music. The conflict between broadcasters and ASCAP . . . had a substantial effect on radio music in 1940–1941.

Compared to the highly professional variety programs, local or national *amateur hour* broadcasts presented unknowns who would sing, tap dance, or do imitations in the hope of making a career. Such programs were used as fillers for years. Although the quality was uneven, the audiences that had cheered hometown talent supported contestants from all over the country. The most famous amateur variety show, *Major Bowes and His Original Amateur Hour,* began on New York station WHN in 1934 and moved to NBC-Red in March 1935. Within a few months, it was the most popular program on radio—at one time reaching a near-unbelievable rating of 45 when 20 was more typical! It presented amateurs who went on to fame—including Frank Sinatra, who made his radio debut in this program's first year—and others who went down to defeat and anonymity. Bowes became known by his catch-phrases and for his abrupt, even brutal manner with a gong as an aural equivalent of the "hook" used to remove inept or stage-frightened performers. The program continued on radio until 1952 and went on television from 1949 to the late 1960s, with Ted Mack serving as MC after Bowes's death—and bears a family resemblance to the *Gong Show* of the mid-1970s.

Many other national and local programs were built around a single performer, almost always a male singer or comic, usually backed by a musical group and supplemented by weekly guest performers. Most of these variety stars were products of vaudeville, burlesque, legitimate theater, or music halls. One was Bob Hope, who began his weekly show on CBS in 1935.

Such variety programming remained a network favorite, with little change, until inauguration of the army draft just before World War II gave a military slant to programs of the early 1940s. The *Army Show* (later the *Army Hour*), on NBC-Blue, *This Is Fort Dix* over Mutual, the Navy Band hour, and *Wings over America* were typical. The formats resembled earlier radio variety shows, with bits of song, humor, and chatter, but the participants frequently were military person-

nel, and the programs often originated from military camps and bases.

Drama

By far the most important network dramatic programming, in hours broadcast per week, was the woman's serial drama, or soap opera. Starting in 1935, the weekly hours of such fare increased sharply until, in 1940, the four networks combined devoted 75 hours a week to such programs, nine of every ten sponsored daytime network hours. These programs lasted 15 minutes, came on at the same time each weekday, and had soap and food manufacturers as sponsors. Typical of the longer running programs were *Back Stage Wife* ("what it means to be the wife of a famous Broadway star—dream sweetheart of a million other women"), which began in 1935; *The Guiding Light* (about a kindly cleric); *Lorenzo Jones* (inventor of useless gadgets); *Our Gal Sunday* ("Can this girl from a mining town in the West find happiness as the wife of a wealthy and titled Englishman?"); and *Road of Life* (doctors and nurses, although it began as the tale of an Irish-American mother's attempt to raise her children). In each case, domestic life was emphasized with its ups, and more usually, downs. Many of the actors and actresses played the same parts for decades. For a portion of each day, they performed a live, convincing, emotion-filled episode with little rehearsal, but their evenings were free for the stage or other professional activities. Behind many of the serials was the husband and wife team of Frank and Anne Hummert, who originally wrote all their own work but eventually employed dialogue writers to work within their character development and story lines. Elaine Carrington and Irna Phillips also wrote "soapers"—sometimes several at the same time.

The typical serial format was wonderfully simple: a brief musical introduction played on the studio organ, a narrator opening the day's episode with a recap of what had happened before, two segments of action separated by a commercial break, and a closing word from the narrator suggesting the problems ahead. Dialogue and organ music were somber and simple; story progress was very slow, giving time for character development and allowing a listener to miss an episode or two painlessly. Audiences were loyal, and many programs lasted 15 or more seasons, until radio's programming character changed in the 1950s. Listeners to soap operas were among the first studied by social psychologists, and much criticism was levied at the genre in 1940 and 1941, as it was nearly impossible to schedule anything else between 10 A.M. and 5 P.M. These complaints dropped off as the number of serials decreased during the war years.

"Prestige" drama increased in the 1930s. These programs usually were "anthologies" offering different stories with new casts each week, sometimes adaptations from other media, but often original radio plays. Writers such as poet Archibald MacLeish, later Librarian of Congress, and unknown authors such as Norman Corwin and Arch Oboler gained recognition almost overnight. Prestige series included the *Columbia Workshop* of experimental drama on CBS, started late in 1936, and the more conventional *Lux Radio Theater,* which presented such stars as Helen Hayes, Leslie Howard, and an unknown player named Orson Welles in hour-long versions of current films.

Welles at twenty-three was the guiding light behind a new CBS series in fall 1938, the *Mercury Theater on the Air.* As writer, director, and star, he built up a company of actors whose names were famous for decades: Joseph Cotton, Agnes Moorehead, Everett Sloane, Ray Collins. His Sunday evening, October 30, 1938, Halloween program probably ranks as the most famous single radio show ever presented. It was an adaptation by Welles and Howard Koch of H. G. Wells's science fiction story "War of the Worlds." The location was changed to northern New Jersey, the time was moved to the present, and, even more important, the narrative was changed to reflect radio's format. Listeners who tuned in to the program's beginning, or who lis-

tened carefully to the between-acts announcements, understood these circumstances. But those who tuned in late—and many had a habit of listening to the first few minutes of ventriloquist Edgar Bergen and his dummy Charlie McCarthy on NBC before tuning over to CBS for the play—were due for a surprise. The program in progress seemed to feature a band performing in a hotel. A few moments later, an announcer broke in with a "news bulletin" saying that a gas cloud had been observed on the planet Mars. Then back to the music; another interruption, asking observatories to keep watch; more music; an interview with a "noted astronomer" on the possibility of life on Mars (unlikely); more music—and, suddenly, a bulletin saying that a large meteorite had fallen in the vicinity of Grovers Mill, New Jersey. The pace built in a series of news bulletins and on-the-spot reports of the opening of the cylindrical "meteorite," the emergence of the Martians, the assembly of Martian war machines, the rout of U.S. military forces, and government reaction. Reports of casualties, traffic jams, transmissions from hapless military pilots, ominous breaking off of on-the-spot reports, the later report of the "death" of the field reporter, and use of familiar names and places—all gave it reality. As the Martian war machines headed toward New York to discharge their poison gas over the city—to the sounds of fleeing ocean liners, the last gasps of a newsman atop the broadcasting studio, and the cracked voice of a solitary ham radio operator calling "Isn't anybody there? Isn't anybody?"—many listeners did not wait to hear the mid-program announcement that it was all a hoax. By 8:30, thousands of people were praying, preparing for the end, and fleeing the Martians.

These reactions were not silly, although it may look that way today. The pacing of the program undermined critical faculties. It convinced the listener that a reporter had traveled the miles from Grovers Mill "in ten minutes," when less than three minutes actually had elapsed. Already sure that mobs were fleeing, listeners who looked out their windows and saw lots of people going about normal pursuits assumed that everyone was trying to get away from the Martians, just as the radio said. If no one was in sight, they assumed that everyone else had fled and left them behind. Few heard the three announcements of the program's fictional nature or the last half-hour, which was mostly a monologue by Welles, as a scientist who believes that he is one of the few survivors and who observes the demise of the Martians from the effects of earthly germs and bacteria. If they had heard this obviously dramatic material, many persons might have caught on. In the East, especially near the "landing site," thousands of people—a small proportion of the population but a large number nevertheless—called police, fled their homes, or otherwise reacted as though the invasion were real.

This panic had a number of causes, notably the way the program's "Halloween prank" nature was glossed over in the introduction. Afterwards researchers learned that many listeners did not try to double check the "news" on another station or telephone friends; and that others, who found normal programming elsewhere on the dial, decided that these stations had not yet received the word. The panic was also a reaction to the "Munich Crisis" just one month before, when Americans had been glued to their radios expecting the world to go to war. . . .

Welles was amazed but only slightly abashed at the program's impact. The FCC let it be known that it would not consider such "scare" programs and formats as broadcasting in the public interest. Although "War of the Worlds" was rebroadcast recently in the United States as a "period piece" without much effect, its original adaptation broadcast in other countries brought the same sort of panic. Several persons were killed in a riot in South America, when resentment over having been fooled boiled over. This drama showed better than any other program or episode the impact of radio on society— "if it was on the radio, then it must be true."

Thrillers and situation comedies filled more network time per week than any other form of drama. Adventure programs, starting in the early 1930s . . . were heard both in the evenings, as crime-detective shows for adults, and in the late afternoons, as action-adventure serials for children. These live, mostly network shows could be technically complicated, with large casts, sound effects, and split-second timing. Programs included the true story–recreating *Gangbusters* starting in 1935, whose loud opening of sirens, machine-gun fire, and marching feet gave rise to the phrase "coming on like Gangbusters"; *Mr. Keen, Tracer of Lost Persons;* and *I Love a Mystery,* which had one of radio's most loyal audiences. The last was written by Carlton E. Morse, writer of the enduringly popular *One Man's Family. Mr. District Attorney,* a program starting in 1939 which opened with the DA reciting his oath of office, provided a generation with the concept of the law as protector as well as prosecutor.

Programs aimed at children included *Jack Armstrong—The All-American Boy; Tom Mix,* a cowboy-adventure program; *Captain Midnight* and *Hop Harrigan,* both with pilot-heroes; *Terry and the Pirates,* based on the Milton Caniff comic strip; and a number of other serials that made the American "children's hour" far different from the period of silence that the British offered for several decades. Two of the most important children's adventure programs were not serials. *The Lone Ranger* and *The Green Hornet,* which began over Mutual in 1938, were written and acted by the team at WXYZ, Detroit. . . . Indeed, the publisher-hero Green Hornet was identified as the Lone Ranger's grandnephew! *The Green Hornet* used a classical music theme and a hard-punching opening: "He hunts the biggest of all game! Public enemies who try to destroy our America. . . . With his faithful valet, Kato, Britt Reid, daring young publisher, matches wits with the underworld, risking his life that criminals and racketeers, within the law, may feel its weight by the sting of—the Green Hornet!" Until FBI chief Hoover objected, the Green Hornet's targets were "public enemies that even the G-Men cannot catch." When the United States entered World War II, the faithful valet-chauffeur Kato was quickly changed from Japanese to Filipino.

Radio's half-hour situation comedies were a staple for years. *Li'l Abner* began over NBC in 1939, originating in Chicago as many programs then did; Fanny Brice, about whom the musical *Funny Girl* was written, created her immortal *Baby Snooks,* the child demon who created crisis after crisis for her father, and her baby brother Robespierre; *Blondie,* a 1939 CBS entry based on the Chic Young comic strip, featured the tribulations of Dagwood and Blondie Bumstead—another example of broadcasting's penchant for weak father figures; and *Henry Aldrich*—the misadventures of a crack-voiced adolescent—after appearing for some years as a segment on other programs, aired on its own over NBC-Blue in 1939.

Except for daytime serials and thriller programs, most network drama—anthology, or serial like *One Man's Family* and *Those We Love*—occurred in the evening. Only the largest stations produced their own dramatic programs regularly, most being content with network offerings, although many stations supplied dramatic or sound effects for commercials and special programs.

To an audience reared largely on movies, amateur theatricals, and traveling companies, radio provided something new and fascinating. The resulting loyal audience was very attractive to advertisers. Since it could perceive radio only by ear, the audience had to use its imagination to fill in the setting and the action. This it did well with the help of numerous musical and sound-effect conventions. Everyone understood transitions of time and space; the absence of carpet in radioland homes told the listener when somebody was entering or leaving a room. A filter that removed some of the audio frequencies placed a voice on the telephone; a bit more filter and some reverberation or

"echo" would transport a ghost to fantasyland. But without the audience's imagination, radio drama never would have succeeded. . . .

Political Broadcasting

Radio as a political instrument in the United States came into its own with the first administration of Franklin D. Roosevelt. Taking with him a habit from his New York governorship, F.D.R. began a series of "Fireside Chats" with the American public on the problems of Depression-hit America. There were 28 such broadcasts—8 in each of his first two terms, and 12 in the third, wartime term, nearly all of them half-hour programs broadcast in prime time—and they generally received ratings near the top. Roosevelt had a natural approach to radio, and his words came across more as a conversation between friends than a political speech. In the third "chat," when he stopped for a moment and drank from a glass of water, it seemed perfectly natural and correct.

In the 1936 presidential election campaign, a desperate Republican party tried a number of innovative uses of radio. The GOP nominee, Kansas governor Alfred Landon, submitted to a lengthy radio interview just prior to his nomination. More than 200 stations carried the convention in Cleveland, and the convention floor bristled with microphones. Once the campaign got underway, frequent spot radio commercials emphasized aspects of the GOP platform. In October, Senator Arthur Vandenberg presented a "debate" on CBS in which he asked questions of an absent President Roosevelt and then played carefully selected recordings of earlier F.D.R. speeches and promises. The program violated CBS policy against recordings, and many of the network's affiliates either refused to carry it or cut out during the program when they realized its unfair approach. Finally, when the networks refused to sell the Republicans time after the convention, the GOP used Chicago station

WGN to present an allegorical play depicting its campaign promises.

On the other hand, the Democrats used nothing special—only F.D.R. That consummate political speaker had huge audiences listening to his broadcast speeches. On election night, the networks initially interrupted regular programs with ballot bulletins from time to time, supplementing with commentary. CBS went full-time to election results at 10:30 P.M., while Mutual reported its first election that year.

The second Roosevelt administration showed increasing use of radio, not just by the President and his cabinet but by numerous federal agencies as well. The Office of Education, for example, produced 11 educational network programs; the Federal Theater Program—part of the Depression-spawned Works Progress Administration—produced more radio programming in its short life than any other agency; the departments of Agriculture and Interior supplied recorded programs to individual stations. Many local stations also benefited from the forecasting services of the U.S. Weather Bureau, and produced local programs featuring county agricultural agents.

The 1940 election campaign saw F.D.R. run again, this time against Republican Wendell Willkie, a little-known utilities executive before a whirlwind public relations campaign had propelled him into the limelight. Willkie pushed himself so hard that his voice weakened during the campaign—perhaps one of the reasons why Roosevelt consistently got higher ratings. Surveys conducted during this campaign suggested that most voters now considered radio more important than newspapers as a source of political news and tended to listen most to the candidate they favored; in other words, radio strengthened voters' predispositions. On election eve the Democrats mounted a special radio program of speeches, party propaganda, and entertainment by stage, screen, and radio stars. Full-time election coverage, as in 1936, came after the regular prime-time entertainment, although bulletins were provided throughout the evening. Human interest pieces and voter interviews were more common than in previous years.

Political broadcasting was not limited to the presidential campaign. Louisiana Senator Huey Long made anti–F.D.R. populist speeches until his 1935 assassination. Like Roosevelt, he had an informal approach, inviting listeners to call a friend or two and tell them Huey Long was on the air, and then delaying the meat of his address for the next several minutes. Catholic radio priest Coughlin . . . after promising to leave the air in 1936 if his third-party candidate got less than nine million votes—he got less than one million—came back to rail against the New Deal. He became increasingly rightist, criticizing Jews and defending many of the tenets of Nazism, until pressure from the Church hierarchy and other sources forced him off the air. . . .

UNDERSTANDING RADIO
Marshall McLuhan

Marshall McLuhan (1911–1980) was one of the most popular and controversial scholars of this century. Although he was a professor of English at the University of Toronto for much of his career, his notoriety came in the field of communications. His work in the 1960s exhorted an entire generation to "understand media."

England and America had had their "shots" against radio in the form of long exposure to literacy and industrialism. These forms involve an intense visual organization of experience. The more earthy and less visual European cultures were not immune to radio. Its tribal magic was not lost on them, and the old web of kinship began to resonate once more with the note of fascism. The inability of literate people to grasp the language and message of the media as such is involuntarily conveyed by the comments of sociologist Paul Lazarsfeld in discussing the effects of radio:

> The last group of effects may be called the monopolistic effects of radio. Such have attracted most public attention because of their importance in the totalitarian countries. If a government monopolizes the radio, then by mere repetition and by exclusion of conflicting points of view it can determine the opinions of the population. We do not know much about how this monopolistic effect really works, but it is important to note its singularity. No inference should be drawn regarding the effects of radio as such. It is often forgotten that Hitler did not achieve control through radio but almost despite it, because at the time of his rise to power radio was controlled by his enemies. The monopolistic effects have probably less social importance than is generally assumed.

Professor Lazarsfeld's helpless unawareness of the nature and effects of radio is not a personal defect, but a universally shared ineptitude.

In a radio speech in Munich, March 14, 1936, Hitler said, "I go my way with the assurance of a somnambulist." His victims and his critics have been equally somnambulistic. They danced entranced to the tribal drum of radio that extended their central nervous system to create depth involvement for everybody. "I live right inside radio when I listen. I more easily lose myself in radio than in a book," said a voice from a radio poll. The power of radio to involve people in depth is manifested in its use during homework by youngsters and by many other people who carry transistor sets in order to provide a private world for themselves amidst crowds. There is a little poem by the German dramatist Berthold Brecht:

> *You little box, held to me when escaping*
> *So that your valves should not break.*
> *Carried from house to ship from ship to train.*
> *So that my enemies might go on talking to me*
> *Near my bed, to my pain*
> *The last thing at night, the first thing in the morning,*
> *Of their victories and of my cares.*
> *Promise me not to go silent all of a sudden.*

One of the many effects of television on radio has been to shift radio from an entertainment medium into a kind of nervous information system. News bulletins, time signals, traffic data, and, above all, weather reports now serve to enhance the native power of radio to involve people in one another. Weather is that medium that involves all people equally. It is the top item on radio, showering us with fountains of auditory space or *lebensraum*.

It was no accident that Senator McCarthy lasted such a very short time when he switched to TV. Soon the press decided, "He isn't news any more." Neither McCarthy nor the press ever knew what had happened. TV is a cool medium. It rejects hot figures and hot issues and people from the hot press media. Fred Allen was a casualty of TV. Was Marilyn Monroe? Had TV occurred on a large scale during Hitler's reign he would have vanished quickly. Had TV come first there would have been no Hitler at all. When Khrushchev appeared on American TV he was more acceptable than Nixon, as a clown and a lovable sort of old boy. His appearance is rendered by TV as a comic cartoon. Radio, however, is a hot medium and takes cartoon characters seriously. Mr. K. on radio would be a different proposition.

In the Kennedy-Nixon debates, those who heard them on radio received an overwhelming idea of Nixon's superiority. It was Nixon's fate to provide a sharp, high-definition image and action for the cool TV medium that translated that sharp image into the impression of a phony. I suppose "phony" is something that resonates wrong, that doesn't *ring* true. It might be that F.D.R. would not have done well on TV. He had learned, at least, how to use the hot radio medium for his very cool job of fireside chatting. He first, however, had had to hot up the press media against himself in order to create the right atmosphere for his radio chats. He learned how to use the press in close relation to radio. TV would have presented him with an entirely different political and social mix of components and problems. He would possibly have enjoyed solving them, for he had the kind of playful approach necessary for tackling new and obscure relationships.

Radio affects most people intimately, person-to-person, offering a world of unspoken communication between writer-speaker and the listener. That is the immediate aspect of radio. A private experience. The subliminal depths of radio are charged with the resonating echoes of tribal horns and antique drums. This is inherent in the very nature of this medium, with its power to turn the psyche and society into a single echo chamber. The resonating dimension of radio is unheeded by the script writers, with few exceptions. The famous Orson Welles broadcast about the invasion from Mars was a simple demonstration of the all-inclusive, completely involving scope of the auditory image of radio. It was Hitler who gave radio the Orson Welles treatment for *real*.

That Hitler came into political existence at all is directly owing to radio and public-address systems. This is not to say that these media relayed his thoughts effectively to the German people. His thoughts were of very little consequence. Radio provided the first massive experience of electronic implosion, that reversal of the entire direction and meaning of literate Western civilization. For tribal peoples, for those whose entire social existence is an extension of family life, radio will continue to be a violent experience. Highly literate societies, that have long subordinated family life to individualist stress in business and politics, have managed to absorb

and to neutralize the radio implosion without revolution. Not so, those communities that have had only brief or superficial experience of literacy. For them, radio is utterly explosive.

To understand such effects, it is necessary to see literacy as typographic technology, applied not only to the rationalizing of the entire procedures of production and marketing, but to law and education and city planning, as well. The principles of continuity, uniformity, and repeatability derived from print technology have, in England and America, long permeated every phase of communal life. In those areas a child learns literacy from traffic and street, from every car and toy and garment. Learning to read and write is a minor facet of literacy in the uniform, continuous environments of the English-speaking world. Stress on literacy is a distinguishing mark of areas that are striving to initiate that process of standardization that leads to the visual organization of work and space. Without psychic transformation of the inner life into segmented visual terms by literacy, there cannot be the economic "take-off" that insures a continual movement of augmented production and perpetually accelerated change-and-exchange of goods and services.

Just prior to 1914, the Germans had become obsessed with the menace of "encirclement." Their neighbors had all developed elaborate railway systems that facilitated mobilization of manpower resources. Encirclement is a highly visual image that had great novelty for this newly industrialized nation. In the 1930s, by contrast, the German obsession was with *lebensraum*. This is not a visual concern, at all. It is a claustrophobia, engendered by the radio implosion and compression of space. The German defeat had thrust them back from visual obsession into brooding upon the resonating Africa within. The tribal past has never ceased to be a reality for the German psyche.

It was the ready access of the German and middle-European world to the rich nonvisual resources of auditory and tactile form that enabled them to enrich the world of music and dance and sculpture. Above all their tribal mode gave them easy access to the new nonvisual world of subatomic physics, in which long-literate and long-industrialized societies are decidedly handicapped. The rich area of preliterate vitality felt the hot impact of radio. The message of radio is one of violent, unified implosion and resonance. For Africa, India, China, and even Russia, radio is a profound archaic force, a time bond with the most ancient past and long-forgotten experience.

Tradition, in a word, is the sense of the total past as *now*. Its awakening is a natural result of radio impact and of electric information, in general. For the intensely literate population, however, radio engendered a profound unlocalizable sense of guilt that sometimes expressed itself in the fellow-traveler attitude. A newly found human involvement bred anxiety and insecurity and unpredictability. Since literacy had fostered an extreme of individualism, and radio had done just the opposite in reviving the ancient experience of kinship webs of deep tribal involvement, the literate West tried to find some sort of compromise in a larger sense of collective responsibility. The sudden impulse to this end was just as subliminal and obscure as the earlier literary pressure toward individual isolation and irresponsibility; therefore, nobody was happy about any of the positions arrived at. The Gutenberg technology had produced a new kind of visual, national entity in the sixteenth century that was gradually meshed with industrial production and expansion. Telegraph and radio neutralized nationalism but evoked archaic tribal ghosts of the most vigorous brand. This is exactly the meeting of eye and ear, of explosion and implosion, or as Joyce puts it in the *Wake*. "In that earopean end meets Ind." The opening of the European ear brought to an end the open society and reintroduced the Indic world of tribal man to West End woman. Joyce puts these matters not so much in cryptic, as in dramatic and mimetic, form. The reader has only to take any of his phrases such as this one, and mime it

until it yields the intelligible. Not a long or tedious process, if approached in the spirit of artistic playfulness that guarantees "lots of fun at Finnegan's wake."

Radio is provided with its cloak of invisibility, like any other medium. It comes to us ostensibly with person-to-person directness that is private and intimate, while in more urgent fact, it is really a subliminal echo chamber of magical power to touch remote and forgotten chords. All technological extensions of ourselves must be numb and subliminal, else we could not endure the leverage exerted upon us by such extension. Even more than telephone or telegraph, radio is that extension of the central nervous system that is matched only by human speech itself. Is it not worthy of our meditation that radio should be specially attuned to that primitive extension of our central nervous system, that aboriginal mass medium, the vernacular tongue? The crossing of these two most intimate and potent of human technologies could not possibly have failed to provide some extraordinary new shapes for human experience. So it proved with Hitler, the somnambulist. But does the detribalized and literate West imagine that it has earned immunity to the tribal magic of radio as a permanent possession? Our teenagers in the 1950s began to manifest many of the tribal stigmata. The adolescent, as opposed to the teenager, can now be classified as a phenomenon of literacy. Is it not significant that the adolescent was indigenous only to those areas of England and America where literacy had invested even food with abstract visual values? Europe never had adolescents. It had chaperones. Now, to the teenager, radio gives privacy, and at the same time it provides the tight tribal bond of the world of the common market, of song, and of resonance. The ear is hyperesthetic compared to the neutral eye. The ear is intolerant, closed, and exclusive, whereas the eye is open, neutral, and associative. Ideas of tolerance came to the West only after two or three centuries of literacy and visual Gutenberg culture. No such saturation with visual values had occurred in Germany by 1930. Russia is still far from any such involvement with visual order and values.

If we sit and talk in a dark room, words suddenly acquire new meanings and different textures. They become richer, even, than architecture, which Le Corbusier rightly says can best be felt at night. All those gestural qualities that the printed page strips from language come back in the dark, and on the radio. Given only the *sound* of a play, we have to fill in *all* of the senses, not just the sight of the action. So much do-it-yourself, or completion and "closure" of action, develops a kind of independent isolation in the young that makes them remote and inaccessible. The mystic screen of sound with which they are invested by their radios provides the privacy for their homework, and immunity from parental behest.

With radio came great changes to the press, to advertising, to drama, and to poetry. Radio offered new scope to practical jokers like Morton Downey at CBS. A sportscaster had just begun his fifteen-minute reading from a script when he was joined by Mr. Downey, who proceeded to remove his shoes and socks. Next followed coat and trousers and then underwear, while the sportscaster helplessly continued his broadcast, testifying to the compelling power of the mike to command loyalty over modesty and the self-protective impulse.

Radio created the disk jockey, and elevated the gag writer into a major national role. Since the advent of radio, the gag has supplanted the joke, not because of gag writers, but because radio is a fast hot medium that has also rationed the reporter's space for stories.

Jean Shepherd of WOR in New York regards radio as a new medium for a new kind of novel that he writes nightly. The mike is his pen and paper. His audience and their knowledge of the daily events of the world provide his characters, his scenes, and moods. It is his idea that, just as Montaigne was the first to use the page to record his reactions to the new world of printed books, he is the first to use radio as an essay and novel form for recording our common awareness of a totally new world of universal human participation in all human events, private or collective.

To the student of media, it is difficult to explain the human indifference to social effects of these radical forces. The phonetic alphabet and the printed word that exploded the closed tribal world into the open society of fragmented functions and specialist knowledge and action have never been studied in their roles as a magical transformer. The antithetic electric power of instant information that reverses social explosion into implosion, private enterprise into organization man, and expanding empires into common markets, has obtained as little recognition as the written word. The power of radio to retribalize mankind, its almost instant reversal of individualism into collectivism, Fascist or Marxist, has gone unnoticed. So extraordinary is this unawareness that *it* is what needs to be explained. The transforming power of media is easy to explain, but the ignoring of this power is not at all easy to explain. It goes without saying that the universal ignoring of the psychic action of technology bespeaks some inherent function, some essential numbing of consciousness such as occurs under stress and shock conditions.

The history of radio is instructive as an indicator of the bias and blindness induced in any society by its pre-existent technology. The word "wireless," still used for radio in Britain, manifests the negative "horseless-carriage" attitude toward a new form. Early wireless was regarded as a form of telegraph, and was not seen even in relation to the telephone. David Sarnoff in 1916 sent a memo to the Director of the American Marconi Company that employed him, advocating the idea of a music box in the home. It was ignored. That was the year of the Irish Easter rebellion and of the first radio *broadcast*. Wireless had already been used on ships as ship-to-shore "telegraph." The Irish rebels used a ship's wireless to make, not a point-to-point message, but a diffused broadcast in the hope of getting word to some ship that would relay their story to the American press. And so it proved. Even after broadcasting had been in existence for some years, there was no commercial interest in it. It was the amateur operators or hams and their fans, whose petitions finally got some action in favor of the setting up of facilities. There was reluctance and opposition from the world of the press, which, in England, led to the formation of the BBC and the firm shackling of radio by newspaper and advertising interests. This is an obvious rivalry that has not been openly discussed. The restrictive pressure by the press on radio and TV is still a hot issue in Britain and in Canada. But, typically, misunderstanding of the nature of the medium rendered the restraining policies quite futile. Such has always been the case, most notoriously in government censorship of the press and of the movies. Although the medium is the *message,* the controls go beyond programming. The restraints are always directed to the "content," which is always another medium. The content of the press is literary statement, as the content of the book is speech, and the content of the movie is the novel. So the effects of radio are quite independent of its programming. To those who have never studied media, this fact is quite as baffling as literacy is to natives, who say, "Why do you write? Can't you remember?"

Thus, the commercial interests who think to render media universally acceptable, invariably settle for "entertainment" as a strategy of neutrality. A more spectacular mode of the ostrich-head-in-sand could not be devised, for it ensures maximal pervasiveness for any medium whatever. The literate community will always argue for a controversial or point-of-view use of press, radio, and movie that would in effect diminish the operation, not only of press, radio and movie, but of the book as well. The commercial entertainment strategy automatically ensures maximum speed and force of impact for any medium, on psychic and social life equally. It

thus becomes a comic strategy of unwitting self-liquidation, conducted by those who are dedicated to permanence, rather than to change. In the future, the only effective media controls must take the thermostatic form of quantitative rationing. Just as we now try to control atom-bomb fallout, so we will one day try to control media fallout. Education will become recognized as civil defense against media fallout. The only medium for which our education now offers some civil defense is the print medium. The educational establishment, founded on print, does not yet admit any other responsibilities.

Radio provides a speed-up of information that also causes acceleration in other media. It certainly contracts the world to village size, and creates insatiable village tastes for gossip, rumor, and personal malice. But while radio contracts the world to village dimensions, it hasn't the effect of homogenizing the village quarters. Quite the contrary. In India, where radio is the supreme form of communication, there are more than a dozen official languages and the same number of official radio networks. The effect of radio as a reviver of archaism and ancient memories is not limited to Hitler's Germany. Ireland, Scotland, and Wales have undergone resurgence of their ancient tongues since the coming of radio, and the Israeli present an even more extreme instance of linguistic revival. They now speak a language which has been dead in books for centuries. Radio is not only a mighty awakener of archaic memories, forces, and animosities, but a decentralizing, pluralistic force, as is really the case with all electric power and media.

Centralism of organization is based on the continuous, visual, lineal structuring that arises from phonetic literacy. At first, therefore, electric media merely followed the established patterns of literate structures. Radio was released from these centralist network pressures by TV. TV then took up the burden of centralism, from which it may be released by Telstar. With TV accepting the central network burden derived from our centralized industrial organization, radio was free to diversify, and to begin a regional and local community service that it had not known, even in the earliest days of the radio "hams." Since TV, radio has turned to the individual needs of people at different times of the day, a fact that goes with the multiplicity of receiving sets in bedrooms, bathrooms, kitchens, cars, and now in pockets. Different programs are provided for those engaged in divers activities. Radio, once a form of group listening that emptied churches, has reverted to private and individual uses since TV. The teenager withdraws from the TV group to his private radio.

This natural bias of radio to a close tie-in with diversified community groups is best manifested in the disk-jockey cults, and in radio's use of the telephone in a glorified form of the old trunk line wire-tapping. Plato, who had old-fashioned tribal ideas of political structure, said that the proper size of a city was indicated by the number of people who could hear the voice of a public speaker. Even the printed book, let alone radio, renders the political assumptions of Plato quite irrelevant for practical purposes. Yet radio, because of its ease of decentralized intimate relation with both private and small communities, could easily implement the Platonic political dream on a world scale.

The uniting of radio with phonograph that constitutes the average radio program yields a very special pattern quite superior in power to the combination of radio and telegraph press that yields our news and weather programs. It is curious how much more arresting are the weather reports than the news, on both radio and TV. Is not this because "weather" is now entirely an electronic form of information, whereas news retains much of the pattern of the printed word? It is probably the print and book bias of the BBC and the CBC that renders them so awkward and inhibited in radio and TV presentation. Commercial urgency, rather than artistic insight, fostered by contrast a hectic vivacity in the corresponding American operation.

PART VII

TV Times

Watch TV in your own home. *Orion Publishing Group.*

The first television broadcasts in North America began in 1939. Radio, at the height of its "Golden Age," had its preeminence challenged. However, just as World War I put the development of broadcast radio on hold, so World War II delayed for almost a decade the dream of television as the new mass medium. By the early 1950s, television was in the throes of a remarkable growth. Sales of television receivers boomed. Radio would never be the same again. Given what we have already discussed regarding the relationship between new media and old, it should come as no surprise to learn that the early content of television drew from both the motion pictures and radio. Distinct directions soon followed, most notably the filming of comedy and adventure series. *I Love Lucy* was one of the first programs to follow this convention, and with the help of "canned laughter," it broke the format of the live broadcast that was the staple of "radio days."

The mass audience that was enamored of radio in the 1930s adapted with enthusiasm to television during the 1950s. After the war, production and consumption increased as the first waves of the baby boom broke over the social landscape. People became more mobile as a variety of new job opportunities opened up. Yet family life remained strongly home centered, especially on evenings and weekends, when, thanks to a shorter work week, people had increased leisure time and more money to spend on it. Television, with its affordability, mix of national and local programs, and panoramic view of the new consumer culture via advertising, became a technology central to social life.

Although television during the 1950s managed to draw people always from radio sets and movie theaters, it was not always technologically reliable. Snowy pictures, sound problems, and interrupted signals were often a problem, especially in areas at the periphery of major cities and the expanding suburbs. However, the next several decades saw improved signal delivery systems, replacement of the vacuum tube by the transistor (during the 1950s, set breakdowns resulting from tube failure were a regular occurrence, and every neighborhood had its TV repair shop), the emergence of reliable, affordable color sets, and the introduction of cable transmission. As of this writing, we are on the threshold of yet another transformation, the establishment of high-definition television (HDTV). Whatever its final format, HDTV will dramatically increase screen resolution, providing viewers with a visual experience comparable to that of 35mm and 70mm films. Promoters and most experimental users of this technology confidently predict that significant shifts in programming and patterns of viewing will result. We leave it to readers informed by the essays that follow to speculate on what this might entail.

The unique aspect of television is a concern of Edmund Carpenter, an anthropologist who during the 1950s collaborated with Marshall McLuhan on a major research project and on a journal dealing with human communication, entitled *Explorations*. Like McLuhan, Carpenter argues that a medium constructs its messages as much through its form as through specific content. ("The medium is the message" was McLuhan's provocative maxim for overstating this notion.) Media are never neutral; they impart what Harold Innis—who also influenced Carpenter—called a bias to communication. In his essay, Carpenter likens media, especially television, to languages. Television is contrasted with radio, film, theater, and the book, particularly through a consideration of the way in which each medium gives a distinct shape to what appears to be the same story. His analysis of *The Caine Mutiny* in this respect is revealing. It should encourage readers to think of books they have read that were made into movies or television programs and to think about how viewing films in the theatre compares with viewing them on television.

The social impact of television during the 1950s is the subject of our next excerpt. Lynn Spigel explores the way television, suburban life, and the new postwar patterns of consumption developed in concert. As she notes, the resulting shift in domestic space and the aspirations of a newly emerging middle-class were often mirrored in the programs. Since a number of the programs that she mentions are available via syndicated rerun or on video, we urge readers to have a look. In what ways do they reflect a social world that is quite different from today? What themes are still relevant and consistent with a 1990s sensibility?

Our next selection deals with television news. In it, Mitchell Stephens shows us how radio, then television, imitated and eventually altered the newsgathering roles of other media. Radio news originally adopted the reporting style of newspapers. However, the sometimes complex sentences of newspaper reporting had to be reduced to make reading on the air effective. World War II was a major arena for this evolution. It created enormous audiences for broadcast news. Stephens argues that the Vietnam War played a similar role in giving television news its distinct format of almost instant televisual reporting, as a consequence pushing radio farther into the background of local broadcasting and music formats.

Television news has led to certain expectations and dependencies for viewers. Stephens argues that this is not all to the good. He challenges McLuhan's optimistic view that television extends our eyes and ears into a greater awareness of events in the "global village." He warns of the dangers and limitations of linking news to newscaster celebrities and formulaic visual presentations.

Over the past two decades, traditional entertainment programming on television has been augmented by a new format: the music video. As Pat Aufderheide notes in her selection, rock videos derived initial inspiration from commercials. The new directions they explored were in turn reappropriated by advertisers, blurring the line dividing the genres. As she points out, the emotions invoked in MTV videos foster a search for identity among young people, creating the desire to belong to communities defined by particular styles of popular culture. The power of this imaging has not been lost on politicians, who now incorporate music video techniques into campaign advertising.

Our last selection is rather unusual: a dinner conversation between two renowned and controversial commentators on media and popular culture, Neil Postman and Camille Paglia. Postman champions the book and the sense of culture he associates with it. Paglia argues that television—and the image culture gathered around it—dominates our time. But they concur in the need for critical literacy in both media. An interesting project might be to continue their debate, adding examples from your own experience as well as from other essays in this book.

In scale, television far surpasses what was possible during the newspaper and radio eras. Each medium, however, built on its precursors and tried to bypass their inherent limitations. Today, television provides a compelling demonstration of simultaneity and co-presence, which began almost 150 years ago with the telegraph. The moon landing, the Olympics, and the fall of the Berlin Wall all provide instances of shared global experience, which should be continually reflected upon in light of the history and nature of a medium whose influence on our lives continues to deepen.

34 THE NEW LANGUAGES

Edmund Carpenter

Edmund Carpenter is an anthropologist known for his diverse and lively studies of the impact of media on societies, primitive and modern. He is a former collaborator with Marshall McLuhan on the Explorations *project and journal (1953–1958), a major interdisciplinary forum devoted to the study of human communication.*

Brain of the New World,
What a task is thine
to formulate the modern
. . . to recast poems, churches, art

Whitman

English is a mass medium. All languages are mass media. The new mass media—film, radio, TV—are new languages, their grammars as yet unknown. Each codifies reality differently; each conceals a unique metaphysics. Linguists tell us it's possible to say anything in any language if you use enough words or images, but there's rarely time; the natural course is for a culture to exploit its media biases.

The same is true of the other new languages. Both radio and TV offer short, unrelated programs, interrupted between and within by commercials. I say "interrupted," being myself an anachronism of book culture, but my children don't regard them as interruptions, as breaking continuity. Rather, they regard them as part of a whole, and their reaction is neither one of annoyance nor one of indifference. The ideal news broadcast has half a dozen speakers from as many parts of the world on as many subjects. The London correspondent doesn't comment on what the Washington correspondent has just said; he hasn't even heard him.

The child is right in not regarding commercials as interruptions. For the only time anyone smiles on TV is in commercials. The rest of life, in news broadcasts and soap operas, is presented as so horrible that the only way to get through

life is to buy this product: then you'll smile. Aesop never wrote a clearer fable. It's heaven and hell brought up to date: Hell in the headline, Heaven in the ad. Without the other, neither has meaning.

Of the new languages, TV comes closest to drama and ritual. It combines music and art, language and gesture, rhetoric and color. It favors simultaneity of visual and auditory images. Cameras focus not on speakers but on persons spoken to or about; the audience *hears* the accuser but *watches* the accused. In a single impression it hears the prosecutor, watches the trembling hands of the big-town crook, and sees the look of moral indignation on Senator Tobey's face. This is real drama, in process, with the outcome uncertain. Print can't do this; it has a different bias.

Books and movies only pretend uncertainty, but live TV retains this vital aspect of life. Seen on TV, the fire in the 1952 Democratic Convention threatened briefly to become a conflagration; seen on newsreel, it was history, without potentiality.

The absence of uncertainty is no handicap to other media, if they are properly used, for their biases are different. Thus it's clear from the beginning that Hamlet is a doomed man, but, far from detracting in interest, this heightens the sense of tragedy.

Now, one of the results of the time-space duality that developed in Western culture, principally from the Renaissance on, was a separation within the arts. Music, which created symbols in time, and graphic art, which created

262

symbols in space, became separate pursuits, and men gifted in one rarely pursued the other. Dance and ritual, which inherently combined them, fell in popularity. Only in drama did they remain united.

It is significant that of the four new media, the three most recent are dramatic media, particularly TV, which combines language, music, art, dance. They don't however, exercise the same freedom with time that the stage dares practice. An intricate plot, employing flash backs, multiple time perspectives and overlays, intelligible on the stage, would mystify on the screen. The audience has no time to think back, to establish relations between early hints and subsequent discoveries. The picture passes before the eyes too quickly; there are no intervals in which to take stock of what has happened and make conjectures of what is going to happen. The observer is in a more passive state, less interested in subtleties. Both TV and film are nearer to narrative and depend much more upon the episodic. An intricate time construction can be done in film, but in fact rarely is. The soliloquies of *Richard III* belong on the stage; the film audience was unprepared for them. On stage Ophelia's death was described by three separate groups: one hears the announcement and watches the reactions simultaneously. On film the camera flatly shows her drowned where "a willow lies aslant a brook."

Media differences such as these mean that it's not simply a question of communicating a single idea in different ways but that a given idea or insight belongs primarily, though not exclusively, to one medium, and can be gained or communicated best through that medium.

Each medium selects its ideas. TV is a tiny box into which people are crowded and must live; film gives us the wide world. With its huge screen, film is perfectly suited for social drama, Civil War panoramas, the sea, land erosion, Cecil B. DeMille spectaculars. In contrast, the TV screen has room for two, at the most three, faces, comfortably. TV is closer to stage, yet different. Paddy Chayefsky writes:

> The theatre audience is far away from the actual action of the drama. They cannot see the silent reactions of the players. They must be told in a loud voice what is going on. The plot movement from one scene to another must be marked, rather than gently shaded as is required in television. In television, however, you can dig into the most humble, ordinary relationships; the relationship of bourgeois children to their mother, of middle-class husband to his wife, of white-collar father to his secretary—in short, the relationships of the people. We relate to each other in an incredibly complicated manner. There is far more exciting drama in the reasons why a man gets married than in why he murders someone. The man who is unhappy in his job, the wife who thinks of a lover, the girl who wants to get into television, your father, your mother, sister, brothers, cousins, friends—all these are better subjects for drama than Iago. What makes a man ambitious? Why does a girl always try to steal her kid sister's boy friends? Why does your uncle attend his annual class reunion faithfully every year? Why do you always find it depressing to visit your father? These are the substances of good television drama; and the deeper you probe into and examine the twisted, semi-formed complexes of emotional entanglements, the more exciting your writing becomes.[1]

The gestures of visual man are not intended to convey concepts that can be expressed in words, but inner experiences, nonrational emotions, which would still remain unexpressed when everything that can be told has been told. Such emotions lie in the deepest levels. They cannot be approached by words that are mere reflections of concepts, any more than musical experiences can be expressed in rational concepts. Facial expression is a human experience rendered immediately visible without the intermediary of word. It is Turgenev's "living truth of the human face."

Printing rendered illegible the faces of men. So much could be read from paper that the method of conveying meaning by facial expression fell into desuetude. The press grew to be the main bridge over which the more remote interhuman spiritual exchanges took place; the immediate, the personal, the inner, died. There was no longer need for the subtler means of expression provided by the body. The face became immobile; the inner life, still. Wells that dry up are wells from which no water is dipped.

Just as radio helped bring back inflection in speech, so film and TV are aiding us in the recovery of gesture and facial awareness—a rich, colorful language, conveying moods and emotions, happenings and characters, even thoughts, none of which could be properly packaged in words. If film had remained silent for another decade, how much faster this change might have been!

Feeding the product of one medium through another medium creates a new product. When Hollywood buys a novel, it buys a title and the publicity associated with it: nothing more. Nor should it.

Each of the four versions of the *Caine Mutiny*—book, play, movie, TV—had a different hero: Willie Keith, the lawyer Greenwald, the United States Navy, and Captain Queeg, respectively. Media and audience biases were clear. Thus the book told, in lengthy detail, of the growth and making of Ensign William Keith, American man, while the movie camera with its colorful shots of ships and sea, unconsciously favored the Navy as hero, a bias supported by the fact the Navy cooperated with the movie makers. Because of stage limitations, the play was confined, except for the last scene, to the courtroom, and favored the defense counsel as hero. The TV show, aimed at a mass audience, emphasized patriotism, authority, allegiance. More important, the cast was reduced to the principals and the plot to

its principles; the real moral problem—the refusal of subordinates to assist an incompetent, unpopular superior—was clear, whereas in the book it was lost under detail, in the film under scenery. Finally, the New York play, with its audience slanted toward Expense Account patronage—Mr. Sampson, Western Sales Manager for the Cavity Drill Company—became a morality play with Willie Keith, innocent American youth, torn between two influences: Keefer, clever author but moral cripple, and Greenwald, equally brilliant but reliable, a businessman's intellectual. Greenwald saves Willie's soul.

This is why the preservation of book culture is as important as the development of TV. This is why new languages, instead of destroying old ones, serve as a stimulant to them. Only monopoly is destroyed. When actor-collector Edward G. Robinson was battling actor-collector Vincent Price on art on TV's *$64,000 Challenge*, he was asked how the quiz had affected his life; he answered petulantly, "Instead of looking at the pictures in my art books, I now have to read them." Print, along with all old languages, including speech, has profited enormously from the development of the new media. "The more the arts develop," writes E. M. Forster, "the more they depend on each other for definition. We will borrow from painting first and call it pattern. Later we will borrow from music and call it rhythm."

The appearance of a new medium often frees older media for creative effort. They no longer have to serve the interests of power and profit. Elia Kazan, discussing the American theatre, says:

> Take 1900–1920. The theatre flourished all over the country. It had no competition. The box office boomed. The top original fare it had to offer was *The Girl of the Golden West*. Its bow to culture was fusty productions of Shakespeare.... Came the moving pictures. The theatre had to be better or go under. It got better. It got so spectac-

ularly better so fast that in 1920–1930 you wouldn't have recognized it. Perhaps it was an accident that Eugene O'Neill appeared at that moment—but it was no accident that in that moment of strange competition, the theatre had room for him. Because it was disrupted and hard pressed, it made room for his experiments, his unheard-of subjects, his passion, his power. There was room for him to grow to his full stature. And there was freedom for the talents that came after his.[2]

Yet a new language is rarely welcomed by the old. The oral tradition distrusted writing, manuscript culture was contemptuous of printing, book culture hated the press, that "slagheap of hellish passions," as one 19th century scholar called it. A father, protesting to a Boston newspaper about crime and scandal, said he would rather see his children "in their graves while pure in innocence, than dwelling with pleasure upon these reports, which have grown so bold."

What really disturbed book-oriented people wasn't the sensationalism of the newspaper, but its nonlineal format, its nonlineal codifications of experience. The motto of conservative academicians became: *Hold that line!*

A new language lets us see with the fresh, sharp eyes of the child; it offers the pure joy of discovery. I was recently told a story about a Polish couple who, though long resident in Toronto, retained many of the customs of their homeland. Their son despaired of ever getting his father to buy a suit cut in style or getting his mother to take an interest in Canadian life. Then he bought them a TV set, and in a matter of months a major change took place. One evening the mother remarked that "Edith Piaf is the latest thing on Broadway," and the father appeared in "the kind of suit executives wear on TV." For years the father had passed this same suit in store windows and seen it both in advertisements and on living men, but not until he saw it on TV did it become meaningful. This

same statement goes for all media: each offers a unique presentation of reality, which when new has a freshness and clarity that is extraordinarily powerful.

This is especially true of TV. We say, "We have a radio" but "We have television"—as if something had happened to us. It's no longer "The skin you love to touch" but "The Nylon that loves to touch you." We don't watch TV; it watches us: it guides us. Magazines and newspapers no longer convey "information" but offer ways of seeing things. They have abandoned realism as too easy: they substitute themselves for realism. *Life* is totally advertisements: its articles package and sell emotions and ideas just as its paid ads sell commodities.

Several years ago, a group of us at the University of Toronto undertook the following experiment: 136 students were divided, on the basis of their over-all academic standing of the previous year, into four equal groups who either (1) heard and saw a lecture delivered in a TV studio, (2) heard and saw this same lecture on a TV screen, (3) heard it over the radio, or (4) read it in manuscript. Thus there were, in the CBC studios, four controlled groups who simultaneously received a single lecture and then immediately wrote an identical examination to test both understanding and retention of content. Later the experiment was repeated, using three similar groups; this time the same lecture was (1) delivered in a classroom, (2) presented as a film (using the kinescope) in a small theatre, and (3) again read in print. The actual mechanics of the experiment were relatively simple, but the problem of writing the script for the lecture led to a consideration of the resources and limitations of the dramatic forms involved.

It immediately became apparent that no matter how the script was written and the show produced, it would be slanted in various ways for and against each of the media involved; no show could be produced that did not contain these biases, and the only real common denominator was the simultaneity of presentation. For each communication channel codifies reality differently and thus influences, to a surprising degree, the content of the message communicated. A medium is not simply an envelope that carries any letter; it is itself a major part of that message. We therefore decided not to exploit the full resources of any one medium, but to try to chart a middle-of-the-road course between all of them.

The lecture that was finally produced dealt with linguistic codifications of reality and metaphysical concepts underlying grammatical systems. It was chosen because it concerned a field in which few students could be expected to have prior knowledge; moreover, it offered opportunities for the use of gesture. The cameras moved throughout the lecture, and took close-ups where relevant. No other visual aids were used, nor were shots taken of the audience while the lecture was in progress. Instead, the cameras simply focused on the speaker for 27 minutes.

The first difference we found between a classroom and a TV lecture was the brevity of the latter. The classroom lecture, if not ideally, at least in practice, sets a slower pace. It's verbose, repetitive. It allows for greater elaboration and permits the lecturer to take up several *related* points. TV, however, is stripped right down; there's less time for qualifications or alternative interpretations and only time enough for *one* point. (Into 27 minutes we put the meat of a two-hour classroom lecture.) The ideal TV speaker states his point and then brings out different facets of it by a variety of illustrations. But the classroom lecturer is less subtle and, to the agony of the better students, repeats and repeats his identical points in the hope, perhaps, that ultimately no student will miss them, or perhaps simply because he is dull. Teachers have had captive audiences for so long that few are equipped to compete for attention via the news media.

The next major difference noted was the abstracting role of each medium, beginning with print. Edmund M. Morgan, Harvard Law Professor, writes:

> One who forms his opinion from the reading of any record alone is prone to err, because the printed page fails to produce the impression or convey the idea which the spoken word produced or conveyed. The writer has read charges to the jury which he had previously heard delivered, and has been amazed to see an oral deliverance which indicated a strong bias appear on the printed page as an ideally impartial exposition. He has seen an appellate court solemnly declare the testimony of a witness to be especially clear and convincing which the trial judge had orally characterized as the most abject perjury.[3]

Selectivity of print and radio are perhaps obvious enough, but we are less conscious of it in TV, partly because we have already been conditioned to it by the shorthand of film. Balázs writes:

> A man hurries to a railway station to take leave of his beloved. We see him on the platform. We cannot see the train, but the questing eyes of the man show us that his beloved is already seated in the train. We see only a close-up of the man's face, we see it twitch as if startled and then strips of light and shadow, light and shadow flit across it in quickening rhythm. Then tears gather in the eyes and that ends the scene. We are expected to know what happened and today we do know, but when I first saw this film in Berlin, I did not at once understand the end of this scene. Soon, however, everyone knew what had happened: the train had started and it was the lamps in its compartment which had thrown their light on the man's face as they glided past ever faster and faster.[4]

As in a movie theatre, only the screen is illuminated, and, on it, only points of immediate relevance are portrayed; everything else is eliminated. This explicitness makes TV not only personal but forceful. That's why stage hands in a TV studio watch the show over floor monitors, rather than watch the actual performance before their eyes.

The script of the lecture, timed for radio, proved too long for TV. Visual aids and gestures on TV not only allow the elimination of certain words, but require a unique script. The ideal radio delivery stresses pitch and intonation to make up for the absence of the visual. That flat, broken speech in "sidewalk interviews" is the speech of a person untrained in radio delivery.

The results of the examination showed that TV had won, followed by lecture, film, radio, and finally print. Eight months later the test was readministered to the bulk of the students who had taken it the first time. Again it was found that there were significant differences between the groups exposed to different media, and these differences were the same as those on the first test, save for the studio group, an uncertain group because of the chaos of the lecture conditions, which had moved from last to second place. Finally, two years later, the experiment was repeated, with major modifications, using students at Ryerson Institute. Marshall McLuhan reports:

In this repeat performance, pains were taken to allow each medium full play of its possibilities with reference to the subject, just as in the earlier experiment each medium was neutralized as much as possible. Only the mimeograph form remained the same in each experiment. Here we added a printed form in which an imaginative typographical layout was followed. The lecturer used the blackboard and permitted discussion. Radio and TV employed dramatization, sound effects and graphics. In the examination, radio easily topped TV. Yet, as in the first experiment, both radio and TV manifested a decisive advantage over the lecture and written forms. As a

conveyor both of ideas and information, TV was, in this second experiment, apparently enfeebled by the deployment of its dramatic resources, whereas radio benefited from such lavishness. "Technology is explicitness," writes Lyman Bryson. Are both radio and TV more explicit than writing or lecture? Would a greater explicitness, if inherent in these media, account for the ease with which they top other modes of performance?[5]

Announcement of the results of the first experiment evoked considerable interest. Advertising agencies circulated the results with the comment that here, at last, was scientific proof of the superiority of TV. This was unfortunate and missed the main point, for the results didn't indicate the superiority of one medium over others. They merely directed attention toward differences between them, differences so great as to be of kind rather than degree. Some CBC officials were furious, not because TV won, but because print lost.

The problem has been falsely seen as democracy vs. the mass media. But the mass media are democracy. The book itself was the first mechanical mass medium. What is really being asked, of course, is: can books' monopoly of knowledge survive the challenge of the new languages? The answer is: no. What should be asked is: what can print do better than any other medium and is that worth doing?

NOTES

1. *Television Plays.* New York: Simon and Schuster, 1955, pp. 176–178.
2. "Writers and Motion Pictures," *The Atlantic Monthly,* 199, 1957, p. 69.
3. G. Louis Joughin and Edmund M. Morgan, *The Legacy of Sacco and Vanzetti,* New York, Harcourt, Brace & Co., 1948, p. 34.
4. Béla Balázs, *Theory of Film,* New York, Roy Publishers, 1953, pp. 35–36.
5. From a personal communication to the author.

MAKING ROOM FOR TV

Lynn Spigel

Lynn Spigel is associate professor in the Department of Critical Studies, School of Cinema-Television, University of Southern California, and the author of several studies of television, including Make Room for TV.

Nicholas Ray's 1955 film, *Rebel without a Cause*, contains a highly melodramatic moment in which family members are unable to patch together the rift among them. The teenage son, Jim, returns home after the famous sequence in which he races his car to the edge of a cliff, only to witness the death of his competitor. Jim looks at his father asleep in front of the television set, and then he lies down on a sofa. From Jim's upside-down point of view on the sofa, the camera cuts to his shrewish mother who appears at the top of the stairwell. In a 180-degree spin, the camera flip-flops on the image of the mother, mimicking the way Jim sees her descending the stairs. This highly stylized shot jolts us out of the illusory realism of the scene, a disruption that continues as the camera reveals a television screen emitting a menacing blue static. As the camera lingers on the TV set, Jim confesses his guilt. Moments later, when his mother demands that he not go to the police, Jim begs his henpecked father to take his side. Finally, with seemingly murderous intentions, Jim chokes him. The camera pans across the TV set, its bluish static heightening the sense of family discord. With its "bad reception," television serves as a rhetorical figure for the loss of communication between family members. In fact, as Jim's father admits early in the scene, he was not even aware of his son's whereabouts during this fateful night, but instead had learned of the incident through an outside authority, the television newscast.

As this classic scene illustrates, in postwar years the television set became a central figure in representations of family relationships. The introduction of the machine into the home meant that family members needed to come to terms with the presence of a communication medium that might transform older modes of family interaction. The popular media published reports and advice from social critics and social scientists who were studying the effects of television on family relationships. The media also published pictorial representations of domestic life that showed people how television might—or might not—fit into the dynamics of their own domestic lives. Most significantly, like the scene from *Rebel without a Cause,* the media discourses were organized around ideas of family harmony and discord.

Indeed, contradictions between unity and division were central to representations of television during the period of its installation. Television was the great family minstrel that promised to bring Mom, Dad, and the kids together; at the same time, it had to be carefully controlled so that it harmonized with the separate gender roles and social functions of individual family members. This meant that the contradiction between unity and division was not a simple binary opposition; it was not a matter of either/or but rather both at once. Television was supposed to bring the family together but still allow for social and sexual divisions in the home. In fact, the attempt to maintain a balance between these two ideals was a central tension at work in popular discourses on television and the family.

The Family United

In 1954, *McCall's* magazine coined the term "to-getherness." The appearance of this term be-tween the covers of a woman's magazine is significant not only because it shows the impor-tance attached to family unity during the post-war years, but also because this phrase is symp-tomatic of discourses aimed at the housewife. Home magazines primarily discussed family life in language organized around spatial imagery of proximity, distance, isolation, and integration. In fact, the spatial organization of the home was presented as a set of scientific laws through which family relationships could be calculated and controlled. Topics ranging from childrearing to sexuality were discussed in spatial terms, and solutions to domestic problems were over-whelmingly spatial: if you are nervous, make yourself a quiet sitting corner far away from the central living area of the home. If your children are cranky, let them play in the yard. If your hus-band is bored at the office, turn your garage into a workshop where he'll recall the joys of his boy-hood. It was primarily within the context of this spatial problem that television was discussed. The central question was, "Where should you put the television set?" This problem was tackled throughout the period, formulated and reformu-lated, solved and recast. In the process the televi-sion set became an integral part of the domestic environment depicted in the magazines.

At the simplest level, there was the question of the proper room for television. In 1949, *Bet-ter Homes and Gardens* asked, "Where does the receiver go?" It listed options including the liv-ing room, game room, or "some strategic spot where you can see it from the living room, din-ing room and kitchen."[1] At this point, however, the photographs of model rooms usually did not include television sets as part of the interior decor. On the few occasions when sets did ap-pear, they were placed either in the basement or in the living room. By 1951, the television set traveled more freely through the household spaces depicted in the magazines. It appeared in the basement, living room, bedroom, kitchen, fun room, converted garage, sitting-sleeping room, music room, and even the "TV room." Furthermore, not only the room, but the exact location in the room, had to be considered for its possible use as a TV zone.

As the television set moved into the center of family life, other household fixtures tradition-ally associated with domestic bliss had to make room for it. Typically, the magazines presented the television set as the new family hearth through which love and affection might be rekindled.[2] In 1951, when *American Home* first displayed a television set on its cover photo-graph, it employed the conventionalized iconog-raphy of a model living room organized around the fireplace, but this time a television set was built into the mantelpiece. Even more radically, the television was shown to replace the fireplace altogether, as the magazines showed readers how television could function as the center of family attention. So common had this substitu-tion become that by 1954 *House Beautiful* was presenting its readers with "another example of how the TV set is taking the place of the fire-place as the focal point around which to arrange the seating in the room."[3] Perhaps the most ex-treme example of this kind of substitution is the tradition at some broadcast stations of burning Yule logs on the television screen each Christ-mas Eve, a practice that originated in the 1950s.

More typically, the television set took the place of the piano.[4] In *American Home*, for in-stance, the appearance of the television set cor-relates significantly with the vanishing piano. While in 1948 the baby grand piano typically held a dominant place in model living rooms, over the years it gradually receded to the point where it was usually shown to be an upright model located in marginal areas such as base-ments. Meanwhile, the television set moved into the primary living spaces of model rooms where its stylish cabinets meshed with and enhanced the interior decor. The new "entertainment centers," comprised of a radio, television, and phonograph, often made the piano entirely obsolete. In 1953, *Better Homes and Gardens* suggested as much when it displayed a television set in a "built-in music corner" that "replaces the piano," now moved into the basement.[5] In that same year, in a special issue entitled "Music and Home Entertainment," *House Beautiful* focused on radio, television, and phonographs, asking readers, "Do You Really Need a Piano?"[6] One woman, writing to *TV World* columnist Kathi Norris, answered the question in no uncertain terms:

Dear Kathi:

Since we got our television set, we've had to change the arrangement of furniture in our living room, and we just can't keep the piano. I need new pictures, but can't afford to buy them with the expense of television, so I was wondering if I might somehow find somebody who would trade me a picture or two for a perfectly good piano.[7]

This woman and, I suspect, others like her were beginning to think of television as a replacement for the traditional fixtures of family life.[8]

As the magazines continued to depict the set in the center of family activity, television seemed to become a natural part of domestic space. By the early 1940s, floor plans included a space for television in the home's structural layout, and television sets were increasingly depicted as everyday, commonplace objects that any family might hope to own. Indeed, the magazines included television as a staple home fixture before most Americans could even receive a television signal, much less consider purchasing the expensive item. The media discourses did not so much reflect social reality; instead, they preceded it. The home magazines helped to construct television as a household object, one that belonged in the family space. More surprisingly, however, in the span of roughly four years, television itself became *the* central figure in images of the American home; it became the cultural symbol par excellence of family life.

Television, it was said, would bring the family ever closer, an expression which, in itself a spatial metaphor, was continually repeated in a wide range of popular media—not only women's magazines, but also general magazines, men's magazines, and on the airwaves. In its capacity as unifying agent, television fit well with the more general postwar hopes for a return to family values. It was seen as a kind of household cement that promised to reassemble the splintered lives of families who had been separated during the war. It was also meant to reinforce the new suburban family unit, which had left most of its extended family and friends behind in the city.

The emergence of the term "family room" in the postwar period is a perfect example of the importance attached to organizing household spaces around ideals of family togetherness. First coined in George Nelson and Henry Wright's *Tomorrow's House: A Complete Guide for the Home-Builder* (1946), the family room encapsulated a popular ideal throughout the period. Nelson and Wright, who alternatively called the family room "the room without a name," suggested the possible social functions of this new house-hold space:

Could the room without a name be evidence of a growing desire to provide a framework within which the members of a family will be better equipped to enjoy each other on the basis of mutual respect and affection? Might it thus indicate a deep-seated urge to reassert the validity of the family by providing a better design for living? We should very much like to think so, and if there is any truth in this assumption, our search for a name is ended—we shall simply call it the "family room."[9]

This notion of domestic cohesion was integral to the design for living put forward in the home magazines that popularized the family room in the years to come. It was also integral to the role of the television set, which was often pictured in the family rooms of the magazines' model homes. In 1950, *Better Homes and Gardens* literally merged television with the family room, telling readers to design a new double-purpose area, the "family-television room."[10]

But one needn't build a new room in order to bring the family together around the television set; kitchens, living rooms, and dining rooms would do just as well. What was needed was a particular attitude, a sense of closeness that permeated the room. Photographs, particularly in advertisements, graphically depicted the idea of the family circle with television viewers grouped around the television set in semicircle patterns.

As Roland Marchand has shown with respect to advertising in the 1920s and 1930s, the family circle was a prominent pictorial strategy for the promotion of household goods. The pictures always suggested that all members of the family were present, and since they were often shot in soft-focus or contained dreamy mists, there was a romantic haze around the family unit. Sometimes artists even drew concentric circles around the family, or else an arc of light evoked the theme. According to Marchand, the visual cliché of the family circle referred back to Victorian notions about domestic havens, implying that the home was secure and stable. The advertisements suggested a democratic model of family life, one in which all members shared in consumer decisions—although, as Marchand suggests, to some extent the father remained a dominant figure in the pictorial composition. In this romanticized imagery, modern fixtures were easily assimilated into the family space:

> The products of modern technology, including radios and phonographs, were comfortably accommodated within the hallowed circle. Whatever pressures and complexities modernity might bring, these images implied, the family at home would preserve an undaunted harmony and security. In an age of anxieties about family relationships and centrifugal social forces, this visual cliché was no social mirror; rather, it was a reassuring pictorial convention.[11]

Much like the advertisements for radio and the phonograph, advertisements for television made ample use of this reassuring pictorial convention—especially in the years immediately following the war when advertisers were in the midst of their reconversion campaigns, channeling the country back from the wartime pressures of personal sacrifice and domestic upheaval to a peacetime economy based on consumerism and family values. The advertisements suggested that television would serve as a catalyst for the return to a world of domestic love and affection—a world that must have been quite different from the actual experiences of returning GIs and their new families in the chaotic years of readjustment to civilian life.

The returning soldiers and their wives experienced an abrupt shift in social and cultural experiences. Horror stories of shell-shocked men circulated in psychiatric journals. In 1946, social workers at VA hospitals counseled some 144,000 men, half of whom were treated for neuro-psychiatric diseases.[12] Even for those lucky enough to escape the scars of battle, popular media such as film noir showed angst-ridden, sexually unstable men, scarred psychologically and unable to relate to the familial ideals and bureaucratic realities of postwar life (the tortured male hero in *Out of the Past* [1946] is a classic example). The more melodramatic social problem films such as *Come Back Little Sheba* (1952) and *A Hatful of Rain* (1957) were character studies of emotionally unstable, often drug-dependent, family men. Such images, moreover, were not confined to popular fiction. Sociological studies such as William H. Whyte's *The Organization Man* (1956) presented chilling visions of white-collar workers who were transformed into powerless conformists as the country was taken over by nameless, faceless corporations.[13] Even if his working life was filled with tension, the ideal man still had to be the breadwinner for a family. Moreover, should he fail to marry and procreate, his "manliness" would be called into question. According to

Tyler May: "Many contemporaries feared that returning veterans would be unable to resume their positions as responsible family men. They worried that a crisis in masculinity could lead to crime, 'perversion' and homosexuality. Accordingly, the postwar years witnessed an increasing suspicion of single men as well as single women, as the authority of men at home and at work seemed to be threatened."[14] Although the image of the swinging bachelor also emerged in this period—particularly through the publication of *Playboy*—we might regard the "swinger" image as a kind of desperate, if confused, response to the enforcement of heterosexual family lifestyles. In other words, in a heterosexist world, the swinger image might well have provided single men with a way to deflect popular suspicions about homosexuality directed at bachelors who avoided marriage.[15]

Meanwhile, women were given a highly constraining solution to the changing roles of gender and sexual identity. Although middle- and working-class women had been encouraged by popular media to enter traditionally male occupations during the war, they were now told to return to their homes where they could have babies and make color-coordinated meals.[16] Marynia Farnham and Ferdinand Lundberg's *The Modern Woman: The Lost Sex* (1947) gave professional, psychological status to this housewife image, claiming that the essential function of woman was that of caretaker, mother, and sexual partner. Those women who took paid employment in the outside world would defy the biological order of things and become neurotics.[17] One postwar marriage guidebook even included a "Test of Neurotic Tendencies" on which women lost points for choosing an answer that exhibited their desire for authority at work.[18] The domestic woman needed to save her energy for housekeeping, childrearing, and an active (monogamous) sex life with her husband.[19] The ways in which people interpreted and applied such messages to their own lives is difficult to discern, but their constant repetition in popular media did provide a context in which

women could find ample justification for their early marriages, child-centeredness, reluctance to divorce, and tendency to use higher education only as a stepping stone for marriage.[20]

Even if people found the domestic ideal seductive, the housing shortage, coupled with the baby boom, made domestic bliss an expensive and often unattainable luxury. In part, for this reason, the glorification of middle-class family life seems to have had the unplanned, paradoxical effect of sending married women into the labor force in order to obtain the money necessary to live up to the ideal. Whereas before the war single women accounted for the majority of female workers, the number of married women workers skyrocketed during the 1950s.[21] Despite the fact that many women worked for extra spending money, surveys showed that some women found outside employment gave them a sense of personal accomplishment and also helped them enter into social networks outside family life.[22] At the same time, sociological studies such as Whyte's *The Organization Man* and David Reisman's *The Lonely Crowd* (1950) showed that housewives expressed doubts about their personal sacrifices, marital relationships, and everyday lives in alienating suburban neighborhoods. Although most postwar middle-class women were not ready to accept the full-blown attack on patriarchy launched in Simone de Beauvoir's *The Second Sex* (1949; English translation, 1952), they were not simply cultural dupes. Indeed, as the work of feminist historians such as Elaine Tyler May and Rochelle Gatlin suggests, postwar women both negotiated with and rationalized the oppressive aspects of the family ideal.

The transition from wartime to postwar life thus resulted in a set of ideological and social contradictions concerning the construction of gender and the family unit. The image of compassionate families that advertisers offered the public might well have been intended to serve the "therapeutic" function that both Roland Marchand and T. J. Jackson Lears have ascribed to advertising in general. The illustrations of domestic bliss and consumer prosperity presented a soothing alternative to the tensions of postwar life.[23] Government building policies and veteran mortgage loans sanctioned the materialization of these advertising images by giving middle-class families a chance to buy into the "good life" of ranch-style cottages and consumer durables. Even so, both the advertising images and the homes themselves were built on the shaky foundations of social upheavals and cultural conflicts that were never completely resolved. The family circle ads, like suburbia itself, were only a temporary consumer solution to a set of complicated political, economic, and social problems.

In the case of television, these kinds of advertisements almost always showed the product in the center of the family group. While soft-focus or dreamy mists were sometimes used, the manufacturers' claims for picture clarity and good reception seem to have necessitated the use of sharp focus and high contrast, which better connoted these product attributes. The product-as-center motif not only suggested the familial qualities of the set, but also implied a mode of use: the ads suggested television be watched by a family audience.

A 1951 advertisement for Crosley's "family theatre television" is a particularly striking example. As is typical in these kinds of ads, the copy details the technical qualities of the set, but the accompanying illustration gives familial meanings to the modern technology. The picture in this case is composed as a *mise-en-abyme:* in the center of the page a large drawing of the outer frame of a television screen contains a sharp focus photograph of a family watching television. Family members are dispersed on sofas on three sides of a room, while a little boy, with arms stretched out in the air, sits in the middle of the room. All eyes are glued to the television set, which appears in the center lower portion of the frame, in fact barely visible to the reader. According to the logic of this composition, the central fascination for the reader is not the actual product, which is pictured only in miniscule proportions on the lower margin of

the page, but rather its ability to bring the family together around it. The ad's *mise-en-abyme* structure suggests that the Crosley console literally contains the domestic scene, thereby promising not just a television set but an ideal reflection of the family, joined together by the new commodity.[24]

Even families that were not welcomed into the middle-class melting pot of postwar suburbia were promised that the dream of domestic bliss would come true through the purchase of a television set. *Ebony* continually ran advertisements that displayed African-Americans in middle-class living rooms, enjoying an evening of television. Many of these ads were strikingly similar to those used in white consumer magazines—although often the advertisers portrayed black families watching programs that featured black actors.[25] Despite this iconographic substitution, the message was clearly one transmitted by a culture industry catering to the middle-class suburban ideal. Nuclear families living in single-family homes would engage in intensely private social relations through the luxury of television.

Such advertisements appeared in a general climate of postwar expectations about television's ability to draw families closer together. In *The Age of Television* (1956), Leo Bogart summarized a wide range of audience studies on the new medium that showed numerous Americans believed television would revive domestic life. Summarizing the findings, Bogart concluded that social scientific surveys "agree completely that television has had the effect of keeping the family at home more than formerly."[26] One respondent from a Southern California survey boasted that his "family now stays home all the time and watches the same programs. [We] turn it on at 3 P.M. and watch until 10 P.M. We never go anywhere."[27] Moreover, studies indicated that people believed television strengthened family ties. A 1949 survey of an eastern city found that long-term TV owners expressed "an awareness of an enhanced family solidarity."[28] In a 1951 study of Atlanta families, one respondent said, "It keeps us together more," and another commented, "It makes a closer family circle." Some women even saw television as a cure for marital problems. One housewife claimed, "My husband is very restless; now he relaxes at home." Another woman confided, "My husband and I get along a lot better. We don't argue so much. It's wonderful for couples who have been married ten years or more. . . . Before television, my husband would come in and go to bed. Now we spend some time together."[29] A study of mass-produced suburbs (including Levittown, Long Island, and Park Forest, Illinois) found similar patterns as women expressed their confidence that television was "bringing the romance back." One woman even reported, "Until we got that TV set, I thought my husband had forgotten how to neck."[30]

Typically also, television was considered a remedy for problem children. During the 1950s, juvenile delinquency emerged as a central topic of public debate. Women's magazines and child psychologists such as Dr. Benjamin Spock, whose *Baby and Childcare* had sold a million copies by 1951, gave an endless stream of advice to mothers on ways to prevent their children from becoming antisocial and emotionally impaired. Not only was childrearing literature big business, but the state had taken a special interest in the topic of disturbed youth, using agencies such as the Continuing Committee on the Prevention and Control of Delinquency and the Children's Bureau to monitor juvenile crimes.[31] Against this backdrop, audience research showed that parents believed television would keep their children off the streets. A mother from the Southern California survey claimed, "Our boy was always watching television, so we got him a set just to keep him home."[32] A mother from the Atlanta study stated, "We are closer together. We find our entertainment at home. Donna and her boyfriend sit here instead of going out now."[33] Such sentiments were popularized in a *Better Homes and Gardens* survey in which parents repeatedly mentioned television's ability to unify the family. One parent

even suggested a new reason for keeping up with the Joneses. She said, "It [television] keeps the children home. Not that we have had that problem too much, but we could see it coming because nearly everyone had a set before we weakened."[34]

NOTES

1. *Better Homes and Gardens,* September 1949, p. 38.
2. In some cases, the television set was actually placed in the fireplace. Here, the objects were made to share the same system of meaning so that the familial values traditionally attributed to the fireplace were now also attributed to the television set. *See,* for example, *House Beautiful,* May 1954, p. 72. . . .
3. *House Beautiful,* September 1954, p. 153.
4. Television sets were often adorned with objects that connoted intellectual pursuits and high art, values traditionally associated with the piano. See, for example, *Ladies' Home Journal,* April 1951, p. 132. . . .
5. *Better Homes and Gardens,* March 1953, p. 72.
6. *House Beautiful,* January 1953, p. 76.
7. Kathi Norris, "How Now," *TV World,* August 1953, p. 54.
8. While the home magazines recommended substituting the television set for the piano, other evidence suggests that piano ownership might still have been significant for postwar families. Sales figures for the entire market show that the sale of pianos actually rose from 136,332 in 1940 to 172,531 in 1950, and by 1960 sales had increased to 198,200. Although these sales statistics alone cannot tell us how significant this rise was for the domestic market per se, they do caution us against assuming that the piano was actually phased out during the postwar years. See *Statistical Reference Index,* Music USA: 1982 Review of the Music Industry and Amateur Music Participation/American Music Conference, Report A2275-1 (Bethesda, MD: Congressional Information Service, 1983), p. 4. Also note that the National Piano Manufacturers Association saw radio as largely responsible for a 300 percent increase in

sales during the late 1930s. The Association claimed, "Millions of listeners, who otherwise might never have attained an appreciation of music, are manifesting an interest in musical culture and endeavoring to become participants themselves." Cited in Davis, "Response to Innovation," p. 138.

9. George Nelson and Henry Wright, *Tomorrow's House: A Complete Guide for the Home-Builder* (New York: Simon and Schuster, 1946), p. 80.

10. *Better Homes and Gardens*, August 1950, p. 45.

11. Roland Marchand, *Advertising the American Dream* (Berkeley: University of California Press, 1985), pp. 248–54.

12. Elaine Tyler May, *Homeward Bound: American Families in the Cold War Era* (New York: Basic Books, 1988), p. 78.

13. William H. Whyte, Jr., *The Organization Man* (1956; Reprint, Garden City, NY: Doubleday, 1957).

14. Tyler May, *Homeward Bound*, p. 88.

15. See Barbara Ehrenreich, *The Hearts of Men: American Dreams and the Flight from Commitment* (Garden City, NY: Doubleday, 1983).

16. As Maureen Honey shows in her study of women's wartime magazine fiction, the Office of War Information gave suggestions to the magazine editors on ways in which to encourage married middle-class women to work. Honey, however, shows that magazines suggested wartime work for women was temporary, to be discarded when the GIs returned. Still, as Honey also shows, many women did not want to leave their jobs when men returned home. See *Creating Rosie the Riveter: Class, Gender and Propaganda During WWII* (Amherst: University of Massachusetts Press, 1984). . . .

17. Marynia Farnham and Ferdinand Lundberg, *The Modern Woman: The Lost Sex* (New York: Harper and Bros., 1947).

18. Jean and Eugene Benge, *Win Your Man and Keep Him* (New York: Windsor Press, 1948), p. 10. Cited in Tyler May, *Homeward Bound*, pp. 80–81.

19. Although feminine ideals and attitudes toward sexuality had changed considerably since the nineteenth century, the ideal woman of the 1950s shared a common problem with her Victorian ancestors—she was placed in the impossible position of taking on several incompatible roles at the same time. The efficient housewife was somehow supposed to transform herself into an erotic plaything for her husband at night. Even mothering was presented in terms of divided consciousness. . . .

20. In the early 1950s, the median marriage age ranged between twenty and twenty-one; the average family started having children in the beginning of the second year of marriage and had three to four children. For birthrates, see Rochelle Gatlin, *American Women Since 1945* (Jackson, MS: University Press of Mississippi, 1987), pp. 51, 55, 61. . . .

21. For labor force statistics, see Gatlin, *American Women Since 1945*, pp. 24–48. . . .

22. A 1955 survey showed that while most women worked for financial reasons, 21 percent worked to fulfill "a need for accomplishment" or to keep busy and meet people; even the women who worked for economic purposes cited the benefits of companionship and a sense of independence. A 1958 survey showed that almost two-thirds of married women cited their jobs as their chief source of feeling "important" or "useful," while only one-third mentioned housekeeping. See Gatlin, *American Women Since 1945*, p. 33. . . .

23. Marchand, *Advertising the American Dream*, pp. 335–59. . . .

24. *American Home*, October 1950, p. 25. For other examples of the product-as-center motif, see *House Beautiful*, November 1949, p. 1; *Ladies' Home Journal*, October 1948, p. 115; *House Beautiful*, February 1949, p. 1.

25. For examples, see *Ebony*, March 1950, p. 7; *Ebony*, August 1953, p. 3; *Ebony*, December 1955, p. 103. Advertisements in *Ebony* also showed white viewers and white actors on screen.

26. Bogart, *Age of Television*, p. 101. As a cautionary note, I would suggest that in his attempt to present a global, synthetic picture of the television audience, Bogart often smooths over the contradictions in the studies he presents. This attempt at global synthesis goes hand in hand with Bogart's view that the television audience is a homogeneous mass and that television programming further erases distinctions. He writes, "The levelling of social differences is part of the standardization of tastes and interests in which the mass media give expression, and to which they also contribute. The ubiquitous TV antenna is a

symbol of people seeking—and getting—the identical message" (p. 5). Through this logic of mass mentalities, Bogart often comes to conclusions that oversimplify the heterogeneity of audience responses in the studies he presents.

27. Edward C. McDonagh, et al., "Television and the Family," *Sociology and Social Research* 40 (4) (March–April 1956), p. 117.

28. John W. Riley, et al., "Some Observations on the Social Effects of Television," *Public Opinion Quarterly* 13 (2) (Summer 1949), p. 232. This study was cosponsored by Rutgers University and CBS.

29. Raymond Stewart, cited in Bogart, *Age of Television,* p. 100.

30. Harry Henderson, "The Mass-Produced Suburbs: I. How People Live in America's Newest Towns," *Harper's,* November 1953, p. 28.

31. For more on this and other aspects of the public concern over juvenile delinquents, see James Gilbert, *A Cycle of Outrage: America's Reaction to the Juvenile Delinquent in the 1950s* (New York: Oxford University Press, 1986). . . .

32. McDonagh, et al., "Television and the Family," p. 116.

33. Stewart, cited in Bogart, *Age of Television,* p. 100.

34. *Better Homes and Gardens,* October 1955, p. 209. . . .

36 TELEVISION TRANSFORMS THE NEWS
Mitchell Stephens

Mitchell Stephens is a professor of journalism and mass communication at New York University. He has written books and numerous articles that deal with the nature and social implications of news.

Radio gave newsmongers back their voices; television restored their faces. Indeed, the television newscast seems to resemble that most ancient of methods for communicating news: a person telling other people what has happened. But this resemblance, as with much of what we see when we first examine this most powerful of news media, can be misleading.

A method for transforming moving pictures into and out of electronic signals, using a rotating disk with spiral perforations, had been devised as early as 1884 by Paul Nipkow of Germany. By the 1920s experimenters in Britain and the United States had succeeded in sending such signals through the air to receivers, and the rotating disk was soon replaced by an electronic scanning system. The technology of television was perfected by radio networks. And by 1941

CBS was broadcasting two fifteen-minute newscasts a day to a tiny audience on its New York television station.[1]

The problem faced by the producers of early television news broadcasts, most of whom were veterans of radio, was how to fill the screen. Those first newscasts on CBS were "chalk talks," with a newsman named Richard Hubbell standing, pointer in hand, in front of a map of Europe. Picture quality was so poor that it was difficult to make out Hubbell, let alone the map. When Pearl Harbor was attacked, CBS did not ignore its handful of television viewers, but for visuals they had to make do with a shot of an undulating American flag, blown by a fan in the studio.[2]

The development of television was placed on hold by the Second World War, but by 1949

Americans who lived within range of a couple of the approximately one hundred television stations that now dotted the country could *watch* the *Kraft Television Theater* or *Howdy Doody,* and choose between two fifteen-minute newscasts—*CBS TV News,* with Douglas Edwards, and NBC's *Camel News Caravan,* with John Cameron Swayze. The visuals on these newscasts consisted mostly of what would become known as "talking heads": shots of the somber Edwards or the boutonniered Swayze reading to the camera. (Don Hewitt, the director of the CBS newscast, was constantly searching for a way to increase the newscaster's eye contact with the camera, but Edwards drew the line at Hewitt's suggestion that he learn to read his script in Braille.)[3]

What film there was of news events was supplied by newsreel companies. (Television journalism was seen initially as an amalgam of radio news and movie newsreels.) Coverage of events was severely limited by the scarcity of film crews, by the bulkiness of their 16mm or 35mm cameras, by the time-consuming process of developing the film and transporting it to New York, and by the limitations of the genre— the newsreel emphasized on-scene photography, not on-scene reporting. Since filmed reports might not be aired for days after they were shot, film tended to be reserved for planned events and timeless features. Nonetheless, viewers were captivated simply by the opportunity to witness, from their living rooms, a ribbon cutting, a submarine christening, the dedication of a dam, a beauty contest or, on the first installment of Edward R. Murrow and Fred Friendly's hallowed *See It Now* in 1951, live shots of the Brooklyn Bridge and the Golden Gate Bridge side by side.[4]

Even with this primitive equipment, television journalism obviously possessed a power to re-create the sights and sounds of events that went well beyond anything even the most verbally skilled of their predecessors might have achieved, and it was not long before they were more fully exploiting that power. In 1949 a for-

mer radio journalist and former movie cameraman set out to cover a balloon race for France's first television news program. They were reporting on the race from the vantage point of their own balloon when storm winds swept it onto a high-tension wire. The two newsmen escaped with camera rolling, and film of their balloon exploding and burning provided the first great example of the potential of this new news medium in France. "*Le journal télévisé*" originally was broadcast three times a week; by the end of the year, it was aired twice a day.[5]

In the United States CBS and NBC began producing their own film reports in the 1950s. Camera crews were stationed in the largest cities; their film flown to New York by plane.[6] Correspondents in Washington and a few other cities might also appear live via a cable hookup. The quadrennial political conventions were covered; the earliest stirrings of the space program were covered, as were the initial struggles of the civil rights movement.[7] Occasionally, the "anchorman" (a term apparently first used to describe Walter Cronkite's central role in CBS's convention coverage in 1952) himself ventured out of the studio on a story. In 1956 Hewitt's aggressiveness, Edwards's fame and some fortuitous timing secured a place for Edwards and a film crew in a Navy plane circling the Italian liner *Andrea Doria* as it sank off the coast of Nantucket. The film, combined with Edwards's eyewitness narration, which led off CBS's newscast that evening, provided further evidence of the potential power of this medium.[8]

That power was realized in the 1960s. John Kennedy defeated Richard Nixon on television; Lee Harvey Oswald was shot on television; presidents dissembled, protesters protested, in front of the cameras, indeed with their eyes fixed upon the cameras. In August of 1965 a CBS reporter, Morley Safer, accompanied a group of United States Marines in Vietnam on a "search and destroy" mission to a complex of hamlets called Cam Ne. The Marines, who faced no resistance, held cigarette lighters to the thatched roofs and proceeded to "waste" Cam Ne. And this, too, appeared on television.[9]

Television news was no tool of radicals. Safer's report, the exception rather than the rule in television coverage of Vietnam, caused considerable consternation among the management at CBS; the network would make an effort in the following days to air more positive stories about the war.[10] Television journalists in the United States were subject not only to the moderating influence of their own allegiance to a working definition of the ethic of objectivity, but to the moderating influence of their corporate owners, their government regulators (the Federal Communications Commission) and their corporate sponsors. (The film cameras that fed the *Camel News Caravan* had dared not happen upon any NO SMOKING signs.)[11]

In England, the nonprofit British Broadcasting Corporation—controlled by a board of governors appointed by the government and financed by an annual license fee on radio and television sets—maintained a similarly moderate tone. In France, where television has until recently been entirely under government control, television journalists placed a stricter interpretation upon their obligations to their superiors and became more open partisans of government policies. French President Charles De Gaulle once explained that "my enemies have the press, so I keep television."[12]

Nevertheless, television news, where it was free from direct censorship, was too sensitive an instrument to ignore the tremors radiating through the United States and Western Europe in the 1960s and early 1970s. And the workings of television news were not yet transparent enough to public relations experts employed by the established institutions that its reports might have been prevented from amplifying some of those tremors. Perhaps on television in these years the "human spirit," to use Harold Innis's terms, was breaking through before a new "monopoly of knowledge" had a chance to consoli-

date itself. Society, in the United States at least, has not since appeared on the television screen in such a state of disarray.

The morning after CBS aired Morley Safer's filmed report on Cam Ne, the network's president, Frank Stanton, was awakened by a telephone call. "Frank, are you trying to fuck me?" a voice said. "Frank, this is your president, and yesterday your boys shat on the American flag." This brief, unsolicited piece of journalism criticism, contributed by the president of the United States, Lyndon Johnson, is an indication of the political pressure under which television news operates. That Stanton, a good friend of the president, is reported to have "had it in for Safer" for a time after the call is an indication that journalistic principles may occasionally have sagged under the pressure.[13] Johnson's deep concern with one piece of news film on one network newscast also helps demonstrate another point: the extent to which television news had come to fascinate, if not obsess, the nation. President Johnson stationed three television sets in his office, so he could monitor coverage on all three networks. Many an evening, after Walter Cronkite would finish anchoring the *CBS Evening News,* Cronkite would find his secretary waiting to hand him the telephone: "White House on the line."[14]

And now, though it has been around for decades, television news continues to fascinate leaders and citizenry alike; it continues—like those French newsmen in a balloon—to make news as it covers news. Our interest in this "pretty toy" has, if anything, increased as it has brought us images of inner-city riots and of men hopping on the moon; images, in color and via increasingly portable videotape equipment, from the scene of famines and earthquakes, from John Dean's doorstep; images, via satellite, from Iran; images, live and then replayed endlessly on videotape, of a space shuttle disintegrating. We remain fascinated, too, by the irreverence with which television seems to treat the news—by its mix of bantering sportscasters, cavorting weathercasters, over-exposed celebrities, beatings, stabbings, crashes, and sobbing mothers invited to explain to a microphone how it feels to have lost all.

The perfect expression of this fascination may have been a scene during the intensely covered New Hampshire presidential primary in 1984 when television news cameras reported on the phenomenon of television news cameras reporting on the presence of so many television news cameras. And enthralled as we are with this seemingly omnipotent product of our seemingly omnipotent technology, we tend to overstate some of its accomplishments—pretty and ugly.

To begin with, despite the presence of satellites and twenty-four-hour cable news services, the television audience is hardly unique in its interest in news in general, or in events over the oceans in particular; nor is this audience, to recap another point, . . . uniquely well informed about all aspects of the world. A television camera is trained on the president of the United States every moment that he spends in public, but in the larger television "markets," at least, such cameras are rarely in a position to supply news of neighborhood occurrences to the residents of what is left of such neighborhoods.

Some of the criticism television journalism inspires is equally short-sighted. Journalists did not become encumbered by celebrity for the first time when Barbara Walters was offered a million dollars to work for ABC television news; Horace Greeley was well enough known to obtain the Democratic nomination for president, and James Gordon Bennett, Henry Morton Stanley, Nellie Bly, Joseph Pulitzer and William Randolph Hearst are all examples of journalists who achieved considerable renown without appearing on television. Nor did news and entertainment meet and mate for the first time on often giggly, often frivolous, local television newscasts in the United States, their affair dates back at least as far as criers and minstrels. Television news, in other words, did not inject a

foreign substance—playfulness—into the news; news has been enjoyed for as long as it has been exchanged.

Like the penny papers of the 1830s, the yellow journals of the 1880s and 1890s and the tabloids of the 1920s, television has succeeded in attracting a new audience to the news. Once television sets became affordable, news became available to audiences of many millions, including even those lacking the energy, skill or maturity to read a newspaper or concentrate on a radio narrative. (Television newscasts are, if anything, easier to watch than news events themselves, in the sense that it is easier to turn the set on than to walk outside and into the street.)

From this perspective, it is remarkable that television journalists have not adopted more sensationalistic techniques to cater to this largest of mass audiences. Local newscast producers in the United States have discovered the drawing power of murders, fires, gossip and fluff; but as a rule they include somewhat less blood, sex and depravity in their newscasts than can be found in some entertainment programs, and somewhat less than Joseph Pulitzer, for example, squeezed into his *New York World* in 1883.[15]

Crime is reported with great industriousness on television, but these stories of misbehavior tend to be told in the friendly but earnest equitone that has, give or take the occasional quip, become the voice of the medium worldwide; television journalists rarely resort to the overheated prose—teeming with adjectives, admonitions and sobriquets—of the tabloid journalist. And while celebrity scandals, quack diets and unidentified flying objects have occasionally found their way onto the television schedule, we have not yet seen the freaks and dismemberments that characterize some supermarket tabloids.

Perhaps *viewing*, rather than reading about, a freak or a real individual screaming for mercy would be too sensational even for a news audience; simply glimpsing a forlorn mother's sobs can be difficult enough to bear. Perhaps television cameras are not yet sufficiently swift and dexterous to capture life's rawest moments, moments newspaper reporters can recall with the still formidable magic of words. Perhaps that triumvirate of governors—corporate owners, corporate sponsors and government regulators—directs news producers away from the more extreme examples of the seamy and sordid. Or perhaps such techniques have simply never been needed in the comfortable environs of broadcast news: the *World* was losing about $40,000 a year when Pulitzer purchased it and began fighting for circulation; most commercial television stations in the United States turn a substantial profit (though networks have been hurt in recent years by competition from cable television and home videotapes). Television may be so simple and seductive a news medium that it attracts an economically viable audience without resort to the more exaggerated forms of sensationalism. Or perhaps such techniques are simply waiting to be discovered by some aggressive television journalists in some future ratings war. Whatever the explanation, as popular forms of journalism go, television newscasts have remained relatively tame.

The charge that these newscasts treat events with particular superficiality is more difficult to refute. Television newswriters have room for fewer words than their newspaper counterparts—their stones are measured in seconds, not column inches. Moving pictures (particularly the ever-more-popular moving graphics) certainly contribute information of their own, but to the extent that depth of coverage correlates with volume of words, television stories are undeniably shallower than most newspaper stories. And since their words are intended for a less acute, less painstaking sense—hearing—television newswriters must forswear the more complex formulations a newspaper reporter might hazard. But these are differences of degree.

Journalists, whatever their medium, tend to swim close to the surface—concerned with the splashes and waves more than the underlying currents. Whether communicating by print, newsletter or cry, journalists are not often endowed with the time or the endurance to delve deeper. More thorough discussions may accompany breaking news coverage—in extended newspaper series or columns, in television documentaries or interview programs, in magazine articles. But here too the hurry and fascination with the moment that permeates most newsrooms, and is indeed inherent in the journalistic enterprise, appears to discourage longer perspectives and more searching analyses.

Recently, a writer visiting an Eskimo village in Canada's Northwest Territories was asked by one of the residents how long he planned to stay. Before the writer could answer, the Eskimo suggested, in English: "One day—newspaper story. Two days—magazine story. Five days—book."[16] It is not clear whether that Eskimo was familiar yet with the three-hour, hit-and-run operations mounted by television news crews, with their complex equipment and harried schedules, but he hardly required acquaintance with a television reporter to grasp the journalist's tendency toward superficiality.

Television is also routinely accused of having debased contemporary politics. But newspapers had faced similar accusations before television cameras began to steal the attention and abuse. When reporters were first beginning to cover Parliament in England in the late eighteenth century, one of its members, William Windham, fumed that politicians were being treated like "actors." "What was to become of the dignity of the House," Windham demanded, "if the manners and gestures, and tone and action of each member were to be subject to the license, the abuse, the ribaldry of newspapers?"[17]

Television favors candidates who are attractive, skilled at producing a newsworthy fifteen-second statement and able to afford airtime for political commercials. Modern newspapers have favored candidates whose views are easily capsulized in headlines, and in the days before circulation measured in the hundreds of thousands, publishers demonstrated a less subtle bias—toward parties and candidates willing to help subsidize their operations.

Our impatience with television's view of politics represents, in part, a longing for an era when the news regularly achieved the depth, impartiality and seriousness of the civics lesson—an era that never was.[18] Journalists throughout history have been as prone to oversimplification as the politicians about whom they write. Certainly, there is substantial room for improvement in television's coverage of politics, but such efforts should not be based on a false nostalgia.

Of course, television has had some profound effects on journalism. Particularly noticeable are the changes it has imposed upon newspapers. With broadcast newscasts now routinely beating them to breaking news, newspapers increasingly are emphasizing news features and more analytical approaches to events. They are moving away from pure news reporting toward some hybrid of news, opinion, history and pop sociology. (Network television newscasts may now have to move in the same direction in the face of competition from lengthier, more frequent local and cable television newscasts.)[19] Television (along with radio) also deserves some credit for the modern American newspaper's return to less constricted writing styles—at the expense of the five Ws lead, the inverted pyramid and even the sobriquet. The anecdotes or turned phrases that now lead off so many front-page stories are there to compensate for the breaking news lost to broadcast journalists, but they are also there in imitation of broadcast journalists, who have long recognized that their wordings, written to be read aloud, had to sound conversational.[20] Television's influence on newspapers is nowhere more apparent than in the national daily *USA Today*—a colorful confection of graphics and short, breezy stories.

But perhaps the most significant effect the television newscast has had on journalism has been the added distance it has placed between news purveyor and audience (in this it has continued the work of the newspaper). Television news is deceptive; it looks so friendly. The vast pool of live, videotaped and computer-generated images available to television newscasts have never succeeded in forcing the "talking head" of the newscaster from the screen. Audiences apparently prefer having their news delivered by a familiar, affable, *human* presence—these apparent throwbacks to criers or busybodies. Yet, the television screen is too flat and impenetrable for this to be much more than mimicry. No news medium offers less of the *actual* interaction and neighborly contact characteristic of spoken news than does television.

It is possible that the increasing number of channels made possible by cables and satellite dishes will drive television newscasts toward the smaller, demographically segmented audiences now sought by many radio stations. But for now, television speaks predominantly to the large communities of nation or metropolitan area. The chances of a member of those communities being heard—still a vague possibility for newspaper readers through a letter or a canceled subscription—have almost entirely disappeared with television. This is one-way news.

Television viewers live in a world of mediated reality. Increasingly they talk and think about people they have not met, places they have not been. Television has, in McLuhan's terminology, "extended" dramatically our access to news but, as cars weaken the legs they have "extended," reliance on television news may have weakened our ability to hear and tell our *own* news. We borrow facts, perceptions, even opinions from newscasters, and we borrow the newscasters themselves—with whom we fancy ourselves on a first-name basis—as surrogate busybodies, surrogate friends. It is important to remember, as we allow one of these well-known, well-dressed personalities to present our news, that the exchange of news has not always been a spectator sport, that the pursuit of news once encouraged even nonjournalists to move, observe, investigate, remember and talk, that for an individual to be fully informed, it was once necessary to leave the house.

One accomplishment of television seems impossible to overstate: it brings a wealth of news into our homes with astounding speed and immediacy. The development of television news has capped centuries of improvements in the means of news dissemination and news gathering, centuries in which the perennial shortage of reliable information about current events has been transformed into a surplus. We can learn more and see more of a President Reagan or Princess Diana than most of Thoreau's contemporaries could have dreamed of learning and seeing of President Pierce or Princess Adelaide. But we pay a price.

Selected Bibliography

Barnouw, Erik. *A Tower in Babel, A History of Broadcasting in the United States.* I. New York: 1966.

———. *The Image Empire, A History of Broadcasting in the United States.* III. New York: 1970.

———. *Tube of Plenty: The Evolution of American Television.* New York: 1975.

Epstein, Edward Jay. *Between Fact and Fiction: The Problem of Journalism.* New York: 1975.

Gates, Gary Paul. *Air Time: The Inside Story of CBS News.* New York: 1979.

Halberstam, David. *The Powers That Be.* New York: 1979.

Lanson, Gerald, and Mitchell Stephens. "'Trust Me' Journalism." *Washington Journalism Review,* November 1982, pp. 43–47.

———. "Jello-O Journalism: Reporters Are Going Soft in Their Leads." *Washington Journalism Review,* April 1982, pp. 21–23.

MacDonagh, Michael. *The Reporter's Gallery.* London: 1913.

Miguel, Pierre. *Histoire de la Radio et de la Télévision.* Paris: 1984.

Reasoner, Harry. *Before the Colors Fade.* New York: 1981.

Notes

1. Barnouw, *Tube of Plenty,* 5, 48–49, 86; Gates, 55.
2. Gates, 55.
3. Barnouw, *Tube of Plenty,* 102, 112–113; Gates, 59–60, 66, 76.
4. Barnouw, *Tube of Plenty,* 102, 168–171; Gates, 59–60, 67–68.
5. Miguel, 193–194.
6. Barnouw, *The Image Empire,* 42.
7. For an account of some of these early efforts, see Reasoner.
8. Gates, 73–74, 79.
9. Halberstam, 448–490; Gates, 165–170.
10. Epstein, 213–214; Halberstam, 491.
11. Barnouw, *Tube of Plenty,* 170.
12. Cited, Paul Lewis, "French TV Battle Grows as Rightist Wins Contract," *New York Times,* February 25, 1987.
13. Halberstam, 490–491. This story is also told in Gates, 128, although Gates does not specifically connect Johnson's call to Safer's report on Cam Ne.
14. Barnouw, *Tube of Plenty,* 388.
15. Some examples of headlines from the first week after Pulitzer took control: Screaming for Mercy, Love and Cold Poison, While the Husbands Were Away; *New York World,* May 12, 16, 17, 1883.
16. Cited, Herbert Mitgang, "Barry Lopez, a Writer Steeped in Arctic Values," *New York Times,* March 29, 1986.
17. Cited, MacDonagh, 293–295.
18. In the first half of the eighteenth century, English periodicals featured the work of Addison, Steele, Swift, Defoe and Johnson. But it was during this apparent "golden age" that Defoe complained that his fellow journalists left readers "possessed with wrong notions of things, and wheedled to believe nonsense and contradictions," and that Dr. Johnson suggested that the press "affords . . . too little" information "to enlarge the mind."
19. See Lanson, "'Trust Me' Journalism."
20. For a critique of one aspect of this change in writing style—the use of "soft leads"—see Lanson, "Jell-O Journalism."

37 MUSIC VIDEOS
Pat Aufderheide

Pat Aufderheide is associate professor in the School of Communication at American University, in Washington, D.C.

Music videos are more than a fad, or fodder for spare hours and dollars of young consumers. They are pioneers in video expression, and the results of their reshaping of the form extend far beyond the TV set.

Music videos have broken through TV's most hallowed boundaries. As commercials in themselves, they have erased the very distinction between the commercial and the program. As nonstop sequences of discontinuous episodes, they have erased the boundaries between programs.

Music videos have also set themselves free from the television set, inserting themselves into movie theaters, popping up in shopping malls and department store windows, becoming actors in both live performances and the club scene. As omnivorous as they are pervasive, they draw on and influence the traditional image-shaping fields of fashion and advertising. Even political campaigning is borrowing from these new bite-sized packagers of desire.

If it sounds as if music video has a life of its own, this is not accidental. One of music video's distinctive features as a social expression is its open-ended quality, aiming to engulf the viewer in its communication with itself, its fashioning of an alternative world where image is reality. Videos are perhaps the most accessible form of that larger tendency known as postmodern art. That aesthetic-in-formation, signaled variously in the work of such artists as Andy Warhol, Nam June Paik, Thomas Pynchon, Philip Glass, and Keith Haring, is marked by several distinctive features. Among them are the merging of

commercial and artistic image production, and an abolition of traditional boundaries between an image and its real-life referent, between past and present, between character and performance, between mannered art and stylized life.

When art, even self-consciously lightweight commercial fare, crosses that last boundary, it forces consideration of its social implications. And music videos have triggered plenty of such speculation, especially so since its primary audience is the young. Literary critic Fredric Jameson has suggested that the emerging postmodern aesthetic evokes an intense euphoria, a kind of "high," one that partakes in an experience rather than responding to an artist's statement. It is a provocative, and troubling, observation applied to music videos as they infiltrate the various domains of consumer culture, both on screens and on streets. A euphoric reaction is different in quality from the kinds of energizing, critical response once called up by rock music, hailed by Greil Marcus as triggering the critical capacity of negation, "the act that would make it self-evident to everyone that the world is not as it seems," and enthusiasts of rock culture wonder if music video heralds a new, more passive era for the young. Critic Marsha Kinder, for instance, finds the dreamy structure of videos a disturbing model for viewers who are stuck in real time. Not all agree; critic Margaret Morse suggests that the populist, self-assertive energy of popular culture may be reclaimed in music video's use of lip-synching; viewers may make that voice their own by singing along. Even Jameson, while positing a new relationship between artwork and audience, suggests that euphoria may have expressive qualities we cannot yet judge.

Whatever one's view, the rapid spread of the music video look is motive enough to take the phenomenon seriously. But it is particularly important because it is in the vanguard of reshaping the language of advertising—the dominant vocabulary of commercial culture—in a society that depends on an open flow of information to determine the quality of its political and public life. And so consideration of its form also implies questions about the emerging shape of the democratic and capitalist society that creates and receives it.

Music video was pioneered on television with three-to-seven-minute films or tapes whose visual images were coordinated loosely (or not at all) with a pop song's lyrics. Until recently, almost all music videos on TV were rock songs from the dead center of mainstream pop. With the growing appeal of the form, one sees music videos of country singers, easy-listening musicians, black rock stars, sometimes even rhythm and blues groups. If there are no waltz or tango music videos as yet, they are on their way. When music video has completed its present phase of being either acerbically challenged or heralded by hip pop culture critics (J. Hoberman of the *Village Voice* put a music video on his list of top-ten films of 1984), it will be ready for the easy-listening, easy-viewing audience. Indeed, VH-1, a music video channel aimed at adults aged twenty-five to forty-nine, has launched the process and wobbles toward viability. But long before there is a music video channel for Lawrence Welk tastes, the format will have pervaded nonmusical features of daily life. Indeed, one of the striking features of music video is its mutability.

This analysis of music video circa 1985 performs an unnatural act on the form, by taking a kind of photograph of a process defined by constant mutation. Most examples will have disappeared from viewers' memory; performers will have taken on new personas; and the form may

have relocated itself on, the social landscape. But its energy in this pioneering stage guarantees its importance in the emerging national pop culture—where the distinctions between public and private, between social standard and individual taste, are eroded to a rock beat.

Music video's roots are in the mass marketing of popular songs, not only as populist entertainment but as talismans of subcultural autonomy and rebellion in successive generations of American youth. Top-40-hits radio programs cemented a pop cultural consciousness in the 1930s. In fact, national mass media were instrumental in shaping a national self-consciousness stratified by generation—unlike regional and folk culture, which unified the generations, transmitting legacies while incorporating the new. As new groups and sounds were created in the image of rebellious self-assertion, they were also pop-ified, which usually meant whitening them as well. (English outsiders could market black rhythm and blues to mainstream white audiences as the R & B masters never could.) The 1960s generation celebrated its uniqueness in rock concerts, wore the badges of rock groups, and never moved to communal farms without stereo equipment.

Putting together the music with pictures was an early innovation. The Max Fleischer cartoons of the 1930s and 1940s were cut precisely to songs sung by the likes of Cab Calloway and Louis Armstrong. As early as 1943, the Panoram Soundies had brief success. These were jukeboxes placed in nightclubs and diners, where viewers could punch up songs and watch performers on the miniscreen atop the jukebox. A European device called Scopitone brought the gimmick back in the 1960s, though it never caught on, some say because it generally featured mainstream European singers without the oppositional appeal of American pop idols. More influential were commercials borrowing a hip edge from rock sounds, and the commercial-fed work of film artists like Richard Lester, who turned the Beatles into a visual experience. In *A Hard Day's Night,* Lester made the Beatles' screen personae and lifestyle, as well as their performances, the subject of film episodes backed by music cuts. Rock videos were shown in the 1970s in European clubs, and some English underground groups rode them to celebrity. This was a moment in English pop music when the performer's persona had become as important as the sound of the music, and so the form nicely fulfilled its function.

The transatlantic success of music video awaited the moment at which cable TV became an option for a substantial number of Americans. Then targeted audiences became commercially attractive. Amid wild talk of whole cable channels devoted to pet care and chess, programmers brainstormed channels that would deliver the same kind of programming—to a big but still targeted audience—around the clock. Movies were a surefire idea, and music seemed an ideal vehicle to attract highly prized consumers: young people. They had value not merely because the young buy records, but because buyable popular culture is central to their lives. Pop culture commodities are now the tools to express personal taste, even talismans of identity and identification with a subculture. No one needs to sell young people on the key role of fad and fashion in designing their identities; indeed, channeling such information to them provides a service welcomed for its news of what's happening.

Still, no one foretold the success of music video. At Warner, which gambled on the format in 1980, the prospect of a cable channel wholly dedicated to rock videos, on air twenty-four hours a day, was received with major reservations. Even though the program time was to be filled with free videos given to the channel as promos by record companies, Warner hesitated before backing the concept. Even its strongest in-house advocates only promised record companies that they would see increased sales in two years.

But when MTV—Music Television—started up in 1981, its success was almost instantaneous. MTV became a hot media item in itself, and record companies were reporting rising sales within months. Music videos have fueled the current boom in the record industry, a fact reflected in music industry awards for videos. The channel took a little longer to start paying out. MTV stayed in the red for two years before Warner was confident enough of its future to spin it off as a separate company. It showed a profit in 1984, claiming access to 24.2 million viewers, with independent services estimating only slightly less, making it the highest-rated music cable service on the air even after ratings leveled off in 1984.

Nielsen ratings for 1985 showed a dramatic 30 percent drop from 1984; the rating was disputed by MTV, which argued with some reason that Nielsen's cable estimates are flawed. But some falloff is indisputable and may reflect the proliferation of similar services in other areas, both nationally and internationally. And so, mutating again, MTV added rock-oriented and nostalgia-laden sitcoms to its nonstop round of para-information, and also changed the faces of its video jockeys. Meanwhile, MTV's signal is being picked up abroad, among other places by TV pirates in Latin America. In Europe, clubs pirate videos on similar services, and in the Soviet Union, illicit music videos are hot tape items.

Other music cable channels quickly imitated and improvised on MTV's example, but no cable channel on the scale of MTV has been able to compete, partly because MTV has aggressively attacked rivals legally and with such marketing practices as signing producers to exclusives and paying contracts. Ted Turner accomplished the most spectacular failure, with a service he billed as a more wholesome, family-oriented version of MTV. After abysmal ratings in early weeks, Turner sold his venture to MTV, where it became VH-1. VH-1 is offered free to MTV subscribers, and all cable channels that carry VH-1 carry both. VH-1's most important role may be to hold down space competitors might otherwise occupy.

Networks and syndicators also attempted to imitate MTV's success. Some, such as the show

Hot, which expired after only twelve weeks, collapsed. Others, such as *Night Tracks* and *Friday Night Videos,* became mass-audience successes, and the cable program service Black Entertainment Television began producing its own music video shows. Music video has also made inroads into prime time (see the articles by Todd Gitlin and Mark Crispin Miller). Twenty-four-hour-a-day music video channels have proliferated in low-cost and low-reach markets, and at this writing there are currently about eleven such channels on UHF and low-power frequencies. Many broadcasters expect an all-music TV channel to exist in the top hundred markets within the next few years, although 1985 was financially rocky for several of the low-power sources.

However packaged, the music video format always amounts to wall-to-wall commercials for something. The videos tout particular rock groups and albums. The production "credits" usually include only the name of the group and the record. (This is the viewer's first clue that music videos purvey a peculiar amalgam of celebrity and anonymity; from the outset, they are represented as authorless adventures. The exception comes when a video is made by someone with star status, who has "brand name" recognition.) The videos have become products in themselves, sold in compilation or long-form versions in video stores. Cross-plugging, weaving other products into the atmospherics, is ever more common, and cross-financing goes on too. (RC Cola, for instance, financed a Louise Mandrell video, which then, with its appropriate images of RC-sipping, debuted at the National Soft Drink Association convention in 1985.) When a song cut comes from a movie soundtrack, the video is a virtual movie trailer. Between videos on a program, video jockeys (VJs) tout both the service and, through music industry "news," other music products and tickets for performances. And then there are the commercials.

Advertisers have been quick to take a cue from music video's appeal, just as the videos have built in a stylistic base created by commer-

cials. An advertisement for Clairol Heated Rollers, for instance, features close-ups of muscles and aerobically coordinated bodybuilders backed by a strong rock beat. The "bodybuilder" rollers become one of many trigger visuals for a gestalt. A commercial for the Duster car, like the Clairol ad, features the colors black, white, and blue, a color scheme that in its artificiality locates the action within television's alternative universe. On an outsized indoor-outdoor jungle gym, the Duster car becomes an actor among a group of peripatetic dancers.

It is easy to see why commercials imitate music videos, sometimes even mimicking their opening "credits." It is not merely that advertisers like the pleasure-happy attitude that the videos promote, although Okidata computer software appeals directly to that attitude with a commercial featuring a cartoon character who sits at a terminal muttering "Where's the fun?" It is also that music video never delivers a hard sell, never identifies the record or tape or group as a product. Instead, it equates the product with an experience to be shared, part of a wondrous leisure world.

Commercials have always sold the sizzle, not the steak—that is, depended on atmosphere. But they have usually promised consumers that the product will enhance an experience ("adds life," "takes the worry out of being close") or permit one ("don't leave home without it"). But music videos are themselves primary experiences. Music videos give the product a new location on the consumer's landscape, not as messengers of a potential purchase or experience, but as an experience in themselves, a part of living.

Two decades ago, science fiction writers imagined a commercial-mad future, where consumers were perpetually dunned with demands to buy. Even the prescient Philip K. Dick, in *The Simulacrum,* imagined roving electronic commercials that attached themselves to beleaguered consumers. But the reality of permanent and pervasive commercials turns out to be quite different. Once commercial reality becomes primary in daily life, the direct appeal to buy can be submerged. Products come to seem "natural." Any product—a record, tape, videocassette, article of clothing, car, perfume—takes its place as an aspect of the gestalt. The raw material for postmodern pastiche art is everywhere.

With nary a reference to cash or commodities, music videos cross the consumer's gaze as a series of mood states. They trigger moods such as nostalgia, regret, anxiety, confusion, dread, envy, admiration, pity, titillation—attitudes at one remove from primal expression such as passion, ecstasy, and rage. The moods often express a lack, an incompletion, an instability, a searching for location. In music videos, those feelings are carried on flights of whimsy, extended journeys into the arbitrary.

In appealing to and playing on these sensations, music videos have animated and set to music a tension basic to American youth culture. It is that feeling of instability that fuels the search to buy-and-belong, to possess a tangible anchor in a mutable universe while preserving the essence of that universe—its mutability. It allows the viewer to become a piece of the action in a continuous performance.

Music videos did not discover the commercial application of anxiety, of course. The manufacturer of Listerine was selling mouthwash on anxiety sixty years ago. Nor did music videos succeed in making themselves widely appealing by somehow duping passive audiences into an addiction to commercial dreams. Music videos are authentic expressions of a populist industrial society. For young people struggling to find a place in communities dotted with shopping malls but with few community centers, in an economy whose major product is information, music videos play to the adolescent's search for identity and an improvised community.

As media image-making comes to dominate electoral politics, music video has invaded that domain too. Consultants to both the Democratic and Republican parties have used music video to explore the mind-set of younger generations. "You can see the tensions among kids rising in their music," said pollster Patrick Caddell, "as they struggle to figure out what they will become." Or, he might have added, what they are. Republican strategist Lee Atwater decided, "We've got a bunch of very confused kids out there." That hasn't stopped politicians from using music videos as ads; videos were also enlisted (without marked results) in voter registration campaigns in 1984. The collision of music video with traditional political mobilizing brings one world—that of the consumer, concerned with individual choice—smack up against another—that of the citizen, charged with responsibility for public decisions. It is this collision that led fashion analyst Gerri Hirshey, noting the passionate investment of the young in their "look," to write: "If one's strongest commitment is to a pair of red stiletto heel pumps, style has a higher price tag than we'd imagine." In one sense, politics is fully ready for music video, if the success of Ronald Reagan—whose popularity rests on a pleasant media image to which "nothing sticks" while critics search in vain for a corresponding reality—is any guide.

The enormous popularity and rapid evolution of music videos give the lie to conspiracy theorists who think commodity culture is force-fed into the gullets of unwilling spectators being fattened for the cultural kill. But it should also chasten free-market apologists who trust that whatever sells is willy-nilly an instrument of democracy. Music videos are powerful, if playful, postmodern art. Their raw materials are aspects of commercial popular culture; their structures those of dreams; their premise the constant permutation of identity in a world without social relationships. These are fascinating and disturbing elements of a form that becomes not only a way of seeing and of hearing but of being. Music videos invent the world they represent. And people whose "natural" universe is that of shopping malls are eager to participate in the process. Watching music videos may be diverting, but the process that music videos embody, echo, and encourage—the constant re-creation of an unstable self—is a full-time job.

TWO CULTURES—TELEVISION VERSUS PRINT

Neil Postman and Camille Paglia

Neil Postman is currently chair of the Department of Communication Arts and Sciences at New York University. Of his many books, three relate directly to the history of communication: The Disappearance of Childhood, Amusing Ourselves to Death, *and* Technopoly. *Camille Paglia teaches at the University of the Arts in Philadelphia. Her three books——*Sexual Personae, Sex, Art, and American Culture, *and* Tramps and Vamps——*as well as numerous essays on media-related themes, are not without controversy.*

"What I see as dangerous here," he said, "is the discontinuity of emotion that television promotes, its unnatural evocation, every five minutes, of different and incompatible emotions."

"You leave a restaurant," she said, "and get killed by a falling air conditioner. A tornado hits a picnic. There is no sense to reality. Television is actually closer to reality than anything in books. The madness of TV is the madness of human life."

So went the conversation between two cultural critics. Neil Postman and Camille Paglia, taking up an argument that has vexed nearly everyone in this century—the struggle for preeminence between words and pictures, today between books and television. This conflict is uniquely American—a debate so dense with prejudices that it has turned almost all of us into liars: "I don't watch TV" is now so common a dissembling among those who read that it has become a kind of mantra. And "I read that book" is a euphemism acceptable among recent generations to mean simply that one has heard of the title.

Neil Postman is one of the most original writers in defense of the book. A professor of communication arts at New York University and the author of *Amusing Ourselves to Death: Public Discourse in the Age of Show Business,* Postman is a scholar, raised in the pretelevision world, whose eloquence owes much to the classical declarative prose of Strunk and White. He

argues that reading is an ordered process requiring us to sit at a table, consume ideas from left to right, and make judgments of truth and falsehood. By its nature, reading teaches us to reason. Television, with its random, unconnected images, works against this linear tradition and breaks the habits of logic and thinking. Postman has said that the two most dangerous words in this century are "Now . . . this"—that strange verbal doo-dad uttered by television anchors to ease the transition from a report on a natural disaster to a commercial about your need—desperate need, in fact—for an electric toothbrush.

Those who argue from the other side usually make a weak and unconvincing case. With the possible exception of Marshall McLuhan, anyone writing about television has done so with apologies. Recently, a new critic has emerged named Camille Paglia. She is a professor of humanities at the Philadelphia College of the Arts and is currently finishing a critical history of culture that ranges from the cave paintings of Altamira to the Rolling Stones concert at Altamont. Volume One, entitled *Sexual Personae: Art and Decadence from Nefertiti to Emily Dickinson,* was recently nominated for a National Book Critics Circle Award. Paglia was born after World War II, an accident to which she ascribes great significance. To hear her talk is to confirm her theory about the influence of the modern media: She speaks in a rush of images, juxtapositions, and verbal jump cuts. She argues that instead of criticizing television, most academics and other cultural critics simply turn up their noses dismissively at its enormous power—a kind of intellectual denial. Television, Paglia says, *is* the culture. And, she asks, by what and whose criteria is the latest Madonna any less meaningful an icon than the last? To those who argue that kids who watch television can't recall any of the facts mentioned on it, she wonders whether we have ever *watched* television. Perhaps we are doing something else when we stare at the screen: perhaps the remembrance of facts has nothing to do with television's significance or effect.

Since no two thinkers have in recent time made such compelling cases, *Harper's Magazine* decided to introduce them. We sent each author a copy of the other's book and asked each to read it. One cold winter night in December, we asked them to dine in the private Tasting Room of New York City's Le Bernardin restaurant—a small, glass room located inside the kitchen of Chef Gilbert Le Coze. Throughout the conversation Bruno Jourdaine served a *menu dégustation* beginning with seviche of black bass and poured glasses of St. Veran Trenel (1988). We began the dinner with a blessing in the form of two readings from the Bible.

> *"Thou shalt not make unto thee any graven image."*
>
> —*Exodus 20:4*

> *"In the beginning was the Word, and the Word was with God, and the Word was God."*
>
> —*John 1:1*

CAMILLE PAGLIA: But John got it all wrong. "In the beginning was nature." That's the first sentence of *my* book. Nature—violent, chaotic, unpredictable, uncontrollable—predates and stands in opposition to the ordered, structured world created by the word, by the law, by the book-centered culture of Judeo-Christianity. The image—which is pa-

gan and expressive of nature's sex and violence—was outlawed by Moses in favor of the word. That's where our troubles began.

Remember that when the Ten Commandments were handed down on Mount Sinai, Moses had just led the Jews out of Egypt. They had followed Joseph down there several hundred years before and had become resident workers, then slaves. Over time, Judaism had gotten a little mixed up with the local Egyptian cults—a syncretism not unlike Santería in the Caribbean, with its blend of voodoo and Catholicism. When Moses tried to get his people to leave Egypt, there was resistance: "What are we *doing?* Moses, you're crazy. What homeland are you talking about?" The Ten Commandments were an attempt to clarify what is Hebrew, what is Jewish.

The Second Commandment implies that the Hebrew God has no shape, that He is pure spirit. Egyptian gods often appeared in animal form. The pagan cults of Egypt, Babylon, and Canaan worshiped such idols—for example, the Golden Calf. So Moses is saying, "We do not worship the gods of nature but a God who is above nature, a God who *created* nature. The ultimate God."

And the prohibition against graven images didn't forbid just pagan idols. It banned *all* visual imagery, of anything on earth or in the heavens. Moses knew that once a people begin to make images of any kind, they fall in love with them and worship them. Historically, the Second Commandment diverted Jewish creative energy away from the visual arts and into literature, philosophy, and law.

NEIL POSTMAN: It is curious that of the first three, so-called establishing commandments, two of them concern communications: the prohibitions against making graven images and taking the Lord's name in vain. Yet this makes sense if you think about the problems of constructing an ethical system 3,000 years ago. It was critical to tell the members of the tribe how to symbolize their experience. That is why Moses chose writing—using a phonetic alphabet, which the Jews no doubt borrowed from the Egyptians—to conceptualize this nonvisual, nonmaterial God. Writing is the perfect medium because, unlike pictures or an oral tradition, the written word is a symbol system *of* a symbol system, twice removed from reality and perfect for describing a God who is also far removed from reality: a nonphysical, abstracted divinity. Moses smartly chose the right communications strategy. With the Second Commandment, Moses was the first person who ever said, more or less, "Don't watch TV; go do your homework."

Most important, the written word allows for the development of a God who is, above all things, *mobile*. To invent a God who exists only in the word and through the word is to make a God that can be taken anyplace. Just as writing is portable speech, Moses' God is a portable God, which is fitting for a people setting forth on a long journey.

PAGLIA: That is why Jewish culture is one of the founts of Western tradition and why Western culture is so intellectually developed. Jewish thought is highly analytical, as is Greco-Roman philosophy. Both are very Apollonian. But the Greco-Roman tradition is also one of pagan idolatry. Early Christianity, which first proselytized among the poor, outcast, and unlearned, needed to use visual imagery, which became more and more pronounced in the Middle Ages and early Renaissance. Out of this came the renegade priest Martin Luther, who correctly diagnosed a lapse from authentic early Christianity in medieval Catholicism. Catholics are never told to read the Bible. Instead, they have to listen to the priest commenting on excerpts from the Bible, usually just the New Testament.

POSTMAN: Luther called the invention of the printing press the "supremist act of grace by

which the Gospel can be driven forward." And it was. As a result of Luther's Reformation, the intellectual geography of Europe flipped. Until then Venice, in the south of Europe, was the leading printing center and one of the world's intellectual capitals. Then the Catholic Church got nervous about it, because of the possibilities of further heresy, and began to restrict the printing press. And then, within a year of each other, Galileo died and Newton was born. The intellectual power of Europe moved from the south to the north. England, Scandinavia, Germany became the realm of the word, and the south returned to spectacle. Catholicism resorted increasingly to ornament and beautiful music and painting. To this day we think of Spain, Italy, and southern France as centers of great visual arts, from the Escorial to the Sistine Chapel. The north, home of the austere Protestant, concentrated on the word, until it found its greatest fulfillment here in the first political system built on the word alone: no divine right of kings, no mysticism, just a few pages of written text, the American Constitution.

PAGLIA: The polarity in Europe got more and more rigid. In the north, book, book, book; but in the Counter-Reformation of southern Europe, unbelievably lurid images—like Bernini's St. Teresa having a spiritual orgasm. My first childhood memories are of images, fantastic images, created by the Catholic Church. The statues are polychromatic, garish. In my church stood a statue of St. Sebastian, nude, arrows piercing his flesh, red blood dripping down. Who can wonder where *my* mind came from? Here were spectacular pagan images standing right next to the altar. In the beginning, you see, were sex and violence.

Early Christianity was very masculine. Just two male gods and a neuter—the Father, the Son, and the Holy Ghost. But the popular imagination couldn't tolerate that, so in the Middle Ages it added the Virgin Mary.

Go reread the Bible and see how small a role Mary plays in the Gospels. Almost none. She is a survivor of the great goddess cults of antiquity. I interpret the most essential elements of Italian Catholicism as pagan. Martin Luther saw the latent paganism of the Catholic Church and rebelled against it. The latest atavistic discoverer of the pagan heart of Catholicism is Madonna. This is what she's up to. She doesn't completely understand it herself. When she goes on *Nightline* and makes speeches about celebrating the body, as if she's some sort of Woodstock hippie, she's way off. She needs *me* to tell her. But this is what she's doing—revealing the eroticism and sadomasochism, the pagan ritualism and idolatry in Italian Catholicism.

Protestantism today continues to be based on the word and the book. That's why Protestant ministers in church or on television always stress the Bible. They shout, "*This* is all you need." And they wave it, they flap it, they even slam it around. The Protestant needs no priest, no hierarchy. There is nothing between you and God. Protestants want a close and chatty relationship with Jesus: "Have you accepted Christ as your *personal* Savior?" And they sing, "He walks with you and He talks with you." For Protestants, Jesus is a friend, the Good Shepherd.

The Italian Catholic Jesus can't speak. He's either preliterate—a baby in the arms of Mary—or comatose—a tortured man on a cross. The period when Christ is literate, when he can speak, is edited out of southern Catholicism.

. . . baked sea urchin . . .

POSTMAN: It helps to understand your point if we remember what happens every time Moses leaves. He comes back and the whole tribe has lapsed into idol worship. He is always complaining to Aaron, "What the hell did you do while I was gone?" The image is so seductive. Catholics are known for keeping little images on the dashboard of their cars, and nowadays you find them among Jews as well. Many reform temples now have more and more interesting visual designs. The Second Commandment held for a long time. Jews weren't known for their achievements in the visual arts until this century.

This proves my point about the life of the word and the image: Humans are not biologically programmed to be literate. In John Locke's essay on education, he insists that the body must become a slave to the mind. One of my students, upon hearing that quotation, said, "I know just what he means." And she told me how she can only read lying on her side while holding the book against the wall and, as a result, only reads the right-hand page of any book. This is the challenge of literacy: to get children accustomed to sitting still, to abiding in a realm that is unnaturally *silent*. That is the world of the word. How can silence compete with television?

PAGLIA: But, Neil, people who are naturally disposed to reading may not be as physically active as others. There is an important difference here. I teach dancers. They are sometimes poor readers or even dyslexic. But they are brilliant at other, older forms of feeling and expression. Some people are inclined to the sedentary life that reading requires, others are not. That is why the entire discourse on sex and gender in academe and in the media is so off, because teachers and writers are not nearly as athletic or rambunctious as others.

POSTMAN: The literate person does pay a price for literacy. It may be that readers become less physically active and not as sensitive to movement, to dance, and to other symbolic modes. That's probably true. It's a Faustian bargain. Literacy gives us an analytic, delayed response in perceiving the world, which is good for pursuits such as science or engineering. But we do lose some part of the cerebral development of the senses, the sensorium.

PAGLIA: And some people have more developed sensoriums than others. I've found that most people born before World War II are turned off by the modern media. They can't understand how we who were born after the war can read a book and watch TV at the same time. But we *can*. When I wrote my book, I had earphones on, blasting rock music or Puccini and Brahms. The soap operas—with the sound turned down—flickered on my TV. I'd be talking on the phone at the same time. Baby boomers have a multilayered, multitrack ability to deal with the world. I often use the metaphor of a large restaurant stove to describe the way the mind works. There are many burners, and only one of them is the logical, analytical burner. And, Neil, I think we agree that our contemporary education system neglects it.

One reason American academic feminism is so mediocre is that these women can't think their way out of a wet paper bag. They have absolutely no training in logic, philosophy, or intellectual history, so they're reduced to arguing that we should throw out Plato and Aristotle because they're dead white males, or some such nonsense. That's so dopey and ignorant. People born before World War II can't understand those of us raised in the fragmented, imagistic world of TV. We can shut off one part of the brain and activate another. Scientists, psychologists, and IQ testers haven't caught up with these new ways of perception.

POSTMAN: Camille, I think we actually agree on the evidence. Only you think it is all just fine and will be a liberating development. Television and the other visual media will enlarge the sensorium and give people a fuller repertoire of means of expression. Marshall McLuhan used to refer to people like me and others as POBs: Print-Oriented Bastards—literates who had their right hemispheres amputated or atrophied. You should adopt the term, Camille; your analysis is absolutely correct. Only I tend to see this development as ominous.

Bertrand Russell used to utter a lovely phrase. He said that the purpose of education was to teach each of us to defend ourselves against the "seductions of eloquence." In the realm of the word, we learn the specific techniques used to resist these seductions: logic, rhetoric, and literary criticism. What worries me is that we have not yet figured out how to build defenses against the seductions of imagery. The Nazi regime was only the most recent example of seducing, through words and images, one of the most *literate* populations on earth. I remember Hitler's rantings. Now, I won't ask you how old you are.

PAGLIA: I'm forty-three. I was born in 1947. And you graduated from college in 1953. I checked! I wanted to know, because I think this information is absolutely critical to how one views the mass media. I graduated from college in 1968. There are only fifteen years between us, but it's a critical fifteen years, an unbridgeable chasm in American culture.

. . . shrimp and basil beignets . . .

POSTMAN: Well, I remember the imagery of the 1940s, when an entire political machine was pressed into the service of imagistic propaganda. In America it is somewhat different. There *is* a machine producing such images, but it is capitalism, and the output is the commercial. The process is the same. Have you seen the commercial for Hebrew National frankfurters? It shows Uncle Sam while a narrator declares how good and healthy frankfurters are because Uncle Sam maintains such high standards. Then Uncle Sam looks up as the narrator adds that Hebrew Nationals are even better than other frankfurters because they must answer to a higher authority.

PAGLIA: I love that ad! It's wonderful. Hilarious.

POSTMAN: Here is what bothers me. Symbols *are* infinitely repeatable, but they are not inexhaustible. If you use God to sell frankfurters, or if you use the face of George Washington to sell discount car tires, you drain the symbol of the very meanings, Camille, that you so astutely discover and explicate in your book. You look at a painting and analyze its levels of meaning, its ambiguities, its richness. But what happens if people see the same image a thousand times, and always to sell tight jeans?

PAGLIA: I would argue exactly the opposite. In the Hebrew National ads the invocation of Uncle Sam and God reinforces their symbolic meaning and helps young people have a historical perspective on their own culture.

Ads shaped the imagination of my generation. The Hebrew National image of Jehovah—that he's invisible, a voice inspiring his children to high standards—is faithful to tradition. It's a fabulous ad. And, by the way, it's true—kosher franks *are* better! I believed this ad and bought the franks! I love ads as an art form. To me, there is no degradation in this particular ad at all.

POSTMAN: Perhaps you're not taking it seriously enough, Camille. By age twenty, the average American has seen 800,000 television advertisements, about 800 a week. I am not talking about radio, print, or any other kind of advertisement. I am *referring* only to television advertisements. Television commercials are now the most powerful source of socialization, and the schools ought to take them seriously.

Some advertisements are good, of course. I don't think Madonna would serve too well. But I think of Jimmy Stewart selling soup. In that advertisement, the producers used his voice only because that voice is sufficient to symbolize what he stands for—the embodiment of the thoroughly decent American. So the use of that imagery is fine. But

in the Hebrew National advertisement, a sense of the sacred is being eliminated, or exploited by redirecting it to the profane world.

PAGLIA: If Jehovah had never expressed Himself about table manners, I would support you. But the Bible shows that Jehovah instructed the Jews at great length about what foods to eat and how to prepare and serve them.

POSTMAN: And, of course, Jehovah also forbade shellfish—everything we're eating tonight!

PAGLIA: This is the point. Kosher ritual preparation is dictated by the Bible. Nothing in the Hebrew National ad distorts or lies about Jewish tradition.

POSTMAN: Suppose you saw a commercial that showed Jesus looking at a bottle of Gallo wine and saying, "When I turned the water into wine in Cana, it wasn't nearly as good as this Gallo Pinot Noir." What does that do to the meaning of Jesus Christ for Christians? You seem very enthusiastic about the use of these images, but I think the *secularization* of these symbols and religious icons is dangerous.

PAGLIA: To you, coming from the Judeo-Christian tradition, this looks secular. If you look at it from my perspective, popular culture is an eruption of paganism—which is also a sacred style. In your book, you skip from 1920 to television. I think you leap over a critical period—the great studio era of Hollywood movies in the 1930s and 1940s. Cinema then was a pagan cult full of gods and goddesses, glamour and charisma. It was a style devoted to the sacred and the numinous. So it's not that the sacred has been lost or is being trivialized. We are steeped in idolatry. The sacred is everywhere. I don't see any secularism. We've returned to the age of polytheism. It's a rebirth of the pagan gods.

What I argue in my book is that Judeo-Christianity never defeated paganism but rather drove it underground, from which it constantly erupts in all kinds of ways. Ancient Greco-Roman culture harnessed the dynamic duality of the Apollonian and the Dionysian principles. We've inherited the Apollonian element of the Greco-Roman tradition. The history of Western civilization has been a constant struggle between these two impulses, an unending tennis match between cold Apollonian categorization and Dionysian lust and chaos.

That's why you can always tell whether a critic was born before or after World War II by the way he or she speaks of the twentieth century. To you who grew up knowing life as narrative exposition and who saw the end of an era with Fitzgerald and Hemingway—and you're right, there was a great shift, and the novel is now dead as a doornail—it's the Age of Anxiety. But the death of the novel was also the beginning of movies. I date the modern age from the first sound pictures in 1928. I call the twentieth century the Age of Hollywood.

There's a huge generational difference here. For those of us born after the war, our minds were formed by TV. Take Susan Sontag, born in 1933. There are fourteen years between her and me. It doesn't seem like much, but it's like an abyss between us. In the 1960s she was writing briefly about popular culture, but then she backed off and has spent the rest of her life saying, "I'm serious, I'm serious. Gotta find that ultimate Eastern European writer!" A few years ago, she boasted in *Time* that she had no TV and had to rent one when a guest came to visit. My TV is constantly fluttering. It's a hearth fire in the modern home. TV is not something you *watch*; it is simply on, all the time.

. . . seared scallops in truffle vinaigrette . . .

POSTMAN: If you keep this up, Camille, I'm going to need either more wine or a cigarette. Do you mind if I smoke?

PAGLIA: Not at all. Neil, in your book you mentioned tests in which people didn't remember any facts from a news program they had watched thirty minutes earlier on TV. But they weren't testing the right part of the brain. Watching TV has nothing to do with thought or analysis. It's a passive but highly efficient process of storing information to be used later. The proper analogy is to interstate driving or football. You know, baseball was *the* sport of the pre–World War II era. Academics love it. It's the ultimate academic sport—linear, logical, slow. Football, especially as *remade* for TV with slow motion and replays, is the sport of my generation. There's a lot of writing about baseball but hardly any good stuff about football. When a quarterback pulls back from the line and quickly checks out the field, he's not thinking, he's *scanning,* the very thing we do when we watch TV. It's like the airline pilot sweeping his eyes across his bank of instruments or the driver cruising down the interstate at high speed, always scanning the field, looking for the drunk, the hot rod, the police, or the slow old lady in the Cadillac—watch out for *her*. None of these people—the quarterback, the pilot, the driver—is *thinking*. They're only reading the field and working by instinct, deciding in an instant where to throw the ball or steer the jet or car. The decision is made by intuition, not by ratiocination.

POSTMAN: It's called pattern recognition.

PAGLIA: Oh, really? Perfect! And that's why you can't picture Susan Sontag driving a car. You know what I mean? Can you imagine Susan Sontag behind the wheel? Forget it. It's like a *New Yorker* cartoon: *Susan Sontag buys her first car!*

POSTMAN: Of course, I agree: Reading a book and "reading" television are two completely different cerebral activities. I can remember hearing print-oriented people complain that the problem with a show like *Charlie's Angels* is that it didn't honor the Aristotelian unities of time, place, and action. Or that it didn't have any *true* character development.

PAGLIA: You liked *Charlie's Angels*?

POSTMAN: As a matter of fact, I did, but I am bringing it up as an example of how people misread television. Print-oriented people can't understand such a show because they try to judge it by the measures of literature. I came to understand *Charlie's Angels* when I realized that the entire show was about *hair*.

Do you remember that at the end of the show there was a two-minute segment in which the disembodied voice of Charlie explained to the angels *what the entire show had been about*. I imagine that the show was written by a bunch of former English majors. And I see them confounded by the fact that they have just written a show that is basically about hair and doesn't fit any of the categories that they have been taught count. So at the end, they shoehorn in a vestigial narrative. Once I saw an episode in which, in order to explain everything, the voice at the end had to mention characters and action that hadn't even been *in* the program: "She killed him because years ago he had stolen money and given it to a third person . . ." Those sixty seconds before the credits—when the show was actually already over—were meant to give a show about hair a sense of logic or coherence.

PAGLIA: *TV Guide* once said about the actresses on *Knots Landing*—my favorite prime-time show—that "they act with their hair." I love it! Soap operas also are mainly about hair, you know. Very pagan—the worship of beauty. And do you realize that the Farrah Fawcett hairdo of *Charlie's Angels* can still be seen today in every shopping mall in America? Though that show has been off the air for ten years, it has this incredible ongoing influence. Farrah herself has moved on to battered-wife roles, but her old Seventies hairstyle is still the dominant look for boy-crazy girls in American high schools. Awesome, really.

POSTMAN: We agree on the influence of popular culture as expressed through visual images. Everyone has a right to defend his or her own culture, and I feel sure there will be a cost to the kind of culture I value. It may be that your sensorium has been enlivened while mine has atrophied. But let's look at my tradition and see what it has accomplished. Consider that in 1776 Thomas Paine sold, by the most conservative estimates, 300,000 copies of *Common Sense*. That is the equivalent of selling 30,000,000 copies—a feat attainable only today by Danielle Steel or Tom Wolfe. Camille, do you think we will pay a price for this more fully developed sensorium?

PAGLIA: In your book you say that there was a high literacy rate during the American Revolution. But does that mean people actually *read* books? Political and literary books? Or was it that they could just sign their names? Your portrait of the highly literate nineteenth century also sort of ignores the trashy sentimental novels, ladies' fashion magazines, and the dime western. I agree with you that our country was founded as an Enlightenment experiment. The framers of the American Constitution were true intellectuals. But I think your book puts undue stress on that period, which was, as I see it, a kind of privileged moment. Comparing our period with that one—when there was a high degree of cultural awareness and political activity—makes us think we're slipping into a decline. But maybe we're just returning to the norm. I think the world as it is now is the way it always was.

. . . black bass in coriander nage . . .

POSTMAN: I'm not certain it was only a privileged moment, although you are right in suggesting that a high literacy rate creates a somewhat abstracted view of the world. Our culture paid a price for literacy, and it will pay a price for its transformation into a visual culture. We are, for example, rapidly losing any sense of sacrality. The reason the Ayatollah Khomeini struck most Americans as either a complete riddle or a lunatic is that he was actually a *truly religious person.* And we can no longer understand what such a person is like.

PAGLIA: Exactly. Whenever Qaddafi would spend days in his tent, the Western media would sneer and ridicule him. I couldn't believe it. Does no one understand the ethical meaning of the desert in Bedouin culture? It's like our Walden Pond. Hasn't the media ever seen *Lawrence of Arabia?* There are two lessons in the Salman Rushdie case. First, artistic freedom is a value only in the democratic Western tradition. Second, to millions of people in the world, religion is a matter of life and death.

POSTMAN: Camille, I think these observations support my argument that what I call the secularization of imagery depletes religious symbolism: not only the frequency of the image but also the ignominious tie between the image and commercialization. That is why we in the West can't understand why someone would risk his life in an attempt to kill Salman Rushdie. To us, it's crazy. To the martyr, it is the path to heaven.

PAGLIA: Rather than your total secularization, I see the repaganization of Western culture. In the realm of politics, I think pop culture—the vehicle of the pagan eruption—plays a crucial role. Popular culture has the function of purging politics of many of its potential demagogues. Elvis Presley, an enormously charismatic figure, was able to build his empire in the politically neutral realm of pop culture.

POSTMAN: Are you saying that Hitler might have been a Hollywood star in America?

PAGLIA: Today, you have other ways for extraordinarily charismatic people to create their worlds. There are other ways to rule the universe. Before popular culture, the only realm that allowed that kind of power of personality was politics.

POSTMAN: I see the confluence between television and politics a little differently. The first television president was, obviously, John Kennedy. But the first *image* president was Ronald Reagan. They were very different figures. Kennedy, Jimmy Carter, even Mario Cuomo are very much identified with regions of the country. They were and are developed personalities that play well on television. But Reagan and even Bush are different. Remember how no one knows what state Bush is from and how Reagan's being from California seemed irrelevant. These are personalities onto whom a full spectrum of voters are able to project their personal image of a president. Whatever a president is supposed to be, then that is what Reagan or Bush is.

PAGLIA: As a television persona, Reagan was avuncular and nostalgic—a return to the happy, innocent, pre–World War II era of baseball, before the chaos and disasters of the Sixties. He was simple, kindly, even-tempered, sometimes goofy. He got into his pajamas right after dinner. He ate jelly beans. He called his wife "Mommy." He never aged. His hair never got gray. To liberal writers and academics, these things seemed stupid and ludicrous. They were off reading his policy papers, missing the whole point of his popularity. Our president is both the political and the symbolic head of our government, serving in jobs that in England, for example, are separately represented by the prime minister and the queen. The president symbolizes the nation in psychodramatic form.

POSTMAN: A nation as heterogeneous as ours gropes to find comprehensive symbols and icons to pull us together. Ronald Reagan was such an image. Every Christmas you hear people say, "Happy Holidays." We try to be so polite and inclusive. We are a fragile polity desperate for unifying images. But, paradoxically, we can destroy ourselves by exhausting the available icons.

PAGLIA: Another such image is the national weather map, which is shown, naturally, on TV. Here's this patchwork country of Chinese and Chicanos and African-Americans and Jews and Italians, and then there's this map with beautifully sweeping curved lines of air pressure stretching from sea to shining sea, pulling us together. The weatherman and the president are our two titular heads.

These images and their meaning become obvious once you know how to read TV. One more example. Remember, during the 1988 election, how everyone was calling George Bush a wimp? And he *was* a wimp, constantly trotting after Reagan and in his shadow. What a ninny, I would think; he'll never win the election. Then came the day when Ronald Reagan made his last visit to the Republican convention, and Bush named Dan Quayle as his running partner for vice president. It was the most stunning moment of TV transformation I've ever seen, but no one in the media picked it up. After Reagan left, remember the outdoor scene when Bush named Quayle? The press hysterically rushed off to report the story of how silly, stupid, and rich Quayle was. But the story was not that George had picked a jerk. The story was

that George Bush, emerging as a new man, had picked a *son*. Bush had made a complete *rite de passage* on television and for television. Remember how Quayle was jumping around, acting like a puppy—even grabbing Bush by the shoulder? Later that day at the indoor press conference, Bush was amazingly stern and confident. He cut reporters off, he was completely in charge. He was this totally new person, a man no one had seen before. It was then I knew he was going to be president. I called people up and told them, but no one believed me. If you didn't know how to read TV or weren't watching, you missed it completely.

POSTMAN: And my point, Camille, which you are overlooking, is that Roger Ailes engineered that entire effect. We were all manipulated into having just that very perception.

PAGLIA: What I am talking about is nothing that Roger Ailes could have created. It was a side of Bush that predated Roger Ailes. We all have many personas, and we can pick and choose which to make public. But we cannot create them. Roger Ailes could not have saved Michael Dukakis.

. . . roast monkfish on savoy cabbage . . .

POSTMAN: Granted. If you read Bush's résumé, it is one of the most macho documents of recent times—first baseman at Yale, youngest Navy pilot, shot down in combat, head of the CIA. But when Ailes saw him acting like a ninny on television—and television does have a way of showing the authentic soul—I agree, he went to work on the indecisive wimp and promoted the image of the macho guy so that you and others would pick it up. And then that image was repeated and repeated, washing away any memory of a past impression.

PAGLIA: In your book you speak of television as being a medium of flashing images with only an eternal present and no past. I disagree. It's just the opposite. TV is a genre of reruns, a formulaic return to what we already know. Everything is familiar. Ads and old programs are constantly recycled. It's like mythology, like the Homeric epics, the oral tradition, in which the listener hears passages, formulae, and epithets repeated over and over again. There is a joy in repetition, as children know when they say, "Mommy, tell me that story again." TV is a medium that makes us feel "at home."

If you go back to the Fifties, when movies lost their cultural centrality to TV, you'll see that the great sacred images—the huge, cold images of cinema—were being miniaturized, familiarized, and domesticated by the television screen. The box became part of the family, and the shows reflected it: *Father Knows Best* and *Leave It to Beaver*. Ads are the same way. I put one of my favorite ads in my book—Luciana Avedon crooning, "Camay has coconut-enriched lather." I adored that ad! Of course, ads you hate are like torture. You want to die. So TV is about repetition and compulsion. It's like prayer, like the Catholic Rosary, repeated over and over again. That's what ads are: soothing litanies that make us feel safe and familiar and at home in the strange modern world.

POSTMAN: So idolatry has triumphed. I think Luther would join Moses in saying that the cult of the word is defenseless in the face of the image.

PAGLIA: Moses got his people out of Egypt, out of the land of the pagan image. That was the only way. Judaism could not have flourished in Egypt. Today, either you live in a cabin in northern Canada or you try to control TV. And I believe we *should* try to control it, by the way. Liberals are wrong when they say, "Parents should just turn off the TV set." You can't. TV is everywhere. It's bigger than politics. It's bigger than the Church.

POSTMAN: This is where education comes in, Camille. I believe that educational theory should be what I call "ecological"; that is, education should supply what the rest of the culture is not supplying. In this case, I think the only defense against the seductions of imagery is a literate education. If children are educated in the traditions of the word, then perhaps they will be able to make discriminating choices in the chaotic realm of the image.

PAGLIA: To me the ideal education should be rigorous and word-based—logocentric. The student must learn the logical, hierarchical system. Then TV culture allows the other part of the mind to move freely around the outside of that system. This is like the talent you need for internal medicine. An internist has to be intuitive. He knows there are about a half dozen different systems in the body, all interrelated. His mind has to weave in and out and around them and more or less guess what's wrong. This is the mental flexibility that a word-based education and a TV-based culture can develop. All parents should read to their children, from infancy on. Education is, by definition, repressive. So if you're going to repress, then repress like hell. I don't believe in the Dewey or Montessori methods— "We want to make this pleasant." There is nothing pleasant about learning to read or to think. The teachers used to shake me and yell at me to stay in line or sit still in my seat. I didn't like it, but I recommend it.

POSTMAN: In *Aspects of the Novel,* E. M. Forster wrote that if you say the king died and the queen died, you don't have a story. But if you say that the king died *because* the queen died, you have a story. I find that television undermines these simple word-based connections. The whole idea of language is to provide a world of intellectual and emotional continuity and predictability. But many of my students no longer understand, for example, the principle of contradiction. I was talking to one student the other day about a paper in which he asserted one thing to be true in the first paragraph and the exact opposite to be true three paragraphs later. He said, "What's the problem?"

This habit derives from television, which tells you that there was a rape in New York and then it tells you there was an earthquake in Chile and then it tells you that the Mets beat the Cardinals.

PAGLIA: Well, Neil, that's life.

POSTMAN: That's insanity.

PAGLIA: Not to me. In your book you say TV is Dadaist in its random, nihilistic compilation of unrelated events. I say it's surrealist—because *life* is surreal! You leave a restaurant and get killed by a falling air conditioner. A tornado hits a picnic. There's no sense to reality. It simply happens. Television is actually closer to reality than anything in books. The madness of TV is the madness of human life.

POSTMAN: Here is what I would like: When our young student is watching Dan Rather say that 5,000 people died in an earthquake in Chile and then Dan says, "We'll be right back after this word from United Airlines," I would like our student to say, "Hey, wait a second, how could he ask me to make such an emotional switch?"

PAGLIA: My answer is this: Buddha smiles. He sees the wheel of reincarnation and accepts the disasters of the universe. That's the way it should be. There's no way we can possibly extend our compassion to 5,000 dead people. By juxtaposing such jarring images, TV is creating a picture of the world that is simply true to life. We are forced to contemplate death the way farmers do—as just another banal occurrence, no big deal. Nature can crack the earth open and swallow thousands,

and then the sun shines and the birds sing. It's like going from an airplane crash to a hemorrhoids ad. In TV, as in nature, all have equal weight.

. . . carousel of caramel desserts

POSTMAN: What I am focusing on is our emotional response to those things. We all know that nurses who work in hospitals make jokes. They see the absurdity of death routinely. But they don't see anywhere near the number of deaths the television viewer sees. What I see as dangerous here is a discontinuity of emotion that television promotes, its unnatural evocation, every five minutes, of different and incompatible emotions.

PAGLIA: By moving from disaster to commercial, TV creates the effect of Greek tragedy: emotion, then detachment; contemplation of loss, then philosophical perspective. At the end of *Hamlet,* there are four corpses strewn all over the stage.

POSTMAN: But no one is laughing—although I will admit that in the graveyard scene, when Hamlet makes the "Alas, poor Yorick" speech, he *is* laughing. But my point is, just after Horatio's final soliloquy, at least on television, we would then see the Hebrew National spot, or perhaps a commercial for Danish pastry.

PAGLIA: To make that radical switch from disaster to detachment is, I think, a maturing process. If you fully responded emotionally to every disaster you saw, you'd be a mess. In fact, you'd be a perpetual child, a psychological cripple. Wisdom by definition is philosophical detachment from life's disasters.

POSTMAN: Injecting humor into otherwise insane catastrophes is comic relief. It is what we must do unless we want to go mad. But the effect I am talking about on the television news is different.

PAGLIA: I know that you see "amusement" as a bad thing wherever it shows up. You said in your book that teaching has finally been reduced to a branch of popular entertainment and that students won't sit still for anything that's not as funny as Big Bird on *Sesame Street*. And you cite Plato, Cicero, and Locke as educational philosophers who would insist on seriousness. I respectfully disagree. Plato's dialogues, which follow the Socratic method, a conversational give-and-take such as we're having here, are in fact very entertaining. There's a lot of comedy in Plato. Socrates is always pretending to be the most ignorant person there, and so on.

I think Jesus was a brilliant Jewish stand-up comedian, a phenomenal improvisor. His parables are great one-liners. When an enemy, trying to trap him, asks him about paying taxes, Jesus says, "Show me the coin of the tribute. Whose image is on it?" "Caesar's," the guy replies. "Then render unto Caesar the things that are Caesar's and unto God the things that are God's." I think that line got applause and laughs.

POSTMAN: You studied with Harold Bloom too long.

PAGLIA: Bloom used to say, "Teaching's a branch of show biz!" One last point—there are the koans, the teachings of the great Buddhist masters. They often took the form of slapstick. The novice comes in and says, "Tell me about life, master," and the elder whacks him on the head. Or says something surreal, like "Beanstalk!" So we do have many examples of teaching by great sages using humor or stand-up improv—Plato, Jesus, Buddha.

POSTMAN: No one is saying not to use humor in the classroom. I guess we are talking about

magnitude. It is one thing to use humor to reveal an idea you are developing. But now it is used simply to win the student's attention. Consequently, drawing an audience—rather than teaching—becomes the focus of education, and that is what television does. School is the one institution in the culture that should present a different worldview: a different way of knowing, of evaluating, of assessing. What worries me is that if school becomes so overwhelmed by entertainment's metaphors and metaphysics, then it becomes not content-centered but attention-centered, like television, chasing "ratings" or class attendance. If school becomes that way, then the game may be lost, because school is using the same approach, epistemologically, as television. Instead of being something different from television, it is reduced to being just another *kind* of television.

PAGLIA: Our dialogue has reached one major point of agreement. I want schools to stress the highest intellectual values and ideals of the Greco-Roman and Judeo-Christian traditions. Nowadays, "logocentric" is a dirty word. It comes from France, where deconstruction is necessary to break the stranglehold of centuries of Descartes and Pascal. The French have something to deconstruct. But to apply Lacan, Derrida, and Foucault to American culture is absolutely idiotic. We are born into an imagistic and pagan culture ruled by TV. We don't need any more French crap from ditsy Parisian intellectuals and their American sycophants. Neil, we agree on this: We need to reinforce the logocentric and Apollonian side of our culture in the schools. It is time for enlightened repression of the children.

PART VIII

New Media and Old in the Information Age

The ENIAC, an early digital computer. Computers like this one helped to lead the way in developing computers as essential tools for research, business, and military applications. *The University of Pennsylvania Archives.*

Our final section deals with the computer, now in its fifth decade of development. Hazarding judgment on the consequences of this medium for our own time and for an immediate future most of us will live to see is no easy task. The evolution of the computer is the evolution of a technology which, like movable type printing, has influenced and in turn been influenced by other technologies—hence the title of this section. Computers got their start in large organizations, aiding administration, scientific research, and the military. Following the development of microchip technology in the 1970s, computer circuitry permeated industry and became a mainstay of household appliances, such as stoves, television sets, and children's games. With the emergence of the personal computer, an individual working at home now has access to information-processing capacities that previously had been the sole preserve of large institutions. Today, we are witnessing the rapid proliferation of networks—best typified by the Internet, corporate intranets, and the World Wide Web—permitting an expanding range of administration, research, education, social activity, and commerce.

To understand the implications of all of this, we can draw on insights from past media revolutions. We know, for instance, that new media frequently bypass difficulties, bottlenecks, or barriers encountered in older media. In the late Middle Ages, print helped to democratize the reading public. It lessened the control over literacy exercised by church scribes and the religious orders. The resulting changes profoundly reorganized the ways in which knowledge circulated in society. Likewise, in the promotion of electronic communications, such as broadcasting, analysts have seen an equivalent bypassing of the institution of the book (and the newspaper) in accessing information. Perhaps one of the most controversial areas of the bypass effect with computers is the use of hand-held calculators in the classroom to circumvent traditional memory-based mathematical operations. As Walter Ong has pointed out, there are intriguing parallels with Plato's critique of writing as an "artificial" aid, one that Plato argued could lead to the erosion of mental capacities, specifically memory.

Despite the dramatic implications of the computer, we must not forget that aspects of it have been formed from traditional ways of structuring information found in previous media. The computer program is a case in point. Morse code was also a program, one that standardized the transmission of telegraphic messages. Likewise, vernacular grammars and Arabic numbers were programs that facilitated the use and accelerated the influence of the printing press. The index in printed books is yet another example. The index gave rise to the text as a work of reference. The resulting dictionaries, encyclopedias, and manuals of grammar helped to promote the use of standardized classification systems for knowledge. These reference works can be directly compared to contemporary computer databases for the storage of medical, legal, and business information.

In terms of not just the storage, but the movement of military, industrial, and commercial information, the computer can be compared to the telegraph's creation of a "wired world." The computer-based linking of stock markets and currency exchanges on a global basis recalls the telegraph's role in transforming the commodity price and marketing system of a century ago. And just as the earlier systems of railway traffic regulation and forward ordering depended on telegraphy, so our tightly linked systems of air traffic monitoring and inventory control are tailored to the coordinating capabilities of the computer.

Consistent with the previous observations is the view of communications historian James Beninger. In our first selection, "The Control Revolution," Beniger proposes that the computer's greatest impact so far has been on other media. He argues that the capacity of the computer to digitize the output of all other communication and information media, will make it into a new "generalized medium" in the twenty-first century. This is because computers can treat previously discrete forms of communication as technically the same. Thus, numbers, words, pictures, and sounds can be coded digitally by the computer, stored, or transmitted, then reproduced on demand in a virtual facsimile of the original. This convergence of our previously discrete semiotic systems of textual and audiovisual materials signals major changes in how such materials will be categorized, catalogued, and stored in the future.

In the next essay, William J. Mitchell looks at the development of the computer as a communications tool and concludes that it is still in an early phase of its development. He likens computers as media to a frontier society, slowly evolving rules and establishing conditions of use whereby the flows of information among computers become something like an information utility working in the background, not unlike the public utilities on which modern cities depend for their water, electric power, and transportation.

As this new information utility expands its reach, new interfaces will become familiar features of everyday life, much as ATMs have replaced significant aspects of personal banking. Some of these interfaces may have an impact on social life, for instance in the way online socializing through discussion forums, chat sites, and newsgroups suggests new pathways for informal interactions, perhaps even the possibility of virtual communities of interest. Mitchell believes that the combination of these social and commercial developments may result in new environments paralleling both our conventional urban-suburban life styles and our relationships with mass media. Some of these developing features of computer-facilitated communication are strikingly different from the world of older mass media. In particular, interaction now possible in web sites such as multi-user dungeons (MUDs) are an indication of how this new medium encourages role playing and participation in ways quite different from the experiences we have with television, radio, and books.

In the next essay, Mitchell's colleague at MIT, Janet Murray, explores the Web site as the newest publishing vehicle, allowing individual artists and entrepreneurs to challenge convention practices for how we tell stories and for what counts as entertainment. She shows how the new medium of the Internet has begun to create shadow versions of our older media, especially recorded music and television, providing parallel forms of content, commentary, and promotion. As the carrying capacity of the Internet improves, Murray outlines a future overlap, perhaps an eventual integration, of all electronic media, permitting not just easier access to news, information, and entertainment but hybrid forms of all three. For instance, she suggests that programming will be able to provide expanded narratives around conventional television dramas, that will allow a viewer to access different parts of a story or to choose to follow a drama from the viewpoint of a single character—all ways in which Murray believes we will encourage the emergence of experimental storytelling, much as film did earlier in the century.

In the next essay, Derrick de Kerckhove looks at how artists and technologists are collaborating to develop controlled environments of virtual sensory experiences, often referred to as VR or Virtual Reality. The results to date, he suggests, are moving us away from industrial models of design, long the handmaiden of mass production, and toward a new sensibility, which he calls cyberdesign. Although de Kerckhove's argument about cyberdesign presents some difficulties for readers who are less familiar with the issues of the arts and technology, like Murray and Mitchell, he is drawing our attention to how quickly and dramatically the shift to a new medium reorganizes the sensory spaces in which we live, work, and create.

Robert Logan, our fifth contributor, warns us that the continued development of electronic media brings about more than new sensibilities. It also enfranchises new groups in society, whose additional command of computer literacy is already providing them with considerable advantages. Logan calls these groups and individuals the new computerate class, and he predicts that their presence will have effects on commerce and culture that rival in some ways the effects that literacy had for the merchant class of the late Middles Ages and Early Modern period. If the Information Age comes to depend more and more on its relationship to intellectual capital, as many scholars predict, the presence of computer-literate skills will continue to enfranchise those who have them and—quite possibly—to disenfranchise those who do not.

In our final essay, Mark Poster makes a related point in a brief but eloquent explanation of how public opinion and our capacity for public discussion in general have depended upon our media systems. He reminds us that the Internet, as the first large-scale demonstration of the potential of the computer as media, is not that different from earlier media in at least one respect: It does not automatically support a society's established democratic practices. Although it is a powerful and provocative form of electronic communication, the Internet does not yet have a settled shape, and for that reason it will continue to raise important issues of security, the ownership of intellectual property, and local and community values.

The computer, like the other communications media we have explored in the previous sections, enables new forms of social action at the same time that it disables others. Poster suggests as much, and it has been a recurring theme in many of the contributions. The conclusions that Harold Innis drew from his analysis of the role of writing in the early civilizations of the Middle East seem applicable to the contemporary convergence of computers with electronic media. Media, Innis proposed, can never be truly neutral. By their very application they structure the interaction of individuals. They also give shape to the form of knowledge and to its circulation in society. In turn, of course, each society can shape and give direction, within limits, to the media that develop. This perspective is a fitting final formulation for students of media, a reminder that our exploration of media revolutions must always be joined to an appreciation of their ongoing social consequences.

39 THE CONTROL REVOLUTION

James Beniger

James Beniger is a professor of communications at the University of Southern California. His book The Control Revolution *is widely regarded as an important theoretical and historical investigation of technology's role in the management of industrial society.*

Few turn-of-the-century observers understood even isolated aspects of the societal transformation—what I shall call the "Control Revolution"—then gathering momentum in the United States, England, France, and Germany. Notable among those who did was Max Weber (1864–1920), the German sociologist and political economist who directed social analysis to the most important control technology of his age: bureaucracy. Although bureaucracy had developed several times independently in ancient civilizations, Weber was the first to see it as the critical new machinery—new, at least, in its generality and pervasiveness—for control of the societal forces unleashed by the Industrial Revolution.

For a half-century after Weber's initial analysis bureaucracy continued to reign as the single most important technology of the Control Revolution. After World War II, however, generalized control began to shift slowly to computer technology. If social change has seemed to accelerate in recent years (as argued, for example, by Toffler 1971), that has been due in large part to a spate of new information-processing, communication, and control technologies like the computer, most notably the microprocessors that have proliferated since the early 1970s. Such technologies are more properly seen, however, not as causes but as consequences of societal change, as natural extensions of the Control Revolution already in progress for more than a century.

Revolution, a term borrowed from astronomy, first appeared in political discourse in seventeenth-century England, where it described the restoration of a previous form of government. Not until the French Revolution did the word acquire its currently popular and opposite meaning, that of abrupt and often violent change. As used here in Control Revolution, the term is intended to have both of these opposite connotations.

Beginning most noticeably in the United States in the late nineteenth century, the Control Revolution was certainly a dramatic if not abrupt discontinuity in technological advance. Indeed, even the word *revolution* seems barely adequately to describe the development, within the span of a single life-time, of virtually all of the basic communication technologies still in use a century later: photography and telegraphy (1830s), rotary power printing (1840s), the typewriter (1860s), transatlantic cable (1866), telephone (1876), motion pictures (1894), wireless telegraphy (1895), magnetic tape recording (1899), radio (1906), and television (1923).

Along with these rapid changes in mass media and telecommunications technologies, the Control Revolution also represented the beginning of a restoration—although with increasing centralization—of the economic and political control that was lost at more local levels of society during the Industrial Revolution. Before this time, control of government and markets had depended on personal relationships and face-to-face interactions; now control came to be reestablished by means of bureaucratic organization, the new infrastructures of transportation and telecommunications, and system-wide communication via the new mass media. By both of the opposite definitions of *revolution,* therefore, the new societal transformations—rapid innovation in information and control technology, to regain control of functions once contained at much lower and more diffuse levels of society—constituted a true revolution in societal control.

Here the word *control* represents its most general definition, purposive influence toward a predetermined goal. Most dictionary definitions imply these same two essential elements: *influence* of one agent over another, meaning that the former causes changes in the behavior of the latter; and *purpose,* in the sense that influence is directed toward some prior goal of the controlling agent. If the definition used here differs at all from colloquial ones, it is only because many people reserve the word *control* for its more determinate manifestations, what I shall call "strong control." Dictionaries, for example, often include in their definitions of control concepts like direction, guidance, regulation, command, and domination, approximate synonyms of *influence* that vary mainly in increasing determination. As a more general concept, however, *control* encompasses the entire range from absolute control to the weakest and most probabilistic form, that is, any purposive influence on behavior, *however slight.* Economists say that television advertising serves to control specific demand, for example, and political scientists say that direct mail campaigns can help to control issue-voting, even though only a small fraction of the intended audience may be influenced in either case.

Inseparable from the concept of control are the twin activities of information processing and reciprocal communication, complementary factors in any form of control. Information processing is essential to all purposive activity, which is by definition goal directed and must therefore involve the continual comparison of current states to future goals, a basic problem of information processing. So integral to control is this comparison of inputs to stored programs that the word *control* itself derives from the medieval Latin verb *contrarotulare,* to compare something "against the rolls," the cylinders of paper that served as official records in ancient times.

Simultaneously with the comparison of inputs to goals, two-way interaction between controller and controlled must also occur, not only to communicate influence from the former to the latter, but also to communicate back the results of this action (hence the term *feedback* for this reciprocal flow of information back to a controller). So central is communication to the process of control that the two have become the joint subject of the modern science of cybernetics, defined by one of its founders as "the entire field of control and communication theory, whether in the machine or in the animal" (Wiener 1948, p. 11). Similarly, the pioneers of mathematical communication theory have defined the object of their study as purposive control in the broadest sense: communication, according to Shannon and Weaver (1949, pp. 3–5), includes "all of the procedures by which one mind may affect another"; they note that "communication either affects conduct or is without any discernible and probable effect at all."

Because both the activities of information processing and communication are inseparable components of the control function, a society's ability to maintain control—at all levels from interpersonal to international relations—will be directly proportional to the development of its information technologies. Here the term *technology* is intended not in the narrow sense of practical or applied science but in the more general sense of any intentional extension of a natural process, that is, of the processing of matter, energy, and information that characterizes all living systems. Respiration is a wholly natural life function, for example, and is therefore not a technology; the human ability to breathe under water, by contrast, implies some technological extension. Similarly, voting is one general technology for achieving collective decisions in the control of social aggregates; the Australian ballot is a particular innovation in this technology.

Technology may therefore be considered as roughly equivalent to that which can be done, excluding only those capabilities that occur naturally in living systems. This distinction is usually although not always clear. One ambiguous case is language, which may have developed at least in part through purposive innovation but which now appears to be a mostly innate capability of the human brain. The brain itself represents another ambiguous case: it probably developed in interaction with purposive tool use and may therefore be included among human technologies.

Because technology defines the limits on what a society *can* do, technological innovation might be expected to be a major impetus to social change in the Control Revolution no less than in the earlier societal transformations accorded the status of revolutions. The Neolithic Revolution, for example, which brought the first permanent settlements, owed its origin to the refinement of stone tools and the domestication of plants and animals. The Commercial Revolution, following exploration of Africa, Asia, and the New World, resulted directly from technical improvements in seafaring and navigational equipment. The Industrial Revolution, which eventually brought the nineteenth-century crisis of control, began a century earlier with greatly increased use of coal and steam power and a spate of new machinery for the manufacture of cotton textiles. Like these earlier revolutions in matter and energy processing, the Control Revolution resulted from innovation at a most fundamental level of technology—that of information processing.

Information processing may be more difficult to appreciate than matter or energy processing because information is epiphenomenal: it derives from the *organization* of the material world on which it is wholly dependent for its existence. Despite being in this way higher order or derivative of matter and energy, information is no less critical to society. All living systems must process matter and energy to maintain themselves counter to entropy, the universal tendency of organization toward breakdown and randomization. Because control is necessary for such processing, and information, as we have seen, is essential to control, both information processing

and communication, insofar as they distinguish living systems from the inorganic universe, might be said to define life itself—except for a few recent artifacts of our own species.

Each new technological innovation extends the processes that sustain life, thereby increasing the need for control and hence for improved control technology. This explains why technology appears autonomously to beget technology in general (Winner 1977), and why, as argued here, innovations in matter and energy processing create the need for further innovation in information-processing and communication technologies. Because technological innovation is increasingly a collective, cumulative effort, one whose results must be taught and diffused, it also generates an increased need for technologies of information storage and retrieval—as well as for their elaboration in systems of technical education and communication—quite independently of the particular need for control.

As in the earlier revolutions in matter and energy technologies, the nineteenth-century revolution in information technology was predicated on, if not directly caused by, social changes associated with earlier innovations. Just as the Commercial Revolution depended on capital and labor freed by advanced agriculture, for example, and the Industrial Revolution presupposed a commercial system for capital allocations and the distribution of goods, the most recent technological revolution developed in response to problems arising out of advanced industrialization—an ever-mounting crisis of control.

NEW CONTROL TECHNOLOGY

The rapid development of rationalization and bureaucracy in the middle and late nineteenth century led to a succession of dramatic new information-processing and communication technologies. These innovations served to contain the control crisis of industrial society in what can be treated as three distinct areas of economic activity: production, distribution, and consumption of goods and services.

Control of production was facilitated by the continuing organization and preprocessing of industrial operations. Machinery itself came increasingly to be controlled by two new information-processing technologies: closed-loop feedback devices like James Watt's steam governor (1788) and preprogrammed open-loop controllers like those of the Jacquard loom (1801). By 1890 Herman Hollerith had extended Jacquard's punch cards to tabulation of U.S. census data. This information-processing technology survives to this day—if just barely—owing largely to the corporation to which Hollerith's innovation gave life, International Business Machines (IBM). Further rationalization and control of production advanced through an accumulation of other industrial innovations: interchangeable parts (after 1800), integration of production within factories (1820s and 1830s), the development of modern accounting techniques (1850s and 1860s), professional managers (1860s and 1870s), continuous-process production (late 1870s and early 1880s), the "scientific management" of Frederick Winslow Taylor (1911), Henry Ford's modern assembly line (after 1913), and statistical quality control (1920s), among many others.

The resulting flood of mass-produced goods demanded comparable innovation in control of a second area of the economy: distribution. Growing infrastructures of transportation, including rail networks, steamship lines, and urban traction systems, depended for control on a corresponding infrastructure of information processing and telecommunications. Within fifteen years after the opening of the pioneering Baltimore and Ohio Railroad in 1830, for example, Samuel F. B. Morse—with a congressional appropriation of $30,000—had linked Baltimore to Washington, D.C., by means of a telegraph. Eight years later, in 1852, thirteen thousand miles of railroad and twenty-three thousand miles of telegraph line were in operation (Thompson 1947; U.S. Bureau of the Census 1975, p. 731), and the

two infrastructures continued to coevolve in a web of distribution and control that progressively bound the entire continent. In the words of business historian Alfred Chandler, "The railroad permitted a rapid increase in the speed and decrease in the cost of long-distance, written communication, while the invention of the telegraph created an even greater transformation by making possible almost instantaneous communication at great distances. The railroad and the telegraph marched across the continent in unison ... The telegraph companies used the railroad for their rights-of-way, and the railroad used the services of the telegraph to coordinate the flow of trains and traffic" (1977, p. 195).

This coevolution of the railroad and telegraph systems fostered the development of another communication infrastructure for control of mass distribution and consumption: the postal system. Aided by the introduction in 1847 of the first federal postage stamp, itself an important innovation in control of the national system of distribution, the total distance mail moved more than doubled in the dozen years between Morse's first telegraph and 1857, when it reached 75 million miles—almost a third covered by rail (Chandler 1977, p. 195). Commercialization of the telephone in the 1880s, and especially the development of long-distance lines in the 1890s, added a third component to the national infrastructure of telecommunications.

Controlled by means of this infrastructure, an organizational system rapidly emerged for the distribution of mass production to national and world markets. Important innovations in the rationalization and control of this system included the commodity dealer and standardized grading of commodities (1850s), the department store, chain store, and wholesale jobber (1860s), monitoring of movements of inventory or "stock turn" (by 1870), the mail-order house (1870s), machine packaging (1890s), franchising (by 1911 the standard means of distributing automobiles), and the supermarket and mail-order chain (1920s). After World War I the instability in national and world markets that Durkheim had noted a quarter-century earlier came to be gradually controlled, largely because of the new telecommunications infrastructure and the reorganization of distribution on a societal scale.

Mass production and distribution cannot be completely controlled, however, without control of a third area of the economy: demand and consumption. Such control requires a means to communicate information about goods and services to national audiences in order to stimulate or reinforce demand for these products; at the same time, it requires a means to gather information on the preferences and behavior of this audience—reciprocal feedback to the controller from the controlled (although the consumer might justifiably see these relationships as reversed).

The mechanism for communicating information to a national audience of consumers developed with the first truly mass medium: power-driven, multiple-rotary printing and mass mailing by rail. At the outset of the Industrial Revolution, most printing was still done on wooden handpresses—using flat plates tightened by means of screws—that differed little from the one Gutenberg had used three centuries earlier. Steam power was first successfully applied to printing in Germany in 1810; by 1827 it was possible to print up to 2,500 pages in an hour. In 1893 the New York *World* printed 96,000 eight-page copies every hour—a 300-fold increase in speed in just seventy years.

The postal system, in addition to effecting and controlling distribution, also served, through bulk mailings of mass-produced publications, as a new medium of mass communication. By 1887 Montgomery Ward mailed throughout the continent a 540-page catalog listing more than 24,000 items. Circulation of the Sears and Roebuck catalog increased from 318,000 in 1897 (the first year for which figures are available) to more than 1 million in 1904, 2 million in 1905, 3 million in 1907, and 7 million by the late 1920s. In 1927 alone, Sears mailed 10 million circular letters, 15 million general catalogs (spring and fall editions), 23 million

sales catalogs, plus other special catalogs—a total mailing of 75 million (Boorstin 1973, p. 128) or approximately one piece for every adult in the United States.

Throughout the late nineteenth and early twentieth centuries uncounted entrepreneurs and inventors struggled to extend the technologies of communication to mass audiences. Alexander Graham Bell, who patented the telephone in 1876, originally thought that his invention might be used as a broadcast medium to pipe public speeches, music, and news into private homes. Such systems were indeed begun in several countries—the one in Budapest had six thousand subscribers by the turn of the century and continued to operate through World War I (Briggs 1977). More extensive application of telephony to mass communication was undoubtedly stifled by the rapid development of broadcast media beginning with Guglielmo Marconi's demonstration of long-wave telegraphy in 1895. Transatlantic wireless communication followed in 1901, public radio broadcasting in 1906, and commercial radio by 1920; even television broadcasting, a medium not popular until after World War II, had begun by 1923.

Many other communication technologies that we do not today associate with advertising were tried out early in the Control Revolution as means to influence the consumption of mass audiences. Popular books like the novels of Charles Dickens contained special advertising sections. Mass telephone systems in Britain and Hungary carried advertisements interspersed among music and news. The phonograph, patented by Thomas Edison in 1877 and greatly improved by the 1890s in Hans Berliner's "gramophone," became another means by which a sponsor's message could be distributed to households: "Nobody would refuse," the United States Gramophone Company claimed, "to listen to a fine song or concert piece or an oration—even if it is interrupted by a modest remark, 'Tartar's Baking Powder is Best'" (Abott and Rider 1957, p. 387). With the development by Edison of the "motion picture" after 1891, advertising had a new medium, first in the kinetoscope (1893) and cinematograph (1895), which sponsors located in busy public places, and then in the 1900s in films projected in "movie houses." Although advertisers were initially wary of broadcasting because audiences could not be easily identified, by 1930 sponsors were spending $60 million annually on radio in the United States alone (Boorstin 1973, p. 392).

The mass media were not sufficient to effect true control, however, without a means of feedback from potential consumers to advertisers, thereby restoring to the emerging national and world markets what Durkheim had seen as an essential relationship of the earlier segmental markets: communication from consumer to producer to assure that the latter "can easily reckon the extent of the needs to be satisfied" (1893, p. 369). Simultaneously with the development of mass communication by the turn of the century came what might be called *mass feedback* technologies: market research (the idea first appeared as "commercial research" in 1911), including questionnaire surveys of magazine readership, the Audit Bureau of Circulation (1914), house-to-house interviewing (1916), attitudinal and opinion surveys (a U.S. bibliography lists nearly three thousand by 1928), a Census of Distribution (1929), large-scale statistical sampling theory (1930), indices of retail sales (1933), A. C. Nielsen's audiometer monitoring of broadcast audiences (1935), and statistical-sample surveys like the Gallup Poll (1936), to mention just a few of the many new technologies for monitoring consumer behavior.

Although most of the new information technologies originated in the private sector, where they were used to control production, distribution, and consumption of goods and services, their potential for controlling systems at the national and world level was not overlooked by government. Since at least the Roman Empire, where an extensive road system proved equally suited for moving either commerce or troops, communications infrastructures have served to control both economy and polity. As corporate bureaucracy came to control increasingly wider markets by the turn of this century, its power was increasingly checked by a parallel growth in state bureaucracy. Both bureaucracies found useful what Bell has called "intellectual technology":

> The major intellectual and sociological problems of the post-industrial society are . . . those of "organized complexity"—the management of large-scale systems, with large numbers of interacting variables, which have to be coordinated to achieve specific goals . . . An *intellectual technology* is the substitution of algorithms (problem-solving rules) for intuitive judgments. These algorithms may be embodied in an automatic machine or a computer program or a set of instructions based on some statistical or mathematical formula; the statistical and logical techniques that are used in dealing with "organized complexity" are efforts to formalize a set of decision rules. (1973, pp. 29–30)

Seen in this way, intellectual technology is another manifestation of bureaucratic rationality, an extension of what Saint-Simon described as a shift from the government of men to the administration of things, that is, a further move to administration based not on intuitive judgments but on logical and statistical rules and algorithms. Although Bell sees intellectual technology as arising after 1940, state bureaucracies had begun earlier in this century to appropriate many key elements: central economic planning (Soviet Union after 1920), the state fiscal policies of Lord Keynes (late 1920), national income accounting (after 1933), econometrics (mid-1930s), input-output analysis (after 1936), linear programming and statistical decision theory (late 1930s), and operations research and systems analysis (early in World War II).

In the modern state the latest technologies of mass communication, persuasion, and market research are also used to stimulate and control demand for governmental services. The U.S. government, for example, currently spends about $150 million a year on advertising, which places it among the top thirty advertisers in the country; were the approximately 70 percent of its ads that are presented free as a public service also included, it would rank second—just behind Procter and Gamble (Porat 1977, p. 137). Increasing business and governmental use of control technologies and their recent proliferation in forms like data services and home computers for use by consumers have become dominant features of the Control Revolution.

THE INFORMATION SOCIETY

One major result of the Control Revolution had been the emergence of the so-called Information Society. The concept dates from the late 1950s and the pioneering work of an economist, Fritz Machlup, who first measured that sector of the U.S. economy associated with what he called "the production and distribution of knowledge" (Machlup 1962). Under this classification Machlup grouped thirty industries into five major categories: education, research and development, communications media, information machines (like computers), and information services (finance, insurance, real estate). He then estimated from national accounts data for 1958 (the most recent year available) that the information sector accounted for 29 percent of gross national product (GNP) and 31 percent of the labor force. He also estimated that between 1947 and 1958 the information sector had expanded at a compound growth rate double that of GNP. In sum, it appeared that the United States was rapidly becoming an Information Society.

Over the intervening twenty years several other analyses have substantiated and updated the original estimates of Machlup (1980, pp. xxvi–xxviii); Burck (1964) calculated that the information sector had reached 33 percent of GNP by 1963; Marschak (1968) predicted that the sector would approach 40 percent of GNP in the 1970s. By far the most ambitious effort to date has been the innovative work of Marc Uri Porat for the Office of Telecommunications in the U.S.

Department of Commerce (1977). In 1967, according to Porat, information activities (defined differently from those of Machlup) accounted for 46.2 percent of GNP—25.1 percent in a "primary information" sector (which produces information goods and services as final output) and 21.1 percent in a "secondary information" sector (the bureaucracies of noninformation enterprises).

The impact of the information society is perhaps best captured by trends in labor force composition. As can be seen in Figure 1 and the corresponding data in Table 1, at the end of the eighteenth century the U.S. labor force was concentrated overwhelmingly in agriculture, the location of nearly 90 percent of its workers. The majority of U.S. labor continued to work in this sector until about 1850, and agriculture remained the largest single sector until the first decade of the twentieth century. Rapidly emerging, meanwhile, was a new industrial sector, one that continuously employed at least a quarter of U.S. workers between the 1840s and 1970s, reaching a peak of about 40 percent during World War II. Today, just forty years later, the industrial sector is close to half that percentage and declining steadily; it might well fall below 15 percent in the next decade. Meanwhile, the information sector, by 1960 already larger (at more than 40 percent) than industry had ever been, today approaches half of the U.S. labor force.

At least in the timing of this new sector's rise and development, the data in Figure 1 and Table 1 are compatible with the hypothesis that the Information Society emerged in response to the nineteenth-century crisis of control. When the first railroads were built in the early 1830s, the information sector employed considerably less than 1 percent of the U.S. labor force; by the end of the decade it employed more than 4 percent. Not until the rapid bureaucratization of the 1870s and 1880s, the period that . . . marked the consolidation of control, did the percentage employed in the information sector more than double to about one-eighth of the civilian work force. With the exception of these two great discontinuties, one occurring with the advent of railroads and the crisis of control in the 1830s, the other accompanying the consolidation of control in the 1870s and especially in the 1880s, the information sector has grown steadily but only modestly over the past two centuries.

Temporal correlation alone, of course, does not prove causation. With the exception of the two discontinuities, however, growth in the information sector has tended to be most rapid in periods of economic upturn, most notably in the postwar booms of the 1920s and 1950s, as can be seen in Table 1. Significantly, the two periods

of discontinuity were punctuated by economic depressions, the first by the Panic of 1837, the second by financial crisis in Europe and the Panic of 1873. In other words, the technological origins of both the control crisis and the consolidation of control occurred in periods when the information sector would not have been expected on other economic grounds to have expanded rapidly if at all. There is therefore no reason to reject the hypothesis that the Information Society developed as a result of the crisis of control created by railroads and other steam-powered transportation in the 1840s.

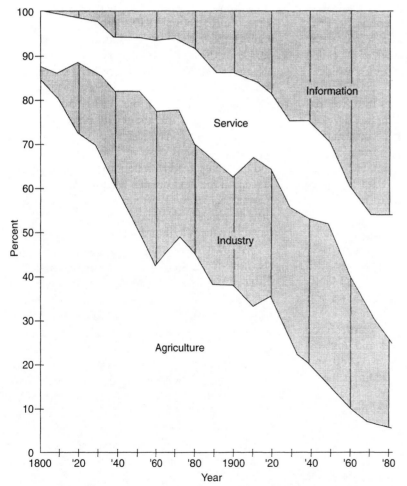

FIGURE 1 U.S. civilian labor force chart.

TABLE 1 U.S. EXPERIENCED CIVILIAN LABOR FORCE BY FOUR SECTORS, 1800–1980

Year	*Sector's Percent of Total*				Total Labor Force (in millions)
	Agricultural	Industrial	Service	Information	
1800	87.2	1.4	11.3	0.2	1.5
1810	81.0	6.5	12.2	0.3	2.2
1820	73.0	16.0	10.7	0.4	3.0
1830	69.7	17.6	12.2	0.4	3.7
1840	58.8	24.4	12.7	4.1	5.2
1850	49.5	33.8	12.5	4.2	7.4
1860	40.6	37.0	16.6	5.8	8.3
1870	47.0	32.0	16.2	4.8	12.5
1880	43.7	25.2	24.6	6.5	17.4
1890	37.2	28.1	22.3	12.4	22.8
1900	35.3	26.8	25.1	12.8	29.2
1910	31.1	36.3	17.7	14.9	39.8
1920	32.5	32.0	17.8	17.7	45.3
1930	20.4	35.3	19.8	24.5	51.1
1940	15.4	37.2	22.5	24.9	53.6
1950	11.9	38.3	19.0	30.8	57.8
1960	6.0	34.8	17.2	42.0	67.8
1970	3.1	28.6	21.9	46.4	80.1
1980	2.1	22.5	28.8	46.6	95.8

Sources: Data for 1800–1830 are estimated from Lebergott (1964) with missing data interpolated from Fabricant (1949); data for 1860–1870 are taken directly from Porat (1977); data for 1980 are based on U.S. of Labor Statistics projections (Bell 1979, p. 185).

A wholly new stage in the development of the Information Society has arisen, since the early 1970s, from the continuing proliferation of microprocessing technology. Most important in social implications has been the progressive convergence of all information technologies—mass media, telecommunications, and computing—in a single infrastructure of control at the most macro level. A 1978 report commissioned by the President of France—an instant best-seller in that country and abroad—likened the growing interconnection of information-processing, communication, and control technologies throughout the world to an alteration in "the entire nervous system of social organization" (Nora and Minc 1978, p. 3). The same report introduced the neologism *telematics* for this most recent stage of the Information Society, although similar words had been suggested earlier—for example, *compunications* (for "computing + communications") by Anthony Oettinger and his colleagues at Harvard's Program on Information Resources Policy (Oettinger 1971; Berman and Oettinger 1975; Oettinger, Berman, and Read 1977).

Crucial to telematics, compunications, or whatever word comes to be used for this convergence of information-processing and communications technologies is increasing digitalization: coding into discontinuous values—usually two-valued or binary—of what even a few years ago would have been an analog signal varying continuously in time, whether a telephone conversation, a radio broadcast, or a television picture. Because most modern computers process digital information, the progressive digitalization of mass media and telecommunications content begins to blur earlier distinctions between the communication of information and its processing (as implied by the term *compunications*), as well as between people and machines. Digitalization makes communication from persons to machines, between machines, and even from machines to persons as easy as it is between persons. Also blurred are the distinctions among information types: numbers, words, pictures, and sounds, and eventually tastes, odors, and possibly even sensations, all might one day be stored, processed, and communicated in the same digital form.

In this way digitalization promises to transform currently diverse forms of information into a generalized medium for processing and exchange by the social system, much as, centuries ago, the institution of common currencies and exchanges rates began to transform local markets into a single world economy. We might therefore expect the implications of digitalization to be as profound for macrosociology as the institution of money was for macroeconomics. Indeed, digitalized electronic systems have already begun to replace money itself in many informational functions, only the most recent stage in a growing systemness of world society dating back at least to the Commercial Revolution of the fifteenth century.

Selected References

For works of primarily historical interest, generally those published before 1960, citation is to the year of *first* publication except for ancient texts. When the text used was not this edition, page numbers and other references are to the edition (including year of publication) listed after the publisher. In the citation "Kant 1788," for example, the year refers to the first German publication; references are to the English-language edition published by Bobbs-Merrill in 1956. Citations to works in languages other than English are to translations whenever available.

Abbott, Waldo, and Richard L. Rider. 1957. *Handbook of Broadcasting: The Fundamentals of Radio and Television,* 4th ed. New York: McGraw-Hill.

Bell, Daniel. 1973. *The Coming of Post-Industrial Society: A Venture in Social Forecasting,* New York: Basic Books.

———. 1979. "The Social Framework of the Information Society." Pp. 163–211 in *The Computer Age: A Twenty-Year View,* ed. Michael L. Dertouzos and Joel Moses. Cambridge, Mass.: MIT Press.

Berman, Paul J., and Anthony G. Oettinger. 1975. *The Medium and the Telephone: The Politics of Information Resources.* Working Paper 75–8 (December 15). Cambridge, Mass.: Harvard University Program on Information Technologies and Public Policy.

Boorstin, Daniel J. 1973. *The Americans: The Democratic Experience.* New York: Random House, Vintage.

Briggs, Asa. 1977. "The Pleasure Telephone: A Chapter in the Prehistory of the Media." Pp. 40–65 in *The Social Impact of the Telephone,* ed. Ithiel de Sola Pool. Cambridge, Mass.: MIT Press.

Burck, Gilbert. 1964. "Knowledge: The Biggest Growth Industry of Them All." *Fortune* (November): 128–131ff.

Chandler, Alfred D., Jr. 1977. *The Visible Hand: The Managerial Revolution in American Business.* Cambridge, Mass.: Belknap Press of Harvard University Press.

Durkheim, Emile. 1893. *The Division of Labor in Society,* trans. George Simpson. New York: Free Press, 1933.

Fabricant, Solomon. 1949. "The Changing Industrial Distribution of Gainful Workers: Some Comments on the American Decennial Statistics for 1820–1940." *Studies in Income and Wealth,* vol. 11. New York: National Bureau of Economic Research.

Lebergott, Stanley. 1964. *Manpower in Economic Growth: The American Record since 1800.* New York: McGraw-Hill.

Machlup, Fritz. 1962. *The Production and Distribution of Knowledge in the United States.* Princeton. N.J.: Princeton University Press.

———. 1980. *Knowledge: Its Creation, Distribution, and Economic Significance,* vol. 1. Princeton, N.J.: Princeton University Press.

Marschak, Jacob. 1968. "Economics of Inquiring, Communicating, and Deciding." *American Economic Review* 58(2): 1–8.

Nora, Simon, and Alain Minc. 1978. *The Computerization of Society: A Report to the President of France.* Cambridge, Mass.: MIT Press, 1980.

Oettinger, Anthony G. 1971. "Compunications in the National Decision-Making Process." Pp. 73–114 in *Computers, Communications, and the Public Interest,* ed. Martin Greenberger. Baltimore: Johns Hopkins University Press.

Oettinger, Anthony G., Paul J. Berman, and William H. Read. 1977. *High and Low Politics: Information Resources for the 80's.* Cambridge, Mass.: Ballinger.

Porat, Marc Uri. 1977. *The Information Economy Definition and Measurement.* Washington: Office of Telecommunications, U.S. Department of Commerce.

Shannon, Claude E., and Warren Weaver. 1949. *The Mathematical Theory of Communication.* Urbana: University of Illinois Press.

Thompson, Robert Luther. 1947. *Wiring a Continent: The History of the Telegraph Industry in the United States, 1832–1866.* Princeton. N.J.: Princeton University Press.

Toffler, Alvin. 1971. *Future Shock.* New York: Bantam Books.

U.S. Bureau of the Census. 1975. *Historical Statistics of the United States, Colonial Times to 1920.* 2 vols. Washington: U.S. Government Printing Office.

Wiener, Norbert. 1948. *Cybernetics: or Control and Communication in the Animal and the Machine.* Cambridge, Mass.: MIT Press, 2nd ed., 1961.

Winner, Langdon. 1977. *Autonomous Technology: Technics-out-of-Control as a Theme in Political Thought.* Cambridge, Mass.: MIT Press.

40 SOFTCITIES

William J. Mitchell

William J. Mitchell is Dean of the School of Architecture at MIT and author of several works on image technology and architecture. His most recent book is City of Bits.

The early days of cyberspace were like those of the western frontier. Parallel, breakneck development of the Internet and of consumer computing devices and software quickly created an astonishing new condition; a vast, hitherto-unimagined territory began to open up for exploration. Early computers had been like isolated mountain valleys ruled by programmer-kings; the archaic digital world was a far-flung range in which narrow, unreliable trails provided only tenuous connections among the multitudi-nous tiny realms. An occasional floppy disk or tape would migrate from one to the other, bringing the makings of colonies and perhaps a few unnoticed viruses. But networking fundamentally changed things—as clipper ships and railroads changed the preindustrial world—by linking the increasingly numerous individual fragments of cyberturf into one huge, expanding system.

By the 1990s the digital electronics and telecommunications industries had configured themselves into an immense machine for the on-going production of cyberspace. We found ourselves rapidly approaching a condition in which every last bit of computer memory in the world would be electronically linked to every other. And those links will last forever. Because its electronic underpinnings are so modular, geographically dispersed, and redundant, cyberspace is essentially indestructible. You can't demolish it by cutting links with backhoes or sending commandos to blow up electronic installations, and you can't even nuke it. (The original ARPANET was, in fact, explicitly designed to withstand nuclear attack.) If big chunks of the network were to be wiped out, messages would automatically reroute themselves around the damaged parts. If some memory or processing power were to be lost, it could quickly be replaced. Since copies of digital data are absolutely exact replicas of the originals, it doesn't matter if the originals get lost or destroyed. And since multiple copies of files and programs can be stored at widely scattered locations, eliminating them all with certainty is as hard as lopping Hydra heads.

Cyberspace is still tough territory to travel, though, and we are just beginning to glimpse what it may hold. "In its present condition," Mitch Kapor and John Perry Barlow noted in 1990, "cyberspace is a frontier region, populated by the few hardy technologists who can tolerate the austerity of its savage computer interfaces, incompatible communications protocols, proprietary barricades, cultural and legal ambiguities, and general lack of useful maps or metaphors." And they warned, "Certainly, the old concepts of property, expression, identity, movement, and context, based as they are on physical manifestation, do not apply succinctly in a world where there can be none."[1]

This vast grid is the new land beyond the horizon, the place that beckons the colonists, cowboys, con artists, and would-be conquerors of the twenty-first century. And there are those who would be King.

HUMAN LAWS/CODED CONDITIONALS

Out there on the electronic frontier, code is the law. The rules governing any computer-constructed microworld—of a video game, your personal computer desktop, a word processor window, an automated teller machine, or a chat room on the network—are precisely and rigorously defined in the text of the program that constructs it on your screen. Just as Aristotle, in *Politics*, contemplated alternative constitutions for city-states (those proposed by the theorists Plato, Phaleas, and Hippodamos, and the actual Lacedaemonian, Cretan, and Carthaginian ones), so denizens of the digital world should pay the closest of critical attention to programmed polity. Is it just and humane? Does it protect our privacy, our property, and our freedoms? Does it constrain us unnecessarily or does it allow us to act as we may wish?

At a technical level, it's all a matter of the software's conditionals—those coded rules that specify *if* some condition holds, *then* some action follows. Consider, for example, the familiar ritual of withdrawing some cash from an ATM. The software running the machine has some gatekeeper conditionals; *if* you have an account and *if* you enter the correct PIN number (the one that matches up, in a database somewhere, with the information magnetically encoded on your ATM card), *then* you can enter the virtual bank. (Otherwise you are stopped at the door. You may have your card confiscated as well.) Next the program presents you with a menu of possible actions—just as a more traditional bank building might present you with an array of appropriately labeled teller windows or (on a larger scale) a directory pointing you to different rooms: *if* you indicate that you want to make a withdrawal, *then* it asks you to specify the amount; *if* you want to check your balance, *then* it prints out a slip with the amount; *if* you want to make a deposit, *then* yet another sequence of actions is initiated. Finally, the program applies a banker's rule; *if* the balance of your account is sufficient (determined by checking a database), *then* it physically dispenses the cash and appropriately debits the account.

To enter the space constructed by the ATM system's software you have to submit to a potentially humiliating public examination—worse than being given the once-over by some snotty and immovable receptionist. You are either embraced by the system (if you have the right credentials) or excluded and marginalized by it right there in the street. You cannot argue with it. You cannot ask it to exercise discretion. You cannot plead with it, cajole it, or bribe it. The field of possible interactions is totally delimited by the formally stated rules.

So control of code is power. For citizens of cyberspace, computer code—arcane text in highly formalized language, typically accessible to only a few privileged high-priests—is the medium in which intentions are enacted and designs are realized, and it is becoming a crucial focus of political contest. Who shall write the software that increasingly structures our daily lives? What shall that software allow and proscribe? Who shall be privileged by it and who marginalized? How shall the writers of the rules be answerable?

FACE-TO-FACE/INTERFACE

The most basic built-in rules of virtual places control when you can act, what kinds of actions you can take, and who or what you can affect by your actions. Old computer graphics hackers, for example, fondly remember *Spacewar,* the first computer game; it provided a diagrammatically depicted, deep-space bartlefield in which players could take turns moving simulated spaceships, launching missiles, and amiably attempting to blow each other to bits.[2] On timesharing systems, players did not have to share a single console but could operate individually from their own. And when networks began to develop, so did remote *Spacewar* between players who might be hundreds of miles apart. But

the game stayed the same. The relationships that mattered were not those of the players' bodies in physical space (as, for example, in a pistol duel) but those of their surrogates in cyberspace, and the rules that counted were the coded-in ones of the virtual place in which the surrogates met.

On the early bulletin boards and commercial networks, "forums" or "rooms" that allowed participants to "chat" quickly became a main attraction.[3] Here the rules structured not a shoot-'em-up arena but a space for (mostly) risk-free, multiparticipant conversation. The place that you entered was presented as a scrolling text window. It had a descriptive or evocative name (like a bar, coffee shop, or other such hangout), and you could survey the scene by looking at a list of current participants. At any point, you could type in a short text comment; this appeared in the window, preceded by your chosen online handle, so that a stream of comments scrolled by on each participant's screen—a geographically distributed, highly stylized, cocktail party with electronically masked participants and a mouse in your hand instead of a drink.

Forum habitues would often bar crawl from room to room until they found one that seemed to have the right buzz. If they struck up an interesting conversation, they could agree to go off into private rooms to continue, and eventually might even contemplate the big step of choosing times and physical locations to go face-to-face with new-found friends.[4] So these virtual places performed, in a vivid new way, the traditional urban function of creating opportunities for chance encounters between strangers. And the associated conventions allowed those encounters to evolve, step by step, toward friendship and intimacy. Not surprisingly, some of these convivial spots became hot hangouts in cyberspace.

In the early days of computer networks it seemed a slightly far-fetched metaphor to describe these sorts of interaction sites as "places," since bandwidth was narrow and communication was mostly restricted to typing and receiving text. But SIMNET changed that.[5] A military project dating from the interregnum when ARPA was DARPA, SIMNET first came online in 1986 as a network of M-1 tank simulators, and it has since been elaborated to include other types of vehicles. The viewports of the "tanks" are video screens displaying simulated three-dimensional terrain over which a mock tank battle takes place. Since the computer-generated display is updated in real time as controls are manipulated, dozens of widely scattered tank crews have the vivid impression of maneuvering around the same patch of countryside. Perhaps fittingly, this prototypical electronic landscape—this Garden of Eden of cyberspace—is a realistically simulated battlefield.

The technology of distributed interactive simulation (DIS) systems grew out of SIMNET, and by the early 1990s it was being hyped as the latest thing for the theme park industry.[6] Pretty soon you could line up to play *BattleTech, Virtuality,* or *Fightertown*—interactive games unfolding in networked simulator pods that immerse you in tacky but fairly convincing virtual worlds.

As bandwidth burgeons and computing muscle continues to grow, cyberspace places will present themselves in increasingly multisensory and engaging ways.[7] They will look, sound, and feel more realistic, they will enable richer self-representations of their users, they will respond to user actions in real time and in complex ways, and they will be increasingly elaborate and artfully designed. We will not just look *at* them; we will feel present *in* them.[8] We can expect them to evolve into the elements of cyberspace construction—constituents of a new architecture without tectonics and a new urbanism freed from the constraints of physical space.

ON THE SPOT/ON THE NET

Why do some places attract people? Often, it is because being on the spot puts you in the know. The merchants' coffeehouses of eighteenth-cen-

tury New York, for instance, provided opportunities to get the latest shipping information, to meet potential trading partners, and to exchange other important commercial information.[9] Depending on your trade, you might find the need to locate in the financial district, the garment district, or SoHo, on Harley Street, Fleet Street, or Lincoln's Inn Fields, in Hollywood, Silicon Valley, or Detroit. You might be attracted to the literary salon, the corner saloon, or the Cambridge high table. It's not just a matter of where the jobs are, but of where you can exchange the most up-to-date, specialized information with the most savvy people; you may be able to do the same work and pursue similar interests if you are out in the sticks, but you are likely to feel cut off and far from the center of things.

In cyberspace, list servers soon evolved to perform some of the same functions. These are programs for broadcasting e-mail messages to all the "subscribers" on specified address lists. They are like electronic Hyde Park Corners—places in which anybody can stand up and speak to the assembled crowd. Lists may assemble formal groups such as the employees of a business, or the students enrolled in a class, or they may be constructed through some informal, self-selection process. As with physical assemblies, some lists are public and some secret, some are open to anybody and some are rigorously exclusive.

Electronic "newsgroups" were also quick to develop. Newsgroup software allows participants to "post" text messages (and sometimes other sorts of files), much as you might pin printed notices to a physical bulletin board. The notices—queries, requests, responses, news items, announcements, tips, warnings, bits of gossip, jokes, or whatever—stay there until they are deleted, and anyone who enters the place can read them. Usually there is a host—a sort of Cyber de Staël or Virtual Gertrude presiding over an online rue de Fleury—who sets topics, coaxes the exchanges along when they flag, and occasionally kicks out an unruly or objectionable participant.[10] By the 1990s there were countless thousands of these places, advertising every interest you might imagine and some that you surely would not. If you wanted to be in touch and up with the latest in your field, it was increasingly important to have ready access to the right newsgroups. And your physical location no longer mattered so much.

When there is a sudden need, ad-hoc newsgroups can spring almost instantly into existence. Within hours of the January 1994 Los Angeles earthquake, there was a Usenet newsgroup called *alt.current-events.la.quake.* Long before the rubble had been swept from Wilshire Boulevard and before telephone service had unjammed, it was providing a place to post damage reports and find news about friends and relatives. It was the best place to be if you wanted to know what was going on.

The virtual communities that networks bring together are often defined by common interests rather than by common location: Unix hackers, Amiga enthusiasts, Trekkies, and Deadheads are scattered everywhere. But the opposite can also be true. When networks and servers are organized to deal with information and issues of local concern to the people of a town or to the students, staff, and faculty of a university, they act to maintain more traditional, site-specific communities. So, for example, the City of Santa Monica's pioneering Public Electronic Network (PEN) is available only to residents of Santa Monica, to people who work in the city, or at thirty-five public-access terminals located within the city boundaries.[11] And the Athena educational network was put in place on MIT's Cambridge campus to serve the MIT community.

STREET NETWORKS/WORLD WIDE WEB

Ever since Ur, urban places have been linked by movement channels of various kinds: doorways and passageways have joined together the rooms of buildings, street grids have connected buildings to each other, and road and rail networks have allowed communication between distant cities. These familiar sorts of physical connections have provided access to the places where people lived, worked, worshipped, and entertained themselves.

Now there is a powerful alternative. Ever since the winter of 1994, I have had a remarkable piece of software called Mosaic on the modest desktop machine that I'm using to write this paragraph.[12] (Right now, Mosaic is open in another window.) Mosaic is a "client" program that provides convenient access to World Wide Web (WWW) servers located throughout the Internet. These servers present "pages" of information, which may be in the form of text, graphics, video, or sound. Pages typically have "hyperlinks" pointing to related pages elsewhere in the Web, allowing me to jump from page to page by clicking on highlighted text or images.

The "home page" of any WWW server invites me to step, like Alice through the looking glass, into the vast information flea market of the Web—a cyberspace zone now consisting of countless millions of interconnected pages. The astonishing thing is that a WWW page displayed on my screen may originate from a machine located *anywhere* on the Internet. In fact, as I move from page to page, I am logging into computers scattered around the world. But as I see it, I jump almost instantaneously from virtual place to virtual place by following the hyperlinks that programmers have established—much as I might trace a path from station to station through the London Underground. If I were to diagram these connections, I would have a kind of subway map of cyberspace.

NEIGHBORHOODS/MUDS

MUD crawling is another way to go. Software constructions known as MUDs, Multi-User Dungeons, have burned up countless thousands of log-in hours since the early 1980s.[13] These provide settings—often very large and elabo-rately detailed ones—for online, interactive, role-playing games, and they often attract vast numbers of participants scattered all over the Internet. They are cyberspace equivalents of urban neighborhoods.

The particular joy of MUDville is the striking way that it foregrounds issues of personal identity and self-representation; as newcomers learn at old MUDders' knees, your first task as a MUD initiate is to construct an online persona for yourself by choosing a name and writing a description that others will see when they encounter you.[14] It's like dressing up for a masked ball, and the irresistible thing is that you can experiment freely with shifts, slippages, and reversals in social and sexual roles and even try on entirely fantastic guises. You can discover how it *really* feels to be a *complete* unknown.

Once you have created your MUD character, you can enter a virtual place populated with other characters and objects. This place has exits—hyperlinks connecting it to other such settings, which have in turn their own exits. Some heavily frequented MUDs are almost incomprehensibly vast, allowing you to wander among thousands of distinct settings, all with their own special characteristics, like Baudelaire strolling through the buzzing complexity of nineteenth-century Paris. You can examine the settings and objects that you encounter, and you can interact with the characters that you meet.

But as you quickly discover, the most interesting and provocative thing about a MUD is its constitution—the programmed-in rules specifying the sorts of interactions that can take place and shaping the culture that evolves. Many are based on popular fantasy narratives such as *Star Trek,* Frank Herbert's *Dune,* C. S. Lewis's *Chronicles of Narnia,* the Japanese animated television series *Speed Racer,* and even more doubtful products of the literary imagination; these are communities held together, as in many traditional societies, by shared myths. Some are set up as hack-'n-slash combat games in which

bad MUDders will try to "kill" your character, these, of course, are violent. Darwinian places in which you have to be aggressive and constantly on your guard. Others, like many of the Tiny-MUDs, stress ideals of constructive social interaction, egalitarianism, and nonviolence—MUD-derhood and apple pie. Yet others are organized like high-minded lyceums, with places for serious discussion of different scientific and technical topics. The MIT-based *Cyberion City* encourages young hackers—MUDders of invention—to write MUSE code that adds new settings to the environment and creates new characters and objects. And some are populated by out-of-control, crazy MUDders who will try to engage your character in TinySex—the one-handed keyboard equivalent of phone sex.

Early MUDs—much like text-based adventure video games such as *Zork*—relied entirely on typed descriptions of characters, objects, scenes, and actions. (James Joyce surely would have been impressed; city as text and text as city. Every journey constructs a narrative.) But greater bandwidth, faster computers, and fancier programming can shift them into pictorial and spatial formats.[15] Lucasfilm's *Habitat,* for example, was an early example of a graphic MUD that had its first incarnation, in North America, on the QuantumLink Club Caribe network (a precursor of America Online) and Commodore 64 computers. Later, it spawned a colony, *Populopolis,* that reputedly attracted a lot more paying customers on the NIFtyServe network in Japan.[16]

As a citizen of *Habitat,* you could customize your character, known as your Avatar, by selecting from a menu of body parts and choosing a sex.[17] (That was a one-bit choice, since *Habitat* was marketed as fairly conservative family entertainment.) Players conversed with one another in comic strip speech balloons. A region—one of as many as 20,000 similar ones in the original *Habitat* at its zenith—was a place that you can walk your character around, and it had doors and passages to other regions. These regions were filled with functional objects such as ATM machines to provide cash, bags and boxes to carry things in, books and newspapers to read, weapons, flashlights, and garbage cans. You could walk, take elevators, or teleport to other regions and explore them; you could exchange conversation, buy and sell goods, and even swap body parts. And, if you got tired of your character, you could reconfigure it, give it some drugs, or take it to the Change-o-matic sex-change machine.

As the creators of *Habitat* soon found, their task became one of reinventing architecture and urban design for cyberspace. They commented:

> For 20,000 Avatars we needed 20,000 "houses" organized into towns and cities with associated traffic arteries and shopping and recreational areas. We needed wilderness areas between the towns so that everyone would not be jammed together into the same place. Most of all, we needed things for 20,000 people to do. They needed interesting places to visit—and since they can't all be in the same place at the same time, they needed a *lot* of interesting places to visit—and things to do in those places. Each of those houses, towns, roads, shops, forests, theaters, arenas, and other places is a distinct entity that someone needs to design and create.[18]

Only limitations in bandwidth and processing power inhibit taking the next step—the realization of whizzier World Wide Webs, super-MUDs, and other multiparticipant, urban-scale structures consisting of hyperlinked, three-dimensional, sensorily immersive spaces. And these limitations are temporary. The online environments of the future will increasingly resemble traditional cities in their variety of distinct places, in the extent and complexity of the "street networks" and "transportation systems" linking these places, in their capacity to engage our senses, and in their social and cultural richness.

But no matter how extensive a virtual environment or how it is presented, it has an underlying structure of places where you meet people and find things and links connecting those places. This is the organizing framework from which all else grows. In cyberspace, the hyperplan is the generator.

NOTES

1. Mitchell Kapor and John Perry Barlow, "Across the Electronic Frontier," Electronic Frontier Foundation, Washington, DC, July 10, 1990.
2. It seems to have first appeared on a DEC PDP-1 at MIT in 1962. It was the progenitor of increasingly fancy space shoot-'em-ups that appeared as computers became faster and graphics more sophisticated.
3. The *Picospan* software, authored by Marcus Watts to support interaction on the WELL, provided a very influential early model for this sort of virtual place.
4. Miss Manners has tackled the question of how to handle this progression. She advises: "Miss Manners would not go so far as to say that a computer bulletin board exchange constitutes a proper introduction, but she has heard worse ones. Notwithstanding, it does not confer any social obligation." *The Washington Post*, Wednesday, August 18, 1993, B5.
5. Apparently SIMNET was inspired by *Battlezone*, an Atari arcade game from the early 1980s. For discussions of SIMNET, see Warren Katz, "Military Networking Technology Applied to Location-Based, Theme Park and Home Entertainment Systems," *Computer Graphics* 28: 2 (May 1994): 110–12; Michael Harris, "Entertainment Driven Collaboration," *Computer Graphics* 28: 2 (May 1994): 93–96; and Bruce Sterling, "War Is Virtual Hell," *Wired* 1: 1 (1993): 46–99.
6. See Katz, "Military Networking," for an introduction to DIS technology.
7. The aspects of synthetic experience, and technologies currently available to provide them, are surveyed in Warren Robinett, "Synthetic Experience: A Proposed Taxonomy," *Presence* 1: 2 (Spring 1992): 229–47.
8. The phenomenon of feeling present in a virtual place has been discussed extensively in the literature of simulation and virtual environments. See,

for example, Carrie Heeter, "Being There: The Subjective Experience of Presence," *Presence* 1: 2 (Spring 1992): 262–71.

9. For discussion of New York's communication advantages and their role in its growth to commercial dominance, see Eric H. Monkkonen, *America Becomes Urban: The Development of U.S. Cities and Towns 1780–1880* (Berkeley: University of California Press, 1988).

10. Though, as Miss Stein might well have judged had she encountered a newsgroup, "Remarks are not literature."

11. The City of Palo Alto was also quick to create an online information service, but took the very different approach of setting up a World Wide Web server on Internet. You can access it by Mosaic or Lynx *http://www.city.palo-alto.ca.us*, or you can get information by e-mailing to *wwwadmin@city.palo-alto.ca.us*. There is a city government phone directory, a city council agenda and meeting schedule, and so on.

12. On the development, introduction, and remarkable initial success of NCSA Mosaic, see John Markoff, "A Free and Simple Computer Link," *The New York Times*, Wednesday, December 8, 1993, D1, D5. Mosaic is essentially a point-and-click, graphic interface to the World Wide Web, an international system of database servers organized to allow remote requests for information from any computer on the Internet. The original work on World Wide Web was done by Tim Berners-Lee at CERN in Geneva in the late 1980s. Mosaic was developed at the National Center for Supercomputer Applications at the University of Illinois, Urbana-Champaign. By early 1994, more than 50,000 copies of Mosaic were being downloaded monthly from NCSA's public server.

13. The first MUD, written at the University of Essex by Roy Trubshaw and Richard Bartle, was based on the fantasy board game Dungeons and Dragons—hence the name. There are numerous arcane variants on the generic Multi-User Something idea—TinyMUDs, MUSEs, MUSHs, MUCKs, MOOs, and so on. The differences do not matter for our purposes here. On the experience of MUD crawling, see David Bennahum, "Fly Me to the MOO," *Lingua Franca* 4: 4 (May/June 1994): 1, 22–37.

14. This is, of course, closely related to the old literary issue of establishing a voice. "Call me Ishmael" might be the opening ploy in a MUD interaction. So Wayne Booth's classic *The Rhetoric of Fiction* (Chicago: University of Chicago Press, 2nd ed., 1983) serves as a pretty good theoretical introduction to MUDding.

15. As programmers will appreciate, MUDs constitute a natural application for object-oriented programming techniques, and the developments of the MUD idea and of object-oriented programming have been intertwined.

16. Chip Morningstar and F. Randall Farmer. "The Lessons of Lucasfilm's Habitat," in Michael Benedikt, ed., *Cyberspace: First Steps* (Cambridge, MA: The MIT Press, 1991), pp. 273–302. On *Populopolis* see Howard Rheingold, "Habitat: Computer-Mediated Play," in *The Virtual Community* (Reading, MA: Addison-Wesley, 1993), pp. 188–96.

17. In Hindu mythology, an avatar is a deity descended to earth in bodily form; the word is from the Sanskrit for "descend."

18. Morningstar and Farmer, "The Lessons of Lucasfilm's Habitat," pp. 286–87.

41 CYBERDRAMAS

Janet Murray

Janet Murray is a Professor of Writing and an associate of the Media Lab at MIT. Her recent book, Hamlet on the Holodeck: The Future of Narrative in Cyberspace, *is the source for the present excerpt.*

Though the technology of the Star Trek holodeck remains improbably distant and the puzzle mazes, shooting games, and tangled Web sites of the mid-1990s have only begun to tap the expressive potential of the new medium, these first experiments in digital storytelling have aroused appetites, particularly among the young, for participatory stories that offer more complete immersion, more satisfying agency, and a more sustained involvement with a kaleidoscopic world. Although the tools of true procedural authorship are still in their early stages, it has become increasingly easy for interactors to construct their own worlds on the MUDs or to build custom game levels for open-architecture fighting games. For those who are not ready for procedural engagement, the preparation of digital text, audio, and video is increasingly accessible through off-the-shelf software. Web site design is fast becoming as easy as desktop publishing. Just as everyone who can cope with a keyboard and mouse can now make a greeting card, soon everyone who can master word processing will be able to design a simple Web page, complete with hyperlinks to other sites and color graphics.

As more and more people are growing as facile with digital environments as they are with pen and pencil, the World Wide Web is becoming a global autobiography project, a giant illustrated magazine of public opinion. Independent digital artists are using the Web as a global distribution system of underground art, including illustrated stories, animations, hypertext novels, and even short digital films. Although science fiction and fantasy narratives will always remain strong in cyberspace, the documentary elements of the Web—the family albums, travel diaries, and visual autobiographies of the current environment—are pushing digital narrative closer to the mainstream.

At the same time that legions of new Web surfers are busy debating politics or posting digitized pictures of the family schnauzer for the enjoyment of distant dog lovers, media conglomerates are trying to carve up cyberspace into revenue-producing fiefdoms. The entertainment industry has looked upon the world of bits as merely a new delivery channel, a simple wire for carrying their vast inventories of content to another market. They have been slow to understand what people look for in a digital environment, and they are likely to remain conservative in the creation of digital products, seeking only to modify the familiar formats of film and television so that they will somehow become interactive. The shape of narrative art and entertainment in the next few decades will be determined by the interplay of these two forces, that is, the more nimble, independent experimenters, who are comfortable with hypertext, procedural thinking, and virtual environments, and the giant conglomerates of the entertainment industry, who have vast resources and an established connection to mass audiences.

Looking ahead to the next forty years—the working life of the generation that has grown up with videogames and educational computing tools—we can expect a range of narrative formats to emerge as authors look for ways to preserve the customary pleasures of linear narrative while exploiting the essential properties of the digital medium with increasing sophistication. In this chapter we tear our eyes away from the distant horizon of the holodeck to focus on the entertainment products of the more immediate future. If the current multimedia CD-ROMs are the equivalent of the "photoplay," then what will be the next giant steps that will carry electronic narrative down the path from additive to expressive form?

THE HYPERSERIAL: TV MEETS THE INTERNET

One of the clearest trends determining the immediate future of digital narrative is the marriage between the television set and the computer. The technical merger is already under way. Personal computers marketed to college students allow them to switch off the central processing unit and tune in the latest episode of *Friends* on the same screen they use for word processing. The most computer-phobic couch potatoes can now buy a "Web TV" that will allow them to point and click their way across the Internet and even to send and receive e-mail, using an ordinary phone line. American television is rapidly moving toward a high-definition digital standard, which will turn the broadcast TV signal into just another form of computer data. Meanwhile, the Internet is beginning to function as an alternate broadcasting system; already it offers a wide assortment of live programming, including on-line typed interviews, digital radio programs, and even live video coverage of rock music concerts, club openings, and performance art. As television channels and the World Wide Web come closer together, the telephone, computer, and cable industries are racing to deliver the new digital content to the end user faster and in greater quantities. The merger that Nicholas Negroponte has long been predicting is upon us: the computer, television, and telephone are becoming a single home appliance.

From the consumer's point of view, the activities of watching television and surfing the Internet are also merging, thus driving the marketplace to create new frameworks of participation. Television viewers populate hundreds of computer chat rooms and newsgroups, often logging on to these collective environments while watching the shows in order to share their responses with fellow audience members. Broadcasters have experimented with displaying some of these comments in real time, as subtitles beneath the images of an entertainment program, as questions for interviewees, or as quotations at the beginning and end of news segments. The network formed by the cooperative venture between Microsoft and NBC exists as both a Web site and a cable television station; these two separate venues are so intertwined and mutually

referencing that it would be hard to say which one is "the" MS/NBC. They are one entity, even though they now appear on two separate screens. Viewer digital participation is moving from sequential activities (watch, then interact), to simultaneous but separate activities (interact while watching), to a merged experience (watch and interact in the same environment). Although we cannot yet predict the economics of the television–Internet merger, these increasing levels of participatory viewership are preparing us for a near-future medium in which we will be able to point and click through different branches of a single TV program as easily as we now use the remote to surf from one channel to another.

The more closely the new home digital medium is wedded to television, the more likely it will be that its major form of storytelling will be the serial drama. As we have already seen, the daytime soap opera has already been translated into the more participatory Web soap now popular on the Internet. Adding motion video to the format will increase demand for the dramatic immediacy and more tightly plotted action that we expect on TV. It will be hard for the chattily written Web soaps—which are based on a scrapbook metaphor—to compete in the same environment as television serials once the novelty of Web surfing has passed. At the same time, linear television will seem too passive once it is presented in a digital medium, where viewers expect to be able to move around at will.

Probably the first steps toward a new *hyperserial* format will be the close integration of a digital archive, such as a Web site, with a broadcast television program. Unlike the Web sites currently associated with conventional television programs, which are merely fancy publicity releases, an integrated digital archive would present virtual artifacts from the fictional world of the series, including not only diaries, photo albums, and telephone messages but also documents like birth certificates, legal briefs, or divorce papers. Such artifacts appear in the best of the current Web soaps but do not sustain our interest without the motivation of a central dramatic action.

The compelling spatial reality of the computer will also lead to virtual environments that are extensions of the fictional world. For instance, the admitting station seen in every episode of *ER* could be presented as a virtual space, allowing viewers to explore it and discover phone messages, patient files, and medical test results, all of which could be used to extend the current story line or provide hints of future developments. The doctors' lounge area could contain discarded newspapers with circled advertisements, indicating, for example, that Dr. Lewis is looking for an apartment in another state or that Dr. Benton is shopping for an engagement ring. An on-line, serially updated virtual environment would open up a broadcast story in the same way a film expands a story told in a stage play, by providing additional locations for dramatic action or wider coverage of the characters or events merely referred to in the broadcast series. We might see more of the home life of the *ER* doctors, perhaps noticing that Mark Green keeps a photo of the absent Susan Lewis next to a picture of his daughter or that Doug Ross has held on to the medical ID bracelet of a woman who died partly as a result of his out-of-control sexual life. Like the set design in a movie, a virtual set design would be an extension of the dialogue and dramatic action, deepening the immersive illusion of the story world.

All of these digital artifacts would be available on demand, in between episodes, so that viewers could experience a continuous sense of ongoing lives. A hyperserial might include daily postings of events in the major story line—another fight between feuding characters or a set of phone messages between separated lovers—that would be alluded to in the broadcast segments but detailed only in the on-line material. The Web-based material might also contain more substantial development of minor characters and story lines. Maybe Shep, whom Carol broke up with last year, is sending her letters telling her how he is dealing with the stresses of his job as an emergency medical worker, or perhaps the ex-prostitute with AIDS is in danger of losing her apartment. By filling out the holes in the dramatic narrative, holes that prevent viewers from fully believing in the characters, and by presenting situations that do not resolve themselves within the rhythms of series television, the hyperserial archive could extend the melodramatic broadcast drama into a more complex narrative world.

Putting broadcast television into digital form would also allow producers to make previously aired episodes available on demand. A hyperserial site would offer a complete digital library of the series, and these episodes, unlike the same content stored on a VCR tape, would be searchable by content. Viewers could call up individual segments of past episodes (the diner scene in which Mark finalizes his divorce agreement) or view a single continuous story thread (the deterioration of Mark's marriage) that was originally woven into several episodes. Such an encyclopedic representation of the complete series would offer television writers the larger, more novelistic canvas that serial drama has been moving toward for the last two decades. Writers could think of a hyperserial as a coherent, unfolding story whose viewers are able to keep track of longer plot arcs and a greater number of interconnected story threads. Compared to today's television writer, the cyberdramatist could explore the consequences of actions over longer periods of time and could create richer dramatic parallels, knowing that viewers would be likely to juxtapose events told months or even years apart.

There are several ways the complex organizational powers of the computer could be used to support a much denser and more demanding story world. William Faulkner was looking for a similar technological aid when he asked his publisher to use different colors for the print in *The Sound and the Fury* to guide the reader through Benjy's section of the story, a device that would make the time-jumping stream of consciousness of the mentally arrested boy comprehensible without the elaborate charts it otherwise requires from painstaking college professors. Faulkner also included a map of the town of Jefferson in the endpaper of *Absalom, Absalom!* that indicates where some of the events of his novels occurred, including not just the location of some of the more colorful murders but also of the pasture the Compson family sold so that Quentin could go to Harvard. The tongue-in-cheek map ("William Faulkner, Sole Owner and Proprietor") binds the multinovel, multifamily, multicentury saga together, giving us a taste of how Faulkner himself saw his mythical Yoknapatawpha County, not as a mere backdrop for his elaborately spoken stories but as a continuous geographical and historical realm that transcended all the stories told about it. The encyclopedic capacity of the computer allows for storytelling on the Faulknerian scale and invites writers to come up with similar contextualizing devices—color-coded paths, time lines, family trees, maps, clocks, calendars, and so on—to enable the viewer to grasp dense psychological and cultural spaces without becoming disoriented.

In the Victorian era, arguably the pinnacle of novel writing in English, fiction writers often published in weekly or monthly installments that would then be collected and rereleased in bound volumes. Cyberdramatists would be in a similar position and would have the same advantage of writing for two kinds of audiences—the actively engaged real-time viewers who must find suspense and satisfaction in each single episode and the more reflective long-term audience who look for coherent patterns in the story as a whole. But the digital storyteller would also be aware of a third audience: the navigational viewer who takes pleasure in following the connections between different parts of the story and in discovering multiple arrangements of the same material. For instance, a *Homicide* viewer might want to see more of how Pembleton's struggle to regain his mental functioning after a stroke has affected his relationship with his wife and infant. Or we might be offered a chance to get a fuller understanding of the nurse on *ER* whose ineptitude is a risk to patient safety but who is herself a victim of the hospital's policy of rotating senior nurses away from their areas of expertise. In a well-conceived hyperserial, all the minor characters would be potential protagonists of their own stories, thus providing alternate threads within the enlarged story web. The viewer would take pleasure in the ongoing juxtapositions, the intersection of many different lives, and the presentation of the same event from multiple sensibilities and perspectives. The ending of a hyperserial would not be a single note, as in a standard adventure drama, but a resolving chord, the sensation of several overlapping viewpoints coming into focus.

VIRTUAL REALITY
Derrick de Kerckhove

Derrick de Kerckhove is Director of the McLuhan Program in Culture and Technology at the University of Toronto. He was an associate of Marshall McLuhan and is the author of several works, including The Skin of Culture.

Virtual reality has been in the hands of a special breed of artist-engineers from the very beginning. The original VR interface is the HMD unit that was first developed at MIT and the University of Utah during the late sixties and early seventies by computer scientist Ivan Sutherland. However, as Howard Rheingold[1] rightly points out, the idea of getting the watcher into the picture came first to cinematographer Morton Heilig and the realization of the first full-surround multisensory machine was his Sensorama (1960), which is kept under cover in his backyard and still works after over thirty years. The Sensorama is an apparatus that allows a user to experience a film in 3-D, by touch (according to approximately the same principle as was adopted for more recent "sensurround" movies), smell and, of course, auditory stimulations. Another artist-engineer whose concept of VR differed by projecting the user's image into the virtual world is Myron Krueger. Krueger spent years developing his Videoplace environment where the image of the user projected onto the screen creates elegant graphic and sound events. Krueger has only been achieving international recognition as a VR pioneer recently.

It does indeed take a special kind of sensibility to foresee the potential of VR. Heilig never succeeded in finding enough backing to develop what could have been the first VR system. VR was subsequently developed by an institution not known to have been short of money, the U.S. Department of Defense. The HMD was adapted for military flight simulation by people whose practical motivation was to replace costly and potentially fatal training on military aircraft by simulated computerized piloting. Most work on flight simulation consisted—and still consists—in improving the visual, auditory and tactile simulations of landing and take-off, tracking, bombing and air-to-air combat situations.

At the other end of the design spectrum are the many artists, such as Krueger, but also Thomas Zimmerman, Jaron Lanier, Graham Smith, David Rokeby and others who have recognized in VR the best experimental ground for the technological exploration of the human sensorium. The relationship of VR to art is predicated on its potential for sensory expression. There is a whole new field for artists to discover sensory patterns, technically extended sensory projections and their interaction with users. Designers will probably want to pay attention to what artists are doing in this field because soon that is where their best ideas may come from. Today some of the most interesting work in VR is what seems to sprout spontaneously from the artist's studio. Indeed, the inspiration for VR artwork wells from the unfettered probing of the biological ground of our psychological responses.

From a practical point of view, VR is to the drawing table what video recording and instant playback are to celluloid filming. Its responses happen in real time. VR can potentially reduce, if not eliminate altogether, the time and space interval between intention and realization. Eventually VR will go the way of word-processing and desktop publishing that allows the writer the total flexibility of instant and yet erasable publication and distribution. Thus VR is almost a direct technological extension and expression of the mental processes involved in designing. Mental visions are given graphic shapes that can respond at will to changes, almost as things happen in one's own mind. You can work in VR with the added benefit of being able to actually enter the contents of your extended mind and even to share the product of your thought unambiguously with coworkers. VR will eventually allow people to meet and work together in virtual stations that already bear the name of "virtual common."

If there ever was a definite, teleological rather than serendipitous, direction to the development of electronic technologies, VR could well represent its present synthesis. It seems to be the logical outcome and the point of convergence of many other electronic technologies. Behind VR developments there are strong market-potential driven stimuli. For example, at the technical level, VR seems to be ready to take full advantage of the trend to convert analog to digital signals in High Definition Television. VR combines the "live" directness of video technologies with the flexibility of computer intervention. To improve distribution and collaborative use, as well as rendering techniques, VR is pushing rapid developments in signal compression and transmission. Along with improved communication networks and electronic "highways," it can support both broadcast and special services. Coupled with neural network technologies VR can push automation to autonomation, that is, granting controlled levels of autonomy to automated electronic robots.

At a deeper level, VR research brings to convergence the most recent discoveries in psychological as well as technological software. Just as the quest for improved artificial intelligence (AI) and expert systems in computers drove brain research faster and further than if it had been left to the medical and academic institutions, VR is already inspiring an accelerated drive to understand the organic underpinnings and the sensory-laden complexities of human intelligence. Not surprisingly there is also an impetus for adding touch to our visual and auditory expertise in simulations, to make the experience more "real," more direct and ultimately more controllable. Thanks to digitization, it is possible to translate any set of inputs into different sets of outputs. Digitization has become the "common sense" of technology and psychology in computer software.

Once VR technology reaches the level of maturation predicted by actual trends, it is likely to change the levels and processes of any production into objects and products of design. VR will eventually penetrate media in news reporting and make people participate in events as it already does in entertainment. Children's education will be accelerated considerably by full-bodied contact with different types of experiences in knowledge and recreational fields. One day, museums will be jam-packed with VR reconstitutions of environments distant in time and space. Medical practice and research, and care for disabled and handicapped people will be facilitated by applied VR technologies. It is clear that VR in-

dustries will depend first and foremost on the quality and versatility of their designers.

The present state of VR technology is still fairly crude. The image definition is poor and the frame renewal rate is often too slow to give a "real-time" impression of the correlations between one's movements and the effects in the graphic simulations. But the progress of VR is relentless and it will eventually take over the economy—just as television once did—because it stimulates the convergence of market pressures and growing psychological needs. VR is the first technology ever that has hit the popular imagination before it has even reached anything close to maturity. Even as a concept, VR is already powerful enough to help change the thinking of mainstream industry and rejuvenate our exhausted post-industrial economy. We need this new thinking to respond to the challenge of VR.

"Cyberdesign" is design reconsidered by virtual reality. It is an aspect of design about to move from the periphery to the centre of industrial attention. Cyberdesign is what design becomes when it is supported by cyberactive systems. Cyberdesign is a critical addition to the vocabulary of designers because it is about to become a major industry.

Design parameters are the features of design susceptible to change and interaction within cyberactive systems. The designer's task is to provide a choice of integrated parameters that will shape the response of the system. It takes a professional designer to second guess what is needed and what isn't, in ever more complex integrated self-adjusting environments of possibilities. If it is possible to open or close a wall of liquid crystal displays, as one can see in Dutch culturologist Kriet Titulaer's "house of the future," then it is also possible to change its colour or make it interactive with the people moving by. Such features are like elements of a puzzle that the user may sometime want to put together alone. The complexity of parameters to be controlled requires a level of "metadesign," that is, designing a system for use by the buyer/client. The designer's task is to provide a choice of integrated parameters that will shape the response of the system. An example of the complexities involved can be read in the history of word-processing systems that have seen software developers' fortunes rise and collapse over single features.

Cyberdesign could be understood as an offshoot of traditional design but applied specifically to that new figure in the market, the "prosumer."

Alvin Toffler coined that term to highlight the latest trends in marketing, which showed that many potential buyers were not content with being consumers anymore, but they wanted more and more to be in on the act of production.[2] James Joyce had foreseen this development long ago when he asked in jest: "My consumers, aren't they my producers?" What he meant, of course, was that the relationship between production and consumption is one of strong interdependence. What is happening today, however, as a result of the computerization of the social body, is that people want to help produce their own goods. It is not just a matter of "customizing" the product, to make it fit more tightly to the individual needs of the buyer. It is primarily an issue of *empowerment.*

As technology empowers people, consumers develop the need to exercise more control over their immediate environment. As we move towards a consumer-directed rather than producer-directed culture, industry will come to realize that designing features that reflect the power of the consumer will have to be built into the products. The prosumer generation was born during the eighties, the era of yuppies and of computer networks. Computers allowed people to talk back to their screens, to reclaim control of their mental life from television and to take an active part in the organization of their environment, both local and global.

Prosumerism is far from peaking, yet it has already introduced the need for personalized empowerment as a critical feature of many goods destined to mass consumption. To give a small but ubiquitous example, no self-respecting businessperson can be content with a basic telephone.

Add-on functions such as automatic answering, call-waiting, call-forwarding, call-screening and remote message-collecting, etc. are all destined to give added confidence to the user that he or she has increased control over his or her life. Our TV sets themselves have become little production units to respond to the technical sophistication of video-recording and video-editing systems. New computer-assisted desktop publishing, editing, recording and multimedia operating systems land on our desks every two months.

Cyberdesign is the kind of design philosophy that addresses the sensibility of the prosumer. To the extent that sixties and seventies mass markets were predicated on planned obsolescence and packaging, that speed markets of the eighties were ruled by instant communications and high technology, the nineties economy will probably be based on inviting the consumer to take part in production decisions. The leaders will use cyberactive systems and they will inspire a changed approach in many other fields as well, for instance in education, entertainment, self-help services and perhaps even politics—witness the resurgence of populism (service-driven government) in North America.

From the empowerment imperative come other criteria for design that could prove fundamental with tomorrow's mass markets for goods and services. Empowerment translates into improved customizing, greater versatility of products to allow for more choices from a single technology. The inherent selectivity of the desktop industry will allow greater penetration of specialized niche markets. On the consumer side customers want "bells and whistles" with their TV sets, CD players and microwave ovens, not because they need them or actually plan to use them, but because such add-ons empower them. That they could use the features if they were needed is enough justification to spend more. When people buy these systems, they are not buying services, not even status; they are buying power.

Empowerment also brings out the sine qua non condition of *user-friendliness.* The learning process to use the technology should be built into the system and not required from the customer. There are several million people who would have remained computer-illiterate to this day, had it not been for the invention of Apple's Macintosh that you could learn to use in one afternoon. Compare that to the months of laborious practice the users of most IBM systems and their clones required before they finally caved in and adopted the Windows desktop environment. User-friendliness meets the requirements of instant gratification—a legacy from the consuming bulimia fed by the TV era—and of intuitive rather than inductive usage. Perhaps because we have been spoiled by so many different technological helpers, but also because we have lost the habit of making physical efforts, we feel that our machines ought to obey instantly, without asking from us anything but mere attention, and sometimes not even that.

That is why cyberactive systems operate best in real-time. But *real-timeliness* is not just another demand made by our thirst for instant gratification. Of course, the speed at which our orders are carried is a measure of our power, but the taste for real-timeliness comes from the new level of proximity and intimacy that technologies evoke within our bodies and our minds. Certainly, Walkman earphones, VR eyephones, datasuits and datagloves entertain an almost organic relationship with our physical being. We are getting used to conversing with our computer screens as if they were but extensions of our minds, carrying on interactive dialogues that also bear some of the marks of organicity. The consequence is that we are beginning to expect of our machines that they react to our commands with the same intuitive speed as our own limbs and senses.

We think of design primarily as a concern for our eyes; this is an effect of our immediate literate past. There has been some improvement in non-visually based design since we invented the concept of ergonomics, but computer-assisted design research is pushing the limits of sensory simulation and stimulation and it will add awareness of the subtleties of the other senses. Where, not long ago, we used to enter data into our machines or press a button to make them work, now we are beginning to put them on, like virtual bodies.

However, there is one last criterion that somehow seems to have evolved spontaneously, on its own, in the post-industrial culture—something that we might call *inconspicuousness*. Things want to hide, to meld into the background. Functions cease to be evident in some quality machines. This discretion is like a new world of "manners" in design. Although the trend of global economic austerity may account for a recent tendency to avoid external signs of wealth, there may be more to the developing aesthetics of disappearance than an economic base.

There is an inverse proportion between high-tech and visibility: that is, the more high-tech, the more discrete the medium; the lower the technology, the more bells and whistles are needed to prop it up. For example, compare the design of Sony ghettoblasters with the new design of Sony TVs, which have become almost intelligent stations instead of dumb terminals. Even the remote-control systems tend to minimalize all functions to the point of the absurd (I can never find where to adjust the picture for tone or herringbone interferences!).

However, what disappears to the eye, often resurfaces in touch: indeed, in keeping with the metaphor of the central nervous system, the continuity between organic and technological electricity is a matter best handled by feeling. Children who sharpen their hand-eye co-ordination with hand-held videogames experience touch in ways that rival the skills of the professional pianist! Designers will want to know the differences between the articulations of touch as contact and the articulations of touch as remote pressure. Electricity can simulate both to different effects, and industrial designers in Japan are well aware of interaction possibilities with simple commands activated by proximity alone.

Most of the design criteria invoked here are introduced and made relevant by the new technologies. None of user-friendliness, multi-sensoriality, real-timeliness or miniaturization were conceived of in the modernist or even the post-modernist eras. And yet, such criteria are not difficult to identify or to understand. They can be learned "on-the-job" so to speak. Other criteria may not as yet have surfaced and will be discovered as the true nature of cyberactive systems unfolds.

Still, there is also a deeper process at work. It seems as if every major technology, before achieving saturation levels in the cultures has had to go through two basic stages: first to be in stark evidence; second to be interiorized to the point of invisibility. For example, at first electrical wiring was much in evidence everywhere and many cities are still plagued with rather ugly telephone poles and outside wiring, but the tendency, even if it costs much more, is to put it all underground.

The trend to discretion may, in some cases, come from a sort of self-regulated strategy. Electricity is going undercover, so to speak, not only because it partakes of the nature of the human nervous system, but also because a baseline technology works best when it remains unquestioned and undetected. Well-versed in such matters, McLuhan was fond of quoting Joyce's line in *Finnegans Wake:* "The viability of vicinals is invincible as long as they are invisible." A momentous example of this invisibility or transparency of the underlying medium ruling a culture is that of literacy. How long will it take for us to realize the formidable effects the alphabet has had on us since the Renaissance and the Reformation? Of course, as soon as we know how much our basic idea of ourselves has depended on this now less-dominant technology, we will change quite radically. A new generation of cyberdesigners might be called upon to redesign our psychology itself. . . .

There is indeed a psychological change to be expected from the development and mass consumption of VR-related technologies. As they learn to use VR from kindergarten to the workplace and at home for evening and week-end entertainment, people will come to realize that all our technologies, especially the electronically based ones, are not simply external improvements in our immediate environments, but quasi-organic extensions of our most intimate being. VR's true nature is not merely to produce objects, but to extend and expand subjects. When design becomes the standard interface between thinking and doing, the activities that depend on thinking and planning can become direct extensions of thinking and feeling. As we invest our environment with our sensibility in VR, we are brought to the realization that this intelligent and sentient world we are wrapping around ourselves is but an extension of our own minds and souls.

NOTES

1. See Howard Rheingold, *Virtual Reality* (New York: Summit Books, 1991), 55–7.
2. Alvin Toffler, *The Third Wave* (New York: Morrow, 1980).

Proto-Internets and the Rise of a Computerate Class

Robert Logan

Robert Logan is a Professor of Physics at the University of Toronto and a Professor of Education at the Ontario Institute for Studies in Education. He is the author of several works on communications history, including The Alphabet Effect *and* The Fifth Language, *from which the present excerpt is taken.*

The discussion group on the Internet can be likened to an electronic dialogue or Symposium similar to the one described by Plato in his Dialogues, but one in which the participants share a common corner of cyberspace rather than sit at a banquet table. The Internet is obviously not the first forum for the sharing of information. The roots of the Internet or information-sharing networks can be traced to the preliterate storytellers or bards who traveled from settlement to settlement sharing information, carrying news and relating stories from the past which formed the foundations of their culture. Next came the forums of the city-states like those of Babylon which acted as nodes for receiving and sending information. The subsequent manifestation was the imperial communications systems of Mesopotamia, Egypt, Hellenistic Greece, the Roman Empire, and the Roman Catholic Church. In each of these proto-Internets, communications were controlled by and emanated from a central authority (all roads lead to Rome). There was heavy policing of the information transmitted through these systems so that only the Imperial political line or the Church dogma received air time. While these closed systems were opposite in spirit from the openness of today's Internet, they did provide global coverage (at least empirewide coverage) and, relatively speaking, simultaneity. The ancient Roman system of roads and the use of paper documents with a response time of only a month or two to the farthest outposts of the empire provided the fastest distribution of information up to the time of the introduction of the railroad and the telegraph.

The proto-Internets of the Renaissance and early industrial age were the trade routes along which information was carried by traders and merchants along with their goods. These routes became truly global with the arrival of ocean-traveling ships which permitted European powers like England, France, Spain, Holland, and Portugal to set up global trading networks that gathered goods and information from the four corners of the world. The newspapers that emerged in these countries provided readers with news of events from faroff places. With the invention of the telegraph, newspapers were transformed into a global network of correspondents, with the metropolitan newspapers like the *London Times,* the *New York Times,* and *Le Monde* serving as nodes. The link between these nodes where information was collected and disseminated was the international telegraph system, whereas the link to the end users were the daily newspapers, which provided information that was no more than twenty-four hours old. The next proto-Internets to arise were the broadcasting networks that were spawned first by radio and then by television. The feature that all of these proto-Internets lacked was the interactivity of end users, who functioned merely as passive consumers of information.

As McLuhan foresaw, the electrification and then the electronification of information resulted in new patterns of information usage that resemble the oral tradition in many ways. This trend, which began with the introduction of the telegraph and continued with the use of the telephone, radio, and television, is finding its most complete actualization with microcomputers connected through the Internet. Paradoxically, the bulk of the information being transmitted on the Net is still text. Print as a medium is still holding its own. The sale of books and other forms of reading matter continues to increase. The information which is now collected in books has been gathered, written, edited, and typeset using electronic media, but the format of print on paper still seems to be the most sensible format for reading text. Only the briefest messages, such as e-mail, are read exclusively on a video screen. When lengthy files are transmitted from one computer to another, in most cases readers will make a hard copy of the document. The reason is simple; reading from a CRT (or video screen) is an unnatural activity because of the way the brain processes video information. Reading is a left-brain activity, whereas viewing video is a right-brain one. The mosaic pattern of light pulses must be reassembled by the right brain to create an image. There is an inherent conflict in reading directly from a CRT. This is why the book is still a popular medium and will continue to be so. The Internet will not replace the book when it comes to the distribution of lengthy literary material, but it will remain the medium of choice for short text messages and multimedia formats.

Paper-based journals that publish specialized information could easily disappear, however. As archives for information and knowledge, they have long been surpassed by electronic media, and with the Internet they have also been surpassed as distribution vehicles. Rather than printing all its articles on paper and mailing them to their subscribers, journals could distribute their material electronically, leaving it to readers to print out those articles they wish to read closely in hard copy. But what purpose would electronic journals serve if this were done? Why not just have authors distribute their articles individually over the Internet? While this does happen, there is still a reason to have a journal, even if it is in an electronic form. First, the journal serves as a means of creating a community consisting of its readers and its contributors. Second, the function of editing and vetting papers by peers can still be maintained. Disputes between editors and authors can be easily resolved by distributing both authorized and nonauthorized articles. Readers would enjoy the service of having articles submitted for publication vetted by an editorial board and yet have the option of reading or ignoring those articles which were not officially approved by the board for formal publication.

The ease with which text can be read is critical to the success of a medium. This principle is illustrated by the different fates of two media which were introduced at approximately the same time, namely, videotext and desktop publishing. Videotext involved the broadcast of information into the homes of its users, who were able to select what they would view, paying a small fee for each item selected. The service never got off the ground in the U.K. and North America, partly because there was little context to the information provided and also because the video medium was not conducive to the easy reading of large amounts of data. The fact that information could be kept up to date electronically and was therefore always more current than printed information could not overcome the medium's inherent disadvantages. Another drawback of videotext services compared with the Internet was that the users of videotext couldn't make a contribution to the information hoard being compiled and so felt no sense of ownership of the information. The Internet user, on the other hand, can interact with the on-line information by adding to it or commenting on it for other users to read. Thus, users are able to shape the overall direction of a news-group in which they are participating and hence develop a sense of ownership of the information, even if it is shared with other users.

The desktop-publishing medium based on the rapid and relatively inexpensive production of printed material using the laser printer and software packages like PageMaker or Quark has caused a revolution in the print business. Traditional typesetters who could not adjust to the new medium and learn microcomputer-based typesetting were thrown out of work, and printing houses that did not adopt this new technology soon found themselves out of business. Desktop publishing takes advantage of the medium of the laser printer, the electronic image setter, and the microcomputer to reduce the cost of production, make short print runs economical, and increase the frequency with which catalogs and newsletters can be updated. At the same time, it retains the advantages of the crispness of the printed page. Material can be copied directly from laser-printer output or sent to an image setter to produce film for phototypesetting. It is even possible now, using computer-to-plate technology, to bypass the film stage and have the computer directly etch the plate.

The Internet is no longer restricted to text; it is rapidly becoming an important vehicle for the transmission of interactive multimedia data. Multimedia, which combines text, visuals, and audio, owes its current success to CD-ROM, which has served as both a storage medium and a delivery device for this interactive medium. At one time, the CD-ROM medium totally monopolized the distribution of multimedia products. With the Internet and powerful servers, this is no longer the case. As the bandwidth of modems increase, allowing more data to pass from one user of the Internet to another, multimedia presentations will become more practical. The Internet will have a major advantage over CD-ROM. The information on a CD-ROM is frozen and cannot be updated, whereas Internet-delivered multimedia information can be updated dynamically. By coupling a web page server with a database server, web pages can be updated dynamically so that the information being delivered is never out of date. Multimedia presentations on the Internet are, as of the time of this writing, primitive, but the capability for more sophisticated material is there; it is only a question of time before the Internet fully supports multimedia.

From the advent of writing on clay tablets to today's Internet, there has been a continuous speedup of the transmission of information. Harold Innis (Innis 1951) has documented how the transition from clay to papyrus and then paper speeded up the transmission of information, as did the introduction of the printing press. Word processing on computers, followed by desktop publishing, increased the speed with which information could be transmitted and the ease with which it could be edited, changed, and updated. CD-ROM promised to extend this speedy and flexible capability for both text and nontext information such as graphics, sound, and music. CD-ROM has become standard equipment on most microcomputers manufactured today. Despite this, CD-ROM could be squeezed out as the medium for the active transmission of multimedia by the Internet and survive only as an archiving device. My guess is that canned packages like entertainment and educational ti-

tles will find a natural home in the CD-ROM environment and will be produced and distributed much like books, audio recordings, and videotapes of movies. Information that must be kept current, like commercial information and catalogs, corporate annual reports, advertising in the form of infomercials, will likely gravitate to the Internet or other networks like Compuserve, Prodigy, and America On Line. With the recent appearance of recordable CDs, the dynamics could change once again, with recordable CDs being distributed with the most current information, which could be regularly updated through links on the Internet. As in the past, the most likely scenario is some hybrid system making use of the best of Internet and CD technologies.

Just as literacy created a new social class and a new form of privilege and economic opportunity, the use of computers may do the same. Those who will be able to exploit the power of computers will have an important advantage over those who cannot, just as those who were literate had an advantage over those who were not. I predict that the middle class will divide into two subsets, one merely literate and the other both literate and computer literate.

The new social class that will emerge, the computerate class, will be able to realize a commercial and cultural advantage. The consequence will be extremely important for educational planners. Just as the emergence of literacy as a skill affected the patterns of education in literate societies, so, too, will the emergence of computers and the need for computer literacy create major changes in and new demands upon our current education system.

Computing also seems to be restructuring the way in which the existing classes relate to one another and changing the role that class structures play in the economics and politics of society as a whole. Computers allow the integration of many different functions and make each individual worker more self-sufficient. There is also a parallel merger of the three classes. Many of the odious and brute-force tasks of the working class are being performed by robots and other computer-controlled machinery. The percentage of jobs that are unskilled or strictly working-class continues to decrease, while the number of middle-class jobs requiring education, literacy, and computer skills increases. Another effect of computing on the breakdown of class structures is that senior and middle managers are less and less dependent upon support staff.

At the other end of the spectrum, it is easier for middle-class people to become masters of their destiny and enterprise. Information-age enterprises are much less capital-intensive than industrial-era ones. Often, all that is required is intellectual capital and a modest amount of cash capital to start a major business operation. There are a number of middle-class computer whizzes who have become multimillionnaires in a rela-

tively short time. Another sector where the middle class is able to become self-employed and often self-realized is the service sector. While work in this sector does not often lead to a glamorous and aristocratic lifestyle, it has for a number of entertainers, fashion designers, and restaurateurs.

The computer age will continue to see a greater merging of the three traditional classes. The control of information, however, will become more and more the key to success and power. It is natural, therefore, that those who are computer literate will begin to realize tremendous advantages. As to whether or not this advantage will lead to the emergence of a distinct class just when class distinctions seem to be on the decrease is impossible to predict. There is no doubt, however, that computers will be where the action is and they will play an ever more important role in education and educational planning.

44 THE NET AS A PUBLIC SPHERE
Mark Poster

Mark Poster is professor of the history department at the University of California, Irvine. He is the author of numerous works, including The Mode of Information *and* The Second Media Age.

Throughout Western civilization, places such as the ancient Greek agora, the New England town hall, the local church, the coffeehouse, the village square, and even the street corner have been arenas for debate on public affairs and society. Out of thousands of such encounters, "public opinion" slowly formed and became the context in which politics was framed. Although the public sphere never included everyone, and by itself did not determine the outcome of all parliamentary actions, it con-

tributed to the spirit of dissent found in a healthy representative democracy.

Many of these public spaces remain, but they are no longer centers for political discussion and action. They have largely been replaced by television and other forms of media—forms that arguably isolate citizens from one another rather than bring them together.

Now, Internet newsgroups, MOOs, and other virtual communities are being promoted as nascent public spheres that will renew democracy in the 21st century. But these claims are fundamentally misguided: they overlook the profound differences between Internet "cafés" and the agoras of the past.

Disembodied exchange of video text is not a substitute for face-to-face meeting—it has its own logic, its own ways of forming opinion. These attributes will powerfully affect the politics that emerge in our digital era. To understand how our notion of democracy will change—and I believe it will change radically—we need to understand how the Net differs from historical public spheres.

In Western civilization, the public sphere was a place people could talk as equals. Status differences did not exclude frank discussion. Rational argument prevailed, and the goal was consensus. It was a place anyone could argue with anyone else, and the collected assembly acted as judge of the wisest direction for society to take.

As those who read Usenet can tell you, this definition doesn't come close to describing the online world. True, the Net allows people to talk as equals. But rational argument rarely prevails, and achieving consensus is widely seen as impossible. These are symptoms of the fundamentally different ways identity is defined in the public sphere and on the Net.

Traditionally, a person's identity is defined by contact. Identity is rooted in the physical body. This stability forces individuals to be accountable for their positions and allows trust to be built up between people.

The Internet, however, allows individuals to define their own identities and change them at will. A person might be an aging hippie known as *john@well.com* one day, a teenage girl called *kate@aol.com* the next. This kind of protean identity is not consonant with forming a stable political community as we have known it. Dissent on the Net does not lead to consensus: it creates the profusion of different views. Without embodied co-presence, the charisma and status of individuals have no force. The conditions that encourage compromise, the hallmark of the democratic political process, are lacking online. On the Internet, since identities are mobile, dissent is encouraged, and "normal" status markers are absent, it is a very different social "space" from that of the public sphere.

These changes must be examined without nostalgia. True, the Net marks a break with tradition. But that does not necessarily make it incompatible with political thought.

Political discourse has long been mediated by electronic machines: the issue now is that these machines have enabled new forms of decentralized dialog and created unique combinations of human-machine assemblages—individual and collective "voices" that are the modern building blocks of political formations and groupings. If the current media technology (television) is viewed as a threat to democracy, how can we account for a technology like the Internet, which appears to decentralize communication but enhance democracy?

We must remember that the Net is something entirely new, and its effects on democratic politics can't be predicted using historical precedent. The Internet threatens the government (unmonitorable conversations), mocks private property (the infinite reproducibility of information), and flaunts moral propriety (the dissemmation of pornography). The technology of the Internet shouldn't be viewed as a new form of public sphere. The challenge is to understand how the networked future might be different from what we have known.

Suggestions for Further Reading

Part I

Childe, Gordon. *Man Makes Himself.* New York: Mentor, 1951.

Giedion, Siegfried. *Space, Time and Architecture.* Cambridge, MA: Harvard University Press, 1967.

Goody, Jack. *The Logic of Writing and the Organization of Society.* Cambridge: Cambridge University Press, 1986.

Levoi-Gourhan, Andre. *Treasures of Prehistoric Art.* New York: Abrams, 1967.

Marshack, Alexander. *The Roots of Civilization.* New York: McGraw-Hill, 1982.

Pfeiffer, John. *The Emergence of Society.* New York: McGraw-Hill, 1977.

Schramm, Wilbur. *The Story of Communication.* New York: Harper and Row, 1988.

Ucko, Peter, and Andree Rosenfeld. *Paleolithic Cave Art.* New York: McGraw-Hill, 1967.

Part II

Clanchy, Michael. *From Memory to Written Record: England 1066–1307.* Cambridge, MA: Harvard University Press, 1979.

Davis, Natalie Zemon. *The Return of Martin Guerre.* Cambridge, MA: Harvard University Press, 1983.

Eco, Umberto. *The Name of the Rose.* New York: Warner Books, 1983.

Goody, Jack. *The Logic of Writing and the Organization of Society.* New York: Cambridge University Press, 1988.

Havelock, Eric. *The Literate Revolution in Greece and Its Cultural Consequences.* Princeton, NJ: Princeton University Press, 1987.

Illich, Ivan, and Barry Sanders. *ABC—The Alphabetization of the Popular Mind.* New York: Vintage Books, 1989.

Logan, Robert. *The Alphabet Effect.* New York: William Morrow, 1986.

Ong, Walter. *Orality and Literacy.* New York: Methuen, 1982.

Part III

Darnton, Robert. *The Great Cat Massacre and Other Episodes in French Cultural History.* New York: Basic Books, 1984.

Darnton, Robert, and Daniel Roche. *Revolution in Print—The Press in France, 1775–1800.* Berkeley: University of California Press and The New York Public Library, 1989.

Eisenstein, Elizabeth. *The Printing Revolution in Early Modern Europe.* New York: Cambridge University Press, 1983.

Febvre, Lucien, and Henri-Jean Martin. *The Coming of the Book: The Impact of Printing, 1450–1800.* London: New York Books, 1979.

Ivins, William. *Prints and Visual Communication*. London: Routledge & Kegan Paul, 1953.

Joyce, William L., et al., eds. *Printing and Society in Early America*. Worcester: American Antiquarian Society, 1983.

McLuhan, Marshall. *The Gutenberg Galaxy*. New York: Signet, 1969.

Mumford, Lewis. *Art and Technics*. New York: Columbia University Press, 1952.

Postman, Neil. *The Disappearance of Childhood*. New York: Dell, 1982.

Wood, Amanda. *Knowledge Before Printing and After: The Indian Tradition in Changing Kerala*. Oxford: Oxford University Press, 1985.

PART IV

Altick, Richard Daniel. *The English Common Reader: A Social History of the Mass Reading Public, 1800–1900*. Chicago: University of Chicago Press, 1957.

Carey, James. *Communication as Culture*. Boston: Unwin Hyman, 1989.

Knightley, Phillip. *The First Casualty*. New York: Harcourt Brace Jovanovich, 1975.

Marvin, Carolyn. *When the Old Technologies Were New*. New York: Oxford University Press, 1987.

Pool, Ithiel de Sola. *The Social Impact of the Telephone*. Cambridge, MA: MIT Press, 1977.

Schivelbusch, Wolfgang. *Disenchanted Night*. Los Angeles: University of California Press, 1988.

Schudson, Michael. *Discovering the News: A Social History of American Newspapers*. New York: Basic Books, 1978.

Stephens, Mitchell. *A History of News: From the Drum to the Satellite*. New York: Viking, 1988.

Thompson, Robert L. *Wiring a Continent: The History of the Telegraphic Industry in the United States*. Princeton, NJ: Princeton University Press, 1947.

Williams, Raymond. *The Long Revolution*. New York: Columbia University Press, 1961.

PART V

Boorstin, Daniel. *The Image*. New York: Atheneum, 1978.

Chandler, Alfred A. *The Visible Hand*. Cambridge, MA: Harvard University Press, 1977.

Fowles, Jib. *Starstruck: Celebrity Performers and the American Public*. Washington: The Smithsonian Institution, 1992.

Kern, Stephen. *The Culture of Time and Space: 1880–1918*. Cambridge, MA: Harvard University Press, 1983.

Marchand, Roland. *Advertising the American Dream—Making Way for Modernity, 1920–1940*. Berkeley: University of California Press, 1985.

Peterson, Theodore. *Magazines in the Twentieth Century*. Urbana: University of Illinois Press, 1964.

Schudson, Michael. *Advertising: The Uneasy Persuasion*. Los Angeles: University of California Press, 1984.

Williams, Rosalynd. *Dream Worlds*. Los Angeles: University of California Press, 1982.

PART VI

Barnouw, Eric. *A History of Broadcasting in the United States*. New York: Oxford University Press, 3 vols., 1966–1970.

Briggs, Asa. *The History of Broadcasting in the United Kingdom*. London: Oxford University Press, 1966.

Covert, Catherine, and John Stephens, eds. *Mass Media between the Wars*. Syracuse: Syracuse University Press, 1984.

Crisell, Andrew. *Understanding Radio*. New York: Methuen, 1986.

Culbert, David. *News for Everyman*. Westport, CT: Greenwood Press, 1976.

Czitrom, Daniel. *Media and the American Mind: From Morse to McLuhan*. Chapel Hill, NC: University of North Carolina Press, 1987.

Douglas, Susan. *Inventing American Broadcasting: 1899–1922*. Baltimore: Johns Hopkins University Press, 1987.

Lewis, Tom. *Empire of the Air—The Men Who Made Radio*. New York: HarperCollins, 1991.

Part VII

Barnouw, Erik. *Tube of Plenty: The Evolution of American Television*. New York: Oxford University Press, 1970.

Briggs, Asa. *The History of Broadcasting in the United Kingdom*. London: Oxford University Press, 1961–1970.

McLuhan, Marshall. *Understanding Media*. New York: Signet, 1964.

Postman, Neil. *Amusing Ourselves to Death*. New York: Dell, 1986.

Rutherford, Paul. *When Television Was Young: Primetime Canada, 1952–1967*. Toronto/Buffalo: University of Toronto Press, 1990.

Smith, Anthony. *The Shadow in the Cave: The Broadcaster, His Audience and the State*. Champaign, IL: University of Illinois Press, 1973.

Tichi, Cecelia. *Electronic Hearth: Creating an American Television Culture*. New York: Oxford University Press, 1992.

Williams, Raymond. *Television—Technology and Cultural Form*. London: Fontana/Collins, 1974.

Williams, Raymond. *Television and Society*. London: Fontana, 1979.

Part VIII

Beniger, James. *The Control Revolution*. Cambridge, MA: Harvard University Press, 1986.

Hollins, Timothy. *Beyond Broadcasting: Into the Cable Age*. London: BFI Publishing, 1984.

Kuhns, William. *The Post-Industrial Prophets*. New York: Weybright and Talley, 1971.

Poole, Ithiel de Sola. *Technologies of Freedom*. Cambridge, MA: Harvard University Press, 1983.

Poster, Mark. *The Mode of Information*. Chicago: University of Chicago Press, 1990.

Schiller, Dan. *Telematics and Government*. Philadelphia: Temple University Press, 1982.

Weizenbaum, Joseph. *Computer Power and Human Reason*. New York: W. H. Freeman, 1976.

Zuboff, Shoshana. *In the Age of the Smart Machine*. New York: Basic Books, 1988.

Text Credits

From *Human Nature* by Alexander Marshack. Copyright 1978 by Alexander Marschack. Reprinted by permission. From "Tokens: Facts and Interpretation" by Denise Schmandt-Besserat in *Visible Language*, Vol. XX, No. 3, 1986. Reprinted by permission. From *Empire and Communications* by Harold Innis. Copyright 1950, 1986, University of Toronto Press. Reprinted by permission. From *Mathematics of the Incas: Code of the Quipu.* Copyright 1997, Dover Publications. Reprinted by permission. From *The Story of Writing* by Andrew Robinson. Copyright 1995, Thames and Hudson. Reprinted by permission. From *Literacy in Traditional Societies,* Jack Goody (ed.). Copyright 1975 by Cambridge University Press. Reprinted by permission. From *The Literate Revolution in Greece and its Cultural Consequences* by Eric Havelock. Copyright 1982 by Princeton University Press. Reprinted by permission. From *Orality and Literacy* by Walter J. Ong. Copyright 1982 by Methuen & Co. Reprinted by permission of Routledge, London. From *The Name of the Rose* by Umberto Eco, translated by William Weaver. Copyright 1990 by Gruppo Editoriale Fabbri-Bompiani, Sonzogno, Etas S.p.A., English translation. Copyright 1983 by Harcourt Brace & Company and Martin Secker & Warburg, Ltd. Reprinted by permission of Harcourt Brace & Company. From *The Day the Universe Changed* by James Burke. Copyright 1985 by James Burke. Reprinted by permission of Little Brown and Company. From *Art and Technics* by Lewis Mumford. Copyright 1947 by Columbia University Press. Reprinted by permission. From *The Printing Revolution in Early Modern Europe* by Elizabeth Eisenstein. Copyright 1983 by Cambridge University Press. Reprinted by permission. From *Orality and Literacy* by Walter J. Ong. Copyright 1982 by Methuen & Co. Reprinted by permission of Routledge, London. From *Early Modern Literacies* by Harvey J. Graff. Copyright 1987 by Indiana University Press. Reprinted by permission. From *The Media and Modernity* by John B. Thompson. Copyright 1995 by Stanford University Press and Polity Press. Reprinted by permission. From *The Great Cat Massacre and Other Episodes in French Cultural History* by Robert Darnton. Copyright 1984 by Basic Books. Reprinted by permission. From *Communication as Culture* by James Carey. Copyright 1988, 1989, 1992 by Unwin Hyman. Reprinted by permission of Routledge. From *Discovering the News: A Social History of American Newspapers* by Michael Schudson. Copyright 1978 by Basic Books. Reprinted by permission. From *America Calling: A Social History of the Telephone to 1940* by Claude S. Fisher. Copyright 1992 by the University of California Press. Reprinted by permission. From *When Old Technologies Were New* by Carolyn Marvin. Copyright 1988 by Oxford University Press. Reprinted by permission. From *Dream Worlds: Mass Consumption in Late Nineteenth-Century France* by Rosalynd Williams. Copyright 1986 by the University of California Press. Reprinted by permission. From *On Photography* by Susan Sontag. Copyright 1973 by Susan Sontag. Reprinted by permission of The Wylie Agency. From "Photojournalism around 1900" by Ulrich Keller, in *Shadow and Substance,* Kathleen Collins (ed.), 1990. Reprinted by permission of Ulrich Keller. From *Media and the American Mind* by Daniel Cz-

INDEX